D1598419

THE WORLD THE PLAGUE MADE

The World the
Plague Made

THE BLACK DEATH AND
THE RISE OF EUROPE

JAMES BELICH

PRINCETON UNIVERSITY PRESS
PRINCETON & OXFORD

Published by Princeton University Press
41 William Street, Princeton, New Jersey 08540
99 Banbury Road, Oxford OX2 6JX

press.princeton.edu

All Rights Reserved
ISBN 9780691215662
ISBN (e-book) 9780691222875

Library of Congress Control Number: 2022935399

British Library Cataloging-in-Publication Data is available

Editorial: Ben Tate and Josh Drake
Production Editorial: Karen Carter
Jacket Design: Karl Spurzem
Production: Danielle Amatucci
Publicity: Carmen Jimenez and Alyssa Sanford
Copyeditor: Karen Verde

Jacket/Cover Credit: Courtesy of the University of Texas Libraries, the University of Texas at Austin

This book has been composed in Arno

Printed on acid-free paper. ∞

Printed in the United States of America

10 9 8 7 6 5 4 3 2 1

CONTENTS

MAPS

THE WORLD THE PLAGUE MADE

Introduction

PLAGUE PARADOXES

IN 1345, Europe and its neighbours were beset by a terrible plague. In proportion to population, it may have been the most lethal catastrophe in human history. It appeared first in the Black Sea/Volga region, spread throughout the Mediterranean from 1347, and swept Northern Europe in 1348, though it did not reach some Russian regions until as late as 1353. Once known as the "Great Death", "The Great Plague", or simply "*The* Death" or "*The* Plague", it came to be called "The Black Death". Its horrors and terrors defy description, though evocative chroniclers came close. Some variants killed quickly, in a day or two; the main variant took a week or so from the first appearance of symptoms. Sufferers lay in agony, their kin sometimes reluctant to nurse them for fear of infection. Uninfected children died because their parents had done so; infants suckling the breasts of dead mothers. Medics did their best, as shown by their numerous "plague tracts", but could find no effective treatment. Francesco Petrarch, voice of the early Italian Renaissance, wrote: "Our former hopes are buried with our friends. The year 1348 left us lonely and bereft, for it took from us wealth which could not be restored by the Indian, Caspian or Carpathian Sea. Last losses are beyond recovery, and death's wound beyond cure. There is just one comfort: that we shall follow those who went before".[1]

New information about the Black Death requires four revisions to our understanding of it. The case for each is made in part one. Here we briefly consider their possible implications. The first is less a revision than the restoration of an older view. During the twentieth century, most experts were convinced that the Black Death was bubonic plague, caused by the bacteria *Yersinia Pestis* (*Y. Pestis*), which normally infected only wild rodents. Between 2001 and 2011, the notion that the plague was bubonic came under serious attack, but recent

1

science has now decisively reaffirmed it. This confirms that the Black Death kicked off the second of three known bubonic plague "pandemics". "Pandemic" technically means a single vast epidemic, but in common usage has come to mean a series of plague epidemics in the same large space. It is important that we distinguish them from one-off plague epidemics and from regional and local outbreaks—the last at least were, and are, quite common. The First Pandemic was the early medieval "Plague of Justinian", the reigning Byzantine emperor, which hit much the same region as the late medieval Black Death, but eight centuries earlier, in 541. Subsequent strikes, 17 or 18 of them, persisted for two centuries. The Black Death Pandemic, beginning in 1345, persisted for more than three centuries and involved about 30 major epidemics in all. The third, or modern, pandemic went intercontinental from southeast China in 1894, reached all six habitable continents, and declined from 1924. We draw much of our information about plague from this last pandemic, but it was much shorter, more pan-global, and proportionately far less lethal than the previous two. So the Second Plague Pandemic was a rare event, with only one generally accepted precursor and no real successor. If random curveballs from nature ever affected the course of human history over the past two thousand years, the Black Death pandemic is a candidate.

This is even more so because of the Black Death's horrifyingly high mortality, our second revision. The standard estimate for the first strike, 1346–53, is between one-quarter and one-third of the population of Western Europe, say 30%—bad enough in anyone's terms. Many scholars have found this unconvincingly high, given the fact that the Third Pandemic killed no more than 3% in the worst afflicted regions. Yet new and reinterpreted evidence suggests that the real Black Death toll was more like 50%: a sudden halving in the first strike alone. It may seem macabre to dispute the details of so terrible a tragedy: what does it matter if death took a third or a half? But humans are resilient, and the difference could be important to the survivors. If harvests decline 40% and 30% of people die, there is dearth for the living. If 50% die, they have modest abundance. Our third revision concerns the timing of population recovery. None of the later strikes had the spread or lethality of the first one, and, until recently, recovery was thought to be quite rapid, beginning by 1400 and complete by 1500. It now seems that this is about a century out: demographic recovery was not general until about 1500, and was not complete until about 1600. England recovered its pre-plague population in 1625, after 275 years.[2] So, during the fifteenth century, Western Europe still had half its "normal" population—the level before 1345 and after 1600. Yet this is the very century in which Western Europe's global expansion began.

Why Europe? Why did this small continent expand to the point of global hegemony? In 1400, Western Europeans controlled around 5% of the planet's surface. They are said to have controlled about 35% by 1800, reaching 80% by 1900.[3] Territory is a crude measure, and we will see that substantive European control was exaggerated. But, even by 1550, with population recovery still incomplete, Europeans dominated South America's richest bullion sources and had begun to settle in other parts of the Americas. They were also major players in the sub-Saharan African gold and slave trades, as well as in the dynamic mercantile activity of the Indian Ocean, and were beginning to stretch to China too. The wealth of Petrarch's ocean seas proved, after all, to be of some comfort to plague's survivors. This strange intersection of depopulation and successful expansion is plague's first paradox.

Geographic expansion, beginning in the fifteenth century and culminating in global hegemony in the nineteenth, was only one-half of Europe's "Great Divergence" from the rest of the planet. The other half was economic development, culminating in industrialisation in the later eighteenth century. China and India were the global economic leaders in the High Middle Ages (c.900–1300 CE), and the point at which Europe began to catch up on them is disputed. But a case will be made, in part two of this book, for the post-plague era, 1350–1500. This conjunction of terrible epidemics with economic and technological advance is plague's second paradox, which brings us to our fourth and final plague revision. Many authorities still believe that the Black Death pandemic also hit India and China in the fourteenth century, as well as Europe and its neighbours. Part one will suggest that this was probably not the case. This may implicate plague in "the" Great Divergence. To oversimplify for emphasis (and to preempt a possible quip), this book tests a new two-word answer to an old two-word question: Why Europe? *Y. Pestis.*

———

"Why Europe?" is a question that will not go away, though there are many who wish that it would, for some good reasons. Mainstream historians have had enough of European auto-hagiography and "high" histories of politics, diplomacy, and Great Men. Thankfully, their attention has turned to the histories of silenced European majorities, of the layers of subjectivity that refract history, and of the agency and particularity of the vast range of societies out-side Europe. This has yielded an impressive array of new scholarship, which has helped to build this book. Historians have also become understandably suspicious of sweeping generalisations, especially when organised into "meta-narratives"—overarching stories of world history into whose categories the facts can be made to fit. Some feel that the very craft of truth-seeking history is a delusion—"there is no face behind the mask",[4] leaving us with only the masks to study, or that professional history is so embroiled with the late nineteenth-century Eurocentric and nationalist milieu in which it flowered that it cannot transcend it. I see these considerations as reasons for caution, not evasion. Reconstructing history with full accuracy and fully transcending Eurocentrism may well be impossible. But we *can* get closer or farther away. Broad arguments do oversimplify, but they can also contextualise, enable com-parison, and uncover fresh kinds of complexity. Should we leave them to eco-nomic historians, historical sociologists, or populist historians, who are some-what prone to leave out the messy bits of the past, otherwise known as contingent history?

Another argument for ditching the study of Europe's geographic spread and economic growth is that the global ascendancy it delivered was short-lived (say, 1850–1950) and is now long gone. But this is surely no reason for disinter-est from historians whose business is, after all, the past. Further, the death of European ascendancy has been exaggerated. Including Europe itself, four and one-third of the world's six habitable continents (the two Americas, Austral-asia, and Asian Russia) are still dominated by people of European descent, who still often self-define as "European". Europe's great legacy, industrialisa-tion, still pervades the globe, affecting most human lives for good and ill. Of course, whole libraries of explanations for the ascendancy already exist, and most of the more recent have transcended racism and triumphalism. There are many plausible theories about the causes of European imperialism. They in-clude adventurism and evangelism; an urge to deploy surplus European labour or capital; the advent of modern technology giving teeth to long-standing expansionist aspirations; and the competitive system whereby any respectable modern European state had to have an empire. Most focus on the age of "high imperialism", 1860–1914, or on the long nineteenth century, 1783–1914. It is true that the latter period witnessed a massive surge in empire (the subjection of other societies), in settlement (the reproduction of one's own society in dis-tant locales at the expense of the prior inhabitants), and in bulk trade. But these processes built on centuries of earlier expansion, whose origins have yet to be satisfactorily explained.

I do not claim that plague dominates the causal jigsaw. I do suggest that it is the biggest missing piece, whose inclusion casts new light on the whole. While a few prescient historians have intuited a connection, none , to my knowledge, have traced out a plausible causal sequence between Europe's own plague and its geographic spread, let alone tested it. This is less true of economic growth. Since 1860 if not earlier, some scholars have linked the Black Death to the beginning of Western Europe's economic progress and its associated technological development.[5] This view seems cyclical, periodically going in and out of fashion. The last century has been mostly an "out" period. "Most historians writing in the twentieth century . . . relentlessly downplayed the impact of the Black Death, which was relegated to the role of an accelerator of a crisis already in motion".[6] Some continue to explicitly deny the Black Death a major role. In 2014, a leading medieval environmental historian wrote that the Black Death "failed to alter long-term fundamentals".[7] In 2016, a leading economic historian agreed that "In the end, the plague effected no significant long run economic changes".[8] Un-plagued explanations for Europe's modern economic growth currently prevail, though the wheel shows signs of turning again (see chapters 3 and 16).

A sequence of great intellectual movements has been credited with modern Europe's ascent: the Renaissance, centred on the fifteenth century, the sixteenth-century Reformation, the seventeenth-century Scientific Revolution, and the eighteenth-century Enlightenment. This Holy Quartet, particularly the last, still has its advocates.[9] Exceptional culture traits of long standing and benign institutions now feature more. "Scholars who credit inherent qualities in Europe with making possible the emergence of the modern world typically emphasize either culture or institutions".[10] The traits include nuclear families, individualism, curiosity, and creativity. The institutions include strong centralised states, stable law, representative assemblies, and freer markets. There is nothing "politically correct" or "Europhobic" about questioning this causal package. Though now shorn of racism, it remains suspiciously flattering towards Europe. The law of averages, one would think, might include a few more vices and contingencies among the virtues. Most "virtues" did exist, and were important, but we seldom get much of an explanation for their emergence and exceptionality, or hear precisely how they interacted with each other, or with geographic expansion and economic growth. Were they causes or effects of "the" Great Divergence? Or did they, and Europe's real or alleged exceptionality in general, spring from earlier seeds, such as the legacies of classical Greece and Rome, or the Christian religion, or various medieval epiphanies dated to the eighth, tenth, or twelfth centuries? This book seeks to bring the Black Death, and a few other fresh variables, into the conversation—not just for Europe and its geographic spread and economic growth, but for global history.

Prologue

GLOBALISING EUROPE

THE CONSEQUENCES (and, to a lesser extent, the causes) of the Black Death; the causes (and, to a lesser extent, the consequences) of European expansion, plus their interaction, are big enough subjects for any book. But, for my sins, I have become convinced that a still broader approach, indeed a global one, best yields fresh light on them. I should therefore sketch a few idiosyncrasies in my own take on global history. It has at least two forms: extensive and intensive. Extensive global history attempts broad overviews, not necessarily of the whole planet's whole history, but of large chunks of it, or broad patterns in it. It should avoid rigid meta-narratives privileging a single culture group and implying inexorable progress towards the present. But flexible cross-cultural frameworks suggesting broad patterns and processes still have their uses, as long as they do not pretend to be the only respectable way of doing history. Intensive global history, in contrast, brings useful perspectives from anywhere, anytime, to bear on particular historical problems, however big or small, then tests the resulting hypothesis on a wide range of accessible sources, including unpublished theses, arcane journals, and recent science. It may seem ungenerous in second-guessing the specialists on whom it depends, but in fact takes them seriously, and seeks to enhance their depth with its breadth. Intensive global history is this book's main game, but this prologue lays its foundation by experimenting with the extensive variant.

I Rethinking Globalisation and Divergence

Many scholars date the origin of globalisation, a process thought to culminate in a comprehensively interconnected planet, to the very recent past, after

1945.[1] Some historians date it to 1571, when Spanish Manila galleons inaugurated a globe-girdling trade, or to some point in the nineteenth century, when genuinely massive transfers of goods across oceans began. I think that it is too resonant a process to be restricted to the recent past or to the whole planet. For me, the most interesting thing about globalisation is not universality or modernity but *transformative connectivity*. This can create hybrid histories which are more than the sum of their parts, where one plus one equals three. The classic example is bronze, which required connectivity because copper and tin sources are often distant from each other. Biota and cultures can hybridise too. Cold-adapted camels and heat-adapted dromedaries were interbred in Sogdiana or Bactria 2,500 years ago, producing a much bigger beast, able to cope with both cold and heat. Hybrid Afro-Arab (Swahili) and Afro-European broker cultures emerged on the east and west coasts of Africa about 1,000 and 500 years ago, respectively, intensifying Africa's global connections. Globalisation can also create and link subplanetary "worlds", making a newly connected space for history to happen in, a "known world" or ecumene, whose farthest flung parts are known to each other. Such concepts are already in common use—the Islamic World, the Atlantic World. The idea is most useful when stretched beyond any single empire. There were Roman and Chinese "worlds" 2,000 years ago, but they were bigger than the empires—Ireland and Japan were part of the relevant world but not the empire. Three simple typologies help map the scale, engines, and intensities of globalisation, though we should note that the types are artificial fixed points, allowing us to pick up a segment of a fluid reality for closer analysis.

Globalisation has operated at three scales, *fully global* (impacting all six habitable continents); *semi-global* (stretching across most of a whole hemisphere); and *subglobal* (involving two or more subcontinents). I can think of only two instances of the first: modern globalisation and the original dispersal of *homo sapiens* (we self-titled "clever apes") from Africa to all six continents, ending in South America perhaps 12,000 years ago. One example of semi-globalisation is the astonishing spread of Austronesian-speaking, Malayo-Polynesian, far-voyagers from the fringes of Southeast Asia across the Indian Ocean to Africa *and* to the islands of the vast Pacific, probably within the last two millennia and possibly reaching the Americas. Another is the near-encirclement of the North Pole by overlapping Arctic-adapted cultures, using reindeer and sled-dogs, tight-stitched water-proof fur clothing and hide boats, including big whale-hunting *umiaks*, as well as toggle harpoons, bone armour, and bows and arrows. This culminated in the rapid expansion of the Thule

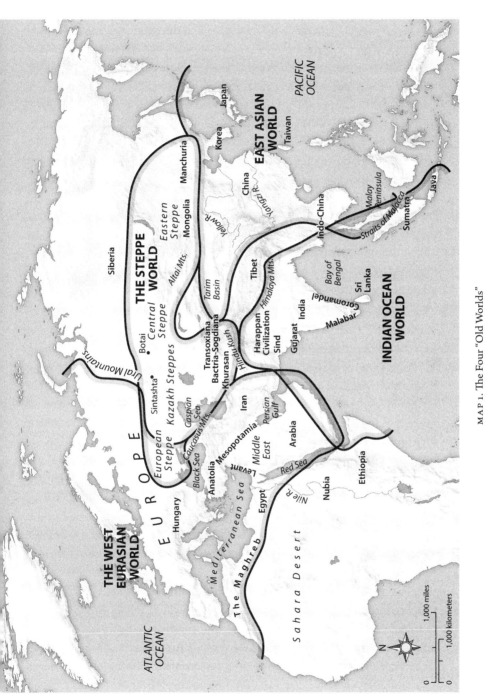

MAP 1. The Four "Old Worlds"

Inuit from Eastern Siberia to Greenland around the twelfth century, shoulder-ing aside Aleuts, Amerindians, Paleo-Inuit and, eventually, the European Norse in Greenland. This book's key cases of subglobalisation are the four "old worlds" that emerged in Afro-Eurasia from 5,000 years ago: East Asia, centred on China; the Indian Ocean world, centred on India; West Eurasia, centred on the Middle East, and the uncentred but connected world of the Eurasian steppes, the grasslands that stretched more than 5,000 miles from Manchuria to the Hungarian plain.

Each world was stitched or woven together by one or more of five engines of connectivity. *Diffusion* of things and thoughts from neighbour to neighbour was the most basic. It was slow and limited, but capable of important transfers. At the other end of the scale was the *expansion* of a single culture group into new territory, which could rapidly extend and intensify connections. Empires became an important form of expansion, but were by no means the only one. Trading, hunting, and slaving systems could expand, sometimes violently, without empire, and there were cases of "pack expansion" like those of tiny Greek city-states throughout the Mediterranean in the last millennium BCE or European nation-states in the nineteenth century CE. But durable expan-sion did require ongoing links, formal or informal, to the source region. If these links faded, expansion became *dispersal*, our third engine. Dispersal could also stand alone, as folk migrations or male warrior migrations with no thought of empire or of return home, like the Anglo-Saxon migration to Britain in the fifth and sixth centuries CE. Dispersal was like a rubber band that stretched and broke, but left its far-flung fragments in place, while expan-sion stretched but did not break. The fourth engine of globalisation was *at-traction*, which acted like a magnet to draw people to prized resources, such as obsidian, or prized manufactures, such as silk. It required *outreach*, our final engine, by which I mean going to get something at source and returning with it, rather than trading for it at some intermediate hub, or waiting for it to percolate through by diffusion. About 1500 BCE, some ancient Swedes lost patience with the slow diffusion of Cypriot copper and went over land to get it themselves, then proving they had done so by making rock drawings of Mediterranean-type ships when they got home.[2]

Even occasional contact could make important *transmissions*, the lowest of four intensities, our last mini-typology. Rare finds of objects from afar, such as Moluccan cloves in an Egyptian pyramid, are interesting because they indicate the breadth of networks, but are not significant in themselves. Yet a handful of transfers of things capable of local reproduction—biota, people, ideas—could make a big difference to the receiving societies. African millets somehow made it to India around 2000 BCE, fitting in to under-utilised ecological niches and permitting denser populations.[3] The highest intensity involved *integration*: links that were so tight, despite distance, that two or more far-flung places were mutually dependent. The reliance of classical Athens on the Crimea for grain is an early example.[4] The lower-middle level of intensity was *interaction*, my proxy for which is fairly regular luxury trade, on which elites might come to depend in order to show that they were elites. *Circulation* was the upper-middle level; its proxy was bulk trade in such items as salt, timber, and grain. Both interaction and circulation could also carry new ideas, material culture, biotechnology, and diseases. We must constantly remind ourselves that globalisation was not necessarily good or inexorable. It could contract as well as expand, weaken as well as intensify, collapse as well as emerge. It could transfer syphilis as well as science. Some diseases, possibly including syphilis, could be transferred long range by mere transmission. Smallpox could just make do with interaction. In all three pandemics, bubonic plague sequences required circulation. Plague pandemics too had hybrid histories. They were co-ventures between random ecological events and the sustained intensity of human connectivity.

Until the fourth millennium BCE, chains of connectivity were prone to stop at big seas, deserts, and the endless steppes. Developments in biotechnology then turned these barriers into bridges. By 3000 BCE, sail-powered ships had come into use; and horses and, somewhat later, Bactrian camels, had been domesticated. From about 2000 BCE, the four Afro-Eurasian worlds began to link up. It is in this context of semi-globalisation that the concept of divergence becomes something more than a beauty contest in which the winner looks rather like the judge.

Around 2000 CE, the "Why Europe?" debate was refreshed and reoriented by publications including *The Great Divergence*, by Kenneth Pomeranz, which argued that Europe did not rise above the economic level of China until about 1800, and that it then pulled ahead only through fortuitous access to (British) coal and (American) colonies and their fertile acres.[5] This challenged, though it has yet to overcome, the prevailing view that a European edge was older and based on unusually growth-friendly institutions or culture traits. This book finds support for the notion that European economic complexity and productivity did not exceed China's until the eighteenth century. But the process of catch-up may have begun earlier, and geographic spread, which may have been a necessary precondition for economic growth, certainly did. It began in the fifteenth century, whether in 1492, when Columbus bumped in to America, or in 1402, when Europeans made their first durable overseas conquest—Lanzarote, an island in the Canary archipelago. The debate on the causes and timing of divergence has generated a large and useful literature. All sides agree, however, that there was only one Great Divergence, that between Europe and the rest of the planet. This consensus needs challenging in its turn.

A divergence, let us say, begins as a major regional innovation in biotechnology or religion, or the hybridising of two such developments. If the divergence provides an advantage in expansion or dispersal, others will try to match it, or be subjugated and have it imposed on them. If it is simply deemed valuable or useful, others will try to acquire it, then try to emulate it by producing it themselves. This requires that they learn about it through interaction, or are educated the hard way through expansion or dispersal. The divergence will then pervade the connected space, maturing into a *convergence*. It is this dissemination to large numbers of people, not the real or alleged achievements of the diverger, that make a divergence "great"—"big" might be a better term. In the linked "worlds" of Afro-Eurasia in the last 5,000 years, there were at least four great divergences—defined as hugely influential innovations that reached from the Pacific to the Atlantic. This sets the bar high. It excludes the impressive spreads of Roman and Buddhist influences, which did not quite make it to both oceans.

II The Equine Revolution

The first of these great divergences was the spread of horse domestication from 3000 BCE. The evidence on this, particularly the science on horse and human genomes, is fast-changing and contested. But, in brief, the story rode something like this. Horses were first tamed at Botai, east of the Urals in Kazakhstan, Central Asia, about 5,500 years ago, for their milk and meat, and possibly for riding. Horse domestication was then taken up, about 3000 BCE, by steppe nomads from further west, now known as the Yamnaya, who had earlier adopted ox-wagons and the herding of cattle and sheep. My guess is that they first took up two-handed riding, grasping horse's manes and necks as well as any bridles. This meant riding was not yet of direct use in warfare—not even one hand was free to use a weapon—but it did yield faster and longer-range scouting and raiding, and allowed warriors to arrive fresh on a battlefield. This may have helped the Yamnaya to disperse rapidly to Eastern and Central Europe by 2500 BCE. Their Indo-European language spread with them.[6] We can date the takeoff of equestrian warfare more confidently, to 2000 BC. At this time, at Sintashta, also in Central Asia, war chariots were developed. These helped peoples descended from or connected to the Yamnaya to mount a fresh set of dispersals by 1500 BCE: to Western Europe, the Balkans, Anatolia, Mesopotamia, Iran, Northern India, and the Tarim Basin in what is now Northwest China, where allegedly European-looking mummies have been found.[7] Stall-feeding over winter and the transplantation of alfalfa grass, which was prime horse feed, took horses beyond steppe-like terrain, though in limited numbers. Horses and chariots reached Eastern China around 1200 BCE, by which time they were in use from the Atlantic to the Pacific.

At least one interpretation of these events still seems influenced by residual Aryanism, a racial theory of which Adolf Hitler is the best known exponent.[8] This has always been a white herring. Indo-European speakers did ride farthest, earliest, and the spread of their language—to Iran, Anatolia, and Northern India as well as Europe—is indeed remarkable. But, despite efforts to credit the Yamnaya with it, recent evidence supports first domestication at Botai.[9] The people of Botai probably did not speak Indo-European, or have Caucasian ancestry.[10] Botai horses were not the ancestors of modern horses, but Yamnaya horses were probably not either. Contrary to earlier hypotheses about a very few equine Adams, the lack of male genetic diversity in modern horses is now attributed to more recent breeding practices involving select stud stallions.[11] In any case, peoples such as the Egyptians had matched steppe nomads in chariot warfare by 1500 BCE. From about 1000 BCE a reverse series of mounted dispersals, from east to west, took place, beginning with the Scythians, whose homeland was long thought to be on or close to the European steppes but is now placed in Siberia/Mongolia.[12] One-handed riding, which enabled the first cavalry, using javelins, lances, or swords, had emerged by this time, and was soon followed by no-handed riding allowing the use of powerful compound bows from horseback. The Scythians may have developed the first horse nomad empires, whose leading role in global history has only recently been given its due. There is some evidence that their federations were very large.[13] Certainly, from 200 BCE, a series of Turco-Mongol horse nomad dispersals and expansions emanated from the eastern steppes into the other worlds of Eurasia, culminating in the thirteenth century CE with the immense Mongol empire. From 1500, Europeans transmitted horses to the Americas. They yielded a brief military advantage, which the Spanish tried to extend by excluding mares from their cavalry,[14] but were soon adopted by Amerindians. Amerindian horse nomad "empires", Araucanian, Comanche, and Lakota Sioux, emerged, and defied European rule until about 1870. It was the horses that counted, not the language or skin colour of the riders.

In suitable environments, mounted archers led military biotechnology for more than 1,500 years after 800 BCE, and remained significant until the nineteenth century. This was only the martial side of equine influence. Horses also revolutionised peacetime transport and many forms of work. They were 60% more efficient than oxen in pulling carts and plowing, and had multiple other uses. The equine divergence surely ranks as great, even as an "Equine Revolution" comparable to the Industrial. People may balk at this comparison, but horses tripled human power, speed, and range for four millennia. They provided half of all work energy in the United States as late as 1850, as much as humans, steam, water, and wind combined.[15] Engines are still calibrated in horsepower. It is hard to think of a biotechnological development between the origin of farming 10,000 years ago and industrialisation 250 years ago that outranks the horse-human alliance.

This first case refines our understanding of the divergence process. It originated, not in the ancient urban clusters of the Middle East, eastern China, or northern India, but on the steppes, among nomads. It was not the achievement of some Isaac Newton among horse whisperers, but of regional ecological variables combined with repeated pulses of collective human innovation. Horses had become extinct across much of their original range, including their American homeland, by about 10,000 years ago, probably due to human hunting. They had significant refuges in Eurasia, from Yunnan to Iberia, but were truly abundant only on the steppes. Pulses of equine divergence kept emanating from the steppes, like a roman candle: two-hand rider dispersals, chariots, one-hand rider and mounted archer dispersals, nomad empires with mobile tent cities. A key military advantage, perfected by the Mongols, was not just horses, but multiple horses for each man, who changed horses for rapid long-range movement, giving a strategic edge, and even in the midst of battle, giving a tactical edge. Yet equestrianism also spread and developed through non-steppe emulation and adaptation, such as horse collars, stirrups, and heavier stall-fed horses that were better able to carry armoured men and to perform agricultural and industrial work. In the end, the globalisation of divergence reduced the relative advantage of the diverger.

III Super-Crops, Super-Crafts

Our second divergence began around 2500 BCE in the great river valleys of eastern China. It featured water control and the mass advent of wet rice cultivation, a super-crop that yielded at least twice as much food per acre as any other cereal. This permitted dense populations, large, rich elites, and social complexity, which in turn generated super-crafts, notably silk production. About 2000 BCE, India experienced a similar development, also based on wet rice cultivation, but with cotton as its super-craft. Chinese porcelain and Indian crucible steel later joined silk and cotton as widely desired manufactures. To oversimplify for brevity, we are looking at a Sino-Indian "super-craft" divergence based on a "super-crop". Large states, often congealing into empires, sheltered regional specialisation and interaction. Social complexity attuned producers to multiple and changing markets. Caste, clan, and lineage encouraged hereditary occupations in which children learned knack as well as skill. Silks and cottons were comfortable lightweight textiles which took dyes better than wool or linen. Coloured clothing could convey anything from uniformity to individuality, and everyone who saw and felt them wanted them, though often only elites could afford them.

Silk, cotton, and porcelain became products that the other old worlds desired and sought to obtain or to emulate. "For over a thousand years, Chinese porcelain was the most universally admired and most widely imitated product in the world", except for silk and cotton, whose global appeal was even older and wider.[16] Silk's value was considered so great that West Eurasians and Central Asians went to China to get it, in small but quite steady streams. Silk fabrics were found outside China, in Bactria, as early as the second millennium BCE, in Egypt by 1000 BCE, and in Europe by 500 BCE.[17] Indian cottons reached the Caucasus around 1500 BCE, and Mesopotamia from 1000 BCE.[18] By the last century BCE, the overland "Silk Roads" were in fairly regular use, operated by alliances of merchants, especially Sogdians from Transoxiana, oases towns, and horse and camel nomads. A three-section sea route had also developed: from South China to the Straits of Malacca; from there to India; and from India to the Persian Gulf or the Red Sea, with ships in all sections riding predictable monsoon winds. Various merchant and seafaring networks operated each section; some Persians and Arabs sailed the whole of it. The system, supplemented by camel caravans from India to Iran, carried Indian cotton to Southeast Asia as well as West Eurasia.[19] In the second century CE, 120 Roman ships sailed to India each year, their cargoes worth five tons of gold.[20]

Porcelain was a relative latecomer, reaching the Middle East by 800 CE and Spain two centuries later.[21] Indian crucible steel, in the form of swords, made the same journey about the same time, and was also imported by China from 700 CE.[22]

The Sino-Indian edge in fine textiles is a proxy for a general edge in manufacturing that lasted for about 2,000 years, to 1800 CE. China and India imported many products, but generally manufactures were not among them. The rest of the world could seldom *make* anything better than they could. This encouraged others to bring them non-manufactured imports, to do the dirty work of acquiring furs, gems, slaves, dyestuffs, and exotic foodstuffs. Even this was not enough, and textiles often had to be paid for with bullion.[23] This may explain the intermittent Sino-Indian disinterest in themselves engaging in long-range trade by sea. There were important exceptions, such as the Chola maritime empire in Southern India, 850–1279 CE, and the great Ming Chinese long-range fleets of the early fifteenth century.[24] But usually the rest of the world came to China and India, bearing its valuables. China and India were able to globalise by attraction.[25]

The superiority of Chinese and Indian crafts was widely recognised, and the drainage of bullion to those countries was widely resented. A Persian wrote, around 1100 CE, that "The people of China are the most skilfull of men in handicrafts. No other nation approaches them in this."[26] An Armenian, around 1300, wrote of China:

> People there are creative and quite clever; and thus they have little regard for the accomplishments of other people in all the arts and sciences . . . And their word is confirmed by the fact that . . . such a quantity of varied and marvellous wares with indescribably delicate workmanship is brought from that kingdom, that no one is capable of matching.[27]

Other West Eurasians agreed, voting with their most valued opinion poll— their bullion—as well as their merchant's feet. From the Roman Pliny the Elder in the first century AD through to the governors of the British East India Company in the eighteenth century, we hear the same complaints about the one-way flow of gold and silver to China and India.[28] As an Ottoman historian put it about 1700: "How much wealth goes to goods from Hindustan while the people of Hindustan buy nothing from the Ottoman provinces! Indeed, what we have to sell is not what they need. . . . they spend nothing in other lands because they have no needs. Hence the wealth of the world gathers in Hindustan".[29]

By about 800 CE, all four Sino-Indian super-crafts had made it from the Pacific to the Atlantic, so this divergence too meets our geographic criteria for "greatness". But a reality check is in order here. Just how significant was the semi-global spread of a one or two thousand tons of luxury cloth, plus a trickle of swords and pots? Good historians since Edward Gibbon have warned us against the siren lure of luxury trades, whose importance can indeed be exaggerated. Yet the following considerations suggest to me that this *was* a "Great Divergence". First, one does the masses no favours by understating the importance of the elites exploiting them. Elites could become culturally addicted to exotic luxuries, displaying them to prove that they were elites, and distributing them to buttress their support. Profit margins were huge; some merchants became rich. Second, the low volumes of luxuries can be deceptive. Some were paradoxically *essential*: they were essences of something, not the final product. Aromatics were essences of smell; spices, essences of taste; dyestuffs, essences of colour. The scent of Tibetan musk, a key ingredient in fine perfumes, "is perceptible even when diluted 3000 times".[30] So a kilogram of musk could become three tons of perfume. A kilogram of pepper could flavour a lot of food; a kilogram of precious dyestuff coloured many yards of cloth. Except for the dyes, this is obviously less true of manufactured articles like silk or cotton than of spices or aromatics. But silk and cotton too could be eked out with lesser textiles, as with fustian, a mix of cotton and linen. They also had a high ratio of impact to weight; 12 metres of silk weighed around a pound (450 grams); 27 metres of cotton fitted inside a coconut shell.[31] Above all, cultural addiction and high cost meant that they were locally emulated, which both spread the divergence and increased its impact.

The initial step was to import cheaper plain silk or cotton textiles, and dye and decorate them according to local taste. The next was to import the raw material, and spin and weave it locally. Finally, if cotton and mulberry plants and silkworms could be acquired, the whole biotechnology could be transferred. Even the second stage employed a surprising number of people, with substantial impact on the local economy. Before industrialisation, 10 tons of imported raw silk required perhaps 1,000 workers to convert into some 10,000 pieces of fine silk clothing annually. The Chinese clung to their silk secrets. Silk was woven in the Middle East as early as the third century CE, but using Chinese yarn. The Byzantines acquired silk worms in the sixth century.[32] By 1000 CE, other parts of the Middle East and even the southern fringes of Europe were developing their own full silk and cotton industries. But Chinese and Indian producers did not stay still, and through later pulses of divergence retained their edge, like the horse nomads of the steppes in mounted warfare. "China did not lose its technological lead" and long continued to produce the best silks, as India did cottons. "The fineness of Indian muslins, the intricacy of chintz prints and the fastness of their dyes baffled other 'craftsmen' around the world."[33] There was a similar sequence in the emulation of Indian-style crucible steel: the technique was transferred to the Middle East and Spain by 1000 CE; most of Europe had to wait until 1400 to come close to matching Damascene and Toledo blades. Persia and Egypt were leading early emulators of porcelain, but no one quite matched China for porcelain until the early eighteenth century, in Saxony, or India for cotton until the late eighteenth century, in Lancashire.

But China and India did not hold all the cards. Their lands were generally poor for horse breeding, and they had constantly to import horses from the steppes. India drew horses in large numbers, very often in return for cottons, through the northern mountain passes from Central Asia, and later across the Arabian Sea.[34] In the Chinese case, silk was exchanged for horses with the steppe nomads along the Silk Road. The importance of the Road has been questioned. "There is little empirical basis for the much-vaunted Silk Road trade".[35] It is true that overland silk routes varied over time, and that traffic was often intermittent and small in scale, and that during the Tang Dynasty (618– 907 CE) most silk went to Chinese garrisons along the eastern half of the Road. But these quantities were so great—almost a million 12-metre bolts a year—that the soldiers must have on-traded much of it to nomads, in exchange for horses among other things, and there is supporting evidence for this. The Tang army had 80,000 horses in 733, many of them imported,[36] and earlier, in the first century BCE, a Han official wrote: "a piece of Chinese plain silk can be exchanged with the Hsiung-nu [Xiongnu horse nomads] for articles worth several pieces of gold and thereby reduce the resources of our enemy . . . horses, dapples and bays and prancing mounts, come into our possession."[37] China's and India's craft divergence helped them match, or at least culturally survive, the steppe equine divergence. A careful 2017 analysis hits back against the Silk Road critics and shows that Chinese silk was reaching the Mediterranean littoral in significant quantities from the last century BCE through the Syrian trading city of Palmyra.[38] In any case, we should recall that luxury trade was a *proxy* for interaction, not the whole of it. Silk Road critics concede that "this modest non-road became one of the most transformative super highways in human history—one that transmitted ideas, technologies, and artistic motifs, not simply trade goods."[39] The technologies transferred from China to

West Eurasia included stirrups, the horse collar, paper-making, block printing and possibly metal-type printing, the marine compass, the wheelbarrow, the crossbow, gunpowder—the list goes on.

Some might still argue that the two millennia of Sino-Indian global precedence featured neither a "great divergence" nor a "world system", on the grounds that there was no global division of labour between core and periphery, or that there was no element of shared and self-perpetuating culture.[40] Yet there was a division of labour, between China and India which did the most prized manufacturing, and the rest of the world, which paid in non-manufactures, especially bullion. All players shared the cultural belief that fine textiles were immensely valuable, and that so were gold and silver, intrinsically the most useless of metals, creating a shared semi-global currency, in standard-weight ingots before coin. These were arguably mere illusions, but they were *shared* illusions. Steppe nomad, Islamic and European expansions were all attracted towards India and China because these countries had super-crafts that they valued, and that they could not make very well themselves.

IV Re-Setting Europe

Europe is the wrong space in which to understand a lot of its own history. It was not in itself a subglobal world, but part of one. Historians have brilliantly demonstrated how the great Mediterranean linked its littorals.[41] But we have neglected the possibility that other seas did likewise, and that a whole constellation of seas could be connected. The Mediterranean is the flagship of a fleet that includes the Black, Red, Caspian, North and Baltic Seas, and also the Persian Gulf and the Bay of Biscay. Straits connect some seas, and rivers link, or almost link, others. Russian river systems connect the Baltic to the Black Sea and the Caspian. The headwaters of the Rhine and Danube lie close together in Central Europe, though one runs to the North Sea, the other to the Black. The Tigris and the Euphrates run down to the Persian Gulf, both with headwaters quite close to the Black and Mediterranean Seas. Perhaps 12,000 years ago, the connective potential of this tri-continental inner-seas world was activated by the development of reliable sea-crossing boats, as yet without sails, and using paddles instead of oars. Our ancestors being who they were, we can trace this through the extinction of island mega-fauna, such as the dwarf hippos of Cyprus.[42] Tellingly, this world has no accepted name; associating it with the modern "West" is deceptive. "West Eurasia", though unfair to North Africa, is the best of a bad job.

West Eurasia was further unified by the spread of the "Levantine farming package", beginning around 10,000 years ago. It included more than a dozen domesticated species of plants and animals, assembled from in and around the Levant.[43] By 7,000 years ago, it had spread south and west to Mesopotamia and Egypt, where it underwrote the emergence of the Fertile Crescent civilisations. By about 6,000 years ago it had also spread to the far reaches of North Africa, Iran, and Northern Europe. Most of West Eurasia now shared a basic repertoire of material culture, including farming and pottery, though with infinite local variations. It also shared, very unevenly, a web of overlapping networks allowing the transfer of things, thoughts, and people. Transmission and interaction were easier and faster within this subglobal world than without. "Between 3400 and 3100 BC, carts and wagons appeared over a large area almost simultaneously in Mesopotamia, central Europe, and on the Russian-Ukrainian steppes".[44] Similar stories could be told for bronze and iron metallurgy. Middle Eastern crops, animals, and metallurgy were eventually transferred to the other three worlds, so this was arguably another great divergence. But it was slow-burning and reciprocal—such domesticates as water buffalo, chickens, and broomcorn millet came the other way.

Two other indicators of West Eurasian cohesion must be noted: God and empire. From 900 BC, a series of tri-continental empires united large overlapping tracts of West Eurasia: Assyrian, Persian, Greek, Roman, Arab, and Turkic, each claiming the mantle of precursors and coopting their techniques and personnel. One can almost imagine a Chinese-style situation in which they were seen as successive dynasties of the same empire. West Eurasia also shared a peculiar propensity towards monotheism. One form was Zoroastrianism, beginning perhaps as early as 1200 BC, which gave rise to Manichaeism and Mithraism. Its stronghold was Iran. It was denigrated by its enemies as "dualist", worshiping the Devil as well as God, but the latter had precedence.[45] Another, emerging about the same time, was Judaism, root of the Abrahamic religions, which came to include Christianity and Islam. From the fourth century, Christianity allied with Roman emperors and elites to become the state religion. On the borders of the Roman Empire, Armenian, Georgian, Ethiopian, and some Arab polities also turned Christian in the fourth century.[46] Until the seventh century, many, perhaps most, Christians lived in North Africa and West Asia. It was the rise and spread of Islam, our third great divergence, that forced the conflation of Christendom and Europe.

Islamic expansion began in the seventh century and by the ninth century covered the Middle East (except Byzantine Anatolia), all of North Africa, all

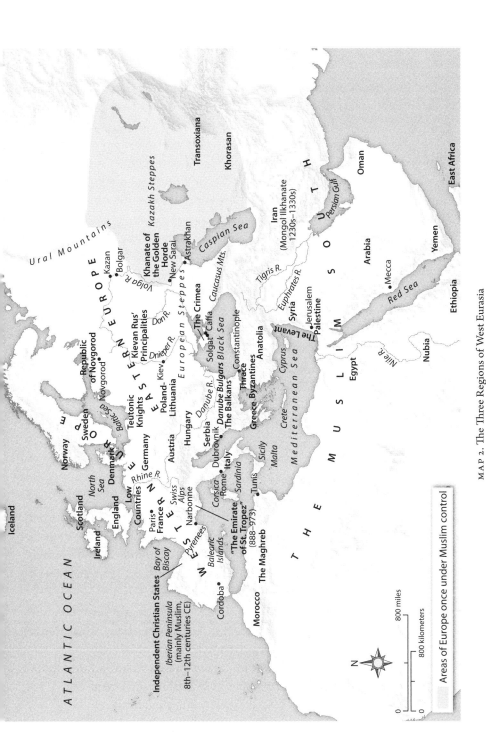

MAP 2. The Three Regions of West Eurasia

ATLANTIC OCEAN

Iceland

EUROPE

Scotland
Ireland
England
North Sea
Norway
Sweden
Denmark
Baltic Sea
Republic of Novgorod
Novgorod

EASTERN EUROPE
Kievan Rus' Principalities
Kiev
Don R.
Dnieper R.
European Steppes
Teutonic Knights
Poland-Lithuania

Ural Mountains
Kazan
Bolgar
Volga R.
Khanate of the Golden Horde
New Sarai
Astrakhan
Kazakh Steppes

Transoxiana

Khorasan

WESTERN EUROPE
Low Countries
Germany
Rhine R.
France
Paris
Swiss Alps
Narbonne
Pyrenees
"The Emirate of St. Tropez" (888–973)
Corsica
Rome
Italy
Sardinia
Austria
Hungary
Serbia
Danube R.
Dubrovnik
The Balkans
Danube Bulgars
The Crimea
Caffa
Solgat
Black Sea
Caucasus Mts.
Constantinople
Thrace
Anatolia
Greece
Byzantines
Cyprus
Sicily
Malta
Crete
Mediterranean Sea
Tunis

Caspian Sea

SOUTH

Iran (Mongol Ilkhanate 1230s–1330s)
Persian Gulf
Oman

Tigris R.
Euphrates R.
Syria
The Levant
Jerusalem
Palestine

THE MUSLIM SOUTH

Egypt
Nile R.
Nubia

Arabia
Mecca
Red Sea
Yemen

Ethiopia

East Africa

Independent Christian States
Iberian Peninsula (mainly Muslim, 8th–12th centuries CE)
Bay of Biscay
Balearic Islands
Córdoba
Morocco
The Maghreb

N

0   800 miles
0   800 kilometers

Areas of Europe once under Muslim control

but the margins of Iberia, most of the big Mediterranean islands including Cyprus and Sicily, and parts of Central Asia and India. It ceased being a single empire at that point, but expansion continued in pulses, stretching to parts of sub-Saharan Africa and Southeast Asia, and deeper into India. Unlike some other expansions, Islam's did not lapse into dispersal when it fragmented politically. It retained cohesion, underwritten by shared law, shared currency (gold dinars and silver dirhams), the hajj pilgrimage to Mecca, and the circulation of scholars, artists, and holy men. Recent genetic research shows there was also constant recycling of camels throughout the Abode of Islam, from India to Morocco, indicating substantial overland trade.[47] Seagoing trade established Muslim merchant communities in coastal China by 800 CE, so muezzins called the faithful to prayer from the Atlantic to the Pacific. This first great West Eurasian expansion intensified connectivity between the four old worlds, easing the transfer and emulation of biotechnologies including the Big Four: Chinese silk and porcelain, and Indian cotton and steel. Islam ringfenced Christian Europe, but also increased its access to the other worlds. Taking into account Muslim Iberia, Muslim Mongol rule in Russia, and Ottoman control of the Balkans and Hungary, almost half of Europe spent time under Muslim rule. The forgotten emirate of St Tropez, based at Fraxinet near the modern resort, controlled Provence and parts of Switzerland for almost a century, 888–973.[48]

Standard explanations for the great Islamic divergence seem to take us only so far. The prophet Muhammad's genius was obviously fundamental: he quickly unified feuding Arab tribes and towns, and equally quickly produced a satisfying religion, though it developed further over time. But he was no Alexander. He died in AD 632, when expansion had barely begun. In the next 80 years his followers conquered a vast swathe of contiguous territory from Spain to Sind, a rapidity matched only by the Mongols in the thirteenth century, and with longer-term effects.[49] A willingness to die in God's wars in the certainty of paradise was available to Christians too.[50] Two major early opponents, the Byzantine and Sassanid Persian empires, had exhausted each other in bitter warfare just when the first Muslims struck, yet they rallied and fought fiercely soon afterwards.[51] Some scholars think that the First Plague Pandemic, 540s–740s, was a factor. There were several widespread strikes during the opening century of Islamic expansion,[52] and a partial nomad exemption to plague may have "facilitated the Arab-Muslim conquest of the Middle East", by affecting them less than the more sedentary Byzantines and Persians.[53] But only half the Arabs were nomads, and the first strike in the 540s is said to have "decimated" pre-Islamic Arabia.[54] Muslim armies also defeated unplagued powers, such as the Tang Chinese at Talas in 751, and were sometimes struck by plague themselves.[55] Islam quickly became reliant on sedentary taxpayers and food suppliers, who were fully vulnerable to plague, and soon built great cities such as Cairo and Baghdad, which were plague-prone too. Islamic conquests continued after the end of the First Pandemic in the 740s. Part three of this book will argue that plague was a factor in late Muslim expansion, after 1350, but its role in the early conquests may have been modest.

One reason for Islam's early success was the underestimated prosperity and sophistication of its base, pre-Islamic Arabia. It was no backwater, but a nodal trading region, with a hundred towns, substantial agriculture, not just in oases, and with gold mines, metallurgy, and ships of its own.[56] Arabs were also sailors, and this may have helped them defeat the Byzantine fleet in the Mediterranean as early as the 650s, though the ships themselves were Egyptian and Levantine.[57] Dromedaries, of which the Arabs were the great masters, were desert-adapted and much faster than Bactrian camels or hybrids, and they gave an advantage well-recognised in the literature. The notion that early Arab ghazis fought from camelback using a new kind of saddle is now doubted.[58] They initially fought on foot, with bows and lances, after dismounting from their transport dromedaries.[59] Less well-recognised is the possibility that the early successes and the plunder gained in them enabled the Arabs to acquire more horses, which until then were quite rare in Arabia. The Mongols achieved great mobility by having numerous spare horses—at least five per man. But fast Arabian dromedaries gave the Arabs a Mongol-like mobility with far fewer horses—one camel and one horse per man would do.

A major prop of Muslim military power from the ninth century was the so-called slave soldier. "The importance, scope and duration of military slavery in the Islamic world have no parallel in human history."[60] Boys were selected from captured or purchased slaves for health, cleverness, and basic skills such as riding; trained and taught the Koran, then freed on graduation as a soldier or administrator. They were not slaves when they soldiered. Their loyalty was to the ruler who freed them, counterbalancing tribal or regional power, and they were well rewarded. Their offspring were not supposed to inherit their status, property, or appanages, so a regular stream of fresh recruits was critical. "Slave" soldiers were something close to a select professional army, and they were generally effective. The Christian military orders, such as the Templars and the Teutonic Knights, may have been intended to match them. These

knights were not supposed to have offspring at all, and when they did so ille-
gitimately the offspring were not supposed to inherit land, which left state or
church appanages intact. This too required the regular importing of fresh recruits. The most famous Muslim example, the Mamluks of Egypt, defeated
both the European crusaders, including the military orders, and the Mongols
in the thirteenth century. In the long term, the system suffered from built-in
obsolescence. After two or three centuries, slave soldiers established their own
lineages and appanages, and acquired local allies. They could then dominate,
or even replace, the relevant sultan. They had often lost their military edge by
this time, though a new regime could begin a fresh round of recruitment.

By no means was all Islamic expansion a matter of conquest. A "monumental eighth–ninth century global trade offensive" by seaborne Arab and Persian
merchants made converts peacefully, as well as boosting commerce.[61] "On
coasts Muslim communities took root in innumerable locations, from Gujarat
to Malabar, Coromandel, Sri Lanka, Bengal, the Malay–Indonesian archipelago and China; and everywhere their raison d'être was trade."[62] The voluntary
conversion of rulers to Islam became quite common from the tenth century.[63]
Another factor behind Islam's success was its power of what one might call
"co-option": the full and willing incorporation of the conquered or converted.
Arabs were soon supplemented by Syrian, Berber, and Persian soldiers, and
later by many varieties of Turkic and European converts. The Koran forbids
forced conversion, and despite spasms of persecution, Islam was relatively
tolerant of related creeds, notably Judaism and Christianity, as long as they
accepted subject status. Conversion of subject populations was usually voluntary and quite slow, often involving the adoption of the Arabic language.[64]
Other conquerors, such as the Spanish in the Americas from 1500, also converted their new subjects, at least nominally, and spread their language. But
these converts were not fully *coopted*: they remained second-class citizens at
best, even if they had some Spanish blood. Arab migrants, whether merchants,
soldiers, or holy men, were males usually unaccompanied by wives or female
kin. They married foreign women and converted them to Islam, with the offspring considered as Muslim as anyone.[65] While Arabs were favoured for a
time and real or alleged descent from the Prophet's own family always conferred prestige, new converts, part-Arab or not, could often join the elite, even
becoming chief ministers. Here was an expansion which subjects could join,
as something close to full citizens.

Some historians suggest that steppe nomad empires and neighbouring sedentary empires like China "mirrored" each other, expanding and adapting in

response to each other. A similar mirroring can be suggested for Christian Europe and its Muslim neighbour, who from an outsider's viewpoint might seem the Terrible Twins of West Eurasia. Unlike China and India, which had the attraction option, they globalised through expansion, and to some extent mirrored each other. The shared origins of Christianity and Islam are obvious, perhaps blindingly so—not just shared monotheism but the self-same God, not just the same subglobal world, but the same Middle Eastern region of origin. Christians originally saw Muslims as "slightly weird co-religionists", and the two shared churches for a century or so.[66] Perhaps less obvious is the way in which, the Americas aside, modern European expansion tracked the earlier expansion of Islam: to West Africa for gold and slaves, East Africa for slaves and ivory, India for cotton and pepper, Southeast Asia for spices, and China for silk and porcelain. Lord McCartney's refusal to kowtow to the Chinese emperor in 1793 echoed that of a Muslim Arab delegation a thousand years earlier.[67] Expanding Europe's local allies were often those seeking to compete with local Muslim polities, or those chafing at the bit of a Muslim elite. The Twins' methods were also similar—a varying mix of conquest, commerce, and conversion.

Our understanding of Europe's divergence needs this backstory of its precursors. It helps un-reify, or "de-exceptionalise", European history, but also enriches it. The various globalisations and divergences overlaid each other like a palimpsest, where texts are written over older texts. The trend to convergence through emulation did not homogenise, though most princes did wear silk, dispense gold, and ride horses. Shared menus of biotechnology could be combined with local variables in almost infinite ways. The stubborn particularity of local, regional, and culture-specific histories persisted. Global history can re-contextualise, challenge, and enhance them, but it can never replace them, nor should it try. There was a ragged trend to greater scale, because new divergences tended to build on the old. But this was not some inexorable march of culture-centric Progress. Divergences initially privileged the divergent culture group, but not necessarily in the long term. The leading beneficiary of the Levantine farming package was not the Levant itself, but the Fertile Crescent civilisations to the south, just as European industrialisation has flourished most in North America, and may yet reach full flower in East Asia. Furthermore, the backstory enables this book to attempt a non-Eurocentric explanation of modern Europe's remarkable spread and growth.

PART I

A Plague of Mysteries

FOR ALL WEST EURASIA's underestimated cohesion, traditional divisions remain important: Western Europe, dominated by Latin Christianity, Eastern Europe, mostly dominated by Orthodox Christianity, and what we will risk calling the "Muslim South", comprising the Middle East, North Africa, and varying chunks of southern Europe (see map 2). It was the Romans who came closest to uniting the three regions. Their empire included most of Western Europe and much of what became the Muslim South, except for Iran and Arabia. In addition, their economic and cultural "world" reached deep into Eastern Europe.[1] In the fifth century CE, Western Europe "escaped from Rome"[2] only to fall victim to other invaders, some from outside West Eurasia, some from its own non-urban margins. Among the former, Huns and Alans led the way, with the related Hepthtalites, or "White Huns", devastating much of Iran. Among the latter, Germanic invaders predominated, great gangs whose names suggest they were newly formed for the purpose: Franks ("Brave Men"), Allemanni ("All Men"), and Goths (just plain "Men").[3] These "barbarian" invasions are well-known. What is less well understood is that they did not stop with the dismemberment of the Western Roman Empire, but continued to afflict West Eurasia for a thousand years, before suddenly ceasing around 1400.

Slavic groups, possibly from the northern Ukraine, dispersed throughout Eastern Europe from the sixth century.[4] Turkic Avars and Bulgars from the steppes carved domains along the Danube and the Volga in the sixth and seventh centuries, reaching a peak in the ninth to eleventh centuries. A succession of Turkic groups invaded the Middle East, or took over regimes they had served as "slave" soldiers, culminating in the empires of the Kwarczmshahs and the Seljuks—the latter inflicted a disastrous defeat on the Byzantines in 1071, which helped prompt the Crusades.[5] In the ninth and tenth centuries, Finno-Ugric Magyars from the steppes seized Hungary, and raided Western Europe as far as Spain and Italy. Scandinavian Viking raids, trades, and settlements flourished at the same time, going east and south down the Russian river system as well as west across the ocean, reaching the Mediterranean and Caspian Seas, as well as Iceland and Greenland. A second pulse of Islamic expansion joined the action, seizing the Balearic Islands, Crete, Sicily, and parts of Southern France in the ninth and tenth centuries.

The greatest invasion of all, and almost the last, was that of the Mongols, led by Chinggis (Genghis) Khan. He united the Mongol tribes, who even so totaled only one million people, in 1206, and created a vast empire stretching deep into all four old worlds. The Mongols and their subject allies, Turks in particular, conquered the Middle East, including Iran; the European steppes, in what is now southern Russia and the Ukraine, and Kievan Rus', in northern Russia between 1220 and 1260. Kievan Rus' was "highly urbanized by the standards of contemporary Europe"—indeed it has been described as a loose confederation of city-states.[6] It was more prosperous, and more integrated into the European economy further west, than was once thought.[7] The Mongols also devastated Hungary, together with parts of Poland and the Balkans, reaching the Adriatic in 1242.[8] They did not invade Western Europe, perhaps because it lacked the necessary vast pastures for their horses,[9] and they bounced off the formidable Mamluks of Egypt, so sparing North Africa as well. The Mamluks continued to prosper (see chapter 8), despite frequent succession crises. By 1345, they controlled Greater Syria, including Palestine (the Christian Holy Land), and also the Hijaz (the Muslim Holy Land). Further west, in the Maghreb, the Moroccan Marinid Dynasty, which had replaced the Almohads in the previous century, mounted a last invasion of Spain in the 1330s. Their rivals included the wealthy Hafsid Dynasty of Tunis, home to the greatest historian of the period, Ibn Khaldun, both of whose parents fell victim to the Black Death.[10]

The Mongol empire soon segmented into four khanates—the great khanate of China and Mongolia, the Central Asian Chagatai khanate, and two in West Eurasia: the Ilkhanate and the Golden Horde. The former was based on Iran, and fragmented in the 1330s into various polities, mostly Turkic. The Horde, based on the European and Kipchak/Kazakh Steppes, was overlord of northern Russia, and often of states in the Balkans too. Though it is hard to tell from the history books, it was Europe's largest and most powerful polity, 1260–1350, and perhaps its most urbanised too. It featured between 100 and 140 towns, including a string of cities up the Volga: from Astrakhan on the Caspian to Kazan in the Middle Volga. Its capital was New Sarai: "conservative archeologists

estimate its population in the first half of the fourteenth century at around
100,000".[11] The Byzantine Empire was already in steep decline before the
Mongol advent. In 1204, an off-course Christian crusade had sacked Constantinople, its great capital—historians still almost come to blows over who
was to blame.[12] The Byzantines survived, and regained the rump of their
empire in 1261, but were thereafter no more than a regional power. The Mongol invasions were undeniably devastating.[13] While many empires deployed
exemplary terror to discourage resistance, they were masters of this dire art.
They are said to have destroyed 180 out of 200 towns in Central Asia, and to
have reduced the population of Hungary by anywhere between 15% and 50%
in only two years.[14] Yet they did not inaugurate a dark age for the conquered
regions. Economic and demographic recovery, with some exceptions in
West Central Asia, began within decades, along with some cultural absorp-
tion of Mongols by their subject peoples.[15] Both khanates converted to Islam
by the early fourteenth century. After initial disruption, the Mongols rewired
and perhaps intensified West Eurasia's overland connections with the other
three old worlds.[16]

While few rank them with the Mongols, some historians see Western Europeans too as high medieval expansionists, or at least as laying the ground-
work for later expansion. "There is a consensus in historical scholarship",
claims a book named *Why Europe?*, "that many of the developments typifying
Europe's 'special path' (*Sonderweg*) arose in the eighth and ninth centuries".[17]
Others say that it was the tenth or the twelfth century in which "the foundations of Europe's future predominance were laid", which rather undermines
the consensus.[18] It might be true that "between 950 and 1350, Latin Christendom roughly doubled in area".[19] But this was mostly due to the voluntary conversion of Slavic, Magyar, and Scandinavian princes, and could be seen as part
of a wider emulation of monotheism by monarchs who equated one god with
one king, or felt a need to fight like with like. We have noted that various rulers
voluntarily took up Islam beginning in the tenth century. The Khazars and the
Uighurs respectively adopted Judaism and Manichaeism in the eighth
century.[20]

Latin Christendom's expansion by force was actually modest and took place
mostly within Europe. Castile reconquered most of Andalusia in the thirteenth century, leaving the rich but small emirate of Granada as the last vestige
of Muslim Iberia. German eastward expansion (*Ostsiedlung, Ostkolonisation*)
has been exaggerated in legend.[21] It did create a remarkable religious state,
under the Teutonic Knights, in northern Poland (Prussia). But this was small,

with a total population of 220,000 in 1300.[22] The knights' expansion was more than matched by that of their chief rival, Lithuania, which was neither western nor Christian. It remained a powerful pagan holdout until 1386, when its prince converted in exchange for the crown of Poland. The adoption of German civic law by Slavic cities did not imply German control. The most substantial attempt at expansion outside Europe was the crusades to the Levant, 1098–1250.[23] In these, Latin Christendom did show impressive power, commitment, and cohesion for so politically fragmented a region, mustering large armies, sustaining them overseas, and establishing four small settler states. But the crusaders failed in the end, defeated by Saladin in the late twelfth century and stamped out by the Mamluks in the thirteenth. The last Latin stronghold, Acre, fell to the latter in 1291. The loss of the Holy Land haunted Latin Christians for centuries, their own special Original Sin. Over a longer period and on a much smaller scale, Europe's other overseas settlement, Norse Greenland, also failed. If Latin Europe did have a "special path", it led nowhere in terms of expansion before 1350.

On the other hand, contrary to old legends of a long "Dark Age", Western Europe did feature economic and demographic growth and political development in the two or three centuries before plague. The influence of the pope and the Holy Roman Emperor had declined by the early fourteenth century, but remained substantial. French court culture had widespread influence. Western Europeans were known to Muslims as "Franks". Historians may now be "jettisoning the intellectual strait-jacket imposed by the feudal construct,"[24] yet at least one core meaning of feudalism is still useful, inside and outside Western Europe: service in return for land tenure. Unfree serfs worked the lord of the manor's demesne in return for small plots of their own. Warriors provided princes with military service in return for manors. Still, feudalism was never the whole story. Much economic development was led by city-states, which are often said to have mounted a "commercial revolution" in the twelfth and thirteenth centuries. Dense urban clusters flourished in Northern Italy and the southern Netherlands (now Belgium). The Hanseatic League of German merchant cities traded vigorously in the North Sea and Baltic, and Italian maritime republics did the same in the Mediterranean and Black Sea, taking the lead over Muslim rivals from the eleventh century.[25] The Muslim South retained an edge over Western Europe in cultural and economic sophistication in the early fourteenth century. But the gap had narrowed substantially compared to 1000 CE, when Cordoba, Cairo, and Baghdad outshone all Christian cities except Constantinople. Furthermore, Western Europe now held a clear lead in people. Its population is thought to have at least doubled between 1100 and 1300. Figures for medieval populations are largely guesswork but, for 1300 CE, 70–80 million for Western Europe, 15–20 million for Eastern Europe (including Russia), and 30–35 million for the Middle East and North Africa may give some idea.

Some historians have argued that Western Europe in the High Middle Ages was a victim of its own demographic success. It was projected into a "Malthusian crisis", they say, in which population outgrew the natural resources accessible to the technology of the day, and demographic collapse became inevitable. The Black Death of 1346–53 merely topped off the crisis, or was even caused by it, with poor nutrition rendering people vulnerable to plague. "The Malthusian position argues that Europe's population by the early fourteenth century . . . was fundamentally unsustainable and the Black Death was simply the agent of an 'inevitable' crisis of human numbers".[26] Historical opinion has turned against this view,[27] but an important study, *The Great Transition* by Bruce Campbell, has revived the idea of a great crisis, if not a Malthusian one. From the late thirteenth century to the late fifteenth, Campbell argues, Europe was afflicted by "a punitive combination of war, commercial recession, extreme weather events and infectious diseases". "Climate's influence was over-arching", in the form of an early Little Ice Age.[28] Others date the main impact of the Little Ice Age to the seventeenth century, when it may indeed have contributed to a climate-led four-horseman apocalypse also involving war, famine, and disease.[29] Key evidence for an early fourteenth-century general crisis, whether climatic or Malthusian, is the "great famine" of 1315–17 followed by the "great bovine pestilence" of 1319–20. The famine killed up to 15% of the population in some afflicted regions, while the pestilence killed up to 62% of cattle.[30] These were indeed heavy blows, but both famine and pestilence were largely restricted to Northern Europe. They could not have paved the way for the Black Death in the rest of West Eurasia, where plague mortalities were similar. Even in the north, the English evidence suggests that both human and cattle populations had recovered their 1315 levels by 1345.[31] On the continent, "a number of studies have indicated that in many regions the population continued to grow in the years immediately before the Black Death".[32]

It might still be true that the most heavily populated parts of West Eurasia were pushing against some ecological limits by 1345. Fertile wastes to convert to prime farmland and such resources as accessible prime timber were becoming scarce in some regions.[33] It is certainly true that economic inequality was extreme. Around 1300, in both England and Piedmont in Italy, "only about 5%

of households enjoyed significant spending power".[34] These tiny elites spent their money on exotic luxuries, on expensive warfare, and on castles and cathedrals rather than economic infrastructure. Peasants, on the other hand, had been "caged" by feudalism, and are said to have become two inches shorter than in the early Middle Ages.[35] Pre-plague Europe, in the main, was starved of capital, infrastructure, and agricultural and industrial equipment, not fertile land or natural resources. At worst, in the most densely populated parts of Europe and the Muslim south, the situation before the Black Death may have verged on that ascribed to China in the eighteenth century and labelled a "high-level equilibrium trap". It was not in fact a "trap" or a "crisis", but a turn to economic "involution", the application of more human labour (and ingenuity) to get more food from the same acreage, leading to little per capita economic growth and much poverty, yet by no means collapse or even population decline. The Black Death was a one-horseman Apocalypse. It did not need fellow riders, or a preexisting "general crisis", to transform the world it struck.

1

The Black Death and the Plague Era

DESPITE 666 YEARS of inquiry, much about the Black Death remains shrouded in mystery. Where was it?—where did it come from, and what parts of the world did it affect? When was it—how long did the second pandemic last, and why did it end? What patterns, if any, do we find in its behavior? How many people did it kill? Even the basic issue of *what* was it remained unclear until very recently. This chapter and the next address these questions. We need to be careful to specify what we are talking about: plague in general; the whole Second Pandemic; or its first terrible strike, the Black Death itself.

I The Black Death

The standard view until 2001 was that the Black Death and all subsequent waves of the Second Pandemic were bubonic plague, whose pathogen is *Yersinia Pestis*. *Y. Pestis* bacteria are common among certain species of wild rodents, such as marmots and gerbils, and their particular fleas. At least 200 species of wild rodents can catch plague, known as "sylvatic plague". Among them, the disease can become enzootic (the rodent equivalent of endemic)—maintained long term, with limited mortality. The habitats of such rodents are known as plague "foci" or "reservoirs". Some have persisted for millennia. Before 1350, natural foci were probably mostly restricted to the Eurasian steppes and their mountainous flanks. Among connected populations of social rodents in such foci today, plague sporadically flares up into epizootics (rodent epidemics). During these, humans occasionally catch plague directly from wild rodents and their fleas, and this was true in the past, but cases are rare and involve few people. "Human plague cases acquired from the bites of wild rodent fleas typically occur singly or in small clusters of cases", and the same is true when people eat infected wild rodents.[1] It is still more rare for plague to spread further—after all, there were only three accepted pandemics in human history. During epizootics, however, a particular population of wild rodents can be decimated or even die out. In these circumstances, their fleas can jump to other hosts if available, including commensal rodents, whose fleas can in turn infect humans. The prime suspect had long been the black rat, *rattus rattus*, and its particular flea, *Xenopsylla Cheopis*. There have been gallant attempts to acquit the black rat, discussed in the next chapter, but for the moment we will assume that it and/or its flea were involved in most plague transmissions to humans.

In human bubonic plague proper, plague spreads through a person's lymph system over a few days after the fleabite and creates the characteristic buboes, typically in the groin or armpits. There are several variants. In primary septicaemic plague, which is rare, the flea bites directly into the bloodstream and kills very quickly, before buboes have a chance to develop. In the secondary pneumonic variant, a bubonic infection reaches the lungs of a victim and can then be spread to other victims by human spittle, as primary pneumonic plague, without the intervention of fleas. These are the three variants usually cited; they were identified as early as 1348.[2] Plague can also be caught by skinning or eating infected animals. In all variants, without modern medicines, most infected people die.

From 2001, the idea that the Black Death was bubonic plague came under increasing fire from revisionist "anti-bubonists". That year, two scholars concluded that: "It is a biological impossibility that bubonic plague had any role".[3] In 2002, for different reasons, another agreed: "the Black Death in Europe, 1347–52, and its successive waves to the eighteenth century was any disease other than the rat-based bubonic plague".[4] Some scientists concurred: "It is almost certain that the Black Death was not a rodent-based zoonosis such as bubonic plague".[5] This view came close to becoming a new orthodoxy, accepted by recent histories of England, Portugal, and the Italian Renaissance for example.[6] A good popular history concluded in 2009 that the "demolition of the case for bubonic plague" had been achieved.[7] Yet the alternative suggestions—anthrax, cholera, typhus, Ebola, some unknown virus—are not convincing. Some scholars continued to insist that it *was* the Bubonic Plague.[8] A third view is that the pathology of the disease is not an issue for historians, and that we should accept that we can never know.[9] But the historical effects of a pandemic depend on its nature, duration, rhythms, and variations, which in turn depend on its pathology, so the matter is not so easily dismissed.

Since 2010, the "bubonists" have struck back decisively. Traces of *Y. Pestis* have been found in an increasing number of samples of DNA from the remains of victims from Black Death burials. A 2010 study concluded that "our data from widely distributed mass plague pits ends the debate about the etiology of the Black Death, and unambiguously demonstrates that *Y. Pestis* was the causative agent of the epidemic plague that devastated Europe during the Middle Ages."[10] The anti-bubonists initially cast doubt on such conclusions.[11] But fresh findings of *Y. Pestis* continue to emerge, as have improved methods of detection.[12] By 2011, it had been found "in ten Black Death burial sites scattered over five countries by using different methodological approaches, and therefore the Black Death undoubtedly was due to the plague agent *Y. pestis*".[13] "Without a doubt, the plague pathogen known today as *Y. pestis* was also the cause of the plague in the Middle Ages".[14] Further finds came from graves excavated in London in 2013.[15] In 2016 another team of scientists concluded that it was "now without any doubt that *Y. pestis* played a major role", and finds continue to be made in late medieval graves.[16] Yet the issues that prompted revision are real. Though wrong, the anti-bubonists have been usefully wrong, a virtue that is also this book's default aspiration. The Black Death did not always behave like the modern pandemic; it killed far more people, for one thing.

Turning back to plague epidemiology, an outbreak jumping from commensal rodents to their humans would likely infect more people than one coming directly from wild rodents. But it could still remain small—a single isolated village, say, which would need to be agricultural to have commensal rats. But if the first infected settlement was linked by human trade to intersecting networks of others, this could expand into a far-flung epidemic. How quickly depended on the mode of trade transport. Chief among the human trades transmitting the pathogen long range was the ship-borne grain trade, carrying hidden rats and/or their fleas. "Although famously omnivorous, black rats prefer grain".[17] The grain-trade sea routes fit well with distribution of plague around the Mediterranean in 1347–48, and with its distribution around coastal northern Europe in 1348–52. The timing of coastal spread matches the average speed of cargo ships—about 40 kilometres a day.[18] A byname for the black rat was "ship rat". One can overstate this case. Medieval trade was typically unspecialised, although the grain trade did come closest. All ships, not just grain ships, would carry grain products to feed their crews and any livestock. Wagons, camel caravans, and riverboats also carried grain in some bulk and might hide rats. We will see that rats could spread plague without human transport. But they did so slowly, and large vessels carrying grain, by sea or downriver, remain the gold standard of plague diffusion. Several recent studies, notably one by Hannah Barker in 2021, confirm this for the launching of the Black Death and also adjust our notions about the location of the launchpad (see map 3).[19]

Ships from the Genoese port of Caffa in the Crimean Peninsula, a major grain exporting region, have long been thought to have first catapulted the Black Death into the Mediterranean, in 1347. The persistent legend that it was literally catapulted into Caffa on a human corpse by a besieging Tartar army has always been unlikely. Barker shows that the Crimean conflict between the Italians and the Tartars of the Golden Horde actually delayed the spread of plague to Europe during 1346, due to trade embargos by both sides. "During this period, numerous people crossed the Black Sea from north to south, but *Y. pestis* did not accompany them. . . . What did not cross the Black Sea from north to south in 1346 was grain".[20] The plague reached the city of Solgat, the regional capital of the Golden Horde in the Crimea, a year before it reached nearby Caffa. It did not get to Solgat by sea, on which the Genoese were dominant, but via the Russian river system, whose middle and lower reaches were then controlled by the Golden Horde. It was reported to have previously reached other Horde cities, from 1345, including Astrakhan at the mouth of the Volga on the Caspian Sea, and New Sarai, 300 kilometres farther up the Volga.

The Volga region, and adjacent lands on the Don and Dnieper Rivers, which flowed into the Black Sea, supplied these cities with grain, which was also exported along with Crimean grain via ports on the Black Sea, shipped by the Italian merchants.[21] Several contemporary sources located the earliest strike in the Volga region, but their "land of Uzbek" has sometimes been mistaken for the land of the Uzbeks, a people who emerged later and farther south and east.[22] They were more likely referring to the domains of Muhammad Uzbek, Khan of the Golden Horde, 1313–41. The Horde's urban spine extended up the Volga north of New Sarai, to Bolgar City and Kazan in the Middle Volga region, which was also a grain producer.[23] In 2019, new techniques of genetic analysis found *Y. Pestis* in human remains excavated in 1979 at Laishevo, 50 kilometres from Kazan.[24] It could be dated only loosely, to the fourteenth century, but was found to be the immediate forebear of the Black Death, differing from it genetically by only the smallest detectable degree, and likely dates to 1345 or soon before. So the Middle Volga replaces the Crimea as the likely point of entry of the Black Death into West Eurasia, with a riverine dispersal southward preceding the maritime one westward. How it got to the

Middle Volga, and where from, are more matters left to the next chapter, where plague history fully engages with plague science.

II Bringing in the Dead

What proportion of the population did the Black Death kill? Let us focus for a moment on the first strike itself, 1345–53, which lasted up to a year in a particular region, and on Western Europe (see map 4). Since 1970, estimates of mortality have varied between 5% and 60% of the population, which is no great help.[25] As noted in the introduction, a death rate of around 30% has long been the standard estimate. Historians are naturally suspicious of higher figures, which seem almost to echo the agonised claims of contemporaries that 90% of their compatriots died. The case for 60% was made by Norwegian scholar Ole Benedictow in 2004.[26] It has been alleged that he was selective in his use of data,[27] and many still prefer the old best guess of around one-third. But, selective or not, the sheer mass of Benedictow's evidence for 60% is impressive, and most of it looks credible. Let us briefly test his case against more recent research.

England has a high density of scholarship on the period and is a useful laboratory for plague history. A 2011 study based on wills finds that "London lost perhaps 55–60 per cent of its population in the first outbreak".[28] The countryside fared no better. "Although the range of mortality between [English] places could be wide," wrote a leading medievalist in 2008, "there was a pronounced tendency for it to cluster between 40 and 60 per cent, with the greatest proportion of manors experiencing death rates of between 45 and 55 per cent."[29] "That the Black Death had an equally devastating effect on more dispersed, rural communities is well documented".[30] A 2007 county history of Suffolk finds that the first strike in 1349 "killed around one-half of the population. . . . Every surviving manorial document from 1349 reveals evidence of the visitation of pestilence, indicating strongly that nowhere escaped its grip".[31] Research on the Bishopric of Durham finds that "mortality during the first outbreak alone averaged approximately 60 per cent".[32] A 2014 publication tells us that, on three manors in Cambridgeshire, populations fell 57%, 70%, and 48% between 1348 and 1350.[33] The death rate for priests in Lincoln was 46.3%.[34] In 2016, archaeologist Carenza Lewis took an ingenious approach to the issue by comparing the number of house sites with pottery fragments in layers dated before and after the Black Death. She organised numerous volunteers to dig almost 2,000 test pits at 55 rural settlements in eastern England, and concluded: "We can now say with some confidence that the pottery-using population across a sixth of England was around 45% lower in the centuries after the Black Death than before".[35] She believes 45% may be an underestimate because settlements that were completely abandoned after 1348 were not included in the study.

We can cross-check these estimates by looking at population levels and taking a longer view, 1350–1500. Medieval statistics are notoriously unreliable, often amounting to a guess based on other guesses. But, in the English laboratory, a team of scholars using recent computer-assisted analysis of a huge multi-manor database has developed a "best guess" for population that looks less unreliable than most.[36] It indicates that the first strike alone reduced the number of English from 4.8 million in 1348 to 2.6 million in 1351, a decline of 46%. Further strikes reduced the English to a nadir of 1.9 million in 1450, a decline on the 1348 figure of 60%. Recovery did not even begin until the early sixteenth century. The Suffolk county history, and a study of the town of Norwich, support these figures.[37] England may not have been typical, but most of its exceptionality lay in the future and I can see no reason to think that it was unusually susceptible to plague.

In fact, recent French, Italian, Catalan, and Scandinavian evidence suggests England *was* typical. Recent revision has lifted France's estimated population in 1328 from 18 million to 21 million.[38] It is generally thought to have been ten million in 1450, a decline of 55%. A 2009 history of France during this period cites considerable evidence of first-strike death rates and concludes that "mortality rates thus appear far higher than the one-in-three figure favoured in older studies, with many surpassing 50 per cent in the worst years . . . urban population decline seems directly comparable in scale to that of the countryside, with drops of around 50 per cent commonly recorded".[39] Recent studies of various Italian regions, from Sicily to Lombardy, support the notion of a halving of populations in the first strike, and little recovery until at least 1450.[40] Tuscan first-strike mortality was "in the order of 50–60%".[41] A 2014 article drew attention to neglected but convincing contemporary estimates for Abruzzo in south-central Italy and Mantua in Lombardy, both indicating 65% mortality in the first strike.[42] "Taken together", concluded a multiauthor 2017 article, North Italian "data indicate a general mortality rate of near or around 60%, similar to France and England".[43] On one modern estimate, Northern Italy's population in 1550 was still 12% below the pre-plague level.[44] One writer in 2010 averaged the first-strike mortality statistics for Spain, Italy, and France, and came up with about 50% which, taking into account normal annual death rates of 2–3% and the escape of a few regions, seems safer than 60%.[45]

England, France, and Italy were densely populated during this time. Scandinavia was just the opposite, with few towns. Yet its plague mortality was similarly high. Recent studies show that in Norway, 56% of farms were abandoned in the early plague era. Farms were often abandoned before the Black Death, and the abandonment rate is not an accurate indicator of population loss.[46] But it is as likely to understate as to overstate, because households became smaller, and because some unpopulated farms continued to be used part-time by surviving neighbours. Norway's population figures are contested, but both high and low sets of estimates show a decline of more than 60% between about 1300 and 1500.[47] Even more farms were abandoned in Sweden, where the yield of a head tax halved immediately after the first strike.[48] Denmark's farm abandonment rates varied regionally, but its population too is thought to have halved.[49] "The total loss of population in the North was probably at the same level as in the rest of Europe".[50]

————

Many historians still claim total or partial exemptions from the plague for particular regions. Most refer to the first strike only, and are not always convincing even for that. Even Benedictow, who debunks most suggestions of exemption, feels that Finland may have escaped, and its plagues did come late. But some 2006 Finnish research states that "plague spread into Finland at least 17 times between the early fifteenth century and 1710".[51] A 2012 analysis notes a consensus that Bohemia missed the first strike, and demonstrates that this is untrue.[52] "At least parts of Bohemia suffered from pestilences of varying but indeterminate intensity" in 1349–50, and from an additional eight strikes by 1415. In 2017, 30 mass plague graves, dating to the fourteenth and fifteenth centuries, were discovered in Bohemia—"the largest set in Europe".[53] So much for Bohemia's plague avoidance. But the 2012 study then proceeded to argue that mortality was modest, using a single strand of evidence: that Prague experienced a boom in public building in the 1350s. It claimed that this constitutes "indirect but overwhelming evidence that Bohemia's largest population centre suffered no mid-century demographic collapse". Indirect evidence can be useful, but not in this case. Counterintuitively enough, many cities well- known to have been hard hit by plague—Paris, London, Bologna, Cairo, Tunis, Granada, Moscow, Novgorod—also had such building booms. Resolving this particular plague paradox is left to a later chapter. The point here is that the "overwhelming evidence" is no such thing.

Suggestions that death tolls in Germany have been "greatly exaggerated" and were as low as 10% for the country as a whole, seem exaggerated themselves.[54] They too use spurts of public-building as a proxy for low mortality. Southern Germany may have escaped relatively lightly.[55] But a late medieval mass grave, complete with *Y. Pestis* DNA, has recently been found in Bavaria. Augsburg was "devastated" by the first strike, and Munich experienced at least 12 strikes to 1496.[56] Farmland was abandoned all over Germany, cereal pollen diminished drastically, and forested areas doubled in some regions in the century after the Black Death, which suggests high rural mortality.[57] Tolls ranging from 40% to 70% for north German cities are accepted by several scholars.[58] The horrific massacre of Jews for allegedly spreading plague is well documented across Germany. One study notes that 218 of 300 German localities perpetrated such pogroms; another counts 303 of 340.[59] The suggestion that Germans killed or expelled their Jews in advance to prevent plague is hard to credit. If you heard that the Black Death was on its way, it would soon be with you whatever you did. A large compilation of evidence shows that numerous German cities were ravaged in 1349–51.[60] Indirect evidence, convincing this time, comes in the form of monasteries suddenly lowering their requirements for replacement priests, even "brothers who had no knowledge of Latin" in Strasbourg, where both plague and pogrom did occur.[61] German death rates were locally diverse, and its overall mortality in the first strike may have been lower than some, especially in the south, but even this region was hit heavily by subsequent strikes.

Claims of partial plague exemption have also been made for Spain. "Plague hit Spain in 1348, and most historians agree that its impact was milder than elsewhere in western Europe. . . . In Castile, the loss of population was probably below 25 per cent and is partly explained by migration to southern Spain".[62] Yet more than 40% of beneficed clerics in the whole of Spain died just in 1348.[63] For the realm of Aragon, there are reports of mortalities of one-half to two-thirds in districts of Catalonia, although for unexplained reasons 25–35% "seems more likely" to the historian who cites them.[64] Taking the longer-term view, a 2017 publication states that "according to the most reliable calculations, in a hundred and fifty years, Catalonia lost 59.69% of its population" and that something similar looks probable for Aragon proper. The Valencia region, with its exceptionally rich irrigated farmland and increasing range of export crops, attracted enough immigrants to remain static.[65] Inland Castile may have suffered less than most regions, though there are some indications to the contrary. At least one Spanish historian finds evidence of great mortality.[66]

Another questions his findings, but also cites a 53% fall in the rents of a monastery in the archbishopric of Toledo between 1338 and 1353.[67] Some Western European regions may have evaded a strike or two, and a few may have had lower than average mortality over the whole period, 1347–1500. These exceptions need to be explained in terms of plague ecology, and the attempt is made later for several regions. But overall the notions of a sudden halving of Western Europe's population around 1350, and of little recovery before 1500, hold up against the evidence.

———

While there are many claims of exemption and lower mortalities, and big gaps in the data, there has never been any question that the second pandemic struck at least parts of Eastern Europe and the Muslim South (see map 6). The domains of the Golden Horde were the first to suffer, as we have seen, and were struck again by at least three more epidemics by 1400. One estimate of the Horde's mortality in the first strike is 45% for its urbanised western regions, with a toll of 75% alleged for the cities of the Crimea.[68] For these regions, "there can be no doubt that the effects of the Black Death on the population . . . must have been equally severe" as in Western Europe.[69] "There is direct and indirect evidence", wrote this expert, Uli Schamiloglu, in 2017, "for the Black Death visiting . . . the Crimea, Saray, Volga Bulğaria, and more generally the towns and cities of the Golden Horde".[70] The Horde's outlying vassals, he thinks, suffered less, because they were more nomadic.

Nomads and semi-nomads are the one possible generic exemption from plague. This exemption was only partial; nomads were less plagued, not unplagued. Even this view was challenged in 2015 by Nükhet Varlık. "Nomads were as much at risk of infection as others—if not more so".[71] She rightly notes that Anatolian nomads interacted regularly with settled folk and that there are well-documented recent cases of North African nomads catching plague. But infection in these incidents was small, even by the standards of the third, modern, pandemic.[72] The peacetime seasonal movement of horse nomad herders does seem likely to have disrupted Second Pandemic plague transmission, for reasons covered in the next chapter—camel nomads may have been a different story. The more common historical opinion, that Tartar, Turkic, Bedouin, and Berber nomads were less plagued than settled people, is based on quite strong contemporary evidence.[73] We will see that there were cases where nomadic groups seem to have had an initial post-plague military advantage over more settled enemies. But it is true that it did not last long, because really successful nomad expansionists clustered into armies, some capable of sieges, and such armies were plague-prone. Nomad conquerors then sometimes became more sedentary themselves, or at least reliant on sedentary subjects for revenue and supply.

Many historians assert that all Eastern Europe was relatively fortunate during the Black Death. "The plague did not strike with the same force as it did in Western Europe".[74] "Poland largely escaped the ravages of the Black Death."[75] This has been attributed to thinner populations, yet this did not help Scandinavia. Much of Poland does seem to have missed the first strike. Early strikes certainly reached its northern coasts, but inland mortality may have been unusually low until about 1400. An archaeological study of northern Poland doubts losses were heavy, though it does find "a close correlation between warfare and settlement desertion and, to a lesser extent, short-lived outbreaks of plague from 1373–1410".[76] But there were no fewer than 81 plague years in Poland by 1550.[77] As for Hungary, the assumption that "the plague was less devastating in Hungary than elsewhere" seems standard, but it is not clear why. The first strike reached it in 1349, killing its queen, and the year was known as "the time of mortality". The second strike, which arrived in 1359, "might well have been more destructive". It killed "many famous barons", four top officials, and many others.[78] "Many Hungarian towns showed an absolute loss of population from the middle of the fourteenth century until the end of the fifteenth".[79] For the rest of Eastern Europe, there is good evidence of similar mortality to the west in the first strike, the Black Death itself. Northern Russia was hit in 1352, beginning in towns close to the Baltic, Novgorod, and Pskov, and reaching Moscow in 1353 (see map 11). "Descriptions suggest that it also had the same ghastly effects on Russian towns as on those further west, killing with frightful efficiency".[80] As elsewhere, the epidemic is often traced through urban chronicles, but was equally severe in the countryside. "That there was a catastrophic decline in the rural population is undoubted".[81] Statistics are hard to come by, but mortality is thought to have been similar to elsewhere. Later strikes were numerous.[82] "The cycles of plague in Russia were roughly equivalent to those in Western Europe".[83]

It has long been clear that plague ravaged the Balkans, and much of the Middle East and North Africa.[84] Dubrovnik (Ragusa), the best-documented Balkan city, was hit by the first strike in 1347. Standard estimates of 25% and 33% have been made for its mortality rate.[85] Yet precise figures give 7,473 dead out of a population of about 15,000 in the city and its immediate surrounds—a toll of 50%. Dubrovnik suffered eight further strikes up until 1400, several more in the fifteenth century, then a last great strike in 1526–27, which took close to a third of its people, but was largely plague free thereafter.[86] Heavy tolls in Greece, Epirus, and Crete can also be documented, during and after the Black Death.[87] Negroponte in Greece, for example, is said to have lost two-thirds of its people in a 1440s strike.[88] The village of Radolibos in Macedonia is also unusually well-documented in the archives of the monastery that owned it. Its population dropped "only" 40%, during 1341–1478, and monasteries were good at repopulating their manors with immigrants. "Several factors suggest demographic change exemplified by Radolibos, was a general trend, not only for Macedonia but also for the Balkans as a whole".[89] In 1347, plague struck Constantinople, and returned ten times by the 1430s.[90] Contemporaries reported that the dead outnumbered the living after the first strike, which we now know is all too possible.[91]

"The Black Death descended on the medieval Islamic world in the mid-fourteenth century with much the same destructive force that it brought to medieval Europe".[92] After the Ottoman conquest in 1453, Constantinople or Istanbul continued to be a plague capital. A strike in 1467 cost the city "at least a third, if not half, of its population".[93] Plague eased in lethality, though not frequency, in Istanbul from the sixteenth century. No fewer than 277 new cemeteries appeared around the city between 1453 and 1595, four times the number of the subsequent 150 years. "It seems that these figures reflect the high mortality afflicted by the numerous great plague outbreaks that took place until the end of the sixteenth century, whereas the next one-and-half century saw less casualties".[94] Outside the city, "the Black Death was a generalized phenomenon in Anatolia beginning in 1347".[95] For Syria, an early source, Ibn Habib, is sometimes said to have reported one-third mortality, but it has been pointed out that he actually wrote "about two thirds of the population died of it".[96] This is by no means the only example of historians arbitrarily reducing high contemporary estimates, automatically assuming that they are exaggerated.[97] After numerous further strikes and some regrowth, the Syrian population in 1500 was less than 60% of the 1346 level.[98] Despite a general downward trend in mortality, very lethal throwbacks continued. Rare hard numbers from a small town near Aleppo indicate "an overall 75% mortality rate" in a 1574 strike.[99] Archaeological evidence of settlement decline shows "marked demographic losses" in Jordan after the first strike.[100] Similar evidence indicates "a great depopulation" in Iraq, "about half of the built-up area was abandoned".[101] "The cycles of epidemics in the Middle East and Europe appear quite comparable".[102]

Egypt was hit frequently, with 17 major strikes to 1513. Again, hard numbers are rare, but the standard assumption of one-third is now being questioned. The numbers of the Mamluk elite fell by a half or two-thirds in the second half of the fourteenth century.[103] A 2005 comparative study by Stuart Borsch concluded that plague in Egypt was as bad as in Europe and "every bit as catastrophic in rural areas as in urban ones".[104] Borsch updated his findings in 2014, concluding that losses were "higher than the one-third estimated by [Michael] Dols", in the classic study of plague in the Muslim South (1977).[105] Cairo, Borsch and colleagues calculate, suffered tolls of 46% and 40% in plagues of 1430 and 1460. "Other studies are revealing that rural population losses were of a similar magnitude".[106] While data on some parts of the Maghreb are scarce, Tunis was clearly hit hard, and plague also reached Morocco and Granada.[107] "In Europe, the plague decimated between 1/8 and 2/3 of the population; similar estimates may be applied to medieval Morocco".[108]

Mecca and Yemen were struck between 1348 and 1351.[109] Early strikes also reached Armenia, Iraq, and Azerbaijan. Some 300,000 people were said to have died in another strike in 1369, in and around the great city of Tabriz.[110] Generally, mortality estimates for these regions are particularly scarce. Dols cautiously accepted the usual guess of one-third, but is right that plague "befell almost the entire Middle East equally".[111] Writing in the 1970s, he could find little evidence for Iran. Most studies of the plague still "fail to mention Iran at all". But Iranian research published in 2018 found 22 major outbreaks in Iran, 1340s–1490s, which "killed people like a fire consuming haystacks".[112] The *Encyclopedia Iranica* notes anecdotal but suggestive evidence of heavy mortality.[113] For example, four out of seven children of a famous poet and religious leader, Fażl Allāh Astarābādī, founder of the Hurufi movement, died from plague in the latter half of the fourteenth century.[114] Like inland Poland, central and southern Iran may have suffered most of their plague losses later than most. The great city of Isfahan had 80,000 to 100,000 people around 1400; only 25,000 a century later.[115] Shared inclusion in the Mongol Ilkhanate and the spread of Persianate culture, along with the conversion of the conquerors to Islam, had integrated Iran with parts of what is now Uzbekistan and Afghanistan. All three countries contributed to the vast province known as Greater Khorasan. Plague reached this region too. There are signs of "a decline in population density" in the later fourteenth century.[116] For the fifteenth century, there are rare numbers for a massive plague strike in an important heartland of Khorasan, the Herat region, which is estimated to have contained 300,000 households. The strike, in 1435, is said to have killed 600,000 people, which would have been about half the population.[117] This strike also hit Samarkand.[118] Another Herat plague took place in 1462, with similarly lethal results.[119] The Second Pandemic, it seems, struck even the furthest reaches of West Eurasia, halving populations deep into the fifteenth century.

III Where Was the Black Death?

Did the Second Pandemic reach beyond West Eurasia? Many writers still assume that plague hit China at much the same time as the west, 1330s–1350s, and some still accept that Europe's Black Death came from eastern China. Pioneer global historian William McNeill fathered the modern version of this view in *Plagues and Peoples* (1976). According to the *Cambridge World History* (2015), McNeill's view was still "broadly accepted", and one of its authors himself asserted that "The Black Death spread from China to Europe in a matter of years".[120] As of 2017, "most scholars believe that the Great Plague or 'Black Death' originated in Southeastern China".[121] Some suggest that it also struck India, West Africa, Ethiopia, and East Africa below the Horn. Was the Black Death a semi-global phenomenon that scythed through all of the great urban cultures of the Old World, beginning in China? This book cannot do justice to this huge question, but cannot evade it either.

Few would suggest transmission across long distances by rodents without unintentional human assistance. Couriers or cavalry, travelling fast and light, are very unlikely to have carried plagued rodents hidden in their saddle bags. Camel caravans, travelling the Silk Routes through Central Asia, are more promising candidates. Camels could catch plague themselves, but the next chapter will argue that they are unlikely to have transferred it very far. Seaborne transmission was common within the West Eurasia, but it too had its limits. Plague did not make it to the Americas (or Madagascar or Australia) until the late 1890s with the mass advent of long-range steamships, though many ships must have started out with it on voyages across the Atlantic over the previous four centuries. Uninfected rats were transferred, as early as 1492.[122] No fewer than 4,000 rats were killed aboard a Spanish ship returning from the Americas in 1622.[123] But *infected* rats were not introduced, because they died before sailing ships could cross wide oceans—the average voyage from Spain to Mexico took 75 days in the sixteenth and seventeenth centuries.[124] "Quarantines" were introduced in Europe from 1377, initially enforced on ships or offshore islets. Thirty days' isolation was tried at first, in Dubrovnik, but it did not work.[125] A longer period of 40 days—from which the word "quarantine" derives—was introduced in Marseilles in 1383. This was more effective, and "the practice spread because it made sense."[126]

It was never entirely effective, because quarantine authorities did not know that they should be sealing off rats and fleas as well as humans and their obvious baggage. But it does support the other evidence that plague, in an isolated and restricted space such as a ship on a non-stop voyage, would burn itself out within 40 days, killing all rats and some humans. It has been argued that the effectiveness of the 40-day quarantine supports the case against the plague being bubonic, because its incubation period in humans is at most ten days.[127] But one should also add the time it takes for fleas to become very infectious (up to 17 days), a delay for the plague to kill off the rats (10 to 14 days), and a fasting period of a few days before fleas jumped to less tasty humans.[128] In all, this does come close to 40 days. Furthermore, as with most infectious diseases, only a small minority of ships from infected regions succeeded in transferring plague. Quarantine records show that in the eighteenth century, during strikes in the Levant and North Africa, plague survived on only 4% of ships reaching Marseilles from the stricken regions—one in 25.[129]

Turning to particular places, recent arguments for the Black Death reaching West Africa from North Africa or Europe face the problems of the vast Sahara and the absence of substantial maritime trade. They are based mainly on the abandonment of large settlements or cities, and plague seldom itself caused such things in West Eurasia. Parts of the region, such as Timbuktu, an important centre of Islamic learning, were highly literate, yet even those arguing for plague's presence concede that: "there seems to be no text or epigraphic inscription describing the occurrence of plague in the second half of the fourteenth century. There is also no mention of a devastating epidemic in later accounts produced by European travellers who came into contact with these parts in the fifteenth century".[130] Indeed, the great Moroccan traveler, Ibn Battuta, who visited Mali in 1352–53, also made no mention of it, even though he noted it frequently while on his way to Mali through the Middle East, Spain, and North Africa.[131] The case for at least a few outbreaks in Ethiopia and coastal East Africa, which did have good maritime connections with the Middle East, is more convincing.[132] But these do not seem comparable to the dozen or more large epidemics that hammered West Eurasia between 1345 and 1500, and the evidence for East African strikes seems strongest for the sixteenth or seventeenth centuries.

The genetic data on the oldest strain of *Y. Pestis* found in East Africa today suggest that the Black Death sent "a long offshoot into East Africa" from

Yemen or Oman, not from India.[133] Like coastal (but not inland) East Africa,[134] India was not short of black rats, and like East Africa, it had a substantial maritime trade with the Red Sea and the Persian Gulf. But wending your way up and down these notoriously tricky waterways after crossing the Arabian Sea normally took 40 days or more.[135] A few exceptional shorter voyages have been recorded,[136] but as we have noted, plague usually required dozens of voyages per transfer. On an earlier journey, Ibn Battuta became ill in India in 1344, but he recovered and did not himself associate his illness with the plague, with which, as we have seen, he became very familiar before writing up his account. Some historians gratuitously made the association for him, an error others have corrected. "There is no concrete evidence that plague infected India" in the fourteenth century.[137] "At present [2011] there is no serious evidence that the Black Death reached India or Southeast Asia".[138] Indeed, there is some serious evidence that it did not. When plague did reach India, in 1615, the Mughal Emperor Jahangir "questioned many learned men and physicians", from whom he concluded "that it was the first time that the disease had occurred in India".[139] A 2018 history of Indian demography concludes, rather reluctantly, that, while "the fourteenth-century Black Death perhaps touched parts of the north-west . . . there is certainly no proof that the infectious disease that caused the Black Death affected the Indian subcontinent". India "did not experience a demographic collapse" in the fourteenth or fifteenth centuries.[140] The particularly problematic case of China must await the next chapter.

IV The Plague Era

"The Black Death" is sometimes used for the first strike alone, and sometimes for the whole pandemic. The former usage is less confusing, but deceptive if taken to imply that major plagues were confined to 1345–53. As noted in the introduction, no subsequent epidemic (also known as a "strike" or "wave") was quite as lethal or universal as the first, but some came close to one or the other. The last major strike in West Eurasia took place in 1835–38, and was restricted to the Ottoman Empire,[141] giving us a "plague era" of almost five centuries. But the pandemic ended earlier in other regions. Detecting patterns is a tricky business. "For the historian, as for contemporaries, the predominant impression left by the local impact of plagues is one of often inexplicable randomness."[142] Six more fourteenth-century strikes hit most of West Eurasia after the Black Death itself, and there were still more in the fifteenth century.

The standard count for Western Europe is 17 epidemics, 1347–1534, and the numbers in Eastern Europe and the Muslim South were similar—perhaps slightly fewer in the former, and slightly more in the latter.[143] Between 1534 and 1683, the standard count is "only" eleven major epidemics for western Europe, to which we could add a widespread strike in Central and Eastern Europe in the early eighteenth century, and a big strike in Russia in the 1770s—making 30 strikes in all for Europe, with an additional two or three in the Muslim South by 1840.

In general, mortalities declined after 1500, strikes diminished in range and frequency, and regional variation increased. There were exceptions to all these rules. A severe epidemic in the mid-seventeenth century covered most of West Eurasia, Turkey to Norway, Russia to Spain, and inflicted mortalities of around 50% in some places. In this period, cities were definitely hardest hit, yet at least a few rural communities and small towns, in Russia, Switzerland, Syria, and England, are also known to have lost half their people.[144] But there is consensus that, overall, the pandemic lost force from about 1500—some say the 1480s, some the 1530s. This correlates with the beginnings of population upturn. So we have a plague era of two halves, roughly 1350–1800, pivoting around 1500. During the early plague era, 1350–1500, plague played few favourites. It tended to kill urban and rural folk alike, although there was a trend over time to more frequent but less lethal plagues in port cities. After the first strike, mortality did vary wildly from place to place, with no obvious geographic and few temporal patterns. Though some recent archaeological research suggests variation by gender and pre-plague health, the differences were slight.[145] In any case, the key health-affecting factors that this research adduces were the Great Famine of 1315–17 and the Great Bovine Pestilence of 1319–20. As noted earlier, both hit hard in Northern Europe only, yet plague mortalities were similar in Southern Europe.[146] Most evidence indicates little variation by gender, class, diet, or—at least for the first strike—age.[147]

One possible exception, suggested by the English laboratory, is that the topmost secular elites suffered least because they could flee faster and farther than anyone else. But elite mortality can be understated because it is sometimes calculated from family trees, excluding the many noble families that died out entirely.[148] The highest English nobility, tenants in chief, are said to have lost only 27% in the Black Death, little more than half the general rate.[149] But plague might have played a nasty trick on them, through another partial exception. Mortalities in districts that had been hit hard in an earlier strike often had low mortality in the next.[150] The few regions and localities that the Black Death itself missed suffered high death rates in the next strike ten or so years later. This may have deceived nobles who had sat out the first strike in one of the few spared regions, into returning to these apparent safe spots, only to find that the second strike was unusually lethal in those locations. An above-average proportion of English tenants-in-chief died in the second strike.[151] These few exceptions aside, the early plague era seems to have been fairly "even-handed" across West Eurasia.

The late plague era was a different matter. After 1500, the disease began to show sharper bias, of several kinds, often killing urban dwellers more than rural, the poor more than the rich, and disappearing at widely different times in different regions. The end of Western Europe's plague era is usually dated to 1650 or 1683, but the last very widespread, though not universal, strike dates to 1703–16. Sometimes thought to have been limited to the Baltic region, it also reached central and eastern Europe, including Poland.[152] Hungary lost 410,000 people,[153] and one small Swedish town lost 75% of its population.[154] There was a famous later regional outbreak, in Provence in 1720–22. Mortalities of 50% and more are well documented for some localities in this outbreak.[155] A less well-known strike hit Messina in Sicily in 1743, killing more than half the population, giving that city a plague era of almost four centuries, 1347–1743.[156] These late strikes ensured that plague remained a lurking nightmare in Western European minds to 1800 and beyond, but it ceased to be a player in the subcontinent's demography by 1720.

In Eastern Europe, Poland seems to have shared the West European pattern, though with a later start. In Russia, the last big local outbreak occurred in and around Moscow in 1770–74, with the city losing 20% of its people.[157] Minor local outbreaks in Russia continued until 1878, when a small strike on the Volga induced some Germans to stop buying caviar for fear of infection, an example of plague's long shadow.[158] But outside the Balkans, Eastern Europe's plague era seems to have ended about 1774. Plague struck the Balkans in 1738 and continued to do so for decades. Most of the area was Ottoman territory in this period, and as this suggests, the southern experience was rather different, though it did share the big shift of the sixteenth century. "After 1517, plague outbreaks affecting Ottoman areas seem to diverge from those affecting the western Mediterranean."[159] As we saw above, Ottoman plague mortality did decline, and Anatolia shared in a widespread sixteenth-century population boom. But from the mid-seventeenth century, the Muslim South was clearly more plague-prone than the rest of West Eurasia. No fewer than 230 plague outbreaks have been counted in the Ottoman capital, Istanbul, over the whole plague era.[160] Most after 1700 had low, even tiny, mortalities, but some did not.

Istanbul lost 15% of its people in a strike in 1705, the same percentage in 1726, and 20% in 1778, with many lesser tolls in between. Similar tolls hit Salonika, and Smyrna suffered even more, losing between 10% and 20% of its population in each of five strikes between 1709 and 1784. There were also substantial strikes in Istanbul in 1812 and, finally, 1836.[161] Egypt was also heavily plagued in the eighteenth century,[162] and the rest of North Africa suffered major strikes in 1792–1821.[163] For the Muslim South as a whole, the end of the plague era measured in major outbreaks seems to have come around 1840.

———

Population levels, of course, are a matter of births as well as deaths. Some economic historians have suggested that the Second Plague Pandemic triggered or consolidated what is known as the "European Marriage Pattern".[164] First detected in 1965 by John Hajnal, it was a tendency to less marriage, later marriage, and fewer births, and was located "west of the line from Trieste to St Petersburg".[165] Many scholars see it as a cause of Western Europe's divergence in economic growth from the rest of the world, permanently reducing the pressure of population on resources, as well as encouraging individualism, nuclear families, and more investment in the education of fewer children. This may or may not be true after 1500—some recent research argues strongly that it was not.[166] What concerns us here is that, for the early plague era, most evidence suggests *increasing* birthrates.

Plague epidemics, including the first, were followed by an upsurge in marriages and births, as bereaved families reshuffled into new ones. Many scholars note this "nuptial frenzy"—an intriguing turn of phrase—and the accompanying "bumper fertility".[167] "The men and women who stayed alive did everything to get married".[168] Rare surviving marriage registers from the town of Givry in Burgundy document the trend quite precisely. Before the Black Death, marriages averaged about 17 a year. After it, in 1349, they rocketed to 86, and stayed higher than average in 1350 and 1351.[169] Statistics from Durham, England, show an even greater increase in marriages from an average of around ten a year to 130 in 1350.[170] This number of marriages among a much-reduced population means an even more spectacular spike in the marriage rate. It was not just a matter of widows and widowers remarrying. "Young people and adults, who had been forced to postpone marriage or resigned to a celibate life, found good vacant tenements everywhere and married in droves all over Europe".[171] An Italian contemporary was indignant at the trend:

When the plague was over, men revived: those who did not have wives took them now. And women who were widowed got remarried. Young, old and spinsters all went this way. Not only these women, but many nuns and sisters threw away their habits and became wives. Many friars ruined themselves to do such things; and men of ninety took spinsters. So great was the rush to remarry that the numbers by the day could not be counted; nor did many wait for Sunday to hold weddings.[172]

Post-plague baby booms were an impressive show of human resilience, creating a "high-pressure" demographic regime where both birth- and death rates were high. Broadly speaking, high birthrates were outmatched by very high death rates during the first few plague strikes. They then ran neck and neck until around 1500, when birthrates at last drew ahead. The high birthrates were annual; the high death rates came from plague strikes every 10 or 20 years, so the tortoise and the hare might be a better analogy than "neck and neck". A population estimate for a year just before a plague strike could give a false impression of long-term recovery. This is supported by new population estimates noted above—for England and Catalonia for example. It is *not* supported by overall population figures. Older estimates give up to 93 million for Europe in 1300 and 78 million in 1400, presumably including Russia, a mere 16% decline.[173] Rather better numbers, now standard (for Europe without Russia), are 79 million in 1300, 54 million in 1350 (after the first strike), with a slight recovery to 57 million in 1400.[174] These indicate declines of 31.5%, to 1350, and 28% to 1400, which suggests they are still based on the old best guess of plague mortality—around 30%—and on the old assumption that recovery began quite quickly. The same assumptions seem to influence the standard estimate for 1500 (76 million), or almost complete recovery. If we replace the old best guess with the new best guess of a 50% decline, and accept that recovery was slow, we would get much lower numbers. The standard figure for the population of England in 1300 is 4.5 million, which is close to that of the multimanor study noted above—4.8 million. But the English component in the standard estimate for Europe in 1500, 3.5 million, is 75% higher than the newer and more convincing one, which is 2 million. If persistent plague mortality on the continent was anywhere near that in England and Catalonia, which seems likely, experts may need to dramatically lower their estimates of Europe's population in the early plague era.

Strong growth did take place in the sixteenth century, and the 1300 population level in Europe might have been restored by 1618, before the seventeenth century was engulfed in a "general crisis" in which plague was only one horseman of an Apocalypse also featuring extensive and intensive warfare, famine, and adverse climate. Regions such as Germany and Poland suffered heavy population declines, in the first and second halves of the century respectively. But, overall, the seventeenth-century "general crisis", which some recent scholarship would argue struck the Muslim South too, slowed growth but did not stop it—Europe's population is thought to have grown about 6% during 1600–1700.[175] The Black Death, on the other hand, halved the population, and the early plague era kept it low for 150 years. We need to recalibrate West Eurasian history to take account of these dreadful new numbers. But first we need to address the remaining plague mysteries by engaging with species unfamiliar to historians, including scientists.

2

The Origins and Dynamics of the Black Death

I Plague Prehistory

Scientific advances over the last 20 years have revolutionised our understanding of the plague pathogen, along two main lines. First, new techniques for extracting and analyzing old *Y. Pestis* DNA from human remains, particularly teeth, have reshaped plague history and pushed back plague prehistory. A plausible evolutionary sequence has been traced out. A form of plague is thought to have diverged from a much milder ancestor, *Yersinia Pseudo-tuberculosis*, perhaps as recently as 3,800 BCE, perhaps earlier.[1] In 2015, *Y. Pestis* was found in the DNA of six human skeletons, who had lived in or around the third millennium BCE. They were scattered across the western steppes and adjacent regions. An ancient epidemic, in the third millennium BCE in Eastern Europe and the Eurasian steppes, has therefore been suggested.[2] But plague likely evolved its full infectivity later. Full plague's earliest known victim was thought to be an Armenian whose death is dated to 950 BCE.[3] Some 2018 research came up with an earlier victim, found near Samara on the Lower Volga and dated to 1800 BCE.[4] Small outbreaks of plague, and even one-off epidemics, are therefore possible before the beginning of the first pandemic in 541 CE. But two prime candidates, the "Plague" of Athens, 430–426 BCE, and the "Antonine Plague" of 165–180 CE, are now generally attributed to other diseases. In any case these were one-off epidemics, not pandemics in our sense of a succession of epidemics over centuries.

The second line of advance in plague science involves "genomic" (whole genome) analysis, which can identify small changes in *Y. Pestis* DNA, old or new, isolated from humans or rodents. These changes are measured in single-nucleotide polymorphisms, or SNPs. Bacterial diseases mutate less rapidly than viruses, and the scientists emphasise that plague remains relatively homogenous. "Recent emergence has led to an overall lack of genetic diversity",[5] so we should not assume sudden major shifts in the behaviour of the pathogen. It is the genetic homogeneity of Second Pandemic *Y. Pestis* that has undermined the thesis that each epidemic after the Black Death entered separately from outside West Eurasia.[6] But SNPs do allow the identification of *Y. Pestis* strains or lineages, their very approximate age, and their relationship to each other in terms of ancestry and descent. Since 1951, three main plague lineages, or "biovars", have been commonly identified: *Antiqua*, *Medievalis*, and *Orientalis*, associated with the First, Second and Third Pandemics respectively. Since 2008, this typology has been convincingly challenged, and is now being replaced, or combined with, a "Branch" typology which is enough for our purposes.[7] Branch O emerged around 200 CE and is thought to have been responsible for the First, Justinianic, Pandemic.[8] In 2013, important research led by Yulong Cui established that Branch O later underwent a "polytomy", a sudden branching out of new variants, at some time between 1142 and 1339.[9] Four new branches sprouted out, designated One to Four, and other research has shown that Branch One was responsible for both the Second and Third Pandemics.

Cui's team thought that the vast Qinghai-Tibet Plateau in what is now China was likely the region in which *Y. Pestis* first evolved. But research since 2017 suggests that "all highly virulent *Y. Pestis* strains had their origin in the Tien Shan mountains",[10] which lie mainly in present-day Kyrgyzstan. Whether or not this is true of prehistoric plague, the ancestors of both the First and Second Pandemics do seem to have come from the Tien Shan, which house active plague foci to this day. The main host is, and probably long has been, the grey marmot (*Marmota baibacina*).[11] This rodent is very susceptible to plague, and epizootics in the present can kill off whole populations of them, which makes plague's persistence over millennia something of a mystery. It has been argued that the plague pathogen survived in the deep burrows of extinct marmots, awaiting marmot recolonisation from elsewhere.[12] Laboratory experiments have shown that *Y. Pestis* bacteria can indeed survive in soil, but only for a year or so. *Y. Pestis* on plagued fleas whose hosts have died have a similar maximum lifespan, and the intervals between epizootics can be much longer than this.[13] Other experiments have found it very hard indeed to infect mice with plagued soil, "suggesting that this route of contamination is unlikely to sustain epizootics".[14] "Maintenance hosts", other wild rodent species that live

MAP 3. West Central Asia: The Origin of the Black Death and Its Transfer to Europe

near marmot niches but are less susceptible to plague, seem a more promising persistence mechanism—caretaking orphaned *Y. Pestis* while the marmot population renews.[15]

Whatever the reasons for its durability as a plague focus, the notion that the Tien Shan was the source of the Black Death has some historical support. These mountains almost surround Issyk Kul, a lake about 180 kilometres long. The fertile Chu River valley running north-east from near the lake prevents complete encirclement. In 1885, in this valley, a Russian archaeologist found "the only evidence we have of a possible plague outbreak in the steppes before the reports from the Crimea in 1346".[16] He examined two cemeteries of Nestorian Christians, whose deaths clustered in 1338–39, and were attributed to "pestilence" on a few headstones. The attribution might refer to another disease, but there are other signs of plague. The 650 recorded deaths averaged around four per year for more than 150 years, but jumped 26-fold, to 106, in 1338–39. Plague is just about the only disease that features this big a leap in mortality. The two Nestorian villages were tributary to the nomadic

Chagatai Khan, who sometimes held court nearby. But they themselves were agricultural sedentary settlements. This, and the scale of the outbreak, suggest to me that it came, not directly from grey marmots, but via commensal rats, a species of which (*Rattus Turkestanicus*, also known as *Rattus Pyctoris*) had been in the wider region since at least the eighth century CE. [17] A study by Philip Slavin, of Issyk Kul as the Black Death's Ground Zero, is not convinced that such circumstantial evidence amounts to much.[18] Yet the timing, location, and scale of the grave inscriptions are all just right. An unconnected but very similar surge in deaths is recorded on Middle Volga gravestones around 1360, and this was certainly associated with plague.[19] It was noted many years ago that Ibn al-Wardi, the best informed of contemporary chroniclers, "makes the clear assertion . . . that the disease came from inner Asia where it had attacked the Uzbeks and the Khitai. The precise location of this region is unclear".[20] We saw in the last chapter that the former was probably the territory of the Golden Horde. The Qara Khitai occupied parts of the Tien Shan region as vassals of the Chagatai, so Al-Wardi may have got it right.

In any case, the Tien Shan has quickly gained considerable acceptance among scientists as the source of the Black Death pandemic. The easternmost ranges extend into what is now westernmost China, so it could still be true that "the Black Death began in China", but only in a technical and deceptive sense. Whether the Black Death *reached* Central or Eastern China is of course another matter, as is the question of how it reached West Eurasia, presumptively at Laishevo, 3,000 kilometres away.

II Mongols and Marmots versus Gerbils and Camels

While the view that the Second Pandemic began in eastern China is still widespread, some scholars have recently inclined against it. A 2011 study found that "a close examination of the sources on the Delhi Sultanate and the Yuan Dynasty provides no evidence of any serious epidemic in fourteenth-century India and no specific evidence of plague among the many troubles that afflicted fourteenth-century China".[21] A 2015 economic history of China noted "a conspicuous lack of evidence for pandemic disease on the scale of the Black Death in China".[22] A 2019 analysis notes lethal diseases in China between 1333 and 1353, but also that "the evidence does not suggest, at least at present, that these mortality crises were caused by plague".[23] But, since 2014, the scholarship on plague in China has taken yet another turn, with a thesis developed separately but mostly compatibly by two able historians, Robert Hymes and

Monica Green. Essentially, they argue that the Black Death was preceded and made possible by a thirteenth-century proto-plague, spread by the Mongol invasions to both China and the Middle East. They were struck by the fact that the time range Cui and Co. posited for the pre–Black Death polytomy, 1142–1339, neatly straddled these invasions. In 2014, Hymes proposed that:

> at least some of the existing rodent reservoirs in China and the rest of Eur-asia were established by the movements of Mongol armies . . . [and] that we may need to place the "beginnings of the Black Death" more than a century earlier than we have been accustomed to . . . the expanding Mon-gols were the agents of plague's spread.[24]

Mongolia had marmots, though not yet plagued ones, and the Mongols were partial to marmot meat and fur. Early in their expansion, suggests Hymes, "the Mongols first encountered plague-bearing rodents, probably marmots, whose flea and bacillus hitchhikers they then transported into [northern] Jin and later [southern] Song China".[25] He puts the encounter at the edge of the Qinghai-Tibet Plateau about 1211, but might accept Green's tweak to 1216 and the Mongol invasion of the Tien Shan region. In her 2020 analysis, Green tagged the four branches of the polytomy as "the Four Black Deaths", and argued:

> That the Mongols, having stumbled upon a population of plague-infected marmots in their initial incursions into the area around the Tian Shan moun-tains, went on to create a connected marmot enzootic landscape, seeding the disease in marmot populations in areas quite distant from the Kyrgyz-stan range [and] that the transmission of plague westward to the regions south and north of the Caucasus can be plausibly assigned to the thirteenth century, instead of the traditional chronology tying it to the Black Death outbreaks of the 1340s.[26]

Building on the work of Chinese scholars, Hymes finds indications of plague in the records of several Mongol sieges of cities in China, notably that of Kaifeng in 1232, as does Green for some sieges in the Middle East, notably that of Bagdad in 1258. Both are well aware that infectious diseases of many kinds were common in sieges. But they note that some of these sieges involved mortalities of 40%, which few diseases other than plague achieve, and that they shared a peculiarity also common to the siege of Caffa in 1347. The disease outbreak began, not inside the city, but among the besieging Mongols, and spread to the citizens only after the siege was lifted—that is, it was brought by the Mongols, and did not develop, as normal, from insanitary conditions and tainted water and food supplies among the besieged. Hymes has found another intriguing line of evidence. At about the same time as the early invasions, a new term suddenly appeared in the Chinese medical literature: *geda*, a bubo-like swelling or nodule in the neck. Hymes's thirteenth-century Chinese sources, however, always find *geda* on the head or neck, and not in the armpits or groin, which is where *Y. Pestis* buboes were most often noted. "Laymen in fourteenth-century Europe and seventeenth-century India and China readily identified these".[27] As a Shanxi gazetteer reported, in 1644, when plague did arrive in China:

> In the autumn there was a great epidemic. The victim first developed a hard lump below the armpits or between the thighs or else coughed thin blood and died before they had time to take medicine. Even friends and relations did not dare to ask after the sick or come with their condolences. There were whole families wiped out with none to bury them.[28]

Hymes goes on to suggest that plague persisted, or repeatedly re-emerged, in China throughout Mongol rule of China, as the Yuan Dynasty, until 1368, perhaps in the form of a long pandemic.

Apart from the siege accounts and some references to epidemics of unspecified infectious disease, the literary sources are strangely silent. Hymes and Green acknowledge this, but it is no small matter for two of the most literate societies in the thirteenth-century world—the Southern Sung in China and the Islamic Middle East. The coincidence of the plague polytomy with the Mongol invasions is neither as clear nor as weighty as they believe. The polytomy was, by definition, quite sudden. It took place *at some point between* 1142 and 1339, not over the whole period, or necessarily at its midpoint. In fact, it is the later end that scientists are now finding the more likely. The earliest fourteenth-century Black Death isolates of *Y. Pestis* are only one or two SNPs away from the polytomy, in a lineage totalling 2,326 SNPs, suggesting proximity in time if not space. Green accepts this in a 2018 essay: "A late thirteenth- or early fourteenth-century date for the polytomy seems reasonable".[29] This is far too late for a thirteenth-century Mongol proto-plague beginning around 1216. Further, the pre–Black Death branching is not the only polytomy in plague's history. Another preceded the Justinianic Pandemic, and yet another has been documented in the twentieth century, with little or no human involvement, and not many human victims.[30] A polytomy might feature human agency, but not necessarily so.

The high tolls recorded in sieges might be the cumulative result of disease, starvation, casualties, and massacres. Indeed, the Mongols were not known for kind treatment of stubborn garrisons. They were infamous for the opposite, and the notion of them sharing their food after a long siege is at least questionable. How that food might have become infected with plague is another issue. The grey marmot is not a tiny animal—adults average about 5.5 kilograms—so live transfer hidden in human cargoes is improbable.[31] Outside burrows, wild rodent fleas, or very infectious commensal rodent fleas would not normally survive long without hosts.[32] *Y. Pestis* bacteria also seem unlikely to have survived in processed marmot fur or cured meat transferred over long distances. Pneumonic person-to-person transmission was possible, but would not transfer plague far because incapacity to travel and death happened so quickly. Aware of all this, Green posits an alternative, more plausible, transfer mechanism, by live commensal rodents (likely rats because mice are poor plague transmitters) or their fleas hitchhiking in the food supplies of Mongol armies. Yet armies without access to the sea preferred to source their food from as nearby as possible, by purchase, pillage, or extortion. They would normally cart in bulky supplies such as grain only when the region in which they were campaigning had none, which was not the case in 1250s Iraq. Green may have found an exception. The Tien Shan was not generally a grain exporter at the time,[33] but the Mongols in the Middle East might have drawn on it for a prized type of millet. But could the *Y. Pestis* bacillus have survived the overland journey of about 3,000 kilometres—120 days by camel, perhaps 200 by the ox wagons of which the Mongols made more use?[34] This matter is considered further below.

Green acknowledges that in West Eurasia "the initial spread of plague, in 1347–1348, was clearly a function of maritime transport and urbanised networks of trade. In contrast, it is likely that plague outbreaks in Mongol areas were only rarely epidemic, let alone pandemic". Hymes is not so sure. There were massive declines in the Chinese population in the thirteenth and fourteenth centuries, and while fully acknowledging that there were other factors, he believes these were large enough to accommodate bubonic plague too. The reliability of the statistics is contested, but they actually seem rather better than those for most of Europe. On Hymes's preferred figures, China's population dropped from 108 million in 1208 to 75 million in 1292, a decline of 30%.[35] This was the period of the devastating Mongol conquests, featuring massacres, floods, and famine as well as non-plague diseases. Depopulation was increased by the Mongol extraction of slaves, vassal soldiers, and artisans.

The population then rose modestly, to 87 million by 1351 before falling again to 67 million in 1392, a decline of 23%. This was the period of the dynastic Yuan-Ming transition, well- known to have been only a notch less catastrophic than the Mongol conquest. These figures seem too low to accommodate, in addition to all the other catastrophes, a plague pandemic of the kind outlined in the last chapter, where populations declined 50% and remained low for 150 years.

———

My own preferred hypothesis also meshes wild rodent and human agency, in this case not marmots and Mongols, but gerbils and camel caravans. Connecting the Tien Shan plague source to West Eurasia 3,000 kilometres away is an unusual historical problem, in that the explanation *needs* to be quite unlikely. Plague, it now seems, only made the journey twice in 800 years, 540s and 1340s, and never after. While the First Pandemic is outside this book's brief, an explanation offered for the Second Pandemic's transmission should have some chance of working for the Justinianic Pandemic as well. The trick is to explain not only how the pandemics began, but also why they were so rare.

Like commensal rats, wild rodents can spread plague overland themselves, but normally only slowly. In early twentieth-century North America and South Africa, sylvatic plague spread at around 25 kilometres per year.[36] Central Asia has an exception to this rule of slow sylvatic spread, the great gerbil (*Rhombomys Opimus*), "the most resistant rodent to *Y. pestis* among the known [plague] reservoirs", suggesting long experience with the disease.[37] The term "great" is relative. It weighs 385 grams or ten ounces. But it does live in great constellations of burrows on the steppes. The burrows have "several hundreds to thousands of entry openings and tunnels up to 100 meters in length, with all tunnels connected; distributed in island-like patterns".[38] Although some studies claim that great gerbils, like grey marmots, seldom stray far from their burrows, others assert that they stray frequently. "One study in Uzbekistan found that 42.8% of female great gerbils and 100% of males switched colonies at least once during a year, potentially spreading *Y. pestis*".[39] Young animals migrate in summer "over distances up to 18 km".[40]

Great gerbils have "highly variable susceptibility to *Y. pestis* infection, which makes this species an ideal reservoir".[41] Plague normally recycles quietly in enzootic form, with limited gerbil mortality. "Usually, about a third of animals in a given plague spot are infected, and roughly half of them will die from the infection".[42] But as with other wild rodents, epizootics occasionally flare up. "In places of epizootic development, 90–100% of gerbils may be infected".[43] What triggers such epizootics is not altogether clear. It could be an unusually high *Y. Pestis* or flea burden, a physical weakening in the gerbils due to low food supplies after big population growth, or the introduction of a slight variant of *Y. Pestis* from another wild rodent species, such as the grey marmot, perhaps also involving intermediate host species like the Eurasian ground squirrel. Grey marmots and great gerbils have different ecological niches, but these closely approach each other in many places around the Tien Shan. A big radiation of plague, seeding new plague foci, and featuring gerbils and ground squirrels, has been documented in the twentieth century. It too featured a polytomy and stretched from the North Caspian region across Western Kazakhstan.[44]

There is other evidence that great gerbil plague epizootics spread faster and farther than others. In the Junggar (Zhungar) Basin in China, adjoining the Tien Shan, 50 years of surveillance before 2005 detected no plague in the local great gerbils. That year, the first case was discovered and plague among Junggar gerbils was widespread within seven years.[45] A study of plague spread among great gerbils in Uzbekistan in 1961–66 found that it moved at an average of 50 kilometres per year, implying a still higher top speed. Uzbekistan, Turkmenistan, and northern Iran today host great constellations of great gerbil burrows, which may be of interest to historians of the First Pandemic. But Kazakhstan hosts even more. The species is not abundant in mountainous Kyrgyzstan, but that country does share a long border with Kazakhstan, which in the fourteenth century was known as the Kipchak Steppe, the eastern half of Golden Horde territory. "In Kazakhstan 39% of territory (1.4 million square km) is the area of plague natural foci".[46] In this huge territory, "burrows of the great gerbil are omnipresent in the landscape".[47] They stretch from Lake Balkash in the southeast to the Uralsk region in the northwest, and modern gerbil epizootics tend to spread on this axis along "plague corridors", or connected constellations of gerbil burrows.[48]

My suggestion, then, is that a gerbil epizootic in the 1320s or 1330s, perhaps also involving a multi-species super-epizootic, spread plague unusually far and wide from the Tien Shan north-westward across Kazakhstan. But this is unlikely to be enough of an explanation in itself for the Black Death reaching both Issyk-kul, in 1337–38, and the Middle Volga in 1345. It seems improbable that great gerbil burrows could be literally contiguous across the whole 3,000 kilometres between these locales, or that the species could transmit plague this far quite this fast. It is here that camel caravans enter the picture. In arid lands, away from the sea and from navigable rivers, camel caravans are the obvious candidate for long-range transmission of plague. It was long assumed that it was they that brought in the Black Death from China, along one of the Silk Routes. A problem with this is that camel caravans carried their crews' food supplies as well as their cargo in modestly sized sacks, packs, or panniers slung on the camels. It was obviously much more difficult for live rats to hide in these than in corners of the holds of ships or big riverboats, or even large wagons, and such containers would noticeably leak grain once a rat had gnawed into them. Live rat fleas without their rats, discussed below, are more plausible, but I think the most likely transmitter was the camel itself.

Camels can catch plague but Bactrian camels at least are quite resistant to it, which may suggest long acquaintance. Kazakhstan is a possible site of Bactrian domestication 4,500 years ago.[49] *Y. Pestis* usually either fails to infect them, or they catch a mild form of plague from which they recover, but a few do die.[50] Consuming infected camel meat is the main way in which humans catch plague from camels. Before modern treatment, plagued camel feasts led to human mortality of up to 90%, which would have brought any caravan to a sudden stop.[51] Camels contract plague from wild rodent fleas, and in the twentieth century Bactrians did so, particularly in Kazakh gerbil country. They do not graze near gerbil burrows, because the gerbils will have eaten the vegetation,[52] but they do sleep on them. "Camels in the desert prefer to lie down for their night's rest on the sand or earth which has been loosened and made friable by rodents (gerbils) round their burrows. The camel sometimes covers with its body a number of the openings of rodent burrows, which contain hundreds of fleas".[53] If the gerbils had been recently exterminated by plague, their fleas would be eager for a new host. Most camels would be uninfected, or receive only a mild infection, so its guest rodent fleas would have no cause to leave it. Even a rare mortally plagued camel could last up to 20 days.[54] It might then lie down and die on the burrows of un-plagued wild rodents, to which its hitchhiking rodent fleas would then jump, thereby seeding a new plague focus. Or it could die in a settlement or caravanserai with commensal rats, which wild rodent fleas would have preferred to human hosts, so kicking off a substantial plague outbreak or epidemic. I suspect that this was the way in which both human plague and new natural foci were spread around the inland parts of the Middle East and North Africa during the Second Pandemic. Most natural foci in these regions today are in camel-using lands.

Camel caravans traveled an average of about 25 kilometres a day,[55] so maximum plague caravan range was about 500 kilometres. But, in a terrible form of leapfrog, another caravan could pick up plague in the new focus and extend transmission another 500 kilometres. More than two sequential coincidences of this kind seem unlikely, so camel caravans, like great gerbils, were probably only medium-range transmitters. But between them, they could have carried plague from the Tien Shan to the Middle Volga. This would not have happened often. Wild rodent super-epizootics were rare, "leapfrog" caravan transmission became less likely with each leap, and the region around Issyk Kul usually used donkeys, not camels, as pack animals.[56] But it could happen once or twice. Despite civil strife in the Chagatai Khanate, the two regions were unusually well connected in the 1320s–1340s, due to the outreach of the prospering Golden Horde. As noted in the last chapter, Laishevo in the Middle Volga region, the likely entry point for plague into Europe, was only 50 kilometres from the Horde's most northerly trading city, Kazan. The Middle Volga is within plagued caravan range of Kazakhstan's most north-westerly plague focus today.

III   Rats on Trial

Grey marmots, great gerbils, and camels, then, may have had key roles in getting the Black Death to the Middle Volga in 1345. But the black rat, *Rattus rattus*, whose crucial transmission role in Asia and Africa in the Third Pandemic is well-documented, remains a prime suspect for plague's circulation in West Eurasia in the Second Pandemic, across 30 epidemics and innumerable local outbreaks. Rats and humans are thought to be distantly related, but went their separate ways 80 million years ago.[57] The genetic evidence suggests that the black rat evolved in India and then spread to many parts of the Old Worlds.[58] Throughout this time, family reunions occurred as black rats became the uninvited partners of human farmers. Black rats could survive in the wild, but they preferred to live in luxury at human expense. Rats domesticated humans, not the other way around. It is unclear when *Rattus rattus* pervaded West Eurasia. It had certainly reached the Middle East by 1500 BCE, perhaps earlier.[59] It is thought to have spread through Europe and North Africa with Roman expansion, and this may be true of rat "saturation", meaning rats in almost all urban and agricultural households. But black rat remains dated to about 1000 BCE have been found in Slovenia.[60] At some point in its wanderings, the black rat picked up its characteristic flea, the sub-tropical *Xenopsylla Cheopis*. When rat and flea encountered *Y. Pestis*, the pathogen found them an excellent pairing of host and vector. During the twentieth century, the black rat was therefore seen as the prime villain of plague transmission in all three pandemics. Since then, science and history have worked hard to rescue it from this infamy.

As noted in the previous chapter, bubonist and anti-bubonist scholars have conducted a fierce but useful debate about the identity of plague. Anti-bubonists argued that the black rat cannot have been the chief vector of the Black Death and its after-strikes, for three main reasons, with which many bubonists agree. Bubonic plague is even more lethal to rats than to humans. Indeed, it tends to wipe out connected populations of them.[61] In the third, modern, pandemic, 1890s–1930s, mass rat deaths were sometimes reported. For the Black Death, there are very few convincing contemporary references to dead or dying rats. One anti-bubonist searched more than 400 plague tracts, without finding a single rat.[62] But black rats were the shadow-selves of medieval humans, like "The Borrowers" of the children's story. At an average of 200 grams or seven ounces, they were half the size of the brown rat, with which Europeans are familiar today.[63] They slept during the day, in nests in roofs, eaves, and lofts. At night, they foraged quietly, within and without their humans' house or barn. They were normally unnoticeable, yet normal when noticed, dead or alive. Their lives, in any case, were short. Most black rats are born and die within a single year.[64] Rats were not suspected as plague vectors until about 1900. Even after they were suspected, "in India only eight of forty local epidemics had obvious mortality of *Rattus*".[65] Sick rats tend to keep to their nests, often in roofs perhaps less fragile than those of India or the slums of Hong Kong around 1900.[66] In any case, how remarkable would dead or dying rats have been amidst the rubbish and crowds, animal and human, of a medieval settlement? How long would they have survived the attentions of the hungry carrion birds, cats, dogs, and pigs that constituted medieval rubbish disposal?

The second rat mystery is that their bones are scarce in the archaeological record. A 1986 study, still frequently cited, claimed "that *Rattus rattus* was rare or absent in most of Europe where Black Death spread and hence was not responsible for the epidemic..[67] Only one rat site associated with medieval Novgorod, a frequent victim of plague, had been found by 2011.[68] The same year, the paucity of rat bones in new London digs made the headlines of newspapers, always sympathetic to the under-rat: "Black Death study lets rats off the hook".[69] In 2013, the allegedly low number of rat finds for medieval Norway, with those few restricted to the coast, was interpreted to mean that "rats cannot have been [the] intermediate hosts for *Yersinia pestis* during medieval plague epidemics in Northern Europe".[70] But rat bones are small and fragile. Until recently, archaeologists were not looking for them in particular and used sieves that were not fine enough to capture their bones.[71] "Up till now [2011], archaeologists have not paid much attention to the bones of small animals during excavations of cultural layers of ancient cities and other settlements".[72] Finds like the remains of six rats in the belly of a mummified cat on the Egyptian shore of the Red Sea dated to the first century AD are rare indeed.[73] Since the late 1990s, however, more sites with rat remains have been found. By 2003, medieval European rat sites totalled 143.[74] By 2009, 16 medieval sites with the remains of 500 individual rats had in fact been found in Norway.[75] But it remains true that rat finds dated to plague periods are quite scarce.

For plagued rats at least, absence of evidence is not evidence of absence. Indeed, absence could be evidence *for* rat-borne plague. Counterintuitively enough, we should expect to find fewer rats during plague periods. Experimental infection of black rats with *Y. Pestis* resulted in 100% mortality.[76] Strikes killed them off, except perhaps for a few refugia, and it might be years or even decades before they again saturated a large region.[77] A plagued century should therefore produce fewer rat bones than an un-plagued one. In England, variations in rat finds over many centuries have been reported. Seventeen rat sites, each representing multiple rats, dating to the third, fourth, and fifth centuries CE have been found, but none for the next two centuries, and only two for the eighth and ninth centuries—roughly the period of the first plague pandemic. The survey does not make the plague connection, but does note that: "No sooner had rats become established than their population seems to have crashed, reflected by the clear paucity of finds dating between the fifth and ninth centuries".[78] In York, "the archaeological record indicates that rats may have undergone extirpation, to be reintroduced in the late ninth century".[79] English rat numbers then recovered, with 41 sites dated from the tenth to early fourteenth centuries. A similar rat gap is reported for mainland Europe.[80] Frustratingly, these sources stop just short of the Black Death. But they do suggest that a downturn in rat finds might be evidence *for*, not against, their major role in pandemics.

In 2011, an archaeologist noted that some rat remains dated to the fourteenth century had been found in recent London digs, "but not in high enough numbers to make them the plague carriers". In particular, none were found in waterfront reclamations where organic preservation is good.[81] But how likely was a halved human population to reclaim land? London's rats would have been wiped out by half a dozen plague strikes between 1348 and 1400, and would have had to breed up and recolonise the city each time. A small clue along these lines is a record of payments to rat catchers by Durham Cathedral Priory in 1347 and 1356, but not between. This hints at eight rat-free years in northern England between the first and second strikes of 1348 and 1360.[82]

The third rat mystery is the problem of how rats, fleas, and pathogens originating in warmer climes survived cold northern European winters. *X. cheopis* becomes immobile at temperatures lower than 8 degrees Celsius.[83] The *Y. pestis* bacillus ceases to grow at temperatures colder than 4 degrees.[84] Northern winters can get much colder than this. It was also thought that black rats themselves did not live in cold climates. This point was a key element of the anti-bubonists' case, but many of those who accept that the Second Pandemic was bubonic, including scientists, still hold firmly to the notion of a black rat–free north.[85] In fact, cold is not a problem for black rats. While they prefer to live with humans, they can also thrive even on subpolar islands, north and south. In 1997, a population of black rats in Britain lived on isolated islands in the Outer Hebrides where they may still dwell.[86] Medieval Northern Europe had rat-catchers, rat traps, rat defences in granaries, and rat legends like that of the Pied Piper—traditionally placed in the north German town of Hamelin in 1284. Like those of the Black Sea and the Mediterranean, the North Sea and Baltic bulk trades, likely carrying rats, correlate well with plague dispersals. Remains of four black rats dating to the twelfth and thirteenth centuries have been identified in the Moscow region, as well as the one in Novgorod dating to the period 1200–1400 and the numerous finds in Norway.[87] In 2020, a rat's remains dating to a major plague strike in the mid-fifteenth century were found in Gdansk, on the Baltic coast, and this rat very likely had plague (not enough DNA could be extracted for certainty).[88] Furthermore, the idea that cold climates exclude rats and plague overlooks the obvious point that the black rat *and* its fleas and their bacteria were commensal. They dwelt in much closer proximity to humans than the larger, bolder, and less intimately commensal brown rat. They did not live outside, but inside the houses and barns of humans and their animals, sharing their warmth—warm air rises. Aliases of the black rat include "house rat" and "roof rat". Here the prosecution rests for the moment, while we consider other possible plague transmitters.

Misled by apparent rat absence in Northern Europe, scholars have searched for alternative transmitters, and it is certainly true that the black rat was not the only plague vector. Cats and dogs were suspected in the fourteenth century—dogs were massacred from Edinburgh to Istanbul.[89] They may have played a small role—cats though rarely dogs have caught plague in modern times. Mice catch plague if artificially injected with it in laboratories, but mouse fleas are poor vectors.[90] In any case, black rats tend to drive out mice.[91] None of these mammals are likely to have been common or long-range vectors. Human ecto-parasites, mainly fleas and lice, are more promising, and are now the vector of choice for many scientists.[92] If there was anything you could count on in the Middle Ages, it was lice. Theoretical modelling and laboratory experiments indicate that lice could convey plague, but that they were poor vectors. "Direct louse-bite transmission has yet to be demonstrated in humans", perhaps for lack of volunteers.[93] Further, unlike rat fleas, who can cover 150 times their own length in a single jump, and who can survive without their host for a time, body lice are less mobile and die within two days if parted from a host.[94]

Human fleas, *Pulex Irritans*, can jump too, and experiments and modelling suggest they also can convey plague.[95] Yet "however plausible, interhuman transmission by *P. irritans* under natural conditions has not been proven".[96] Fleas transmit plague in two ways: blocked (Biofilm Dependent Transmission) and unblocked (Early Phase Transmission, or EPT). *Y. pestis* has acquired the capacity to "block" certain species of flea. The bacteria multiply and cluster into a "biofilm" in the mid-gut of the flea, which prevents it from digesting its blood meal. It repeatedly sucks blood into its foregut, but eventually has to relax its muscles and vomit the blood, now full of *Y. Pestis*, back into its host. Unblocked fleas can transmit *Y. Pestis* sooner, through bacteria on their mouth parts or in their excrement, but do so much less efficiently. Experiments suggest that fleas "transmit few *Y. pestis* by the early phase [unblocked] mechanism", while blocked fleas inject hundreds or thousands of the bacilli.[97] Unblocked fleas feed rarely and briefly; blocked fleas try to feed repeatedly, even jumping to more than one host, before they starve to death.[98] For human fleas, experiments showed that "the *P. irritans* blocking capacity was incredibly low and its ability to transmit plague via EPT is almost nonexistent."[99] Many flea species might occasionally manage unblocked transmission, but few species are prone to block. Chief among them is *X. Cheopis*, the black rat flea. "Compared with most other fleas, *X. cheopis* is an unusually effective and dangerous vector . . . remarkable in its ability to become blocked, and therefore infectious, within as few as 5 days after imbibing *Y. pestis*–infected blood".[100] It is also better than most at unblocked transmission.[101]

Other candidates for major vectors of spread are rat fleas, travelling long distance without their rats, and human spittle, carrying pneumonic plague. Could *X. Cheopis* fleas transmit plague without their rats over any considerable time and distance? Here, we must part company with that formidable plague scholar, Ole Benedictow. He asserts, rightly, that *X. Cheopis* can survive up to one year without its rat, by going dormant in its larval state, or by feeding on debris such as grain dust.[102] But he also insists that blocked fleas were the main vectors of plague, and he cannot have it both ways. "When infected, the rat flea . . . has a well-documented median survival time of only 2 weeks".[103] Another source gives an average survival time of 2.8 days for blocked fleas.[104] Furthermore, rat fleas do not pass on plague to their larvae, and cannot breed unless they feed.[105] Modestly infectious unblocked or partially blocked fleas often clear *Y. Pestis* from their systems through excretion.[106] Those that did not might survive for some weeks in cargoes without rats, conceivably transferring one epidemic.[107] But, even if they could travel far without their original rats, fleas would have to find a new, uninfected, rat population to cause a substantial outbreak. If their destination was rat-free, they could at most cause only a few human deaths. Since the earlier epidemic was likely to have wiped out the local rats, fleas alone could not introduce a second epidemic soon afterwards. Live rats had to circulate to repopulate plagued regions, and if they could do this they could re-introduce plague too.

Our next problem is whether pneumonic plague could emerge as a separate disease, or become the main form of spread after bubonic liftoff. Secondary pneumonic plague develops from bubonic, but the primary form is transmitted by human spittle, without a fleabite. Primary pneumonic plague was rare in the third, modern, pandemic, at most 5% of cases and more often less.[108] But in a small 2006 outbreak in Uganda it was 12%, and in a 2017 outbreak in Madagascar, the pneumonic proportion may have approached 20%.[109] Some scholars argue primary pneumonic plague was the main form of spread in the Second Pandemic, and that this was the key to plague's ability to disseminate rapidly and to strike in cold winters in the north.[110] Yet *X. Cheopis* seems perfectly capable of achieving rapid mass infection on its own. Buildings can host up to ten rats per person.[111] As plagued rats die off, their fleas cluster on the surviving rats. When these rats die off, blocked fleas jump to accessible humans, biting repeatedly in their increasingly desperate efforts to feed. Modelling based on an unusually well-documented late Second Pandemic plague "found that most human cases of plague during the Cairo 1801 outbreak were caused by transmission from the rat population. Our point estimate for this proportion was 82% but the confidence interval reached almost to 100%, suggesting that there is in fact no evidence for human-to-human transmission during this outbreak".[112]

Furthermore, as noted above, pneumonic plague was restricted to coughing range, say two or three metres, and the sufferer was not coughing for long. "Primary pneumonic plague . . . kills within two to three days, and would likely leave an individual too sick to travel within one day".[113] Even with modern rapid transport, "the majority of cases will fail to transmit".[114]

Pneumonic plague might well have increased mortality in crowded medieval halls and houses, especially in winter, but there are good reasons for concluding that it was not a long-range vector, backed by some rare consensus among bubonists and anti-bubonists.[115] There is one well-documented exception, which in fact proves the rule. A plague outbreak in Manchuria in 1910–11 may have been unconnected to the third pandemic, which was going on at the same time, and major pneumonic spread is convincingly attested for it. But here the sick were transferred quickly by rail, and had exceptionally large-scale direct contact with infected non-commensal rodents—tarbagans, a type of marmot. Hunters slept 40 to a hut, surrounded by piles of dead marmots and their fleas. The tarbagan was being hunted en masse because its fur had suddenly quadrupled in price.[116] Pneumonic plague, fleas without rats, and the various other supplementary vectors might together have substantially increased the short-range, short-term, spread of plague. But for long-range and repeat transfers, it seems we should stick to rats.

———

Black rats are homely animals, living in clans of up to 50 and normally venturing no more than a few hundred metres from their nests. But rats breed like rats. In prime conditions, a female can produce five litters averaging eight ratlings each, and females can get pregnant at the age of four or five months.[117] In warm commensal environments, rats can breed throughout the year, during which a mother could theoretically produce hundreds of offspring.[118] Consequently, there is population pressure to fill all accessible niches, and this is coupled with social pressure.[119] Rat clans have two or three leading females and a dominant male, who sometimes expel young rivals. In hitherto rat-free territory, these young settlers will not move fast or far. But they will gradually spread throughout a region to roughly match the human population.[120] A key point is that, though rats and humans live together, their regions are not the same. Black rats face barriers that humans do not. Unlike the Norway or brown rat, the black rat is a reluctant swimmer, and will not cross wide rivers, swamps, or lakes on its own, let alone stretches of sea, though it will swim to or from a ship in port. West Eurasia, that particularly amphibian world, would therefore have comprised a large number of discrete regional rat populations, each of which would have to have been separately settled, resettled, and infected with plague, by rats hitchhiking on human movements.

Black rats are not small enough to hide in the packs of peddlers or pilgrims, or the saddlebags of couriers or cavalry. But they are small enough to hide in the cargoes of ships, large riverboats, and wagons. As noted above, it seems unlikely that they can hide for long in the loads of pack animals. Still, regular and numerous cargoes on any scale greater than mule trains would tend to plant rats throughout a connected constellation of regions. Rats could then gradually pervade each region on their own through unassisted spread. The rate of such spread was slow—20 kilometres a year is the standard guess. But, if rats were introduced to a central point, such as an inland river port, they could theoretically repopulate 400 square kilometres in the first year, 1,600 in the second, 6,400 in the third, and so on. A plague strike would exterminate rats in a particular region, which then had to be repopulated to again be vulnerable to plague. Unassisted infected rat movement could also expand the spread of plague. Rat colonies intersected in towns and villages, and in isolated farms young rats expelled in the normal course of events would seek neighbouring colonies in which to integrate. Lone survivors of plague might also have travelled, seeking mates or company.

Could West Eurasia, as early as the 1340s, really have had a bulk trade circulation system capable of repeatedly introducing both infected and uninfected rats to the various rat regions often enough to cause hundreds of outbreaks? The previous chapter noted that the trade grain was well developed in the Mediterranean, with the northwest Black Sea littoral and Sicily and Apulia, and perhaps Egypt, being the prime exporters. In 1311, Florentine merchants and Genoese shippers took 45,000 tons of grain from Apulia, which would have required hundreds of ships.[121] Numerous port cities elsewhere, including Muslim ports, also imported grain by sea. Northern Europe's grain trade was less well developed, and smaller in scale. But recent research suggests that its regularity and range have been underestimated. England exported wheat and imported rye. Norway, where grain was difficult to grow, imported considerable amounts, exporting cured fish and timber in return.[122] Flanders imported grain from eastern Germany by 1300.[123] "From the twelfth century . . . not only the grain trade but the entire *bulk* trade developed in northern Europe from an incidental activity to a regular trade".[124] The Great Famine stimulated further improvement in grain shipment. Gascon wine exports of up to 100,000 tons annually are reported for the early fourteenth century.[125]

These large maritime circuits were linked to riverine ones, which in turn linked to wagon roads. Christian Russian cities imported grain by river, notably Novgorod, around which even rye cultivation was not easy. Via Moscow and Kazan, the Russian river system linked up with the Golden Horde cities on the Volga, all importing grain downriver where possible. Northern and southern trade circuits were also linked by sea sporadically from the 1270s and permanently from 1318, when a long-range route from Anatolia to England and Flanders became regular, carrying the bulky mineral alum, used for fixing dyes to cloth, and bringing woollens back, along with many other things, perhaps including rats.[126] Some economic historians argue that all trades declined sharply after the Black Death. This view will be challenged in part two, which argues that, after a brief disruption, trade continued and even increased. A plague pandemic required intensive connectivity, or circulation, a continuous bulk trade circulating rats as well as goods and people.

Iceland, long a conundrum in plague studies, is a challenge to this hypothesis. It is said to have been rat-free until the seventeenth century, yet suffered two terrible epidemics in the fifteenth century. The first strike, in 1402–1403, is thought to have killed 50–60% of the human population; while the second, in 1494–95, killed 30–50%. Here we seem to have a clear case of "Plague without Rats".[127] Yet grain was very hard to grow in fourteenth-century Iceland, which therefore was, or tried to be, a regular grain importer. Its grain came from England and northern Germany, which did have rats, as did Norway, the source of the other Icelandic bulk import—timber. Between 1340 and 1347, the number of ships going to Iceland increased to a dozen a year.[128] After plague struck Iceland's trading partners, the trickle of ships declined to almost nothing for most of the second half of the fourteenth century, then recovered from 1397, reaching more than 100 ships a year by 1500.[129] Within a few years of the 1397 trade revival, plague had arrived. It then disappeared for 90 years, before striking again. A 2016 study argues, in my view unconvincingly, that mortality in Iceland's plague strikes has been somewhat exaggerated. But it does concede that "the absence of rat bones from archaeological sites in medieval Iceland is . . . not definitive evidence of the absence of rats".[130] Rat presence—indeed, four introductions of rats—explains the Icelandic pattern far better than rat absence, and we have seen that archaeological traces of rats are hard to find, especially in times of plague. Archaeology in Iceland is far from pervasive—an entire Basque fishing station was discovered only recently.[131] Though material evidence is lacking, it seems likely that rats became established in Iceland in the 1340s, with the emergence of a small but regular grain trade. The downturn in this trade then prevented the arrival of infected rats from the continent until 1402, when trade recovery caused the lethal event. Rats were then wiped out, and reintroduced later in the fifteenth century, but well before 1494, when a fourth rat migration brought plague and a second rat extinction.

We should not exaggerate West Eurasian bulk trade circulation in the 1340s. Few non-urban regions were in regular grain deficit—Norway and Iceland were exceptions. Some regional trade circuits intersected only occasionally. This may explain some of the variations in the scope of plague. The first strike, 1346–53, found uninfected rats almost everywhere, ready to host plague, hence its unmatched spread and lethality in both town and countryside. But it would have wiped out rat populations in most regions. Depending on their mix of trade-assisted rat introductions, unassisted rat re-settlement, and rat barriers, these regions would have returned to rat saturation at very different rates, leading to more variable human casualties in later strikes. The differential repopulation of rat regions may also help explain the inter-strike exemptions noted in the last chapter. Of the few regions and localities that missed the first strike, around 1350, most were hit hard by the second, around 1360. "Not re-infecting the same place for years after the end of an outbreak is another special characteristic of [the] Black Death".[132] Unlike others, the spared regions were still fully saturated by black rats when the next strike came.

Cities were the main traders and the main grain importers, so they would attract infected and uninfected rats. Because unassisted rats took time to move inland from sea and river ports, rural regions would repopulate more slowly than cities. Hence the trend to urban bias in later strikes. The difference between rat regions and human regions might also explain some larger scale regional variations, and even partial plague exemptions. Non-navigable rivers, estuaries, or marshes might subdivide a country into several rat regions, which were infected with plague and repopulated with rats at different times. Some regions in some periods did not import grain, or much else that was bulky. Infected rats might still reach them, but much more slowly than when hitch-hiking on trade. Inland Poland may be a case in point. Benedictow writes that "it would be surprising if the contagion was not passed on upstream by trade relations with inland Poland".[133] This region did export bulk goods, but it did not *import* them and their accompanying rats until the fifteenth century, when its famous grain trade—and regular plague strikes—began. Grain exports were reciprocated by substantial imports of such things as cured fish and woolen textiles. Before this, the main bulk export was not grain but timber, which did not have substantial reciprocal imports reaching far inland. Here was an exception to the rule that bulk trade could transfer plague, because the timber was floated down the Vistula and other rivers as rafts to the Baltic. Upriver traffic against the current was much more difficult, and in seaports such as Gdansk, the rafts were broken up, while the crews walked or rode home, as in pre-steam New Orleans. Riding and walking did not transfer rats. This may explain inland Poland's avoidance of some early strikes.

IV Immunity and Resistance

Rat circulation makes a big dent in solving our plague mysteries, but the puzzle requires a few more pieces. It is generally agreed that, unlike diseases such as smallpox, bubonic plague does not convey immunity to survivors. Depressingly, it was possible to catch plague twice. "Many examples of re-infections by plague have been registered, even within the same epidemic".[134] Leading bubonists and anti-bubonists agree on this.[135] The anti-bubonists pointed to apparent signs of immunity as additional evidence that the plague was *not* bubonic. One such sign involves children seeming particularly vulnerable to plague. This is the pattern of immune diseases, which are age-biased towards those born since the last strike who therefore lack immunity. The anti-bubonists stressed that the major plague epidemics occurred at roughly 12-year intervals. This is indeed consistent with diseases like smallpox, to which immunity is acquired by surviving a dose, and which therefore select for the young, who breed up to critical mass every 10 or 15 years. But the *average* interval between plagues is deceptive. Epidemics often clustered more closely, and were also often much more widely spaced. Marseilles was struck 16 times between 1504 and 1664 but was then plague-free for 56 years, before losing almost half its population in 1720–22.[136] Moscow's last epidemic in 1771 followed a plague-free century.[137] The populations of Naples and Genoa were halved in 1656–57, as in the first strike, but this time after 120 years without plague.[138]

The evidence that plague selected heavily for children in the first strike is not strong, but some cases of child bias in later strikes seem more convincing, notably in late fourteenth-century Siena.[139] But medieval child mortality was extremely high in normal times, around 25% in the first year,[140] and post-plague baby booms of course increased the proportion of children. Swad-dled, cradled infants and homebound children were more vulnerable to rat fleas than mobile adults. There were also child deaths only indirectly related to plague, caused by the death of their carers. One local study of a 1660s plague outbreak in England shows that, where both parents survived, 77% of young children did so too. If their mother died, only 10% survived.[141] These tragic considerations seem to me to resolve this plague mystery.

Resistance is a very different matter from acquired immunity. Random varia-tion might make some individuals less prone to catch a disease or to die from it. They may tend to pass these variations on to their offspring, and so on. On this basis, it is claimed that Europeans today are "almost inevitably, descended from a genetic stock able to withstand the plague".[142] Yet the people of Provence in 1720 proved just as vulnerable as their forebears 370 years earlier. Humans are long-lived and slow-breeding. Their genetic plasticity is nothing compared to rats, which are much better candidates for evolved resistance. Fifty rat generations fit into one human generation of 25 years. Natural se-lection for favourable variations or mutations would therefore operate far faster in rats than in humans.

A similar thought occurred to the Indian Plague Commission in 1908, dur-ing the Third Pandemic, which conducted experiments to test it. Rats from plagued cities proved more resistant than rats from un-plagued ones. In 2009, a group of scientists took this for evidence of complete plague immunity in a subpopulation of rats, and modelled it against documents from the German city of Freiberg in Saxony which suffered a dozen plague strikes between 1553 and 1632, with mortalities ranging from 12% to less than 1%. "In our scenario, the catastrophic epidemics of the fourteenth century would have been re-placed by comparatively small outbreaks once a naturally immunised sub-population of rats had appeared".[143] I think that "immunity" is used here for what I would call "resistance". In any case, the implication is that this evolved resistance was complete and hereditary in a subpopulation of rats. But in that case the immune subpopulation would tend to become the whole population by outbreeding plague-susceptible rats. What then would explain the sudden reversions to high death rates we see in some late plague strikes?

In 2016, other scientists, again prompted by the Indian Plague Commis-sion's data, concluded that it was hereditable "innate resistance" at work, but found it hard to "account for tendency for resistance to persist within cities during non-epidemic seasons, while disappearing from cities after the extinc-tion of plague transmission". They speculated about "lower fecundity among resistant rats as a life history tradeoff that prevents the persistence of high levels of resistance in absence of plague".[144] This might indeed be the case, but it seems to me unnecessary to explain the emergence and disappearance of resistance in rats. Resistant animals like great gerbils have presumably engaged with plague for thousands of years, and even among them resistance can appear and disappear. Rats experienced plague for a shorter time, and more spasmodically. Plague did not select long term and consistently for variations. If rats did evolve resistance, it might therefore be only medium term, disappearing after a few decades without plague strikes.

These hypotheses can be tested in the last stronghold of bubonic plague, Madagascar. Black rats have lived on this great island for at least a thousand years,[145] but plague-infected rats were only introduced in 1898, during the Third Pandemic. Unusually, black rats here are both the wild reservoir *and* the commensal vectors spreading plague to humans.[146] Plague is still endemic in two regions of the central highlands and produces several hundred human cases annually. Some black rats in these regions are highly resistant to plague; yet black rats have no resistance in the coastal lowlands, which are normally plague-free.[147] In 1991, plague from the highlands entered Mahajanga, a lowland coastal city of about 135,000 people. The city had previously experienced four plague strikes between 1902 and 1928; plague had then disappeared for 62 years.[148] From 1991, seasonal outbreaks caused a few human deaths for each of nine years, after which plague disappeared again. The scientists disagree on the hereditability of rat resistance. Some is passed on to a generation or two of laboratory-born offspring, but "resistance is not totally heritable".[149] A mix of resistant and susceptible rats might make plague temporarily "endemic" in a city, as it did in Mahajanga in the 1990s. The rats might then attain functionally complete resistance, as they seem to have done in Mahajanga in 1928 and 1999. New introductions of *Y. Pestis* may occur, as they did in Mahajanga. Resistant rats are not killed off, so that rat fleas seldom jump to humans. But when consistent plague selection for resistance ceases, the rats become susceptible again and the city eventually loses its functional immunity, as Mahajanga did in 1991.

Here, perhaps, we have an explanation for the periods of low-mortality plague in West Eurasian cities, and the devastating late strikes in cities that had long been plague-free. The fit with urban plague histories seems good. Barcelona suffered 31 strikes between 1348 and 1654, 27 of which killed less than 3% of the population. The four serious strikes, killing between 20% and 45% of the townsfolk, were at least 84 years apart, long enough for rat resistance to appear and disappear.[150] London, in the sixteenth and seventeenth centuries, and Istanbul, in the eighteenth and early nineteenth centuries, show similar patterns. Between 1563 and 1679, when plague disappeared from England, London experienced periods of low annual plague mortality, for example in 1606–10 and 1640–47, followed by longer periods when plague was virtually absent, followed in turn by six serious strikes, including the "Great Plague" of 1665.[151] Similarly, there was plague in Istanbul for 94 of the 150 years between 1701 and 1850, but in only seven of these years was mortality substantial.[152] Smaller port cities could also show this pattern. Newcastle had a bad strike in 1588–89, then four mild strikes between 1593 and 1625, then a very bad strike in 1636, which killed 47% of the population.[153] All four cases look rather like Mahajanga—a temporary urban "virtual endemism" eventually leading to high rat resistance, followed by the loss of that resistance and renewed susceptibility to plague.[154]

We can speculate that rat resistance developed in West Eurasian cities after they were repeatedly hit by plague, particularly after 1500. This seems to have happened in many cities apart from the four just mentioned, including Paris, Amsterdam, Genoa, Venice, Naples, Marseilles, Moscow, Alexandria, Tunis, and Algiers. Plague-endemic cities might distribute plague to their hinterlands and trading partners, allowing it to recycle back to them. This is one explanation for the survival of plague between strikes. But such cities might also distribute resistant rats, which would reduce human mortality in the countryside too. Once urban rats became very resistant, plague in the city's humans could also disappear. But if a city did not experience plague for decades, its rats might lose their resistance. This may explain the late high-mortality strikes on Marseilles, Moscow, Genoa, and Naples after plague-free periods of between 60 and 120 years. The medium-term resistance pattern was not restricted to Europe. Tunis enjoyed a plague-free period between 1706 and 1784, with major strikes before and after.[155]

V Plague's Endings

The rise of rat resistance—and the decline of it—seems likely to have played a major role in the decline of plague—and the exceptions to it—throughout West Eurasia. But as we saw in the last chapter, plague history increasingly diverged regionally from 1500. Epidemics ended in Western Europe by 1720 and Eastern Europe by 1780. Major strikes continued to afflict the Muslim South until about 1840. The end of plague is conventionally attributed to human agency, notably the growing power of states to run effective quarantine measures, public health regulations, and border controls. Other factors include a shift in housing from wood to brick and tile, which was less rat-friendly, and to cheaper arsenic in the 1720s, which was not rat-friendly at all. The decline of wooden houses and thatched roofs, ideal black rat environments, and their replacement by brick and tile varied by class, which may account for the trend towards higher casualties among common folk after 1500. All this was no doubt important, but it was not the whole story.[156] Improved public health measures usually get the most credit. They mainly consisted of sealing off plague sites, at scales ranging from the walling-up of plagued houses, through lazarettos and ship quarantines, to *cordons sanitaire* sealing whole borders. Yet Italy had higher plague mortalities in the seventeenth century than Northwest Europe, when "Italian anti-plague institutions were the best in the continent".[157]

This casts doubt on the conventional explanation for plague's persistence in the Muslim South, namely inferior public health systems until these were modernised with the help of European advisors around 1840.[158] The Ottomans did implement public health measures, at least in the cities, as early as the sixteenth century, and they too used arsenical rat poisons.[159] While it may be true that such measures weakened along with the Ottoman state in the eighteenth century, other factors were at work. The second pandemic transmitted plague not only to humans and rats but also to new inland plague foci among suitable species of wild rodents in West Eurasia. Some may have disappeared over time; those that persisted to this day are all in what was once the Muslim South, including the European Steppe/Volga region. It has been suggested that Swiss marmots and even English field voles hosted plague in temporary foci.[160] But "ecological and historical–epidemiological studies have concluded that the presence of a plague reservoir in Western Europe during the Second Plague Pandemic was highly improbable".[161] The subcontinent may have lacked a suitable mix of resistant and susceptible wild rodents, climate, or ecological niches; it did lack camel transmission. At least after 1500, plague likely came to it from the Muslim South, and/or from recycling between resistant and non-resistant rats. The new foci were much closer to dense and sea-trade–connected human populations than the Tien Shan.

Rodent species are the villains of the story so far, but in the early eighteenth century one is thought to have come to the rescue of plagued West Eurasia: the brown or Norway rat. Of course, it did not come from Norway at all—it is now thought to have come from Southeast Asia.[162] Brown rats may have reached central Europe by the 1550s, but are generally believed to have arrived west of the Volga in the early eighteenth century, and to have reached England by 1730, France by 1735, Germany by 1750, and Spain by 1800.[163] The brown is up to twice as big as black rats, and luckily for us does not like them. "Captive studies have shown *R. norvegicus* will kill *R. rattus*".[164] Indeed, it "may completely displace black rats".[165] It seems that this is just what it did in most of Europe, including Russia. The brown rat flea "is a poor carrier of *Y. Pestis*", and brown rats are less tightly commensal than black, preferring fields and sewers to houses.[166] Brown rats probably arrived too late to wholly account for the decline of plague, but may have greatly reduced it. They reached the Muslim South too, but here the regional ecology dealt another bad card. In some conditions, black and brown rats could coexist, as is the case today in Egypt, Morocco, Algeria, Libya, and Iran.[167] The survival of black rats and the existence of local wild rodent foci may explain the persistence of plague in the Muslim South.

This chapter has been speculative, and plausible speculation about the Black Death's origins and spread inevitably goes beyond what is strictly necessary for the main argument of this book. Even if I am wrong and Green and Hymes are right about Mongol plague dispersal, the former acknowledges that it likely caused local outbreaks and one-off epidemics, not pandemics. Even if it did cause a pandemic in thirteenth- and fourteenth-century China, the latter acknowledges that this would have been accompanied by other apocalyptic horsemen: flood, famine, and devastating warfare. These would have destroyed property, infrastructure, stores, and livestock as well as human lives. This was usually not the case in West Eurasian plague strikes, where all but human life survived. So it was West Eurasia, and adjacent parts of West Central Asia, not elsewhere, that suffered not one, not four, but about 30 Black Deaths, over half of them before 1500. Parts two and three of this book consider the effects of these repeated demographic, but not economic, hammer blows.

PART II

Plague and Expansionism in Western Europe

THE BLACK DEATH was instrumental in the fall of two West Eurasian Empires, those of Byzantium and the Golden Horde, and in the rise of two others, the Ottoman and the Timurid. The partial nomad exemption from plague was at work here. As we have seen, the Golden Horde's core territories on the Volga and in Crimea were hit heavily by plague; an outer circle of more nomadic vassals was less effected. This factor is thought to have contributed to the decline of the Khanate from 1359.[1] A rival nomad empire emerged from the Chagatai khanate in central Asia, under Timur (Tamerlane), a new Chinggis Khan. Timur established his dynasty in Transoxiana and Iran by the 1380s, and took plunder and tribute much more widely. Between 1385 and 1395, he defeated the Golden Horde, sacking its great city of New Sarai—destroying the archives that would have made it better known to us—then abandoned the region. The Horde fragmented thereafter, though its successors, notably the Great Horde and the Crimean Tartars, were only somewhat less formidable, and inherited its aspirations to hegemony over the Russian principalities.

Between 1300 and 1350, the Ottoman Dynasty was only one of dozens of jostling Turkic emirates in Anatolia, owing vague allegiance to the declining Seljuk Sultanate. The part-nomad Ottomans were sometimes allies and sometimes enemies of the Byzantines. Plague changed the local balance of power here too. Ottoman chronicles grandly ignored this, playing up pre-plague achievements, and some historians have followed suit. "Historians of the Ottoman Empire rarely assign much importance to the role of plague in the empire's history".[2] Others, however, note that the first strike of 1347–53 had less effect on the Ottomans than on their sedentary rivals. They argue that "the most important fact overlooked in all the theories on the rise of the Ottoman Empire . . . is the impact of the Black Death".[3] The Ottomans conquered parts of the Balkans and Anatolia in the later fourteenth century, defeating a great Christian crusade against them in 1396. Their nomad advantage did not last long; they settled down themselves and came to rely on sedentary subjects for revenue. It was no use at all against Timur, who crushingly defeated them in 1402, and captured their sultan, Bayezid, who Timur is said to have hung in a cage until he died.[4] Timur in turn died in 1405, and under his heirs Timurid power contracted to Iran and Transoxiana. Remarkably, the Ottomans recovered from this blow by the 1420s and resumed their conquests. We examine the relationship of plague and Ottoman expansion in chapter 11.

In Europe, plague wrought different political changes. Titles did not decline in number, but the supply of heirs halved. This intensified the old game of dynastic roulette through reciprocal intermarriage. More lineages went extinct; more titles went to collateral lines. The bolder players inherited scattered territories; the more cautious built up contiguous domains. Burgundy, Aragon, and, eventually, the Austrian Hapsburgs were in the former category: "others have to fight wars, but you, oh Happy Austria, only marry".[5] The French Valois and the Lithuanian Jagiellon dynasties took the contiguous approach. The French crown inherited such territories as Brittany and Provence; the Jagiellons at various times ruled Hungary and Bohemia, as well as Poland and Lithuania. The last two combined long term in 1386 to become the largest realm in Europe. Despite these political shifts, the Black Death did not immediately revolutionise West Eurasia; there was of course substantial continuity before and after 1350. This is among the reasons why so many historians underestimate plague's impact. There is surprisingly little evidence of socioeconomic breakdown for more than a year or two after the first strike; and substantial evidence of impressive human resilience. "For all the tragedy and disruption, the most remarkable aspect of the pestilential year is the resilience of institutions and people."[6] Not even the Black Death could stop people from planting and reaping, or buying and selling—or fighting each other. Below the surface, however, it triggered a fundamental reshuffling in many dimensions, including expansionism.

Historians have long known that disease epidemics can make a big difference in history. The classic example is the tragic "fatal impact" of introduced diseases on the native peoples of the Americas after 1492, which eased the path of European invaders, who were much less vulnerable to most of them. As we have seen, some suggest that Justinian's Plague did early Islam a lesser but similar favour, by weakening Byzantine and Persian enemies more than it did nomadic Arabs. These cases, however, featured outside invasions and *differential* impacts of disease: the invaded suffered much more than the invaders. The Black Death in the early plague era, 1350–1500, had a contrasting effect; it differentiated much less. The nearest it came to advantaging invaders from outside was with Timur. But his empire's point of origin, the Chagatai Khanate, was close to, and well-connected with, West Eurasia, and the Timurid domain shrank rapidly after its founder's death. In the early plague era, with the fleeting nomadic exception, the Second Pandemic's impact on almost all regions and polities in West Eurasia was roughly equal. "The first sweep of the plague provoked as close to a universal chorus as one hears in history".[7] After the initial mega-shock around 1350, later strikes kept population down, and labour shortages continued to incubate various important changes. Some trajectories of change ended with the beginning of population recovery around 1500. Others persisted. Part two retreats to Western Europe, where the evidence is least bad, to develop a thesis about plague-incubated change, while part three asks whether it also applied to Eastern Europe and the Muslim South.

3

A Golden Age?

ECONOMY AND SOCIETY IN THE
EARLY PLAGUE ERA

ECONOMIC HISTORIANS of late medieval Europe are the great exception to the rule of plague evasion. They have long debated plague's economic effects, falling into two schools. The "optimists" argue that the early plague era, 1350–1500, was a "Golden Age", even for common folk; the "pessimists" say that it was a time of "late medieval crisis" or "late medieval depression".[1] In the 1980s, the pessimists prematurely declared victory: "the interpretation of the waning Middle Ages . . . as essentially an economic depression has now become a majority opinion".[2] The optimists struck back in numbers, but pessimism remains strong. Recent versions do allow for "fatalistic yet hedonistic spending sprees",[3] quickly exhausting plague inheritances. But in 2002 "the general belief [was] that the fourteenth and fifteenth centuries experienced a profound period of economic depression".[4] In 2011, this still seemed to be "the general consensus".[5] As of 2018, "the opinion of a late medieval general depression . . . is still alive".[6]

One principle underlying pessimism is an emphasis on aggregate numbers instead of per capita ones. Economic outputs, of course, dropped sharply after the first strike along with the terrible mortality of producers. Aggregate numbers can be important, but per capita numbers often matter more, depending on the issue. Here, the real question is whether agriculture, craft, and trade declined more or less than the populations they served. Some pessimists find it strangely difficult to remember this. For example, a good scholar writes that, between 1348 and the 1370s, "real GDP in current prices shrank by 26 per cent in Spain, 35 per cent in England and 35–40 per cent in Italy and as late as 1500 in all three of these countries remained 15–35 per cent below its immediate pre-plague levels".[7] This is presented as bad news but, given that populations had roughly halved, it actually implies a substantial increase in GDP per capita. When pessimists do remember to think per capita, they tend to retain the old best guesses of a 30% population decline and a quite rapid recovery. The new estimates of mortality and of long-delayed population recovery make a big difference to the optimist-pessimist debate.

But the pessimist case still warrants respect. There is, for example, considerable evidence of a "bullion famine" which is thought to have hobbled commerce, and of adverse climate, which is thought to have hobbled agriculture. There are also ways in which population decline can indeed have negative economic effects. First, it might reduce the labour available for large-scale infrastructure such as flood defences. This did happen, notably around the North Sea. But it was rare for this negative effect to outweigh positive effects. Second, depopulation might reduce trade circulation by shrinking or rupturing exchange networks, or separating two that had hitherto intersected. Third, while relieving the pressure on arable acreage in densely populated areas, plague might make little economic difference in thinly peopled regions that had never had a land shortage in the first place. Fourth, the optimist case often rests on the concept of "Smithian growth" (named for eighteenth-century economist Adam Smith), which relies on regional specialisation and the division of labour. It can be argued that Smithian economic growth needs population growth to enhance demand and increase the labour to be divided.[8]

The principles behind the optimist case start with the fact that the first strike of plague halved populations, but in so doing doubled the average per capita share of just about everything. This "plague bonus" was strongest after the first strike, but later strikes kept populations down and average shares of everything else up. Even when scarce labour prevented the working of two farms or two fishing boats, people chose the better of those available—bigger, newer, more solid, better sited, or more easily worked, a "better half" principle. "It was the meanest properties that were abandoned first".[9] Another principle of optimism derives from plague's own dynamics. If plague struck a circulating, bulk trading, network and destroyed it, or reduced its level of connectivity from circulation to mere interactivity, only that first strike would pervade the network. A series of widespread strikes required the continuation, or very quick recovery, of circulation. So a "long depression" in bulk trade after the Black Death simply does not match the epidemiological evidence.

A final principle of optimism is, or should be, the difference between incomes and disposable incomes. We will see that increases in real wages and real peasant incomes are contested, and were quite modest by some accounts.

MAP 4. Western Europe in the Early Plague Era, 1350–1500

But if your income was £10 a year, and subsistence cost £9, then even a 10% increase in income would double your disposable income. A 30% real increase, which is a conservative estimate of what actually happened, would quadruple disposable incomes. If, at higher levels of affluence, we replace "subsistence" with "normal expenditure", then a similar percentage increase could massively increase an elite's capacity for abnormal expenditure. So, counterintuitively, plague might actually produce *selective increase* in certain categories of the population, even in aggregate. In principle, it could increase the absolute numbers of elites, of those rich enough to pay tax, of regular buyers in the market, and of those affluent enough to educate their children.

I A Plagued Economy

Turning from principles to evidence, we look first at arable farming, well-known to be the backbone of late medieval economies. The best recent pessimist case is by Bruce Campbell, mainly with reference to England but with continental implications. He argues that English yields per seed, per acre, and per worker fell substantially. As noted previously, he blames the weather, an early blast of the Little Ice Age at its worst from 1342 to 1357, for the "lack of any post–Black Death yield dividend".[10] His evidence for declining productivity per worker is slender and his correlation of shrunken harvests and cold weather seems unlikely on his own data. The long cold snap had little effect on English grain yields for its first six years, 1342–48. Yields halved in the plague years 1349 and 1350, but picked up sharply thereafter despite the cold, though still well down on pre-plague levels. This pattern surely correlates much better with the temporary disruption of the Black Death leaving many fields unreaped, and others hastily reaped, than with a 15-year cold snap. Campbell shows that oat yields fell substantially more than wheat yields. Oats are *less* vulnerable to cold than is wheat. Surviving harvesters concentrated on their preferred grains—wheat for bread and barley for beer.[11] On the other hand, Campbell's case for falling English yields per acre and per seed is strong, and finds support from others.[12] It is also true that the number of acres growing grain dropped sharply. But one cannot draw a pessimistic conclusion from this.

There is ample evidence of reduced grain acreages and falling yields per acre and per seed in other parts of Europe after 1348.[13] This is exactly what we would expect from a situation in which labour had suddenly become scarce. Before the Black Death, much farm work was still done by unpaid labour on manors, whose lords held much of the best land in their demesnes. Serfs worked on the demesne for two or three days a week as rental for their own smallholdings. A decline in serfdom had begun before the plague but increased rapidly after it. Many lords therefore had to pay higher wages to more demesne labour, or sell off or lease the demesne in substantial chunks to richer peasants ("yeomen"), who also employed wage labour, especially during harvests. In this context of scarce and/or costly workers, free or unfree, labour inputs common in pre-plague intensive farming were sharply reduced—repeat ploughing, weeding, carting manure, and careful sowing and reaping.[14] All of this lowered yields per acre and per seed. But other post-plague changes limited the fall in yields. The retreat from marginal acres to the best acres must in itself have improved average soil fertility. While grain acreage fell substantially, it did so somewhat less than the mouths it fed. One good recent estimate for England is that "the halving of population between 1348 and c.1450" was accompanied by "only a one-third reduction in the arable area".[15] Livestock were also relatively more abundant, and animals provided manure without human labour when grazed in fields left fallow, or on the stubble after harvest.

There were also various ways of enhancing and reinforcing human labour, and of substituting for it. Work animals (mules, oxen, and horses) became cheaper to buy and cheaper to keep. The displacement of slower oxen by horses increased,[16] as did the use of fewer ploughmen. "The first illustration of the single-handed plough, which could be handled by one man without needing another to drive the team, comes in a Flemish Book of Hours around 1430".[17] After plague, farmers across Europe began using more iron, which had previously been scarce and expensive. In the thirteenth century, a typical peasant household contained only a very few kilograms of iron and other metals. "By the late fourteenth century the descendants of the same family would possess somewhere between twenty and a hundred kilograms of metal".[18] This resulted not only from a post-plague bonus in iron implements per person, but also from more iron production (see chapter 5). Iron replaced wood in spade heads and harrow teeth. Wear and tear made ploughshares big users of iron on farms, hence the biblical need to beat swords into them, and they became larger and more numerous.[19] There was an incomplete but noticeable shift from the sickle to the scythe, which used more iron, in harvesting grain—in England, Germany, Scandinavia, and probably elsewhere.[20] The sickle wasted less of the crop but was slower than the scythe, so scything required less labour.

On eight occasions the estimates both for demesnes and tithes explain that a crop was below normal: "because mown", ie cut with scythes rather than the traditional sickles, and suggests that lord and peasants alike opted for this labour-saving method of harvesting, while running the risk that the sweep of the heavy blade of the scythe would shake loose grains from ripe ears.[21]

There was another counterintuitive post-plague rise—in the size of new barns. Harvest was the great labour bottleneck, and grain had not only to be reaped but also threshed, which was normally done outdoors. Threshing comprised up to a quarter of all harvest work, and bigger barns allowed this to be done slowly, indoors, after the harvest, secure from adverse weather.[22] In Holland, hay barns whose roofs could be jacked up appeared, making it unnecessary to take drying hay in and out when it rained.[23] Such underestimated measures eked out labour with capital. In further contrast to Campbell, other studies find a substantial increase in rural labour productivity across Europe.[24]

Greater productivity per worker in grain growing was coupled with a plague bonus in the means of transport and storage. High plague mortalities increased the per capita availability of carts, wagons, horses, oxen, mules, boats, ships, barns, and granaries, which would also have lost somewhat less grain to rats, who were even more vulnerable to plague strikes than people. The persistence of this increase, even after the vehicles and vessels of 1350 wore out, is documented in chapter 5 in the case of ships. All this enabled a fundamental reshuffling of the Western European economy. Some trade circuits did contract initially. Fewer Florentines needed less Sicilian and Apulian wheat, and there was no need to reconstitute the great grain-supplying companies that had collapsed just before the Black Death.[25] Urban Flanders's grain supply network also shrank for a time, withdrawing from the east to the west of the Elbe River.[26] But, after an initial sharp drop, Sicilian grain exports rocketed from the 1380s.[27] The north European long-range grain trade did not achieve similar scale until the late fifteenth century, but Baltic timber exports grew massively from 1350 (see chapter 12). In the medium term, plague's reshuffling increased trade circulation and even increased the integration of some exporting and importing localities, which in turn underwrote an increase in regional specialisation. The fertile grain regions best placed for export increased their per capita production; less favoured regions, or those with more profitable options, decreased it, and turned to other activities. Most widespread was a shift from arable to pastoral farming, from "corn to horn", but there was also a turn to higher-value crops such as hops for beer and flax for linen in the north, more olives, vines, fruit, cotton, and silk in the south, and to dye plants like woad both north and south.

Specialisation operated at local, regional, and "national" levels. In Suffolk, some manors particularly suited to the crop concentrated on barley, the per capita production of which burgeoned after 1350 throughout northern Europe to meet increased demand for good quality beer. The importance of sheep and cattle, rabbit warrens, cloth production, and fishing all grew, their workers supplied by neighbouring grain manors whose arable acres dropped only 10–15% on pre-plague levels.[28] This pattern of sub-regional specialisation was replicated in Bavaria[29] and, most sharply, in some cantons of Switzerland. Here, the uplands focused on cattle, goats, dairy products, and summer hay, while the lowlands supplied grain, greens, and winter shelter for livestock. In very local "transhumance", communities had long had their own uplands, used only in summer, and lowlands. Now separate upland communities ditched grain, took arable lowland partners, and specialised in herding—"cattle is really all there is".[30] In neighbouring German uplands, the process "went as far as the complete abandonment of cultivation of cereals".[31] Generally, however, "specialisation" fell well short of 100% monoculture; rural localities still produced most of their own food. But, after 1350, more and more began to rely on other localities either as markets for their surplus grain or for imports to meet their grain deficit—not just after bad harvests, but year in, year out, so integrating into systems of mutual dependence. "The shift to pastoral agriculture during the fourteenth century has been documented across Europe".[32] Better-fed livestock increased in size as well as numbers.[33] From England to Portugal, "a statistically-significant increase in the size of domestic livestock . . . occurred in the later fourteenth century".[34] "In many parts of Europe there is now substantial zooarchaeological evidence that livestock and even fowl were improved."[35]

An "international" meat trade in livestock began in the early plague era. Previously only horses had been sold over long distances. Long-range droving was modest at first, but occurred often enough to introduce fresh meat to the diets of even poor townsfolk. Scots cattle were first driven deep into England in 1359.[36] Switzerland supplied cattle to northwest Italian cities, Hungary to south German cities, and, later, Denmark to north Germany and the Low Countries.[37] Regional specialisation within countries increased. In England, East Anglia's arable acreage dropped only 25%, a sharp per capita increase especially marked in Norfolk, while in the less fertile north of England arable acres dropped by more than one-half, a per capita decrease.[38] The freed-up land went to less labour-intensive uses, mainly pasture for sheep. A similar process occurred in Scandinavia. Sweden was hit hard by plague in 1350, and quickly "a regional division of labour emerged". Grain growing retreated from the less fertile acres and was replaced partly by pastoralism and partly by two types of iron production. The pastoralism produced cattle for a growing inter-regional trade in work and meat animals, or salted butter for export. Some iron was produced by seasonal peasant labour in small traditional "bloomeries", giving rise to "a remarkable expansion of bloomery iron production at the end of the fourteenth century".[39] "The peasants . . . produced iron as a seasonal activity alongside farming."[40] More iron was produced in newly abundant water-powered blast furnaces. In the well-irrigated Valencia region, sugar cane, mulberry trees, and rice joined the traditional export crops—vines and olives.[41] Portugal, Malta, coastal Andalusia, the Balearic Islands, the Basque Country, Norway, and parts of the Low Countries also began or increased foreign grain imports, allowing them to specialise more in other products. "Many western agricultural regions reduced grain monoculture, so promoting interregional market exchange of more diverse agricultural products from regional specialists".[42]

There were many local and temporary exceptions to this overall picture of a modest economic "golden age". Some argue that, in England at least, higher prices outmatched higher wages until about 1375.[43] Other exceptions can be correlated with plague exemptions and so, like them, were partial and fleeting. Southern Germany may or may not have had unusually low mortality in the first strike, but its post-plague economic reshuffling followed the general trend, with Bavaria "increasing agricultural specialisation, the growth of crafts and artisanal production, and the rise of local markets".[44] This was also the case in Wurtemburg.[45] Other German regions experienced an unambiguous economic boom, rather to the surprise of those older histories that note it. "The late fourteenth century economic boom thus seems to have spread through most of northern Germany".[46] "The great crisis of the late Middle Ages hardly made itself felt in Cologne".[47]

Another plague exemption is possible for central Castile. This region may have missed the second strike, around 1360,[48] perhaps due to an unusual degree of dependence on mule trains for transport hampering its recolonisation by rats. It lacked navigable rivers and wagon roads and, therefore, cargoes in which rats could hide. Recent economic history correspondingly argues that economic upturn in this region was delayed to the 1390s, but then incautiously extends this conclusion to the whole Iberian Peninsula. "Instead of releasing the Peninsula from population pressure, the Black Death and subsequent mortality crises led to the disintegration of product and factor (namely labor) markets".[49] "Although its death toll was lower, the plague had a more damaging impact on Spain, far from releasing non-existent demographic pressure, it destroyed the equilibrium between scarce population and abundant resources".[50] We have seen that even the first strike death toll was not enough to rupture circulation in most of Europe, including thinly populated Scandinavia. Many farms and some villages were abandoned; towns and cities were not. There were fewer people, but more means of transport and storage. Castile may have missed the second strike, but it was hit by at least four plagues, 1348–99.[51] While it could not save thinly populated regions from a Malthusian crisis that did not exist, plague's "better half" effect could still apply. Even regions in which useable land was available to all farmers had a hierarchy of locations determined by proximity to waterways, roads, and markets; access to wetlands, woodlands, and common pasture; and security from raids and floods. Even in Russia, the most thinly populated European country of all, "neither peasants nor their lords could survive without at least limited contacts with the market".[52] Plague meant that survivors could move up the hierarchy.

Moreover, the early plague era was the very period in which Castile's famous *mesta* system, featuring fine-woolled merino sheep, first developed in terms of international trade. The mesta involved long-range transhumance pastoralism, in which sheep spent winter in lowlands and summer in distant highlands. The royal privileges of the mesta flock owners date back to the thirteenth century, but the full establishment of the system, and possibly the first appearance of merino sheep, was "a daughter of the plague".[53] Sheep numbers in Castile increased from 1.5 million before plague, to 2.7 million in 1467, with a much greater increase per human capita. The centre of the system was Burgos, the northern capital of Castile, which shipped wool to Flanders through the northern Spanish ports, using up to 120 sailing ships a year. In Burgos, incomes increased steadily from 1370. "The fourteenth and fifteenth centuries saw the apogee of Burgos in international trading".[54] Most recent scholarship suggests Portugal's international trade was also flourishing (see chapter 10). There is evidence of post-plague prosperity in southern Castile (Andalusia), and of boom times in the Valencia region.[55] In any case, the Iberian pessimists concede an economic upturn from about 1390. Catalonia, not Castile, may be the Iberian exception. Here, "imperial overstretch" by the expansionist kings of Aragon together with civil strife and an unusual persistence of famines seem to have stymied the post-plague "golden age".[56]

More general pessimist counterarguments involve climate, urbanisation, and circulating bullion. Campbell portrays most of the early plague era as a period of adverse climate, but others contest his statistics,[57] and he himself concedes that the years 1366–1405 were relatively favourable.[58] Temperature declines may have made some crops more marginal in some areas, but this would have been compensated for by post-plague specialisation and trade. Adverse climate could lead to back-to-back harvest failures, and so to widespread famine, and this did happen in the seventeenth century. But, overall, the early plague era featured far fewer famines than the 150 years before.[59]

Urbanisation rates are a more complicated matter. A 2009 estimate of the urban proportion of Europe's population in 1300 and 1400, by Paolo Malanima, shows a fall from 5.3% to 4.3% in cities of 10,000 or more people, and from 7.6% to 6.7% in cities of 5,000 or more.[60] "The decline of the urban population", writes Malanima, "has often been emphasized as the main evidence for the economic depression of the Renaissance".[61] But there are problems with such thinking. First, urban numbers are based on better data than those for the population as a whole. Cities typically kept better records than rural regions. As we saw in chapter 1, the standard figure for Europe's total population, town and country, in 1400 is probably much too high. If we lowered the total number, even modestly, and kept the urban number, we would see an increase in the urbanisation rate, 1300–1400. Other scholars do in fact find a rise in some countries. German urbanisation is thought to have increased from 10% to between 13% and 16%, 1348–1430.[62] Second, the thresholds for city status of 5,000 and 10,000 people should be adjusted to the decline in population. A city that fell from 10,000 to 5,000 people in a region whose rural population had also been halved would retain the same relative influence. Malanima himself notes that, in northern and central Italy, "the number of cities with over 5,000 inhabitants suddenly dropped from 96 to 59" after the Black Death.[63] In any case, he finds that urbanisation rose in the next century, 1400–1500, from 6.7% to 8.6% for cities with more than 5,000 people.

Finally, Malanima thinks that plague epidemics "afflicted above all the urban populations".[64] This was often true after 1500, but not in the early plague era. Cities initially lost no more than the countryside, but then received regular reinforcement from it. "Migrants from the countryside flooded cities after plagues".[65] Before 1348, cities had restricted rural in-migration to protect the jobs of their citizens. Afterwards, they encouraged it by offering various privileges, including tax relief and easy qualifications for citizenship. "Pisa offered 'privileges, fiscal immunities, franchises, and citizenship' to any who would migrate to Pisa . . . Siena extended citizenship to foreigners in an attempt to attract foreign labour to the city".[66] "Numerous towns . . . offered immunities from taxes, sometimes for as long as a decade. These efforts created a competitive market in human beings".[67] Guilds recruited their numbers from rural apprentices, and all cities strove to attract artisans.[68] Urban wages were higher than rural. Housing was more expensive, but less so than before plague doubled the accommodation supply. All this meant that city populations regrew quite quickly after strikes, though not often to pre-plague levels. There were some relative losers, such as Barcelona, Ypres, and Winchester, but more relative winners.[69] Italy's largest cities all declined sharply in size over the fourteenth century, but all except Florence and Pisa by less than 50%.[70] Some exceptionally fortunate cities even grew absolutely: Seville, Valencia, Lisbon, Lubeck, Hamburg, and Exeter.[71] Most cities in 1400 or 1500 still had fewer people than in 1300. But we can be reasonably confident that urbanisation *rates* rose during the early plague era.

Here we may have a solution to a conundrum left unsolved in chapter 1: the Black Death urban building booms in Prague, Paris, London, and elsewhere. After the first strike, surviving princes and urban elites initiated building projects to appease God, memorialise their dead, assert their authority, and wall off their cities more effectively from further strikes. They had more cash, and work animals and building materials were relatively more abundant. Labour was not, but the inflow from the countryside, at its greatest after the first strike, provided workers, as did the agricultural off-season.

Pessimism's final counter-case is the notion of a long "bullion famine", which "locked Europe in a state of commercial recession".[72] This is not credible for the decades immediately after the Black Death: silver and gold did not disappear, people did, and the latter's per capita share of the former increased. Venetian mints were "overwhelmed by bullion" in 1350 and for several years thereafter.[73] "Venice was the most bullion-hungry and credit-hungry commercial market in Europe", and did suffer brief shortages, in 1417–23 for example, but usually as a result of war or blockade.[74] Some suggest a diversion of bullion into decorative uses, such as dinner plate. But gold or silver tableware was easily reconverted to coin, or used as collateral for loans. Implicitly acknowledging such things, pessimists now restrict the "bullion famine" to 1380–1465,[75] and are not wholly convincing even here. "The evidence from France severely undermines the universality of the bullion famine thesis".[76] For England, a detailed 2012 study concludes that "this was not in the main a society held back by an inadequate money supply".[77]

There were periodic and regional shortages of silver to the 1460s, especially in comparison with the silver bonanza thereafter. Silver coins per capita decreased in England, but all coinage, including gold, increased.[78] The availability of credit and credit instruments increased across Europe, and although credit could not replace coinage, it could modestly enhance it. "Written transferable instruments were an additional form of currency in the later Middle Ages".[79] In the last ditch, pessimists argue that because the smallest gold coin was equivalent to five days' unskilled wages, a lack of silver would have impeded local, small-scale commerce. But the payment of large sums in gold would have freed silver for small transactions. The traditional indirect supply of West African gold continued, except for an interruption around 1400, discussed in the next chapter.[80] Neither the European-wide trend towards paying rent and tax in cash rather than goods or labour, nor the sharp decline of interest rates, nor the increase in nominal as well as real cash wages, all of which are generally acknowledged, sit at all well with the notion of a strangling bullion famine.[81] Europeans always wanted more bullion, and circulating gold and silver was sometimes tight in the early plague era, but that was largely because so much—16.5 tons net silver equivalent a year on one estimate[82]—was flowing eastwards for luxury goods. In principle, the pessimists could have a "bullion famine" or a "late medieval depression", but not both. In practice, the balance of evidence suggests that they had neither.

II A Golden Age for Whom?

Increased trade within Europe had its dark side. It helped recirculate rats and plague and, as though this was not affliction enough, increased circulation seems also to have increased the transfer of other diseases. Plague mortalities were "compounded by a number of other disease epidemics in the late fourteenth and fifteenth centuries".[83] Influenza is thought to have become epidemic in Europe only from 1387.[84] Epidemics of smallpox seem to have begun in the 1430s.[85] This process peaked in the late fifteenth century. "Sweating sickness", now thought to be a form of influenza, spread across Northern Europe from 1485.[86] Typhus, a disease that was transferred by lice, spread from the eastern to the western Mediterranean at about the same time.[87] These diseases were less lethal than plague, but could travel farther, as Native Americans were to discover, to their cost. Yet, despite increased mortality, a higher percentage of surviving Europeans began to participate in the market economy and to experience greater prosperity.

Apart from diehard pessimists, experts now agree that real wages rose after the Black Death, at least from 1375, and stayed higher than before the plague until about 1500. For England, "the considerable rise in the purchasing power of wages between the 1370s and the 1420s is indisputable". "By any reckoning, the high level of real wage rates in the fifteenth century meant that wage labouring was substantially better rewarded than at any other period between 1200 and 1850".[88] There is now "a rough consensus" that English wages were on the rise from the 1360s.[89] This applies to Western Europe as a whole. Nominal wages tripled in Florence, increased 157% in Catalan Manresa, and rocketed fivefold in Marseilles, well ahead of price increases.[90] "Nominal agricultural and building wages in and around Palermo increased two to three times; deflating for monetary devaluation, real wages increased c 80–120 per cent".[91] "Almost all over Western Europe there was a sharp rise in real wages . . . after 1350".[92] On the other hand, wage work was irregular, and the experts differ wildly on how much real wage rates rose, claiming anything from 30% to 300%.[93] At the lower end of this range, a person in work for only half the year might have been little better off than before the plague. Furthermore, states, lords, and cities made determined efforts to keep wages low by statute, and people could be forced to work without pay as serfs, or taxed and tithed back into poverty. Increased *average* per capita incomes did not necessarily imply increased *median* incomes—the level around which most people cluster. An average of £100 per head could be achieved by nine incomes of £10, and one of £910. Finally, most people were peasants, not full-time wage workers. So higher real wages do not in themselves prove a golden age for most people.

Like wage workers, most peasants probably did receive more disposable income, in cash or kind, but who did the disposing? Landlords did their best to coopt gains in peasant productivity, by law and by force, and they may have had some temporary success. But, for southern England, "there is now conclusive evidence that they [improved peasant tenures] had gained their initial and decisive impetus in the 1350s and 1360s, as some landlords offered immediate tenurial concessions in the aftermath of the Black Death in their desperation to attract tenants".[94] Throughout England, "the dramatically changed economic conditions after the Black Death increasingly shifted the balance of power away from landlords towards tenants putting a downward pressure on rents, lengthening terms, and leading landlords to assume responsibility for capital maintenance".[95] This was true of most of the rest of Western Europe. Better tenures in various forms have been documented for France, Flanders, Italy, Scandinavia, Spain, and Germany.[96] In Tuscany, Florentine merchants

bought much of the best land and let it to sharecroppers, either locals or immigrants from neighbouring regions. One Tuscan study sees sharecropping as
a poor option for peasants, because half the crop went to the owner, and this is
the standard assumption.[97] But another study notes that sharecropped land was
more than twice as profitable, because it tended to be more fertile and closer to
markets, and because the owner provided animals, seed, tools, and other capital
items, and paid the taxes. "Sharecropping in Tuscany between 1350 and 1500 was
not a harsh form of land tenure".[98] For sharecropping in Italy as a whole, "the mid
fourteenth century constitutes a structural break. Thereafter, landlords increasingly had to commit complementary inputs to their farms and renounce gains
accumulated since 1200".[99] Sharecropping regimes in France and Bavaria show
a fall in the landowners' share, from a half to a third or a quarter.[100]

Studies of England, France, and Aragon have noted that, while a minority
of peasant holdings took up substantially larger landholdings, more remained
no bigger than before, despite cheaper land and leases. The minority was substantial, up to 25%, and it was these peasants who became English yeomen and
their continental equivalents—*coqs de village* in France and *prohoms* in Aragon.[101] Some have attributed the failure of more peasants to take up larger
holdings to their continued poverty, "fatalism", or innate conservatism. But in
regions where wage work was available, keeping your holding small made
sense. If you had to work your own land throughout peak times, notably harvest, you could not work for peak wages. A smallholding provided insurance,
gardens, and a base for farming more livestock, grazing them on your increased
share of common land. Improved conditions were not restricted to grain farming. In the wine-growing regions of Germany, "with the decline in population
it was clear who held the whip-hand: if landlords wished to have their vineyards worked they had to offer more attractive terms to the shrunken pool of
peasants who remained".[102] Another labour-enhancing alternative for vine
owners was a shift, thankfully temporary, from pinot noir to more productive
gamay grapes in Burgundy in the later fourteenth century. "Given the reduction of labour inputs following the plague of 1348 it made sense to convert to
higher yielding, but lower quality, vines".[103] If peasants could not improve
their lot at home, they moved. They migrated to nearby cities or to rural districts offering better wages or tenures. In England, "on most manors by 1500
only a handful of tenants were descended from families present in 1400".[104]
Throughout Europe, "the period 1350–1450 was one of exceptional mobility, not
only amongst wage-earners seeking employment but also among tenants seeking better conditions".[105] This high mobility correlates with a flowering of

surnames, either locational, to distinguish immigrants from locals with the same Christian name (e.g., John of York, useless *in* York); or patronymic, to distinguish locals from immigrants (John Johnson); or occupational (John Smith).[106] Most moves were within the same district, but some were longer range.

The main reinforcements to post-plague wage labour were women. The optimist-pessimist debate heats up when it comes to gender. Even some optimists doubt that the golden age for peasants and workers extended to women. Yet females presumably shared in the increased returns for husbands and fathers, and it seems clear that the proportion of wage workers who were female rose substantially after the Black Death. Peasant women had not been twiddling their thumbs before plague. Apart from "housework", then a very capacious category indeed, they shared fully in all but the heaviest farm work, spun wool and flax for cloth, made clothes, and often hand-milled grain as well. After 1350, common folk bought much more of their cloth and had most of their grain ground in water mills which, as chapter 5 will show, became much more numerous per capita. This released women for wage work, and not just in arable farming.[107] Both pastoral farming and the range of marketable crops increased after 1350, as did the demand for pieceworkers in textile industries. Women were at least as useful as men in these activities. Most evidence indicates women's real wages rose after 1350, even as a proportion of rising men's wages, perhaps from 50% to 70%.[108] There was no gender differential at all in the returns on family farming—grain fetched the same price, or saved the same costs, whether produced by male or female. Gender pessimists might also note new skeletal evidence from Sweden which shows an increase in women's heights of 2.5 centimetres in the century or so after the Black Death, compared to a one-centimetre increase in men's heights.[109]

But there were countercurrents. The height increase discrepancy is probably due to catch-up: Swedish women were even more undernourished than men before the plague. Improvements in pay for English servant women employed on an annual basis were "subdued", probably because they were less protected by custom and community from employer exploitation than were daily wage workers.[110] Gender wage differentials were still substantial, sometimes when women were doing the same work, and in most regions men tended to dominate trades involving women workers, or at least their most profitable portions. Women (and children) comprised 90% of pieceworkers in the growing Florentine silk industry, but men retained the most profitable 10%, and the ownership.[111] Plague-era boosts in the commercial brewing of ale in England and the distilling of brandy in Germany began with women but were taken over by men as they became more profitable.[112] This seems a recurrent dynamic in gender history: women respond to a sudden mega-shift in circumstances, whether a great plague or a great migration to a labour-starved frontier, by increasing their economic centrality. Men then rein in women's gains. This at least shows that male hegemony was not unchallenged. Furthermore, we will see in chapter 6 that there was one type of locality in which plague did help surviving women to improve their long-term lot.

Elites did not take higher wages and absconding serfs lying down. Governments emitted streams of laws banning wage increases and the abandonment of tenancies.[113] "Everywhere, magnates, mayors and monarchs struggled to maintain the status quo".[114] But, as their repetition suggests, the laws were ignored or evaded, or fines were simply paid up as routine. Harsher enforcement followed, and princes also tried to increase their own share of the new prosperity with higher taxes. Peasants and urban workers responded violently. Across Europe there were 621 popular revolts between 1354 and 1425, a tripling of the pre-plague average from two or three to eight a year.[115] Pessimists see these as desperate poverty-driven rebellions. But they look much more like attempts to defend post-plague gains against elite reaction. Historians of France and England note that their great revolts, in 1358 and 1381, were led by the more prosperous peasantry.[116] A famous couplet was associated with the latter revolt: "When Adam delved and Eve span, who was then the gentleman?" It had versions all over Europe.[117] The peasants lost most battles, but until 1500 or so they seem to have won the war. After the 1381 English rebellion was crushed, "attempts to maintain pre-plague wage levels and enforce labour services were largely abandoned, and lords switched to livestock farming as a less labour-intensive alternative."[118] "Political society had always lived in fear of social revolution, and in 1381 it peered into the abyss and took heed".[119] Throughout Western Europe it was not just the threat of revolt that stymied elite reactions, but competition for scarce labour among the elite themselves, leading them to ignore or evade their own labour laws. It was this that made peasant mobility so hard for lords to stop; other lords were aiding and abetting it.

III   Mass Consumption?

We can cross-check the argument that plague triggered a widespread improvement in living standards by looking at consumption. Elites certainly believed that common folk were gate-crashing the luxury market. The lower orders buying non-essentials was a new phenomenon, one that caused indignation among their "betters". "All common people wear their belts mounted with silver. This can be seen well in public, and it is very bad".[120] "People were fewer, but greed was greater".[121] The old elite felt obliged to respond to commoner competition, to keep its distance in appearance and lifestyle. "Their already substantial consumption of meat can be shown, after the Black Death, to have become extraordinary excess".[122] There was a sudden increase in the number and variety of birds consumed by elites, apparent in manorial middens in both England and France. Capons, ducks, and geese were no longer enough to distinguish the high table from the low; swans, herons, peacocks, and the like were now required.[123] But the new competitive dynamic was perhaps most evident in dress, "the very foundation of the luxury trades".[124]

An alternative to sartorial competition with commoners was to stop them from wearing elite dress by law, and many governments tried this. Historians have noted a huge increase in sumptuary laws from 1350 but, as with labour restrictions, their frequent repetition suggests lack of effect. In the 1390s, an English commentator complained that "the pride of the lower orders has so blossomed forth and grown in these days in fine dress and splendid display— in the variety of fashions—that one can hardly distinguish one person from another".[125] In desperation, in 1511, the Venetian Senate ordained that "all new fashions are banned".[126] Despite sumptuary laws, "by the fourteenth and fifteenth centuries an increasing emphasis on conspicuous consumption led to a more rapid turnover of clothing among the upper classes and there was a growing pre-occupation with the cut and shaping of clothes".[127] The old flowing robes were out; tighter, shapelier, more gendered, and more varying styles were in. Whether this amounted to the advent of fashion, valued for change in itself, is an interesting question.[128] One fine doctoral thesis does trace the European origins of fashion to the fourteenth century, but is strangely reluctant to associate it with plague.[129] The change is dated variously to the 1320s, the 1330s, and the 1340s, but the evidence cited suggests the biggest shift came in the 1350s—a good example of scholarly unease with the Black Death as an historical determinant. Birth of fashion or not, an elite need to trump each nouveau riche adoption seems clear for the early plague era. Aristocratic ladies in the Netherlands began wearing expensive frilled veils in the 1350s. They were taken up by rich burghers' wives in the 1380s, followed by the female bourgeoisie in general from the 1460s, at which point noblewomen ditched their veils.[130]

A broadening luxury-buying elite is one thing, increased consumption for the majority is another. Optimists far outnumber pessimists in recent work on this issue.

Rising consumption is well attested for meat, cheese, butter, beer and, in Mediterranean countries, for wine, olive oil, fruit and vegetables; probate inventories, dowries, and archaeological excavations show marked increases in the use of cheap cloth, crockery, wooden utensils and suchlike. The description of the late middle ages as the "golden age" of the peasant and labourer is by and large correct.[131]

This was the era in which "semi-luxuries", or "comforts", as they were known at the time, began to cater to a mass market. "A market for 'low-end' luxury goods grew up over the fourteenth century".[132] These included buckles, badges, and cheap jewelry, gilded to mimic silver, or made of alloyed silver or pewter and, above all, cheaper grades of commercially produced cloth.

It is no great surprise to find this "gilding of the market" in the already-wealthy cities of northern Italy and Flanders. But the upturn extended to lesser towns and rural districts, to middle-ranked economies, and to what had hitherto been marginal and impoverished parts of Europe. Tuscan tax records show "growing prosperity for large swathes of the countryside during the fifteenth century".[133] In one Flemish fishing village, archaeological finds dating to the early fifteenth century show "cloves and pepper, exotic fruits such as pomegranates, ivory combs, cast bronze candlesticks and luxury ceramics; Spanish lustre wares occur in small quantities throughout settlement not—as one would expect—restricted to a few privileged households".[134] England featured a "well-attested rising standard of living in rural society, as well as in towns, between 1349 and the mid-fifteenth century, both among wage-earners and tenant farmers".[135] Rare evidence shows that 44.4% of households in the small town of Edam in Holland held cash in 1462—a century later the proportion had shrunk 12.7%.[136] Even in Scandinavia, cold, thinly peopled even before plague and short of fertile acres even after it, many peasants shared the "golden age", some beyond the margins of grain growing.[137] In 1432, a crippled Venetian ship drifted to the Lofoten Islands in the far north of Norway, and its crew spent several months shivering there. They found the locals, who exported dried codfish, prosperous, wearing London woollens and eating imported grain.[138] The Icelandic economy in the same period "now appears more complex and diverse than previously thought".[139] "European goods became available to a much larger group than before . . . , including a multi-coloured fabric produced specifically for the Icelandic market".[140] The evidence for Danish peasants extends to "strong indications of a late medieval revolution in cloth consumption".[141]

Woollens, linens, and cottons could be either luxuries or comforts, depending on quality. Europe's own cotton cloth industry is usually associated with the eighteenth century, but a related industry long predated this: the production of fustian, which combined imported cotton with local linen fibres and was cheaper than pure cottons. "Historians regard the introduction of fustian weaving as a 'fundamental process of innovation in the second half of the fourteenth century."[142] Some fustian was made in Italy before 1350, but the industry took off afterwards, booming first in northern Italy, then in Germany, where 60 towns were in the business by 1500.[143] The amounts of cotton involved were modest. Cologne imported 18 tons annually between 1414 and 1432. But eked out with linen this made about 5,400 bolts or 243,000 square metres of cloth.[144] Augsburg was a much bigger producer of fustian: 12,000 bolts in 1385 and 85,000 by 1410.[145] These figures must mean that the "lower orders" were invading the fustian market.

More important than cotton was the wool industry. Most commercial production remained regional and dealt in cheaper grades of cloth, but better grades such as broadcloth count as comforts if not luxuries and had long been a major item of international trade. Leading woollens exporters before the plague were Flanders and northern Italy. Both regions experienced problems in the later fourteenth century, due to warfare, disrupted supplies of raw wool, and emerging competition. But overall their woollen cloth industries held up, per capita, in the early plague era. The lead supplier of wool had long been England, and the fate of the English wool industry is another pessimist-optimist battleground.[146] The export of English *raw* wool certainly declined greatly over the early plague era, but this was due to increased domestic demand and increased exports of manufactured wool cloth. Pessimist estimates that sheep numbers declined sharply, and that export volumes of raw wool and wool cloth combined declined slightly, are now convincingly contested.[147] Even on the old numbers, the value of wool exports, raw and manufactured, increased from £250,000 to £500,000 between 1350 and 1450, a per capita quadrupling.[148] New (2014) estimates for English domestic consumption, much higher than the old, are 160,000 wool cloths per year for the early fourteenth century, 120,000 for 1400 (a 50% per capita increase), and 150,000 by the 1440s (a 100% per capita increase).[149] "Production of Colchester russet ... took off immediately after 1350", and was "increasingly attested in foreign markets".[150] The English woollens export trade had major problems from the 1430s to the 1450s, but by 1500 exports exceeded 80,000 cloths per year and reached 150,000 in 1553. Wool cloth was England's "outstanding example of a late medieval boom industry". As for linen, imports into England are estimated to have grown tenfold from 1390 to 1530.[151] Flax and linen production on the continent burgeoned, east and west. One historian has suggested that the early plague era witnessed a European-wide "mass diffusion of linen underwear".[152]

Most people ate and drank better as well as dressed better. Ale brewed without hops did not travel well or last long. Adding hops to barley malt improved its keeping qualities. Hopped beer seems to have been perfected in Germany in the thirteenth century, but the trade really bloomed after the Black Death. The Hanseatic cities of Lubeck and Hamburg were leading exporters. Lubeck needed 10,000 tons of barley a year, plus hops and water, to produce its 80,000 tons of beer exports. Parts of its hinterland of Mecklenburg began to specialise in growing hops.[153] Hamburg exported even more; 43% of its craftsmen were brewers in 1376. Despite plague depopulation, its exports rose from 8 to 18 million litres between 1348 and 1417. Production then spread throughout Germany and to the Netherlands and beyond. Hopped beer made it to England too, but was slow to displace ale. Instead, the local ale industry expanded. Beer could be made from lesser grains, but the best was made from barley malt, and this explains why barley production in England fell far less than other grains.[154] "Before the Black Death, commercial brewing was a marginally profitable trade that attracted little investment". After it, "ale brewing expanded, becoming less domestic and more industrial . . . after the devastation of the Black Death in 1348–49, brewers had fewer customers than before, but those fewer customers drank much more".[155] "Ale consumption per person more than doubled, from 71 to 155 liters per year between 1300 and 1450".[156]

Europe-wide, demand for wine also burgeoned, notably for strong, sweet wines which travelled well.[157] These had an elite market, but small-scale regional trades also grew, along with specialisation and the proportion of farmed land in vines. In the wine-exporting Bishopric of Tuy in Spanish Galicia, for example, the vine/grain split in acreage increased from 60–40 to 75–25 soon after the Black Death.[158] Cargoes from Bordeaux, the great exporter of wine by sea, declined sharply at first. There was an incomplete but "noticeable recovery in the 1360s", and many other regions now joined that of Bordeaux in the continental wine trade.[159] Vines required twice as much labour as grain, but yielded much more per hectare in weight of crop, let alone value.[160]

We have seen that meat production increased all over Europe, but did common folk get much of it? In towns at least, they did, on an unprecedented scale. Available evidence suggests that the average meat consumption of townsfolk at least doubled.[161] Most meat consumption statistics are for towns, but there is some alternative data for the countryside. There is isotopic evidence in rural skeletons of increased meat eating by French and English peasants.[162] From 1350, dripping pans, frying pans, and spits for meat roasting suddenly increase in the archaeological evidence from English peasant households. "The English evidence matches the large-scale rise in meat eating across Europe".[163] In all, R. C. Hoffman's conclusion seems hard to contest:

> Large consumption of meat by the wealthy of the early and high Middle Ages spread down the social scale with increased per capita wealth after the 1350s. Considerable and widespread evidence indicates per capita levels of meat consumption in the fifteenth and early sixteenth centuries not again reached in Europe before the late nineteenth and twentieth.[164]

In the words of an early optimist, Jacob Burkhardt, writing in 1860, plague meant that "the poor had either died or ceased to be poor".[165] In fact the end of poverty was far from complete. But its marked decline is traceable not only through the evidence given above but also through reductions in charity to the reduced number of poor people,[166] archaeological indications of improvements in housing in places ranging from England through Bavaria to northern Castile;[167] and through the increased height of human skeletons.[168]

We must keep this "golden age" in perspective. It came at a horrendous price, of course: the agonised premature deaths of loved ones in repeated plague strikes. It was modest. A few trinkets, a pound or two of meat a week, a larger hut, and sewing your clothes from purchased cloth rather than also spinning and weaving it yourself, was an improvement, but not much by some standards. It varied over time and space. France and other regions experienced devastating warfare over much of the later fourteenth century, delaying the onset of relative prosperity. The Catalan economy declined, at least in relation to neighbouring Valencia. There was a major recession in England in the mid-fifteenth century. Famine still struck, though less often than before the Black Death. The world was not "turned upside down". Aristocratic or urban patrician rule continued, though it was now exercised more carefully in case one's subjects fled. Lords did well too. Inequality diminished, but more because of increased lower-class incomes than a decrease in those of elites. Some sources note that manorial revenues halved, but fail to note that the number of manors inherited doubled. "In England, total noble income from their estates shrank by only 10% from the 1340s to 1370".[169] "The earls of Devon found themselves inundated with new land".[170] Apart from land, lords kept most of their wealth in luxury clothing, jewellery, and plate, and legacies of this too roughly doubled per heir. The increased consumption of luxuries, demonstrated in the next chapter, is not compatible with a decline in elite incomes. Princes taxed the new prosperity as much as they could, and an increased number of fiefs without heirs reverted to them, either directly or through their control of the marriage of heiresses. The church profited from increased bequests. But, whether or not it amounted to "mass consumption" in any modern sense, a modest golden age for most surviving common folk there was, and its leading cause was the Black Death.

The post-plague "golden age" was a 150-year-long era, not a passing moment. But, after 1500 it did come to an end, collapsing into lower real wages, increasing taxes, worsening tenures, or no tenures at all. One factor was population growth, which reduced the leverage of peasants and workers. While pre-plague population levels were not recovered until after 1600, the economy had restructured itself to use less labour by 1500, so strong sixteenth-century demographic growth created surplus labour. Another factor was inflation, stimulated by incoming tides of fresh bullion, from within and without Europe. This was good news for some but bad news for many, because this inflation eroded real wages and hit necessities much harder than manufactures and luxuries. In England and the Netherlands, where the statistics are best, grain prices increased more than sixfold, livestock prices more than threefold, and manufactures only twofold between about 1510 and 1630.[171] Across Europe, "between 1500 and 1800 rent and tax burdens increased dramatically".[172] Meat consumption by common folk fell sharply and average heights declined.[173] "Recent research confirms the occurrence of a general rise in inequality during the early modern period".[174] The economy as a whole still grew a little, and demand for some goods still grew a lot, but the extra was absorbed by population growth and richer elites. The apparent tension between aggregate economic growth and increasing inequality should not give us, in the early twenty-first century, too much difficulty.

An "industrious revolution" may have slowed, though not stopped, the decline in household incomes. Workers can respond to lower incomes by working more hours a day, more days a year, and involving more family members. The European version of this shift is usually dated to the eighteenth century. But the evidence seems to clearly date its main effects to the sixteenth century.

Working days needed to provide the basics for a typical lower-class family increased from 160 a year to 300 a year between 1500 and 1616, much more than any subsequent increase.[175] In the early plague era, common folk had taken part of their economic gains in increased "leisure", though this might take the form of working on their own smallholdings. "It appears that the number of observed saints' days rose after the Black Death".[176] In Holland and England, observed holy days decreased with the advent of Protestantism, from 47 to six over the sixteenth century.[177] Dating the "industrious revolution" to 1500 is also supported by new research showing a discrepancy between declining real wages and more stable gross domestic product per capita, in England, Spain, Holland, and Tuscany.[178] The shift makes cultural as well as economic sense. Meat, wheaten bread, hopped beer, and sugar are not easy habits to give up. The latter two are literally addictive. Making homespun clothes and hand-milling grain are not easy habits to re-adopt. Workers who retained some leverage, such as soldiers, sailors, and harvest workers, successfully continued to demand a lot of meat and alcohol in their rations.[179] Lower-class consumption of comforts, if not luxuries, may have declined rather than disappeared, so contributing modestly to increasing overall demand.

Economics has a concept of price and wage "stickiness", whereby people resist higher prices and lower wages to those to which they have become accustomed, even if inflation or deflation seem to demand them. One could posit a concept of "cultural stickiness", where people strive to preserve their most culturally cherished sandcastles even when the economic tide has turned. The golden age left other residues and legacies among common folk too, discussed further in chapter 6. One was a transnational folk memory of a better "world we have lost", shared by most European countries. Others, more translocal than transnational, were a particular set of regions whose women were less reluctant than usual to migrate permanently, and another set of regions whose men were unusually prone to risk sojourns abroad.

4

Expansive Trades

THE MOST ASTONISHING of plague's many counterintuitive economic effects was the *absolute* increase in some trades as early as 1390—long before the population had even begun to recover. In such trades, half as many people somehow consumed *more* than twice as much per capita. A few historians do note this aggregate increase, though without fully explaining it or tracing its effects. A superb study of the Florentine economy suggests that, after the Black Death, both local business and foreign trade recovered quickly and then expanded after 1348. "The second half of the fourteenth century may in fact have been the most expansive period in the history of the Florentine economy".[1] "Already in the wake of the Black Death of 1348", notes another historian, "trade in Italy had accelerated exponentially, and global networks involved newly widening commercial markets for individual consumption, from localized shops to international fairs and overseas depots".[2] A third confirms this for Aragon's seaborne trade: "the level of 1330–1340 was reached again in 1380–1390 and then exceeded".[3] Similar impressions for Northern European trade can be cited. "It has been estimated that the volume of trade in the Low Countries doubled between 1400 and 1475", when there was little help from population recovery.[4] Chapter 12 suggests that Baltic timber exports also doubled over the fourteenth century, and continued to grow in the fifteenth.

It seems to me that the explanation for aggregate increases must be that the increment in disposable incomes was much greater than that in total incomes, while the percentage of people with disposable incomes also went up—a selective increase. As we have seen, improvements in income did not have to be large to be game-changing. One economic historian has calculated that the disposable income of average peasant grain farmers in England did indeed double after the Black Death, even without the supplement of seasonal wage work or the sale of non-grain products.[5] This was true to a greater degree for skilled workers, for craft masters, and for yeomen farmers—all of whose proportion of the population increased after 1350. It was also true, in still greater degree, for elites. Thus, despite the halving of general populations, the "buying classes"—people regularly in the market for comforts and luxuries—may actually have increased in absolute numbers, and they certainly gained in aggregate wealth. It is this that counters the pessimist argument that "Smithian growth" needs population growth. Not the least of plague's paradoxes is that it may actually have delivered absolute growth in the *commercial* population. Some recent research does in fact suggest a rise in the proportion of people who were at least modestly affluent from 5–10% of the population before 1350 to 25–35% afterwards.[6] The most conservative implication, an increase from 10% to 25% in the buying classes, plus a halving of the population, means 50% more buyers.

Turning to the expanding trades themselves, these fell into two groups: "exotic" and "extractive". Exotic goods, a specialty of southern Europe, came originally from outside Europe: silk, cotton, spices, sugar, and slaves. These were low-volume, high-value, luxury trades. Extractive trades, a specialty of Northern Europe, were natural products, whether luxuries or comforts which, when demand was high, were harvested beyond their local capacity to renew themselves, depleting the resource. They included storable fish (notably salt herring and dried cod), whale products, and furs. Local depletion encouraged a move to fresh hunting or fishing grounds, so extractive trades became expansive trades. The acquisition of bullion outside West Eurasia might also be seen as an expansive trade. Two cities we will come to know as midwives of European expansion, Genoa and Lubeck, were the leading hubs of northern and southern trades respectively. Their roles are explored in chapters 10 and 12. Here, we attempt to assess the trajectories of exotic and extractive trades in the early plague era.

I The Northern Hunt Trades

The peoples of Northern Europe have a long track record of expansionism. Goths, Vikings, Normans, and English all found it hard to stay within their own borders. This has been attributed to racial vigour, and/or to "bracing" climate. An alternative explanation is that the region was not just bracing, but cold, dark, and poor. In between invading others for land or plunder, it had therefore to look to its seas and forests for warmth, light, and food to supplement its farms. Apart from fresh fish, the key sea products were cured herring and codfish, and whales, for their bone and oil. The forests yielded furs, wax, honey, prime timber, and wood products such as potash and pitch. Sea and forest were harvested through what amounted to large-scale commercial hunting, fishing, and gathering—"hunt trades" for short—leading to their depletion in times of high demand. This is a possible motive for the expansion of hunter-gatherer societies, such as the Polynesians and the Thule Inuit, and even for the original dispersal of *homo sapiens* from Africa across the planet. We are less accustomed to seeing depletive hunting as a key dynamic in modern European expansion, and less still to the possibility that it was boosted by plague.

While many northern peoples practiced shore whaling for subsistence, the pioneers of commercial whaling were the Basques of north-eastern Spain and south-western France. Intrepid seafarers, with an ancient tradition of internal cohesion, autonomy, and difference from neighbours, their trade in whale products may have begun as early as the seventh century. They operated from a shore station with a watchtower for spotting the whale and used red-tiled stoves for boiling the blubber into oil. Two or three six-man boats would go out and lance the whale, using drogues or floats to tire it, and special ropes and harpoons, a word that may originate in their (non-Indo-European) language.[7] In the high Middle Ages, whale meat was important: cured and sold as "Lenten fat", in lieu of bacon, in Flanders and northern France. The English liked their whale meat boiled with peas.[8] Whale meat did not preserve very well, however, and the main use became bone (baleen) and oil. The whale's flexible baleen cartilage was used in fishing rods, whips, furniture and coach suspension, umbrellas, and even to keep knights' plumes from drooping—nothing worse than a drooping plume in joust or battle. Whale oil was an excellent lubricant, an ingredient of waterproof paints and varnishes, and above all a prime source of light, cheaper than wax and better than tallow—it was known as "lumera".[9]

The Black Death boost in disposable incomes seems to have increased demand for whale products. There are scattered indirect signs of increased whaling. Basque whaling confraternities, which organised the lookouts, watchtowers, and boat crews, consolidated in the fourteenth century.[10] One authority believes that "the most prosperous period for whale hunting in the Basque Country must have been the fourteenth and fifteenth centuries".[11] Basque whaling *outside* the Basque Country, driven by local depletion of whales, is dated by others to the fourteenth century.[12] "In the late fourteenth and fifteenth century they presumably whaled in the English Channel and Irish waters whence their expeditions were extended north and north-westwards".[13]

The Basques were initially shore whalers, but they did not care whose shore. They established shore stations certainly in Galicia and Asturias, and probably in Portugal, Brittany, Ireland, Scotland, and eventually as far away as northern Norway, Iceland, and Labrador.[14] Basques also fished for cod and hake in increasingly distant waters, and often had some kind of shore base for processing the catch, which may have served for whaling as well. Basque fishing of some sort was causing concern in western Ireland by 1430; and in 1506 was said to have been going on "from times immemorial".[15] Basques began fishing in Icelandic waters around 1410. Like other fisherfolk, the Basques were secretive about their fishing grounds and techniques. Their far-flung fishing stations are known mainly from recent archaeology. Another intriguing line of evidence for their influence in Iceland is the existence of a Basque-Icelandic pidgin language, which featured such endearments as "go shag a horse".[16] As for whaling technology, the only way to acquire its secrets was to hire Basques, which is precisely what other whaling nations did from the sixteenth century, as European whaling continued to expand.

The evidence for increased European consumption of fish after 1350 is more abundant and direct than for whale products. Apart from increased discretionary incomes and the desire for storable protein for winter, meat-free holy days and Lent were kept more carefully after the Black Death, for fear of further enraging an angry God. Fish farming, of carp in particular, in constellations of ponds of up to 100 hectares, flourished in the second half of the fourteenth century, spreading from Bohemia and southern Poland to Western Europe.[17] Sturgeon in French rivers were overfished to the point of "near-total destruction" by the mid-fifteenth century.[18] Carp and sturgeon were expensive; demand soon overshot the supply of cheaper freshwater and coastal fish. The demand was met by expanding exports of cured sea fish. Portuguese and Spanish fishers pumped salted sardines from the Bay of Biscay into the eastern Mediterranean, especially during Lent.[19] Sicilian tuna fishing, for markets farther north, "grew very rapidly after 1350".[20] The west of England's long-range fishing, for a variety of species, burgeoned from the 1370s. The number of shiploads of fish landed at Exeter increased modestly until 1390, then grew sixfold by the 1460s. The first phase, to 1390, met increasing per capita demand and compensated for a decline in fish takes off eastern England. The second, from 1390, suggests increased aggregate demand. This was the typical post-plague pattern in the expansive trades.[21]

The most expansive fish trades were dried cod and salt herring, initially from the North Sea and the western Baltic.[22] These products have been described as the "first mass-produced food commodity".[23] Herring were traded by sea as far south as Pisa by the 1380s, and inland by river to such towns as Nuremburg.[24] "The penetration of cured fish into inland Europe can be traced in cookbooks and kitchen middens from 1350".[25] The great herring fishery off Scania, a large chunk of Southern Sweden subject to Denmark until 1658 but "dominated by Lubeck", produced 40,000–50,000 tons of salt herring a year around 1400.[26] Compare this to the peak of about 5,000 tons reported from Yarmouth, then the base of the leading herring fishery, in 1336–37.[27] The Yarmouth fishery declined from about 1370, the Scanian from 1400. Overfishing may or may not have been the cause, but in any case the herring shoals were pursued further into the North Sea in the fifteenth century, with Dutch fishers becoming increasingly prominent.

Lubeck also dominated the other great fishing industry: freeze-dried cod from Lofoten in Northern Norway. Light in weight but high in protein, this was the ultimate preserved fish, known as stockfish. It was said to remain edible for up to seven years.[28] Commerce in cod dates back to the eleventh century, and dried cod, good rations for seafarers, sustained Viking expansion before that. By the thirteenth century, the fish were brought down the Norwegian coast to Bergen and distributed from there, with Lubeck becoming involved from 1240. But, again, post-plague liftoff is clear. As we saw in chapter 2, the trade did extend to Iceland just before the Black Death, in 1340–47, but only modestly, at a dozen ships a year, possibly bringing un-plagued rats. It then reverted to traditional sources until 1397, when cod fishers first returned to Iceland regularly and in numbers, possibly bringing plagued rats. Cod fishing in Icelandic waters burgeoned thereafter, involving at least 25 English ships in 1419, and 90 Hanseatic ships in 1491—these were the numbers allegedly lost in terrible storms.[29] Hanse ships traded for cod with Icelanders. Other players entered the trade from about 1410—English, Hollanders, and Basques—who did the curing as well as the fishing, at Icelandic fishing stations of "near industrial scale".[30] English vessels alone numbered 149 by 1528, by which time the trade was expanding across the Atlantic.[31]

The plague pattern is corroborated in the cod trade in three ways: by cod prices in Iceland, by isotopic studies of cod bones in London, and by Lubecker processing in Norway. Iceland stockfish prices rose 67% between 1186 and 1350, then remained stable to 1400, reflecting stable output and doubled per capita consumption, then rose 71%, 1400–1550, reflecting still more demand.[32] Cured cod bones in London (distinguishable from fresh cod by the absence of head bones) show a reversion to Lofoten sources in the late fourteenth century, followed by fish from still more distant seas in the fifteenth, "concurrent with the expansion of English fishing into Icelandic waters".[33] The near-cessation of the Iceland trade, 1347–97, came about because Lofoten cured cod was considered better than the Icelandic product and was enough to meet first-phase post-plague demand—a blessing in disguise for Iceland which spared it plague for 50 years. Surging second-phase European demand for the quality Lofoten product pushed fishers yet farther north in the late fourteenth century, to Finmark and Troms.[34] Climbing Norwegian output is confirmed by developments at Bergen. "Lubeck established a massive trade station in Bergen in the 1360s, processing, packaging and distributing Lofoten freeze-dried cod. It had 28 yards, two or three hundred merchants and employed 2,000 men in season".[35] By about 1400, 12,800 tons of cod, three times the value of the same tonnage of herring, were exported annually.[36]

The other great northern hunt trade was in furs. Fur clothes and rugs had practical importance, providing warmth inside, let alone outside, poorly heated medieval houses and halls. They also gave status to elites, who believed they had to look like elites. "Furs dominated the self-presentation of the medieval upper classes", accounting for up to 40% of their clothing budgets.[37] Lesser furs, such as low-grade squirrel, were produced in many countries, but the supply of luxury furs was already diminishing in Europe before the Black Death. These came in two grades: prime squirrel, known as *vair* and *gris*, was considered "fit for great lords".[38] Still more valuable furs included mink, marten, beaver and, above all, sable. "The beaver was virtually extirpated from Western Europe by the fourteenth century".[39] Prime furs were becoming scarce even in Finland, where the first law protecting the relevant animals in their breeding season dates to 1347.[40] Western Europe's furs were increasingly drawn from Northern Russia, especially from the vast domains of the Republic of Novgorod, and distributed by the Hanse. Again, the trade surged after 1350. A recent estimate of total annual exports via the Baltic in the early fifteenth century, much higher than earlier estimates, is 1.5 million furs, mostly squirrel.[41]

The high numbers are somewhat deceptive. It took an average of 120 squirrel skins to make a fur lining for a gown, and even more were needed for fur coats and cloaks.[42] A million skins would therefore make fewer than 10,000 garments. On the other hand, fur garments were durable, lasting for decades, even generations. After 1350, sub-elites if not commoners entered the fur market. I cannot find reliable pre-plague estimates of fur exports to measure the scale of the increase, but three lines of indirect evidence suggest it was large.

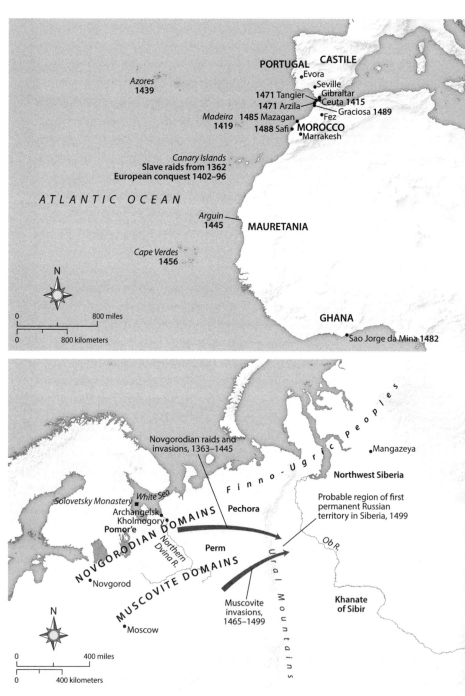

PORTUGAL CASTILE
•Evora
•Seville
1471 Tangier—•Gibraltar
1471 Arzila—•Ceuta 1415
•Fez—Graciosa 1489
Madeira 1485 Mazagan
1419 1488 Safi• MOROCCO
•Marrakesh

Azores
1439

Canary Islands
Slave raids from 1362
European conquest 1402–96

ATLANTIC OCEAN

Arguin—
1445 MAURETANIA

Cape Verdes
1456

N

0   800 miles
0   800 kilometers

GHANA
•Sao Jorge da Mina 1482

Novgorodian raids and
invasions, 1363–1445

Finno-Ugric Peoples

•Mangazeya

Northwest Siberia

Solovetsky Monastery White Sea
Archangelsk•
Kholmogory•
Pomor'e

Pechora

Probable region of first
permanent Russian
territory in Siberia, 1499

NOVGORODIAN DOMAINS

Northern Dvina R.

Perm

Ob R.

•Novgorod

MUSCOVITE DOMAINS

Ural Mountains

Khanate
of Sibir

Muscovite
invasions,
1465–1499

N

•Moscow

0   400 miles
0   400 kilometers

MAP 5. Early European Expansion, 1362–1499. 5.1. Iberian Overseas Expansion before 1492.
5.2. Russian Expansion to Northwest Siberia, 1363–1499

In 1292, there were 214 master furriers or "skinners" in Paris, but 200 in fifteenth-century Cologne, which was at most a quarter the size.[43] Second, fashion again reared its head. From 1400, the middle orders took up lordly furs, prime squirrel, pushing lords towards princely furs, such as sable, to keep their distance.[44] Third, Novgorod began to deplete its traditional trapping grounds, and tried to expand to take over fresh ones, especially for sable (see chapter 14). Unlike squirrels, sables were carnivores, and this was also true of other luxury fur animals like ermine, mink, and black fox. They were therefore much more thinly distributed and easily depleted than squirrel. Sable existed west of the Urals, but not in huge numbers. As early as the eleventh century but especially after 1174, Novgorod sought them over the Urals in Asia, sometimes through middlemen such as the Khanty and Mansi Ugric-speaking peoples, sometimes themselves (see map 5.2). As early as 1363–64, these efforts intensified, culminating in 1445 with "a last vigorous effort to assert Novgorodian rule in Siberia".[45] From 1465, Novgorod's great rival, Muscovy, took up the former's Siberian project with greater success. By 1499, long before its well-known conquest of southwest Siberia in the 1580s, it had secured a permanent lodgment in the northwest. Though virtually unknown, this was modern Europe's first colony in Asia.

II Southern Trades: Sugar, Spice, Silk—and Slaves

Fine textiles, of silk and cotton, were prominent among the southern trades. As noted in the prologue, China and India were the leading producers, but it is unlikely that much of their manufactured product reached Western Europe between the fall of the Roman Empire and 1500. Latins got their silk and cotton mainly from Iran and Greater Syria (including Jordan and Palestine), both as manufactured fabric and as raw fibres for processing in Europe. The effect of Chinese and Indian globalisation on Europe before 1500 was largely indirect, though significant: Europeans emulated Islamic emulation of the Sino-Indian super-crafts. The European industry mainly used imported fibres, but parts of southern Europe could be made to grow mulberry trees, silkworms, and cotton bushes. Increased demand can be tracked by their extension after 1350. There were narrow ecological limits to this domestic substitution, and demand for non-European supplies also increased—first per capita, and then in aggregate.

The centre of European silk production was Lucca, which was already importing 74 tons of raw silk a year in the 1330s.[46] The value of the trade is indicated by the fact that Lucchese silk merchants became the pioneer "trans-national" bankers.[47] Yet again, there was a clear post-plague boom. The indus-try "experienced a rapid growth in Lombardy and other centers of Northern Italy in the fourteenth and fifteenth centuries".[48] The quantity of raw silk in-volved remained low, at between one hundred and two hundred tons a year, but this does not do justice to the value or the "spin-off" effects of the industry. One hundred tons of raw silk was worth 336,000 gold ducats.[49] Making it into garments was extremely labour- intensive: it took a skilled weaver three months to make enough velvet brocade for one sleeveless gown, and the grow-ing and spinning of the silk prior to this were also major tasks.[50] This might have limited its post-plague growth. But, in silk textile production, the labour of women and children was at least as good as men's.[51] By the early fifteenth century, "there were tens of thousands of individuals employed in spinning, weaving and dyeing silk in Genoa, Tuscany, Venice and Naples", as well as in smaller Italian cities such as Vicenza.[52] Furthermore, the spread of water-powered silk twisting [spinning] mills from 1350, particularly in Bologna, slashed labour requirements. "By the fifteenth century twist silk mills, operat-ing day and night at times, were also employed north of the Alps".[53]

Islam had brought silkworms and mulberry to southern Italy and southern Spain as early as the tenth century; the Byzantines had brought them to Greece even earlier. After 1350, new growing areas emerged, in northern Italy, fresh parts of Spain and Greece, and even northern Portugal, but this was pushing the ecological limits.[54] A forlorn relict of a later attempt at an English silk in-dustry sits in the quadrangle of an Oxford college in the form of a crippled four-centuries-old mulberry tree—it was the wrong kind of mulberry in any case. Imports also increased. Europe's main supplier of raw silk continued to be Iran, via the Levant or the Black Sea. Imports from Iran "enhanced increas-ingly from the end of the fourteenth century until the beginning of the six-teenth century".[55] In fact, in the sixteenth and seventeenth centuries, while real wages for silk workers fell, Europe's silk imports climbed still more, now draw-ing on China as well as Iran.[56]

Cotton's tale was similar to that of silk. Greater Syria was Europe's main supplier of cotton, and continued to be after 1350. Venetian cotton imports from Syria were worth 50,000 gold ducats a year in the 1370s; 150,000 in the 1390s. Genoa probably imported similar quantities.[57] Again, further increases in cotton consumption can be traced through the emergence of new cotton-growing areas in Europe. "Secure evidence of cotton growing in the Pelopon-nese appears for the first time in 1365".[58] The island of Malta came to specialise in cotton from the later fourteenth century, now importing its grain.[59] In both silk and cotton, there are hints of the post-plague pattern apparent in the northern hunt trades. The Venetian cotton imports just noted for the 1370s were probably lower than before 1350, those of the 1390s probably higher, indicating the shift from per capita to aggregate increases in consumption.[60]

Increasing demand for cotton, silk—and sugar—could to some extent be met by extending cultivation in the southern fringes of Europe itself. This was not the case with another luxury trade: spices. Pepper, cinnamon, ginger, cloves, and nutmeg grew only in India and Southeast Asia. The main markets in this long-standing semi-global trade were China, India, and the Middle East, with Europe getting the latter's leftovers. Volumes were low; black pepper comprised around half the weight of all spices; and the trade involved just a few annual convoys and caravans, intersecting merchant networks, and competing markets. Prices were therefore volatile. The long routes to Europe went by ship, caravan, or both, from India to the Red Sea and the Persian Gulf; to the Nile and thence to Alexandria; from Mecca's port of Jedda overland to Syria; and from the Persian Gulf overland to Syria or the Black Sea. All routes were sometimes extended to the Levantine coast, where Italian merchants bought spices as an alternative to Alexandria.

Pessimism on post-plague European spice imports is quite strong. The Muslim South naturally tended to satisfy its own demand first (see chapters 8 and 9). Historians have noted ruptures in the spice networks. The Golden Horde disrupted those using the Black Sea from 1343, taking one of the leading ports, Tana, and besieging the other, Caffa. Timur did the same, sacking the inland trading hub of Tabriz in 1392 and plundering Tana in 1395. Some say that imports to the Persian Gulf ceased almost entirely, leaving Europe dependent on the Red Sea, whose Muslim merchants and princes took a handsome cut. Most historians now feel, however, that "assertions that there was a late fourteenth- through fifteenth-century trade decline are incorrect".[61] Venetian and Genoese merchants patiently repaired and improved their ruptured networks: Tana was trading again by 1358, after the rupture of 1343, and by 1399, after the rupture of 1395; Tabriz was again trading strongly by 1404.[62] Chapter 9 will show that the Persian Gulf route continued to operate, though most European imports did come via the Red Sea. Here, during the fifteenth century, control by the merchants of Aden, Cairo, and Mecca was gradually outranked, though not displaced, by that of the Mamluk sultans, who were particularly prone to squeeze the trade. Europeans were not wholly without leverage, however, even against sultans. Genoa controlled the Black Sea slave trade through which the

Mamluks replenished themselves with fresh young recruits, and threatened to stop the flow when Mamluk exactions on their spice trade became too great in 1431.[63] All Muslim brokers valued the bullion Christian merchants paid for their spices (and silks) which in turn enabled the Muslims to cover their trade deficits with India and China. An increasing trickle of Venetian and Genoese merchants made their way to India themselves,[64] perhaps stimulating supply, though we will see in chapter 9 that their efforts were dwarfed by those of their Muslim counterparts.

Despite disagreements among the experts, it is possible to make a reasonable estimate of total Western European spice imports. A sharp drop in prices at Alexandria in the 1360s may suggest a decline in aggregate, though not per capita, European demand, to which Asian merchants had not yet adjusted.[65] But aggregate volumes soon increased.[66] Around 1390, Venice imported about 480 tons of pepper (from Alexandria and Beirut), which we should round up to perhaps 600 tons to allow for lesser routes and suppliers.[67] Imports of other spices were very modest, perhaps around 100 tons combined. This may represent a full recovery of the pre–Black Death peak, itself a doubling of European consumption per capita. Later in the 1390s, volumes suddenly shot up. The best estimate seems to be around 800 tons of pepper and 450 tons of other spices around 1400, including cinnamon, ginger, and perhaps some Middle East–grown saffron. The rarest and most precious spices were from the distant Maluku (Molucca) Islands: cloves, nutmeg, and mace. One source claims Venice imported barely a dozen tons of these spices a year in the mid-1390s. But in 1399, it finds 85 tons of Moluccan spices being imported by Venice, a "most astonishing figure".[68] Volumes continued to rise. "During the first two decades of the fifteenth century, the spice trade entered the Red Sea on an unprecedented scale". Venice installed more and more merchants in Alexandra—200 by 1420.[69]

There was a sharp spike in spice prices in 1410–14, due to developments in China and the Indian Ocean (chapter 9), which deceived older economic histories into positing a decline in prices over most of the fifteenth century, implying softening demand in Europe. But a 2009 study shows that once the spike is taken into account, prices rose.[70] Volumes did too. Their increase over the fifteenth century has been estimated at 30% for pepper and 150% for other spices.[71] The latter is supported by another rough estimate: that "Europe's share of Moluccan spices rose only modestly over the fifteenth century, from less than one-tenth to roughly one-quarter".[72] This "modest" increase in fact represents a 300% increase in per capita consumption and a 150% increase in aggregate imports if Moluccan supply remained the same, even more if it increased. A 30% increase in pepper imports seems about right for the fifteenth century, but is distorted by the later 1390s spike in volumes, just as fifteenth-century prices are by the 1410s spike in prices. Recent work calculates the volume of spices reaching the Red Sea at between 2,350 and 4,230 tons, "mostly pepper". Perhaps half reached Europe. In 1496, Venetian pepper imports alone totaled about 1,800 tons, three times the level of 1390.[73] This was an exceptional year, and 1,200 tons might be closer to the average.[74] Even this was a fourfold increase in European pepper imports per capita between 1350 and 1499, when direct imports began.

This is supported by evidence of spices entering the diets of common folk, spicing up their golden age.[75] One recent study claims that: "What is certain is that a person of even modest affluence consumed impressive quantities of spices", and notes that late fourteenth-century Barcelona, with 30,000 people, supported 115 spice retailers.[76] Pepper was "consumed by many people other than the rich".[77] The two richest men in one remote Tuscan valley were spice sellers, and they could not have become so by selling to elites alone.[78] As with furs and fowl, elites changed habits to keep their distance. "Some spices, such as pepper, had become so widely used that they were of less significance in elite consumption; other, more precious, flavourings were preferred".[79] Elites complained in 1404 "about rural inns where they serve unpleasant and lowly cabbage and leeks seasoned with copious amounts of black pepper".[80] Commoners may have consumed less pepper per head after 1500, but total consumption of it and other spices continued to grow. So too did Christian frustration at their dependence on Muslim intermediaries.

Venice developed a lead over Genoa in the spice trade in the fifteenth century, and vied with it in importing silk and cotton. It sourced its bullion to pay for these goods, often indirectly through south German bankers or through Dubrovnik, from German mines, which were in decline until about 1450, and from mines under Hungarian control. The bullion business was not in itself expansive in this context. Acquired within West Eurasia through the exchange of goods, or of gold for silver and vice versa, it was expensive instead. But bullion was ultimately an extractive product. If you mined it yourself, plundered it, or traded goods for it directly, in distant bullion regions, it was cheap. In this context, the bullion trade *was* potentially expansive. Genoa specialised in a non-Eurasian source of gold: West Africa. This ancient trade began in the sixth century CE, when North Africans acquired enough camels to reliably cross the Sahara.[81] It was associated with trades in salt, horses, ivory, and

black slaves, conducted by African and Islamic networks of traders and cam-
eleers. The slaves and horses walked; the camels were needed to carry water
between oases. The Genoese had trading factories in every major North African port.[82] The leading gold trade outlets changed with the shifting sands and
politics of the Sahara, and the focus of Genoese interest tracked these changes,
from Ceuta in the west to Tripoli in the east and back. While there is evidence
of some direct contact with West Africa in the fourteenth century,[83] the Genoese normally acquired their gold through Muslim middlemen, and brought it
home via Spain. Again, the upturn in demand correlates in time with the Black
Death. "In the second half of the fourteenth century, [West African] gold appeared in considerable quantities both in Spain and in Genoa ... it was used
by the latter in its trade with the Levant".[84] "The spike in demand for gold
production had begun in the later fourteenth century". [85]

At this time, the sub-Saharan empire of Mali was a key player in the trans-
Saharan trade. It had strong connections with Marinid Morocco, through the
city of Sijilmasa among others.[86] About 1374, Morocco split into two parts,
with the north known after its capital as the Kingdom of Fez, whose chief port
was Ceuta, then the leading gold outlet. "The Genoese monopolized the trade
of Ceuta", while Fez was "considered by the Genoese to be their private commercial preserve".[87] In the 1390s, however, the Mali empire began to collapse,
and Sijilmasa was abandoned.[88] During the next few years, Moroccan mints
ceased coining gold and the Kingdom of Fez was wracked by civil war. Fez city
was besieged three times in 1411. "The struggle continued during 1412, and
much of northern Morocco was out of control".[89] Almost two centuries earlier,
in 1235, the Genoese had dealt with a similar situation by sending a hundred
of their own galleys to Ceuta to re-install a friendly regime.[90] Now, with their
manpower depleted by plague, they needed someone else to do the job. As
chapter 10 will show, they settled on the Portuguese, who took Ceuta in 1415.
The trans-Saharan trade reconstituted itself with the displacement of Mali by
the Songhay Empire, and with the temporary stabilisation of Morocco, so the
flow of West African gold to Europe resumed. But it became increasingly clear
to the Genoese and Portuguese that direct relations with the gold-producing
regions would be more reliable and more profitable.

While Venice led in spices, Genoa led in the two remaining expansive
trades: sugar and slaves. The traditional sources of Europe's sugar were Greater
Syria and Egypt, with small supplements from cane grown in Sicily, Southern
Spain, and, especially, Cyprus and Crete. From 1350, demand suddenly shot
up, followed raggedly by supply. In this instance historians have no doubt

about the reason or the timing. "This boom in sugar production, in both Spain and Sicily, reflects the expansion in demand for luxury and semi-luxury foodstuffs that followed the Black Death".[91] "The Sicilian industry only began to succeed significantly after about 1350".[92] Venice controlled Crete, but Genoa tightened its grip on Cyprus, consolidating its control of the export economy though not the whole island, with a large-scale invasion in 1373, which seized the key port of Famagusta.[93] It reorganised and expanded Cypriot sugar production and was also involved in a tenfold expansion of Sicilian sugar production between 1393 and 1416, though the total acreage in cane remained modest.[94] The Genoese then developed sugar industries in Muslim Granada, in Valencia, in Andalusia, and in Southern Portugal.[95] In the fifteenth century, even European common folk ingested modest amounts of sugar. "For palates unused to sweetness, a little sugar goes a long way".[96] The supply was further eked out by syrups and sweetmeats such as sugared fruits, whose production became important in Cyprus and Portugal.[97]

Supply remained a problem, however. One issue was the collapse of the big Egyptian sugar industry after 1400 (chapter 8). Another was the fact that sugar is a greedy crop, quickly exhausting soil fertility, local sources of water, and firewood for processing. It took 50 pounds of firewood to produce one pound of sugar.[98] Sugar was also a labour-intensive industry—because the ripe cane had to be harvested and processed very quickly. Low-level ongoing production was perfectly possible with free peasant labour, if wood and water were available and cultivation was rotated to restore soil fertility. But larger scale expansion required fresh sugar lands and fresh labour, and it was the Genoese who led Europe's hunt for both.

After the Black Death killed half its workforce, Western Europe experienced one of its nastier renaissances—a revived slave trade. Slavery had been in steep decline because serfs and low-paid workers were cheaper. Slaves needed support in childhood and old age, when they earned their owners little or nothing. After 1350, demand for slaves suddenly shot up; and slave prices doubled or trebled.[99] The trade operated under religious constraints, though sometimes honoured in the breach. West Eurasians were generally reluctant to enslave co-religionists, although conversion after enslavement did not necessarily free you. Not only did Muslims prefer Christian slaves, and vice versa, but Latin and Orthodox Christians enslaved each other as did Sunni and Shi'ites. All were in the market for pagan slaves, a diminishing resource in West Eurasia.

Western Europeans regularly enslaved Muslims captured at sea, in raids or in battle in the Mediterranean. But the boot was more often on the other foot.

At one end of the Mediterranean, the Muslim city-state of Bijaya in what is now Algeria began raiding Spain for slaves in the 1360s.[100] At the other end of the inland sea, the Ottomans enslaved Christian war captives in vast numbers. After the defeat by Timur in 1402, their slave-taking went into remission, but re-commenced even more strongly from the 1420s. They are said to have taken 400,000 slaves in 1437–43 alone.[101] In the 1402–20 hiatus, the Timurids were the big slavers, of Christian and Muslim alike, using them to repopulate cities devastated by plague and war. Extrapolating conservatively from estimates for the sixteenth and seventeenth centuries, perhaps 1.5 million Christians fell victim to Mediterranean slave-taking between 1350 and 1800, *excluding* Slavic slaves taken on land in Eastern Europe. At most, half as many Muslims went the other way.[102] But, well into the seventeenth century, a fifth of the populations of Livorno and Malta were Muslim slaves, as were up to half the rowers on Christian galleys.[103]

Slave raids were joined by slave trades, with Latin Christians competing with Muslims in the market for Orthodox Christians from Eastern Europe, mainly Greeks and Slavs, for the peoples of the Caucasus, such as Circassians, and for Turks who had remained pagan on the European steppes. These people were bought in the ports of the Black Sea, mostly controlled by Genoa. The chief Genoese slaving port, Caffa, exported 3,285 slaves in 1374 and 8,545 in 1446, but such numbers are rare.[104] Historians have ingeniously replaced them by looking at laws and surnames. After the second plague strike, ending in 1363, "we suddenly find that the importation of eastern slaves was legalised and regularised by authorities across southern Europe . . . we can thus be fairly certain that the number of slaves in southern Europe increased dramatically".[105] A survey of Italian surnames finds many probably derived from "Russian" (e.g., "Russo") or "Slav" (e.g., "Schiavo").[106] Another source was the trans-Saharan slave trade in pagan black Africans, involving several thousand unfortunate people a year. There are hints of a post-plague surge in this ancient trade,[107] and its Muslim entrepreneurs would sell their surplus to Christians in such ports as Tunis.

There are a few numbers for slaves inside Europe. By about 1390 there were 2,000 slaves in Florence (5% of the population); 7,200 in Genoa (15%); and 5,000 in much-plagued Barcelona (20%).[108] Slaves are thought to have comprised 10% of the population of Lisbon by 1446, and even more in the southern Portuguese city of Evora.[109] Urban slaves were mostly female, working as domestic servants. But the notion that almost all post-plague slaves in Europe were female domestics seems misguided. There were at least 1,700 male slaves in the Valencia region in 1431. Here and elsewhere, most male slaves worked outside the cities in hard and dangerous trades that free labourers avoided:

deep mines, galleys, and plantations.[110] The slaves in Evora may have been used to reclaim land abandoned after the Black Death. In 1472 they were declared "the cause of new lands being opened and woods being cleared and marshes being opened".[111]

Historians dispute whether these numbers were "relatively small" or "astonishing".[112] Certainly, high prices suggest supply was not meeting demand. The problem was that Muslims were out-competing Christians both in reciprocal enslavement and in shared slave markets. The Genoese Black Sea slaving ports all fell to the Ottomans over the fifteenth century. Ever adaptable (see chapter 10), the Genoese moved west, mobilised their Iberian allies, and jointly pushed out into the Atlantic in search of fresh slaving grounds and sugar lands. As early as 1362, the Canary Islands, long known but hitherto mostly neglected, were raided for slaves by Genoese-prompted expeditions. The Canarians (known as Guanches) were of Berber descent, but had lost the arts of seafaring and metallurgy.[113] They put up a fierce resistance even so. One island was seized in 1402, and the last was finally conquered by the Spanish in 1496 (see chapter 7 and map 5.1).[114]

Other Atlantic islands were later discovered by the Portuguese (Madeira, 1419, the Azores, 1439, and the Cape Verdes, 1456). They were uninhabited, but in varying degrees suitable for sugar, as were the Canaries. Most early sugar plantations mixed slave and free labour, but in the 1460s in the Cape Verde Islands, a Genoese in Portuguese service pioneered the slave-only sugar plantation.[115] While slaving in the Canaries was still underway, Portuguese vessels began nosing down the coast of Africa. They were not yet looking for a route to Asia but for slaves, the expeditions being "openly and explicitly a series of raids designed to obtain slaves."[116] In the 1440s, they found that trading for slaves with coastal Africans was easier than taking them, with cheap gold as a bonus, and so the notorious European trade in Africans began.[117] Reaching these coasts and islands from Iberia was easy enough once you tried, but prevailing winds made return difficult. Vessels sailed deeper and deeper into the Atlantic to catch suitable winds for the return home—the *volta do mar largo*. "The closer toward to the equator the caravels sailed, the longer the northwesterly arm of the *volta* became".[118]

———

It seems almost inhumane to find a silver lining in a cloud as dark as the Black Death. In fact, increased prosperity in Western Europe did not eliminate the poor, but turned them from a large majority into a large minority, reducing economic inequality to its lowest levels between about 800 and 1800 CE. For the average person, the silver lining thinned and tarnished after 1500. "Industriousness" could slow that process, but it can also be defined as overwork—long hours of hard labour for both adults and children. As a percentage of the population, the buying classes probably shrank back from their early plague-era peak. But they increased in wealth and absolute numbers as populations began to grow again and demand for exotic and extractive goods continued to track upwards. One estimate suggests a growth rate of 1–2% per year, 1500 to 1800, in the expansive trades—high in preindustrial terms.[119] Yet the earlier post-plague trade boom, 1390–1500, was sharper still, and it was this that boosted Western Europeans' desire to expand beyond their own bounds. By the mid-fifteenth century, with or without Columbus, Europeans were on their way to the Americas in three directions: across the North Atlantic, in pursuit of more cod and whales; into Siberia after prime furs; and across the South Atlantic, seeking winds to take them home from the search for cheap gold, fresh sugar lands, and new slave sources.

5

Plague Revolutions?

THE LAST TWO CHAPTERS have shown that post-plague Western Europe developed the motives for expansion, in the form of temporary increases in per capita affluence and ongoing increases in demand for the goods of the expansive trades. But the desire to expand is one thing; the capacity to do so successfully is quite another. This chapter turns from motives to the *means* for expansion, and plague's effect on them. The inquiry intersects with some long-debated issues. One is whether Europe experienced a "medieval industrial revolution" due to the rise of water-powered milling in particular. This was originally placed in the thirteenth century, and the idea has lost traction in recent times.[1] But there may be a case for broadening the concept, and dating it to the early plague era, 1350–1500. A second theme is the "print revolution", begun by Johannes Gutenberg in Germany in the 1450s with the invention of moveable metal type. This is well-known; some parallel changes in the technology of literacy are not. The third issue is a "military revolution" involving the emergence of gunpowder armies. Historians initially dated this to 1560–1660; while its best-known proponent, Geoffrey Parker, extended it from 1500 to 1800. But some now put it firmly in the period 1350–1500.[2] Here, in all too brief a compass, I attempt to re-assess these matters in the dark light of plague.

I A Late Medieval Industrial Revolution?

The Black Death fundamentally transformed—indeed, inverted—the relationship between labour and capital, creating a strong incentive to replace the former with the latter where possible. This is self-evident enough, but as noted earlier we must also take into account the immediate "plague bonus"—twice as many fixed assets as well as cash, twice the per capita endowment of natural resources, and twice the prime locations—for farms, docks, mills, and so on.

If people could work these extra assets, they did so, in the least labour-intensive ways possible. If they could not, they chose the "better half". We need also to broaden our concept of "labour-saving". It was not just the matter of a wind-mill doing the work of 50 hand-millers, but of shortening training times, taking shortcuts in technique, extending the working days and working lives of the surviving workers, and preserving the lives of soldiers through such means as better armour and fortifications. Perhaps surprisingly, there were few entirely new inventions, but rather a sharply increased uptake of three existing inani-mate sources of energy: waterpower, wind power, and gunpowder.

Driving mills to grind grain was the main role of waterpower before 1350, and water mills continued to grind most grain thereafter. Indeed, they ground a higher percentage of it. While horse-powered and wind-powered mills re-mained significant where millraces were unavailable, hand-milling declined sharply. In England, the fact that "overall mill numbers, whether powered by water, wind, or horse, declined far less than did the population after 1348 sug-gests that many who had milled the grain by hand before the plague patronized other power sources for the task afterwards".[3] Furthermore, waterpower now expanded well beyond grain milling. "Industrial" mills, which mainly sawed timber and powered hammers for fining metal and fulling cloth, existed before the Black Death, but proliferated after it. In England, the number of industrial mills rose from 600 to 2,000 between 1300 and 1540,[4] a sixfold increase relative to population, and at this time England was not the most proto-industrialised part of Europe. France, northern Italy, and parts of Germany at least matched it in the use of waterpower. Mills using the waters of the Rhine and Meuse in France seem to have increased around 50% in absolute numbers in the early plague era, a threefold increase per capita.[5] Initially, industrial mills were con-verted from old grain mills or at least used their sites—a "plague bonus" of surplus buildings and prime sites. The range of industrial milling widened to include such actions as pulping rags for paper, sharpening blades, powering lathes, and pressing nuts and seeds for oil. The key developments in France are all dated to 1348–78.[6]

Apart from sawmills, the most important uses of industrial mills remained the processing of cloth and metal.[7] "Fulling" was the pounding of raw cloth while wet to merge the fibres, and until 1350 was mostly done by the stamping of human feet. This continued to be the case for some luxury textiles consid-ered too delicate for water-powered fulling, but the post-1350 shift towards waterpower is unmistakable. It cut fulling costs by at least two-thirds; and so lowered the cost of cloth, the main item of medieval manufacture.[8] More households could afford to buy cloth, rather than weave it themselves, and more could afford to use powered mills rather than hand mills to grind their grain. It was this that freed more peasant women for the waged workforce. An example of the Black Death's effect on European textile manufacturing is the silk industry in Bologna.[9] By 1341, Bologna had acquired the "Lucchese-invented circular throwing machine . . . a complex cylindrical mechanism powered by hand" via a migrant artisan, the usual means of medieval technology transfer. By 1371, Bologna had 12 *water*powered silk spinning mills, and the number increased rapidly thereafter to create Bologna's main industry. The key product, along with silk veils, was a stronger, thicker silk yarn, a "semi-finished product ready for the loom", which was then sold to other north Italian cities for finishing. My source does not emphasise plague's role, but it seems clear enough. The system, kept secret until 1454, included an "underground capillary network of small conduits called *chiaviche*", a hydraulic innovation apparently peculiar to Bologna, but also depended on water-powered mills along canals. These had previously ground grain but many were rendered surplus, presumably by plague depopulation—grain mills dropped from 70 in the twelfth century to 20 in 1393, with 16 mills now throwing silk and "21 other mills serving the metallurgical, wool and paper industries". The silk industry was concentrated in "a sparsely inhabited area" of the city, likely also made available by plague, and staffed mainly by women and children.

Metals are given precedence in prehistory—the Bronze Age, the Iron Age—but then are somewhat taken for granted until the Industrial Revolution. Yet it seems that, revolutionary or not, the sharpest pre-industrial shift in European metallurgy since the fall of Rome came in the early plague era. The Black Death applied a blast furnace to water-powered blast furnace iron production, which mushroomed after 1350 in regions with the right mix of ore, charcoal, and fast-flowing water. Charcoal, the essential fuel for metallurgy, was shaken to dust by wagon transport,[10] and navigable waterways and fast-flowing water often precluded each other, so iron production tended towards hilly wooded districts with plentiful streams, notably those in Walloon Belgium, parts of Germany, northwest France, and Appenine Italy. Before 1350, iron was mostly produced in small "bloomeries" yielding two or three tons of metal a year. Water-powered bellows and fining hammers existed, but were not common. "The importance of water-powered bellows only increased after the Black Death".[11] Larger-scale blast furnaces emerged, increasing production to 40 or 50 tons a year. Blast furnaces "reduced the thirty to forty smiths and bellows-blowers needed . . . to as few as two or three".[12] A comparable but smaller-scale technology, known as the Catalan forge and using natural water-falls, spread widely from its point of origin in and near the Pyrenees. Between 1400 and 1525, European iron output is thought to have tripled or quadrupled.[13] Certainly, iron from leading exporter, Sweden, sold through Lubeck, increased 132% between 1368 and 1492, and tithe records suggest a sixfold increase in overall Swedish iron production, 1340–1539.[14] These are absolute figures, indicating much greater increases per capita. More water-powered fining hammers "compensated for the rising labor costs that followed the depopulation caused by the Black Death."[15]

Unlike most, historians of technology have long noted the post-plague surge in iron output,[16] but not all of its implications. It drew on techniques used in the processing of other metals, and in return the post-plague surge in metallurgy boosted their production too. Innovations in the processing of lead and silver seem to date mainly to the fifteenth century, but copper production surged earlier, to meet increasing demand for bronze. Sweden was even more important for copper than for iron, and its exports of the former, again via Lubeck, increased almost fourfold, 1368–1492.[17] Returning to iron, recent research demonstrates plague's effect on prices, beginning in England in 1353. Here, and in Sweden, long series of nail prices show that "a new price structure is seen after the Black Death. This shock appears to have triggered the long-term downward pressure on iron prices".[18] The same trend has been traced in Spain, Germany, and the Netherlands. We have seen that more iron implements boosted agriculture, and will soon see that it did the same to shipping, weapons, and armour. Most production was of relatively malleable wrought iron, but cast iron production now began, apparently starting in Italy in 1377.[19] Steel, a byproduct of iron-making, had hitherto been difficult to produce and therefore scarce. Here too, the Black Death quickly stimulated increased quality and quantity, though the latter remained quite modest. As we have seen, the world's leading producer of quality ("wootz") crucible steel had long been India. Indian techniques were emulated in the Middle East and Muslim Spain to produce fine Damascene and Toledo sword blades. Japan was another leading steel sword producer, using very labour-intensive techniques. A comparative scientific study, using new non-intrusive techniques on museum pieces, finds that India and Japan retained an edge in quality, but that "the European method was the cheapest one, both in terms of materials and labour".[20]

Another major post-plague technological shift involved wind power rather than waterpower. Better windmills, and their use for pumping water and sawing wood, emerged in the fifteenth century, particularly in the Netherlands, but developments in wind-powered shipping were more important. Before the Black Death, both the Mediterranean and Atlantic Europe used a mix of sail-only ships and oared ships, which usually also carried sails. Sail-only ships were principally small round vessels, known as cogs, which had one mast and were not very maneuverable. North and south, shippers therefore tended to restrict voyages to seasons and routes where weather and sea conditions were predictably benign.[21] Galleys were used for trickier waters, but had low cargo capacity and heavy crews, and needed to land every few days to take on drinking water. They had sails, and used them when they could—the oarsmen were extremely expensive insurance against lee shores, failing winds, and violent attack. Galleys with around 200 men and a 50-ton cargo capacity were the preferred warship, but any ship could fight or freight. Small galleys, called barges or balingers, were common in the north; and "great galleys" were developed by Venice and Genoa in the south, able to carry 250 tons of cargo. It was initially great galleys that carried pre-plague Europe's longest-range trade, along the "alum route" from Asia Minor to England and Flanders.

The Black Death bequeathed an immediate "plague bonus" in shipping, doubling Europe's cargo capacity per person. Because labour was now so scarce, sailing ships replaced oared ships where possible; and larger sailing ships, with lower crew-to-cargo ratios, were preferred. As old ships wore out, new construction tended to sailing ships rather than galleys, and to bigger sailing ships. In the Mediterranean, Venice and Genoa had long used sail-only vessels, known simply as "ships" (*nau, nao, nave*), with one or two masts. They adopted northern cog-type sail plans, which used less labour, just before the Black Death, but as so often the trend curved sharply upward after 1350.[22] Big versions of the *nave* became known as "carracks", the largest ships afloat, ranging from 400 to 1,000 tons. While Venice mostly stuck with great galleys on the great alum route, the Genoese began using carracks by 1382–83 at the latest.[23] By 1400, Genoa had 64 carracks of over 400 tons each.[24] From 1410, up to 20 of these dominated the alum route, carrying 7,000–8,000 tons of cargo annually, much more than a similar number of great galleys could manage. This boosted trade and encouraged the hybridising of northern and southern shipping techniques. The Basque Country and Portugal, stopping points on the route, were important in hybrid shipbuilding. By 1409, some carracks and some smaller Iberian ships had added a third, lateen, mast, which allowed for extra maneuverability.[25] An exception to the rule of larger sailing ships was the caravel, a small but stable and manoeuvrable vessel, whose role is discussed later in this chapter.

Farther north, plague's effect on shipping can be traced in the average sizes of English seagoing vessels: from 36 tons in 1359 to 65 tons in 1410 to 100 tons in 1450.[26] As the modest tonnages suggest, England was not a major maritime power at the time, and other fleets had much larger ships. In the North Sea, there was a shift from 100-ton cogs to bigger "hulks", beginning around 1380, perhaps because the inherited pre-plague ships had worn out. These were ships of 200–300 tons, with two masts and integral fore and stern castles. At some point in the mid-fifteenth century, northerners replaced their shell-first tradition of shipbuilding with the southern frame-first technique, which was cheaper and delivered a stronger ship. Meanwhile, more complex and adjustable sail plans were appearing north and south, producing the full-rigged three-mast ship by about 1430.[27] Large versions continued to be known as carracks, but soon after 1500 these were joined by a longer, leaner variant known as the galleon. Whether the galleon first appeared in the Mediterranean a little before 1500, or in the Atlantic soon afterwards, is contested.[28]

These developments in Western European shipping are well-known. Some historians recognise that it was the Black Death that slashed maritime freight rates north and south. "Freight rates for bulk cargoes dropped in the course of the [fourteenth] century, despite a sharp rise in seamen's wages, from about 25–30% of the value of a cargo of woad or alum to 8%".[29] One leading expert also notes that "it is impossible to contest the conclusion that shipping grew much more rapidly than the economy as a whole".[30] This of course underwrote the expansion of maritime trade discussed in previous chapters. But one factor needs additional emphasis. Chinese, Indians, and other peoples used sail-only ships too, but generally as specialist craft designed for particular seas, winds, and seasons. Before 1350, this was also the case in European waters, north and south. "Summer winds are, and were, highly predictable in the eastern Mediterranean and Aegean . . . it may be thought of as a 'monsoon wind'." "As in the Mediterranean, there was a summer sailing season in early Atlantic Europe", where gales were eight times more frequent in winter than in summer.[31] The full-rigged ship, in sharp contrast, was a generalist, able to cope with most seas and seasons anywhere on the planet. Weaning mariners from oar insurance in variable seas and seasons was a radical shift—the horrors of a lee shore for sail-only ships are notorious. Longer voyages were coupled with improved navigation techniques: better quadrants, astrolabes, which allowed winter navigation when the sun could not be seen, and the sailing directions known as "portolans". It was the Black Death labour shortage, and the subsequent plagues that kept labour scarcity in place, that pressure-cooked this shift into existence.

II The Print Revolution and the Scribal Transition

In the early 1450s, in Germany, Johannes Gutenberg and his collaborators famously invented printing with moveable metal type. Whether this was a true invention, or one derived from Korea where a similar technology was in use by 1377, a Western European "print revolution" was the consequence. Its wide, long-term resonances cannot be explored here, except to note the cautions of other scholars about "the tendency to associate printing with inevitable progress".[32] But we can establish two things: first, that Gutenberg's invention was a creature of plague, and, second, that the print revolution had an unsung older sibling, which we will call a "scribal transition".

In the 1990s, that perceptive scholar David Herlihy connected printing to plague, and noted that Gutenberg's achievement was "only the culmination of many experiments carried on across the previous century".[33] Recent research on manuscript book production supports this insight. In the two decades immediately following the Black Death, the output of books plummeted, with the deaths of authors and copyists, increased wages for the survivors, and the consequent rise in the costs of production. "But, after this temporary decline, production rebounded, ushering in an even sharper increase in output with an almost tenfold increase over the next hundred years"—before print.[34] Costs decreased as numbers grew.[35] Cheap mass-produced books of woodcut prints emerged in the early fifteenth century, soon followed by "intaglio" printing, involving the etching and engraving of a copper plate.[36] Though used mainly for illustrations, these developments can be seen as intermediate stages in the evolution of moveable metal type printing. "The printing press ... was as much a response to the growing appetite for texts as it was a driver of new consumption".[37] "A vigorous book-using culture was the precursor to the invention of printing rather than its consequence".[38] The rapid dissemination of print technology throughout much of Western Europe supports this perspective, confirming uptake was demand-driven.[39] One factor behind the massive rise in post-plague book production before print was the greater application of waterpower to paper-making, a practice that spread from Italy after 1348.[40] Paper had always been much cheaper than parchment: a Gutenberg Bible printed on parchment required the skins of 300 sheep. After 1350, paper prices fell further throughout Western Europe.[41] Other factors centred on the rise of literacy and an improvement in scribal productivity.

Various shortcuts in book-copying practice appeared after 1350: standard layouts, more abbreviations and more cursive script, tracing multiple copies, like the carbon copies some of us remember, as well as piecework—"dividing text into sections (quires) that were farmed out to multiple scribes and illuminators".[42] The pre-print book boom was important in itself, but also indicated a wider shift—an upturn in the use of writing. The well-known increase in the use of local, vernacular, languages rather than Latin saved scribal training time. The aggregate number of universities more than doubled in Western Europe during the early plague era, and of course the percentage of the population they educated grew even more. Secular schools "mushroomed rapidly in the fourteenth century".[43] As well as letters, they taught numbers, with increasing help from Arabic numerals and the abacus. Several economic historians have demonstrated a general decline in the "skill differential" in wages, for skilled crafts of all kinds, including those requiring literacy. They agree that this indicates a broadening of training and education. More affluent parents invested more in the education of their fewer surviving offspring. The number of skilled workers therefore increased more rapidly, or declined more slowly, than the number of unskilled. In England "this skill premium, on average 115% in the half-century before the Black Death, dropped to . . . only 49% afterwards".[44] Numeracy also increased, measured by a decline in "age-heaping"—the practice of rounding out your age or date of birth to "about 25", or "about 1315". In northern Italy, men's numeracy is thought to have increased from 31% in 1350 to 55% in 1450.[45]

Another cause of the rise of scribes and literacy is a neglected—and plague-prompted—enhancement of human vision: a vision transition. After the Black Death, the surviving scribes and artisans sought to lengthen their working days and working lives. This is likely to have been a cause of the increased demand for whale products noted in the previous chapter. Lamp oil was a leading whale product. Demand for wax candles seems also to have grown. "It seems likely that increased per capita consumption after the Black Death at least compensated for the decline in population, and that the socio-economic conditions of the later middle ages combined with trends in religious practice to drive a growing demand for wax".[46] As with furs, Novgorod was a big producer, Poland another, and the Hanse merchants of Thorn (Torun) alone handled over 40,000 marks worth of Baltic wax a year in the 1360s.[47] Wax was imported from every other possible source too, including the Balkans and

North Africa.[48] Increased artificial light was particularly important in Northern Europe, which had only two-thirds of the south's annual sunshine hours.
Two other changes applied both north and south. Glass windows proliferated
from the late fourteenth century, enhancing natural light in workrooms.[49] Venice, a leading maker of glass, substantially increased its imports of Levantine
soda ash, which helped make the best glass, as early as 1348, and increased
them again from 1386.[50] The proliferation of eyeglasses was even more striking.
Spectacles are thought to have been invented in Italy in the 1280s, but it was
only after the Black Death that they became common.[51] Archaeology shows
that they were now found in fishing villages as well as on the noses of princes
and prelates.[52] Annual exports of thousands of pairs of spectacles by Venice
and Barcelona from 1400 have been documented, and Florence probably exported even more. These cities were particularly hard hit by plague, and had a
high demand for writing in culture and commerce. Eyeglasses not only length-
ened working days for writers, and for other kinds of fine work, but also extended the working lives of older people with failing eyesight.

   "Historians generally agree that literacy expanded significantly during the
fourteenth and fifteenth century, especially in urban areas".[53] We should not
exaggerate this development. We are certainly not looking at the advent of
mass literacy. Men's literacy in England is thought to have increased from 2%
to 11.4% between 1300 and 1500.[54] But this was still close to a threefold "selective increase" in aggregate numbers, and we have seen that productivity per
scribe also increased. Technical manuals proliferated, though most technology
transfer remained a matter of skilled worker migration. In wealthy trading cities, literate men became a large minority.[55] In Genoa and Lubeck at least, merchants began to take over some of the work of professional notaries—"a remarkable change", dating to "the second half of the fourteenth century".[56]
Self-written, co-signed, basic contracts became legal records, freeing notaries
for other work, notably marine insurance contracts, which also emerged at this
time. This facilitated trade and enhanced the cohesion of merchant networks.
More scribes also enhanced public administration and improved the memory
of states, in the form of record keeping.[57] This helped increase tax takes, and
also facilitated the replacement of feudal armies with contracted ones.[58] In
public and private spheres alike, this scribal transition improved the ability of
organisations to maintain relationships across space and time. As the great
Jesuit missionary Matteo Ricci put it, "the whole point of writing things
down . . . is that your voice carries for thousands of miles".[59] Part three of this
text will show that, while the print revolution beginning in the 1450s was

largely restricted to Western Europe, the scribal transition, beginning in the 1350s, extended throughout West Eurasia.

III A Gunpowder Revolution?

The military revolution debate is important for this book not only because plague has scarcely featured in it but also because it has long offered an alternative, plague-free, explanation for Western European expansion. The debate contests and often blurs a pair of developments and a pair of timings. The developments are a gunpowder "revolution" and the emergence of strong "warfare states," rich enough to afford large professional armies and large specialised navies. The timings are "early", 1350–1500, and "late", 1500–1800. Some argue that both gun-led and state-led "revolutions" occurred early. More argue that both occurred late. This book argues that guns proliferated early, while warfare states were late. This section looks at guns and their rivals, while warfare states are left to chapter 7.

Both gunpowder and guns were invented by the Chinese, a side product of their super-craft divergence. Gunpowder had emerged by AD 800, and was applied to warfare a century later. Gunpowder weapons increased from the thirteenth century in the desperate struggle of the Southern Sung against the Mongols. Cannon featured from the mid- thirteenth century at the latest, but were only a part of a wider suite of Chinese gunpowder weapons, which also included incendiary bombs, grenades, "fire lances" (rockets?), and explosive mines..[60] Gunpowder then underwent three global diffusions, the first carried by the Mongols and their Chinese auxiliaries.[61] The Mongols used gunpowder weapons on occasion,[62] but not enough to make theirs the first "gunpowder empire" as has been suggested.[63] From the 1370s, fresh Chinese developments took place under the Ming, now with more emphasis on handguns and small cannon, but with rockets and so on still featuring significantly. Ming gunpowder technology diffused to Southeast Asia, Central Asia, and India during the fifteenth century. It also reached the Middle East, through the Timurids.[64] The earlier, Sung-Mongol, diffusion had more influence on Western Europe. By the later thirteenth century, recipes for gunpowder had percolated as far as England and the Byzantine Empire.[65] By 1327, gunpowder, known as "Chinese snow", was sufficiently common in southern Spain for laws to be passed against fireworks for fear of accidental fires, and the first crude cannon had appeared both here and farther north.[66] But it is generally agreed that guns flourished in Europe only after 1350. Its centres were the Walloon country in Belgium, adjacent parts of northeast France and northwest Germany, perhaps because of their precedence in blast furnaces, and northern Italy, whose town of Pistoia may be the origin of the word "pistol". Together, these regions might be called "Middle Europe", the third hearth of global gun diffusion.

Gunpowder replaced human energy with chemical energy, so saving human labour. After the Black Death, guns and their rivals went through a set of "push-me, pull-you" competitive developments pitting cannon against forts, wrought iron cannon against cast bronze cannon, and breech-loading against muzzle-loading. Similar competitions occurred between gunships and gun galleys, and between improved bows, armour, and handguns (not pistols in this context, but longer guns small enough to be used by one person). These competitive developments produced some "transitional technologies", important in their day but eventually overtaken by rival methods. Among these were wrought iron cannon, made from hoops and staves of wrought iron, hence the term gun "barrel". Cannon ranged in size from monsters useful only to besiegers, firing stone shot of 100 kilograms or more, to small cannon firing as little as half a kilogram. The latter were mounted on the walls of castles, towns (and on ships), in considerable numbers; unlike field or siege cannon they did not have to be moved by men and draft animals, saving still more labour. "Late revolutionists" argue that guns were unimportant in sieges until about 1450, or in field battles until after 1500. But "early revolutionists" note that, as early as 1382, the rebel townsmen of Ghent took 200 small cannon down from their walls, loaded them on carts, and used them to defeat their count in a field battle.[67] They also note that Burgundian siege cannon helped take an English-held fortress in 1377.[68] Cannon could certainly be decisive in sieges from about 1407.[69] In 1415, according to recent research, the English fired 7,466 stone shot into the well-fortified French town of Harfleur—"the huge force of their blows smashed everything that got in their way"—leaving the town vulnerable to assault and forcing its surrender.[70]

Throughout the early plague era, wrought iron cannon competed with cast bronze cannon. The latter were more expensive, but also more reliable, and could handle a stronger charge of gunpowder. Europe was short of the natural saltpetre deposits that provided the best nitrate for gunpowder, and initially scraped its nitrates from dried human and animal urine. From the 1380s, however, saltpetre "plantations" cut the cost of gunpowder. Stronger, drier, cheaper corned gunpowder and other improvements followed.[71] Between 1386 and 1417, the price of gunpowder dropped by two-thirds.[72] This favoured cast bronze cannon, but wrought cannon responded, improving their accuracy by increasing their length, by replacing stone shot with iron balls, which first appeared in 1414, and by developing early "breechloaders", where a breech containing ball and powder could be detached from the gun and replaced by another, allowing faster fire. The raw material of iron cannon balls was more expensive than stone, but iron balls required much less labour.[73] Single-cast bronze cannon could not use detachable breeches, but did adopt iron balls and greater length among other improvements.[74] By about 1500, cast bronze cannon were pushing wrought versions and breechloaders towards redundancy, though small, swivel-mounted breechloaders had a significant after-life—a "transitional technology". Experiments with a third type of cannon, cast from iron not bronze, date to 1429, in Tuscany.[75] Iron was cheaper than bronze, but cannon were difficult to cast from it, and cast iron cannon were not perfected until the 1540s, in England. They were cheaper, but not better, as the English acknowledged. As late as 1595, "less than 20% of English naval guns (188 of 977) were cast from iron".[76]

Both cast bronze and wrought iron cannon also competed with fortifications, which adapted more quickly than the late revolutionists allow. The key adaptation was simply for fortifications to mount guns themselves, which they did as early as the 1360s. Thicker and squatter artillery towers, emerged from 1411, able to sustain and return cannon fire. Earthworks to protect stone walls from bombardment are reported by the 1430s. Bastions had appeared by 1472.[77] These jutted out from the main wall, and cannon mounted in them could not only bring flanking fire to bear on storming parties, but also keep enemy cannon at a distance. Besiegers had therefore to silence the cannon of at least one bastion before they could bring their own cannon to bear on the main walls, doubling their work. "All the characteristics which Parker identifies as original in the *trace italienne* artillery fortifications [built from the 1520s] have medieval precedents".[78] Exceptionally, John Landers makes the link to plague. "The later fourteenth and fifteenth centuries saw the development of particularly elaborate defenses, perhaps as a response to post-plague manpower constraints".[79] In fact, the basic pre-1500 anti-artillery measures, such as squatter towers and bastions to allow flanking fire, were not elaborate, but quite simple, reproducible, and even portable. From 1482, Portuguese carracks carried pre-cut masonry to quickly plant gun forts on the coasts first of Africa and then of Asia.[80]

Guns on ships proliferated after the Black Death, with as many as 225 on a single big sailing vessel.[81] They were small and could not sink or seriously damage a ship.[82] They were anti-personnel weapons, which made it very difficult indeed to take a nave or carrack.[83] At some point in the fifteenth century, bigger "ship-killing" guns were mounted aboard, first on galleys, and then on sailing ships. Until 2014, it was believed that the first large cannon on a galley dated to 1486 or soon before. But a 2.2 ton cannon found on a wrecked galley off the Levantine coast has now been dated to no later than the 1440s.[84] This shifted the balance of power from sailing ships armed with many small cannon back to galleys, now armed with one or two large ones—big enough to dismast or even sink an opposing ship. This led the second coming of the war galley, which remained the preferred warship in enclosed seas like the Mediterranean until about 1600.

To compete, sailing ships had to mount heavy guns too, and we now know that the competition began well before 1486. To the mid-fifteenth century, mounting big guns on a sailing ship was not possible because such cannon affected stability when placed on the top deck, and because breechloaders could not be fired below decks due to their blinding smoke.[85] Cast cannon did not have this problem, but heavier ship-borne ones could not at first be aimed—you fired from the top deck when the gun happened to bear on your target. On ships, muzzle-loading cannon had to be run in and out on sleds to load the gun. The earliest were sleds on rails, or a sled combined with two wheels, with little provision for aiming. Gun carriages appeared on land by 1411.[86] Aiming was not a problem for galleys—one aimed using the whole vessel, which was of course highly maneuverable due to its oars.[87] But it was an issue for sailing ships. Overcoming these problems is usually dated to the 1530s but, as with gun galleys, this now seems a few decades too late. One partial solution was to mount pairs of big guns in the stern of big full-rigged sailing ships—hence the term "gun room" for the aftermost cabin below deck. These could still not be aimed much, except perhaps marginally by using hand-spikes, but did provide some defense against pursuers directly astern. Next, another pair were mounted in the bow, but still had to be aimed by turning the whole ship—a cumbersome process.[88]

Another trajectory of development involved the caravel, a small lateen-rigged sailing ship, initially of only 30 tons or so, with a low free-board so that cannon had less effect on their stability.[89] Caravels were used by the Genoese and Portuguese before the Black Death, but seem to have fallen out of use immediately after it.[90] They reappeared in the late fourteenth century, in bigger though still modest versions of up to 100 tons, perhaps because of their utility in reaching, or rather returning from, the Atlantic islands.[91] They were maneuverable enough to aim their guns at an opposing ship. Perhaps about

1440—almost a century earlier than the late revolutionists would have it—the Portuguese began mounting big cannon, firing shot of around 7 kilograms, broadside, on the main deck of caravels.[92] In 1462, a Portuguese caravel defeated a larger Provencal galley in the Mediterranean by piercing its side with a large round shot. Further Portuguese experiments improved gun caravels, and it is probably this that led to their surprise defeat of a much larger Spanish fleet in 1479.[93] In another battle three years earlier, the Spanish had achieved the opposite result using wrought-iron cannons. These were "propped up over the caprails in the waist of the ships", and so cannot have been large.[94] This suggests that full adoption of big guns on ships by the Portuguese dates to about 1477. "It is clear that the Portuguese had learned the destructive effect on a ship's hull of heavy shot . . . long before they reached Asian waters" in 1498.[95]

Mounting heavy cannon on sailing ships bigger than caravels had been problematic until skeleton-first construction strengthened the hull and permitted gun ports between the ribs.[96] Gun ports used to be dated to 1501 and credited to the French.[97] But gun ports appear in illustrations of ships from the 1470s—they were a relatively easy adaptation from ports for loading cargo such as horses.[98] Guns were mounted broadside on big sailing ships from 1501 at the latest, in the Indian Ocean. Here, the Portuguese fired their guns successively as they came to bear on the target, sinking opposing Indian ships. They could also aim their guns to some extent by pulling on kedge anchors to shift the ship. This information comes from triumphalist Portuguese sources, but is convincing because it is taken for granted. "The kedge anchors that had been laid out on the quarters to allow for the aiming of the guns."[99] Trunnions, small projections near the inboard end of the cannon, soon allowed elevation and some aiming.

The key advantage of broadside mounting was the large number of heavy guns it permitted. Marine archaeology published in 2016 found artefacts from two Portuguese ships wrecked in the Indian Ocean, near Oman, in 1503. They included 35 stone round shot weighing 16 kilograms each, and 47 one-kilogram lead shot for light artillery. Documents indicate that at least 20 big guns and 60 small ones were salvaged from these two ships soon after they sank.[100] "As early as 1518, the standard armament of a Portuguese galleon was 35 cannon".[101] Simultaneous broadsides, which required big crews and sturdy ships, may have come later, and general use of line-ahead formation, which re-designated galleons as "ships of the line", certainly did. But it was "between the 1420s and the 1480s [that] a revolution occurred in the provision and use of shipboard guns".[102] "Between the last quarter of the fourteenth century and the last quarter of the fifteenth, new maritime capabilities were developed that would revolutionize naval warfare".[103]

Handguns, also known as hand-culverins, harquebuses and, later, muskets, appeared as early as 1364, in northern Italy,[104] but were slow to load, hard to fire accurately, of limited power, and too heavy to use without a support of some kind. It was not, initially, that handguns were more effective than bows, but that it took far less time to train a musketeer than an archer. The gun was a labour-saving device, its utility super-charged by the post-plague manpower crisis. With handguns, "masses of untrained men could be made into competent soldiers in six months or less".[105] Handguns competed with improvements in crossbows and armour, transitional technologies arising from the greater availability of steel after 1350. Steel crossbows, using a windlass to load and delivering more energy than the most powerful longbow, appeared—in the later fourteenth century, as we have now come to expect.[106] Steel armour too dates from soon after 1350. Steel was not only more abundant, but by 1400 also benefited from a new quick-quenching method that increased its hardness.[107] Steel armour was expensive, but life-preserving; it gave far more protection than iron armour of the same weight. A steel breast plate dated to 1385 weighed only 2.6 kilograms. "It was nearly impossible for even the strongest longbow or windlass-drawn crossbow to cause serious injury through a breastplate of that sort".[108] A side effect of steel armour was that it made shields less necessary, enabling an armoured man fighting on foot to use his sword two-handed.[109] His sword was plague-improved too. Prior to 1350, Western European swords had steel edges on an iron body. After that date, they were all steel—still not better than world-leading Indian or Japanese steel swords, but cheaper.[110]

Handguns struck back with improvements such as corned powder and lead bullets. The latter are usually dated to after 1450, but are noted by Christine de Pisan in 1408–09.[111] Sailors and townsfolk, with ship's bulwarks and town walls to protect them and to rest guns on, became more formidable opponents for trained soldiers. The term "arquebus" or "harquebus" comes from guns with hooks to steady them on town walls—the German *hackenbusche*.[112] Czech Hussite rebels used wagons for the same protective/steadying purpose, as well as for transport, in the 1420s, when guns won them battles against the German emperor.[113] A key innovation, probably dating to the 1440s, was the "serpentine" firing mechanism, complete with trigger, which brought slow match to the powder charge. This meant that an individual could fire and aim with a gun held to the shoulder, unlike a hand-held match which required support for the gun.[114] "By about the 1460s a gun had been developed that was light enough to be fired by a single individual holding it at his chest or shoulder and at the same time powerful enough to be worth having in battle".[115] Inaccuracy and slow loading remained problems, and musketeers still needed protection while reloading—from barricades, wagons, or pike men until the advent of the ring bayonet around 1700. But the classic harquebus, delivering several times the energy of any bow and able to pierce most armour, had emerged by about 1480.[116] In the mid-sixteenth century, a heavier version known as the musket emerged, and that term later took over from "arquebus" for the smaller weapon too. There were further improvements, but they were few. In the end, one has to concur with the growing number of specialists who date the technology of the European "military revolution", not to the period 1500–1800, but to the early plague era, 1350–1500. What even these specialists rarely acknowledge is the role of plague-prompted labour-saving in pressure-cooking these changes into being.

————

The plague-incubated changes in water-powered industrial technology, especially metallurgy, in wind-powered shipping, and in gun-related warfare were substantial. But were they really revolutionary? Perhaps, in themselves, they were not. Most technologies had appeared before the Black Death, often derived from China, though plague did cause their European proliferation. While technological development did not go into reverse after 1500, as did the golden age for common folk, it did not kick on much, but rather plateaued at the new level—it was no continuous revolution.[117] In England in the 1780s, "labour productivity in the woollen industry had not risen at all from the fifteenth century".[118] The growth rate in European iron production, 1400–1525, was much higher than that in the next 125 years.[119] Even in printing, "some slight qualifications aside, . . . from the 1480s until around 1800 . . . the technology of printing was very stable".[120] "If Gutenberg had returned to Mainz in 1800 he could have resumed work in printing houses with virtually unchanged printing processes".[121] In shipping, the years 1350–1500 saw the most innovation until the nineteenth century. "While the fourteenth and fifteenth centuries saw dramatic changes in ship design the sixteenth through the eighteenth centuries saw only incremental improvements".[122] The one significant exception in firearms was a three-part development which came to a head around

1700: the mass advent of flintlocks, of drills allowing more rapid fire, and of the ring-bayonet, which doubled the firepower of a given number of infantry by eliminating pikemen. But the smoothbore muskets and cannon of the late fifteenth century were fundamentally the same as those of the early nineteenth. Modern tests "failed to reveal any significant improvements in the performance of muskets manufactured from the sixteenth to the eighteenth century".[123] Incremental improvement continued after 1500, major innovation did not.

> The "military revolution" of the 1430s and 1440s is of such a scale and importance as to dwarf all subsequent "revolutions" in military practice . . . followed by an extended period lasting nearly 300 years during which this new standard was never seriously challenged . . . That the pace of technological advance . . . slowed during the sixteenth and seventeenth century is accepted by most specialists.[124]

The plague-incubated technologies did not place Western Europe on some inexorable escalator to continuous "Progress", modernity, and industrialisation. What it did do was force a major step up in technology in general and in metallurgy, marine transport, and military technology in particular. This supplied the core of an "expansion kit", able to project considerable force over a long range with small numbers. The importance of guns to the success of European expansion is a contested matter, with many revisionists arguing that they had little impact. Later chapters consider this issue. The Black Death may not have triggered industrial or military *revolutions*, either in the sense of sudden comprehensive social transformation or in the sense of ongoing innovation. But it did generate a major transition to a new plateau in technology, much of which was at least potentially expansive. Combined with the other changes discussed here in part two, this did amount, collectively, to a "Plague Revolution".

6

Expansive Labour

CASTAS, RACE MOTHERS,
AND DISPOSABLE MALES

IN BROADEST OUTLINE, Western European overseas expansion began in
1402 in the Atlantic Islands and then West Africa, extending to the Americas
and Further Asia from the 1490s. By 1600, Spain had taken over the two largest
Amerindian empires, those of the Aztecs and Incas, and founded settler populations inside or beside them. It had also settled several Caribbean islands, and
established a lodgment in the Philippines, which attracted Chinese traders.
Portugal had acquired many bases on the coasts of Africa, Brazil, and the Indian Ocean, as well as Macau, and had opened direct trade with China and
Japan. At various points in the sixteenth century, France, Britain, and then the
Dutch began trying to plunder and emulate the Iberians. The Dutch took the
lead in the seventeenth century, taking over many of Portugal's assets in West
Africa and Further Asia, and creating their own modest lodgments in the
Americas and South Africa. British and French caught up from the mid-
seventeenth century, and took the lead in the eighteenth. Iberian settlers became substantial minorities in parts of Latin America by 1700, while in the
coastal colonies of North America, British-flagged settlers became majorities.
Just how much real empire existed by 1700 or 1800, as against false claims of
empire or mere trading networks, is a vexed issue (see chapter 15). But between 1500 and 1800, European expansion did substantially reshuffle biota,
bullion, and people across much of the planet.

For all its guns and gunships, European expansion was founded on human
labour. Much came from outside Europe, including about ten million slaves,
1500–1800, eight million of them black African survivors of an enslavement
process that had cost several more million their lives. It was African slaves who

did much of the hardest work of European expansion. Almost everywhere, free local allies were also crucial. Both the "Spanish forces" in the early sixteenth-century conquests in Mexico and the "British forces" in the late eighteenth-century conquests in India were 90% indigenous. "Native allies" saw themselves as acting in their own interests, but in the long term often found Europe's friendship as dangerous as its hostility. These two types of "expansive labour", slaves and allies, are addressed, all too briefly, in chapter 15. Three other categories are treated here, all at least partly derived from inside Europe: solo men, hoping to be sojourners rather than permanent emigrants, settlers in families, and mixed-race people. The chapter extends beyond our time frame hitherto, stretching from 1500 to 1800, and centres on the roles of race and gender in the history of European expansion.

I   Race and Reproduction

Racism is distinct from xenophobia, which dislikes everyone else equally, and ethnocentrism, which measures others in one's own mirror. "Soft racism" held that "inferior races" could be improved, through religious conversion and cultural assimilation, in principle to the point of equality with "superior races", but only with the latter's help and in the latter's judgement. As I have said in earlier work, "racial equality was often a distant prospect, dangled in front of aspirants like the hare in front of a racing greyhound".[1] European missionaries, despite a theoretical commitment to eventual equality, were often reluctant to ordain even their most able converts as priests. "Hard racism" is the illusion that cultures have natures, which change little over time, so that attempts at "civilizing savages" were of limited use. It not only distinguished races/cultures, but usually ranked them, with one's own on top. Racism is mostly discussed in terms of its intellectual history, as racial theory and racial "science", because this is easiest to trace. But it has a social history too: an amorphous set of preconceptions about "Us" and "Them". This popular racial ideology feels little obligation to logic or evidence; it flourishes when and where it is convenient. Racial theory can buttress racial ideology, but the latter sometimes comes first.

Taking the theory-first approach, many scholars date the origins of European racism firmly to the late eighteenth or nineteenth centuries, when racial theories did metastasise. "'Race' was invented in 1775" by Immanuel Kant, or by other thinkers around that time, or in the 1840s with the sprouting of Polygenism—the notion that different races were different species.[2] The 1775 origin may be true of the word "race" in its modern sense, but a prejudice can precede the modern term for it, as with "sexism". Others place racism's origin in the high middle ages. "The mental habits and institutions of European racism and colonialism were born in the medieval world", before 1350.[3] A rise in European exclusionism and the persecution of minorities may date to the eleventh century,[4] but as far as I can see it tended to hate Muslims, Jews, and heretics roughly equally. Furthermore, such groups could be converted and assimilated, at least over a few generations. It is only from 1400 that we see hints of the notion that vice and inferiority were innate in one's ancestry, ineradicable even over generations, converted or not.

Even I am not certain that plague was behind this shift, but the timing is suggestive. The Black Death led to a "striking out against those who appeared to be 'outsiders'."[5] "More than any other event, the coming of the plague occupies a central space in pre-modern histories and periodizations of persecution".[6] As we saw in chapter 4, plague did cause a revival of slavery, though hesitations about enslaving co-religionists persisted. A belief in the innate inferiority of other peoples was useful for keeping slaves enslaved, however devoutly Christian they became. One study concludes, "the concept of whiteness was beginning to take on a positive association while blackness was beginning to signify inherent deficiencies". Slaves were "identified by, primarily, skin colour in both Iberian and Italian legal documents". This trend was "in full development since the end of the fourteenth century".[7] The trickle of black African slaves to Europe via the Saharan trade became a small stream from the 1440s. "In a sense, blacks were by definition impure because of their connection (real or imagined) to slavery".[8] Here was conceptual slippage typical of racial ideology: you were a slave because you were an inferior black, and an inferior black because you were a slave. A supporting legend was "the curse of Ham", according to which Ham indiscreetly glanced at his naked drunken father, Noah of the Ark, while his two brothers were wise enough to look away. For this sin, claimed much later writers, Ham's allegedly black African descendants were sentenced to eternal servitude—there's child discipline for you. Muslims, who in general were relatively non-racist, used this mutation of the Old Testament to justify black slavery from about 800 CE, when they first held significant numbers of sub-Saharan African slaves. Christians took up the idea when they acquired black slaves in numbers.[9]

Racism had an obvious utility for settlers in that it helped justify the exploitation of Africans and natives, free or unfree, however Christian or assimilated. Europeans living on the volcano of an African slave majority had an incentive to emphasise race over class, nationality, or even religion. Catholic Irish indentured laborers in the British Caribbean shared harsh experience with their black co-workers, not with their white Protestant English masters, but usually did not see it that way. "Irish men . . . found that they had far more in common with their former English masters than they did with newly arrived enslaved Africans. More importantly, English settlers, officials, and planters agreed".[10] "The ubiquity of slavery . . . put a premium on whiteness".[11] In the English Caribbean, "white" became "the general name for Europeans" by 1680, a transnational, pan-European, *racial* concept.[12] It did so in other slaving societies too, in Portuguese Brazil and the French America, as *branco* and *blanc*. But uniting against the nightmare of slave insurrection was not the only motive for reproducing whiteness.

In fifteenth-century Iberia, another strand of thought entangled with the emerging stigma of blackness: the doctrine of "the purity [and impurity] of the blood", which asserted that the taint of Jewish or Moorish blood was permanent and hereditary. This featured in the rules of Spanish civic and religious communities from the 1440s. The idea was then transferred to black Africans and Amerindians—another conceptual slippage. "In the course of the first century of colonisation, mixed parentage, such as being mulatto, came to be viewed in the New World as a 'stain' akin to having Jewish ancestors".[13] A case can be made for the origin of racial theory in Spain in the following century, particularly in the work of Juan Sepúlveda, in response to concerns about the mistreatment of Amerindians.[14] I suspect that, as was often the case with racism, the theory underwrote the preexisting attitudes. Racism did not instantly swamp Europe, and it never became universal. Humanitarian theory may have emerged at the same time.[15] Princes and prelates sometimes resisted the doctrine of the purity of the blood, and tried to restrain the excesses of their subjects abroad. Elite non-European visitors to Europe were often treated with respect. As with more recent black sporting heroes, Europeans might exempt esteemed individuals from racial stereotypes. But, especially in the colonies themselves, racism spread because it was useful. Other cultures did racism and expansion, but Europeans had a rare talent for combining the two.

European settlers in the Americas self-defined as "racially European" even before they used "white" as a synonym for it, even in colonies that were not major slavers, and even if it was two or three centuries since the last European-born ancestor. Usually, they were at least grudgingly accepted as European by metropolitan kin. This was no foregone conclusion. Many writers, from the sixteenth century to the nineteenth, argued that European stock degenerated in the colonies. Spanish born in the Americas, claimed one writer in 1570, "turn out like the natives even though they are not mixed with them [by] declining to the disposition of the land".[16] It was an insistence on female settler endogamy, racial in-marriage, that helped colonists claim continuing parity and "purity". Whatever the more numerous European men might do, there was a powerful social proscription against inter-marriage by white women. It scarcely needed laws to buttress it, although there were a few. In 1664, the young colony of Maryland threatened punishment for Englishwomen who "to the disgrace of our nation do intermarry with Negro slaves".[17] "Historians of early- seventeenth-century Mexico have yet to uncover evidence that unions, licit or illicit, between black men and white women were taking place in any significant number".[18] This also applied to Native Americans. In French and British North America, "the very idea that red men should marry white women was anathema to colonial society".[19] The taboo was taken for granted in conceptual language. The remarkable eighteenth-century *casta* paintings of New Spain, which showed 16 possible racial mixtures, include the caption, "Spaniard and *Mestiza* produces Quarteron" (emphasis mine).[20] The *mestiza* partner, daughter of a Spanish father and an Indian mother, was automatically female, not *mestizo*.

Whether the female endogamy imperative among settlers was itself recent or racist is debatable. The Anglo-Saxon settlers of Britain in the fifth and sixth centuries may have practiced it for a couple of centuries.[21] It appears in colonial situations *within* Europe after the Black Death. In 1366, a statute forbade sex between English settlers and native Irish "because mixed unions would tempt the English to lapse into degenerate Irish ways".[22] Venetian Crete and Genoese Chios had about 10,000 and 2,000 Latin (Catholic) settlers respectively around 1400. Orthodox Greeks were the natives here. In Chios, "there were no cases in which the daughters of western immigrants married Greek men".[23] There were some such cases in Crete, but here too the "categories of Latin and Greek served to separate those to whom Venice granted privileges from those to whom it did not"—even if the Greeks converted to Catholicism.[24] "Colonial relations gave rise to the use of ancestry as the principal tool for determining who had the right to benefit from the privileges granted to Latins".[25]

Over time, in settler situations, the female endogamy imperative and European racism intertwined and reinforced each other. We often forget that racism is as much about "Us" as "Them." "Pure blood" and its virtues were the reverse side of the coin of "stained blood" and its vices. Racism enhanced settler self-esteem in the face of those who argued that Europeans deteriorated in non-European environments. If it was race, and not environment, that gave Europeans their characterising virtues, then both virtues and European-ness could be transferred across oceans, long-term. "Racial purity" prevented settlers from "degenerating" into natives, and expansion from lapsing into disconnected dispersal. It underwrote an enduring virtual metropolitan status, and helped lever out metropolitan support and more settlers, who understood themselves to be coming to a "neo-Europe" and not an alien society. I suspect that the perceived need to remain European was also behind the locally born white Spanish American dislike of the term *criollo*, or creole, applied to them by their Spanish-born contemporaries and by historians. In some other places, the term was used for locally born African slaves, but this was emphatically not the case here. Yet it was not that criollo lumped them with non-whites that concerned the settlers, but that it split them from the Spanish-born. In America, "baptismal records used 'Spanish' and 'white' interchangeably".[26] Whites born locally "considered themselves to be Spaniards, and . . . transformed the meaning of Spaniard from a description of origin to one of colour".[27]

In the Americas, European men marrying indigenous women, formally or informally, as distinct from very common casual sex, was quite common compared to the inverse. But it was usually restricted to the initial "frontier period" in which European women were virtually absent. These were sometimes followed by a "founding period" in which a substantial minority of European females arrived, and the basis of "white" natural increase was laid. The offspring of the frontier unions could often "pass as white". Scattered textual evidence does not tell us a lot about the scale of this, but genetic studies do. Note that we are not interested in genetics for itself, but for the otherwise unavailable evidence it can provide on such issues as migration and intermarriage. Such studies reveal the prominence of Canary Island genes in today's Cubans and Venezuelans, and a very substantial survival of matrilineal (Berber-descended) Guanche genes in Spanish Canarians. The Spanish conquistadors in the Canaries in the late fifteenth century were accompanied by few Spanish women, so many married Berber-descended Guanche women, and the "usual restrictions" on purity of the blood did not apply to their offspring.[28] These secretly mixed-race Spanish on-migrated to the Americas from the sixteenth century, where they counted as white and, in effect, *were* "white". White skin was a proxy for enduring European-ness; it seems unlikely that an albino African would have counted.

Initially, European male intermarriage had some official support. In Hispaniola, the first European colony in the Americas after Norse Greenland, some early conquistadors married into elite Taino families. Of 186 wives of Spaniards in 1514, 65 were Amerindian.[29] Officialdom was explicit about the motives.

> If a Spanish settler with the agreement of the priest and administrator marries a cacica (female native ruler), or the daughter and heir of a cacique, he will become cacique and will be regarded and obeyed as such. In this way all the caciques will come to be Spaniards and it will avoid many expenses.[30]

Quite quickly, however, Spanish authorities turned against this policy, and became "increasingly desperate" to attract white women to the Americas.[31] "Spanish administrators frowned on intermarriage throughout Peru".[32] "People of mixed race in Mexico could not inherit *encomiendas* [estates with allocated Indian workers], nor could they enter the priesthood, and from 1576 they were barred from public office".[33]

> Elite . . . mestizos, begin to experience a loss of status in the late sixteenth and seventeenth centuries and were forced into a single "mestizo" category shared with plebeians. The mestizo sons of conquistadors and Spanish nobles had . . . access to positions of relative power in the mid-sixteenth century . . . , but by the end of the century . . . they were socially excluded and relegated to marginal positions similar to those of their poorer cousins.[34]

In English North America, the female endogamy imperative seems even stronger. Historians note the famous marriage of Pocahontas to John Rolfe in 1614, but struggle to find other examples. "There was no melding of the races in Virginia or Maryland during the seventeenth century",[35] and this was also the case in English colonies farther north. There was early official and church support for intermarriage with indigenous women in French Canada, but such marriages were only 65 out of 27,000 recorded, 1608–1765, less than a quarter of 1%.[36] On the fringes of settlement, beyond the parish registers, remarkable hybrid cultures did emerge from long-term European male partnerships with Indian women. On the western Canadian frontier, French and later Scots fur trappers intermarried with locals to produce the Metis, who operated as Europeans or Indians as it suited them, and were not fully subjugated by Canada until 1884–85.[37] On the fringes of Spanish Argentina, a similar Gaucho culture of mixed-race cattle hunters and herders developed earlier.[38] But, at least until nineteenth-century attempts to recast them as icons of independence, such groups were not acknowledged as European or equal by their settler neighbours.

The Portuguese are a more complicated case. Always short on manpower, and even shorter on woman-power, they were more prone to intermarry and interbreed. This is the kernel of truth in their "white legend" of less racism, and in the myth of "racial democracy" cherished by their great offspring, Brazil. Historians are now in little doubt that the Portuguese treated African slaves and Amerindians as badly as did other Europeans.[39] But their treatment of mixed-race people, of Africans in Africa, and of Asians in Asia, ranged across a wide spectrum. In the sixteenth and seventeenth centuries there were two settled patches in Brazil: the sugar-producing northeast, Bahia and Pernambuco, and the southeast, including the first settlement at Sao Vincente (1532) and the regions of Rio de Janeiro and São Paulo. There was some migration after 1532—estimates of visits go as high as 200,000 by 1600—but few were European females, and the settled "white" population in 1600 was only 30,000.[40] These included a large minority of *mamelucos*, offspring of Portuguese fathers and Indian women. A hybrid culture, like the Gauchos and Metis, emerged around São Paulo, founded in 1545, which included mamelucos, whites, and Indian allies: the Paulista *Bandeirantes*.[41] It specialised in slave hunting: capturing and enslaving inland Indians and recapturing escaped African slaves. Throughout Portuguese Brazil, Indians were the main sexual partners and enslaved workers until about 1580, but despite intensive slave hunting, their numbers decreased through high mortality. Influenza and malaria arrived in the 1550s, and smallpox in the 1560s. African slaves took over in the northeast, with the southeast following somewhat later. A trickle of slave partners and daughters (less often sons) were freed—this was also the case in other slaving colonies. Free blacks, usually Afro-European, became a significant group, with whom lower-class white men intermarried.

Historical information from genetic studies on the current population of Brazil, half of which self-designates as white, is affected by large late inflows of millions of Europeans, 1870–1914. But Brazilian studies do suggest an almost complete absence of Amerindian Y-DNA, transmitted by father to son, in the white population, with the interesting exception of Manaus, a late-settled Amazonian province that hosted the Cabanagem rebellion in the 1830s. African male ancestry for "whites" is also scarce—less than 2% in most regions. On the other hand, Amerindian and African ancestry in "white" mitochondrial DNA, transmitted by mothers to both genders, is substantial: up to 33% of the former and 28% of the latter.[42] As in Spanish America, most Amerindian genes were probably taken on early, partly because not many Indian women survived in the settler coastal regions by 1700. But here too there are also signs of a decline in white esteem for mamelucos from 1574, when the Jesuits stopped considering them for ordination as priests—they never even considered Brazilian Indians.[43] Two centuries later, in the 1750s and 1760s, a reformist Portuguese government, seeking to shore up its declining empire, ordained that the descendants of mixed-race marriages "will be left with no infamy whatever . . . and will be eligible for any employment, honour or dignity". But "the white settlers in Brazil rejected the reforms, and they were never put into effect".[44] Still, it does seem that whiteness was more negotiable in Brazil than in other American colonies. It was even more negotiable in Africa and Asia, where one could find "Black Portuguese", and even mixed-race "White Portuguese".

It will be clear by now that these matters are a semantic minefield. "Creole", today's preferred word for people with mixed European and non-white descent who could not pass as white, is historically too ambiguous, since it often meant locally born Europeans. Mestizo for Euro-Indians might be an acceptable term, but the matching "mulatto" (mule) for Afro-Europeans might not. The term *Casta*, for both, seems the best of a bad job.[45] Castas had some cards, and they played them. In certain times and places, whiteness was negotiable even outside Brazil. Families could "breed their way back" to whiteness through strategic marriages. In English America, until the late seventeenth century, a quarter or an eighth of black ancestry did not preclude whiteness, unless of course you were a slave.[46] In sixteenth-century Spanish America, you were allowed up to a quarter of Indian (but not African) heritage without losing your status as "white".[47] Pale-skinned castas could promote themselves to white, particularly if they moved to a place where their family was unknown. Castas ranked above blacks and Indians, and still sometimes penetrated the lower ranks of elites. From 1795, Spanish American castas could belatedly buy whiteness in the form of a state certificate. "Petitioners expressed their expectations that they would be able to 'marry with persons of white birth'."[48] In English Jamaica in 1733, "after decades of unsuccessful attempts to court European residents, the Assembly sought to augment its meager white population by siphoning off elites of color". Some 600 people became white, at a price of £90 each, and with conditions. "Each petitioner . . . had to demonstrate substantial wealth and cultural refinement".[49] These were exceptions that prove the rule. Broadly speaking, Europeans in the Americas passed up the chance to augment their expansive labour with fully integrated mixed-race people or with well-treated local allies—this was the cost of racism. Instead, they placed their hopes on the profits of racism, the production of Neo-European settlers.

II Race Mothers and the Settler Divergence

There were about 8 million whites (take the quotation marks as read from now on) in the Americas by 1800, half of them in fast-growing Anglo-America. Earlier, the balance had favoured Latin America, which had 3.5 million settlers by 1760, compared to some 1.5 million to the north.[50] These people were descended from fewer than 2.5 million migrants who arrived in the Americas, 1500–1800. Migrant numbers are contested, but estimates converge on 750,000 Spanish, 500,000 Portuguese, 650,000 British (reinforced by 100,000 each of Irish and Germans), 150,000 French, and 50,000 Dutch. Women are the needles in these five haystacks.

Settler societies in the Americas grew through reproduction at differing rates, depending on the proportion of female migrants and the healthiness of the region. The general shortage of women and men's preference for white wives meant that women married young, to older men. This increased their reproductive years and led to high birthrates, a "frontier fertility". But some colonies had high death rates as well, especially after yellow fever and *falciparum* malaria, a lethal type, ensconced themselves in the seventeenth century. Both came to the Americas from West Africa—nature's revenge for the slave trade. An attack of either, in childhood in particular, could convey immunity (a milder form of malaria prevalent elsewhere could be caught repeatedly). In addition, because West Africans had been afflicted by these two killers for thousands of years, some resistance had developed. So the terrible African slave death rates in the Caribbean and Brazil cannot be attributed to yellow fever or malaria. But Amerindians and Europeans were vulnerable once these diseases established themselves. This took time, for reasons outlined in the next chapter. Both diseases were mosquito-borne, by species that liked the tropics, sub-tropics, and stagnant water in which to breed.[51] Yellow fever reached Barbados by 1647, and Brazil by 1685. The timing for malaria is uncertain, but was earlier—as noted above, the 1550s have been suggested for northeast Brazil. Settlers in such regions struggled to reproduce themselves. Overlying the disease patterns were wide variations in female migration. In many colonies, early European migration was almost entirely male—95% of Spanish migration to the Americas, 1493–1519.[52] As noted above, it was in this period of "frontier settlement" that Amerindian genes were taken on. If the region remained in this state, mixed-race societies might emerge. But female immigration then often increased for a period, a "founding settlement", before declining to a trickle as natural increase took over. Other colonies again had a more continuous immigration experience, though still usually spasmodic.

Migration estimates rarely allow us to distinguish between male and female migrants, or between familial settler migrants, who had white offspring, and solo men, who generally did not. It was women that mattered in producing settler societies, through the synergy of sexism and racism that created the female in-marriage imperative. There are unusually good estimates for the English colony of New England, a classic example of an unreinforced founding settlement. Its frontier phase was short, the 1620s, and yielded a population of barely a thousand in 1630. A founding migration then took place in the 1630s, of 21,000 people, with a very large female minority of about 40%. "Virtually all growth after 1640 came from natural increase".[53] These New England race mothers had an astonishing number of descendants. One historian writes that the 16 million "Yankees" in 1988 were "all descended from 21,000 English immigrants" of the 1630s.[54]

But what interests us here is that the 21,000 founders suggest a rough "female formula" for family settlements, whereby one simply assumes that females were 40% of total settlers. The small male excess allows for second husbands (old husbands typically died earlier than their wives, despite the risks of childbirth), menservants (who were preferred to female servants in frontier situations), and for unmarried male officials, merchants, clerks, clergy and the like. This represents the white family migrant component of a colonial population. We can cross-check this formula against a few cases of mixed familial settler/solo male populations in which the numbers of settler men, women, children, and solo men are separately enumerated. An example is British Jamaica in 1663, where there were 7,700 settlers, of whom, once we split the children evenly between genders, about 2,800 were female, plus 1,500 male privateers—a total white population of 9,200.[55] Because the settlement had only been in existence for eight years, most of these people must have been migrants rather than locally born. Applying the female formula gives about 7,000 settlers, and implies 2,200 solo men which, given that there must have been a few hundred solos other than the privateers, seems a pretty good fit.[56] There is also a plausible fit with a much larger case, sixteenth-century Spanish migration to the Americas, for which there are good estimates of the female proportion. The founding period here was 1540–1580, when an astonishing 120,000 migrants crossed the Atlantic, far more than the preceding period. They included 30,000 females, or 25%. On our formula, this gives a familial settler flow, both male and female, of 75,000, along with 45,000 solo men to reinforce the conquistadors and miners, which fits with what we know about Spanish America at the time.[57]

Using this very rough formula, I estimate total female migration from Europe to the Americas, 1500–1800, at 135,000 for Spain, 75,000 for Portugal, 200,000 for Britain (including Irish and Germans under the British flag), 25,000 for France, and 10,000 for Dutch. Iberian and British women migrated; French and Dutch women did not. This was the "settler divergence". A French explanation for it, dating to 1740, was that "life in France was so very agreeable, why should anyone wish to stay away for long?"[58] Two good historians also go astray on this issue.

> As [Nicholas] Canny quite rightly remarks: "The apparently anomalous low participation by the French in long-distance overseas migration is explained more by the lack of opportunities for white workers in the French possessions abroad than by any reluctance of the French to translate themselves to foreign destinations."[59]

Similar explanations have been offered for scant Dutch migration. Yet French possessions included Quebec, Ontario, and parts of what is now the US Midwest, while the Dutch founded New York. These were not regions lacking in "opportunities for white workers". Other suggestions, such as higher wages at home or a smaller proportion of common folk with secure land tenures, apply as much to the English, who did settle, as to the Dutch, who did not.[60] We will see in the next section that Frenchmen and Dutchmen did in fact go overseas, in similar numbers to other European nations. What the French and Dutch lacked was settler foremothers. You did not need many women to create a substantial settler population in the very long term. Without continued immigration, a founding settlement would achieve gender parity through births after two generations. But more women did help. New England's 8,000 1630s foremothers produced a population of 700,000 by 1780; compared to New France's 3,000 (in and around the 1660s) and 100,000.[61] Females were a minority in all European migrations to the Americas before 1800, but in the Spanish and British cases, they were substantial ones.

Female reluctance to emigrate was understandable. Emigration was known as "the little death".[62] In the sixteenth and seventeenth centuries, it was more like embarking for another planet than legal international migration today. Women shared the costs of migration—danger, trauma, and discomfort—with men, but not the benefits—the prospects of plunder, promotion, and return. They were aware that shipboard mortality was particularly high for children. I suspect that most women settlers were not forced to leave, but had a choice, a small number of convicts and orphans apart. European states all shared a fear that male-only migration would lead to disorder, miscegenation, and degeneration, and tried repeatedly to induce single women to go to the colonies to marry and convert wild solo males into settlers. They had to resort to orphanages and prisons, and had limited success even here. "Orphans of the king" contributed significantly to settler populations only in French Canada, where they numbered fewer than 2,000. The Portuguese also sent out a couple of thousand orphan girls, plus some prostitutes, but failed to create self-reproducing white populations outside Brazil. Twelve prostitutes reached Angola in 1594, but none had offspring.[63] Historians now tend to see most indentured service as a means of paying one's fare and establishment costs, so indentured migration by women was not necessarily involuntary.[64] Most women migrated in families. No one suggests French and Dutch women were more male-dominated than other European women. Free women migrants consistently tended to the healthier, more family-friendly, overseas places and periods, which suggests they had at least some agency. "There was a noticeable but understandable tendency for [sixteenth-century Spanish] women and children to shun remote, dangerous areas like Florida or Chile in favor of cities considered safe and civilized, such as Santo Domingo, Mexico City and later Lima".[65] French and Dutch women were not anomalous, but normal. Premodern women's Rule Number One was: do not indulge in long-range emigration. Why did some nationalities, but not others, break it?

In previous work I have tried to explain a similar conundrum: the much larger migrations from some, but not all, European countries in the period 1810s–1870s, in which women were much more prominent.[66] Apart from cheaper fares, I isolated three key variables. One was a settler or folk utopianism, detectable in working-class migrant letters back: the notion that migration would restore a utopia for common folk once real at home but long lost. This vision converged with some aspects of immigration guides, known as "booster literature", written by higher classes trying to persuade lower classes to migrate. Both popular and elite versions, for example, emphasised relatively easy access to freehold farms. This was of particular interest to women because it provided insurance against male death, disability, and desertion. It also evaded the standard deficit in women's wages. A dairymaid was paid less that a dairyman, but butter sold by a farmer, male or female, fetched the same price. But folk utopianism diverged from booster literature on other things. In the latter, the freeholds were to be acquired through a long spell of hard and obedient waged work. In the folk version, they were to be acquired very quickly and easily, and to yield abundance without much work, plus other benefits including the universal right to hunt and fish, abundant food, especially meat, as well as more respect for working people. A literary historian has had a similar idea. "The Reformation, and the English and American Revolutions, were all articulated and motivated by millennial prophecies of a Golden Age restored. And so, in its quieter way, was the movement of English-speaking emigrants to the New World".[67]

I too was looking mainly at Anglophone migrations, but came across hints of similar folk utopianism in Scandinavian, French, German, Italian, and even Russian cases.[68] Like everyone else, I did not factor in plague at the time, but I am now inclined to do so. My sources dated to the nineteenth century, and to connect this to the post-plague "golden age" for common folk of 1350–1500 may seem far-fetched. Legends of "ancient liberties", "before the Norman Yoke", need no kernel of truth. But I suspect that a kernel or two gives them extra force and longevity. Peasant cultures have long "social memories",[69] and what other "utopia", with such particular characteristics, might this wide range of European peasantries have had in common? During the post-plague "golden age", peasants did have more meat and better treatment, and infringed more on lordly game laws in forests whose extent had suddenly doubled per capita. Peasant rebels in England in the 1380s and Germany in the 1490s demanded the right to hunt and fish freely.[70]

The second key to levering out settlers was the establishment of a "folk filament" between source and destination, allowing the oral or written transfer of information about the latter from common folk to common folk. The gist of letters could be conveyed to the illiterate by word of mouth. Commoners did not trust official urging or elite recruiters, and remained unmoved by early booster literature, which in any case tended to overdo it. A Portuguese booster around 1600 "forcefully" asserted that diseases in Brazil were so "mild and easy to cure that they almost don't deserve the name".[71] A Scots booster in 1684 claimed that in New Jersey "Sheep never miss to have two lambs and for the most part three".[72] States and company colonisers often held out inducements, such as free passages and tax exemptions, but usually without much effect. A folk filament, and an image of a particular destination that common folk trusted, took time to build up, because it usually required an accumulation of oral accounts from returnees. A study of Spanish sixteenth-century migration shows a "folk filament" at work.

People at home in Extremadura came to know about Peru or Mexico . . . not through vague reports or the very few printed and published descriptions available but as a result of continued contacts maintained through letters, visits, and information and messages brought back by returnees, merchants, and other individuals who moved back and forth with some frequency.[73]

The third key was a cultural shift, a "settler transition", which alleviated the trauma of permanent migration. Here, the insistence on enduring European-ness through female racial endogamy helped, by promising a virtual metropolitan status, a civilised community, rather than a life in the wilds among savages. Also important was previous experience of one successful migration, which took some of the sting from the next. We saw in chapter 3 that the early plague era loosened up European peasantries. Most shifts were short-range, and they were usually associated with an improvement in living standards and status. Yet, as with folk utopias and filaments, these can only have been necessary but not sufficient conditions. Why should they work for Britain and Iberia but not France and the Netherlands? The French went through a full post-plague reshuffle too, though chapter 12 will suggest that this is not as clear of the Netherlands. In any case, when we examine the sources of European family migration, 1500–1800, we find that they were highly regionalised within nations. It was not the Spanish or British that were migration prone, but particular regions within those countries. What these regions had in common was an earlier, shorter-range, successful family migration, producing an unusually family migration–prone regional subculture. It was this that provided the period 1500–1800 with an early form of the wider settler transitions of the nineteenth century.

Christian re-conquest had secured most of Andalusia and all of Portugal by 1248, but the new lands were allocated in big chunks to nobles and military orders to reward them for their efforts in the Reconquista. The noble estates were held in entail to prevent splitting through partible inheritance, so there were limited opportunities for peasant migrants to better themselves. This situation eased after the early plague strikes, when lords offered better tenures. "Repopulation of a new territory usually elevated the status afforded Spanish peasants".[74] A large part of Andalusia, namely Nasrid Granada, was not reconquered until 1492, and within six years "35,0000 to 40,000 new inhabitants from the north were settled on lands taken from the Nasrids".[75] These people were a significant source of settlers for the Americas, though we have no numbers.[76] We do have figures for Andalusia as a whole, however. In the sixteenth century, the region supplied 42% of all emigrants to the Americas, and 60% of women migrants.[77] Its share of the Spanish population in 1591 was only 17.5%.[78] Andalusian women, that is, were 3.5 times as prone to trans-Atlantic migration as other Spanish women.

Portugal is often divided into two main regions, the north (subdivided into uplands and coast), and the south, beyond the Tagus River. But one scholar usefully splits off the north proper (the provinces of Minho, Douro, and Tras-os-Montes) from a central or "north-central", region (Lisbon, Estremadura, and the Beiras). The north proper is generally agreed to be the main source of solo male sailors and adventurers after 1500, and is assumed to be the source of familial settlers as well.[79] In an attempt to recolonise after plague, the Portuguese crown passed a law in 1375, which "sought to bring abandoned land back into cultivation. Wasteland was to be granted to farmers on condition that it would be brought into full production within five years".[80] This is believed to have had only a limited effect, but there was considerable migration from the northern uplands, which were ditching grain in favour of less labour-intensive types of farming. Most were solo men, who moved to the coast, seasonally at first. But some were families, including women, perhaps attracted by the post-plague land grants and tending to the north-central region, which was prospering. Lisbon grew from 14,000 people in 1250 to 35,000 in 1400 despite, or because of, plague (see chapter 10). The south continued to be held in large estates. We will see in the next section that the north proper had a particular long-term social pattern, 1500–1800, resulting from single men's emigration. "This pattern does not appear to hold for the center". There is some rare direct evidence, admittedly from a small sample, of the birthplaces of brides and grooms in Brazil throughout the eighteenth century. As expected, 67% of grooms were from the north, with only 13% from the centre. Brides, by contrast, were 35% from the centre and only 14% from the north.[81]

This is no more than a hint, because the bride sample is tiny. Portuguese men mostly married Brazilian-born women in the eighteenth century, and the marital sample finds birthplaces in Portugal and its Atlantic Islands for 341 men and only 43 women. But another hint from this same source converges with the generally accepted importance of on-migration to Brazil from Portugal's Atlantic islands. Unlike the Cape Verde Islands, Madeira and the Azores were healthy for Europeans. Tiny founding settlements between the 1420s and 1450s, whose participants expected "very wide privileges and franchises",[82] produced significant populations by 1500, when Madeira was "already over-populated".[83] "As early as 1550 the Crown began turning to the Azores for potential settlers".[84] Migration from these islands is well-known to have been more familial, with far more women, than that from Northern Portugal.[85] No fewer than 20 of the 43 brides—almost half—were born in the islands, vastly more than their share of the Portuguese population. Northern Portugal did supply the numerous men, but it is possible that it was Central Portugal and the Atlantic Islands that supplied the relatively few women. Both had "folk filaments", written or spoken, carried by the numerous ships visiting Lisbon and the islands on their way to and from America.

The other big seventeenth-century European migration to the Americas, by the English, does not seem to stem from an earlier shorter-range migration. East Anglia was not, as tradition implies, the only source of the founding New England population, but my impression is that it was a major source of women. The "Puritan" religious reasons are well-known, and in any case involved only 8,000 women. In the eighteenth century, by contrast, British-flagged migration was dominated by two much bigger secondary settlements: of Ulster Scots and Rhineland Germans, each amounting to about 100,000 relatively gender-balanced settlers.[86] Like Andalusia and the Portuguese islands, Ulster had a recent previous experience of migration, namely a large inflow of Scots from the late sixteenth century. By 1700, there were 200,000 "Scotch-Irish" in Ulster, and in the following century they mounted Europe's first *mass* migration overseas. The Ulster linen industry provided its "folk filament", but indirectly. North America featured among its markets, taking up to 21% of exports. But most of these went to the Caribbean, to points north of New York, and to points south of Charleston. Ulster Scots settlement, on the other hand, was concentrated in the region between Charleston and New York, namely the mid-Atlantic and Chesapeake colonies. Moreover, a bounty for linen exports from 1743 applied only if they went through England, and consequently most Irish linen bound for the Americas did just that. Only 10–12% went directly, and most of that went through Dublin. There was little room for Ulster common folk, except as producers, in this trade.

But there was a trade ancillary to linen, one much more intimate and direct as far as Ulster was concerned. This was the flaxseed import trade. Regions producing fine linens, like Ulster, picked their flax before it coarsened and seeded, and therefore needed to import their seed from places that produced coarser flax products.[87] Around 1700, Ulster imported its seed from the Baltic, but warfare ruptured the flow. Ulster increasingly turned to the American colonies for its seed, drawing 81% of it from that source by 1743. The trade was specialised, surprisingly large in scale, and very direct. Seed was required in late winter for spring planting. By the 1760s, some 60 ships sailed each winter from New York, Philadelphia, and Chesapeake ports to small Ulster ports such as Derry and Coleraine, carrying seed and information out and people back. In contrast to the linen trade proper, common folk managed the business. Small traders in America, Ulstermen known as "scow-bankers", were prominent, as were small buyers in Ulster, where farmer-weavers formed collectives of eight or ten, "pledging security for one another". Here we have the "folk filament" that re-activated a preexisting culture of migration and focused it on a particular new destination, as well as providing the physical means of getting there.[88]

German migration was also a matter of secondary settlement, though its folk filament is unclear. During the Thirty Years War, 1618–48, the Rhenish Palatinate in Germany had been repeatedly devastated and eventually depopulated. Between 1651 and 1663, the Elector Palatine made a sustained effort to repopulate his lands. "Many servants and artisans—mostly from Switzerland, but also from Tyrol and the Spanish Netherlands—flocked into the Palatinate, creating a lasting tradition of migration".[89] Most German migrants to the Americas before 1800 came from here, and the same was true of around a quarter of French-flagged settler migration. The tragic fiasco of the French settlement of Guyana in 1763–65, in which most settlers died, involved 14,000 people, of whom 11,500 were from the Palatinate and its French-controlled neighbor, Alsace, which remained German-speaking.[90] With this small borrowed exception, my explanation for the settler divergence is that France and the Netherlands had no migration-prone regions comparable to those of the Big Three. We will see in chapter 14 that the secondary migration principle also holds for Russia, whose migrants, including a significant minority of women from regions of earlier migration, went overland into Siberia.

Prolific New England women aside, it was not so much Britain, Spain, or Portugal that produced the eight million white Americans of 1800, but Ulster, the Rhineland, Andalusia, Madeira, and the Azores, the woman-sending sources of early European demographic expansion. European states often found settlers to be ornery subjects, even before Britain's Thirteen Colonies rebelled in 1775. But they were essential to European expansion in the Americas. Without them, extending the initial lodgments, supplying the plantations and mines, and suppressing Amerindian resistance and African rebellions, would have been very much more difficult, if not impossible. Furthermore, as the French and Dutch found to their cost, "colonies of settlement were a pre-condition to continuing the struggle in the Americas" against European rivals.[91] "By the middle of the eighteenth century, settlers from the Anglo-Saxon world outnumbered the French in North America by around ten to one, an imbalance that would prove critical in determining the future of the continent".[92]

III Disposable Males: European "Crew Culture"

Muslim Middle Eastern expansionists, both medieval and early modern, were prone to female endogamy too. "The technical term for marriage of an Arab man to a non-Arab woman is *hujnah*, which suggests mere "hybridization". The term for the opposite union is *iqraf*, which also means "loathsome infection".[93] The matter was normally handled simply by Arab women not emigrating. Genetic research on Arab spread finds Y-chromosome DNA, transmitted by fathers, but usually little mitochondrial DNA, transmitted by mothers.[94] The big Arab overseas migrant source right up to recent times was the Hadramaut in Southern Arabia. Its male migrants "almost always married local women with or without Hadramaut blood, since Hadramaut women rarely emigrated".[95] There might be concerns about the upbringing of the first generation of offspring born of foreign mothers, but these would not extend into future generations.[96] Early overland migrations, in the seventh and eighth centuries, might have involved families, and one eleventh-century movement certainly did: that of two Bedouin tribes to the Maghreb. Interestingly enough, this too was a secondary migration, like those from early modern European settling regions. The tribes had first settled in Egypt.[97] But these were exceptions. In general, Muslim expansionists produced fairly equal and integrated local allies of mixed descent, but not *racial* reproductions like European settlement colonies.

On the other hand, Muslim societies were seldom short of "disposable males", who could readily be risked in raids or invasions. Mongol and perhaps Viking expansionists may have shared this advantage. An ethos of expansion, like Islam's *ghazi* tradition of holy warriors, may have been one factor here, and so might the unification of groups that had hitherto raided each other. If raiding was culturally or economically endemic, it now had to be conducted against outsiders. A more controversial possibility is the practice of polygamy, or polygyny. Even a small male elite with multiple wives would create "a pool of unmarried men", surplus to local reproductive requirements.[98] Whatever the case with this, monogamous Christendom normally lacked a constant supply of disposable males. This may have been a factor in the failure of the Crusader states, which were never reinforced regularly or adequately. It was plague that changed this equation.

After the Black Death, regions scattered across Europe, in which grain farming was marginal, reduced or even abandoned their arable acres, and relied on imported grain. Such regions tended to be either coastal (including islands) with poor soils or prone to flooding, or mountainous. In the former case, grain could be imported cheaply down rivers and by sea. In the latter, it was imported short-range from nearby valleys and lowlands. These regions shifted from subsistence grain farming to less labour-intensive and more market-oriented activities, notably dairying, and industrial crops, in which the labour of women and children was as useful as that of men. So an important export became male labour. Initially, it was seasonal; the men came home each year. But in grain-importing regions some were not needed for the harvest of spring and winter grain crops, which took place between May and October. This was not possible in regions where grain farming was dominant. Grain-deficit regions provided the manpower for a post-plague transnational labour pool. As populations began to recover, from 1450 in a few places and 1500 in most, their labour exports went up an order of magnitude in scale, range, and duration. The restructured local economies now had an ongoing surplus of male labour. If the region had an existing martial or maritime tradition, these men often became soldiers in someone else's army, or sailors in someone else's fleet.

The classic martial case is the Swiss, Europe's most feared soldiers, around 1500. Demographic recovery was particularly strong and early in the upland cantons, which as noted in chapter 3, shifted from subsistence farming to producing cheese and live cattle for the market.[99] Swiss pikemen and halberdiers had made their reputation in resisting attempts at dominance by the Hapsburgs and the Dukes of Burgundy between 1315 and 1476. They then turned to exporting mercenaries, and most did not return. The Swiss population was only 800,000 in 1500, doubling by 1800. By this time, "at a minimum, the entire mercenary emigration amounted to 1.2 million, with a loss to the cantons of 800,000 men".[100] "The symbiosis of cattle breeding and mercenary service meant that the alpine zone was the major source for migrant soldiers". In one upland Swiss community in 1700, half the younger men were "absent in mercenary service".[101] There were similar shifts in other Alpine regions, notably Northern Piedmont and Tyrol, which also emitted streams of soldiers.[102] Another overproducer of good cheese and good soldiers was the English county of Cheshire, on the Welsh Marches, which had a strong tradition of archery. It too turned towards pastoralism after the Black Death.[103] "Cheshire probably saw a higher proportion of men recruited into later medieval English armies than any other county".[104]

There were other soldier-exporting regions with similar characteristics, some supplying their own monarchs, some the transnational pool of mercenaries, some both. They included Galicia and Upland Castile in Spain, Gascony in France, and parts of Bohemia, Wales, Ireland, and Scotland. The biggest mercenary producer was Germany, whose *landsknecht* combined effectiveness with variable discipline, but here again the story was more regional than national. Swabia, with a socio-economy similar to Switzerland, was one key region.[105] Some lowland German regions also shifted towards linen production combined with dairying—milk was used to bleach the linen. This required less adult male labour than grain, and so enabled the export of disposable males. A classic maritime crew region was the Maltese archipelago, which imported its grain after 1350, and exported cotton and seamen to pay for it. "Records indicate a massive importing of grain to the archipelago from 1400 on".[106] By this time, cotton had acquired "the status of a monoculture on Malta", utilising women's and children's labour, as well as that of Muslim slaves.[107] The islands "provided sailors for the corsair and privateer ships . . . between 1650 and 1750 about half of the able-bodied male population of Malta was at sea".[108] Maltese seafarers were mainly a Mediterranean matter, unlike other leading sailor-producing regions including Holland (see chapter 12), the English West Country, southern Norway, the Basque Country, and Northern Portugal. A string of regions that exported both sailors and soldiers lay along the north German coast and its fringe of islands. The coast was flat, but had "notoriously poor soil".[109] Men from these regions had no doubt worked away from home before the Black Death, and continued to do so immediately after it, but numbers and range increased from the fifteenth century. For a time these crewmen were known as "ship-children" (*schiffskinder*), specialising in the use of crossbows on both land and sea.[110] By the seventeenth century, seafaring dominated, with up to 80% of the men in some localities shipping out. "Nearly all the indigenous men on [the island of] Föhr went to sea".[111] These regions provided manpower first to the Hanseatic, then to the Dutch, and finally to the British fleets.[112]

A leading French source, first of soldiers and then of mariners, was Brittany.[113] Here and elsewhere there are hints that production of surplus men was more local than regional, and that some localities had special relationships with particular long-range trades. Between 1725 and 1770, Brittany supplied 87% of the crews of the French East India Company, totalling 75,000 men. Most came from the districts of Port-Louis and St Malo.[114] Each Breton seafaring community had its own particular fishing grounds in and around Newfoundland, as did Normans and French Basques.[115] In some Breton villages, two-thirds of men were farmers; in others, with poorer soils, only 5% were farmers, "and seafarers comprised three-quarters of the [adult male] population".[116] So maritime regions were not necessarily homogenous, but had more sailor-producing localities than other regions. Martial regions, or rather the relative lack of them, may help explain a long-standing mystery in French military history: the difficulty in recruiting substantial numbers of reliable infantry within its own boundaries before 1600. Most of France grew grain, and so faced the harvest bottleneck; it could spare lower-class men to go soldiering for only a few months. Swiss and German mercenaries were more economically dispensable to their communities, and so able to become professionals. They supplied most of the infantry under the French flag until rising population and productivity enabled France to grow its own foot soldiers. "In 1558, German and Swiss troops comprised 70 per cent of the French Royal army".[117]

———

Soldiers and sailors were not the only products of grain-deficit regions. These also emitted streams of cod fishers, whalers, pirates, smugglers, hunters, fur trappers, loggers, miners, bandits, and the generalist colonisers called "solo men" in the earlier sections of this chapter. Since 1996, I have been using the term "crewmen" to cover all these forms of labour because they had many common characteristics.[118] Married or not, they were away from their womenfolk for years on end, and all operated in teams, gangs, or "crews", formal or informal. Much of the evidence about crew culture relates to mariners. There is a rich literature on pirates, sometimes overly romantic, and some fine newer scholarship on mariners in general. The latter rightly sees pirates as an extreme version of a wider culture. They were one end of a single "fluid spectrum" of maritime labour along which individuals could shift with ease.[119] What we have yet to realise is that mariners were themselves only part of a wider crew culture, and that this was greatly boosted, if not created, by plague restructuring. Intriguingly, the Oxford English Dictionary tells us that the term "crew" did not originate with sailors. Instead, the modern usage of creue, old French for "augmentation" or supplement, emerged in 1455, among the English in

Normandy, at the end of the Hundred Years' War. It meant an unofficial band of armed men, living off the land through predation on the peasantry, who could be recruited as army reinforcements when required. As I have noted in earlier work, crews were prefabricated communities, able to accommodate the constant turnover of individuals and to acculturate new recruits on the job. Once acculturated, you literally "knew the ropes", social as well as technical, informal as well as formal, in any new crew that you joined.

Mariners, we know, had a:

> distinctive work culture with its own language, songs, rituals and sense of brotherhood. Its core values were collectivism, anti-authoritarianism, and egalitarianism, all of which were summarized in the sentence frequently uttered by rebellious sailors: "they were one & all resolved to stand by one another".[120]

English and Dutch sailors used "round robin" petitions to state their grievances, a circle of marks and signatures in which no name came first, making it more difficult to identify a "ringleader".[121] That word is dated in English to 1503 and, like the word "strike", may be a crew legacy.[122] Most scholars now agree on the transnationalism of maritime culture. "Mariners in Seville, Amsterdam, London or Genoa had a vision of the world with a vast range of common denominators, and each one knew the peculiarities of the wage scale, discipline and rations that held sway among their colleagues".[123] Mariners' work was hard, dirty, and dangerous, and diets were deficient in vitamins; scurvy was endemic on long-range voyages. But sailors did insist on large rations of meat and alcohol, perhaps an echo of the post-plague "golden age". Sailors might be members of a large ships company or military unit, but also formed their own smaller fraternities within it, of "messmates", excluding men they did not like—crews within crews.

Crews were more superstitious than religious, and the superstitions were transnational. Spanish sailors did bring a wooden statue of St Anthony on deck to quell storms, but would bite its head off if the storm continued.[124] A belief in "St Elmo's Fire", a light appearing at the masthead thought to indicate better weather, has been traced in English, Iberian, French, Scandinavian, and Italian sailor folklore.[125] New rituals came with expansion, but remained recognisably derived from the older culture. Celebrating crossing the equator is the classic example. "The ceremony temporarily inverted the hierarchy on the ship and many captains were treated with contempt and mockery". This ritual is first documented in 1529, but is now thought to have earlier origins. Typically a sailor dressed up as Neptune and ducked or dowsed all who had not previously "crossed the line"—sometimes you might escape with a fine.[126] Other cross-cultural jolly japes included whipping a random boy to raise the wind in a calm—"the whipping boy".[127] To this list, one should add a propensity to cursing, drinking, gambling, whoring, rioting, and brawling.

Land crews might have no idea about St Elmo, but they shared most of these characteristics, including riotous relaxation. Swiss and German mercenaries held informal meetings sitting or standing in a circle—they too wished to avoid ringleaders. They too had crews within crews, "small self-selected groups" (*Rotte*); the Spanish military equivalent was *Cameradas*.[128] "Landsknechts elected some of their own officers and regarded themselves as an 'order' . . . a well-organised community with the attributes of a union".[129] Other land crews included long-range drovers who flourished after 1350. In the Spanish mesta system, semi-nomadic groups of up to 50 men took flocks of up to 10,000 sheep to upland pastures, ranging over hundreds of miles each summer. They were distinct from sedentary folk, who held them "in suspicion and contempt", though it might be unwise to express such views within earshot. It was said that "they seldom marry, and contribute nothing to the population".[130] Some types of miners also count as crew, especially in new mining districts, which had "an exceptionally large number of young men". "Unlike peasants . . . miners were organised in self-governing communities. . . . In which individual . . . authority was secondary to fraternal companies".[131] Lumbermen, or loggers, moving from site to site to cut prime timber for long-range export, and "navvies" working as teams of contractors far from home, were other variants. German dike-workers in the Netherlands, from 1410, "enjoyed a particularly bad reputation, not least because of their willingness to engage in collective strikes".[132] Like Maltese seafarers, these Europe-only examples confirm that burgeoning crews were not a result of successful expansion but a cause of it.

Crewmen had a varying relationship with authority. They could be semi-domesticated by states or companies into regular armies, operate as a group of independent petty entrepreneurs in a shared enterprise, or act outside the law altogether as smugglers, bandits, or pirates. They were disciplined on the job, and notoriously undisciplined off it, riotously celebrating pay or plunder in an identical way the world over. The harsh discipline on the job, which included flogging, was constrained by custom. Mutinies were frequent—the French navy averaged two a year between 1680 and 1789.[133] Captains were wise to watch their step, because crews were good at violence. They might not "kill men as freely as your cakemakers do flies" like their pirate brethren, but brawls, fistfights, and knife duels were light entertainment.[134] A study of two thousand sixteenth-century Spanish sailors found that "half of them showed the mark of some old wound on their bodies".[135] Even non-military crew were expected to be willing and able to fight, and they were. The average merchant sailor or whaler knew how to handle cannon, handguns, and steel blades of various kinds. A seventeenth-century Basque whaling ship with a crew of 39 carried 14 cannon, 30 muskets, 24 pistols, 30 cutlasses, and 40 grenades.[136] The proficiency in violence of European crew stemmed partly from obvious elements of the occupational culture, and partly from a strange tolerance of risk, discussed at the end of the chapter.

As this love-hate relationship with authority suggests, crew culture was rife with contradiction: individualist yet collectivist, independent yet hierarchical, distinct from wider society yet rooted in it, sometimes idealised in the abstract by that society yet also despised and feared by it. Crewmen were very manual workers, yet often saw themselves as independent contractors. Some crews were paid mainly in loot, or in shares of their work output, a practice that declined over time but in the case of whalers, cod fishers, and fur-trappers, continued deep into the nineteenth century. In any case, wages were often only part of the package for mariners; prize money or a small share of cargo space, a chest filled with trade goods, was often worth more.[137] Crewmen shifted easily between the subcategories, especially overseas. Such shifts were lubricated by shared culture. Perhaps the most shadowy subcategory of all was colonising crew, the solo male migrants who did not settle down and marry white women. Some aspired to do so. The seventeenth-century Chesapeake was dotted with forlorn landholdings with names like "Bachelor's Hope".[138] Others expected to return home, preferably after making their names and fortunes.

Colonising crew activities in the Americas were often violent. The great majority of the conquistadors in Mexico and Peru had no formal training as soldiers, and all were technically irregulars, serving a private military entrepreneur for rations and the prospect of plunder. This was also the case with subsequent armed *entradas*—expeditions searching for plunder and living off Indian communities along the way.[139] There were scores of such expeditions— at least 15 by 1593 into what is now the southern United States alone, some losing nearly all of their men.[140] Slave raids on Amerindians were another crew trade. On one estimate, 200,000 slaves were taken from the Central American coast between 1532 and 1542 alone, too early for locally born whites or castas to have been involved.[141] Crewmen did not feature much in semi-industrial silver mining in the Americas, but they did in placer gold mining, though Indian and African slave labour was used here as well. There was a substantial gold rush in Spanish Columbia in the 1550s, and another in the 1570s.[142] Far larger rushes took place in Brazil, 1695–1760, attracting perhaps 200,000 crewmen. Other colonising crew occupations included coastal shipping, crewing riverboats, privateering, piracy, cattle hunting and herding, fur trading and trapping, cod fishing and logging. By 1670, the British had established a half dozen "new sucking colonies" on the American mainland, cutting dyewood and then mahogany. "The settlement efforts by these 'sailors of the woods' formed the seed of what would eventually become British Honduras and later Belize".[143] Locally born white crewmen, castas, and free blacks eventually took over much crew work in the Americas, but on early frontiers European-born colonising crew were vital.

———

Some crewmen became rootless, with no fixed abode, but most were at least to some extent rooted in their home communities.[144] Between crews abroad and crew regions in Europe were intermediate hubs, the sailors' quarters of great port cities, like Triana in Seville, which could double as crew localities themselves. Like crew regions proper, these quarters had an exceptionally high proportion of households headed by women, either never married, because potential spouses were in distant graves, or the widows or grass widows of sailors. Such households, ranging from 20% to 30% of the total, were two or three times as numerous as in non-crew regions.[145] In inland England, the proportion of women-led households was 8–10%; as early as the 1370s, it was 23.5 % in the port of Hull.[146] This measures households registered as woman-run year on year, and is a rough indicator of the proportion of long-range crewmen. If shorter-range crew, such as cod fishermen who came home once a year but missed the harvest, are added, the proportion could skyrocket. In one small Dutch town in the seventeenth century, 30% of households were formally women-led, but "in daily practice, 66 percent . . . were managed by women".[147] Again, most of the evidence concerns sailors, but martial crew regions such as the Swiss and Austrian Alps have similar figures for women-led households.[148] Some studies paint a bleak picture of the lives of these women and their families. A minority were sent money by menfolk abroad, but it was seldom enough to live on, and many relied on poorly paid work, charity, prostitution, or all three.

Yet one could put a more positive gloss on the lives of crew-women. For one thing, they sometimes controlled significant businesses, often related to the provisioning and cargoes of ships. "In Bilbao in 1568, women seem to have controlled biscuit production altogether," biscuits of course being the seafarers' staple.[149] "The Venetian ambassador described Seville in 1525 as a city 'in the hands of women.'"[150] Until the 1640s, when Portugal delegated cod fishing to the French and English, women controlled about 40% of Oporto's cod retailing.[151] In one small Northern Portuguese crew port around 1615, seven out of eight cod merchants were women, and they were also prominent in the wine trade. Another peculiarity of crew regions was a high rate of illegitimate births that, exceptionally, seem to have involved extra-marital sex by women. Lists of illegitimacy-prone regions could double as lists of crew regions: northern Portugal, the Basque country, the Alpine provinces of Austria, parts of Norway and Scotland. In these regions, illegitimacy rates could rise as high as 25%, compared to a norm of below 5%. These were births registered by disapproving priests and officials, which could be evaded by a visit from a husband in the last nine months.

One great crew region was northern Portugal, where migration from inland to the coast began after the Black Death, continued as grain imports increased, and rose further as the population began to recover in the later fifteenth century.[152] It was the common crewmen of some localities in this region, not the lesser nobility as some sources suggest, that were the backbone of Portuguese imperial manpower. The gender ratio, of all ages, could be as low as 72.5 males to 100 females, suggesting that half the adult men were abroad.[153] Women-led households could reach 43%. Registered illegitimacy rates varied, perhaps according to the tolerance of the local priest as much as to actual sexual practices, but reached as high as 25%. As in the Basque Country, these offspring were readily accepted into the mother's family, and extra-marital relationships were at least tacitly condoned. One source describes a "customary practice" among the wives of seafarers. "Upon the return of her husband, the woman will hang a pair of his pants on the clothesline to alert her lovers to stay away".[154] Women were prominent, if not dominant, in the local economy, and some localities had a special relationship with the distant East Indies. Some crewmen did return with money—and spices, whose distribution went unusually far down the social scale. Others sent back legacies and endowments.[155] The women of the region were considered to be "fiercely independent".[156]

A neighbouring crew region was Galicia in Northern Spain. This grain-deficit region sent its men to the Spanish army and to both Spanish and

Portuguese maritime enterprise. These men "rarely sent for their families", and years of absence became an esteemed masculine tradition. Men who stayed were known as "*remendafoles*", those "without spirit or personality". Here, in one village in 1597, 44.4% of households were headed by women. By the eighteenth century, there were only 60 men for every 100 women in 41 of 50 parishes. "These women adeptly managed without men. In much of Galicia, women held the purse strings and made key decisions about friends and family, and their prerogative to do so was acknowledged by all the parties involved".[157]

There seems more than a hint of what one might call early folk feminism here. Where else did early modern European lower-class women get to run their own household, their own business, and have socially condoned extra-marital affairs if they chose? With exceptions like Andalusia, crew-sending regions and settler-sending regions were not the same, but women in both may have done better than their sisters in most regions of Europe. Despite high illegitimacy rates, the case of the American whaling island of Nantucket suggests that crew regions had lower than normal birthrates,[158] which meant fewer years spent pregnant and less risk of death in childbirth. Whether this contributed to the "Western European Marriage Pattern" is an interesting issue, but not one we can pursue. A tragic side of crew regions remained. Male and female births in these communities were roughly equal, but the number of men who died at home was sometimes as low as 44%. Such under-manned graveyards dot the crew regions of Europe.

———

Crewmen are slippery subjects in more ways than one; they are certainly not easy to count. Overall statistics on crews going overseas are rare, and those we do have sometimes count different things, such as the number of sailor voyages, which may register the same man several times, rather than the number of individuals. Whalers and cod fishers are sometimes not included, on the grounds that some of their activities were in what are now considered European waters. Spitzbergen, which attracted up to 12,000 Dutch whalers a year between 1650 and 1720, was almost 2,000 miles from Holland and completely unknown to Europeans until 1596.[159] It is better seen as part of an Arctic frontier of European expansion than a part of old Europe. Some estimates for the Americas are for total migration, crew and family settlers alike, and as noted above it is difficult to separate them out. However, calculations based on crude formulas, and such particulars as ships' tonnages and crew-ton ratios, average recruitment, and the sizes of overseas armies and garrisons, which are known for various times and places, means it is just possible to make a semi-educated guess: 8 million Western European overseas crewmen, 1500–1800.

The details may be for aficionados, but I need to show here that, high as the number may seem, it is at least plausible. Modest annual flows cumulate over centuries, as with the African slave trade. We do have one firm figure. Between 1602 and 1795, the Dutch East Indies Company sent out 973,000 men, about half of them Dutch. Total Dutch-flagged long-range crew, 1600–1800, has been put at over 2.8 million, but this includes some double counting, and 2 million might be a safer number.[160] An estimate of 1.5 million for Portuguese emigration is generally accepted, and it is likely that about a million of these migrants were crew rather than settlers. Spanish, French, and British are likely to be somewhere between the Dutch and Portuguese figures, to which we should add Scandinavian-flagged mariners—hence my 8 million. A grim consideration gives more weight to these numbers. At least half of all crewmen did not return, as our crew region cemeteries suggest, and most of them did not enjoy a new life in the colonies but died prematurely instead. Some 80% of 2,000 Spanish were thought to have died in the conquest of the Incas in the 1530s.[161] No less than 62% of Dutch crews to Asia, 600,000 men, did not return home, and there were never more than 20,000 live Dutch in the Indies at any one time. Death rates may have been as high among the 300,000 Portuguese crew who ventured to the East Indies in the sixteenth and early seventeenth centuries. Only half the 5,200 soldier recruits who left Lisbon for Goa, 1629–34, actually arrived. Most of the rest quickly died in the Goa royal hospital, in which 25,000 Europeans expired, 1604–1634.[162] Things did not necessarily improve much over time, as new diseases ensconced themselves in South-East Asia and the Caribbean. "In the terrible year of 1775, more than 70% of the [Dutch] Company's soldiers died within a year after their arrival from Europe".[163] In 1655, the first major English campaign in the Caribbean, which failed to take Hispaniola but took Jamaica as a consolation prize, lost 80% of its 10,000 men, mostly to disease.[164] The last English campaigns in the same region, in the 1790s, lost 45,000 soldiers plus at least 12,000 sailors.[165]

Such terrible mortalities might not have been predicted in the very first overseas expeditions. But they quickly became all too obvious from the accounts and small numbers of returning survivors. Yet crewmen continued to stream out. No doubt some were coerced, but it seems most were not. Merchant sailors, cod fishers, and whalers were normally volunteers.[166] Spain recruited its army from volunteers in the sixteenth century, and did not begin conscripting sailors until about 1640.[167] Even the notorious British press gangs, until recently believed to have supplied half the navy's crewmen in the eighteenth century, are now thought to have provided as few as 16%.[168] Once aboard, arrears of pay, the prospect of booty, and *espirit de crew* could turn a conscript into a belated volunteer. The mariner literature notes many examples of a "culture of risk".[169] "The prospect of dying was something mariners were accustomed to".[170] Sailors "come very near to losing their lives, and at the very moment of their escape turn round and laugh as though it were a good joke".[171] "No Man can have a greater contempt for Death. For every day he constantly shits upon his own Grave, and dreads a storm no more, than He doe a broken head, when drunk".[172] Irregular soldiers in the many late sixteenth-century Spanish *entrada* north of present-day Mexico also showed their crew colours. They "displayed extreme tolerance for risk, extraordinary physical stamina, and a callousness that verged on the sociopathic".[173]

I suspect that crewmen's willingness to knowingly and voluntarily accept a fifty-fifty chance of premature death was influenced by plague, at least until the 1650s. Portugal suffered frequent strikes in the fifteenth century, especially from 1477 to 1496, just before Vasco da Gama set out for the East Indies, and this was followed by "the serious epidemic of 1505–1507".[174] Spain suffered a "severe plague epidemic between 1517 and 1519", while Hernan Cortes was marching on the Aztecs; men soon flocked to join him.[175] Devon, a key source of early English seafarers, experienced a dozen strikes between 1498 and 1636.[176] After 1500, as we saw in chapter 1, plague became biased towards big port cities. A plague in Lisbon in 1569, for example, is thought to have killed 30% of the population, and there was another in the 1570s.[177] Between 1493 and 1649, Amsterdam experienced 24 plague outbreaks.[178] Strikes in other great port cities, like London and Seville, were frequent until 1665. Dicing with death was a fact of life in such places, and if you sailed for Goa or Batavia at least you threw the dice yourself. Once abroad, crewmen risked many diseases, but bubonic plague was not among them. Europe's crews were vital to its expansion. They were inured to risk because they had to be. They were also armed and dangerous. The mastery of relevant transport, courage, skill at violence, and brutality of these "Sea-Mongols" matched that of the horse-borne kind, and European crew carried pox if not buboes as well. They were literally the cutting edge of European expansion, as disposable as razor blades.

7

States, Interstates, and the European Expansion Kit

BETWEEN 1350 AND 1500, plague prompted changes that gave Western Europe the potential for expansion. The early plague-era economic boom, ragged and temporary as it was, provided the motives: increasing demand for exotic and extractive goods. In these expansive trades, growth continued after 1500, though it was less widely shared. Technologies were plague pressure-cooked into potential means for expansion. Plague also incubated expansive labour: prolific settlers and crews of disposable males, the latter inured to mobility, risk, and violence, and surplus to the economic and reproductive requirements of their home localities. But what of the organisational capacity to deliver on the motives, and to mobilise and deploy the means? Were they sufficient to effectively control the expansion kit, and did it in turn have a sufficient edge over non-Europeans to enable successful long-term expansion? Or were there political variables, independent of plague, that might provide alternative explanations? As usual these questions intersect with existing debates, with which we need to engage without being submerged.

I Warfare States

A long-standing explanation for Western European expansion is the rise of its large, powerful, and centralised territorial states—Spain, France, and England are the archetypes. Warfare was the main business of these "proto-national" states, and the two reinforced each other. In the much-quoted words of Charles Tilly, "war made the state, and the state made war".[1] This claim meshes with the wider "Military Revolution" thesis mentioned in chapter 5, which incorporates the gunpowder transition but also stresses non-technological factors. Only proto-nations, it argues, could afford the big, professional armies and big navies of specialist warships that came to characterise European warfare. It was, it says, the globally exceptional amount of warfare between these rival proto-nations, not plague, that gave Europe a military and organisational edge over the rest of the world. "Recurring great power wars drove military innovation and state-building in Western Europe, which subsequently gave these states a competitive advantage that they used to dominate non-European polities." As of 2018, "the military revolution narrative remains the presumed foundation of why the world is the way it is and how it got that way".[2] One variant of the thesis, associated with John Brewer, emphasises the rise of the "military-fiscal state", able to spend many years of future income on its current wars (see chapter 16).[3] Another variant, proposed by Phillip Hoffman, sees these wars as a "tournament" between absolutist European monarchs, addicted to war, the "sport of kings", and encouraged by the fact that they themselves faced little risk of losing their lives or thrones. Constant practice and constant cribbing from each other drove "continuous innovation".[4]

The state-led Military Revolution thesis has proved useful to those who see exceptional institutions as the key to Western Europe's divergence, creating a favourable environment for continuous economic growth, technological innovation, and geographic expansion.[5] As noted in chapter 5, some date the Military Revolution and the rise of warfare state to 1500–1800, others to 1350–1500. I sided with the latter on the gun-led component; it was a product of the early plague era. There is a case for saying the same of the state-led component. "Throughout fourteenth-century Europe the state made its entry in force. . . . Feudalism died. Absolute monarchy everywhere took its first steps".[6]

Plague does seem to have given both states and warfare a boost. Campaigns from Syria to Spain halted briefly around 1350, but Western Europeans were soon at each other's throats again, and wars actually increased in frequency and length if not scale. England, for example, sent five expeditions to Ireland during 1361–76, invaded Castile twice, overcame a great peasant revolt in 1381 and a great Welsh rebellion in 1400–1409, fought a couple of civil wars and five wars against the Scots, and lost its hundred-year struggle with France, all by 1453. Similar bloody stories could be told for the other proto-nations. One study counts well over 200 wars across Europe in the fifteenth century.[7] On the other hand, armies, and therefore the economic destruction they caused, halved in size. But, judging by expenditure, war was indeed the main business of late medieval states as well as early modern ones.

Plague's contribution to these early warfare states was considerable. The scribal transition delivered bigger and better state bureaucracies. Armies halved but tax takes did not. Already beset, from 1337, by war with the English, French government revenues were badly disrupted by plague, but only for two or three years. "By 1351, the crown had managed to accumulate rather sizable revenues and to stabilise taxation following the disaster of the plague".[8] Further defeats, internal feuding, and repeated debasements of the currency created later revenue crises to the 1420s, but in the longer run the French state's income increased greatly.[9] On the other side of the same war, the English government collected, in 1352–54, 95% of its pre-plague taxes despite the near-halving of the population.[10] Intensifying state demands were a factor, but the main explanation was a sudden drop in the proportion of people too poor to pay any tax at all, which in parts of England had amounted to 60% of households before the Black Death.[11] This proportion at least halved after 1350, and similar declines in the percentage of untaxed households have been noted for Navarre and parts of France.[12] Taxpayers were one of the "selective increases" paradoxically created by plague. States could spend more money per soldier on their smaller armies, and mobilise them more often.

Yet big states did not always look very strong in the early plague era, and were by no means the only war-makers, or the leading gunpowder innovators. The Holy Roman Emperor, despite also being king of Hungary and having the help of the pope, was no match for the rebel Hussites, pioneers of the use of guns in field battles, in the 1420s and 1430s. After defeating several "crusades" against them, and rampaging as far north as the Baltic, the Hussites were finally undone in 1436 by a split in their own ranks. As for potential proto-nations, they were not on some inexorable path to success. Some promising prospects—Aragon, Burgundy, and Hungary—fell to dynastic failure and military defeat between 1474 and 1526. Those that did make it had their weaknesses. Centralised states are supposed to monopolise war and law within their borders, yet fourteenth- and fifteenth-century French monarchs could not stop literally scores of small wars among their lordly subjects.[13] In fifteenth-century English law courts, allegedly an institutional fount of that country's ascent to greatness, "only about one-third of those indicted eventually stood trial—the remainder never appeared and were outlawed". Of those who *were* tried, 80% were acquitted, 10% executed, and 10% escaped.[14] Quite apart from the Wars of the Roses (1465–85) between contenders for the throne, there were small wars between English lords, using cannon and handguns—three in 1469–71.[15]

Handguns, after all, were *less* expensive, and required less training, than either steel crossbows or heavy cavalry. Cannon, especially heavy ones, were more expensive, but the main cost of field artillery and siege trains was their overland transport. Mounting cannon on town walls evaded this cost. The original hearths of Middle European gun transition, Wallonia and adjacent parts of Germany, plus northern Italy, were not the heartlands of successful proto-nations. Instead, they featured autonomous towns, whether or not they were nominally independent. Plagued towns, "long on cash and short of man-power", led the process of replacing labour with guns, and led the very rapid dissemination of firearms after the Black Death. Venice, "perpetually seeking to magnify the effectiveness of limited manpower",[16] was one leader, but the most striking case was the merchant republic of Dubrovnik (Ragusa). The Adriatic city was actually in Eastern Europe, but was in effect a "turntable", equally oriented towards all three macro-regions of West Eurasia. Guns arrived in 1351, and by 1363 it was making its own. "By 1378, guns had become regular weapons in the defense of the city, and Ragusa had soon acquired the status of a major centre of firearms production".[17] It exported guns to Southern Italy and Spain, a technology transfer from Eastern to Western Europe.[18] Even in Hungary, then a strong proto-national kingdom, "the dissemination of fire-arms can best be traced in town account books from the 1390s".[19] French cities were as active as kings in buying and making guns.[20]

The French crown's cannon were bigger and more mobile, but proto-national siege trains were a response to gun-defended cities, not an independent state-led development. Eventually, states did maintain large regular armies and specialist navies that no one else could afford, but not until about 1650. David Parrott and others have recently confirmed that the centralised warfare state is largely an illusion until this time.[21] War did help make powerful nation-states, but they developed much too late to explain the gunpowder transition of 1350–1500. Moreover, state rivalries continued after 1500 while, as we saw in chapter 5, major technical innovations did not, though semi-constant warfare did prevent any technical decline. The state-led military transition to big armies and navies of 1650–1800 must take second place to, and was partly built on, the plague-led gunpowder transition of 1350–1500. The period between 1500 and 1650—which was roughly the late plague era in Western Europe—was transitional in more ways than one.

The role of big proto-national states in early expansion can also be exaggerated. Two of the most successful, the Dutch and the Portuguese, were also the smallest, each with no more people than the Venetian Republic. It is well-known that most of the earliest attempts at expansion were undertaken by private groups, not states. The Spanish conquistadors Cortes and Pizarro are only the best-known. States did have a trick or two up their sleeves, however. Many early non-state attempts at expansion failed; states latched on to those that succeeded. States were also important in ensuring that successful expansions did not lapse into dispersals but remained connected to metropoles. But one could argue that expansion made the centralised states as much as they made it. Overseas bullion empowered the monarchies of Spain and Portugal, helping them to dispense with representative assemblies to authorise taxes. Conversely, overseas trade enriched Dutch and English merchants, inducing older elites to incorporate them into their representative assemblies and giving increasing power to single mega-cities, Amsterdam and London.

II Transnationalisms, Networks, and Shape-Shifters

None of the above is intended to suggest that proto-nations were not growing in importance from about 1450. Yet, until at least 1650, they had to share their world with several other species of organisation, rather as *homo sapiens* had to share theirs with other species of humans before 30,000 BCE. Both *sapiens* and nation-states ultimately dominated, but the students of both are prone to extend the period of their primacy, pushing it back in time. Before 1650, proto-nations had to coexist with, indeed depend on, other types of state, and on non-state organisations. To fund, fight, and supply their wars—and their expansions—even the biggest territorial states depended on transnational networks of merchants, brokers, financiers, and entrepreneurs—and on city-states.

The role of one merchant network, the Portuguese *conversos*, forced to convert from Judaism in the 1490s, in the development of the trans-Atlantic trade has deservedly received much recent attention. They constituted "a nation without a state, a collectivity dispersed across the seas". They were Catholic in the Portuguese empire (though they retained portraits of "Saint" Moses) and, later, Jewish again in more tolerant Amsterdam.[22] Though sometimes persecuted in Iberia, and though many migrated to the Low Countries and elsewhere, they were important as traders, merchants, and financiers in both Portuguese and Spanish expansion. The conversos were by no means the only merchant network flourishing in the plague era, 1350–1650, and the others were also "often fluid in their identities".[23] There were other Jewish networks, and Christian and ethnic ones as well—Scots, Breton, Basque, Huguenot.[24] In the mid-fifteenth century, French entrepreneur Jacques Coeur built a network almost from scratch, specialising in the spice trade, with 300 factors on land and sea, many from his small home region of Berry.[25] Other networks were based in particular cities or city-states. In major ports, foreign merchants clustered into self-administered enclaves, nodes in their network, known, like university students, by their place of origin as "nations". But their very essence was "transnational", to use the anachronistic but convenient term.[26] "These self-organised networks transcended the borders imposed by empires, forced the frontiers negotiated between polities and fostered a cross-cultural, multireligious and trans-national world".[27]

Plague boosted trade and therefore trade networks. They could operate with, around, and even against big states. They could dissolve into parts, which might take different sides in a conflict. Recent scholarship has at last done justice to networks, but less so to their key role: brokering a similarly transnational floating pool of resources. The resource pools included salt, grain, and strategic raw materials such as prime timber for ships, copper for bronze cannon, and flax for rigging. These were exported by particular regions, but traded internationally, even between states at war. Bullion and credit were other transnational resources, in which German and north Italian cities and banking clans specialised. Above all was a transnational pool of manpower, not just the crewmen discussed in the last chapter, but also various types of experts: German gunners, Basque whalers and shipwrights, Genoese bankers, navigators, and naval entrepreneurs. After the Black Death, more capital and opportunity chased less labour and expertise. In these circumstances, the success of states, big and small, depended on their ability to coerce or attract labour, including foreign labour. The Great Game in post-plague politics was "man-powering." After the plague, territorial states and even empires had to enter the manpower game too, often using city-state and merchant brokerage networks as their agents—and being used by them.

Military transnationalism in the sixteenth century is a case in point. State forces depended on the transnational pools for finance, provisions, equipment, as well as crewmen and ships. In 1490, only 6,000 of 25,000 Venetian mariners were actually Venetian. In 1522, Sweden bought an entire fleet from the city of Lubeck.[28] At the Battle of Marignano in 1515, the Milanese army was mainly Swiss, the French army mainly German.[29] Swiss and German mercenaries, and others ranging from Scots to Albanians, were themselves organised into networks and subcultures. In the case of the Swiss, hiring out troops was a mainstay of the economy. The "Spanish" army at the Battle of St Quentin in

1557 was only 12% Spanish; most was German.[30] Spain's Mediterranean fleet was largely Genoese in the sixteenth century. In the 1570s, Spain tried to do without the Genoese navy, but could not manage it.[31] English armies in the fifteenth century were supplied by neo-feudal private contracts, and often comprised as many Welsh and French as English. Foreign mercenaries were the mainstay of Henry VIII's continental adventures. Private and transnational military suppliers and hired transnational crewmen were the norm in European warfare, fourteenth to seventeenth centuries, and Parrott notes that "this is even more true of European military activity beyond the borders of the Continent".[32]

————

City-states are often said to have declined after 1450 or 1500, and they did decline from 1650. But some enjoyed a long "Indian summer". They had previous experience in the great game of man-powering, being intrinsically cash-rich and labour-poor. They were pre-adapted to the post-plague labour crisis, and some were also old hands at expansionism, though mainly within Europe. Florence acquired nine neighbouring Tuscan cities between 1349 and 1406.[33] Its military innovations included "a separate unit in 1350 of fifty *barattieri*, or ribalds, whose job involved mocking the enemy through acts of *infamia*, an important aspect of Tuscan warfare at this time"—a factoid not lost on the makers of *Monty Python and the Holy Grail*.[34] "In the forty years between 1380 and 1420, Venice more than doubled its territory and population", using the former to achieve the latter.[35] It suffered defeats, trade diversions, and numerous plagues between 1347 and 1631, with mortalities of 60% in the first and 30% in the last, but was repeatedly able to recover. Militarily, it was a match for territorial states, able to muster as many as 72,000 mariners, militia, and soldiers in the 1420s despite plague losses.[36] Venice remained a major power for more than three centuries after the plague. This was camouflaged by its struggle against the Turks in the eastern Mediterranean for much of this period, which reduced its influence elsewhere.

Other city-states specialised in less formal empires than Venice and in more fluid practices and identities. Three important cases are discussed mainly in other chapters but need brief mention here: Dubrovnik (chapter 11), Lubeck (chapter 12), and Genoa (chapter 10). Like Venice and Florence, all three doubled as merchant networks, but unlike the Portuguese conversos, had a state when they needed one. All three were shape-shifters, changing both their allegiances and the balance of their activities as circumstances required. We saw above that Dubrovnik, an inter-regional hub of West Eurasia, was an important gun-maker and distributor. It was also the classic post-plague shape-shifter, or perhaps "flag shifter", known sarcastically as "Ragusa of the Seven Flags".[37] It did pay tribute to at least four rulers, Venice, Hungary, Serbia, and the Ottomans, at various times—often to two at once. It also carefully maintained good relations with the papacy and, until their conquest by the Ottomans in 1517, with the Mamluks. Larger powers shifted their merchant ships to its flag to alleviate the effects of war on trade. In 1560, Dubrovnik had approximately 150 ships totalling 36,000 tons, already large for a small city. In the 1570s and 1580s, this shot up to 250 ships and 66,000 tons. The extras were probably Venetian and Genoese vessels sailing under the Dubrovnik flag while their cities were embroiled in wars with Ottomans (Venice), Dutch, and English (Genoa was an ally of Spain). The fleet reverted to 36,000 tons in the early seventeenth century when these wars were over.[38]

Flag-shifting helped Europe's trade survive its numerous wars. If two states were in conflict, their merchants would shift their cargoes and even their ships to neutral flags. Flag-shifting, plus transnational part ownership of single ships, meant that "at a certain point it is impossible to speak of a 'Genoese' fleet or a 'Ragusan' fleet in any terms other than under which standard it sailed".[39] Some English fought the Spanish Armada in 1588 while others supplied Spain with munitions.[40] In the single year 1587, the Spanish seized 94 Dutch ships pretending to belong to the Hanseatic League.[41] More often, states turned a blind eye to, or actively connived in, trading with the enemy, even insuring them against the state's own attacks. The Dutch and Portuguese were at war in the 1620s, but the latter were still able to "buy [insurance] policies from the same state that was preying on their shipping".[42] Recent studies have demonstrated the camouflaged internationalism of the Brazilian-Portuguese sugar trade from its inception in the mid-sixteenth century.[43] All this did not prevent war from having an adverse impact on trade, but it did reduce it.

Lubeck had several identities simultaneously: it was an imperial city of the Holy Roman Empire, an independent city-state, and leader of the Hanseatic League, with its own small empire nestled within the League, itself "a strong, yet changeable and fluid body".[44] Lubeck's own empire in Scandinavia and the Baltic was informal and "patchwork", economically controlling small but rich patches of other states, its influence underlying that of their own governments rather than displacing them. Lubeck also pioneered what I call "urban colonisation" in Northern Europe, whereby a city developed "virtual hinterlands" highly adapted to the colonising city's needs, sometimes to their mutual benefit. It illustrates that monochrome political maps of early modern Europe, claiming that each region had only one allegiance, are deceptive. Genoa was another shape-shifter, frequently changing allegiances and appearing to some historians as a "failed state", to others as a loose set of merchant-warrior clans whose tentacles reached across West Eurasia. Chapter 10 will argue that key features of the "military-fiscal state"—public debts, reserve banks, and maritime insurance—were not invented by Amsterdam and London in the seventeenth century, but inherited from Genoa and other north Italian city-states, which developed them in the fourteenth century in response to plague. The same applies to "virtual clans" in which merchant survivors of plague reshuffled into groups of fictive kin, sometimes taking on the same name. These were arguably the ancestors of the joint-stock company, whose origin is also often credited to England and the Netherlands. Finally, Genoa was adept at entwining its own patchwork empire with others, both profiting from and reinforcing them.

In all, four types of transnational imperialism emerged in the early plague era: "entwined empires", where two or more empires intermeshed; "urban colonisation", whereby a city built up "virtual hinterlands" in other countries; "patchwork expansion", in which patches of formally or informally controlled territories were linked by strategic hubs and networks; and subcontracted expansion, at first featuring individual adventurers but tending to more permanent corporate colonisers. Centralising states still had a significant role, but these myriad transnationalisms were at least as important for early expansion. In particular, they enabled tiny powers like Portugal and the Dutch Republic to create great empires. Their dwarfishness was part illusion. We will see that Genoa marshalled the skills and capital of much of the Mediterranean to midwife early Portuguese expansion, and that Amsterdam used Lubeck's legacy to mobilise the grain, metals, timber resources, and manpower of northeastern Europe in the service of Dutch expansion. The fluidities inside Europe allowed resources to funnel transnationally to where the prospects of expansion were most promising.

Big states struggled to wean themselves from dependence on transnational pools, merchant networks, and cross-cultural brokers, and the seventeenth-century decline of city-states is a measure of their eventual success. They sought to nationalise segments of the resource pools, or at least develop an exclusive relationship with them. They tried to better manage their own forests in the service of their fleets. They educated their own experts, organised their own finances, and borrowed internally rather than externally. They are thought to have been helped in this by the rise of individualism over kinship, real or virtual, as the organising principle of mercantile relationships from the seventeenth century. They acquired new crew regions—Brittany and Gascony for fifteenth-century France, Ireland and Scotland for sixteenth- and seventeenth-century England. They supplemented crews with non-crew soldiers and sailors, using press gangs and various quota systems. They sought to tame their crewmen, using standard uniforms, regular wages, and strict discipline. But they never quite succeeded, at least before 1800. A shadowy transnationalism continued to lurk in the background of Western Europe's disunity.

Since Machiavelli in the early sixteenth century, many writers have attributed Western Europe's advantages over the rest of the world, real and alleged, not only to its large centralised states but also to its competitive state system. Plague was, I think, even more important. Europeans may have "escaped from Rome" in the fifth century, but they did not escape from Europe until a thousand years later—too long a lead time for the former to explain the latter.[45] Yet it remains true that, after plague's revolution, 1350–1500, state rivalries kept European powers up to their new speed. As we saw in chapter 5, technology (especially military technology) did not advance much, but it did not fall back either, unlike the Chinese case, as we will see. But the post-plague surge in transnationalism also had its legacies, and synergy joined rivalry. The five major Western European colonial powers (Portugal, Spain, the Netherlands, France, and England), for all their fierce internecine wars, mounted strikingly parallel expansions, 1500–1800. All five had colonies in South America, and a significant stake in the China trade, in which Sweden and Denmark also joined in the eighteenth century. All except Portugal had settler colonies in North America, as did Sweden. The New Netherlands swallowed, and built on, New Sweden, and was in turn swallowed, and built on, by New England. All five, except Spain, had lodgments in India, as did Sweden and Denmark. All, including the two lesser players, went slaving in West Africa, though Spain usually let other people deliver its slaves. All, except Portugal, held Caribbean sugar islands, again including the two minor flags. All the big five, except France, had possessions in South East Asia. The Dutch muscled aside the Portuguese and British here in the seventeenth century, but not the Spanish in the Philippines, and the British came back in the eighteenth century. All the big five were involved, heavily at varying times, in the Newfoundland Banks cod fishery. All, except Portugal, were involved in the fur and whaling trades, both of which went global from the late eighteenth century, extending to the whales, sea otters and fur seals of the Pacific. There is a sense in which expansive early modern European states hunted as a squabbling pack, rather like today's football clubs, stridently emphasising separate identities and rivalry and battling hard on the field, while at the same time drawing on a shared pool of money, techniques, coaches, and players.

III The Western European Expansion Kit

By about 1480, the various plague-incubated developments we have outlined congealed into a mature expansion kit, whose most obvious elements were gunpowder weapons and maneuverable gunships. Motley crews of disposable males provided the initial manpower, later reinforced by settlers, *castas*, slaves, and local allies. Centralising states and merchant networks provided an intermittent but ongoing trickle of resources from the transnational pools. Newly epidemic diseases had emerged which, unlike plague, could cross wide oceans. Part three will broaden and deepen the story, but before embarking on it we need a preliminary assessment of the European expansion kit. For several decades, "military revisionists" have pushed back strongly against "military revolutionists". "European military superiority was clearly not the key variable".[46] Weaknesses in the Military Revolution thesis have been exposed. Big regular armies and specialist navies were seldom used to conquer non-European enemies. "Before the 1750s the improved devices and institutions of the 'military revolution' were neither seriously applied nor tested overseas".[47] What might be called "musket denigration" is prominent in this line of thinking. Guns scarcely featured in some early conquests, it is said, and in any case were too slow-loading and inaccurate to be of much use. "There is a growing tendency among historians to downplay the decisiveness of gunpowder weapons in European hands at least in the era between about 1500 and 1800".[48] A good summary of the revisionist position, published in 2018, notes that European forces overseas were usually small and irregular. Local allies, it argues, were the real keys to European success.

> The military innovations said to be decisive in Europe were almost entirely absent elsewhere before the Industrial Revolution. Instead, early modern European expansion in the Americas, Asia, and Africa was largely carried out by tiny forces of adventurers and chartered companies, who adapted local tactics, and usually did not possess any significant technological advantage over their opponents.[49]

In any case, Chinese, Indians, and some other Asians had guns, gun forts, and gunships too. "In the East, the technological gap between European and local forces was often quite slight or non-existent, particularly in firearms". "Beyond the brute necessity of crossing the oceans . . . even the West's main military-technological advantage, the gun-armed sailing ship, failed to alter the strategic balance".[50]

Up to a point, I count myself among the revisionists. In my earliest work, on nineteenth-century indigenous resistance to European expansion, I posited a "myth of conquest" which exaggerated European victories and downplayed defeats. If defeat was blatant, it was explained away by mis-attributing it to the weaknesses of native allies, to the exceptional absence of good European leadership, or to its exceptional presence on the other side in the form of renegades. Alternatively, it was credited to native "natural advantages", such as vast numbers, or the ability to creep like rats through woodland, or to swim like fish. Such accounts, I suggested, were not merely biased, but reliably biased, and could therefore be used against themselves in concert with other evidence.[51] There is still much work to be done along these lines in rethinking "colonial small wars." But I did not deny that European military technology had an edge over most opponents, which is precisely why some non-Europeans were quick to adopt, adapt, or develop antidotes to it. Ironically, denying this edge can end up belittling the achievements of those who strove against it. A plague-incubated European military edge, of course, does not imply any intrinsic or general European superiority. The Mongols had a military edge over the rest of the world in the thirteenth century. No one suggests that this somehow made them the apex of civilisation.

Revolutionists certainly exaggerate the decisiveness of European military superiority before 1800, but are revisionists right to discount it altogether? The sixteenth- and seventeenth-century East Asian answer to this question was an emphatic "No". European muskets, cannon, and gunships did have an edge over those of the Ming diffusion, according to the Ming themselves. The rapid and large-scale uptake of European-style muskets by the Japanese from 1543 is well-known. The Ming and the Koreans took up European-style muskets at much the same time. The former produced a manual explaining volley fire, using them in 1560.[52] The latter recorded a test of the musket's accuracy a century later. A unit of 200 Korean musketeers fired at targets 72 metres distant, 1.6 metres high, and only 10 centimetres wide. Their leader recorded the results, which averaged 25% hits.[53] If the targets had been man-sized, the average would have been much higher. This accords with the European evidence—muskets were quite accurate up to 80 yards or so. They delivered a lead ball at 15 times the kinetic energy of even a steel crossbow, and were able to penetrate even steel armour.[54] The revisionist position may be influenced by an unintended inheritance of an old bias. Military elites all over the world valued their skill at arms and horsemanship, gained over decades of training and honed in hunts and jousts. They were often disinclined to dwell on the new reality: that an emaciated peasant with a wooden leg, a musket, and a few months' training was a match for any of them. They were therefor inclined to downplay the efficacy of guns, and they had a disproportionate influence on the documentary record. Muskets did remain slow-loading and prone to misfire, but in many (though not all) situations they were more formidable than any other individual weapon.[55] Non-Europeans—Africans, Amerindians, and Polynesians, as well as Asians—were quick to perceive this and to seek to acquire European guns. These peoples were not fools.

Chinese ships first clashed with European galleons at the mouth of the Pearl River in 1521–22, and at first the Chinese cannon were outmatched. The Ming soon dealt with the Portuguese using fireships, surprise attack, and weight of numbers. But the Chinese commander, Wang Hong, was impressed by the foreign guns: "Since ancient times, no weapons have ever surpassed these powerful and violent ones". On his initiative, the Chinese state adopted and adapted Portuguese-style handguns and small cannon, producing 4,000 in 1528 alone.[56] In the seventeenth century, the Chinese repeatedly showed that they could emulate European gun technology when they needed to. But they did not need to very often, and between clashes relaxed back towards their own gun styles. Most of their wars were against steppe nomads, which required large numbers of mounted archers. It is not true that guns were of no use against nomad horsemen. They could be decisive in defending or attacking fixed positions, which nomads did occasionally take up, and in breaking a cavalry charge. Steppe nomads themselves sought to acquire guns from the sixteenth century. Crimean Tartars had plenty of mounted archers, but "against the harquebuses also a 'harquebus army' is needed".[57] But guns were somewhat less important against nomads than when fighting rival gun armies, and may have required different types of weapons, such as very small cannon, light enough to be carried by a camel. In the 1680s, Russians found that Chinese troops at first "had no use for 'small firearms', employing largely cannons and cold weaponry and preferring 'bow combat'," though they quickly came back up to speed (see chapter 14).[58]

The Chinese were impressed by Portuguese galleons, as well as guns, as early as 1517, on the basis of their actions in Southeast Asia, notably the taking of Melaka, a Chinese ally, in 1511:

> On each side of their ships are placed four or five guns, and from within the ship's hold they can secretly fire them. If another ship comes near, the bullets burst asunder the planks and the water leaks right in. With them one can rampage across the seas and other countries cannot stand up against them.[59]

European galleons continued to have an edge over Chinese warships. In Tonio Andrade's words, "world historians are shy about judging European's technological superiority, but seventeenth-century Chinese historians weren't. . . . There are many descriptions in Chinese sources about the superiority of Dutch ships".[60] To give another example, "the red-hairs build their ships tall as mountains and sturdy as an iron bucket, so solid that they cannot be destroyed . . . Ultimately, there is no way to stand up to them. With great ease they traverse the oceans without worry of being defeated or damaged".[61] Galleons proved harder for non-Europeans to emulate than cannon and muskets.

Despite their guns and galleons, Europeans before 1800 were never a real threat on land to the big powers of East Asia. But Asian acknowledgment of their military edge is more than a mere debating point. European-style technology, though not Europeans themselves, *were* major threats in the case of the late sixteenth-century Japanese invasion of Korea, and the mid-seventeenth century resistance of the Taiwan-based Koxinga clan to the Qing (Manchu) takeover of China (see chapters 14 and 15). There was no European empire in East Asia before 1800, and not much afterwards. But European expansion and globalisation did affect the region, and its influence in turn ricocheted back to Europe.

"Biological warfare" was another component of the expansion kit, particularly in the Americas. Amerindians had their own diseases, but were vulnerable to new European and African pathogens. One case of deliberate infection, with smallpox-infected blankets by the British in North America around 1760, seems quite well documented, and others are rumoured.[62] But disease transfer was normally unintended and far from automatic. It is often presented as a single tragic wave of near extinction, which eliminated 90% of Amerindians within a few decades of contact. The differential impact of European diseases was indeed tragic, and sometimes did give Europeans an advantage. But the idea of a single inexorable wave of "Fatal Impact" is dangerously deceptive, reducing Amerindians to hopeless, hapless, helpless victims, doomed from first contact. As we have seen, plague itself did not make it to the Americas, and West African yellow fever did not arrive until the mid-seventeenth century, and then hit Europeans and Amerindians alike. In the sixteenth century, the chief differential villains were measles, typhus and, above all, smallpox.[63] The full set did not become prevalent in Europe until about 1490. Influenza, the most lethal strains of which could kill up to 22% of a well-connected population,[64] did not become pervasive in Europe until 1510–80, and some think it did not make it to the Americas until 1647.[65] Other diseases—scarlet fever, mumps, whooping cough, and typhoid—played relatively minor roles, and cholera did not arrive until the nineteenth century. The big three diseases confer long if not total immunity on those who survive them.[66] A major epidemic of any one would therefore prevent a second until a critical mass of non-immune children, born since the last, had built up, which took about 15 years. Suggestions like the notion that the Huron were devastated by three strikes of smallpox in the 1630s are therefore unlikely.[67]

Measles were sometimes only mildly lethal, but could kill up to 15% of an interactive population; typhus, perhaps 20%; and smallpox, 25%. Higher figures are sometimes given, but they may confuse *case* fatality, the proportion of deaths among those infected, with overall fatality—some people always escape entirely. Amerindians initially had no chance of acquiring immunity to these diseases through surviving a strike, but the idea that they had less genetic resistance is now doubted.[68] Smallpox had an incubation period of 9–12 days, during which the infected person could walk or ride but was not infectious, and an eruptive period of 7–10 days, during which the victim was infectious but could not travel unless carried—a maximum of 22 days, after which the victim was either immune or dead. Measles took no more than 18 days to run its course; typhus, up to 23 days. Since a voyage to the Americas in the sixteenth century took at least 50 days, a sequence of infections of non-immune people was required. Because an increasing number of Europeans had acquired immunity, transfers could become rarer over time. So smallpox did not arrive until 1518,[69] measles perhaps in 1530,[70] and typhus or typhoid in 1545, after hundreds of voyages had failed to transfer them.[71] None of these diseases became established in the Americas until the mid-seventeenth century, so each strike had to be separately introduced across the Atlantic. All this scales back, but does not eliminate, the terrible effects of introduced diseases on Native Americans. A devastating sequence of all three diseases in a decade or so remained possible, and may actually have occurred in Hispaniola. Differential disease was an important component of the European expansion kit in the Americas, and in other regions that did not share the Old World's disease regime, but it was not a reliable one.

———

Can we briefly test the effects of the European expansion kit, including crewmen, metropolitan support, weapons and microbes, on early cases of conquest? One possibility is the Canary Islands, which the Spanish and Portuguese tried to conquer both before and after the kit was fully developed. As noted in chapter 4, the Berber-descended Guanche people of these islands had lost the art of metallurgy, and they numbered only about 50,000 at contact.[72] Slaves were taken from 1362, and some smaller islands were conquered in the early fifteenth century. But, utilising their mountainous interiors for protection, using wooden spears and swords, and throwing stones with great force and accuracy, the inhabitants of the larger islands proved formidable opponents. Several Portuguese and Spanish expeditions, of up to 2,000 men, came to grief.[73] The conquest was finally completed between 1478 and 1496. "By this time", says the latest analysis, "firearms, though still relatively primitive, were coming into wider circulation and helped swing the balance of power in favour of Europeans".[74] It is likely that increasing disease transfers also played a role. Information for the Canaries is scant, but there is enough for a somewhat more intensive test in the famous case of the Spanish conquest of central Mexico, 1519–21.

The Spanish conquest of the Aztec Empire in Mexico in fact consisted of two separate campaigns, with opposite outcomes. In the first, prompted by news of gold acquired by pillaging and bartering expeditions to the Yucatan coast in 1517, Hernan Cortes gathered 600 Spanish crewmen, few of whom were regular soldiers or martial *hidalgo* gentry, and 200 Indians in Cuba, and sailed for Mexico in 1519. All accounts agree that he had very few horses and handguns; the most reliable count is 13 harquebuses and 14 horses. He also had 14 small cannon. These numbers increased as reinforcements straggled in, but not by much. The expedition may at first have seemed unthreateningly small—central Mexico's population was over 1 million[75]—and some Aztecs wanted to receive it peacefully. But fighting soon broke out, the Spanish acquired Indian allies from among the Aztec's rivals and tributaries, and won several victories against much larger Indian armies. They negotiated their way into the Aztec capital of Tenochtitlan. But, in June 1520, they were bloodily ejected, and forced to retreat to the coast, tail between legs, with a total loss of 900 Spanish, leaving only a few hundred alive. Thus, despite the early victories, the first invasion was a catastrophic failure. The second invasion, 1520–21, was a different story. It was larger—at least 1,300 Spanish and 96 horses—better planned, better equipped, and better supported. It succeeded in taking Tenochtitlan in August 1521, after 50 days' siege. This came nowhere near to a "Spanish conquest of Mexico", which in fact was never completed—groups such as the Yacqui and Huichol were still functionally independent when Spanish rule ended in 1821. But it did conquer Mexico's leading power, confiscate its accumulated gold, and establish the base for a lucrative patchwork expansion.

Revisionists now dismiss the role of guns, and in some cases of horses too, in explaining Spanish victories.[76] They must be right about handguns in the first invasion; they were simply too few. The horses probably were significant; even a few men on huge horses are a danger to any pedestrian crowd without steel weapons; police still use them for crowd control. The Aztecs displayed the heads of both slain horses and men as trophies.[77] In the longer term, horses were an ephemeral advantage because Indians acquired them too. The 14 cannon must also have been useful, but only if they were carried or dragged by Indian allies. It was these allies, say the revisionists, who were really decisive. They were indeed one key variable, particularly the Tlaxcalans, who saw the Spanish as their last chance to escape Aztec hegemony.[78] But they cannot have been the only one—they featured as much in the failed campaign as in the successful one. What chapter 5 described as "transitional technologies" were another key. All-steel swords were one such technology, and steel crossbows were another. Cortez landed with 32 crossbows, as against 13 harquebuses, in 1519. Steel breast and back plates were not important here, because lighter and more comfortable Aztec cotton armour provided protection against indigenous weapons, which had obsidian points and edges, and the Spanish quickly adopted it.[79] But cotton armour did not protect against steel swords or lances, cannon shot, harquebus bullets, or crossbow bolts.

Spanish accounts typically exaggerate enemy numbers and losses, but were accurate about their own casualties. These were often high, as a percentage of the small Spanish forces involved, but included many wounded, often not badly enough to stop them fighting, and very few were killed. The account of the conquistador Bernal Diaz is peppered with disproportionate casualty lists. "One of our men was killed in the fighting, and sixty were wounded". In another engagement, only two Spaniards were killed, "one of whom had been fatally struck in the throat, the other in the ear", but 70 were wounded.[80] In Old World battles, the proportion of killed to wounded was vastly higher than this—one dead to three or four wounded might be typical. Similar imbalances occurred in engagements with the Incas. "Only one Spaniard was killed but almost all were wounded".[81] The standard explanation is the Amerindian desire to take live prisoners for sacrifice.[82] But similar disproportions appear in Portuguese accounts of engagements with Asian Indian coastal polities, which did not practice human sacrifice, around the same time. In 1509, the Portuguese, who did not use shields, suffered 16 killed and 220 wounded in taking one port city, and other similar imbalances could be cited.[83] In all cases, even allowing for exaggeration, opposition losses appear to have included a much higher proportion of killed, as well as higher overall casualties. This suggests that European armour was better, at least in the sixteenth century, even than that of the sub-continental Indians. "Full plate armor of the type used in Europe during this era was extremely rare. It was not manufactured in India".[84] In America, the Spanish did not need their breastplates; cotton armour sufficed. So battles seem rather like some horribly unfair computer game in which the Iberians had nine lives while opponents had one.

In the first invasion, Cortes had scrambled for men, horses, guns, and money, none of which were abundant in Cuba, borrowing his own modest cash contribution.[85] In the second, successful, invasion, he had many more guns, beginning with 80 harquebuses and 18 cannon. There were also 2,000 Indian allies, whose number rose to at least 20,000 during the siege of Tenochtitlan.[86] He received repeated reinforcements for his initial 1,300 Spanish and fresh supplies of guns and ammunition. Just after the war ended, he had at least 105 cannon.[87] The allies carried the key parts for 13 brigantines, with both sails and oars, which had been partly prefabricated. Each mounted a bronze cannon in the bow, and the boats were crucial in dominating Lake Texcoco, in which the island city of Tenochtitlan sat, leading to success in the siege. Some of the enhanced support came all the way from Seville, where Hernan's father, Martin Cortes, had good contacts, and used them in 1520. His son "had henceforth at his disposal the best commercial network in Spain".[88] While the cannon in the first campaign were borrowed from local ships, the bronze cannon on the gunboats in the second came from Seville. Harquebuses were scarce and expensive in Cuba, but not in Spain, where 32,000 had been used in the conquest of Granada.[89] By 1522, Hernan Cortes had 1,500 infantry with hundreds of harquebuses, and 500 cavalry. He had yet another ally—differential disease.

The first epidemic of smallpox in the Americas reached the Caribbean in late 1518, but was not transferred to Mexico until 1520, after the first invasion had failed. It is likely to have killed around 20% of the Aztecs, especially in crowded Tenochtitlan. While their Indian allies were also affected, the Spanish were mostly immune.[90] In short, Cortes had a very limited version of the European expansion kit in his failed invasion, but a much fuller version in his successful one.

———

Galleons could normally cope with any waters in the world, and they could eventually reach their destination—a necessary condition of expansion. They were self-sustaining in terms of propulsion, and their guns made them pretty much invulnerable to any vessel other than their own kind. They enabled Europeans to scout the world's coasts, looking for opportunities, like eagles or vultures, depending on perspective. Heavily gunned fortified ports were almost invulnerable to attack from land, and could be supplied by sea. Gun forts allowed the Portuguese to cling like leeches to the flanks of great land powers, and proved very hard to take. Portuguese Melaka resisted eight attacks by hugely superior forces in the sixteenth century.[91] Many guns substituted for few men. As early as 1515, the Portuguese forts in Morocco boasted about 2,000 cannon, those in India, 1,500.[92] There was never any chance of the European warfare states' large armies crossing oceans en masse; sailing ships before 1800 were not up to that. The troops transferred on a single fleet never exceeded 10,000, and were normally far fewer. As chapter 6 noted, these little armies were also prone to high mortality. So plague-like pressure on European manpower overseas persisted even after domestic populations recovered. Guns, gunships, and gun forts enabled the global projection of at least coastal power. They emerged less from any special European gift from Athena than from the fact that plague forced Europeans to learn to project power with small numbers. Europeans exaggerated their imperial successes; the notion of world empire before 1800 is more smoke than fire. But there was still some real fire. For some peoples, at some times, it burned hot.

PART III

Western Europe or West Eurasia?

WE TURN at last to the unspoken question haunting part two. Plague caused profound changes in Western Europe, 1350–1500. Did it also do so in Eastern Europe and the Muslim South, which part one argued were equally plagued? The standard answer is that it did not. For Eastern Europe, the explanation is that it was ecologically less well-endowed, more thinly populated, and generally "backward". For the Muslim South, it is that the region was ecologically and culturally less adaptable, the latter due to the prevalence of Islam. There is an "Orientalism" problem here, a residue of Western Eurocentric observer bias, which we will have to navigate. But we should note that for the plague era to have different outcomes in different regions is perfectly possible. Even in Western Europe, there were variations in plague effects, though due more to politics, warfare, and contingency than to differences in ecology or religion: Catalonia declined; nearby Valencia throve. The three great regions of West Eurasia were well connected, but they did differ substantially in geography, climate, religion, and culture. The Black Death was no clean slate; its consequences were mediated by preexisting circumstances as well as contingency and human agency. What we are testing for is not a mirroring of Western European history in Eastern Europe or the Muslim South, but the possibility of some under-recognised similarities among many well-recognised differences.

To gather the strands of part two into brief summary, the pattern in Western Europe involved two overarching developments over two plague eras. In the early plague era, massive depopulation was accompanied by increased productivity per worker, increased disposable income, and increased demand for exotic luxuries and for extractive goods prone to depletion. To 1500, common folk had some share in the relative prosperity, at the horrendous cost of each generation of survivors losing many kin to plague. Scarce labour was the big new constraint, and this incubated changes in shipping, technology, and warfare, as well as in society and culture. This produced the "expansion kit". Guns, gun forts and gunships were an eye-catching part of this, but by no means the whole of it. It also included upturns in the size and fluidity of transnational pools of resources and in the networks that brokered them; man-powering changes involving regions producing settlers and/or crews; and other shifts ranging from revived slavery to a broadened sense of citizenship. There was a scribal transition that enabled better bureaucracies and a murkier shift in attitudes to race and risk, as well as the variable impact of non-plague diseases, whose differential transfer sometimes favoured long-range expansionists. Various forms of expansionism flourished in the post-plague hothouse: patchwork expansion, entwined empires, and urban colonisation.

From 1500, with the renewal of population growth, the late plague era began. Labour lost its leverage and rising prices reduced real wages. The limited golden age for common folk eroded. But elites grew in size and wealth, and aggregate demand for luxuries and extractive goods continued to rise, at least modestly. In various regions that had abandoned or diminished grain farming, increasing populations made more disposable males available as crewmen, for service and violence inside and outside Europe. While centralising states grew in strength, they continued to depend on transnational networks and resource pools, and economic partnerships even between enemies, until at least 1650.

Four chapters of part three (8, 9, 11, and 13) seek to integrate the Muslim South into our understanding of plague-boosted early modern economies and long-range expansionism. To "zoom in" to these histories is, of course, a dangerous game for a generalist. But the alternative—accepting the continued exclusion of Muslims (and others) from the history of early modern expansion and globalisation—is even worse. Almost as dangerously, chapter 14 attempts a similar exercise for Russia. The other two chapters (10 and 12) revert to Western Europe, but in cases that need broader, West Eurasian, context.

8

Plague's Impact in the Muslim South

THE "MUSLIM SOUTH", though always based on the Middle East and North Africa, was a space that changed over time. In the fifteenth century, it lost Granada and its indirect hold over the Russian principalities. But, due to Ottoman expansion, by 1526 it had gained a vast chunk of Southeast Europe—a long-lasting 450,000-square-mile modern Asian empire in Europe, about five times the size of Britain.[1] By this time, the entire Muslim South except Morocco and "Greater Persia" (see below) was at least loosely controlled by the Ottomans. In the early plague era, 1350–1500, the Muslim South included other important polities. As we saw in part one, plague pervaded the region from 1346, though it crossed seas more easily than deserts.

There is little optimism about the effects of plague on the core of the Muslim South, the Middle East. Pessimism predominates, and debate is mostly about the causes of decline. "While [economic] historians have long speculated that the Black Death had long-term positive effects on Europe effects on the Middle East have largely been perceived as negative".[2] Older studies, such as those of Eliyahu Ashtor, combined formidable scholarship with questionable preconceptions about the cultural and institutional conservatism of Islam. In 1992, Ashtor summarised his position: "the reasons underlying the economic decline were similar in all Middle Eastern countries". They included population decline due to plague, as well as devastating warfare.

> A third reason was misrule, prevalent throughout the Levant . . . The almost natural opposition to innovation certainly constituted another factor . . . The misrule of the feudal lords and a strong conservatism had a much greater impact in the Muslim countries than in Christian Europe.[3]

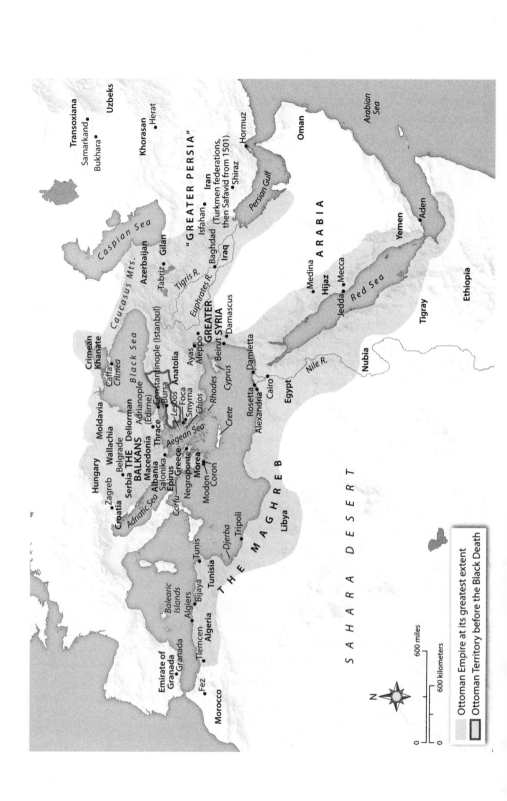

Transoxiana
Samarkand •
Bukhara • Uzbeks
• Herat
Khorasan

"GREATER PERSIA"

Iran
Isfahan • Baghdad (Turkmen federations,
then Safavid from 1501)
Iraq • Shiraz
Hormuz

Oman

Arabian Sea

Caspian Sea

Azerbaijan
• Gilan
Tabriz •

Caucasus Mts.

Tigris R.

Euphrates R.

A R A B I A

Medina •
Hijaz
Jedda •
Mecca •

Red Sea

Yemen
• Aden

Ethiopia

Crimean Khanate
Caffa • Crimea

Black Sea

Constantinople (Istanbul)

GREATER
SYRIA
• Aleppo
Ayas •
Beirut •
Damascus •

Cyprus

Damietta •

Nile R.

Nubia

Tigray

Hungary
Moldavia
Zagreb •
Croatia
Wallachia
Belgrade •
Serbia THE
BALKANS
Deliorman
Adrianople
(Edirne)
Thrace
Macedonia
Albania
Salonika •
Epirus
Corfu •
Adriatic Sea
Greece
Negroponte
Morea
Modon •
Coron •

Anatolia
Bursa •
Foça
Smyrna •
Chios
Lesbos
Aegean Sea

Rhodes

Crete

Rosetta •
Alexandria •
• Cairo

Egypt

Libya

Tripoli

Djerba

T H E   M A G H R E B

Tunis •
Tunisia
Bijaya •
Algiers •
Algeria
Tlemcen •
Balearic Islands

Emirate of
Granada
• Granada
Fez •
Morocco

S A H A R A   D E S E R T

N

0   600 miles
0   600 kilometers

More recent literature is increasingly uneasy about such reasoning, but still asks: "why did the same exogenous demographic shock produce such sharply divergent outcomes?"[4] Timur Kuran's recent answer emphasises "institutional bottlenecks" caused by Islamic law and culture. Laws of inheritance inhibited the individual accumulation of capital; the law lacked a concept of corporations; the *vakf* (an endowed charitable establishment), long seen "as the primary 'vehicle for financing Islam as a society'," "locked vast resources into organizations likely to become dysfunctional over time".[5] Kuran is no Orientalist. He acknowledges that Islamic institutions had been commerce-friendly earlier, but argues that they failed to adapt to new circumstances from the fifteenth century. Most of his more convincing evidence, however, dates from 1700,[6] when the Ottoman Empire, and the economy of the Muslim South as a whole, did undergo relative decline. But the same was true of Southern Europe, notably Spain and Italy, whose problems were not Islamic. These issues merge into an economic historians' debate about the "Little Divergence"— why did southern Europe, and well as the Muslim South, fall behind northwestern Europe? We revisit this matter in part four; here, we focus on the period 1350–1500, extending into the sixteenth century as appropriate. The focus on institutions, of course, is itself an issue. Part two implied that it was mainly plague reshuffling, rather than economically benign institutions, that produced late medieval prosperity. Muslim institutions may in fact have played *more* of a role in plague adaptation than did their Christian cousins.

I The Mamluk Empire and the Maghreb

Much of the evidence for post-plague Muslim decline comes from Egypt, stronghold of the Mamluk Empire which also ruled Greater Syria (including Jordan, Lebanon, and Palestine) and the Hijaz in western Arabia. Older scholarship blamed the Mamluks themselves for "the stagnation and internal decay that prevailed during the entire Mamluk era".[7] Alternatively, it blamed plague. Egypt, still perhaps the richest part of West Eurasia in 1340, was "economically prostrate" by the early sixteenth century. "We can date this striking economic deterioration from the Black Death".[8] More recent research suggests a more complicated picture: a typical post-plague economic boost to 1400; followed by untypical agricultural and manufacturing decline in Egypt, but less so, if at all, in Greater Syria; all somehow coupled with a strong increase in long-range trade and urban prosperity in both regions, both before and after 1400.

A brief general plague boost, 1350–1400, is suggested by the higher real wages found by leading economic historian Sevket Pamuk. "My real wage calculations for Egypt point to a significant increase in real wages after the Black Death and then a decline in the fifteenth century".[9] Urban signs of plague boosts familiar from Western Europe appeared in Cairo: a strong building boom;[10] women gaining more economic centrality;[11] the emergence of new elites, and their increased consumption, decried by old elites as they "began to dress like a mamluk".[12] Visiting in 1383, Ibn Khaldun found Cairo's markets and shops "bursting with bounties and merchandise".[13] Indirect signs persist into the fifteenth century. The Mamluk civil service had a department monitoring the deaths and legacies of the rich, with a view to maximising the state's share. "Only" a fifth to a third of the population of Cairo were of interest, suggesting a large buying class of 20% or 33%.[14]

How much the early plague boost helped unwaged rural commoners is not clear, though there is scattered evidence of higher living standards, such as the use of sugar. In Jordan, "wheat, sugar, and olive oil were staples of the average man's diet".[15] In Egypt, even the poor *fellahin* used sugar to help their plague medicine go down.[16] From about 1400, however, things went downhill in rural Egypt. The root problem was the collapse of the irrigation system. Egyptian agriculture had always been unusually dependent on very large-scale irrigation, which distributed the annual Nile flood to winter crops of wheat and flax and held it in reservoirs for the summer crop of wheat and sugarcane. The irrigation system, and transport canals in the Nile Delta, required immense inputs of labour.[17] Egypt was hit hard by the early strikes of plague, and a further strike in 1405 is said to have been as lethal as the first.[18] Terrible mortalities in the strikes of 1430 and 1460 prevented any population recovery. Perhaps even before the 1405 strike, the irrigation system began to deteriorate and fragment through lack of manpower.[19] Grain prices rose sharply from 1401.[20] By the 1430s, we find Egypt importing grain, like coals to Newcastle.[21] Like grain, flax and sugarcane relied on the irrigation system. Both were agro-industries, producing spun and woven linens and milled and refined sugar. They too declined sharply around 1400—not before. Unlike Greater Syria, Egypt did not then produce much silk or cotton;[22] fine linen and refined sugar were its leading exports. This goes a long way towards explaining the decline of Egyptian manufactured exports, which Ashtor attributes to technical stagnation and Mamluk mismanagement.[23] One doubts whether the Mamluks could have done much about the irrigation crisis. They had an incentive to try—they owned a large minority of the sugar mills—and one sultan did attempt to give the industry a state boost during 1425–33, with little success.[24] But this was a rare case in which the human labour deficit exceeded the capacity of more abundant capital and work animals to compensate.

Others too blame the Mamluk elite for Egypt's economic woes, on more reasonable grounds. The sultans' leading lieutenants, the *amirs*, were funded by allocations of rural land, rotated to discourage their putting down regional roots, but also discouraging re-investment. Their "slave-soldier" system required regular intakes of apprentice Mamluks, and this expense rose even more than average after the Black Death, because these slaves were select— one source suggests a sixfold increase in cost.[25] As elsewhere, rivals for rule gave away state land to build support; and succession crises were endemic. The period 1341–82 was particularly unstable. The Mamluks were in effect a regular army, better able to coerce their peasants than European states, and may have squeezed their peasants to the point of strangulation. Between 1348 and 1420, tax revenues declined only 12%, a massive per capita increase like those in Western Europe.[26] Increased taxes were sustainable before 1400, because average disposable incomes also rose, but not afterwards. Peasants in the Nile Valley began fleeing to join the nomadic Bedouin pastoralists, who now grazed their livestock on what had once been prime arable land.[27] The contribution of Egyptian agriculture to state revenue fell very steeply in the fifteenth century. There may have been some recovery in the Nile Valley late in the century, possibly based on a shift from manpower to animal power, notably ox-powered pumping of subsurface water. But it was recovery to a lower level than before.

Sultans after 1382 restored some stability, and also took positive economic measures, particularly in terms of trade. They established new royal law courts in Alexandria and Damascus, "where justice was rendered by government officials and not by *qāḍīs* [religious judges]", which helped reassure Christian merchants of judicial fairness.[28] They needed reassurance, because what the sultans wanted was to ensure that no one but themselves exploited merchants. As we saw in chapter 4, volumes of eastern imports through Egypt to Europe increased from 1390, and the sultans used rising trade revenues to offset falling land revenues. They taxed spices in particular at both Red Sea inlets and Mediterranean outlets. From 1397, they also forced merchants to buy royal spices at high prices.[29] This enraged the Venetians and Genoese, but normally not enough to stop them coming. It has been suggested that Alexandria, the key port in this trade, was in decline in the fifteenth century.[30] It is possible that the silting mouths of the Nile diverted some trade to the nearby ports of

Rosetta and Damietta, which were thriving.[31] Others say that despite some physical decay, perhaps buildings abandoned due to plague depopulation, Alexandria was "still the most important gateway" in the trade with Europe, "closely connected to and supervised by Cairo", and that overall trade was thriving.[32] Ashtor himself calculated that by the later fifteenth century, Europe imported 660,000 gold ducats worth of goods from the Mamluk Empire each year, and exported only 260,000, paying for the rest in bullion—a massive trade surplus of 400,000 ducats in Egypt's favour.[33] Much would then have gone east to buy exotics, but some remained in the hands of urban elites, and we can be sure that the sultans took their cut.

The Mamluks took military measures to improve their control of the Far Eastern trade's entry and exit points. In 1375, they conquered the rump of Cilician Armenia and its port of Ayas, a Mediterranean outlet that drew on the Persian Gulf and competed with Mamluk Alexandria and Beirut. Aden in Yemen was traditionally the chief Red Sea inlet for the Asian trade. Mamluk-Yemeni relations were hostile at various times, for instance around 1351, 1507, and 1515,[34] but their interaction was usually successfully brokered by the great Cairo-based Karimi merchant network, whose influence, revealed in the Geniza letters, had pervaded Muslim global trades since the twelfth century. Like the Genoese, the Karimi merchants cooperated and competed, intertwined with states, and received a plague boost lasting until at least the 1420s.[35] From the late fourteenth century, a variation on the Red Sea route emerged, which avoided Aden, probably touching at East African ports instead, and then went straight to Jedda, the main port of Mecca, Medina, and the Hijaz. The Mamluks may have had a hand in this, but initially most taxes went to the Sharif of Mecca, who had considerable autonomy.[36] From 1423, the Mamluks took measures to increase their share, including military intervention and the establishment of a bureaucracy in Jedda.[37] They also began sponsoring merchants other than the Karimis. These new networks included the Khawāja, who specialised in slave trading, by both sea and land. They were even more closely integrated with the state than the Karimis.[38] In these ways, the Mamluks are generally thought to have muscled aside the Sharifs of Mecca and the Karimis and monopolised the Red Sea trade. In fact, the Sharifs and the Jedda merchants continued to get a share, and the Karimis did as well—they were still the most influential traders on the Malabar coast of India in 1519.[39] The Mamluks did increasingly squeeze their golden geese, Christian and Muslim alike, but not to the point of killing them.

Greater Syria was not dependent on the Nile flood, and on my reading of the evidence did not share Egypt's agricultural decline. Its lead city, Damascus, was hit hard by the Black Death in 1348 and revisited by plague a dozen times before 1500.[40] Some suggest it suffered economic decline too, before recovering from around 1382,[41] but there are countervailing indicators. Its imports of mastic, a luxury breath-freshening chewing gum from Chios, were massive in the 1360s and 1370s.[42] "In Damascus, trading in spices went on at the same pace as in the previous period (1250s–1340s), if not faster".[43] An older study of Damascus castigates "the stagnation and internal decay that prevailed during the entire Mamluk era", yet claims that the city gradually declined from 1400 due to its sacking by Timur, who took its craftsmen to his capital of Samarkand.[44] It also notes evidence that city and region recovered quickly, hosting a "very flourishing" textile industry and marketing an extraordinary range of crops later in the fifteenth century. A recent study confirms this rapid recovery and continued prosperity.[45] In 1464, the governorship of Damascus sold for 45,000 dinars; in 1487, the figure was 90,000. This may suggest corruption (Europe also practiced the sale of offices); it does not suggest economic decline.[46] Damascus was a hub of many caravan routes, and of the spice trade, a role it shared with Aleppo, which had also recovered quickly from a lethal visit from Timur. "In the fifteenth century, Aleppo was called 'little India' because of its huge ginger and pepper imports from Hind".[47] Spices and other eastern exotics were re-exported to Europe, along with local products, through ports such as Beirut and Sidon. In the early sixteenth century, Aleppo's fertile hinterland and "concentration of wealth and general prosperity made it a magnet for a wide range of occupational groups, from upwardly mobile peasants, to religious and political refugees, to retirees from state service".[48]

Greater Syria was normally self-sufficient in grain, importing it only in years of poor harvests. But plague seems to have led to an internal reallocation of grain land to cotton. "One may wonder whether the expansion of cotton fields in later medieval Syria was carried out at the expense of grain fields".[49] Syria was Europe's leading supplier of cotton; its product was considered the best available.[50] We have seen that the value of Venice's imports of Syrian cotton increased from 50,000 gold ducats a year in the 1370s to 150,000 in the 1390s.[51] Sugar exports to Europe continued strongly to about 1415 and then declined, but may have shifted to supplying Egypt. Raw cotton exports to Europe continued, but so did exports of "Arabesque carpets and metalwork".[52] There was a plague-prompted reshuffling in Jordan's agricultural regions, and the

Mamluk state may have played a positive role through *vakf* (*awakf*) endowments. A careful recent study reconsiders traditional views on Mamluk decline and concludes that:

> The process of creating rural *awakf* from former state lands may have been a form of land development, sponsored by the state to respond to and recover from agricultural crises, such as drought, famines, and plague. Seen in this light, the fifteenth century was more a period of rural transformations than decline of the state. [53]

The vakf, it seems, was a more flexible institution than Timur Kuran allows. Other evidence from the Mamluk domains, and from throughout the Muslim South, supports this, and indicates a surge in the number of vakf after 1350.[54] They could protect the property of a family from state sequestration, and so allow the accumulation of capital. Their endowments could support religious, educational, and charitable institutions, and also economic infrastructure, such as markets, caravanserais, and roads. They invested and lent money, and were established by guilds and fraternities as well as by states and wealthy families. They were more easily established on unoccupied land, which was much more common after the Black Death.

Still, Egyptian land revenues were never easy to replace, a situation worsened by a currency crisis in the early fifteenth century, and there remains considerable evidence of increasing exploitation by the late Mamluks.[55] This stemmed more from dire necessity than an intrinsically flawed regime. The Mamluks fought an expensive war against the Turkmen in 1468–73,[56] then faced the expansive Ottomans. Relations between the two empires had been quite good up to 1453,[57] but a major war took place in 1485–91. "Against all odds the Mamluks engaged in three pitched battles and defeated the Ottoman army in every case".[58] This confirms that Mamluk decline has been exaggerated. But the war was expensive, as was subsequent heavy spending on guns and infantry. The Ottomans cut off the supply of replacement Mamluks from the Black Sea by the 1480, and conquered their rivals in a second war, in 1516–17.

Two sets of long available figures may sum up the limits, the substance, and the variation of plague effects on the Egyptian and Greater Syrian economies. The pre-plague populations of Egypt and Greater Syria are estimated at between 4 million and 8 million, for the former, and between 900,000 and 1.2 million for the latter.[59] Taking the lower bound in both cases, the ratio was 4.5 to 1 in favour of Egypt, and we can assume that the ratio also applied to the two economies. The contribution of Egypt and Greater Syria to Ottoman revenues in 1526 was 25% and 10% respectively,[60] a ratio of only 2.5 to 1. Like Western Europe, Syria became richer in the early plague era. Egypt became poorer, a great exception to the rule of post-plague prosperity. It did so, not because of Mamluk misrule or inflexible Islamic institutions, which would surely have applied to Syria too, but because its distribution of the Nile floods deteriorated sharply in the fifteenth century. "No land ever depended on water management more than Egypt".[61]

The Maghreb

Egypt was an exception to the rule of post-plague economic prosperity, but it seems that the rest of North Africa was not. Granada and northern Morocco were part of an informal Genoese-led trading system, but the relationship was more symbiotic than exploitative (see chapter 10). Despite the need to hold off Spanish re-conquest, Granada was prosperous and commercially active, 1350–1480, exporting manufactured products such as silk textiles and fine ceramics. Archaeologists have recently traced Granadan luxury ceramics, which involved a cobalt glazing technique originating in Tunisia, to much of the Mediterranean littoral. Some of Granada's commerce was mediated by the Genoese, but recent research shows it also had its own merchant networks, and at least a few of its own ships.[62] Government revenues reached one million silver *reales*, which helped finance a post-plague building boom.[63] The second half of the fourteenth century was a time of "thriving cultural growth and the construction of the madrassah of Granada and some of the most splendid buildings of the Alhambra".[64] The city of Granada was "the Damascus of Spain", a "distinguished commercial center for traders", characterised by "its inexhaustible flow of silk and sugar".[65] Outside the city, "despite whatever chaos the plague years brought, agricultural and the system of international export remained intact, and in the second half of the fourteenth century, the income of those who cultivated the land actually rose".[66]

The situation in Morocco is more difficult to read. The country was wracked by civil strife and foreign invasions between the 1390s and the 1570s (chapters 4 and 10), but may have had spasms of prosperity despite this. "Morocco actually experienced a period of efflorescence under its Marīnid rulers in the fourteenth/fifteenth centuries".[67] Evidence is scarce, with one important exception: the geography of North Africa written by the interesting culture-crosser Leo Africanus. He was one of the few who converted from Islam to Christianity, while many went the other way. He wrote in the

1520s, but referred back to the late fifteenth century, and used insider information and personal observation. Leo left no doubt of the size and wealth of the
city of Fez, "the metropolitan not onely of Barbary, but of all Africa" around
1500. It had 100 public baths, 200 grammar schools, 400 mills, 600 fountains,
and so on. But the kingdom of which it was capital had fallen on hard times.
"The king of Fez hath very large dominions, but his revenues are small, to wit,
scarce three hundred thousand ducats." Some territories were now "defaced
and ruined by reason of wars"; others paid their tribute to the Portuguese or
to the rebel Sa'idis.[68] As in Catalonia, endemic warfare may have trumped
plague boosts in Morocco, but only to the extent that it declined relative to
booming neighbours.

In the rest of the Maghreb, the leading power in the early plague era was the
Hafsid Dynasty, based at Tunis. The Hafsids revived from the 1360s after an
earlier decline. Their region was the heart of the ancient "Ifriqiya" of Carthage
and Rome. The Hafsids repelled Marinid invasions, 1340s–1360s, then extended their sway to Tlemcen, Bijaya, Algiers and most of the Algerian coast,
and to Libyan Tripoli.[69] In a possibly plague-induced reshuffle, they lost some
control over the interior to Berber and Arab nomads, led by religious reformist
sheiks. But they kept a tight grip on the irrigated coastal strip, the cities, and
the commerce. Tunis city's immediate hinterland no longer supplied it with
grain, a sad comedown for a breadbasket of the Roman world, but like other
cities it imported grain from those regions under Hafsid control that had reliable surpluses. Its hinterland now specialised in olive oil for export. "On all
sides of the citie within fower or fiue miles," reported Leo, "there growe such
plentie of oliues, that the oyle thereof sufficeth not onely the citie, but is carried also in great quantitie into Egypt".[70] Tunis was a hub of commerce. It ri-
valled Fez as the "incontestable capital" of the Maghreb, and it too had a post-
plague building boom. "One sign of the continued flourishing of Tunis in the
fourteenth and fifteenth centuries, despite many instances of political instability and plague, was the multiplication of infrastructure projects".[71] The city was
re-peopled after plague strikes by Bedouin and Berber migrants from the interior, by slaves, and by Muslim and Jewish refugees from Spain, who also
reinforced its trade networks.[72] The urban population, perhaps with some
exaggeration, was put as high as 100,000 before the Black Death.[73] Plausible
later estimates are 30,000 in 1361, and 45,000 in 1500, despite many plague
strikes.[74] Like some fortunate cities in Western Europe, it seems Tunis actually
grew during the early plague era, though not to its pre-plague size.

The Maghreb's fertile coastal strip produced silk and cotton as well as more conventional crops, and pastured horses, cattle, and sheep.[75] The last were particularly important in the Bijaya region, which exported wool to Europe until about 1450, after which it lost out to Castilian wool. But Bijaya, known to Europeans as "Bougie", adapted, and turned to the export of fine lambskins, known as" budge", a name that became generic in Europe for that product. Its increased wool surplus was accompanied by increasing imports of wheat. Bijaya was the centre of a "vast network of roads" connecting rich agricultural villages. Leo estimated its population at around 30,000 in 1500, and implied that it had once been much greater. "The houses, temples, and colleges . . . are most sumptuously built. . . . Neither Monasteries, Innes, nor Hospitals . . . are heere wanting: and their market place is very large and faire . . . The citizens were exceeding rich, and used with their warlike gallies continually to molest the coasts of Spaine".[76] Bijaya, which unusually for the region had good timber in its interior, was a major shipbuilder.[77] Tlemcen, Tripoli, and other ports also seemed prosperous, and cities were not the only post-plague grain importers. The large and fertile island of Djerba, about halfway between Tunis and Tripoli, specialised in dates, olive oil, and raisins, but also manufactured cloth from wool brought from inland by Arab traders, and sold this and its own produce to a wide range of foreign merchants living on the island. Leo assessed its annual tribute payments around 1500 at about 100,000 ducats, a staggering amount for an island of 500 square kilometres.[78] This general trend to more regional specialisation along the coast looks very like plague adaptation.

Hafsid Africa's trade relations with Egypt, Muslim Granada, and the Middle East continued, and relations with Europe intensified, taking the form of both trade and raid. Its most famous citizen, Ibn Khaldun, bemoaned the region's maritime decline, but there are hints of a revival from the 1370s, including the use of "naves," sail-only ships, as well as galleys.[79] As indicated in the case of Bijaya, state-backed raids on Malta and the Spanish coast began at the same time, and continued throughout the fifteenth century, foreshadowing the "Barbary corsairs".[80] Tunis, Tlemcen, and Tripoli were also outlets for the trans-Saharan caravan trade in gold and slaves. By the late fifteenth century, the Hafsid sultan could boast "that he was the richest Muslim prince of his time".[81] In the sixteenth century, Hafsid decline and competing Spanish and Ottoman invasions damaged the economy of the coastal Maghreb. But it seems that it experienced a humanly painful but economically positive plague reshuffling, 1350–1500, just like Western Europe.

II Ottoman Heartlands: The Balkans and Anatolia

The heartlands of the Ottoman Empire were Anatolia and the Balkans, strange as the inclusion of the latter in "the Muslim South" may seem. Ottoman control in both regions was substantial by 1400, but far from complete, and it contracted with Timur's occupation of Anatolia in 1402–1404. Yet, from the 1410s, "the re-launched Ottoman Empire sprang from a south-eastern Balkans power base".[82] The Ottomans forced some ex-vassals back into allegiance, directly annexed others, tightened their economic grip, and completed their conquest of Anatolia and most of the Balkans by the 1470s—Transylvania and Croatia remained under Hungary until 1526. The taking of Constantinople in 1453 is seen as a major turning point. Chapter 11 deals with the Ottoman arts of plague management; here we assess the effect of plague on the heartland economies. In an inversion of the notion of Muslim economic decline, signs of prosperity in the Balkans have been dated to after 1450 and credited to Ottoman rule.[83] The Ottomans were indeed good economic and demographic managers once conquest was over. But it seems that post-plague prosperity predated their rule. Beneath the fog of war, there are indications of the Black Death rebalancing of people, on the one hand, and money, fixed capital, and fertile land on the other. New thesis research argues that "more money and more people with money signal the unarguable advance of the late medieval rural economy in the Balkans".[84]

A proxy for conditions in the Balkans, and an important example of the positive economic effects of plague, is the city-state of Dubrovnik or Ragusa. As we saw in chapter 7, the city paid tribute to several powers while retaining its autonomy, but had to tread particularly carefully with the Ottomans. Though sometimes claimed for Italian or Illyrian histories, it was primarily Slavic by the fourteenth century—Eastern Europe had thriving city-states too.[85] As noted in chapter 2, the city was hit hard by the first strike of plague, losing half of its 15,000 people. But, as a result of legacies and the post-plague boom in trade, its 30 or so merchant patrician clans had, in the words of Susan Mosher Stuard, "at least four times the disposable wealth about 1450 that they had possessed about 1300. The figure is conservative".[86] The patricians worked hard to repopulate their city, engaging in "zealous if not frenzied marrying and childbearing" themselves and bringing in spouses from other Dalmatian urban elites.[87] Respect for elite intermarriage was sternly enforced. In the 1490s, one Dubrovnik scholar was imprisoned for six months for insulting his mother-in-law.[88] The city fathers also attracted artisans from the hinterland with offers of five years' tax exemption.[89] They bought more slaves too, though they are sometimes said to have stopped on-selling them from about 1420.[90] By 1500, the patricians had recovered their own numbers, to about 2,000, no doubt helped by wet-nursing, which freed elite women for more pregnancies.[91] Unusually, the general population also may have recovered. The city-state and its hinterland contained 88,000 people in 1498, though some of these people came from small territorial acquisitions.[92]

Dubrovnik had long functioned to connect the inland Balkans to wider markets, using riverboats where possible, but also pack caravans of up to 1,000 horses, to bring in hides, wool, and bullion to process in the city—its silver belts were famous.[93] It provided imported luxuries and its own manufactures, especially cloth, in return, together with salt from its Adriatic pans. The inland trade clearly boomed in the early plague era. "One reason for this was surely the favourable economic situation in the neighbouring countries".[94] By the 1460s, Dubrovnik had some 30 trading posts, staffed by its own merchants, throughout the Balkans, and shared control of the great silver mines of Srebrenica with the Hungarian king.[95] Parts of Albania and Epirus seem to have become virtual Ragusan hinterlands, supplying grain and livestock.[96] At sea, Dubrovnik responded instantly to the Black Death manpower crisis by ditching galleys and turning to sail. By 1400 it had built 120 new ships with 2,700 crew—an average of only 25 men per ship. It then built another fleet of 100 larger sailing ships by 1500.[97] The city and its ships and networks became an important interface between the Ottomans and Christian Europe. In addition to its Balkan posts, it had 11 "consulates" in Sicily, to ensure its grain supply, and many more in mainland Italy, as well as in Alexandria and Istanbul.[98] Its merchants were also important traders, brokers, and moneylenders in Lubeck and London, where its Italianate name, Ragusa/Aragouse, and its big carracks gave rise to the term "Argossy" for a big and opulent ship.

Dubrovnik's entwining with the Ottomans was preceded by, and overlapped with, entanglements with other powerful monarchies, Hungary and Serbia, especially in the mining and distribution of gold and silver in which these two kingdoms were rich. Hungary's great international export trades in wine and cattle began soon after the Black Death.[99] Market towns emerged, perhaps no more than villages with periodic markets, but numerous. There were 50 by 1390, 299 by 1441, 630 by 1490, and 709 by 1526—note the much faster growth rate before 1490.[100] Zagreb, the leading town of Croatia, then subject to Hungary, flourished between 1350 and 1450, repopulating itself with Slavic, German, and Italian artisans and merchants. Zagreb experienced its "'golden age' precisely in the latter half of the fourteenth century".[101] Hungary was the main European gold producer, and there was no early silver famine here—the value of silver in terms of gold fell sharply between 1350 and 1375.[102] As in Western Europe, the early plague era saw a steep decline in serfdom. "In the fifteenth century free peasants were very numerous in Hungary, while serfdom had virtually disappeared".[103] "The economic conditions of the peasant population seem to have generally improved in the fifteenth century".[104] The nobility tried to turn back the clock, but a major peasant revolt in 1437 stymied their efforts for a time. They kept trying, using their control of the national assembly to impose exploitative laws, and finally succeeded after suppressing another great revolt in 1514.

In 1350, it looked as if the southern Balkans might become a Serbian empire under Tsar Stefan Dušan, but he died in 1355 and his territories in Macedonia and Albania broke free.[105] After their defeat at Kossovo in 1389, the Serbs paid tribute to the Ottomans and fought bravely for them against Timur, but then became more independent. Raška, the heart of their domain, featured a large colony of Dubrovnik merchants. With their help, silver mining intensified. "A rise in the price of silver . . . attracted new investors, stimulating production both in the traditional mining regions like Novo Brdo to the south, and in new mines further north near Belgrade and the Drina River".[106] Around 1425, Serbia was brought to heel again by the Ottomans, then annexed in 1438–39.[107] The princes of Wallachia and Moldavia were a little more successful in retaining autonomy. They encouraged trade and established their own mints in 1365 and 1377. Using the Danube and other rivers, as well as their Black Sea ports, Genoese traders were important in these countries, as was the Armenian merchant diaspora from 1367.[108] Wallachia also traded overland with Transylvania and other northern regions. The involvement of many minor merchants "suggests some sort of mass market",[109] while the precious dyes in luxury textiles indicate a wealthy elite.[110] In these Romanian principalities too, the nobility struggled to nail down its peasants in the fifteenth century, with mixed success until 1500, and turned to a forgotten slave trade to supplement their labour force. The mass advent of Romani (Gypsies) in Europe dates to the second half of the fourteenth century, when the manpower crisis would have made them welcome, at least as slaves. Initially, they settled "especially in the territories held by Venice", which was particularly short of labour.[111] "By the fifteenth century, Gypsy slavery had become widespread throughout the Romanian provinces".[112] From this time, though they remained Christian, Wallachia and Moldavia were normally vassals of the Ottomans, in whose empire slavery was common and legal. Romani remained enslaved in Romania until 1856.

Even the senescent Byzantine Empire got a shot of plague's brutal economic Viagra, despite endemic dynastic civil wars and the strengthening Ottoman embrace. Belatedly, "the aristocracy now became much more involved in trade than it had ever been before, a trend that continued into the fifteenth century".[113]

> There can be no doubt that the Black Death led to a large long-term increase in nominal and real wage levels in the Byzantine territories. Urban real wages at the end of the fourteenth century were above their pre-Black Death levels by as much as 100 per cent. This large jump in the urban wage levels was paralleled by and confirmed further by the doubling of slave prices across the Byzantine territories during the second half of the fourteenth century.[114]

The people of the Byzantine domains and former domains were known as "Romanians", or "Greeks", and the last in particular was a fluid category. It could indicate Greek speakers and Orthodox Christians as well as ethnic Greeks, many of whom lived in Thrace and Anatolia. The Ottomans made the Thracian city of Edirne (formerly Adrianople) their European capital and economic hub from around 1370. With their help the city quickly recovered from conquest. "Edirne was another Ottoman city that prospered during the fourteenth and fifteenth centuries".[115] Rural Thrace continued to export grain, but now added rice and cotton.[116] Recent research argues strongly that prosperity, commerce, and development in late medieval Bulgaria have been greatly underestimated.[117] In Greece in its modern sense, the post-plague pattern also seems strong—before, as well as after, Ottoman conquest. Salonika, the Byzantine Empire's second city, "recovered more quickly from the troubles of the mid-fourteenth century than has been previously thought".[118] Salonika was an important trade centre, until it was sacked by the Turks in 1430, and became renowned for producing woollens, using water-powered mills. The flowering of this industry was once credited to the sixteenth-century immigration of Sephardic Jews from Iberia,[119] bringing western skills, but is now dated to the late Byzantine period.[120]

Other Byzantine towns tended to autonomy or foreign rule, but also flourished economically. Demand for the famous wine of Monemvasia in Laconia surged, new vineyards were planted and, to 1460, "Monemvasia exhibited all the characteristics of a vibrant city-state".[121] The Venetian-controlled ports of Modon and Coron exported the same kind of wine, exceeding two million litres annually in the 1350s.[122] In the rest of the Morea (the Peloponnese), and in the Greek islands, we see the usual post-plague trend towards more valuable crops in the places least suitable for grain farming.[123] The islands specialised: Paros (cotton), Patmos (olive oil), Andros, Tinos, and Kithnos (silk).[124] On Crete, "in the last quarter of the fourteenth and during the fifteenth century the economic situation of the island improved distinctly, like that of the rest of 'Románia' . . . mainly due to the general development of agriculture, especially of cotton and sugar-cane plantations".[125] After 1350, Corfu grew only a quarter of its own grain, and turned first to wine and cotton, and then in the sixteenth century to the production of olive oil for export. Like the other Greek islands, it also exported increasing numbers of sailors to European as well as Ottoman fleets.[126] In all, contrary to the standard view, Southeast European survivors reshuffled and prospered after the Black Death along the same lines as Western Europe, even before the Ottomans provided them with a centralised state.

Anatolia's economic response to plague seems similar to that in the Balkans. Here too, full Ottoman conquest did not occur until about 1480. Here too, the ravages of wars and plagues were followed by rapid economic recovery. Here too, the region had more economic potential than one might think. "Anatolia was an agriculturally rich region."[127] Wheat for humans and barley for horses were the leading cereals, and here too rice production increased in the early plague era.[128] The numerous Turkic emirs were well aware that their revenues depended on the prosperity of their domains, and sought to enhance trade. Anatolia exported horses, wool (including mohair), leather, alum, and copper to Europe, as well as manufactured cloth and carpets.[129] Most manufactured goods for local markets were still being made locally in the seventeenth century.[130] Turkic nomads made up about a quarter of the population (falling to 16% by 1580)[131] and, economically at least, were well integrated with settled districts. Farming reshuffled to the more fertile lands, and the relative price of Anatolian grain was low, which along with the rapid repopulation of towns from the countryside indicates increased agricultural production per capita. "In most regions . . . there was a shortage of labour, which became particularly pronounced at harvest times". Nomads helped out with the harvest, as well as providing hides, wool, and work animals in large numbers.[132] Conditions improved further under Ottoman management.

Bursa, captured by the Ottomans in 1326, became their Anatolian economic capital in the late fourteenth century. It was sacked by Timur in 1402, but had recovered by about 1430. It had more than 27,000 people around 1450, and 42,000 in the 1480s, impressive growth for the time.[133] Its main businesses, 1350–1500, were the spice trade, for which it provided an alternative hub to Alexandria, Damascus, and Aleppo; the slave trade; the import of raw silk from Iran; and the manufacture of silk cloth for export. From 1453, along with its European twin, Edirne, it added the provisioning of Istanbul to its main games.[134] Some spices came from the Red Sea route, via caravans of up to 3,000 camels from Mecca, to which silk was exported (as currency for pilgrim travel expenses) in return.[135] Other spices likely came from the Persian Gulf, on caravans (of mules as well as camels) from Iran which also carried up to 25 tons of raw silk each.[136] Spice imports were large from 1432, and have been estimated at 2,500 tons per year in the 1480s.[137] This included some locally grown saffron, but still seems improbably high—as much as the whole of European consumption. Yet duties did total 140,000 gold ducats in 1487, indicating a large trade.[138] Skilled slaves were imported, and they and free labour made the silk into highly regarded cloth, which was then widely exported. "It was reported in the late fifteenth century that more [silk] cloth was manufactured in Bursa than in the whole of Italy".[139]

Anatolian prosperity persisted into the early sixteenth century. "Rising receipts from tax farms, customs, and agriculture all point to decent growth early in the century".[140] Until then, peasants shared in it, as in Europe. Archaeology indicates increased meat-eating, and larger domestic meat animals.[141] Rural servitude had mostly disappeared, taxes were moderate, and though the Ottoman state owned most land, peasant tenures were secure as long as they cultivated their land.[142] They had "a relatively high standard of living".[143] Real wages for urban workers were also high.[144] As the sixteenth century wore on, however, this modest "golden age" for common folk declined, as in Europe. The key factor was population increase, which was very strong in most of the sixteenth century. Increased taxes, rebellions, and adverse climate also contributed from late in the century. But, as far as Anatolia is concerned, "the decline of the Middle East" seems largely mythical, at least for the period 1350–1580.

III Greater Persia

The Mongol Ilkhanate and its Timurid successor empire integrated Iran with parts of West Central Asia. These Central Asian regions became known as "Turan", twinned with Iran; Muslim in religion and Persianate in culture. This integration continued despite the Timurids losing territory to the Uzbeks, and to the "Black Sheep" (Kara Koyunlu) and "White Sheep" (Aq Qoyunlu) Turk-men confederations over the course of the fifteenth century. The Timurids' residual heartland, Khorasan, was known as the "gem in the centre of the neck-lace linking Iran and Turan".[145] There is still little evidence for the very first strike, the Black Death itself, in Greater Persia, and this was assumed to be true of later strikes as well. We now know that it experienced repeated major plagues from the 1360s until at least 1462, and probably longer (chapter 1). It also experienced a second catastrophe, Timur's conquests and devastations, 1380–1400. He sacked the region's great cities as he had done those of Greater Syria and Anatolia. Separating these depopulations from those of plague is not easy. What is clear is that after both kinds of disaster, the region showed an "astonishing recuperative capacity".[146]

Tabriz was a leading city of Northwest Iran (Azerbaijan). It suffered at least three plague strikes before being sacked by Timur in 1392. Yet, by 1404, a Cas-tilian traveller, Ruy Gonzalez de Clavijo, found it "rich in goods and abound-ing in wealth".[147] Its fertile hinterland, four days' ride long, specialised in rice, which it exported.[148] Azerbaijan's other main city, Sultànïya, had fewer people but as much trade, redistributing prime raw silk from the Caspian province of Gilan and importing silk and cotton textiles from Shiraz and Khorasan.[149] Other cities also became more prosperous, if not more populous, despite visi-tations of plague and Timur. Isfahan in central Iran is thought to have had a population of 80,000–100,000 in the late fourteenth century. It was sacked by Timur in 1388, and an alleged 70,000 of its citizens were massacred. Yet it had recovered enough by 1407 to lose 20,000 people to plague.[150] It recovered again to 50,000 in the 1470s, when both city and region were thriving econom-ically. It may then have suffered a further plague, since it had only 25,000 people in 1500.[151] Herat, in present-day Afghanistan, may even have increased in population as well as prosperity during the early plague era. It was the eco-nomic and cultural hub of Khorasan, and became the Timurid capital in 1409.[152] It had been sacked by Timur in 1383, and suffered at least two terrible plagues 1435 and 1462. Yet it remained the "brilliant center of Timurid imperial culture in the fifteenth century",[153] repeatedly rebuilding its population to be-tween 45,000 and 60,000—possibly more than its pre-plague level. Like other urban recoveries, this of course required an increasingly productive agricul-tural base. The Herat region was renowned for its grapes, fruit, grains, rice, and honey, as well as its "industrial crops": madder, indigo, henna, and hemp.[154] Its fifteenth century was "a golden age of agricultural and horticultural achievement".[155]

Post-plague reshuffling from less to more productive regions was one key to Greater Persia's powers of recovery. Herat's 400 villages declined to 200–250 during the early plague era, while the survivors' productivity increased.[156] But another key was the role of activist states. Like that of the Ottomans, the record of the later Timurids was good in this regard. Their islands of settled agriculture depended on irrigation, with water management systems on a lesser scale than the Nile Valley, but still substantial, based mainly on *qanats*—underground irrigation channels. These systems often broke down after plagues or invasions, and the Timurids made it their business to repair and extend them. They also made use of tax relief and vakf. Maria Subtleny has uncovered a "dramatic expansion of vakf in Khorasan during the period of Timurid rule" and argues that "agricultural activity during the Timurid period was organised to a large extent through the institution of vaqf".[157] Other scholars too see "care for agriculture . . . as one of the characteristic features of Timurid rule".[158]

While one recent article suggests prolonged plague disruption,[159] the balance of evidence is that trade also prospered in Persia in this era, as it did throughout the Muslim South. The mass export of horses by sea from the Persian Gulf to India, as many as 10,000 per year, is documented in the next chapter. It implies a large return trade. It also contradicts the standard assumption that the Gulf trade was in decline at this time, with most shipping diverted to the Red Sea. It may well be true that most of the Further Asian exotics that reached Western Europe came through the Red Sea—one source plausibly suggests 75–80%.[160] But this was because the Middle East itself was absorbing the goods that came through the Persian Gulf. Like other spices, pepper was "in as much, if not higher, demand in the Middle East as it was in Europe".[161] Clavijo repeatedly noted the abundance of spices and other exotics in the towns he visited, on two occasions mentioning that the range was greater than in Alexandria. The Muslim South also absorbed about half of the Red Sea inflow, which as we saw in chapter 4 was burgeoning from the early fifteenth century. Still more goods came overland, on a surprising scale. An amphibious route, along the Caspian to Astrakhan and then by caravan over the steppes, maintained the ancient Transoxiana link with Russia, with silks going one way and furs the other—sables were popular among Muslim elites.[162] Camel caravans, bearing cotton textiles, came annually from India. Iran is thought to have been a major producer of cotton cloth in and around the tenth century, but then gave up trying to emulate Indian super-artisans.[163] Persians, remarked a seventeenth-century European observer, could "make Calico Cloth very reasonable; but they make none fine, because they have it cheaper out of the Indies than they can make it".[164] Historians agree that Iranians and Turanians gave up on fine cottons because "neither could compete with Indian producers in terms of quantity, quality, variety and price".[165]

Caravans between China and the Timurid domains have long been known. One, of 800 camels, reached Samarkand in 1404. But recent research shows that the scale of this trade has been underestimated. It counts 98 caravans between 1387 and 1550, and there may have been many others. The exchange peaked in 1407–49, when the arrival of caravans must have been an annual event.[166] This was in addition to a significant maritime trade. Between the 1390s and the 1430s, several dozen Chinese ships reached Hormuz (and Aden and even Jedda), with even more voyages going the other way. The inflow of Chinese super-crafts, silks and porcelains, was substantial. Two large collections survive, in the Topkapi Palace in Istanbul and the Ardebil Shrine in Western Iran. Of the former's collection of 10,000 ceramics, 8,000 are Chinese, many dating from the fifteenth century. Of the latter's 595 dated blue and white Chinese pieces, almost one-third date to between 1403 and 1435.[167] Local crafts went the other way, an exception to the general rule of few manufactured imports by China. A single Ming Chinese prince had 3,400 pieces of Persian and Indian jewelry collected from early fifteenth-century maritime voyages.[168] Furthermore, unlike Indian cottons, Persian artisans did emulate Chinese silks and porcelains with products that were "not mere imitations of Chinese models but imaginative reinterpretations".[169] It was this innovative and resilient post-plague economy, with its wealthy patrons and its links across the old worlds, that underwrote what scholars describe as the "Timurid Renaissance" during the fifteenth century, with great achievements to its credit in science, literature, art, and craft.[170]

Very little Chinese silk or porcelain made it through the Middle East to Europe in this period. Even the wealthy Medici acquired their first piece only in 1487. "When Vasco da Gama left Lisbon for India in 1497, he was given specific instructions by King Manuel I to find spices, Christians, and 'porcellanas.'"[171]

IV Shared Revolutions?

This chapter opened with the question of whether plague really had "sharply divergent outcomes" in Western Europe and the Muslim South as is generally assumed. The answer seems to be that it did not. Overall, plague reshuffling increased capital, prime land, and productivity per survivor and sharply increased disposable incomes in both regions. Consumption of spices was probably even higher per capita in the Muslim South than in Western Europe, and consumption of Indian and Chinese textiles and porcelain was far higher. For some Muslim-ruled countries, such as Anatolia and parts of the Balkans, there are even signs of a temporary "golden age" for common folk, 1350–1500. The plague bonus among nomadic pastoralists might have been less, but it did increase the flocks, herds, and prime grazing lands of the survivors, who also supplied sedentary farmers with seasonal labour. As in Europe, peasant life worsened after 1500, and the real wages of urban workers declined 30–40% by 1600, and stayed low to 1750.[172] Elite demand across the Muslim South continued to increase. Egypt remained a major exception to these rules, and there were other differences. There is some truth in the notion that the balance of manufactured exports shifted in favour of Europe. Christians caught up with Muslims and overtook them in some crafts—in glass-making for example. Post-plague Europe had more water-powered manufacturing, and an incentive to undercut Muslim producers in the form of the trade deficit. But, on the whole, the similarities between economic responses to plague are more striking than the differences.

One difference was water-powered mills. There are numerous examples of Islamic use of these, before and after the Black Death. A recent search of Arabic sources shows water mills all over the Muslim South in the fifteenth century, but argues that they had "largely disappeared from Islamic core areas (Iraq, Syria and Egypt)".[173] There is some exaggeration here. Jordan and Palestine still used water-powered sugar mills, and the latter also had cloth fulling mills.[174] Water mills were quite common in Anatolia, and the Mamluks were building them in Syria in 1375.[175] It remains true that waterpower was less important south than north, and some still attribute this to Muslim "backwardness".[176] But the simple fact was that the Muslim South was more arid, with fewer fast-flowing streams, and that priority in sparse water supplies had to be given to irrigation.[177] In 2013, historian Richard Bulliet suggested another factor.[178] Animal power was much cheaper in the Muslim South than in Europe.

Natural fodder resources are so ubiquitous, despite being sparsely strewn across the landscape, that there is rarely any need for farmers to choose between growing crops for human sustenance and growing crops for working animals to consume. . . . most mills . . . were operated not by water, as in Europe, but by a camel, ox, or donkey that had grown to working age at virtually no expense and could be replaced quite cheaply. The same applied to mechanical irrigation devices and wells operated by animals.[179]

Other scholars confirm that an animal-powered mill cost between one-quarter and one-eighth of a water mill.[180] This factor must have been enhanced by the plague, which doubled the ratio of work animals and grazing land per surviving farmer.

Mechanised printing did not appear in the early modern Middle East, due to the religious importance of handwriting and copying, and to Arabic's cursive script. But two other European "plague technologies" were taken up: guns and glasses. As we saw in chapter 5, the increased use of guns in Western Europe after the Black Death was rapid and widespread. Gunpowder weapons appeared in Muslim Granada before the Black Death, and may have been independently derived from the first, Sung Chinese, diffusion. The Timurids acquired their gunpowder weapons through the third, Ming Chinese, diffusion. Timur used gunpowder mines in India in 1398, and may have had handguns, known as *tufangs*. His successors were casting large bronze cannon in Herat by 1444.[181] But most Muslims received their gun technology though the second, European, diffusion. This of course was also true of Europe outside the Middle European hearths of firearm innovation. "When experts travel from Italy to England, this is taken as a sign of openness to new ideas; when they travel from Italy to Turkey, suddenly it is a crippling dependence on foreign technologies".[182] The time, place, and pace of mass uptake of an innovation, with "second movers" having the advantage of others doing their research and development, can matter more than the point of origin. Mounted archers continued to be crucial for Muslim and Eastern European armies, and it took time to learn to integrate these with field cannon and musket-armed infantry. The plague-prompted European gun diffusion reached the coastal Middle East by the 1360s, but percolated inland at differing speeds and intensities.

The Mamluks were long thought to have been especially resistant to firearms, but there is now "abundant evidence of an early adoption of firearms in the Mamluk Sultanate".[183] Cannon appeared in the 1360s, and were used by both sides in a Syrian rebellion in 1391, "causing considerable damage and great casualties". Harquebuses protected pilgrim caravans to and from Mecca by 1432.[184] These uses do suggest that the state was not yet heavily involved in firearms. Intensive training gave the Mamluk elite an edge in cavalry combat, like the Genoese in crossbows, and in both cases this may have slowed the wholehearted adoption of guns. But the Mamluks were using cannon in sieges by 1419,[185] and had a sufficient grasp of cannon-making technology to transfer it to India from about 1460.[186] The late Mamluks recruited "a new army comprising non-Mamluk infantry equipped with firearms" and built up a large artillery train by 1500.[187] They had 200 cannon in their last battle with the Ottomans in 1517.[188] The White Sheep Turkmen, like the Mamluks, were enemies of the Ottomans and allies of the Venetians. In the 1460s, the Venetians supplied their formidable leader, Uzun Hasan, "with cannons and arquebuses and artillerymen to operate them and advise on their use".[189] The Safavid movement was using guns even before it took power in Iran in 1501, possibly from 1478, and certainly by 1488.[190]

It was the Ottomans, however, who perfected the integration of guns and horse archers. They were using light cannon in field battles by the 1380s, the same decade as the first such usage in Northern Europe. Around 1400, they were the first to establish a regular infantry army and a permanent artillery train. By 1444, they had developed a system whereby light cannon, protected by wagons or some sort of barricade, and by harquebusiers, could form a solid centre around which cavalry wings could manoeuvre—a "ready-made moveable fortress".[191] The Ottomans derived this *tabor*, or wagon lager, from the Bohemian Hussites via the Hungarians—an Eastern European military innovation. But they became its master practitioners. To trespass on chapter 11, between 1444 and 1526 they successively outgunned Christian crusaders, White Sheep Turkmen, Venetians, Safavids, Mamluks and, finally, the Hungarians. "Portugal and the Ottoman Empire led the world in cannon technology at the beginning of the sixteenth century".[192] We will not find a "Little Divergence" between Western Europe and the Middle East in plague-forged gun technology.

"The transmission of eyeglasses to the Muslim world is traditionally dated to the late sixteenth century". Recent evidence, however, shows that they reached Mamluk Egypt very soon after the Black Death. They appear in the 1350s, in the verse of an aged perfumer: "I used to have eyes upon my cheeks / and today they have come to be upon my nose".[193] Spectacles were being imported into the Middle East in large quantities by the beginning of the fifteenth century. "Barcelona's municipal records mention the export of 2,160 pairs of eyeglasses to Alexandria and Beirut in 1403 . . . In 1482 some 1,100 pairs of Florentine eyeglasses were sold to a merchant to be traded in various Ottoman cities".[194] In the single year of 1540, 24,000 pairs were exported from Venice to the Levant. The Muslim South did not experience the print revolution and it did not have quite the same incentive to improve vision as Northern

Europe—Baghdad has twice the sunshine hours of London. But this remark-able mass uptake of eyeglasses suggests they did share Western Europe's "scribal transition", and other evidence supports this.

Even before the Black Death, throughout the Muslim South, "evidence of the premium placed on literacy is everywhere".[195] Plague had a similar effect on educational institutions north and south. As in Europe, there was a surge in the founding of "universities"—*madrassas*, or colleges attached to mosques. One, founded in Cairo in 1360, had 506 students, large libraries, and taught languages, law, and medicine as well as theology.[196] A single Timurid viceroy built three such establishments.[197] Less well-known are the *maktabs*, or schools providing basic education, but these too must have flourished in pro-portion to population after 1350. The 100 endowed places for orphans in one Tabriz establishment would now educate double its previous percentage of the population. Paper became cheaper in the Middle East too, either locally produced or imported from Europe or India.[198]

> Islamic society of the period 1000–1500 was profoundly a culture of books. We can get a rough indication of just how many books were in circulation from the estimate that there are currently more than 600,000 known Mus-lim manuscripts, and these are but a small fraction of the total that must have existed then.[199]

One effect of this Muslim "scribal transition" was to facilitate commerce— the literacy rate often corresponded to the intensity of trade.[200] Another was to increase the availability and effectiveness of bureaucrats. Improved record-keeping and accounting were key factors behind "the signal success of the Timurid agrarian economy".[201] The Mamluks also improved their bureau-cracy.[202] But, again, the leaders were the Ottomans. From 1389, the Ottomans built the administrative machinery of a centralised state on a grander scale than anyone else in West Eurasia. By 1501, the central state could issue almost 500 orders-in-council in a single month. Its capacity for censuses and surveys was unsurpassed. Ottoman archivists boasted of never having lost a document even in the late nineteenth century.[203] "Scribes were indispensable in carrying out the administrative tasks during Ottoman campaigns".[204] Not just their regular army, but also their *timariot* contract levies, dating from the 1380s, de-pended on scribes. Each holder of a *timar* had a modest fief, with only two to five retainers accompanying him into battle. To field the usual 40,000 timariots involved at least 10,000 timar contracts. Each was checked by state scribes against lists from the archives at the beginning of a campaign, and if the timariot failed to show up, or did so understaffed or underequipped, his fief went to someone else. The documents "inevitably record delays and other hitches in the procedure, but the overall impression is one of remarkable efficiency".[205] This scribal state intertwined with the proliferation of vakf to create a machinery for both disaster recovery and expansion.

There was another component to the Muslim South's recovery/expansion kit. Sufis, also known as dervishes (and as marabouts in the Western Maghreb),[206] were wandering mystics and holy men, distinct from the establishment religious scholars, the *ulema*. From the thirteenth century at the latest, some began to settle down into lodges or "convents" (*zawiya*) in which they and their followers lived.[207] These in turn cohered into far-flung orders or brotherhoods, not unlike monastic orders. Entitled "shayks" (sheiks) in their lifetimes, some Sufis became "saints" posthumously; their lodges became shrines, places of pilgrimage. Their religious role remained important, but they also acquired other functions: as healers, spokesmen for common folk, economic organisers, maintainers of infrastructure, and community leaders and founders.[208] They were particularly effective in these functions when backed by vakf foundations established to give their lodge an income. Sufism surged right across the Muslim South after the Black Death. "In the late medieval period . . . Sufism became increasingly popular and politically important".[209] It lost the stigma of unorthodoxy, and many important brotherhoods, such as the Naqshbandi, date their origins to the early plague era.[210]

Since the 1970s, historians have noted that "colonising dervishes" led Muslim colonisation of the Balkans in the fifteenth and sixteenth centuries by Turkmen from Anatolia with the encouragement of the Ottoman government.[211] Sufi-led resettlement also occurred in the Middle East itself. "Hospices of colonizing dervishes had a distinctive significance for economic history. established on the main migration paths of those who colonized the new settlements".[212] More recently, a similar role for Sufis in settlement has been noted in sixteenth-century Mughal India. "As both living blessed men and dead saints, Sufis served as the symbolic founder-figures of new urban or tribal communities, becoming attached to narrative traditions of community genesis that at times required them to be imagined as the earliest residents in an area even when factually they were not".[213]

What seems less appreciated is the correlation of the surge in Sufism with the early plague era; its role in recolonising plague-depopulated lands, as well as in colonising newly conquered ones; and the use of "monastic colonisation" beyond the Muslim South.

Relations between Sufis and states varied. In Hafsid Tunisia, the former took control of inland regions after the Black Death, as we have seen. Elsewhere too, some Sufis were involved in rebellions. But many allied with states, and helped them recover from wars and plagues. The Timurids engaged in "legitimizing Sufi activity and teaching".[214] In one case, the Shi'ite Safavids, a Sufi movement, *became* the state, with its takeover of Iran in 1501.[215] Their Shahs were known to Europeans as "The Grand Sophy", or Sufi. The Safavids were a long-term thorn in the side of the Ottomans, but the latter were eager allies of other Sufis. Ottoman land grants to Sufis surged after the Black Death,[216] particularly in areas that needed to be repopulated or resubordinated in both the Balkans and Anatolia. "By endowing dervish lodges for popular Sufi figures, powerful emirs reestablished their legitimacy through an alliance with the local Turcoman population".[217] "The shaykhs acted as a sort of volunteer bureaucracy for the state".

> Among their most common activities were: providing guidance on religious issues, accommodation and hospitality services to travellers, public works such as the construction of bridges, fountains and homes, and assistance in agriculture and animal husbandry . . . For these reasons, the rulers were very sympathetic to the shaykhs and donated land for the construction of their lodges and foundations (*vakf*), met their routine expenses and dispensed alms (*sadaka*) and gifts to them.[218]

The combination of Sufi-led resettlement, increased numbers of vakf, and economically activist states enabled more rapid recovery from plague and war, and suggests that Muslim institutions actually adapted at least as well to post-plague circumstances than Western European ones. They encouraged the tendency of survivors to move from less productive to more productive places, and backed them with capital or tax relief and the restoration of infrastructure. The package also delivered "soft power" in the service of expansion, encouraging economic integration and, sometimes, religious conversion. This capacity for recovery through states, Sufis, and vakf may have had deep roots in Islam, but adapted and expanded as a consequence of plague.

While I cannot blunder far into yet more historiographical minefields, it has to be said that these cultural and religious developments in the Muslim South look rather similar to those in Europe at the same time, where they are known as the Renaissance and the Reformation. One trend in recent scholarship re-dates the beginning of the Italian Renaissance from 1250 or 1300 to 1350 or 1400, demoting Dante Alighieri and the early Petrarch to precursors and allowing for possible triggering by the Black Death.[219] According to leading expert Peter Burke, the Renaissance was "first clearly detectable toward the middle of the fourteenth century".[220] Another trend broadens it beyond its traditional home in Italy to such regions as the southern Low Countries in the fifteenth and sixteenth centuries.[221] There is a case for a Cracow-centred Polish Renaissance too, and Russian Novgorod also experienced "a burst of cultural creativity".[222] A third trend finds renaissances outside Europe, notably the Timurid one mentioned above, to which we could add the surges of artistic output and learning in Granada, Tunis, and Cairo.[223] The case for a Timurid renaissance in Iran's plagued fifteenth century, "an astonishing upsurge of cultural and intellectual life," seems particularly strong.[224] These multiple renaissances all interacted: "the Renaissance was a hybrid of European initiatives with transplantations of extra-European culture".[225] Yet they look less like a dispersal from one source than separate but similar responses to the same development: the Plague Revolution.

All agree that elite patronage was crucial to the Renaissance, and elites as we have seen had more disposable wealth after plagues—think of the more than fourfold increase in Dubrovnik. New elites competed with older elites to patronise artists and scholars, as did great cities, whether they were independent or not. Individual patrons were joined by collective ones: monasteries, guilds, city governments themselves.[226] The traditional talent pool was halved by the Black Death and pruned anew by subsequent strikes, so talent quests expanded, both spatially and down the social scale.[227] The population of Florence, at around 100,000 in 1348, was halved by the first strike, and is thought to have then recovered modestly to 60,000 by 1401. It was reduced by four further plagues to 37,000 in 1427, and recovered only slightly to 40,000 in 1480.[228] Yet Florence produced about half of the great Italian painters of the fifteenth century, many of them newcomers to the city.[229] The vision transition must have meant that artists too had longer working days and working lives. Richer patrons, urban and elite rivalry, and extended talent quests would have been shared throughout West Eurasia, clustering where great cities did, as in northern Italy, the southern Low Countries, and the Timurid domains. Italy might still be the flagship of the fleet, but we may need to consider the possibility of a West Eurasian renaissance triggered by plague.

The origins of secular modernity are often located in the Renaissance, yet the great majority of its paintings still had religious themes.[230] One might think that the randomness of plague, striking down saint and sinner alike, would have caused doubt in God's good will or even his existence. But that is an anachronistic idea from a secular age. Faith intensified during the plague era, and the afterlife became even more important to the living and dying. Doubts did emerge, but about religious establishments, not the god they mediated. In England, John Wyclif and his followers, known as Lollards, attacked the corruption and materialism of the Catholic Church from 1375 to 1417, when they were suppressed. Wyclif had some influence on Jan Hus, though this may have been exaggerated. While other Czech leaders were important, Hus is the best-known founder of the remarkable Hussite movement, which in early fifteenth-century Bohemia preached the same anti-Church message and advocated direct worship by the laity, with minimal priestly mediation.[231] Both Wyclif and Hus were particularly irritated by the sale of indulgences offering years off Purgatory and remission of sins, sometimes associated with pilgrimages to shrines. The English had a set rate for adultery—six annual visits to St Andrew of Rochester. Adultery with your godmother required a trek all the way to Compostela in northern Spain.[232] "Purgatory was one of the most successful and long-lasting theological ideas in the Western Church", writes a leading expert, "there is no doubt that [it] was much encouraged by the trauma of the Black Death in 1348–9".[233] After the plague, the papacy, beset by schism and needing money for its wars, increased the sale of indulgences, which vexed Martin Luther as it had Wyclif and Huss.

Less well-known than Lollards and Hussites are comparable movements in Eastern Europe, notably the Strigolniki, or "shorn ones", of Novgorod. "The heresy of the strigol'niki . . . occurred in the aftermath of recurrent plague years". Whether they were heretics or reformers of the Orthodox church is a matter of debate, as it is with the Lollards and Hussites.[234] There was also a Lollard spin-off in Dalmatia. "In the 1380s, a certain Gualterius (Walter), a disciple of . . . John Wycliffe, spent some time in Split and with his preaching provoked the resistance of the people against the secular and ecclesiastical authorities".[235] When full Protestantism emerged in the sixteenth century, it was surprisingly strong in Poland, Hungary, and Transylvania, excoriating "you fat little monks, all stuffed with your prebends", before succumbing to the Counter-Reformation in the seventeenth century.[236] These developments in Western and Eastern Europe, along with the rise of Sufis, vakf, and the Safavid Shi'ite religious state in Iran, may suggest a plague-triggered West Eurasian-wide "proto-reformation". Reformation specialists may well find such thinking too general and too simple, and I do not mean to deny the importance of such remarkable individuals as Luther in the creation of Protestantism in the sixteenth century.[237] Yet the sudden death of half its believers is surely likely to have had profound effects on any religion, and it may be that plague was a necessary, though not sufficient, prerequisite of reformation.

Returning to our main theme, the Muslim South's "expansion kit" was significantly different from Western Europe's. Ottomans were great exploiters of Balkan crew regions and European and non-European mercantile networks, but there are few signs of crew regions in West Asia or North Africa. As noted in chapter 6, Islamic societies had their own ways of generating "disposable males". Another difference was the absence of Muslim gun galleons before the seventeenth century, due to the absence of much in the way of an Atlantic coastline. But the Muslim South did have guns, and we will see that it also had gun galleys, gunboats, and gun forts. It also had motives for expansion in the form of burgeoning demand for exotic goods, and for slaves. Its recovery/ expansion institutions, including vakf, Sufis, and activist states were, if anything, ahead of those in Western Europe. Why, then, did the Muslim South not expand beyond West Eurasia too? This book's answer is that it did.

9

Early Modern Ming-Muslim Globalisation

CHINA HAD ITS OWN mid-fourteenth century crisis, less lethal but more destructive of property than the Black Death. As chapter 2 noted, it involved epidemics of diseases other than plague, floods, and famines, but centred on the efforts of the Han Chinese to throw off the Yuan Mongol yoke, from 1351, and on further bloody wars to decide which rebel faction would take over. By 1368, the faction led by Zhu Yuanzhang had won, and he established himself as the first emperor of the Ming Dynasty, taking the name Hongwu, the Martial Emperor. The Ming set about reconstruction with energy and ample manpower, rebuilding the Great Canal that integrated Northern China with the rice-producing south; encouraging the resettlement of devastated regions; and boosting agriculture to well above thirteenth-century levels by 1393.[1] In 1402, the uncle of Hongwu's successor usurped the throne as the Yongle emperor, and it was he who sponsored an exceptional Chinese exercise in global outreach. The best-known aspect of this was the voyages of the great admiral Zheng He. Between 1405 and 1433, Zheng's fleets of 50–100 ships, with up to 27,000 people aboard, repeatedly toured the Indian Ocean, touching in Southeast Asia, Sri Lanka, India, East Africa, the Persian Gulf, and the Red Sea. Some of the ships were as large as any European carrack, though they were still primarily monsoon-runners. The voyages were "precisely organised and successfully carried out due to careful consideration of the conditions and periodical patterns of the Asian tropical and subtropical monsoon".[2] Polities all around the Indian Ocean happily accepted nominal Ming suzerainty in return for the chance to trade for Chinese silk and porcelain; fragments of the latter scattered around the Indian Ocean serve as Zheng He's visiting cards. In 1433, however, these great official voyages ceased. Coupled with the Ming's

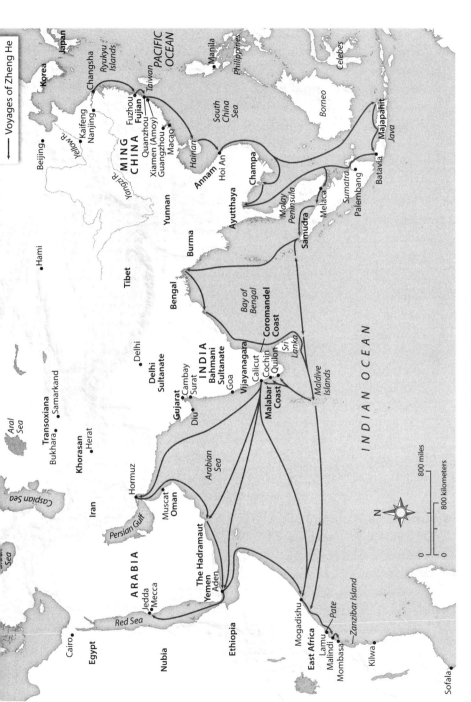

MAP 7. Ming-Muslim Globalisation

numerous bans on private maritime trade, 1371–1567, and the disdain towards commerce and foreigners detectable in official annals, this has been taken to indicate a Chinese "inward turn", an abandonment of interest in the rest of the world. This is often used to answer the question "Why not China?", an inversion of "Why Europe?" One aim of this chapter is to assess the extent and nature of Chinese engagement with West Eurasian expansion.

The other aim is to outline the forgotten first episode of that expansion, an episode which joined hands with the Ming outreach: Muslim mercantile expansion from the later fourteenth to the sixteenth centuries. It was Southern Arabia and the Persian Gulf, not Iberia, which launched this first West Eurasian early modern expansion, and I suggest that it did so at least partly in response to plague-boosted demand for spices, silks, cottons, and porcelains. This expansion predated the maritime entry of Western Europeans into the Indian Ocean by at least a century, then competed and coexisted with it, and it established the context in which European imperialism in the Indian Ocean operated.

I Early Modern Muslim Mercantile Expansion

Southern Arabia, which includes Yemen, the Hadramaut, and Oman, complicates our preconceptions about the Arabian Peninsula—that it was largely infertile desert, dots of oases joined by lines of camel transport. While a recent description of the region as the southern "fertile crescent" may be pushing it,[3] Southern Arabia did have fertile irrigated land and, where it was touched by the monsoons, rain-fed upland pastures.[4] It contained Arabia's best horse breeding lands and had long produced such items as frankincense and dried dates for export. It had an ancient maritime tradition—indeed, it may have invented sailing boats.[5] Its sewn-plank dhows had been riding the monsoons as far as China since the eighth century if not earlier, and it had sprinkled a network of Muslim enclaves around the Indian Ocean. Southern Arabia's chief port cities were Aden and Hormuz, located at the throats of the Red Sea and the Persian Gulf. Regarding Southern Arabia's Indian Ocean trade during 1350–1400, "the notion of a broad decline in this period is [in 2006] a consensus view among economic historians".[6] But a growing number of experts contest this, and instead posit a "dramatic increase of overseas trade in the fourteenth and fifteenth centuries",[7] though they do not connect it to plague. "The fourteenth and fifteenth centuries saw the expansion of Islam on the shores of the Indian Ocean, and the growing presence of Muslim mercantile communities, whether in East Africa, India, or Southeast Asia".[8] These views can be tested by looking first at the Persian Gulf and the Red Sea, then at East Africa, and then at the western Indian coast.

A discussion of Hormuz, an island city in the Persian Gulf of around 50,000 people, could easily have appeared in the last chapter. It was a Dubrovnik-like proxy for the commercial prosperity of Iran in the early plague era, indeed for the whole Middle East. New Hormuz was established on Jarun Island around 1300 and took over the name from Old Hormuz on the Iranian mainland opposite. Ruled by a king, and nominally a vassal of whoever controlled Iran, it was in fact an independent maritime city-state, even an empire city. It traded regularly by sea with East Africa, India, and Southeast Asia—and, from the early fifteenth century, with China—and it distributed imports from these countries throughout the Middle East by sea and caravan. The taxes Hormuz paid to Iranian rulers, together with its own efforts in maintaining caravanserais and inland partner towns, ensured the inland network was seldom ruptured, even in time of war.[9] The island itself produced nothing except salt; even drinking water had to be imported.

I can find no direct evidence of plague in Hormuz, for or against. But given that it was dependent on bulk grain imports, some from Iran and Iraq, which did have plague, it is unlikely to have escaped. It also drew grain from fertile patches on the Arabian side of the Persian Gulf, particularly Oman. There is no direct evidence of plague in Oman either, but the country did have black rats, and numerous cats, which might reflect a desire to control rats.[10] There are signs of plague's counterintuitive economic effects. In Hormuz, even lower-class citizens were prosperous—"the people of the country are all rich";[11] the army included foreign mercenaries and "slave soldiers", indicating both wealth and labour shortages; and Hormuz's heyday was the period 1350–1500. "New Hormuz experienced an economic boom during the fourteenth and fifteenth centuries, according to historical and archaeological research". Chinese and Russian visitors wrote that fifteenth-century Hormuz was "a port without equal on the face of the earth", "a vast emporium where there were peoples and goods of every description from all parts of the world".[12] "Hormuz extended its maritime empire to all the islands of the Persian Gulf", and to its littoral and beyond.[13] "They hold the Gulf coast for seventy leagues [over 200 miles], and all the territories for twenty-eight leagues landwards".[14] The important Omani ports of Qalhât, Sohar, and Muscat were subject to Hormuz, whose reach extended throughout Oman—a surprisingly productive country, with 40 walled towns, irrigated agriculture, sugarcane, and rain-fed horse breeding uplands.

Its cereals, dried fish, and dried dates supplied Hormuz city and its fleets. Rice was imported from India.[15] Other resources came from the Iranian coast, parts of which were also subject to Hormuz's "maritime hegemony". This hegemony was enforced by monopoly over imports of Indian shipbuilding timber to Southern Arabia and the Gulf.[16]

Hormuz was a major distribution hub for imports of Indian cottons and spices. It exported a lot of bullion to India in return—mostly silver derived from its re-export trade with the rest of the Muslim South, which in turn derived some from Europe. The kingdom was not just a re-exporter, but had two important exports of its own: pearls and horses. It accessed the rich pearl-fishing grounds of the Persian Gulf through Qatar and Julfar, where the fishing fleets were based, and distributed fine pearls globally, an ancient trade.[17] The Omani horse trade, which reached 10,000 horses annually by the sixteenth century, was probably even more valuable.[18] Muscat and other ports, as well as Hormuz, were big horse exporters. The trade used light but large specialised ships, and Indian demand was strong.[19] As noted in the prologue, India was not good at breeding large cavalry horses. The Delhi Sultanate controlled the overland routes for horse imports from Iran and Turan. Powers farther south, like the Bahmani Sultanate and Hindu Vijayanagara, depended on seaborne imports for military parity with Delhi and each other.

Hormuz-Oman's twin at the eastern end of Southern Arabia was Aden-Yemen. This country was struck by the Black Death in 1351. I can find nothing about its subsequent plague history, but it clearly shared West Eurasia's general post-plague "golden age". Yemen was ruled by the Rasulid Dynasty from 1229 to 1454. Especially from circa 1350, "the Rasulid era was the golden age of premodern southern Arabia, a time of wealth, luxury, sumptuous buildings, and courtly cultivation of the arts".[20] The wealth came from overseas trade. In 1411–12—before Zheng He's first visit to it—Aden's port duties are said to have "amounted to as much as 1,470,000 dinars".[21] The figure is implausibly high for port duties, but not for the value of trade as a whole. Aden too exported horses from its hinterland to India, with the trade regulated by the state.[22] As with Hormuz, the return trade included Indian teak for ship timber, which Southern Arabia had long lacked[23]—this trade was still more tightly state-controlled. It enabled Aden, like Hormuz, to rule over a small maritime empire, though the Rasulid capitals were inland. "Rasulid rulers utilized maritime expertise and naval power to further their commercial and strategic interests and ultimately to stake out their territories both on the lands they ruled and on the waters that enveloped them".[24] As we saw in the last chapter, Yemen had increasingly to share its trade with Jedda from the late fourteenth century, and clashed sporadically with the Mamluks. The Rasulids clashed with their own tribal vassals as well. In 1454, one of these, the Tahirids, overthrew the dynasty. But Aden remained an important hub—it was still "a burgeoning port" in 1484, and remained so regardless of who controlled it.[25] The Cairo-based Karimi merchant network continued to entwine with Yemeni trade, as well as with that of the Mamluks.

Interesting support for the notion of Aden-Yemen's precedence in West Eurasian expansion is the fact that it is the place and time that the great addictive trades actually began. They are generally associated with Western Europe, with tobacco and tea, and with later centuries. Coffee, an Ethiopian plant, is thought to have been first cultivated for export in fifteenth-century Yemen, perhaps as early as 1418.[26] Trade in the drink with the rest of the Muslim South took off later in the century, "and expanded throughout the sixteenth century along with the proliferation of coffee-related artifacts such as Chinese porcelain cups".[27] Red Sea and Persian Gulf Muslim merchants were the means through which the whole of West Eurasia, Europe included, received its seaborne imports from the Indian Ocean and beyond until 1500. Hormuz and Aden were the Venice and Genoa of the region, and unlike the latter they had direct access to the Indian Ocean. We have seen that imports of Far Eastern exotics quickly recovered their aggregate pre-1350 levels, then began to increase in volume from about 1390. The Indian Ocean trades were ancient, sporadically achieving ongoing interaction from the first century BCE, and Muslim merchants from in and around Southern Arabia had been key players in it since the eighth century. But the system was not one that could quickly or easily respond to increased demand. Merchants could not simply press a button to increase supply; they had to voyage out and try to effect an increase themselves.

This is just what Arab and Persian merchants did from the later fourteenth century. They had plague-boosted motives for expansion, but not much in the way of obvious plague-boosted means. While Mamluks and Ottomans were quick to guns, Southern Arabians were not. In any case, the full military expansion kit did not emerge anywhere in West Eurasia until about 1480, a century after Southern Arabian mercantile expansion began. The Muslim merchants were merchant warriors too, and they had few qualms about assisting local allies in wars in India, or in increasing the power of their Southeast Asia city-states through local jihads. But they had no military edge over the locals. In addition, the shortage of local ship timber was a potentially crippling disadvantage, as the Ottomans were to learn in the sixteenth century, and we can presume that local labour was also in short supply. But Southern Arabia did have one plague-boosted advantage: an increased number of Sufi spiritual leaders, who usefully combined conversion with commerce and settlement. Indeed, the region had a particularly migratory variant: the Alawi Hadrami sayyids.

As noted in chapter 6, the Hadramaut, sometimes included in Yemen, had an ancient tradition of migration. *Sayyids* was one name for descendants, real or alleged, of the Prophet's own family. The early modern Hadrami variant doubled as Sufis and leaders of overseas migration. The classic study, by Eng-seng Ho, dates its main impact to the sixteenth century, but it seems clear that it developed earlier. Ho lists eight key sayyids; two founding figures died in 1161 and 1255; the remaining six died between 1416 and 1522, which must mean that they first achieved prominence in the late fourteenth century. The large crop of religious leaders may have been a response to plague. The Hadrami sayyids specialised in "revivified dead land".

> Pious, successful migrants put their money in real estate to foster learning among their offspring; many built mosques; others sank wells, thereby creating new agricultural lands, population settlements, and pilgrimage destinations . . . Each land they descend upon is brought to life, as if making thrive the most ruined of countries.[28]

As elsewhere in the Muslim South, plague-honed recovery techniques proved serviceable for expansion too. An upturn in Middle Eastern male migration, accompanied by substantial capital, is traceable in East Africa, India, and Southeast Asia, perhaps as early as the 1360s. Hadramis were prominent, but others were involved, notably Persians, and they too doubled as, or were accompanied by, Sufis.[29] They were not accompanied by their own womenfolk, marrying and converting local women instead.[30] But the new wave's links to their homelands and to Mecca were stronger than before, through constant reinforcement and return trips. So this was more of an expansion than a dispersal, though it had little political coherence.

Southern Arabian Muslims established their first post in East Africa by 717.[31] From about 900 they hybridised, more culturally than ethnically, with Bantu-speaking Africans to form the remarkable Swahili cross-culture, which had good links to inland African trade circuits as far as the African Great Lakes.[32] A chain of Swahili city-states emerged along the coast, from Mogadishu in Somalia to Sofala in Mozambique, with Kilwa, Mombasa, Malindi, and the island of Zanzibar in between. East Africa exported gold, ivory, and slaves, among other goods. Much of the gold came from the kingdom of Great Zimbabwe and was shipped from Sofala in short hops up the coastal ports to the north, which provided the shortest route to Middle Eastern and Indian destinations. Ivory was an important product because it was the best material for precise miniature engravings, which could convey a story without words, rather like modern cartoons.[33] African elephant tusks were larger and better for engraving, and for popular ivory bracelets, than those of Indian elephants, so they had a market in India as well as in West Eurasia. The profits on gold and ivory helped Arab and Swahili merchants fund imports of Further Asian exotics.

Trade and mercantile migration experienced an upturn from the fourteenth century."Most of the major waves of Yamani [Yemeni] migration to the Swahili region took place between AD 1300–1500".[34] As mentioned in chapter 1, plague may have come along too. Kilwa held the lead among the Swahili city-states at this time, though its hegemony was loose and partial. In the later fourteenth and later fifteenth centuries, it experienced two spells of decline. The first has been associated with the Black Death reaching the region. One or two strikes are possible—there are hints of plague's positive economic effects. But both of Kilwa's downturns look more like the result of other factors. Decline was restricted to Kilwa town itself. Recent archaeology shows evidence of increased building, settlement, and harbour work in the surrounding region. Another substantial town nearby, Songo Mnara, was "founded in the late fourteenth century".[35] The second decline, from 1450, probably stemmed from a downturn in the gold trade due to the collapse of Great Zimbabwe, which also reduced the importance of Sofala.[36] In 1506, a Portuguese expedition found only 4,000 people in Kilwa, though the town was still fairly prosperous.[37] Farther north, in Zanzibar, Mombasa, Malindi, Lamu, and Pate, 1360–1500 was an era of booming trade and increased urban settlement. "The expansion in settlement numbers and the size of towns reached its greatest extent in the 1400s and represent an increase in trade that was not superseded until the nineteenth century".[38] One recent thesis finds that "the growing trade of the fourteenth and fifteenth centuries generated a steady growth of Mtwapa", a port city allied to nearby Mombasa.[39] Another finds evidence of "a major commercial shift" in inland Africa around 1400, in the form of the appearance of new words for trade in the Greater Yao language. [40] This surge in trade likely stemmed less from local plague effects than from the fresh injection of Southern Arabian merchants and capital, responding, I think, to increased West Eurasian demand for African goods.[41]

While one source claims that "slaves were not an important article of export from East Africa before 1500",[42] others suggest slave exports were significant. A Turkish text from 1521, before Europeans had much involvement, "reveals the great scale of the slave trade".[43] Plague-decimated Arabs and Persians are likely to have been in the market for manpower. A crucial voluntary source of skilled maritime labour—and of prime ship timber—was Gujarat. This region had broken free from the Delhi Sultanate soon after 1400. It produced cotton and indigo itself, and was the leading transshipment hub for other goods. "The growing European demand for goods from the East . . . [and the] rise of Red Sea ports and increasing demand for spices resulted in reorganization of Gujarati ports".[44] Cambay was dominant in our period (1350–1500), but was outranked by Surat in the sixteenth century, with many smaller ports also featuring. Muslim merchants and associated Sufis had come to Gujarat earlier, but two recent works demonstrate a clear upturn in arrivals after 1360. One shows that in the century before that year, 17 mosques and Sufi tombs, often associated with markets, were built in the region, whereas 69 were built over the next century, a fourfold increase.[45] "Why is it", the other expert asks, "that the first set of prominent sufis who acquired a significant regional following and whose tomb-shrines defined the region's Muslim sacred space for subsequent generations, were migrants to Gujarat in the fifteenth century and not before?"[46] My answer would be that Gujarat became a halfway house for post-plague Arab and Persian mercantile expansion.

Fresh Middle Eastern migration is also traceable in other Indian regions. The Malabar (southwest) Coast of India was the great producer of black pepper, and was politically fragmented, except for a period under Vijayanagara overlordship in the mid-fifteenth century. Its major port in the late fourteenth century was Quilon, whose trade was shared by long-established Syrian Christian, Jewish, and Muslim merchant networks. Over the fifteenth century, inland princes known as the Zamorins extended their control over the coast in alliance with the Karimi merchants, and their ports, Cannanore, Cochin, and especially Calicut, displaced Quilon. Malabar's old Muslim trade networks included the Mapilla, engaged in small-scale local trade, and the Marakkars, who were actually from Coromandel on the east coast, but became important suppliers of rice to Malabar and eventually established themselves there too.[47] These groups remained significant. The Karimi had controlled the oceanic trade since about 1250, but had originally tended to return home after each voyage—one made the trip five times before 1304.[48] From about 1400, however, we see signs of the Karimis increasingly merging and blurring with a wider category, *paradesi* or "foreign" Muslim merchants, who tended to stay longer, or settle permanently.[49] Calicut "hosted four thousand foreign Muslim traders in the fourteenth century".[50] By 1504, "all the trade was in the hands of the Muslims, whose total number reached almost 15,000, with most of them already born locally".[51]

Developments similar to those in Gujarat and Calicut, though on a lesser scale, are indicated for Sri Lanka (a key source of cinnamon). Gujarat remained so important that it was easily mistaken for the author of this expansion. By 1509, Europeans noted that Gujaratis "have factors everywhere . . . as do the Genoese in our part of the world".[52] But "Gujarati merchant" was a generic term, meaning "Gujarat-networked merchant".[53]

> Many of the "Gujarati" merchants were not actually from Gujarat; rather, the term referred to any who had come from Sri Lanka or India's west coast and beyond. These merchants normally had trade links to Middle East ports such as those on the Saudi Arabian Peninsula and in the Red Sea region (Aden and Hormuz), with access to Mamluk Egypt, and an assortment of Persian Gulf ports . . . All the Gujarati merchants were Muslims.[54]

The merchants lacked labour and ship-timber, but not cash. They were among "the most munificent employers of manpower in South Asia".[55] "All Arabian and Persian dhows . . . were either built in India or were built of timber brought from there".[56] Sewn-plank dhows reached no more than moderate size, but bigger ships of up to 400 tons, hybrids of Arab, Southeast Asian, and Chinese techniques, their planks fastened with wooden dowels rather than sewn, were built from Gujarati teak for Arab and Persian owners, made and crewed by Gujarati labour.[57] Like West Europeans, early modern Muslim expansion made good use of "native allies", including the biggest of all: China.

II Chinese Outreach

Zheng He's seven great voyages, once little known to Europeans, have understandably captured imaginations in recent decades. The motives for them, and for their sudden demise in 1433, are contested. Some suggest that Yongle, being a usurper, "craved" the submission of distant princes to buttress his legitimacy.[58] It seems unlikely that recognition by small and distant states could have mattered so much to a Chinese emperor. Another view is that Zheng was engaged in "proto-maritime colonialism", using force or the threat of it.[59] It is true that Zheng was a formidable soldier—a great eunuch war-leader like the

Byzantine Narses; that his fleet carried many guns and thousands of soldiers; and that he used force with brutal efficiency on several occasions during his voyages, particularly the earlier ones. But the troops doubled as traders, and when 170 of them, having gone "ashore to trade", were "accidentally" killed in western Java in 1406, the local prince was fined rather than executed.[60] A Sri Lankan ruler and Chinese pirates in Sumatra were not so lucky, but given that the seven voyages involved hundreds of landings, the level of violence seems low. In 1442, after the voyages had ended, the ruler of Hormuz sent an envoy to plead that Chinese "colonialism" resume. He "humbly hoped that the Court would show great kindness and would, like before, send envoys in order to keep the avenues open".[61] A third explanation for the voyages is that the Ming wanted to demonstrate that they too, like the Mongols in their prime, were a global hegemon. Their variant at least posed as being benign, but willing and able to act as the world's policeman.[62] Finally, some assert that "the profit motive is clear, and [the] overwhelmingly commercial character [of the expeditions] is too conspicuous to be overlooked".[63]

This matter merges with broader debates about China's "inward turn". State bans on private maritime trade, between 1371 and 1567, were the main Ming manifestation of this. These, and the end of the Zheng voyages, are linked to attitudes of disdain towards commerce. Such attitudes do appear among the Confucian-Legalist scholars, selected by examination, who provided the Ming bureaucracy. China can seem an academic's paradise, a country run by classicists and historians—what's not to like? But the influence of such scholars on the official record was greater than on the realities. They resented wealthy merchant families—a rival elite like the court eunuchs, of whom Zheng He was one—all the more when some became rich enough to hire famous scholars to write their epitaphs.[64] The frequent repetition of the bans "suggests that they were not very effective".[65] Indeed, it is not clear that they were normally bans at all, but rather attempts to tax and control trade.[66] There were occasional attempts at rigorous enforcement, but even during these, private trade simply went illegal, turning to piracy, smuggling, and offshore markets. The early Ming did have problems with "Japanese pirates", some of whom were in fact Chinese, but these had settled down by 1400.[67] Fishermen, who provided a fifth of all taxable income in at least one coastal prefecture near Shanghai in 1417, switched easily between fishing and legal and illegal trade.[68] A recent study shows that major piratical incidents averaged around one per year between about 1400 and 1550, then erupted to 30 a year during a final spate of real enforcement 1550–67.[69] As a Ming official observed at the time: "Pirates and merchants are the same people. When trade is open, the pirates become merchants; but when trade is illegal, merchants become pirates. To start by prohibiting merchants is to end by struggling to contain pirates".[70]

It remains true that the Chinese preferred to keep maritime trade at arm's length, leaving the messy business of exchange to a system of air locks or transit lounges. One way of doing this was by designating particular Chinese ports for particular trades. Another was to locate exchange on offshore islands. The importance of the Ryukyu Islands in this respect has long been known. Ryukyu was an autonomous tributary state which acted as an outport for China, an offshore transshipment hub—with the deliberate help of the Ming. Between 1385 and 1435, the Ming government provided ships and trained sailors to Ryukyu. After 1435, the islands were rich enough to build their own ships and recruit their own (Chinese) sailors in Fujian, which required the consent of the Ming state.[71] What is less well-known is the role of small offshore islands just off the Chinese coast, of which there are 7,000, mostly unpopulated.[72] Recent research is suggesting that these had a role as a kind of cordon sanitaire, a chain of transit lounges, between the mainland and maritime trade. This was unrecorded by Ming officials, but appears in indirect evidence. On these islands, foreign embassies waited for their credentials to be checked, and private traders, legal, illegal, or semi-legal, exchanged goods with agents (*yahang*) "shuttling" back and forth from licensed ports.[73] Some islands were not so tiny. A recent Chinese study argues that the sea bans were never enforced on Hainan, which is bigger than Sicily.[74] From 1517, the Portuguese inserted themselves into this shadowy island fringe, one bunch of traders among many, before moving to the Macao peninsula in 1557. The sea bans are increasingly looking like means of controlling private trade, while keeping it at arm's length, rather than stopping it, with the brief spells of genuine enforcement, especially 1550–67, as the exceptions that prove the rule.

One form of trade was always legal: tribute missions. On the face of it, these were diplomatic missions in which foreigners willingly acknowledged Chinese supremacy, travelled to China, and exchanged gifts with the emperor. They are now known to have doubled as trade missions, involving a lot of private trade alongside the official gifts, and encouraging still more.[75] Maritime tribute missions were quite numerous in the first decade of Ming rule, the 1370s (41 missions). They then declined to a nadir of 14 missions in the 1390s. Between 1398 and 1402, there were none at all.[76] Piracy in the Straits of Malacca around 1400,[77] and possibly competition from rising West Eurasian demand, may also have contributed to what looks like a low point in long-range maritime imports into China around 1400. My impression is that this is the problem the Zheng voyages were intended to address.

Recently, an intriguing prologue to the Zheng voyages has been posited: a diaspora of Chinese Muslim refugees to Southeast Asia. The Yuan Dynasty had made much use of Muslim soldiers, merchants, and officials, generating hostility to Muslims among the Han Chinese.[78] Muslims were particularly prominent on the southeast coast. Here, in 1357–67, during the chaos of the Yuan-Ming transition, some Persian-descended Muslims rebelled and were defeated. Muslims were subsequently persecuted by local warlords and fled overseas to mainland and island Southeast Asia, where their Chinese-style Islamic gravestones appear from the 1370s.[79] Initially, this was by no means good for Chinese trade with the region. On the contrary, trade "collapsed due to the destruction of the Arab network at the fall of the Yuan dynasty in 1367".[80] Tribute missions declined from the 1380s, ceasing completely around 1400 as we have seen, and persecution of Muslims continued up to about the same time. But Ming relations with Chinese Muslim groups from farther inland, including Zheng He's homeland of Yunnan, were rather better. The Yongle emperor effected a general Sino-Muslim reconciliation soon after he took the throne in 1402, proscribing any mistreatment of Muslims in 1407. That year he also set up an "Office of the Barbarians of Four Quarters", perhaps the world's first Institute of International Relations, training translators in various languages, including Persian.[81] The Zheng voyages do seem designed to engage with Muslims in particular. Not only was Zheng himself Muslim—his father and grandfather are said to have made the *hajj* pilgrimage to Mecca—but so were several of his senior subordinates and some of his crew.[82]

The impression that Zheng's voyages were intended to reboot international trade is reinforced by the fact that they were by no means the only element of Ming global outreach. Four visits to Bengal by Chinese squadrons, but apparently not Zheng himself, in 1412–23, generated 14 reciprocal missions to China from Bengal by 1439.[83] Other Chinese maritime expeditions went to Borneo and the Philippines, bringing the total to 18 expeditions apart from Zheng He's seven.[84] Least recognised are a set of overland expeditions, one of which we encountered in the last chapter. Twenty Chinese caravans are known to have reached the Timurid domains between 1387 and 1550, most between 1407 and 1449. At least 78 caravans went the other way.[85] One or two Chinese missions to the Central Asian trading hub of Hami led to 63 "tribute" missions in return, 1403–27.[86] Another eunuch, Isiha, led six expeditions into the Amur region in China's far north, boosting trade in furs and ginseng, but not attempting conquest, and withdrawing from advanced positions when trade became self-sustaining.[87] Once foreigners and overseas Chinese took up the task without prompting, the Ming state ceased all its outreach expeditions, not just Zheng's great fleets: job done. They also cut back on expensive hospitality and gifts for official tribute missions, reducing their size and number, and allowing the Institute of Interpreters to run down—trade could now be left, with or without an official sneer, to the private sector.[88] This was not an "inward turn", but the end of a strategic and temporary state intervention to restore the Chinese system of globalisation by attraction. Like the other trade missions, the seven Zheng voyages triggered far more reciprocal maritime missions to China: an average of about 35 per decade 1400–1440. Another decline then began, because private trade was now back up to speed.

What needs explanation is less the global outreach than the Chinese appetite for overseas goods, which as we saw in the prologue rarely included manufactures. Furs, spices, dyestuffs, aromatics, and exotic foods were important to Chinese elites, and their restoration to the height of Yuan levels provided evidence of Ming parity with their precursors. What Western scholars may have missed is that the Ming showed a special interest in non-food crops, perhaps for internal elite consumption, but also for export. "From early in the dynasty, the government adopted a series of measures to promote non-food crops".[89] These included regulations urging that land not needed for rice be planted in mulberry trees and cotton bushes, tax breaks for doing so, and large-scale state transplantation of mulberry to expand silk production. Porcelain production, complex, state-managed, and large in scale, may have taken longer to reboot after the chaotic transition. Exports of porcelain to mainland Southeast Asia declined, 1430–1570, and were replaced by local production.[90] But the notion of this long and general "Ming gap" in porcelain exports is contradicted by the rise in Middle Eastern imports noted in the last chapter, except for the much shorter period, 1436–64, when there may have been production problems, or a policy of destroying second-rate pieces to maintain standards and price.[91] Recent archaeology suggests periods during the Ming when "rejected pieces were deliberately smashed as part of a strict management system".[92] I suspect a diversion of exports from short-range to long-range, possibly because the latter buyers were more likely to pay in silver. Ming repair, maintenance, and extension of the inland road, river, and canal networks lay behind the capacity of silk- and porcelain-producing regions to supply increasing quantities of silks and porcelain to Fujian and Guangdong merchants for export.

Trade delivered foreign silver, though its impact on the vast Chinese economy can be exaggerated. The Ming initially preferred paper currency, but rampant inflation of this did lead them to show a strong, if reluctant, interest in silver. The financial demands of expensive land campaigns in mainland Southeast Asia and the Mongol steppes may also have been a factor here—there was nothing intrinsically peaceful about the Ming, and bullion was best for the payment of armies. China's own silver mines were limited, but the Ming managed to squeeze more out of them: from 1.1 tons in 1390 to 3 tons in 1403 to 10 tons in 1409.[93] These amounts, themselves paltry, declined thereafter as these mines were exhausted—new mines were later developed in Yunnan.[94] A desire for bullion is thought to have been a factor in China's overland attempts at conquest in mainland Southeast Asia, which had diminishing success from the 1430s.[95] A study of Chinese monetary history at this time finds "a growing trend toward un-coined silver as a means of exchange in private markets. From 1430s, the Ming government itself increasingly adopted a de facto silver standard in fiscal payments and national accounts".[96] Other experts also refer to the Ming "thirst for silver"; "the insatiable Chinese demand for one precious substance: silver".[97] Muslim traders had long delivered bullion for Chinese super-crafts, some of it originating in Europe. Sometimes, from 1435, they again did so by voyaging to China themselves.[98] More often they used trading hubs in Southeast Asia.

III Joint Ventures in Southeast Asia

Southeast Asia, even more amphibian than West Eurasia, is fascinating for its rich interfaces between global, regional, and local histories. On the "Indo-Chinese" mainland, powerful states rose and fell, in "strange parallel" with similar states farther west.[99] At their "Zomian" margins, small polities elbowed room for themselves, dividing bigger neighbours to avoid being ruled.[100] In island Southeast Asia, two maritime empires, Malay Srivijaya and Javanese Majapahit, jostled for supremacy over smaller networks of maritime traders and raiders. Local agency is not easy to disentangle from that of the Middle Eastern and Chinese newcomers on whom we have to focus. Between about 1380 and 1500, joint ventures involving all these groups not only lubricated trade but also reorganised it and substantially increased production, changing the lives of local people in response to distant demand.

In coastal Java around 1413, Zheng He's crew found Middle Eastern and Chinese Muslim mercantile communities co-habiting comfortably. "One class consists of the Muslim people . . . from every foreign kingdom in the west who have flowed to this place as merchants . . . [Another] class consists of . . . people from Guangdong and from Zhangzhou and Quanzhou and such places, who fled away and now live in this country . . . many of them follow the Muslim religion".[101] Sometimes they also co-habited comfortably with the local people, making themselves essential to non-Muslim princes by handling their long-range trade. At other times and places, the sources speak of "jihads" spreading Islam through violence.[102] Java itself produced benzoin incense and aromatic aloe wood, but was also important as a regional agent of the spice trade. It exported rice to other islands, allowing them to concentrate on spice production. Its Muslim traders sought the rare and precious spices of the Maluku (Moluccan) Islands—cloves from Tidore and Ternate, and nutmeg and mace from the few small islands of the Banda group.[103]

It was presumably these traders who stimulated increased production of Moluccan spices, revealed to us by the sudden fourfold surge in European imports in the late 1390s. "An annual average of nine tonnes of cloves and two of nutmeg may have been brought to Europe in the years 1394–97, rising sharply to thirty-two and ten tonnes respectively in 1399–1405".[104] Plague-boosted European demand was a *necessary* condition of this; willingness to pay high prices for Moluccan spice may have been increased by the belief that nutmeg and mace helped prevent plague.[105] But demand was not a *sufficient* condition—why wait 50 years after the Black Death to boost imports of these alleged plague prophylactics if you had a choice? The likelihood is that the various trade networks, with new Southern Arabian merchants prominent among them, somehow engineered an increase, beginning about 1380, which first met increased demand in the Muslim South, and only then overflowed into Europe. This correlates in time with the first introduction of Islam into the Banda Islands, traced by archaeology through the sudden disappearance of pig bones in middens.[106]

The black pepper trade was on a much larger scale than that in Moluccan spices. The success of the Zheng voyages in restarting long-range trade can be traced to what all sources agree was a big rise in Chinese pepper imports between 1410 and 1430—it was this competition that produced the spike in European prices, 1410–1414, noted in chapter 4.[107] The rise in pepper exports thereafter to West Eurasia as well can only be explained by a substantial increase in production, and we find clear signs of this. In India, production was extended north from Malabar into Kanara at some point in the fifteenth century.[108] A more dramatic extension of production was to Sumatra early in the same century, where black pepper plantations throve. Allusions to Southeast Asian pepper exports before 1400 may refer to long pepper, a different and less well-regarded product.[109] Zheng's Chinese may have been involved in this; China had a track record in reshuffling useful biota. But another important player was Samudra-Pasai, a precursor of the Aceh sultanate, located in west

Sumatra. Samudra-Pasai was the oldest Muslim state in Southeast Asia, established in the thirteenth century.[110] A "cosmopolitan centre of Islam", it had links to the Chulia Muslim trade network in the Bay of Bengal, whose merchants had grown extremely rich by the early 1420s.[111] Gravestone evidence demonstrates a surge in connections with Gujarat, from before 1406 to 1448,[112] and given this region own links with Southern Arabia and pepper-producing Malabar, a correlation with the transfer of pepper plantations seems likely. Black pepper was later also grown in Java, and Javanese rice imports allowed upriver regions to focus on pepper, just as rice imports enabled the expansion of Indian pepper plantations in and around Malabar. Soon after 1500, Southeast Asian pepper production matched that of India, indicating at least a doubling of global production during the fifteenth century.

From 1403, more and more trade came to pass through a new hub of Ming-Muslim globalisation: Melaka (Malacca). In the 1390s, Majapahit, itself in decline, had managed to throw a last vestige of the Srivijaya regime out of the Sumatran port of Palembang. A thousand or so refugees settled first in what is now Singapore, then in 1403 moved up the west coast of the Malay Peninsula to Melaka, a small fishing port. The port was sheltered, and strategically positioned near the Straits of Malacca, at the intersection of several monsoon routes—south to the Spice Islands, east to China, west to the Bay of Bengal. Zheng He found it to be a ramshackle but bustling little port in 1407, and thereafter often visited it.[113] Over the next century, it grew into the first of the many new cities produced by West Eurasian expansion, in its case with the help of local agency and Ming global outreach. By 1500, it contained at least 50,000 permanent inhabitants and perhaps as many as 150,000, depending on how many ships were in its harbour, awaiting their particular monsoon. A staggering variety of merchants lived in or visited Melaka, and the list of goods on sale there was endless, but its key re-exports were silks and porcelains from China, cotton and pepper from India, spices from Southeast Asia, and bullion from wherever it could get it—gold was said to be abundant.[114] Imports of Indian textiles alone, for redistribution in Southeast Asia in exchange for spices, are estimated at the equivalent of 19.3 tons of silver per year.[115] While Melaka, under its Malay sultan, welcomed all sorts and all religions, "Gujarati Muslims, in particular, were enticed by Malacca's convenient location and low rates of tax. . . . From the 1420s at least these Gujarati merchants therefore moved to the city in great numbers".[116]

Like merchant "nations" in European ports, each trading group had its own establishment, from which four port-masters (shah-bandars) were selected. The

Gujarati-networked shah-bandar was "the most important of all". More than 4,000 important resident Muslim merchants comprised "the Gujarati faction . . . even if it originated further west and even if the sailors involved were Arab, African, or Turkish".[117] Gujarati-networked merchants "established a monopoly on Melakan trade with the western shores of the Indian Ocean".[118] After the Zheng voyages ended in 1433, a small community of resident Chinese merchants remained important in Melaka, but the city-state's own rulers converted to Islam—perhaps as early as 1414. "Chinese Muslims may well have facilitated Muslim integration into the Chinese market. The Chinese no longer had to send their own ships further than Southeast Asia, but could pick up all they needed at Melaka and lesser Southeast Asian ports". But "most of the fresh impetus came from the Middle East".[119] We should rank this post-plague mercantile expansion from the seagoing south of the Middle East at least equally with the Chinese, the Indians, and local agency among the causes of Melaka's rise.

Melaka's rise represented a reorganisation of global trade, a consolidation and enhancement of the segmentation which actually rendered the trade more efficient than going all the way to China and back. In the first segment, Arab and Persian merchants from Aden and Hormuz sailed to Gujarat, picked up crew and perhaps bigger ships, and either took up their return cargo there or sailed on to Malabar for pepper and then to Melaka—the second segment. There, they linked up with the various local networks that delivered spices, and with ships from China carrying silk and porcelain. Melaka was a new part of a network of Muslim city-states around the entire Indian Ocean. The network was not controlled by a single state, but its main metropoles were Hormuz and Aden, and links to the Middle East were maintained by hajj pilgrimages to Mecca (perhaps 15,000 people a year from India alone),[120] and by the migrations of Sufis and Sayyids, as well as by interaction through trade.

It was this semi-coherent patchwork expansion, a very informal empire, that delivered the goods for plague-boosted West Eurasian demand in the fifteenth century. It not only foreshadowed Western European expansion in the Indian Ocean, but also incentivised and configured it, as well as fiercely contesting it. Western Europeans at the time knew of Middle Eastern maritime expansion, which prompted Vasco da Gama's "discoveries" in 1498. A few dozen European merchants, spies, and adventurers made their way around the Indian Ocean, often disguised as Muslims in acknowledgment of who was in charge.[121] They were aware of its interdependence with the Muslim South. Soon after 1498, the Portuguese were planning "to take Malacca out of the hands of the Moors, [so that] Cairo and Mecca would be entirely ruined".[122]

They did take Melaka in 1511 and they did temporarily disrupt the Muslim Red Sea trade from about 1509. But it was back up and running by the 1520s, and increasing from the 1540s (chapter 11). The Middle Eastern network adapted to European disruption, took new shapes, and continued to operate. The Portuguese did manage to hijack valuable parts of it, including Hormuz, which they captured in 1515, and to prey on the remainder. Most of the major Portuguese fortified ports around the Indian Ocean were former Muslim city-states: Sofala, Malindi, Kilwa, and Mombasa; Hormuz and Muscat; Goa, Diu, Cannanore, and Cochin; Samudra-Pasai and Melaka. The Portuguese empire in the Indian Ocean was a cuckoo in a Muslim nest, and in the seventeenth century the Dutch took over their nest in turn, becoming the third wave of early modern West Eurasian expansion to wash around the ocean's coasts.

The Indian Ocean was no maritime Garden of Eden before the entry of the European serpent in 1498. Coastal India, Southeast Asia, and the China Sea sheltered numerous groups prone to piracy, some Muslim, many not.[123] Gujarat and Melaka were quite formidable maritime powers, and had acquired numerous guns by the time they clashed with the Portuguese—3,000 pieces of artillery in the case of Melaka in 1511.[124] But these were mostly weapons from the Ming Chinese gunpowder diffusion, which had not been forged in the fires of plague. For all the military revisionism noted in chapter 7, the high Portuguese quotient of success in maritime and amphibious warfare in Further Asia remains stubbornly apparent. Adam Clulow writes, with only modest exaggeration, that "in virtually every encounter at sea, ships from Europe inflict overwhelming defeats on fleets opposing them".[125] It was this edge in maritime violence that enabled the Portuguese to muscle in on the Muslim network. They were initially less adept than their Middle Eastern precursors at the arts of conversion and cooperation, and had to watch while Melaka declined under their rule as its Muslim merchants departed to more hospitable regimes. On India's pepper-producing Malabar Coast, the Portuguese were at first seen as welcome new buyers, but soon fell out with the Zamorin of Calicut and his Karimi merchant allies. They were defeated at Calicut in 1510, and thrown out in 1525.[126] But, from their other bases at Cochin and Cannanore, they soon learned that acquiring pepper required allied local merchant networks or their own inland links, and they began subsidising inland pepper producers to supply them. Goa, farther north, replaced Cochin as the main Portuguese base in India, and soon after, they turned to Brahmin bankers for credit and Gujarati merchants for connections. It was business as usual in Hormuz, under the Portuguese from 1515, supplying spices and cloth to Persia and horses and silver to southern India. The trade was valued at about a million florins a year around 1520, of which the Portuguese took 10%, still carried mainly in 50–60 Muslim ships.[127] After temporary disruption, the Muslim trades went on as before, paying off, resisting, or evading the Portuguese.

Despite their edge in maritime violence then, the Portuguese—and the Spanish, Dutch, English, and French who followed them into Further Asia—had no choice but to rely on local allies, and to cozy up to big states such as China, Japan, and the Delhi Sultanate. As with their Middle Eastern precursors, European numbers were modest—a maximum of 10,000 Portuguese in Asia at any one time in the sixteenth century,[128] and 20,000 Dutch in the seventeenth,[129] though as we saw in chapter 6, maintaining anything like these levels required much larger flows. Given the tension between Muslims and Christians, non-Muslim merchant networks, such as the Kelings of the Bay of Bengal, were natural allies for the Portuguese. The Portuguese "carefully distinguished between the *mouros da terra* ("native Moors"), and the *mouros de Meca* ("Moors from Mecca"—which is to say the Middle East); they saw the latter rather than the former as their principal adversaries".[130] Sometimes they even allied with the former, as in Hormuz and with at least some Persian merchants in Gujarat.[131] The Portuguese in particular also bred and converted their own collaborators (chapter 15). In Southeast Asia, following Muslim precedent, European expansion's crucial ally was not local but Chinese.

Chinese communities, Muslim or not, appeared in Southeast Asia ports from the late fourteenth century. Small fresh migrations took place regularly thereafter, though technically illegal. Some migrants returned, few brought their womenfolk, and some stayed and intermarried with the locals. Hokkiens from Fujian were especially prominent. Their region was poor, isolated in terms of inland communications, and had a rather distant relationship with the state. Fujian's ports—Quanzhou (Zaitun, from which the word "satin" is derived) and Xiamen (Amoy)—lost out to better-connected official ports of trade, leading Hokkien merchants and migrants to go out and get it.[132] Fujian was the closest China came to having a crew- and settler-producing region. The important Siamese upriver port of Ayutthaya hosted one Chinese trading community, mostly Hokkien, three or four thousand strong, in the seventeenth century, and 30,000 strong in the eighteenth. A similar community developed at Hoi An in Vietnam.[133] These overseas Chinese helped run the last leg of the semi-global Eurasian trading system, along with a few European ships and many Chinese ships owned by merchants still living in China. They provided an outer layer of transit lounges for China's maritime interaction with the world, similar in function to the coastal islands noted earlier. But overseas Chinese were not highly regarded at home. "In the eyes of the Chinese government—and perhaps in the eyes of the people—the Chinese diaspora who abandoned ancestral graves to live abroad in violation of imperial law was not Chinese at all".[134] These migrants therefore lacked the active backing of their own state for their overseas enterprises. They saw the establishment of Spanish Manila in the Philippines (1571) and Dutch Batavia in Java (1619) as opportunities to obtain the support of someone else's state.

The Spanish in Manila were even more undermanned than the Portuguese and Dutch—their numbers are generally estimated at a mere 2,000 at any one time before 1760. They made considerable use of Filipino troops and labour.[135] But they also needed artisans and petty entrepreneurs—a middle class of colonists which was neither Spanish nor Filipino. Chinese settlers, in numbers ranging from 10,000 to 40,000 between 1586 and 1762, delivered this. "It was the Spaniards and Chinese who wielded the most power as they remade Manila in ways that fit their objectives".[136] The marriage worked, but it was not happy. The Chinese absorbed some Filipino resentment that would otherwise have been directed at the Spanish, were discriminated against by the Spanish, and periodically rebelled and were massacred—on at least four occasions in the seventeenth century.[137] Yet there was no keeping back the Hokkiens, and Sino-Spanish colonisation of the Philippines re-established itself each time. Chinese co-colonists helped lay the foundation for the immensely profitable exchange of Chinese silk and Spanish American silver. After 1571, Manila "became the single largest foreign port for Chinese goods for the next two centuries".[138] Many other aspects of Spain's partial dominion in the Philippines were also underwritten by their Chinese partners. A similar story can be told for Batavia and the Dutch East Indies. The former, headquarters of the Dutch East India Company from 1619, has been described as a "Chinese colonial town".[139] It was the Chinese who actually managed, and often financed, the expansion of pepper plantations from the fifteenth century to the seventeenth in Island Southeast Asia, for both European and Muslim enclaves.[140] When the Dutch established sugar in Java in the late seventeenth century, the actual mill owners were mostly Chinese. From the late eighteenth century, the British in Malaya also relied on Chinese co-colonists. European empire in Southeast Asia was a joint venture between European states, or their chartered company proxies, and Chinese private enterprise.

10

Entwined Empires

THE GENOESE PARADOX AND
IBERIAN EXPANSION

ONE EUROPEAN STATE that kept a very close eye on the Muslim South and its mercantile expansion was the republic of Genoa. Claims were made for it in part two: that it was a key player in the expansive trades, that it was Europe's leading innovator in plague adaptation, and that it was a "midwife" of Iberian expansion. This chapter substantiates these claims, and considers their implications, groping its way through a history and historiography peppered with paradox. The Genoese were shape-shifters, with a city-state (or three) *and* a merchant diaspora. They had a reputation for secrecy, yet left in their notarial records a key source for historians. Many scholars claim post-plague decline, but dates of onset vary suspiciously. Benjamin Kedar's 1976 argument is still accepted by some. "By the close of the 1340s Genoese merchants, hitherto the most enterprising in Europe, were fast losing heart and confidence and curtailing the geographical orbit of their activities".[1] Decline is also dated to defeat by Venice in 1381, or to a "takeover" by France around 1400, or to the fall of Constantinople in 1453. "The attempt to crush Venice ended up ruining Genoa . . . Genoa's power would steadily wane for the next seventy years, until its virtual extinction in 1453".[2] Yet the succeeding period has been called the "Century of the Genoese", a time when "Genoa had become the motor of Europe".[3] The city is "on the one hand hailed as the cradle of global financial capitalism, and on the other described as a 'failed state." Alternatively, it is not hailed much at all, despite having sporadically fascinated and frustrated institutional historians. "Genoa remains the land that scholarship forgot, especially regarding the fourteenth century".[4] "Despite Genoa's pivotal importance . . .

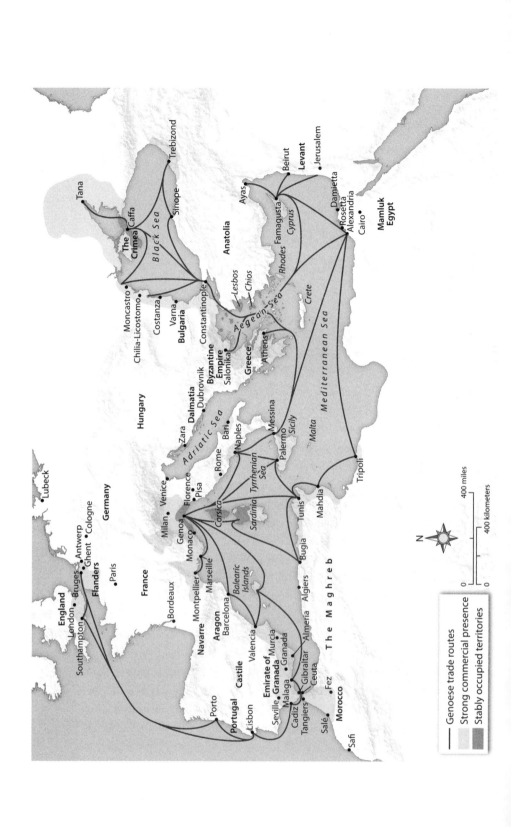

England
London
Southampton
Bruges
Ghent
Antwerp
Cologne
Flanders
Germany
Lubeck
Paris
France
Bordeaux
Porto
Portugal
Lisbon
Castile
Navarre
Aragon
Montpellier
Marseille
Monaco
Genoa
Milan
Venice
Florence
Pisa
Rome
Barcelona
Valencia
Balearic
Islands
Seville
Malaga
Cadiz
Tangiers
Gibraltar
Ceuta
Fez
Salé
Safi
Morocco
Emirate of
Granada
Granada
Murcia
Almeria
Algiers
The Maghreb
Bugia
Tunis
Mahdia
Corsica
Sardinia
Tyrrhenian
Sea
Naples
Messina
Palermo
Sicily
Malta
Tripoli
Bari
Zara
Dubrovnik
Dalmatia
Adriatic Sea
Hungary
Rome
Salonika
Byzantine
Empire
Athens
Greece
Constantinople
Lesbos
Chios
Aegean Sea
Crete
Rhodes
Mediterranean Sea
Anatolia
Bulgaria
Varna
Costanza
Chilia-Licostomo
Moncastro
The
Crimea
Caffa
Sinope
Trebizond
Tana
Black Sea
Ayas
Cyprus
Famagusta
Beirut
Jerusalem
Levant
Damietta
Rosetta
Alexandria
Cairo
Mamluk
Egypt

it remains seriously under-researched".[5] It is as though history does not quite know what to do with Genoa and the Genoese.

Genoa was dwarfed in size, stability and, according to most, significance, by its rival, Venice. Both cities were dominated by martial merchant clans, some descended from local landed nobles. They competed in Western Europe's major trade circuits, and had close connections to Eastern Europe and the Muslim South. Venice and Genoa fought seven wars, 1257–1433, four of them soon after the Black Death: the War of the Bosphorus, 1350–55; the War of Chioggia, 1378–81; and two less important clashes in 1403–1404 and 1431–33. Venice was renowned for political and institutional stability; Genoa was notorious for the opposite. It averaged a coup or rebellion every 5 years between 1257 and 1528.[6] By 1557 Venice and its north Italian hinterland contained 1.75 million people, while Genoa and Liguria held only 250,000—even this was a marked recovery from a low point of about 140,000 in 1350, after the first strike of plague.[7] There was a similar disparity between the two overseas formal empires. But Genoa's size does not measure its power. It won the War of the Bosphorus, and came very close to physically taking the city of Venice in the War of Chioggia. Though its siege failed, historians now concede that Genoa achieved its strategic war aims of dominating the Black Sea and alum trades.[8] While Venice then concentrated on building up both its Italian base and its formal overseas empire, Genoa turned to more subtle forms of expansionism.

I Genoese Imperialisms

Each year, the Doge of Venice cast a ring into the Adriatic to signify that Republic's marriage to the sea. Genoa's love life was more diverse. Between the 1260s and the 1520s, it made formal or informal "marriages", often tumultuous, with a half dozen empires and several other powerful states. Who wore the trousers in these relationships varied, but it was usually the Genoese that held the purse strings. Other historians have noted this capacity for "imperial symbiosis", currently the preferred term.[9] But "symbiosis" implies equal benefits for only two parties, and this was not always the case with Genoa's relationships, hence my preference for "entwining". Entwining empires was only one of several forms of imperialism and colonialism, pioneered by the Genoese, that flowered in Europe after the Black Death. As noted in chapter 7, others included "patchwork expansion", which combined patches of empire, formal and informal, with strategic strongpoints and with trade networks; "urban colonialism", in which a city reproduced itself at a distance, and/or converted overseas territories into "virtual hinterlands"; and private, non-state, colonial-ism. Before the Black Death, these expansionisms had yielded Genoa a loose and ragged, but profitable, patchwork empire stretching from the North Sea to the Black Sea. The biggest paradox of all is how a tiny, plague-ravaged city-state not only retained this empire after the Black Death, but extended and diversified it. Post-plague expansion came in two phases, roughly 1350–1450 and 1450–1550. The first featured Genoese military aggression; the second tended to let other peoples do the fighting. The phases overlapped; they were not a clear-cut turn from one region or one form of imperialism to another. But there was a gradual shift in balance from east to west, gathering pace from 1450.

Each year in the century after 1380, several Genoese carracks sailed up the English Channel to Southampton and Bruges or Antwerp, carrying more Mediterranean goods than all other shippers combined. The number of Geno-ese carracks, each of 400–1,000 tons, peaked at 20 and averaged nine a year, 1425–60.[10] Italian merchants dominated the most valuable trades of Bruges and Antwerp, and the Genoese comprised about half the Italian merchants in each city.[11] They were also the largest group of foreign merchants in Paris.[12] French merchants took over from the mid-fifteenth century, but Genoese fleets in French employ periodically raided England, sacking numerous ports during the Hundred Years' War, and returned in 1513 to introduce the English to "ship-killing" heavy cannon mounted in war galleys.[13] Yet "it was the Geno-ese . . . who were most active in the trade with England".[14] Genoese commerce with England included about half the wool trade until the 1480s. It declined after this, as in France, but Genoese bankers continued to be influential in London throughout the sixteenth century.[15] They are thought to have helped finance the voyages of John Cabot, himself probably Genoese, to North Amer-ica on behalf of the English crown.[16] In war, shipping, trade, and finance, the Genoese were major players in *Northern* Europe let alone in their own Greater Mediterranean.

Genoa's formal hinterland, Liguria, was a small, mountainous, crew region. Its informal hinterland stretched deep into neighbouring Piedmont and Provence, but its influence here was increasingly contested after 1350 by the Counts of Savoy and French princes. Genoa struggled to turn its biggest for-mal possession, Corsica, into an overseas "hinterland" from 1120 to 1769, founding coastal towns and introducing settlers and chestnut trees, but faced recurring rebellions and outside invasions.[17] Corsica was to Genoa as Ireland was to Britain: a useful but troublesome colony. Genoa vied with Venice for dominance of the trades in spices, silk, and cotton from Egypt and the Levant, with mixed success. From about 1430, Venice took an increasing lead, though the Genoese kept trying. Genoa was much stronger than Venice in the Western Mediterranean. In these waters, its chief rival was Aragon and its great Catalan port of Barcelona. Aragon and the Genoese clashed in the 1350s and fought three more wars between 1420 and 1458. Genoa suffered some defeats, but captured the king of Aragon and destroyed his fleet in 1435.[18] In southern Spain and North Africa, Genoese commercial hegemony was less contested. When it *was* contested, in 1355 by the Muslim city-state of Tripoli, the Genoese sacked the city, claiming that unauthorised adventurers were to blame, including Philip Doria, Admiral of Genoa. Doria and his men, "after remaining four months in Tripoli, plundering freely, were permitted to return to Genoa laden with loot, and received only a nominal punishment".[19] Both Muslim Granada and northern Morocco have been described as "virtual colonial territory of Genoa"[20] in the early plague era, and much the same could be said of Castilian Seville and, later, Aragon's Valencia. All the major ports of North Africa, from Alexandria to Ceuta, contained Genoese trading posts.

The Genoese had long entwined with the Byzantine Empire. They held Pera (Galata), across the Golden Horn from Constantinople. It was the main port of Constantinople, taking 85% of the customs revenue.[21] Pera was linked to two key Genoese assets in the Aegean. One was Foca or Phocaea on the Anatolian coast, the chief producer of alum, where the Genoese leased not only the alum mines but also the local government—first from the Byzantines and then from the Ottomans.[22] Genoese preeminence in alum production and trade predated the Black Death, but tightened and expanded after it, with the acquisition of the next most important alum producer, the island of Lesbos in 1355.[23] Chios, another Greek island, was acquired by the Genoese in 1346 and held until 1566.[24] It was the main producer of mastic, which freshened the breath of elites in both Europe and the Muslim South.[25] With alum and mastic, Genoese control of production as well as distribution allowed them to set the price, a technique other Europeans would later put to profitable use in the Spice Islands.

Another Genoese city, Caffa, was established in the Crimea, also in the 1260s, and became notorious as the maritime launch pad of the second plague pandemic in 1347, but recovered to 20,000 people by 1386.[26] Caffa drew on the Russian river system for slaves, furs, wax, timber, on the Black Sea littoral for hides, salt, grain, and on the Caucasus and the Pontic Steppes for more slaves, distributing cloth, wine, and spices in return. It was the capital of a "virtual empire"[27] on the Black Sea coast held in sometimes uneasy condominium with the Golden Horde and its successor states—another imperial entwining.

In a treaty in 1381, the Horde acknowledged "Genoese authority over 18 places and villages in southern Crimea".[28] Genoese trade reached far inland by river to the central Balkans, Poland and Muscovy, and southwards to Trebizond, Tabriz, and beyond.[29] Pera and Caffa were quite close in size and wealth to Genoa itself. They were the famous "Other Genoas". "And there are so many Genoese, and they are so scattered across the world, that wherever they are they make another Genoa".[30] They were cornerstones of an eastern patchwork expansion, firmly controlled by Genoese—not by Genoa. Pera and Caffa each had their own assembly, and were largely autonomous, but expected the help of the mother city in a crisis.

To about 1430, the Genoese continued their eastward expansion, using a mix of violence and diplomacy. In the Black Sea, they seized more ports, such as Balaclava in 1357 and Soldaia in 1365. Between 1360 and 1387, Genoese naval operations imposed a similar hegemony over coastal Bulgaria.[31] Caffa and Genoa took the lead in these developments, but there were private initiatives too. The seizure of Cyprus in 1374 was carried out by a group of merchant clans, which raised 14,000 men. Lesbos was acquired from the Byzantines by a single clan, the Gattilusio, who also obtained Imbros, Samothrace, Lemnos, and Thasos, and the city of Aenos (modern Enez in Turkey), a little private empire which they held until 1462.[32] Another clan, the Zaccaria, former holders of Chios and Foca, controlled most of the Morea in mainland Greece, 1404–32. [33]

Genoa's most perilous eastern entwining was with the rising Ottoman Empire. Its role in the birth of that empire was more ferryman than midwife. In 1352, Genoa signed a treaty with the Ottomans and helped them cross the Dardanelles to Europe for the first time.[34] In 1387, another treaty gave the Genoese trading rights throughout the Ottoman domains.[35] They took sides in the Ottoman wars of succession that followed Timur's invasion. In 1421, Giovanni Adorno ferried the formidable Sultan Murad II across the straits to fight his uncle. Halfway across, he is said to have insisted that the Sultan waive a debt that Adorno owed him. The Genoese were suspected of, and hated for, helping the Ottomans to defeat two great Christian counterattacks against the Ottomans, at Nicopolis in 1396 and at Varna in 1444.[36] When the Turks finally took Constantinople in 1453, Pera remained neutral and untouched. Yet it was Genoese carracks, led by the Doria clan, that temporarily broke the Ottoman siege and allowed some supplies into Constantinople.[37]

———

It was the merchant clans that gave the Genoese their flexibility. One, the Grimaldi, acquired the principality of Monaco in 1297 and holds it to this day. The Spinola and the Doria were of similar standing, and there were a few dozen others. All combined war, piracy, trade, and banking in proportions that varied over the centuries. It was these clans, not the city itself, that owned most galleys and contracted most crossbowmen. By hiring them out in between their own wars, the Genoese maintained a semi-professional army and navy at other people's expense. Each major merchant clan was itself a network, with kin or agents in each overseas colony and major trade station. Their propensity to internecine feuds was real enough, but was constrained. The losers in civil strife might lose political power in the city and be exiled, but they were not executed or subjected to confiscation of property, so their economic power survived.[38] In a real crisis, such as the War of Chioggia, most came to the aid of the mother city.

The Genoese network of networks operated at several levels: clan, long- and short- term alliances of clans, classes of clans (old and new, noble and non-noble), and the whole. Contrary to the orthodoxy, it appears to have been *less* individualistic, and more kin-based, than the Jewish-Muslim merchant networks revealed by the Geniza letters.[39] Generic rivalry occurred between old and new clans—new aspirant elites emerged regularly. The old elite tended to monopolise existing trading partners, so new elites had to find fresh ones, creating an endemic expansive impulse. A change of government through a coup or rebellion could enlist the modest resources of the state in the interests of the new elite. Outlaw clans came in handy, permitting the Genoese to trade with and fight the same polity at the same time. The Gattilusio, who were "acclaimed as inherently and irreducibly Genoese when it suited the government . . . could also be presented as thoroughly foreign, as convenience dictated".[40] In 1453, the Genoese of Pera were able to convince the triumphant Ottoman Sultan that they hated the Doria as much as he did, so they remained unpunished for the temporary breaking of the siege. This also explains the continuance of Genoese influence in England, despite such peccadilloes as the sack of Southampton—France's Genoese mercenaries had nothing to do with *Genoa*. Genoa did not like the English making their own ventures into Mediterranean trade, and took two Bristol ships which made the attempt around 1457, but blamed this on pirates over whom, of course, the Genoese republic had no control.[41]

This politically flexible Genoese "merchant diaspora" had a state when it needed one, and had an even greater role than other diasporas in deploying the transnational pools of skills, labour, money, and raw materials noted in chapter 7. It developed this in various ways, one of which was the export of leaders. Genoa provided admirals for France, Castile, Aragon, the Holy Roman Empire, the Papacy, and the Ottomans. "Six members of the Genoese Pessagno family served as admirals for the kingdom of Portugal in the fourteenth century".[42] Genoese also provided high military or financial officers for several other states, including England and Morocco. Initially, I looked for educational and cultural roots for this apparent overproduction of talent. Genoese elite education was indeed unusually secular, practical, and transnational.[43] A strong tradition of military entrepreneurship did exist—its last practitioner was arguably Napoleon Bonaparte, a Corsican of part-Ligurian descent who missed out on being born a Genoese citizen by one year. But the main purpose of appointing these leaders was to plug in to the Genoese network and its special ability to access transnational pools. Hiring a Genoese leader was like buying a Sky television decoder.

Despite their diffuse but real power and their shape-shifting agility, the Genoese met their match in the Ottomans, and were wise enough to realise it. From 1420, the Sultans recovered from post-Timur stress disorder, and acquired their own navy. They also plugged into existing merchant networks (Greek, Armenian, Jewish, and Muslim) and developed close trade relations with Dubrovnik—and with Venice between wars. This left the Genoese with reduced leverage. They hung on in Pera, which was still described as a "Colony of the Genoese" in 1586, and in Chios until 1566.[44] But the Ottomans mopped up the rest of their Aegean and Black Sea possessions, including Foca and Caffa, between 1455 and 1482—with the temporary exception of Cyprus, taken over by the Venetians in 1489 and conquered by the Ottomans in 1571. Long before this, around 1400, a decline in Genoese access to slaves and in the receipts of Pera had become noticeable.[45] Noting the added advantages of access to fresh sugar lands and of leaving the Venetians to go head to head with the Ottomans, the Genoese shifted balance westwards. Before we join them, we need to consider the effects of plague on Genoese power and resilience.

II Genoese Plague Responses:
The Origin of Modern Capitalism?

Far from declining after 1350, Genoa proved to be Europe's leading plague manager. Like other city-states, it was to some extent pre-adapted to post-plague conditions. But its small size, big aspirations, and social and political peculiarities made it especially dynamic. "Despite the ravages of plague, warfare and civil strife . . . Genoa's elite quickly became adept at mobilizing and organizing men, material and money above all else in service of both the peaceful and warlike faces of their Mediterranean ambitions".[46] Specific manpowering techniques included strategic withdrawals from labour-intensive activities, and maximising Genoa's own scant population, both by attracting immigrants and by increasing the willingness of its citizens and subjects to fight for it and invest in it. The Genoese seemed to have pulled out of the land mercenary business soon after 1350, and abandoned the use of labour-intensive galleys for trade, though not warfare, soon after that.[47] They focused on weapons and ship-building at the expense of other industries.[48] Silk manufacture, which employed a moderate 11.6% of the city's workforce in the mid-fifteenth century, and the trademark cotton industry—the word "jean" derives from "Genoa"—were the main exceptions.[49]

Other man-powering measures were more positive, notably the effort to attract outsiders. "To become a citizen of Genoa . . . involved none of the difficulties encountered in Venice, but simply a promise to fulfil the obligations of citizenship".[50] In fact, Venice too eased its citizenship rules, but not on the same scale as Genoa.[51] Taking what seems the best of varying estimates, the pre-plague population of Genoa city in 1347 was about 80,000, reduced to 40,000 in the first strike.[52] It then recovered to 60,000 in 1395, despite further strikes and numerous war deaths. A similar pattern of rapid partial recovery after plague strikes continued to 1580, after which the city was free from plague until 1657, when a last devastating strike occurred. Clearly, Genoa was drawing in people. Ligurians outside the city were granted rights to be "treated just as the people of Genoa and their goods are in Genoa, the district, and everywhere else in the world".[53] There are also signs of an improvement in the treatment of Genoa's Greek subjects in Chios and the Crimea.[54] As in Dubrovnik, sharply increased dowries ensured noblewomen quickly found husbands, and the use of wet nurses—whose own children had usually died—increased.[55] This enhanced birthrates by reducing the gap between pregnancies. The Genoese even had a post-plague state pro-natal policy. Settlers in Corsica were offered baby bonuses[56].

All of this came on top of a long-standing Genoese edge in the competition for crew. They had "a well-organized industry run by contractors" to supply galley crews, and a comparable system run by merchant bankers to recruit crossbowmen and hire them out as mercenaries.[57] While latter activity diminished after 1350, first the French and then the Spanish continued to hire fleets from Genoese clans. There were attempts to "domesticate" particular sections of the transnational manpower pool, to establish special relationships with particular crew regions: Greek islands, Swiss cantons, and Bulgarian districts, though such relationships are better documented for Venice. Genoa continued its traditional tolerance towards Jewish and Muslim merchants, and was quick to welcome an Armenian diaspora, driven out of Cilician Armenia by the Mamluks from 1366. By the early fifteenth century, Armenians provided much of the population of Caffa.[58]

The effort to motivate and mobilise core manpower and expertise in Genoa itself was a complex mix of war, politics, economics, and collective identity. The War of the Bosporus, 1350–1355, required a huge financial as well as military effort from a society recently halved by plague, but with plague-boosted disposable incomes. The challenge was met by transforming the public debt into shares, seldom refundable but interest-bearing and saleable privately, and by increasing both the number of investors and the amount invested. Seven thousand Genoese contributed to the initial 300,000 lira loan for this war, and an even greater amount was subscribed for the War of Chioggia, taking the public debt to 3 million lira by 1400—one source implies this was equivalent to 108 tons of silver.[59] This helped make the Genoese "precocious innovators in the field of borrowing". It also "effectively redefined the political body", generating an "increasing equation of citizen with lender". [60] If your retirement fund was invested in public debt, you could not afford the collapse of the state. A simultaneous political shift had a similar outcome. From 1363, political tumult saw noble clans forced to share high public office.[61] Rich non-noble families then rose to prominence, including the Adorno and Campofregoso. Sources note the "gradual but increasingly forceful rise of both families during the second half of the fourteenth century".[62] This was no democracy, but the civic role of lesser "commoners"—small businessmen and master artisans— did increase.[63] Membership of the key councils was shared equally between nobles and commoners.[64] The nobles resented this, but their economic power remained, including their substantial share of the public debt. Neither they, nor the people at large, could afford the fall of the state. But the notion that "Genoese civic identity was predicated on individual benefit" needs qualification.[65] In the War of Chioggia, both classes showed that they fought for more than their purses. An old but plausible estimate for the deaths of Genoese citizens in that conflict is 8,000[66]—something like a fifth of the adult men in Liguria at the time, a World War I mortality rate. "Given the degree of internal division within Genoa and the divisiveness of Genoese society, the city's forces at sea usually showed remarkable unity of intent and action".[67] Genoa had few people, but was able to mobilise and motivate an increasing proportion of them.

When solidarity lapsed, which was still quite often, the Genoese pulled in foreign mediators in the form of hired *podesta* (chief magistrates), or by "giving themselves" to princely overlords, notably the rulers of Milan and the kings of France. Once seen as an indicator of decline, these measures seem to have had little real impact on Genoa's independence, let alone that of the Genoese diaspora.[68] The frequency with which podesta and overlords were sacked supports this, as does other evidence. Doge Antoniotto Adorno managed a handover to France in 1396, but continued "to pull the strings from behind the scenes".[69] In any case, this first spell of French "rule" ended in 1409, and the second lasted only three years, 1458–61. A longer spell began in 1494 or 1499, and ended in 1512 or 1528—again, dates differ suspiciously.[70] In 1528, a coup led by the great admiral Andrea Doria took over the government. It consolidated an alliance with Hapsburg Spain and reduced the number of merchant clans to 28. The Genoese fiscal achievement peaked thereafter, when they "overwhelmingly dominated the Spanish crown's finances".[71] But the roots of the system lie in the decades immediately after the Black Death.

While they seldom associate it with plague, some scholars have long suspected a Genoese role in the origins of (modern European) capitalism and in the emergence of growth-friendly financial institutions, such as central banks, currency exchanges, joint-stock companies, permanent tradeable public debt, and the book settlement of private debt, which in effect modestly increased the money supply. Goods were eventually paid for, and profits taken, in bullion, but at any given moment, the money supply was a few percent greater than the amount of bullion in circulation. Bills of exchange had a similar effect. While the role of such institutions can be exaggerated, and artificially separated from other factors, it did exist and was significant. Other scholars persist in locating the birth of modern fiscal institutions in the Netherlands from about 1600, followed by England from 1688. Post-plague northern Italy, and Genoa in particular, is a more likely place and time of origin.

In 1407, the Genoese established a central bank, the Bank of St George, and the public debt was transferred to it. The debt has been estimated at the equivalent 191 tons of silver in 1500, *before* Genoa began receiving bullion from the Americas via Spain, a 77% increase on 1400.[72] Despite Genoa's reputation for political instability, and despite low interest rates, the bank and its tradeable shares (*luoghi*) enjoyed public confidence—inside and outside Genoa. "A multitude of small investors, Genoese and others, entrusted their savings to the bankers for modest returns".[73] Genoa had long participated in an overland trade through Switzerland and France to the Low Countries, featuring "exchange fairs" at which goods were traded and debts in different currencies were settled. Before the Black Death, the most important were located in Champagne, and the goods involved were carried by mule trains. Once the maritime route north began to use capacious carracks after 1380, the overland route ceased to make sense for cargoes of any bulk, but became even more important for "business": the settlement of debts, the placing of investments, and the transfer of bullion—preferably gold because it was 12 times easier to carry than the same value of silver. The rise of regular mounted courier services, often dated to around 1500 and associated with the German von Taxis family,[74] in fact began with the *scarsella genovese* (named for the leather letter bag), in the later fourteenth century.[75] Averaging 50 kilometres a day, these could transport information from Genoa to Bruges faster than a carrack or great galley, a pioneering separation of communication and transport in which each served the other. The Genoese participated increasingly in the banking side of the overland route, and the location of the key exchange fairs moved south towards them, first to Geneva and Lyon in the fifteenth century, then to Besançon and Piacenza in the sixteenth.[76] Partly through the fairs, and partly through the attractions of the Bank of St George, "the capital of the Italian cities was all drained towards Genoa".[77]

One problem with the bulk maritime trade to Northern Europe was the risk of attack by pirates and privateers. Maritime insurance emerged, in Genoa from 1350, though historians seem reluctant to explicitly implicate plague. "The first known policies were written in Genoa in the mid-fourteenth century".[78] "The timing of the emergence of maritime insurance in the mid fourteenth century was linked to an increase in individual disposable capital".[79] The number of insurance contracts signed before notaries in Genoa increased from the 1370s. It peaked in 1428–32 and declined from 1440 because the law now recognised private insurance contracts, and notaries were no longer needed.[80] As mentioned in chapter 5, the same scribal transition, saving the time of surviving notaries, occurred earlier with more familiar types of contract. Maritime insurance did not reduce risk-taking; indeed, it increased the collective willingness to take risk by sharing it. Early insurers were private individuals taking a small share of the risk, not specialised companies.[81] There are hints from elsewhere that early maritime insurance might have been seen as a form of gambling,[82] which itself may have surged after the Black Death. Playing cards appeared in Italy and Spain in the last quarter of the fourteenth century.[83]

Formal lotteries are known only from the 1440s, but seem already "fully developed, which suggests that that lotteries had been ongoing for some time".[84] Whatever the case with this, in post-plague Genoa, insured and insurers were drawn from the same group, and the contracts reinforced group ties.[85] Groups were certainly in flux among the Genoese at the time, and this too may have interesting implications for the origin of capitalism.

The Black Death, and to a lesser extent each subsequent plague, shattered families, large and small, which then regrouped. At the simplest level, widows and widowers remarried, and orphaned children were adopted. There is also widespread evidence of regrouping on a larger scale, notably in the form of religious fraternities, some based on shared occupations and so blurring with craft guilds. "Fraternities had existed before the Black Death but multiplied considerably after it".[86] Fraternities were "a form of surrogate family", "they acted as artificial families, tied not by blood but by common rule".[87] Actual extended families, tied by blood or some substitute for it, could play this game too, and in Genoa they did so.

Even before plague, for the Genoese elite, "family" was a malleable concept, extensible through marriage, adoption, apprenticeship, service, and godparentage. The Genoese noble merchant clans came to be known as *alberghi*, a usage first documented in 1267. Literally "inns", these occupied neighbourhoods within the city itself.[88] But it was after the Black Death that these "family consortia . . . became the linchpin of the city's social structure".[89] The new elite of wealthy commoner families that emerged after 1350, seen by some as a "new nobility", may have felt the need to match the old nobility in numbers and security as well as wealth. One expert defines the *albergo* as "a social network formed by a new Genoese nobility that went beyond their own family".[90] New alberghi were formed of *groups* of families. "Much more than a simple alliance between families; they represented a fusion of the families composing it".[91] They either took the name of the leading family or adopted an entirely new name. "Abandoning the ancestral name was a serious step and an indication of the strong desire to form a new unit with the same solidarity as the old kindred group".[92] The old nobility seems to have responded by incorporating lesser families into their alberghi. In 1455, the Spinola "family" included at least 135 households. Such urban tribes proliferated after 1350. "Around seventy existed in the 1370s, about a hundred in 1400". By 1467, 95% of households in Genoa were organised into alberghi. As noted above, the number was reduced by Doria fiat in 1528 to 28 clans, to which most townsfolk belonged.[93] This probably worked to reduce the power of the common folk and increase that of the elite.

A comparable evolution occurred in a similar entity, the *mahona* or *maona*, used from 1235 for groups participating in a shared enterprise outside the city. It differed from business partnerships (*commenda*) in that it was intended to be permanent, and as with alberghi came to adopt a shared surname. The most prominent example was the Giustiniani, a fusion of a dozen non-noble merchant families established to run Chios in 1362—which it did for more than two centuries. The first Chios mahona was established in 1349, then reformed in 1362. By 1566 it had more than 600 shareholders.[94] The Giustiniani also had an albergo in Genoa. Other less successful mahona emerged in the later fourteenth century, attempting to govern Cyprus (1374, reformed 1403) and Corsica (1378).[95] Of the six identifiable mahona, five post-date the Black Death. Mahona were non-state organisations, but were officially recognised by the city commune, and since 1913, scholars have seen in them an origin for European mercantile chartered companies, such as the English and Dutch East India Companies. Some alberghi too had formal rules requiring members "to act and comport themselves in all things as if they were born of the said name".[96] But these rules and recognitions merely registered a post-plague socioeconomic reshuffling: they did not drive it, and this is also true of another type of group—long-term alliances of several clans that were not formal mahona, but informal syndicates that had no official existence. They were linked by intermarriage, god-parentage, and the exchange of sons as apprentice merchants, to whom one should "act like I would in the future for a son of yours".[97] "A certain convergence of interests, strengthened by ties of marriage, occur[ed] between the Campofregoso and the Doria and Grimaldi on the one hand and the Adorno . . . Spinola, Malaspina, and Del Carretto on the other".[98] This reflected "the pervasive role of clans in Genoa", and a greater preference than Venice for informal rules, rather than the use of expensive and cumbersome law courts.[99]

Informal syndicates also formed to a lesser degree in other North Italian cities, such as Florence, after the plague. They do seem a plausible ancestor for the modern company or firm, though not one likely to be popular with those economists who prefer a rational individualist lineage. They echo the semantic association of kin and company—*com panis*, those with whom you shared bread, at a shared table or *board*. Something functionally similar can be detected among the German banking clans of Augsburg and Nuremburg.[100] I am not convinced that "institutional" is the right descriptor for some of these developments. They seem more a matter of social or cultural history, or even historical anthropology. There may be a neo-tribal strand of fictive kinship in the origin of companies and multinational corporations, and perhaps modern European capitalism itself, incubated by plague rather than Progress.

III Iberian Entanglements: Portugal

In the century after 1415, Portugal settled four Atlantic archipelagoes, established a string of trading forts along the West African coast, each allied to local African polities, and acquired significant coastal territories in Angola and western Morocco. This last proved temporary but, across the Atlantic, after several private ventures, the Portuguese crown consolidated control of patches of coastal Brazil from 1549. The northeastern region (Bahia and Pernambuco) became the world's leading sugar exporter around 1570. Along with the Bretons and Basques, the Portuguese also pioneered Newfoundland cod fishing from 1499, sending up to 100 small ships there annually until about 1550, after which they delegated the trade to others, having more profitable things to do.[101] Portugal acquired some 50 forts and ports in East Africa, India, and Southeast Asia, including the great cities of Melaka (1511) and Hormuz (1515). Portuguese merchants reached China in 1516, and established a base in 1557 at Macao, with Ming consent, followed by a trading post in Japan at Nagasaki in 1571.

As many have noted, Portugal was an unlikely base for this remarkable expansion.[102] In 1415, it had no more than 900,000 people, but may have begun its demographic recovery earlier than most. It was not itself well-endowed with natural resources or growth-friendly institutions. It was once quite common to suggest that Genoese connections solved the mystery, but this view seems to have lost traction in recent decades. Certainly, Genoa seldom features in the explanations for Portugal's first overseas conquest, of Ceuta in Morocco in 1415. Instead, these debate Portuguese motives: reviving the Reconquista (after 166 years); consolidating the new royal dynasty, established in 1385; or keeping the military nobility out of mischief. It has been suggested that "the Genoese were clearly not happy with this military campaign in Ceuta, for it had ruined their commercial operations there".[103] In fact, as we saw in chapter 4, their commercial operations, especially the acquisition of West African gold, had already been compromised, by civil war in Morocco and the consequent disruption of the trans-Saharan trade. Though Portugal might not have been the top priority of Genoese merchants in 1415,[104] their influence there was substantial. "Italians, particularly the Genoese, probably handled the bulk of Portugal's maritime trade, as well as supplying credit and banking services".[105] The Pessagnos were still hereditary admirals, and other merchant clans had also established themselves. Virtually every ship in the Portuguese mercantile fleet was used for the Ceuta expedition, which was hardly possible without Genoese cooperation.[106] One source explicitly states that the Genoese backed the expedition financially, and another implies it.[107] Of course, the Genoese played both sides and continued to feature prominently in Muslim Fez as well as Christian Ceuta.[108] The flow of gold did revive—the disruption dates "from the late 1390s until the second decade of the fifteenth century".[109]

What the Portuguese then did was establish a mini-empire in the eastern Atlantic, a springboard for expansion, partly predating and largely enabling their American and Asian adventures. They did so with substantial Genoese help. The springboard had three regional components: West Africa, the Atlantic islands, and Morocco. In the last, early efforts to expand beyond Ceuta were mostly unsuccessful, but between 1471 and 1515, the Portuguese managed to conquer most of Morocco's Atlantic coast including 10 port towns, such as Mazagan, Safi, Mogador, and Agadir. These towns produced textiles in demand in West Africa, which were used in the trans-Saharan trade. About 40% of gold and slaves received were paid for with Moroccan textiles. "Moroccan cloth was considered a luxury item in [West] Africa."[110] Inland of these Moroccan towns were fertile regions, producing a grain surplus, interspersed with more arid regions, producing horses. The Portuguese allied with nomad pastoralists from the latter, and with their help exacted grain as tribute, which provided about half the 9,000 tons annually that they took from Morocco at peak.[111] "The great grain-producing plains of Morocco . . . became a very important part of . . . the Atlantic world the Portuguese created".[112] This was important because Portugal itself had an increasing grain deficit. Horses helped West African polities defend themselves from slave-taking cavalry from further inland, so there was huge demand for them as well as for cloth. The Portuguese acquired their horses in Morocco, "either by purchase or through tribute", to trade for slaves farther south.[113] The Moroccan ports, each with its Genoese traders, were also convenient outlets for the trans-Saharan trade, cutting the distance caravans had to travel, and they supplemented the gold and slaves extracted from Portugal's West African trading posts, notably Arguin (Mauretania) established in 1445, and Sao Jorge da Mina (El Mina, Ghana, 1482). (See map 5.1.)

> Although the Portuguese [later] relied mainly on Arguin and Sao Jorge da Mina for their supplies of African gold, until the year 1510 commerce with towns along Morocco's Atlantic littoral yielded supplies of both gold dust

and minted gold coins whose value . . . sometimes exceeded that taken in trade at these more famous locations. Between the years 1495 and 1498, for example, the value of gold acquired at Safi exceeded by 37 percent that of the gold dust taken at Mina.[114]

The Portuguese military edge over the Moroccans eroded from 1515. A large Portuguese army was crushed at Alcazar in 1578 by a new, reformist, Moroccan dynasty (see chapter 13). Portugal's first empire, in Morocco, collapsed. Historians note, rightly, that it had become extremely expensive in men and money. But it did fulfill that springboard role.

Portuguese voyages along the West African coast began in 1419, seeking slaves and cheap gold. The Genoese were involved from the outset. That ship's compasses were known in Portugal as "Genoese needles" encapsulates their contribution.[115] A Genoese syndicate set up the first slaving company, in 1444, at Lagos, Portugal's southernmost port. [116] Genoese capital was probably behind Fernao Gomes, who leased the crown monopoly on the "Guinea" (West African) trade for a time from 1469.[117] By 1500, the Genoese "dominated the early supply of slaves from Senegambia to Lisbon and Cabo Verde"—the Cape Verde Islands off the Guinea coast.[118] These islands became an important hub of both the slave trade and a hybrid "Black Portuguese" cross-culture, discussed in chapter 15. The Genoese introduced sugar plantations to the islands, which they had helped to settle in the 1450s and 1460s. It was here, in 1462, that they are thought to have made their most dubious contribution to global history, the first sugar plantation worked mainly by black slaves. The Genoese clan "credited" with this invention was the De Nolli, minor nobles from the Ligurian town of that name who around 1450 brought their three ships from the Eastern Mediterranean into the Atlantic in Portuguese service. They intermarried with the Portuguese elite, participated in the slave and gold trades, and established a base on one of the Cape Verde Islands.[119] Here, "early Cape Verde colonists, led by their Genoese ruler, created an Italian-style colony on the fringe of European and African societies".[120]

The Genoese established a more successful sugar industry in Madeira from 1446, which they continued to dominate. "In 1472, Portuguese cultivators on Madeira protested against Genoese hegemony in the sugar trade".[121] Around 1500, Madeira briefly became the leading sugar exporter, with 200 mills and an output of around 3,000 tons. But the fertile island's lowland timber resources were quickly exhausted, for ship timber and sugar-making fuel, and its sugar output declined thereafter. The Sao Tomé Islands in the Gulf of Guinea, settled from 1480, had a similar career as a sugar exporter in the mid-sixteenth century, with 60 larger sugar mills producing the same amount as Madeira at peak. Sao Tomé, like the Cape Verdes, also served as a hub of the slave trade and a base for the "Black Portuguese". The Genoese also introduced sugar plantations to the Azores, but these islands proved unsuitable and so were instead turned to grain-growing. Three times the size of Madeira, they were very fertile, producing two to three times the yield per seed of grain in Portugal.[122] They became "the Granary of Lisbon and Madeira".[123] The Azores and Madeira had mainly white settlers and, as we saw in chapter 6, provided very much more than their share of Brazil's settler foremothers.

Between about 1440 and 1480, as Genoa's westward shift in the Mediterranean gathered pace, "many Genoese men sailed to Portugal, and most never returned to Italy", Christopher Columbus among them.[124] Like the De Nolli, Columbus married into the Portuguese nobility, and others did likewise. Four merchant clans, including the Doria, intermarried with the influential Portuguese Da Costas for instance.[125] From 1492, the Genoese shifted balance again, leaning more towards Spain than Portugal, but as usual retaining some ties, just in case. They financed the establishment of Macao,[126] and their influence in the *Estado Da India* (the Portuguese patchwork "empire" in Asia) persisted into the seventeenth century. In 1625, despite a ban on foreign merchants, eight Genoese living in Goa offered a large loan to the *Estado*.[127]

None of this is to deny Portuguese agency in its own expansion. Portugal itself was of course a crucial base, partly because of its own plague adaptations. A recent pessimist interpretation of the post-plague economy is contradicted by several lines of evidence.[128] One is the expansion of maritime activity from as early as 1360.[129] Another indicator is the increasing role of sales taxes from 1372. These boosted royal revenues by 41% by 1401.[130] A third is the increasing demand for Setubal salt, the best in Europe, for the expanding northern fisheries.[131] A fourth is the growth of Lisbon *before* 1500 which, given the diminished general population, indicates increased centralisation, specialisation, and commercialisation. Lisbon had 14,000 people in the thirteenth century; 35,000 in 1400, and perhaps 50,000 by 1500, despite numerous plagues, before burgeoning to 165,000 by the early seventeenth century.[132] Finally, as increasing grain imports suggest, there was a shift to more valuable farm products such as livestock, flax, olives, and grapes. By 1500, 43% of agricultural output came from livestock and 16% from wine, with only 38% from cereals.[133] The post-plague livestock were bigger as well as more numerous.[134] The shift was particularly marked in Minho in the north, allowing it to become one of the great crew-producing regions.[135] None of this was enough to fund the huge Ceuta expedition, of 20,000 men and at least 200 ships—the loans were still being paid off in 1440[136]—but it did help.

The plague-incubated development of Portuguese expansive technology is noticeable from the 1370s, when guns, gun forts, and steel armour appear, along with larger caravels. There were also various improvements in military organisation. "From 1380 to 1415 fundamental developments occurred in the Portuguese way of war".[137] This Portuguese expansion kit does not seem to have reached maturity in time to help in the earlier Moroccan campaigns. Both sides had some guns at the taking of Ceuta, but it is Portuguese numbers and Moroccan divisions that seem decisive. As noted in chapter 7, a Portuguese expedition of 2,000 men to the Canary Islands in 1424 was disastrously defeated by the Canarians, who had no guns or steel at all. In 1436–37 the Moroccans, with few guns, heavily defeated a Portuguese attack on Tangier.[138] In the 1460s, four further attacks on Tangier also failed. But in 1471, the Portuguese took Arzila nearby, having "blasted the gates with terrifying artillery fire", and Tangier surrendered.[139] Most Portuguese victories in Morocco occurred between 1471 and 1515.

Indeed, tiny Portugal's military edge at this time may have been global. Portuguese galleons were adapted from Genoese carracks, and Genoese financiers were involved in the establishment of strategic industries such as the Lisbon docks and armoury.[140] Middle European bronze guns were acquired once there was West African gold to pay for them. But Portugal itself took the lead in caravels and guns on ships, defeating a larger Castilian fleet in 1478, as noted in chapter 5. The Portuguese were apparently the first to use canister shot in cannon and are said to have led Europe in cannon technology by 1500.[141] Thousands of expensive cast-bronze cannon supplemented their small garrisons in Morocco and Asia by 1525.[142] By that time, they had 21 gun galleons in the Indian Ocean, an oceanic fleet not even the Ottomans could match, as the next chapter will show. Portuguese expeditions inland often failed. Between 1550 and 1638 for instance, five were defeated by the inland kingdom of Kandy in Sri Lanka.[143] But Portuguese fortified ports could not be taken. Some were acquired through negotiation with local rulers who welcomed an alternative merchant network (chapter 9). But others fell to amphibious Portuguese assaults, using ship's boats mounting breech-loading swivel guns able to fire faster than Indian guns, while another "transitional technology", steel armour, gave an additional edge (chapter 7). In the early decades in Asia, there was a certain mad-dog quality to the Portuguese, similar to that of the Spanish in Mexico and Peru at the same time. But the Portuguese soon learned that they had to have local allies and inland merchant networks, and so tempered their aggression.

Patches of coastal Brazil and Angola apart, Portuguese expansion was less an empire than a semi-global necklace of fortified trading ports, Ceuta to Macao, and it brought home only about 3,000 tons of Further Asian goods a year. But as a profiteering globaliser, reshuffling goods, slaves, biota, and bullion around the planet, it can be underestimated. Value was high, even if volumes were not. The Portuguese extracted about 80 tons of gold from West Africa between 1480 and 1620, and by the later sixteenth century were acquiring similar annual quantities of gold from the Zimbabwe region as well.[144] Profits on the West African gold were around 500%.[145] Asian spice profits were huge too. Pepper sold in Lisbon brought eight times its Indian price, and the Portuguese imported between 1,000 and 2,000 tons a year. The markups on the several hundred tons of other spices were higher still. "During the first half of the sixteenth century, Portugal was the wealthiest country in Europe. . . . by 1518, overseas trade accounted for 68 percent of its national revenues".[146] Brazil produced sugar from 1557, and was the leading exporter between about 1580 and 1650. Private profits here were a modest 30%, but that was after the crown took a similar sized cut.[147]

Much of this wealth, however, went to other European powers, in return for manufactures such as cannon and cloth, and it whetted rival appetites for a share in the trade. From 1578, Portugal fell on hard times, not so much as a result of dynastic union with Spain, 1580–1640, which is now thought to have been quite benign, but through defeats by rivals, old and new. The defeat at Alcazar cost 15,000 men, the Mughal conquests of Gujarat and Bengal in the 1570s restrained operations in India, and Japan expelled the Portuguese in 1639. Above all, from 1592, the Dutch made a determined attempt to take over the Portuguese empire, a matter left for chapter 12. Relative decline was quite sharp from 1620, yet the Portuguese empire showed a remarkable resilience, due to its own peculiar hybridity rather than any ongoing help from the Genoese. But its early sins and successes were co-created by its own plague adaptations and by Genoese midwifery, itself a part-product of plague.

IV Iberian Entanglements: Spain

A unified Spain emerged in 1479 through the marriage of Isabella of Castile and Ferdinand of Aragon ten years earlier. In 1516, Charles V Hapsburg inherited both kingdoms and Aragon's claims in southern Italy. He already held the extensive domains of the Dukes of Burgundy, including the Low Countries, and the old Hapsburg lands in and around Austria, the management of which was delegated to his brother Ferdinand. In 1519, Charles bribed his way to election as Holy Roman Emperor with two tons of gold.[148] Through the marriage of his son Phillip, of Armada fame, to Queen Mary Tudor, the Hapsburgs were one baby away from acquiring England too. Through various inheritances and alliances, they also controlled most of Italy, and even had an eye on the throne of Denmark-Norway.[149] Outside Europe, the Spanish conquered the Canaries and the larger Caribbean islands between 1480 and 1510, and then the Aztec and Inca empires in the 1520s and the 1530s. From 1565, they acquired a strategic position in the Philippines where they exchanged Chinese silk for American silver. Spain's North African empire proved temporary and is less well-known, but at various times between 1497 and 1574 it included most of the Maghreb's Mediterranean coast between Melilla, near Ceuta, and Tripoli.[150] Around 40% of Western Europeans owed some sort of allegiance to Charles V.[151] He abdicated in 1556, allocating the imperial crown and the Austrian lands to Ferdinand and the rest to Phillip. But this did not end the Hapsburg European Union; dynastic cooperation continued until 1648.

The role of the Genoese as Spain's bankers, after their formal alliance with Spain in 1528, is amply acknowledged in the literature. What is less well understood is that this entwining began earlier and went wider. The Mediterranean grain trade revived quite quickly after the Black Death. Whereas Venice and Florence had been Genoa's peers in this trade before 1350, their hinterlands provided a higher percentage of their grain than was the case with mountainous Liguria. So Genoa had the incentive to take the lead in the revived post-plague trade, drawing its wheat from the Black Sea littoral and southern Italy. "Given its scope and international character, the grain trade may have been the most important of Genoese enterprises".[152] Genoese merchants had a strong presence in southwest Andalusia and its chief port, Seville, as well as Murcia, and in Granada and its ports of Malaga and Almeria. These regions turned naturally to the Genoese for grain as they shifted to more valuable export crops. Granada began importing Sicilian grain via the Genoese in 1378, and Seville at about the same time.[153] Both became dependent on these supplies, "not just as occasion required, but continuously".[154] Somewhat later, Valencia also became dependent on Genoese grain.[155] Many decades before the formal Spanish alliance of 1528, the Genoese had southern Spain by the bread.

Southern Andalusia (Castile), Granada (Muslim and independent to 1492), and the Kingdom of Valencia (subject to independent Aragon to 1479) were at first eggs in separate political baskets. Genoese relations with all three regions intensified after the 1370s and went far beyond grain supply. "Throughout southern Spain in the late Middle Ages, the most significant merchant group was the Genoese".[156] They encouraged, funded, and organised the new export crops: sugar, silk, rice, wine, olive oil, and dried figs and raisins. There were forty Genoese merchants in Muslim Malaga in the mid-fifteenth century, and another group headed by the Spinola clan had close relations with the Nasrid emirs inland in Granada city itself.[157] The Genoese presence in Seville was even larger, and doubled between 1450 and 1500 to as many as 400 merchants.[158] The Seville Genoese were not very prominent in loans to the Spanish crown, which were mostly handled by merchants from Genoa itself; they had plenty of other business.[159]

The kingdom of Valencia had perhaps the most plague-boosted economy in Western Europe. Government revenues increased by 230% between 1315 and 1415.[160] Genoese trade with Valencia was already strong in 1379, but a fly in this ointment was sporadic conflict with its overlord, Aragon. This ceased in 1458, and economic links thrived, with most Valencian exports going to Genoa from about 1470 for consumption or redistribution.[161] Valencia city doubled in size between 1418 and 1497.[162] In all,

> economic growth in the southern region of the Iberian Peninsula can be mainly linked to Genoese trade. Indeed, Genoese merchants played a key role in joining up diverse trading areas (for example, they included Seville, Granada, and Valencia in their trading network). They organized production activities in areas like Granada and Valencia, while at the same time playing an important role in the transmission of technical knowledge.[163]

Genoa developed a similar relationship with what became Spanish domains in southern Italy, the Kingdom of Naples and Sicily. The relationship dates back to 1250, but intensified with the Genoese-mediated revival of the post-plague grain trade from the 1370s, of which Sicily and the Apulia region of Naples were key suppliers.[164] The Genoese also encouraged the extension of dairying, sugar and cotton cultivation in Sicily and of silk in Calabria, another Neapolitan region. Links grew despite tension with Aragon, which took over Naples in 1442, and developed even further under united Spanish rule from 1503. Increasingly, resident Genoese shared even rural power with Spanish and Neapolitan elites. At peak, in the 1630s, "the Genoese controlled 1200 fiefs out of 2700 rural centers of the Kingdom of Naples". They held "almost all" of the kingdom's debt of 80 million ducats. In the great city of Naples itself, the Genoese headed one-third of the guilds and owned one-third of the banks.[165]

What we seem to have here is a strange, informal and trans-sub-national, economic entity, a Genoese urban colonisation of southern Spain and southern Italy. As its alternative Black Sea source was taken over by Istanbul, Genoa became increasingly dependent on southern Italian grain, but that region's economy was also dependent on Genoa. Southern Spain too was dependent on Genoese-transported wheat, plus the higher-value agricultural exports that this enabled, which went to or through the Genoese. In both its great semi-colonies, Genoese influence helped economic development, and its own economy adapted in response over time. From about 1570, Genoa revived its own manufacturing, partly though "putting out" in Liguria, whose population grew strongly in the sixteenth century. Silk looms quadrupled to 10,000, employing 35,000 people, between 1531 and the 1570s.[166] It exported iron and steel products, paper, and cotton, wool, and silk textiles, as well as ships. Almost all of these products went to Spain.[167] The raw wool came from the Spanish *mesta* system;[168] the silk and cotton from southern Italy. The net impression is of an integrated triangular economy, with Genoa at the apex, intertwined with the broader fiscal role in Spain.

Urban colonisation can be "symbiotic", benefiting both parties, or more oppressively colonial. What was the case here? In southern Spain, it seems to have tended towards symbiosis. There were Spanish complaints about "Genoese leeches" in Seville,[169] but like Valencia, the city thrived under leech leadership, doubling in size during the fifteenth century—before the inflow of American bullion—then booming from 14,000 people in 1500 to 122,000 in 1590.[170] Granada also did quite well from its Genoese relationship, though it suffered heavy economic damage in the Spanish conquest of 1482–92. Southern Italy may be a different story. One fine recent study claims that Genoese "symbiotic imperialism led not to stagnation but rather to prosperity in southern Italy", but seems conflicted. An earlier version suggested that "the Genoese relationship to the Kingdom of Naples can be described as predation".[171] The same author also provides evidence for two tests of the issue. First, from about 1570, under Genoese influence, Naples turned from making its own silk textiles to exporting raw silk to Genoa—a case of "deindustrialization" like that by the British in nineteenth-century India. Second, grain was exported to Genoa even during south Italian famines. The Spanish viceroy of Naples objected, but was overruled by the Spanish king in favour of the Genoese.[172]

Urban colonisation depends on open sea-lanes, and their defense was very much a Genoese-Spanish joint venture. I suspect this is one factor behind the surprisingly large effort Spain put into the conquest of North Africa, where it may have lost up to 200,000 men in the sixteenth century (counting wastage in garrisons). It lost 58,000 men in four major battles, and there were many more. Galley warfare required sequences of ports for the frequent uptake of supplies and water, hence its need for a string of ports rather than the one or two major bases that sufficed for galleons. Spain's first conquest, 1505–1512, was relatively easy. Even at this stage, before the formal alliance of 1528, the Spanish were supported by the Genoese, whose fleet defeated the famous Barbarossa brothers at La Goletta in 1512.[173] But the Barbarossa then acquired Ottoman support, and struck back. Bloody amphibious warfare lurched back and forth along the Maghrebi coast until 1580. "Genoese control over the naval forces of the Mediterranean rivaled Genoese control over Spanish finances", and the Hapsburgs were delighted to receive their help.[174] In the lead-up to the formal alliance of 1528, Emperor Charles V wrote: "do anything to persuade the said Andrea Doria to enter my service, whatever it may cost me".[175] The Spanish-Genoese had their victories. They retook Tunis in 1535, ejected a Franco-Ottoman invasion of Corsica in 1559, narrowly fought off an invasion of Malta in 1565, and helped win the great fleet battle of Lepanto in 1571. But, on balance, the war ended in a limited Muslim victory. Spain's holdings in North Africa were restricted to a few modest westerly ports, and Ottoman-backed corsairs raided freely from the regencies of Algiers, Tunis, and Tripoli. Over the course of the seventeenth century, this gradually eroded the maritime capacity of Italy's and Spain's Mediterranean coast.

Whatever the case with the sharing of benefits, the Genoese-led Italian-Spanish triangular economy has important implications. It was strong and long-lasting, from the 1370s to the 1630s. The expanding Spanish wool trade in the north and other evidence, noted in chapter 3, demonstrate why, contrary to legend, the plague-adapted "Spanish" economy was quite healthy during its early imperial adventures in the sixteenth century. It helps explain the strength of Genoese attachment to the Spanish empire, and their persistence in funding it—by the seventeenth century they were in too deep to readily detach themselves. Furthermore, the Seville end of the triangular economy made a good springboard for Spanish Atlantic expansion, in which the Genoese were also prominent, from well before 1528.

The Spanish conquest of the Canary Islands, 1477–92, was "made possible by financing from Genoese bankers".[176] The same syndicates were among the financiers of the first voyage of their kinsman Columbus in 1492.[177] The Seville Genoese had fingers in every Spanish imperial pie. They "helped finance the sugar plantations in the Atlantic islands, the voyages overseas, the colonisation of the

Americas, and the exploitation of the major silver mines in Mexico and Peru".[178] "In the early years of trade with America, they were by far the most important group of investors".[179] They dominated the slave trade to the Canaries and established sugar plantations there, then transferred both to the Caribbean. They paid the Spanish crown 25,000 ducats for the formal right to supply of slaves to the Americas in 1517, but their first slave exports pre-date that.[180] They may have set up sugar mills in Hispaniola by 1503, and had certainly done so by the 1510s. They extended sugar planting and milling to Mexico from the 1520s[181] The "best commercial network in Spain", mentioned in chapter 7, which backed the conquest of Mexico from 1520, was of course Genoese. But their main role in American bullion was on the eastern side of the Atlantic.

Between 1500 and 1650, the Spanish extracted a minimum of 181 tons of gold and 16,800 tons of silver from the Americas.[182] Smuggling made the true figures at least 20% higher. The gold exceeded the take from West Africa; while the silver, worth ten times as much, is said to have increased world output fourfold. The early flow was mainly gold, from the Caribbean, Mexico, and Peru.[183] This was a diminishing resource; finite alluvial deposits from Hispaniola's rivers, and plunder and melting down of the gold accumulated over generations by the Aztecs and Incas for ornaments. As with other extractive and expansive trades, declining output in the 1530s stimulated the search for alternative sources. More alluvial gold was found in Colombia from the 1550s, and that region experienced a series of modest rushes thereafter.[184] By far the main source of bullion to 1650 was the silver mountain of Potosi, discovered in the Andes in 1545, close to an Inca silver mine.[185] Native Andean knowledge, skill, food supplies, and labour, both coerced and paid, were crucial for the rapid development of Potosi. But it has to be said that the early modern Spanish, not known for technical innovativeness, were no slouches when it came to extracting bullion. The Spanish began adapting a better refining process using mercury ("quicksilver") amalgamation as early as 1554, and perfected it by 1571.[186] In 1572, they used Andean labour to construct dams able to supply water for dozens of large water-powered mills.[187] These and other measures increased Potosi's silver output sevenfold by 1585.[188] By 1611, Potosi had a population of 160,000, despite being in a "desolate, arid landscape" 4,000 metres above sea level,[189] surely larger than any industrial city in Europe. Spanish planning and Amerindian labour handled the production, but the distribution of all this silver required help from the Genoese.

The contribution of American bullion to Spanish crown revenues peaked at 32% in 1559,[190] and was more often around 20% of a rising revenue. But it was liquid and disposable, not earmarked for the uses expected by domestic tax-payers, some of whose money came from private silver inflows in any case. Most was spent on wars, against the French and against German, Dutch, and English Protestants, as well as the Ottomans. It was distributed throughout Europe, paying armies and fleets, subsidising allies, buying weapons, horses, and supplies. Genoese often acted as brokers in these payments, but also vacu-umed the savings of southern suppliers back up through the exchange fairs and bank deposits noted earlier in this chapter. This cash was then lent back to the Spanish crown, giving it a second bite at the same coin. Two economists consider this to be "global finance at its best".[191] Initially, lending to the Spanish state was shared with German bankers who drew bullion from new or rejuve-nated mines in central and south-eastern Europe.[192] Even so, the leading German bankers, the Fuggers and Welsers, lent Spain 9.7 million ducats between 1521 and 1555, compared to 19.6 million from the Genoese.[193] Thereafter, Genoese dominance of, and dependence on, the management of Spanish American bullion intensified.

A tiny number of Genoese syndicates, or clan alliances, perhaps as few as three, handled the lending of recycled American bullion to Spain. But constant warfare—Philip II was at war every year of his reign, 1556–98—meant that that silver flowed out even faster than it flowed in. Between 1557 and 1596, the crown suspended interest payments to the Genoese four times, who each time denied it fresh loans until it negotiated a settlement. Any crack in the united front, such as a one clan accepting payments denied to the others in return for fresh loans, would have let the crown off the hook. There was no crack, despite the fact that some clans involved were hereditary enemies. The loans were organised by overlapping syndicates. Clan A and Clan B might be feuding and unable to work with each other, but each was in a separate syndicate with Clan C, which prevented A or B using the situation to go one up on their rival.[194] Here, the Genoese showed how they could combine division and unity. These financial crises were suspensions, not defaults or state bankruptcies as they are sometimes described,[195] and the Genoese lent an additional 20 million ducats between 1598 and 1607, 88% of all Spanish borrowing.[196] By this time, however, interest on long-term debt was closing on half of Spanish government spending[197]—more than twice the silver revenue coming in from the Americas. There was then a brief hiatus in warfare, which recommenced with a vengeance in 1618 with the onset of the Thirty Years' War. The financial system creaked on until about 1640, when it and Spain began a sharp decline. The Genoese began trying to lean away from Spanish loans from about 1608,[198] but they were entwined too tightly with Spain to wholly extract themselves, and they shared the decline.

Massive inflows of bullion ultimately harmed the Iberian economies through what is deceptively known as "Dutch disease", on the grounds that it occurred in the mid-eighteenth century Netherlands too.[199] Like the temperature of Goldilocks's porridge, optimal bullion flows had to be just right, neither too little nor too much. Dutch disease, perhaps better described as fiscal gout, arose from abundant bullion making it easier to buy manufactures from others than to make them yourself. It has been suggested that this also affected gold-rich fifteenth-century Hungary.[200] Why innovate when abundant bullion allowed you to easily and selectively buy the innovations of others? "Let them invent their trinkets; the Spanish will choose those that are worth using".[201] This eroded your manufacturing sector while boosting those of others, whose economies were also helped by more limited and digestible intakes of your bullion. Bullion inflows also stimulated inflation, which was sharper in agriculture than in manufacturing, as noted in chapter 3. This harmed the Iberian domestic economies, while French, British and, until the mid-eighteenth century, Dutch, all preyed on, and entwined with, the Iberian empires overseas, their economies lubricated by Iberian American bullion.

This chapter has dwelt on the Genoese role in early Portuguese and Spanish imperial history. My intention is not to downplay Iberian agency, but to suggest the following causal sequence. First, contrary to some views, the Iberians shared in plague's boost to the economy, at least from 1390, and they developed an "expansion kit" under the pressure of more capital, more war, and less manpower. Second, through a combination of their preexisting peculiarities and agile plague adaptations, the Genoese led Europe in expansive techniques in the early plague era, including growth-friendly institutions. They were Europe's first "military-fiscal state" or, perhaps, "military-fiscal culture". Third, in the fifteenth century, pushed out of the eastern Mediterranean by the Ottomans, the Genoese entwined intensively first with Portugal and then with Spain, playing midwife to the global expansions of each. Finally, Iberian expansion pioneered, prompted, and helped enable the later expansions of the Dutch, French, and British.

11

The Ottomans and the
Great Diversion

THE OTTOMANS BEGAN as a small group of Oghuz Turks living in Anatolia. They were unknown to history until 1301. By the 1530s, they held easily the largest empire in West Eurasia, encompassing Anatolia and Iraq; the former Mamluk domains of Egypt, Greater Syria, and the Hijaz; and the coasts of the Black Sea, Yemen and the Maghreb, as well as the Balkans and most of Hungary. Over the next century or so, raiders' tributary to the Ottomans took thousands of slaves as far north as England, Ireland, and Muscovy. In 1683, "the Turks" came so close to taking Vienna that the Holy Roman Emperor fled his capital.[1] As noted in chapter 8, they then held a 450,000-square-mile domain in Europe, and they retained most of it until the mid-nineteenth century. Yet they are still often excluded from European history—except as its nineteenth-century "sick man". People still need reminding that Istanbul is, and always has been, in Europe. While Eurocentric misapprehensions about the Ottomans persist in some quarters, a wealth of countervailing scholarship has emerged in recent decades. This chapter redeploys some of it to re-assess the role of plague in Ottoman expansion, and the role of the Ottomans in European expansion.

I The Recovery State

As we have noted, the Ottomans preferred to attribute their remarkable rise to their own virtues and divine favour, and not to "mere accidents" such as plague. Plague did give them a nomad advantage over rivals such as the Byzantines, but it was short-lived. By the early fifteenth century, when three sons of the unlucky Sultan Bayezid I died of it, the Ottomans were as plague-prone as anyone else, and became more so from about 1520.[3] Nükhet Varlık argues convincingly that Ottoman expansion and economic integration helped spread and recycle plague from that time. But she also asserts that the Ottoman "rise occurred in spite of it".[4] "Because of it" might be closer to the mark. The real plague boost for the Ottomans was not the passing and partial nomad plague exemption, but the creation of a new labour-starved playing field in which their extraordinary skill at getting other people to work and fight for them was refined and extended to the point where it became a decisive advantage. They were the ultimate plague managers, ranking higher than even the Genoese, and as we have seen, their disaster recovery techniques doubled as elements of their expansion kit.

The case for dating a gearshift in Ottoman expansion to the decades immediately after the Black Death looks strong (see map 6). The Ottomans did score successes before plague, between 1301 and 1346. They took Byzantine Bursa in 1326, but only after 12 years of blockade—they could not yet take cities outright. They gained the voluntary allegiance of Byzantine lords and groups of Turkic nomads. Their main success against rival Muslim beyliks before 1350 seems to be the subjection of the coastal emirate of Karesi in 1345–46, during a succession crisis.[5] But, before the 1350s, the Ottomans appear little different from other leading beyliks, such as Germiyan and Karaman. Their entry into Europe in 1352–54, when they acquired their first European base, Gallipoli, marks the gearshift. They secured Thrace in the 1360s. They subjected Bulgaria in 1376, and the formidable Serbs after the Battle of Kossovo in 1389.[6] In the 1390s, they added six Anatolian beyliks to their domains and defeated a major European crusade against them at Nicopolis in 1396.[7] It was in this immediate post-plague period that elements of Ottoman statecraft first appear and cohere: the Janissaries, elite slave infantry, perhaps as early as 1365; tax-farming—a way of realising future income for current wars, in the 1380s; and their first naval arsenal in the 1390s. The important *devshirme* system, the "handpicking" of slave soldiers and slave bureaucrats, a tax in sons on Christian subjects, was in place by 1395 at the latest.[8] "Ottoman rulers began developing their distinctive slave and clerical institutions in the late fourteenth century".[9] It was the clerical institutions, which utilised the post-plague scribal transition, that enabled other developments. The centralised Ottoman state, often known as "The Porte" from 1453, after a gate in the Topkapi Palace, possessed Europe's first modern bureaucracy.

From the 1360s, as noted in chapter 8, the Ottomans had two bases, in Anatolia and the Balkans, and they used each to expand the other.[10] The ghazi tradition of holy war against Christians was exploited to recruit Turks, helped by an Ottoman monopoly on Turkish access to the Balkans after 1352 due to their alliance with (some) Genoese. If you were a ghazi keen for profit or paradise on the new Balkan frontier, you had to place yourself under the Ottoman banner. This factor was once over-emphasised in the historiography, which now puts more stress on the co-option of Christians, but it was typical of the Ottomans that the two could coexist. One historian claims that the empire was "cofounded" by the Ottomans and two Christian or ex-Christian groups, who initially saw themselves as equals. But the Ottomans proved to be "the only one of the cofounders with the ability to attract a steady stream of new manpower".[11] After 1360, when other Turkic beyliks became vassal allies, their troops quickly augmented Ottoman armies in the Balkans. Their archers led the Ottoman attack at Kossovo in 1389.[12] In fact, several military historians now see that hard-fought battle as a draw. But the Ottomans were quickly able to rebuild their army, whereas the Serbs were not. When they did recover, many Serbs in turn fought for the Ottomans, led by the son of the king slain at Kossovo. By 1427, "Stephen Lazarevic had been a reliable Ottoman vassal for some thirty-five years", campaigning in Anatolia as well as the Balkans.[13] The Serb folk hero, Marko Kraljevic, sometimes fought for the sultan, sometimes against him. Christian troops made up a substantial part of the Ottoman army that took Constantinople in 1453.[14]

Having an alternative, Balkan, base, was one key to Ottoman recovery from defeat by Timur in Anatolia. Ex-vassals in the Balkans and Anatolia were reconquered from the 1420s; a second European crusade was defeated at Varna in 1444; and Constantinople soon fell. Venice fought its first war with the Ottomans in 1463–75, and lost Negroponte (Euboea) to them. A second war in 1499–1503 cost its mainland Greek possessions of Modon and Coron. In Asia, the Ottomans defeated the Aq Qoyunlu Turkmen in the 1470s, the Safavid Iranians in 1514, and conquered the Mamluks in 1516–17. In 1526, they added most of Hungary to their empire and threatened Vienna in the 1530s. The vast Hapsburg empire of Charles V was Europe's solution to the Ottoman threat, and it proved only a partial one. An Ottoman military edge was one factor in this, as we will see in section III below; the sheer scale of Ottoman manpowering was another.

Ottoman labour recruitment and disaster recovery were systematic, but the systems were multiple, varying over time and space, and mixing innovation with the adapted traditions of others. Slave-taking was crucial, but essentially the Ottomans in the early plague era took anyone they could get any way they could get them, and they could get a bigger share of the plague-diminished pool than any other West Eurasian power. Anatolian peasant infantry, archers at this stage, known as *azabs*, were conscripted for early campaigns to supplement the *timariot* cavalry—a product of the contract system described in chapter 8. There were tens of thousands of azabs in Ottoman armies until the late fifteenth century, after which they were sidelined for a while by more professional troops.[15] As noted in chapter 6, the Muslim South does not seem to have had its own crew regions. But, especially in the early plague era, the Ottomans drew heavily on plague-enhanced Christian crew regions, such as Albania, Bosnia, and the Greek Islands. Many Christians converted to Islam in the Balkans after 1500, and unconverted Christian troops declined, though special categories such as "Martolo" garrisons and "Voynuk" recruiters remained important.[16]

From 1500, Ottoman armies became more Muslim, professionalised and specialised, but little less varied. High population growth in Anatolia, combined with a cultural imperative to acquire a landholding before marriage, boosted the number of bachelors—from 3% to 44% in one region.[17] These were drawn on for soldiers from about mid-century and trained quickly in the use of muskets, but became a problem for the state during the Celali rebellions of 1595–1610. After the conquest of Egypt in 1517, the Ottomans were not going to let a good military system go to waste, and began to recruit their own mamluks, using the same sources as *the* Mamluks, notably Circassians. This is sometimes mistaken for the perpetuation of the old Mamluks themselves.[18] Within five years, these new troops assisted in the conquest of Rhodes. After 1517, the Ottomans campaigned mainly on two broad fronts: against Europeans in the west and against Safavid Iran in the east. The main army set out annually from Istanbul in either case, but also needed auxiliary light cavalry. In the west, these came from the neo-Mongol Crimean Tartars, heirs of the Golden Horde, who typically provided 40,000 men and many more horses. In the east, the same function was fulfilled through carefully nurtured alliances with Kurdish and Turkmen groups, who provided 33,000 horsemen in 1609.[19]

The Ottoman navy was even more cosmopolitan than the army, and sometimes almost as big. The Ottomans used warships from 1374, but their fleet burgeoned from 1453, because they now needed to protect the maritime supply of Istanbul. By 1500, they were said to be able to muster 250 gun galleys, about the same as all Christian powers combined, and during the sixteenth century increased their shipyards and naval arsenals to 110. In 1585, a Venetian official observed that "The naval forces which the Great Turk uses to defend his empire are vast and second to none in the world".[20] Like their Venetian rivals, they were slow to shift to galleons, though they did so from the 1640s more effectively than was once believed.[21] Manning the fleet was a perennial problem, but less so for the Ottomans than for their enemies because their man-powering system was bigger and better. Slave rowers were never considered ideal by anyone, because they would not double as fighters and were prone to mutiny, but in the early plague era, and in shorter-term labour crises thereafter, they were used en masse by the Ottomans.[22] The idea that Turks themselves were allergic to seafaring is false; there were many in the fleet, but Greek sailors were probably even more numerous. "The huge participation of the Greeks in the Ottoman navy" began in the fifteenth century and increased over time.[23] The probable role of plague in boosting the streams of crewmen from such regions has been overlooked. Around 1400, the women of Naxos were "celibate for lack of men", the latter having gone to sea as professional oarsmen after the island began importing its grain.[24] "Greek" was a fluid identity, a transnational culture, able to shift balance between two or more flags, like the Basques and Cossacks. Greek mercantile and brokerage networks, sometimes the same ones, became vital to both the Venetian and Ottoman Empires.[25] To other Europeans, Orthodox Greeks in Ottoman service were fellow Christians. To Muslims, they were fellow Ottoman subjects. Greek networks brokered a wider non-elite pool of Greek sailors, and this in turn was part of a wider transnational pool of martial and maritime European crew. By 1600 the Ottoman merchant fleet, with Greeks even more prominent than in the navy, totalled 80,000 tons, the biggest in the Mediterranean.[26]

The importance of various Jewish networks to Ottoman commerce is well-known; and, like other powers, the Ottomans also used the vast Armenian network, especially in the silk trade. Elite Ottoman Muslims themselves were thought to have avoided overseas trade and to disregard commerce, other than provisioning the armed forces and the capital, but this is now contested, as is any notion of unsophisticated economics. Ottomans acquired trading rights in Venice in 1419, were using bills of exchange in Cracow, Prague, and Budapest by the late fifteenth century, and established a trading post in Ancona in 1514.[27] At the outbreak of one war in 1570, 75 Muslim merchants were arrested in Venice.[28] Between wars, Venice and the Ottomans traded intensively. We have seen that during wars the trade moved to Dubrovnik-flagged ships, and that the early relationship of the Ottomans with the Genoese, 1350–1450, was also close. Around 1500, the Ottomans shared with the Venetians and Genoese in a development that reduced dependence on preexisting networks: training your own multilingual culture brokers, known as dragomen.[29] They were also dexterous in playing off the merchants of Christian city-states, and later nation-states, against each other until the eighteenth century, when the French came to dominate.

The post-plague economy of the Ottoman domains has also been described in chapter 8. With the help of "colonising dervishes" and *vakf* foundations, the activist state quickly revived regions depopulated by plague or disrupted by war. This continued into the sixteenth and seventeenth centuries. For example, agricultural production in the Basra region of southern Iraq, whose conquest was consolidated in 1552, doubled by 1590 under Ottoman management.[30] The economy did suffer from devaluations, fiscal crises, inflation, and the rising cost of transferring tax revenues to the centre. It may also have been subject to "Dutch disease", an inflow of bullion so large that it encouraged foreign imports over local manufacture. But "the narrow range of imports from Europe did not significantly affect Ottoman industries".[31] The net European deficit in trade with the Ottomans was about 50 tons of silver per year, 1600–1650.[32] Balkan silver production, now controlled by the Ottoman state, is thought to have reached another 50 tons in 1600.[33] Much of this bullion, of course, flowed out again, to Yemen for coffee, Iran for raw silk, and Further Asia for spices and super-crafts including porcelain. But the total money stock of the empire in 1600 is estimated at 1,000–1,500 tons of silver, so enough remained to lubricate the economy.[34] Inflation was high in the half-century around 1600, but declined thereafter.[35] All in all, the Ottoman economy was usually quite strong deep into the eighteenth century.

The *devshirme* "hand-picking" system of recruitment delivered talent as well as manpower, civil as well as military. When the system was at its height in the fifteenth and sixteenth centuries, promising boys 12 or 13 years old were selected from Christian households and taken to Istanbul for training—six years for Janissaries, up to 14 years for officials.[36] They began as "slaves of the palace" and were converted to Islam, but were well paid, well treated, and had good prospects. Europe recruited workers through slavery; the Ottomans used it to recruit leaders as well. Some rose to become viziers and grand viziers, ministers and prime ministers, of the empire. Of 49 grand viziers between 1453 and 1623, only five were Turks, one was Armenian, the rest European, including voluntary converts as well as ex-slaves.[37] It was not their being European that counted, but that many were peasants—the widest talent pool available, on which other powers rarely drew for leaders. Inside influence, bribery, and the sultan's whim did sometimes count, but no other West Eurasian government was as meritocratic, and this was not lost on European contemporaries. One mid-sixteenth century commentator noted that "our system is very different; there is no room for merit, but everything depends on birth".[38] Recent revisionism may have taken positive interpretation of the devshirme too far, to the point where it looks like an Ottoman Rhodes Scholarship.[39] It is seared deeply and negatively into Balkan folk history, with poignant images of young boys being taken away forever on donkeys in pairs of panniers, two by two.[40] The whole point was to "hand-pick" the best, whether they or their parents liked it or not. The system did become less coercive from the later seventeenth century, with people volunteering their children, and janissaries insisting, against the rules, that their sons be recruited too. The system was then in decline, succumbing to built-in obsolescence like other soldier-importing regimes. Still, by far the best chance for a European peasant lad to rise to high authority was through the Ottoman devshirme.

A related source of Ottoman military talent was the European renegade. The archetype was the sailor taken as a slave at sea by corsairs. Such men often "turned Turk" and converted to Islam, though it is hard to see this as entirely voluntary when the option was unpaid hard labour. There seems to have been a selection process here too: not all slaves were freed on conversion, and those who were tended to be either skilled adults, or malleably young. Of a large sample of 978 renegades, 55.5% were younger than 15 years of age when captured and 78.4% were younger than 20.[41] Many were captured in land raids, not at sea. One raid on southern Spain in 1566 penetrated 20 miles inland and took 4,000 Christians. In the seventeenth century, the corsairs shifted from gun galleys to small, fast gun galleons, with the help of Dutch and English renegades, and extended their depredations into the Atlantic. In 1627, they raided Iceland and took 400 slaves,[42] and raids also occurred in the Canary Islands, Ireland, and Cornwall. The corsairs took around 25,000 English over the course of the seventeenth century, many of whom "turned Turk".[43] It now seems that there were also fully voluntary renegades.

> The period from 1500 to 1650 represents the golden age of the renegade; their numbers were so great that the flow from Christianity to Islam has been characterized as a "hemorrhage [sic] of men" and a "religious nomadism" . . . many renegades were inspired by reports, which circulated widely, that Islamic society knew no "social discrimination or privileges" and that opportunity existed for all, regardless of background.[44]

The Ottomans did not have everything their own way in post-plague warfare; they suffered some severe defeats, and some victories were immensely expensive. They also underwent repeated ecological, economic, and political crises, as well as more plagues than anyone else. The Ottomans recovered from defeat better than their enemies did from victory. They lost 180 of 220 galleys at their great naval defeat of Lepanto in 1571 by a Hapsburg-Venetian alliance.[45] But they quickly produced a fresh fleet of 280 galleys and took the strategic port of Tunis from the Hapsburgs in 1574. The conquest of the island fortress of Rhodes in 1522, stubbornly held by the Knights of St John, should have been a crippling victory. Sultan Suleyman "the Magnificent" himself estimated it cost him 103,000 men—"this appears not to be an exaggeration".[46] Yet a fresh Ottoman army of similar strength conquered Hungary in 1526. The empire also suffered from various non-military crises, notably acute inflation, droughts, and floods in the late sixteenth century. But "by the time the Ottomans went off to war in Hungary in 1593, they appeared fully recovered from the disasters of the preceding decades".[47] Renewed ecological crisis in the early seventeenth century, symbolised by the freezing over of the Bosphorus in 1621, "bottomed out" in the 1640s.[48] The secret of Ottoman success was not the capacity to avoid disaster, but the capacity to recover from it, a resilience incubated by plague.

II Ottoman Urban Colonisation and Slavery

We have seen that the Ottomans came late to gun galleons, like the Venetians and Russians. Another gap in the Ottoman expansion kit was shared with the Dutch and French: the paucity of settling regions and the weakness of long-range settlement.[49] But the Ottomans did go in for short-range settlement, or re-settlement, sometimes in a big way. There was substantial Sufi-led, vakf-supported, Muslim colonisation in parts of Bulgaria and Thrace in the sixteenth century. Its scale is not easy to establish, because Muslim settlers are hard to separate from the Christians in these regions who converted to Islam. A usual estimate is 50,000–100,000 actual migrants, mostly Turkmen sheepherders known as "Yuruks" from Anatolia. There were also reshufflings of Europeans, notably Vlachs and Albanians, to depopulated parts of the Balkans, and similar resettlements in Anatolia. Conversion was voluntary, which was not always the case with the settlement. "It is the law of the sultans that they should order *surgun* [compulsory settlement] that it might cause the region (*il*) to prosper once again".[50]

The great example of Ottoman re-peopling and, less obviously, economic engineering, is Istanbul. Istanbul had about 40,000 people after the siege of

1453.[51] "Immediately . . . the repopulation of the city was one of the primary concerns of Mehmed II"—the victorious sultan.[52] The number of inhabitants doubled in the next decade or so, but a plague strike in 1467 killed at least a third of them.[53] Within ten years, the population had again been rebuilt to 80,000; another strike in 1492 killed 30,000.[54] There were at least five more high-lethality strikes in the sixteenth century. Yet the population repeatedly recovered to its 1525 level of around 400,000,[55] a tenfold increase over 1453 despite recurrent plagues. The size was exceptional and the rapidity of growth even more so. Coerced settlement was significant, especially in the later fifteenth century, and the 20% of the population who were slaves were always coerced. But after 1500, most migrants to Istanbul came voluntarily, because of the opportunities it offered relative to a countryside in which population was now rising, notably, the opportunity of being well-fed. Byzantine Constantinople is thought to have had 300,000 people in 1200, but had not been a large city since 1204, when it was sacked by crusaders. In the following 250 years, the neighbouring regions adjusted to *not* having to supply a mega-city. So the sudden tenfold increase in Istanbul's population demanded the extension and transformation of its hinterlands through "urban colonisation".

Istanbul's empire within an empire had inner, middle, and outer circles. The inner circle of virtual hinterlands, some overseas, included the original Ottoman base, Bithynia in Anatolia, centred on Bursa, the old capital. As noted in chapter 8, this city and its twin, Edirne in Thrace, added supplying Istanbul to their main industries after 1453. Bursa shipped grain and timber through ports on the Sea of Marmara. Parts of Thessaly and Macedonia soon joined the inner circle.[56] Istanbul continued to grow, and a larger middle circle of virtual hinterlands developed between 1480 and 1520, comprising the Black Sea littoral and Egypt. The Ottomans "converted the entire Pontic coastland into a vast and valuable hinterland".[57] The Danubian principalities of Wallachia and Moldavia, despite sporadic bids for political freedom, were increasingly integrated into the Istanbul economy, as was the fertile Crimean Peninsula. They supplied Istanbul with wine, timber, meat, and butter, as well as some of its daily bread. Under Ottoman management, guided by local expertise, Egypt's irrigation systems were reconstituted and it again became a grain exporter in the sixteenth century, with Istanbul as its most important market.[58] The Ottoman state was sensitive about Istanbul's food supply—shortages caused riots and mutinies. Water transport was crucial, because sheer bulk made sufficient overland supply impossible.[59] It was this that forced the Ottomans to put so much effort into naval control of the eastern Mediterranean. If an enemy controlled that sea, Istanbul would starve, a problem familiar to Londoners in the two twentieth-century world wars.

Urban colonisation transformed at least some of the hinterlands as well as sustaining Istanbul, rendering them more specialised, commercialised, and productive. This might or might not be good for the inhabitants. Istanbul consumed at least 200,000 cattle and 1.5 million sheep a year.[60] Many of the cattle came from Wallachia, which the Ottomans controlled increasingly firmly from 1462. Wallachia then suffered massive depopulation during a period of general growth, perhaps halving from 400,000 people between 1460 and 1600. The decrease may have been due to the marginalisation of small peasant farms by a turn to large-scale production for the Istanbul market. Tightening serfdom and gypsy slaves retained a core labour force. From about 1600, "Wallachia was becoming virtually an Ottoman colony",[61] not only in the sense of being part of the empire, which had been the case sporadically since the late fourteenth century, but also in the sense of becoming an economic colony, or virtual hinterland, of Istanbul. A similar process of increasing exploitation took place in Moldavia, where the tribute due to the Porte grew from 4,000 gold pieces in 1487 to 260,000 in the seventeenth century. "Cattle, sheep and grain could only be exported to Constantinople . . . [which] devastated the lucrative trade with the German lands and Poland".[62] A particularly privileged Greek network managed the transition: "Phanariotes" based in Istanbul and claiming descent from Byzantine elites, from whom the governors of Moldavia and Wallachia were usually drawn.[63] Urban colonialism worked better when it was less coercive, which reduced the risk of rebellion, and it worked best of all when handled by your own kind, who were pre-adapted to supply the wants of their particular urban carnivores. This applied to Deliorman in Northeast Bulgaria. A 2011 doctoral thesis shows that this region was still plague-depopulated in 1500, and that it was replenished by a substantial immigration of "Yuruk" shepherds from Anatolia. Deliorman was good sheep country, and "sheep-breeding on a large scale" was "the primary economic occupation of the incoming settlers".[64] Exports were aimed at one big market—Istanbul.[65] There must have been other sheep regions too, transformed like Deliorman by Istanbul's new demand, which the normal sheep surpluses in 1450 simply could not have met.

Trade between an empire city and its informal colonies had other peculiarities: smoother flows than normal commerce, a high degree of export-oriented specialisation in the colony, lavish consumption patterns in the city, and an intimacy that made the relevant product *seem* local to metropolitans. In

Istanbul, one of the four mutton supply seasons was known as "Deliorman". "The famous butter of Caffa [was] much prized in Istanbul". Caffa, formerly Genoese, was now known as "little Istanbul".[66] Rice was a staple for most classes in the city; an elite luxury outside it.[67] "The trade between Egypt and the rest of the Ottoman Empire was remarkably stable, free from the violent fluctuations that characterized exports to Europe".[68] In 1533–34, three-quarters of the trade of Amastra, another Black Sea port, was with Istanbul. Parts of Thessaly, Macedonia, and Thrace came to specialise in tobacco, rice, and cotton, while other parts specialised in grain.[69] Around half the output went to Istanbul. This was an exceptional proportion of exports to output for the period—Poland's famous grain trade did not exceed 12% of output.[70] It suggests considerable agricultural efficiency.

Istanbul's reach was vastly extended by its outer circle of suppliers, which consisted of two sets of long-term Ottoman allies: the Crimean Tartars and the Barbary "regencies" of Algiers, Tunis, and Tripoli. I initially assumed that, after the sixteenth century, these polities supported the Ottomans only when it suited them, and that the alliance was loose. But it appears that this was only partly true. The Barbary Corsairs might continue to prey on Ottoman allies, such as the French, but this was a Genoese-like sleight; the Porte could deny responsibility. In some respects, its hold on the regencies was strong. The Ottomans supplied artillery, ship-building timber, and janissary garrisons, and were "firmly in control".[71] The Porte sent subsidies on occasions, but regularly received tribute. The Crimean khan similarly hosted a janissary brigade, and received firearms and, in this case, an annual stipend, but could be deposed if he crossed the sultans. He reliably supplied upwards of 40,000 light cavalry for the Sultan's European campaigns.[72] The janissaries underwrote Ottoman control, but also helped defend the khan and the regents from heavily gunned Russian and Spanish attacks. Still more important in cementing the alliances, however, was mutual economic dependence. Khanate and regencies supplied slaves in numbers not available elsewhere, and Istanbul supplied an irreplaceable market for them.

Soon after the Ottoman conquest of the Black Sea littoral, including the Crimea itself, the Crimean Tartars dwelling on the inland steppes allied with the new regime and began supplying it with slaves taken in their raids. This was an old game, but the scale and regularity of this "mutually beneficial economic relationship" was new.[73] The main Black Sea slave trade port, Genoese Caffa, had exported about 1,500 slaves a year until the Ottomans took the town in 1475. Caffa's trade burgeoned, and 17,500 slaves were apparently sold there

in the single year of 1578. The number seems huge, but is supported by Ottoman slave tax receipts of 4.5 million *akçes* (around 40,000 gold ducats). "Since
the highest tax collected on any one sale was 255 *akçes*, at least 17,500 slaves
were sold there in that year".[74] Caffa under the Ottomans probably functioned
as a "staple" at which most Black Sea slaves were taxed. The general estimate
of its annual exports in the sixteenth and seventeenth centuries is between
10,000 and 20,000 people, with recent scholarship favouring the latter.[75]

Some of Caffa's slaves were drawn from the Caucasus, particular from Cir-
cassia and Karbadia. Crimean and other Tartar groups raided the fringes of
the Caucasus Mountains, but most slaves from the region were taken by local
folk and sold to traders. "The Caucasus remained a key source of manpower
for the Ottoman Empire until well into the nineteenth century".[76] The Ottomans nurtured alliances with some chiefs, paying them subsidies to counter
Russian and Safavid influence, a strategy familiar to European slavers in West
Africa.[77] Another source of Caffa's slaves were Russians and Poles taken by the
Crimean Tartars in annual raids, great and small. "There were forty-three
major Crimean and Nogai attacks on Muscovite territory just in the first half
of the sixteenth century; Lithuania and Poland experienced seventy-five incursions over the period 1474–1569".[78] The Russians considered Caffa "an abyss
into which our blood is pouring"; "a heathen giant who feeds on our blood".[79]
"A compilation of estimates shows that Crimean Tartars captured about 1.75
million Ukrainians, Poles and Russians from 1469 to 1694". Including Circassians and the like, the numbers totalled "around 2.5 million between 1475 and
1700".[80]

The Ottomans first intervened on the Barbary Coast of North Africa in
1487, when they sent help to the embattled fellow-Muslims of Granada and
drew on Barbary seafarers for the navy from 1494.[81] But really close relations
with the region began around 1516, when the Ottomans allied with the Barbarossa brothers, independent sea captains of Turkish and Greek descent from
Lesbos who had arrived earlier to assist local Muslim rulers against Spanish
attacks. The most famous was Hayreddin Barbarossa, who became commander of the Ottoman fleet and ruler of Algiers.[82] In addition to guns and
janissaries, the sultan gave the corsairs the right to recruit troops of their own
in Anatolia,[83] and this helped them establish what amounted to maritime city-
states in Algiers, Tunis, Tripoli, and some lesser ports. A separate corsair fran-
chise was Saleh or Sallee, on the Atlantic coast of Morocco. It was subject to
Morocco, itself briefly an Ottoman client in the 1550s, but enjoyed several decades of independence in the seventeenth century. Barbary corsairs seized 963

ships, mostly Dutch and French, between 1613 and 1622, about 100 a year, which provides an idea of the scale of their activity.[84]

Ottoman Algiers was the biggest of the corsair states. The city's own population was about 20,000 in 1500,[85] but it rose rapidly to perhaps 100,000 in 1600, "despite the ravages of the plague".[86] About 12% of these people were Turkish, 8% free European renegades, and 25% European slaves. The first two categories made up the elite. Local Moors and Berbers comprised only 16% or so of the population, the rest of whom were Moriscos and Jews expelled from Spain, and black Africans.[87] This was a "Euro-Ottoman" hybrid culture, like the Afro-Portuguese. Between 1550 and 1650, half the governors were of Christian origin.[88] Algiers had 36 galleys in 1581 and about 70 ships in 1634, now including galleon-types of up to 40 guns. Tunis had five galleys and 40 sailing ships at this time; Tripoli somewhat fewer.[89] "Prosperity was very evident . . . Tunis in particular grew back to its former size . . . as did Tripoli. Algiers developed from a small port into one of the great cities of the empire".[90]

How far the janissary and renegade elites of the Barbary regencies saw themselves as Ottoman I do not know. But a leading scholar has suggested that the broader "Ottoman military-administrative elite", usually of slave and/or non-Turkish origin, did develop a transnational collective identity. One could describe this as a "civic imperialism" (in contrast to an ethnic one) to which other empires since Rome could rarely aspire. By about 1550, this elite "was made up of these new Turkish-speaking Muslim officers who called themselves not Turkish but 'Roman' [*Rumi*] or 'Ottoman.'"[91] Anatolia had long been known as *Rum*. Like the Crimean Tartars, the corsairs were reliable allies of the Ottomans in time of war. Barbarossa sent galleys to assist the conquest of Rhodes in 1522.[92] The corsairs contributed squadrons to the Ottoman fleet throughout the sixteenth and seventeenth centuries. They were still sending ships as late as the 1820s, to fight Greek rebels and Lord Byron.[93] But their regular contribution was supplying slaves to Istanbul, of two kinds. As noted above, they enslaved the crew and passengers of European ships and raided European territory for more slaves. Sicily was raided 136 times between 1570 and 1606, and the last raid, on Sardinia, took place in 1815.[94] The best estimate of the total number taken between 1530 and 1780 is one to one and a quarter million.[95] Some were ransomed, some "turned Turk", and some laboured as slaves on the galleys, docks, and hinterland farms of the Barbary cities. But a great many went to Istanbul.

This was also true of the second stream of slaves via the Maghreb, black Africans from the trans-Saharan caravan trade. The corsair cities, particularly

Tripoli, were the outlets for this ancient trade, which continued deep into the nineteenth century, when the slaves were carried to Istanbul in steamships. "Black slaves from Africa south of the Sahara were much in demand in the Ottoman empire in the sixteenth and seventeenth centuries".[96] Estimates vary, but they cluster around 5,000 a year after 1350. This level continued to 1778, when evidence from the British and French consuls suggests an inflow of 4,000 slaves to Tripoli alone, of whom 3,000 were re-exported to "the Levant", most of them probably to Istanbul.[97] If 4,000 a year was the average, Muslims brought 2 million slaves across the Sahara between 1350 and 1850 of whom perhaps 1.5 million would have ended up in the Ottoman Empire. The Ottomans seem to have drawn at least as many black African slaves from East Africa. Two large caravans a year brought two or three thousand slaves each from the Southern Sudan.[98] Despite sporadic hostility, Ethiopia is said to have sold 10,000 slaves annually to the Ottoman Red Sea ports from 1557.[99] A recent estimate of black African slaves from all sources reaching the Ottoman Empire in the earlier nineteenth century is about 17,000 a year,[100] though this may have been an increase to compensate for the diminishing supply of Europeans. A reasonable estimate of overall Ottoman enslavements, 1350–1800, would be close to seven million.

The scale is comparable to Western Europe's Atlantic slave trade; the lethality, permanence, and racism are not. Ottomans enslaved and manumitted white and black alike; slaves could buy their freedom and seem mostly to have merged with the lower orders of the general population once freed. But there remains a hint of "white legend" in received interpretations of Ottoman slavery, which allege that, apart from the devirshime, it was largely domestic and not economically central. Yet it was clearly the means of repopulating Bursa in the late fifteenth and early sixteenth centuries. As we saw in chapter 8, this crucial auxiliary of Istanbul grew and prospered from the 1430s, despite visitations by plague and Timur. It reached 35,000 people by 1500 and 42,000 by 1530, doubling to almost 90,000 people by 1600.[101] Two experts calculate Bursa's annual intake of slaves, from tax receipts, at a remarkable 6,000 a year around 1500, many employed in industry. Slaves comprised around one-third of the population, and freed slaves another third[102]—a city sustained by state-mentored slavery.

As populations grew and free labour became cheaper in the sixteenth century, there was a shift away from slavery in Bursa. It is also true that domestic slaves, mostly female, were important for status for the city folk who could afford them—about 12% of the population of Bursa were slave-owners, more in Istanbul. But slavery continued to provide an Ottoman "reserve army" of labour. In Aleppo and Edirne, more than 60% of slaves were male between 1600 and 1750.[103] The rich farmlands of the Crimea, producing wine as well as wheat, were worked by slaves, estimated at 400,000 in the mid-seventeenth century, compared to 187,000 free Muslims—a proportion not matched by the most slave-prone states of the US South in the mid-nineteenth century.[104] Intensively worked plantations in other regions also had slave labour forces. Gypsy slaves worked farms in Istanbul's Balkan virtual hinterlands, and European slaves worked on farms and docks near the Barbary cities. One private owner had 2,000 slaves on his Chios plantations in the seventeenth century.[105] Private slave-owners in Istanbul contracted out slaves to the Ottoman navy— an estimated 11,000 in 1570—and these would not have been domestic servants.[106] The Porte commissioned the Crimean Tartars to obtain rowers for the fleet for the Cretan war with Venice; in 1644 alone they obligingly provided 20,000 unfortunate Russians.[107] A bonanza of 108,000 Hungarians were taken in 1683.[108] The Ottomans ran one of the two great slaving systems of the early modern world; Western Europeans the other. Both were adapting manpowering systems and attitudes to labour generated in the early plague era, getting others to do much of the dirty work of slave-taking and using slavery to augment their economic clout.

III The Ottomans and Expansion beyond West Eurasia

The direct participation of the Ottomans in expansion beyond West Eurasia has long been underestimated, but recent research makes a case for seeing them as a colonising power, like the Portuguese, in the Indian Ocean world. Their record here does at least confirm that the West European military edge was in fact West Eurasian, with the Ottomans featuring far and wide as disseminators of plague-incubated firearms technology. The Ottomans also had sub-Saharan African connections, partnerships, and tributaries—a modest sub-Saharan African "empire", but larger than Western European ones before the nineteenth century. After their 1551 conquest of Tripoli, the Ottomans inherited trade links with the Sahelian sultanate of Bornu, a powerful state supplying the trans-Sahara trade with salt, gold, and slaves (see map 12). From the late sixteenth century, Bornu payed annual tribute to the Ottomans, in slaves and gold, and received guns and gunners in return, giving Bornu's ruler "much better firepower than his rivals". This allowed the extension of his domains and slaving operations, just as European alliances and guns did farther west in Africa.[109]

In 1503, the Portuguese made their first attack on the Persian Gulf. They sacked Muscat and briefly seized Hormuz in 1507–1508, and soon showed similar interest in the Red Sea.[110] Their numbers were small, at most 2,000 Portuguese in any one expedition. But a thin stream of risk-inured crewmen, perhaps influenced by the plagues ravaging their homeland at the time, kept coming, and they were supplemented by Indian auxiliaries. Between about 1508 and 1514, according to a Muslim source, "no cargo was delivered at the port of Jeddah because of the European corsairs sailing the Indian Ocean".[111] The rival Muslim empires temporarily shelved their differences to face this threat. From the outset, their main problem was the absence of ship timber on the southern coasts of the Middle East. Ships were prefabricated on the Mediterranean coast or the Nile, then hauled in parts across the desert. Painfully, the Muslim allies assembled a small fleet of a dozen galleys and sailing ships in 1508, sailed to India, and won a naval battle off Chaul "with bronze cannon similar or even better than those of the Portuguese".[112] The next year, however, the Portuguese counterattacked and defeated the allied fleet. In 1513, 17 Portuguese galleons entered the Red Sea, threatening Aden, Jedda and, therefore, Mecca itself. They found the narrow sea difficult for non-specialist ships, and were forced to retreat with heavy losses to disease, but tried again in 1517. With the conquest of the Mamluks that year, this had become a solely Ottoman problem. Their concentration on it fluctuated according to other commitments and to the vision of the administrators, soldiers, and admirals who were most influential at the time. But it was sometimes considerable. It had fairly consistent objectives and strategies. The objectives were the protection of the Red Sea, the security of the Hajj pilgrimage, and rebooting the spice trade. The strategies were the long-range expression of hard or soft power.

Galleys were the warships of choice for the Red Sea, and being lighter, they were much easier to transport there. An Ottoman fleet of 15 galleys and 12 smaller oared *fustas* clashed with the Portuguese off Jedda in 1517 and had the better of them, despite the Portuguese now having eight galleys of their own, plus 15 galleon-types.[113] The Ottomans built a naval base at Suez, managed to assemble a few galleons, and maintained a galley squadron in the Red Sea thereafter. By 1528, with the seizure of a base near Aden and the defeat of a Portuguese squadron, they had limited the Portuguese threat to the Red Sea itself. Revitalising the flow of goods from Further Asia was more difficult. Some Muslim ships got through, either by evading the Portuguese or by buying *cartaz* passes from them, but at least 30 were taken in the 1520s.[114] At this time, the Ottomans allied with Bahadur Shah, the Muslim ruler of Gujarat, and supplied him with guns and engineers, which enabled him to repel three Portuguese attacks on his port of Diu (see map 10). Bahadur then made the mistake of conceding Diu to the Portuguese in 1535, as part of a peace settlement—his other port of Surat was more important. It was he who made the famous statement: "War at sea is the business of merchants; it does not concern the prestige of kings".[115] The Portuguese killed him in 1537, aboard one of their ships. But he did take the precaution of sending his vast treasure— said to amount to 3.6 million gold coins—to Mecca for safekeeping.[116] In 1538, the Ottomans used this money to mount an attack on the Portuguese in India.[117] It involved 10,000 men and 76 ships, mostly galleys, again laboriously carried overland in pieces to Suez. The fleet took one Portuguese fort near Diu, but depended on local allies for supplies, and was forced to withdraw when the alliance broke down.[118] On the way back, however, the fleet seized Aden, then a Portuguese ally, and began the conquest of all Yemen, which the Ottomans held, with difficulty, for a century. Despite this, the Portuguese made a last effort in the Red Sea in 1541, with eight galleys and 70 fustas built in India, and only five galleon-type vessels—a very Ottoman-like fleet. Their oars enabled them to travel all the way to Suez on this occasion, but they were outgunned by the Ottoman defences.

Portuguese long-term occupation of Hormuz in the Persian Gulf began in 1515, but here they kept the local dynasty on as a vassal, in what has been described as a "Portuguese-Hurmuzi condominium".[119] Shortly before this, Hormuz had lost some of the patchwork of territories that it once had, and the Portuguese helped to partially restore it, in Muscat and Bahrein for example. In 1552–54, an Ottoman fleet of 25 galleys and four galleons left the Red Sea and attacked Hormuz and Oman. It sacked Muscat, but failed to take Hormuz and was forced to withdraw. But the Ottoman conquest of Iraq in the 1530s, and their development of the port of Basra from 1547, had already provided an alternative Persian Gulf inlet for the Further Asian trade.[120] Hormuz was taken and dismantled by Safavid Iran in 1622, which established a new port at Bandar Abbas. The Portuguese clung on for a time to other Omani ports.

The Ottomans were more successful in extending their territories along the African shore of the Red Sea south of Egypt, where their first lodgements date to 1517. In 1542, they sent musketeers and cannon to assist a Muslim attempt to conquer Christian Ethiopia. The Portuguese countered by sending 400 gunmen to help the Christians, but were heavily defeated. The Ottomans then withdrew, the local Muslim leader was killed, and with Portuguese help, inland Christian Ethiopia survived.[121] But the Ottomans conquered much of the coast of Sudan, Eritrea, and the Tigray province of northern Ethiopia by the 1550s, and retained the major ports, Suakin and Massawa, for centuries.[122] They repelled Ethiopian efforts to retake Tigray between 1562 and 1582.[123] After initial conflict, they allied with the inland Funj sultanate, so extending their informal sway, and worked out other accommodations with local allies.[124] In these parts of East Africa, Ottoman colonialism did look similar to that of Europeans—small coastal garrisons with little inland power but taking a large cut of trades in ivory, gold, and slaves.

The Ottoman use of long-range soft power was more successful still. They provided Indian Muslim states with guns and experts to help them resist the Portuguese, and from 1547, they developed alliances in Southeast Asia, in particular with the rising Sumatran sultanate of Aceh. The allies made repeated unsuccessful attempts to take Portuguese Melaka.[125] An Ottoman attempt to take the Portuguese ports in East Africa in the early 1580s also failed, after coming close to success.[126] But Ottoman soft power helped the heirs of the first early modern (Muslim) mercantile expansion to survive, and to adapt to, European incursions. Aceh, Surat, and Basra became hubs in this new version of the Muslim trading system, which by 1560 ran its own spice trade in competition with Europeans. The Ottomans disseminated gun technology throughout the system—Francis Drake found 20 Ottoman gunners in the clove island of Ternate in 1587.[127] "Ottoman muskets were also held in high esteem in Safavid Persia, Mughal India, and Ming China, where a treatise in the late 1590s considered Ottoman handguns better than Portuguese muskets".[128] This helped keep trade flowing, with or without European consent. Eight or nine spice ships a year from Aceh reached the Red Sea in the 1570s; others reached Basra.[129] The Ottomans cleverly used different techniques in the two inlets. The state monopolised the Red Sea spice inlet, at marginal cost since it had to protect the Holy Places in any case, and extracted profits of 50–100% from the trade. It left the Basra inlet to the free market, but taxed this trade at 40%. From the 1560s, this is said to have given them "a far larger share of the Indian Ocean spice trade than the Portuguese Crown ever had", estimated at 500,000 gold ducats, close to the revenues of Egypt.[130]

The long conflict between the Ottomans and the Portuguese in the Indian Ocean, 1500s–1560s, provides another test of "expansion kits". The two were roughly equal in cannon, fortification, siege warfare, and musketeers. The Ottomans were ahead in "soft power", partly because most allies were fellow Muslims, and partly because their statecraft was more sophisticated. The Ottomans had the edge in gun galleys, though the Portuguese tried hard, while the inverse was true of gun galleons. The Portuguese advantage in the latter derived from the striking fact that it was easier to sail heavy gunships thousands of kilometres from Portugal than to transfer them over a hundred kilometres of desert—the Ottomans are said to have considered a Suez Canal, in 1568, to overcome this problem.[131] Excellent ship timber was available in Gujarat, and the 1508–1509 expedition may have taken advantage of this. Portuguese accounts indicate that this Muslim fleet included two sturdily built "galleons", while most were lighter types. In 1509, Portuguese cannon sank the lighter ships, but not the galleons. There is also a broad hint from the Portuguese viceroy that the galleons were built in Gujarat.[132] But the Ottomans were unable to guarantee permanent access to Gujarati timber or shipyards. The "Catch 22" for the Ottomans was that they could not establish a permanent lodgement in India without galleons, nor build galleons without such a lodgement.

———

The direct participation of the Ottomans in global expansion was significant, but in the end it was outranked by their indirect impact on the statecraft, war-making, and imperial trajectories of other West Eurasian powers. It is only recently that the Ottomans have begun to receive their due in these respects. A major contributor to this reassessment, Gabor Agoston, states that "instead of focussing on the putative military superiority of European arms, future studies must consider the reverse proposition: the impact of Ottoman military strength and prowess on developments among the Ottomans' rivals and contemporaries".[133] As he suggests, and later chapters of this book will demonstrate, there was indeed substantial uptake of Ottoman techniques and technology by other Muslim West Eurasian expansionists, and by the Russians. Agoston does not engage with the issue of the Ottoman impact on West European expansion, and is dismissive of notions of a "military revolution". Yet he might agree that there was at least a major military transition between 1350 and 1500, and that it owed as much to the Ottomans as to anyone.

It is true that the Ottomans initially accessed gun technology by hiring foreign experts, but as chapter 8 noted, this was also true of most of Europe. The Ottomans took up guns in the Balkans in 1381, perhaps with the help of Dubrovnik, and used cannon in battle at Kossovo in 1389, only seven years after the first such use in Northern Europe, though without great effect.[134] In the 1440s, they adopted the Hussite tabor, or wagon lager, used against them early in the decade by Czech mercenaries in the service of Hungary.[135] They were quick to adopt corned powder in the early 1420s, and while their gun-powder was no better than that of European powers, they made more of it—around 1,000 tons a year by 1600, almost four times Spanish production.[136] The Ottomans are said to have been obsessed with massive siege guns, and to have produced smaller guns with bronze so poor they were melted down rather than re-used by the victors of Lepanto.[137] The former notion has been convinc-ingly debunked by Agoston: they produced cannon of all sizes, mostly small and medium, up to 1,322 a year by the late seventeenth century.[138] Chemical analysis has shown that the bronze in their cannon was very good as early as 1464.[139] Their forts too had anti-artillery features, from as early as the 1440s.[140]

As a papal envoy remarked in the sixteenth century, "no nation has shown less reluctance to adopt the useful inventions of others".[141] But the Ottomans were also themselves military innovators. In the 1390s, they established West Eurasia's first permanent artillery corps, as well as its first regular infantry army since the Romans—the Janissaries. They proved themselves to be among the leaders in cannon-enhanced siege warfare, including sapping and mining.[142] In 1444, their coastal batteries managed to sink a ship of the crusader fleet, perhaps the first such event, and their galleys sank a Venetian ship in 1499, perhaps another first.[143] The Venetians acknowledged the superiority of Ot-toman vessels and artillery at this time.[144] The Ottomans were also pioneers in the use of "gunboats" of several varieties, including light galleys, for riverine amphibious warfare, first on the Danube and then on the Tigris and Euphra-tes.[145] On land, at the Battle of Varna in 1444, they used a defensive barrier of entrenchments, iron stakes, and cannon chained together, before adopting the more mobile *tabor*, or perhaps merging the two techniques—the system was credited to them as far away as India.[146] Their individual firearms also rated highly—their musket barrels were imported by Christian European powers. It may have been the Ottomans who developed the crucial serpentine trigger mechanism in the 1440s and, in 1526, first used volley fire.[147] Apart from mili-tary hardware, we have seen that the Ottomans were pioneers in statecraft, recovery techniques, man-powering, and organisation for war: strategy, logis-tics, and preparation. Within their own domains, they paid for local supplies to avoid damage to the economy, and carefully stocked and restocked depots with provisions and equipment. When the Hapsburgs finally retook Budapest in 1686, they found 247 cannon on the walls, and another 213 spares, laid by to equip another fortress or a field army.[148]

Ottoman economic interaction with West Europe was substantial, and things and thoughts percolated north as well as south. We know that the

Ottoman tastes in coffee, carpets, tulips, and artistic motifs were among them, and I suspect a similar but untold story for statecraft and war-craft, its Muslim origins shrouded by Orientalism. While the Ottomans did most of their land-fighting against Austrians, East Europeans, and Iranians, they also fought the Spanish in the long and bloody "forgotten war" in North Africa, 1510–80, in which many Spanish crewmen learned their trade. Ottoman war-craft was also taken up wholeheartedly by Sa'idid Morocco about the same time, giving the Portuguese military a similar harsh tempering, in a war that has been described as a "school for cutthroats".[149] "Iberians used Morocco as a training ground to experiment and gain experience with tactics they were to use elsewhere in the Atlantic world and the Indian Ocean".[150] The English also had a touch of this brutal military education during their tenure of Tangier, 1661–84. Above all, it was the Ottomans who swept the Genoese westward, and closed down all southward options for European expansion.

Decline set in from the eighteenth century, but in the fifteenth to seventeenth centuries the Ottomans were the world's leading "gunpowder empire". Their gun fighting, man-powering, networking, and administrative skills were second to none, and all with hardly a Western European institution in sight. What they did share with Europe was plague-boosted consumer demand, urbanisation, and disposable capital, and the various plague-driven enhancements of gun technology, scribal labour, and man-powering techniques. The Ottomans did attempt long-range maritime colonialism in the Indian Ocean in the sixteenth century, but were not too bothered when the ecology of their southern coasts constricted it. They had plenty on their plate within West Eurasia. Indeed, Europe coveted what they had. Egypt was "a prize for which the Spanish and the Portuguese would have gladly traded all their claims in the Americas", at least before Potosi erupted silver.[151] France would no doubt have preferred the Levant to Canada, and Russia, Istanbul to Siberia, but the Ottomans gave none of them this choice. Their main contributions to West Eurasian expansion outside its boundaries were indirect: a raising of the bar in war and statecraft, and a "Great Diversion" from south to west and east—the long way. In both respects, they were the anvil on which European expansionism was forced to hammer itself out.

12

The Dutch Puzzle and the
Mobilisation of Eastern Europe

THERE WAS AN IMPORTANT exception to the rule that resources per capita doubled after the Black Death: timber. Wood for fuel was not the main problem. Peat and coal were alternative fuel sources. Coppiced trees, cut to produce several slender trunks, regenerated in 20 or 30 years, as did small trees, and were used for fuel as well as joinery and the like. Over 90 years, coppiced oaks produced 2.5 times the wood of mature oaks.[1] But mature trees were needed for ships and for large buildings, which required massive timber frameworks even if built of stone or brick. These trees took up to 120 years to grow. Trees without close access to water transport were of little use to preindustrial timber trades. While pre-plague Western Europe was not generally in "Malthusian crisis", it was running short of accessible prime timber, and this was one shortage that continued after 1350. "Plantation forestry . . . [was] first introduced for wood production in the late fourteenth century almost simultaneously in both France and Germany"[2] Other forest products may also have been in short supply—pitch, tar, potash, and so on were literally the essence of forest, burned down. They were sometimes sustainable by-products of rotating slash-and-burn agriculture, but also came from the permanent clearance of forest for cultivation. Pitch and tar were important for caulking ships; together with flax or hemp for cordage they were known as "naval stores". Large mature forests took decades to regenerate. Northwest Europe had long drawn timber from Norway. From 1350, pre-plague shortages encountered the post-plague boom and Western Europe drew more and more of its timber and forest products from Eastern Europe via its Baltic coast. Western European resource dependence on the east is usually associated with the rise of the Polish grain trade, which emerged in the late fifteenth century and flourished in the sixteenth and earlier seventeenth centuries. In fact, it began more than a century earlier, with forest products.

The evidence for this is quite recent and has yet to be fully factored in to European history. Most timber objects decompose over centuries, but there is an exception. As well as long balks for ships and large buildings, prime timber was used for large, high-quality oak boards known as wainscots, one of whose uses in turn was room panelling. Until replaced by canvas in the seventeenth century, these were a favourite surface for the artists of the Low Countries Renaissance, whose best work was carefully preserved. Dating of timber from its growth rings is an old game, but from about 2002, non-intrusive techniques were developed for finding its place of origin as well. Some 540 works of art from the early plague era have been tested, and the wood for 80% came from the Baltic.[3] The dominant source was inland Poland, with timber floated in rafts down the Vistula River and processed into balks and wainscots at Gdansk (Danzig). Tests on English wood also demonstrate a shift from Norwegian to Baltic sources. "For the fourteenth, fifteenth and early sixteenth centuries, all tested boards . . . in England show that imported timber came from Poland".[4] The scale of the timber trade burgeoned, as did that in forest products. "There can be little doubt that there was a rise in both timber and by-product imports over the century, despite the drop in population". "Over the fourteenth century the timber trade possibly doubled in volume".[5]

Many areas across Europe, depopulated by the Black Death, reverted to forest, and from some point in the fifteenth century these forests must have matured, alleviating the prime timber bottleneck. Yet, from the mid-fifteenth century, timber prices rose, suggesting that demand was increasing still further, overtaking increased supply.[6] Western Europe's maritime powers took measures to preserve and replant ship timber from this time. "Venice passed the earliest forest ordinances in the fifteenth century. The Low Countries followed in 1517, Spain in 1518, a number of German states in the 1530s and 1540s, England in 1543, Sweden in 1558, and Tuscany in 1559, among others".[7] But they remained dependent on the Baltic in varying degrees. A galleon required 2,000 mature oaks, equivalent to 20 hectares of forest. English and Dutch drew much of their oak for keels and pine for masts from the Baltic beginning in 1350. Portugal's accessible prime timber was already depleting by 1450; and it quickly used up that of its early colony, Madeira. It therefore took a keen interest in Baltic ships and timber from the later fifteenth century.[8] Spain was somewhat better supplied with hull timber, but "all western European powers relied on pines from the Baltic region for masts".[9] Western Europe's expansion floated

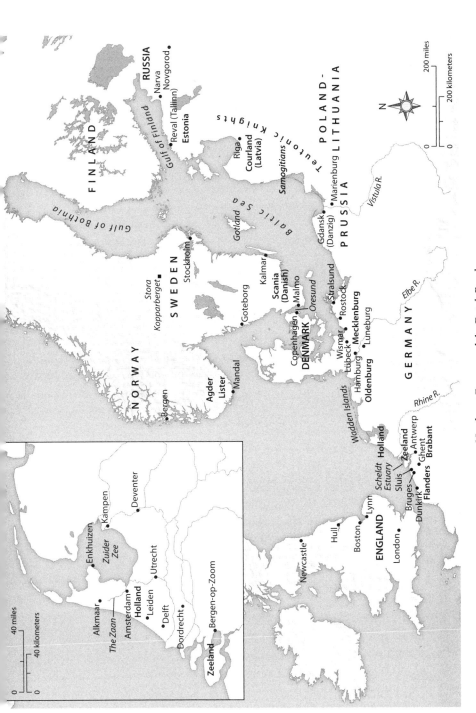

MAP 9. Northeast Europe and the Dutch Puzzle

on Eastern European timber, and this was only one of the ways in which the former drew on the latter.

I Plague and Empire in Eastern Europe

We saw in chapters 1 and 2 that inland Poland was one of the few regions that does seem to have avoided some early strikes of plague, before being ravaged like the rest in the fifteenth century. There were early strikes on the Baltic coast, but at least some did not move south despite navigable rivers. A possible reason, noted in chapter 2, is that bulk upriver imports, unlike timber rafted downriver for export, were very modest before 1400. Over time, imports of cured fish and English woollens grew, perhaps transferring rats, and unassisted rat spread also occurred, with inland Poland joining the main stream of West Eurasian plague history from about 1390. As these increasing imports suggest, there are some signs of positive plague economic effects in Poland and its neighbours.

The Baltic littoral was a region of multiple allegiances—autonomous port cities, the Hanseatic League, powerful prelates, Polish and Lithuanian monarchs, and stubbornly polytheist independent tribes such as the Samogitians. The closest thing to a coastal overlord was the Teutonic Order of crusading knights, an organisation similar to the Mamluks in that the elite did not let its offspring inherit, but instead reproduced itself through regular soldier imports from distant parts. After the Black Death, the Order had difficulty finding fresh recruits from Western Europe and relied increasingly on mercenaries and a curious military tourism: seasonal visits from western knights eager for plunder and years off purgatory.[10] Between 1345 and 1380, the Knights and their guests made almost a hundred raids on the still-polytheist Lithuanians, who responded with 40 counter-raids.[11] Between and even during wars, the Order continued to trade with Christian and pagan alike.[12] They were the "sworn enemy and constant trading partner" of Lithuania, the latter facilitated by a series of secret treaties, 1350s–1370s.[13] The Order had a similar love-hate relationship with Novgorod, spending 200 kilograms of silver there annually on furs, despite several wars. It was also heavily involved in the ancient trade in amber, used for the rosary beads that helped the illiterate to remember their prayers. The Order was a partner in the trade of Gdansk and beneficiary of a modest coastal grain trade. Economically, "the latter half of the fourteenth century was very much a 'golden age'" for the Order's domains.[14] Though the Order disintegrated in the later fifteenth century, one of its heirs, the Duchy of Courland in what is now Latvia, launched a brief bid for global empire in

the seventeenth century, building 44 warships and 79 merchantmen and establishing colonies in Gambia, for slaves, and Tobago, for sugar.[15]

The seed of the Knights' demise was planted in 1385–86, when Poland and
Lithuania were dynastically united under the Jagiellons. The union heavily
defeated the Knights at the Battle of Tannenberg in 1410, where both sides had
artillery, and inflicted further defeats over the next half-century.[16] Polish-
Lithuanian influence on the Baltic coast increased, in cooperation with local
port cities. Gdansk remained the leading timber port, and sometimes put its
timber together itself. "In the fifteenth century Gdańsk became not only an
exporter of timber but also the largest Baltic producer of ships sold to the
Dutch and Portuguese".[17] Gdansk itself is said to have had 500 ships flying its
flag by 1450.[18] Around this time, the town boasted a great water mill, driving
18 millstones, four town halls, 130 granaries, and 24 goldsmiths.[19] As the most
accessible timber close to the Vistula was depleted, other rivers and other
river-mouth ports such as Riga and Reval joined the trade in forest products.
An Eastern European post-plague boom, then, was continuing in the Baltic
littoral. But how far did it spread southwards, and down the social scale?

There is some evidence of growing trade and at least urban prosperity
throughout Eastern Europe—the Balkans and Hungary were considered in
chapter 11, as parts of the Ottoman Empire. In the northeast, exports of English
woollens, as against raw wool, multiplied more than tenfold between the 1350s
and the 1490s. "Eastern [European] markets could take up to 60 per cent of
English cloth exports".[20] Absent in inland East Europe before 1350, cured fish
was common at markets as far south as Cracow by 1390. "Dried fish was a
widely traded commodity in late-medieval East Central Europe".[21] Royal charters gave towns some protection from local nobles and prelates, and 22 new
town charters were issued between 1350 and 1450 in Poland, "mostly in the
more prosperous upland region of the south".[22] Poland's most famous trade,
in wheat and rye boated downriver to Gdansk and then exported to the Low
Countries, did not take off until about 1480. It was only 6,000 tons in 1460,
rising to 20,000 by 1500, then really rocketing to 90,000 tons in 1560, and a
quarter-million in 1618.[23] Goods came from the south as well as the north.
Poland-Lithuania defeated the Golden Horde in 1362, recovered from a reverse
result in 1399, and gained access to the Black Sea for a time. Various merchant
networks, such as the Armenians, brought silks and spices north. "The Polan-
ders use more spices than any other nation".[24]

Assessing plague effects embroils us with two long-standing issues in Eastern European history. One is "second serfdom", first posited by Friedrich

Engels. The appropriateness of the term "serfdom", let alone "second serfdom", is now contested, and it may be true that it is too sharply distinguished from other forms of coercing workers and restricting their movement.[25] Something like it did occur, but not immediately after 1350, or 1400, as is generally assumed, so it cannot be harnessed to plague. As in Western Europe, Polish and Lithuanian peasants gained better lands and better tenures in the early plague era, and here too they did so with the connivance of nobles desperate for labour. In Poland, legislation banning peasant movement and increasing compulsory labour on the lord's demesne began in 1496 and was not fully developed until 1588.[26] It correlates with the rise of populations and the grain trade, not with the early plague era. Manorial farming, centred on the commercial cultivation of the lord's demesne, did increase in the fifteenth century, but demesnes expanded by taking up plague-vacated lands, not by kicking out much-needed peasants. Rents were paid in cash or kind as much as in compulsory labour, which was in any case modest as yet. "A workload of one day per week . . . is widely regarded as usual for fifteenth-century Poland".[27]

The condition of Polish peasants before and after 1500 remains contested. One recent study argues that it was grim in the fifteenth century, and improved in the sixteenth. But this focuses on the more prosperous tenants, the Polish equivalent of yeomen, and may mistake a 1460s recession for a century of stagnation.[28] Another study indicates that the average peasant family growing grain would have had 31.5% of their crop available to sell in the first half of the fifteenth century, after their own consumption, seed corn, taxes, tithes, and rents, suggesting a very modest prosperity. By the second half of the sixteenth century, the "surplus" had dropped to 19.3%—closer to bare subsistence given the need to buy such things as salt and tools.[29] Moreover, compulsory labour demands rose, first to two days and then to three a week over the sixteenth century.[30] The proportion of independent peasants halved in the sixteenth century, because lordly demesnes were now increasing at their expense.[31] The Polish population was then rising, so wage labour was available anyway, but what the grain lords wanted was *cheap* labour.

I suspect prospects for peasants varied over space as well as time, in a "niche" or "trans-local" history similar to that of crew-producing regions. The grain trade depended on close access to navigable rivers, and in arable riverlands peasant life became grimmer in the sixteenth century and onwards. The timber trade also depended on rivers, but its catchment was wider. Logs could be floated down fast streams that were not otherwise navigable, and valuable processed forest products, such as the birch tar favoured for caulking ships, could stand the cost of wagon transport better than grain. Peasants in timber trade lands were really farmer-foresters, like seventeenth- and eighteenth-century settlers in North America. In each case, observers sneered at primitive-looking slash-and-burn farming practices, but these provided fields made fertile by the ash, as well as forest products. Such acres could yield two or three times the grain per seed of normal acres.[32] Forest peasants also had access to game, berries, furs, wax, and honey, the last three in increasing demand after the Black Death. Wood-trade lands burgeoned from 1350; grain-trade lands, from 1500. Since the former were better for peasants, this supports the notion that Polish peasants shared in both the early plague era "golden age" to 1500 and its decline thereafter. Even unskilled real wages were high in Polish towns in 1500—higher than England, according to one scholar—but they too declined from 1575, and peasants increasingly tied by law to the land had less access to them in any case.[33] From 1650, Poland fell victim to the rapacity of its nobles and neighbours, and except for Courland the country did not feature in European expansion, though its grain and timber did. We will see in chapter 14 that Poland's socioeconomic experience in the plague era was broadly shared by its Russian rival and neighbour, which did expand.

———

The second long-standing issue in Eastern European history has already been touched on: exploitation, even semi-colonisation, by Western Europe, posited by Immanuel Wallerstein and others. I think that some informal colonisation did occur, but that it was very particular, involving tight economic links between a single city and certain regions, not countries as a whole, let alone the entire subcontinent. Furthermore, it is not clear that all the "colonised" were exploited. The key early urban coloniser was not Gdansk, but its senior partner, Lubeck. "Lübeck and Gdansk were the two hubs of the . . . timber trade".[34] Though Gdansk's own merchants retained some autonomy, resident merchants from Lubeck were its "economic powerhouse".[35] Both cities were members of the Hanseatic League. Lubeck usually appears in the literature as "first among equals" in the League, which was a loose alliance of north European port originating in the thirteenth century. Like Genoa, the Hanse spasmodically fascinates institutionalists, but its formal institutions too do not seem strong. No one even knows how many member cities it had at any given time—between 70 and 100. Lubeck did usually lead the Hanse. But the League also camouflaged Lubeck's own informal empire. Lubeck had been founded on the site of a Slavic town with close river access to the Baltic in 1158. From 1230, it was tightly allied with Hamburg, "in effect its outport on the North Sea".[36] It had become a formidable maritime power by the 1280s, when it was able to coerce Norway into its economic orbit through its control of grain supplies to that kingdom. In Flemish, German, and English trades, however, it tended to be overshadowed by Cologne before 1350. Lubeck's population, small in any case at about 25,000 in 1348, was hard hit by the Black Death. A reasonable estimate of its mortality is 40%, though far higher figures were claimed, and its junior partner Hamburg is said to have suffered even more, with 55%.[37] Yet the upturn in Lubeck's fortunes from 1350 was as sharp as Genoa's, from an even smaller base, and there were other similarities between the two.

Like Genoa's, Lubeck's merchant tribes reshuffled and sought reinforcements after 1350, but in different ways. Its merchant networks were initially kin-based, but after the first strike of plague were shored up by the proliferation of guilds and religious fraternities, which often intersected. Around 1520, there were 70 fraternities in Lubeck, most founded since the 1360s, in addition to 50 guilds.[38] These consolidated plague-depleted families and incorporated newcomers. After a post-1348 surge in immigration,[39] the tradition of exclusion re-asserted itself from 1360 until a fresh strike of plague in 1367 caused the merchant elite to open up again. The same cycle of closing and opening occurred at least twice more, pivoting on the plague strikes of 1388 and 1405, "forcing it to turn to those without ancestral connections".[40] Lubeck was hit by plague six times in the fourteenth century, and five times in the fifteenth, yet its population always recovered quickly. It exceeded 25,000 in 1460, when the city contained 5,385 households, plus temporary dwellings, of which 58% belonged to the middle and upper classes—most of the lower classes supporting this over-sized elite lived elsewhere.[41] The overseas trading posts known as *Kontors* may have delivered another kind of post-plague virtual clan, with rather crew-like qualities. They were staffed by men only, who were discouraged from marrying local women but did consort with them. They had brutal initiation rituals, bouts of hard drinking, and oaths of brotherhood.[42] An exceptional archive of 6,400 Lubeck wills, all dating to before 1500, shows an intersection between fraternities, kontor partners, and urban neighbourhoods. Most guardians and executors came from these networks, not from actual kin.[43]

Most of the reinforcements were presumably Germans, but one intriguing group was merchants from Dubrovnik and other Dalmatian ports. Between 1365 and 1510, almost 10% of Lubeck town councilors were Dalmatian. The

Dubrovnik connection may have allowed Lubeck to outflank the networks of Cologne, Venice, and Genoa in the English and Flemish trades. Certainly, it allowed Lubeck to continue trading when at war with England in 1467–74 by substituting German Lubeckers with Dalmatian ones, who could operate under the radar of English hostility. Such wartime trade substitution, of course, was Dubrovnik's specialist role in the Mediterranean.[44] Lubeckers themselves were martial merchants, and as in Genoa the lower classes sometimes showed a strong sense of citizenship, which made the militia formidable. But, after plague, locals were no longer enough. Lubeck turned to the general German mercenary market, including the crewmen known as "ship-children" who fought ashore or afloat.[45] These men came from infertile North German coasts and islands which now increasingly imported their grain. Like Lubeckers themselves, "ship-children" initially specialised in crossbows, but as early as 1352 there was a turn to guns, which soon also appeared on Lubeck's ships.[46] Financially, Lubeck was reinforced by a precocious turn to mortgages and annuities to deliver credit, an innovation it shared with Hamburg.[47]

Still, 25,000 people was a tiny base for even a small and informal patchwork empire. Lubeck produced little except ships and beer, and most of its assets were outside the city itself. Between about 1360 and 1420, it established control over parts of its immediate hinterland, defeating or buying out local lords.[48] Its burghers owned 240 villages scattered across Northern Germany.[49] Lubeck's most important inland asset was its senior partnership with the salt-producing city of Luneberg, dating from 1379, which it consolidated in 1391–98 by financing linking canals. Local lords and princes contested Lubeck's dominance of Luneberg salt exports to 1410, but Lubeck's military power and money proved too much for them.[50] Wismar and Rostock also joined this inner circle, a ring around the throat of Denmark. It was sometimes known as the Wendish League, after the Slavic people of the region. Lubeck also had partnerships with German-speaking port cities further east: Gdansk, Riga, and others, all the way to Reval or Tallinn on the Gulf of Finland.[51] As we have seen with Gdansk, these towns had territorial overlords, a degree of autonomy, and membership of the Hanse, and sometimes chafed at Lubeck's bit. But Lubeck was "not defied without urgent reasons", and not just because it was leader of the League.[52] In 1408, Lubeck's lesser townsfolk rebelled against the elite and controlled the town for a decade. Their regime was outlawed by the rest of the Hanse, but Wismar, Rostock, and Hamburg remained closely allied with Lubeck despite this.[53] Their relationship with Lubeck trumped that with the Hanse as such.

The best known Hanseatic kontors were in London, Bruges, and Novgorod, but there were some 50 lesser stations in the network—Hull, Boston, and Lynn in eastern England, for example.[54] Lubeck's influence in these trading posts varied. It delivered Bruges its grain, and could bring that much bigger city into line by withholding supplies, as it did in 1391 and 1436.[55] It certainly dominated the Hanse in Scandinavia. In the early plague era, Lubeck and its allies increasingly established hegemony over the richer districts. The Norwegian crown merged into the Danish in 1380, and the 1397 Kalmar union with Sweden too was at least partly intended to contest Lubeckian control.[56] But, at sea, Lubeck and Company was usually a match for all Scandinavia until the sixteenth century. Polish timber allowed its ship tonnage to increase greatly after 1350. In 1399, there were 1,760 ship departures from Lubeck alone, and the Hanse fleet eventually numbered a thousand ships, a quarter owned by Lubeck, which were bigger than average.[57] Bigger cogs were later joined by new-style "hulks", which were bigger still, with stern rudders, two masts, and more efficient building techniques. Until the early sixteenth century, these were armed merchantmen, not warships, but their solid forecastles and after-castles, their size, their handguns, and their cannon allowed them to double as both.[58]

Lubeck's rivals contested its trade privileges, its control of the Baltic, including the Scanian herring fishery, and its access to Oresund, "the Sounds," linking the Baltic and North Seas. Lubeck could send some products by river, canal, and short land portages to Hamburg, but not very bulky products such as timber. As the prime herring fisheries shifted from the Baltic to the North Sea in the fifteenth century, it needed access to these as well. Lubeck won a war with Denmark over these issues in 1361–70, which "set the seal on the Hansa's supremacy over Denmark".[59] When Denmark did succeed in imposing tolls in the Sounds, Hanse cities were exempt.[60] Lubeck and Company had the better of several more wars with Denmark up to 1522–23, when it placed its candidates on the thrones of both Denmark and Sweden. Until the sixteenth century, Sweden usually sided with Lubeck in conflicts with Denmark-Norway because that town and its allies had a "relentless grip on the [Swedish] national economy".[61] Sweden's main towns and export industries were dominated— and developed—by the Lubeckian Hanse. German merchants and craftsmen comprised about a third of the population of Stockholm and Kalmar. A Swedish law of 1350 allocated half the town council seats and one of two burgomasters to Germans.[62]

From this time, Sweden's economy moved towards regional specialisation, and began to export more cattle and mine products.[63] Lubeck imported and redistributed hides, butter, and almost all of Sweden's copper and iron output which, as we saw in chapter 5, increased sixfold between 1340 and 1540.[64] The flow of copper increased even more. Hanseatic capital was behind these increases. Hanse merchants in overseas towns were "trans-locals", engaging in local politics and charity as well as trade and industry, but retaining cohesion, not intermarrying, and returning home on retirement.[65] We noted in chapter 4 that Lubeck led the post-plague surge in the cod and herring trades. Its share of the herring trade around 1400 was 60–75%, and it was Lubeck that "succeeded in developing a high quality product by means of uniform barrels and content, strict rules for processing, control and quality markings".[66] Its share of the cod trade was even higher, with 2,000 people working in its cod processing and trading kontor in Bergen. "Lubeckers are virtually synonymous with Hansards in Bergen".[67]

Lubeck used violence against rival polities, and even against its regional semi-colonies when they contested its control of commerce. In 1455, the natives of Bergen, led by their bishop, tried to assert authority over the kontor, but were attacked by its merchants, who killed the bishop and 60 of his supporters.[68] But "soft power" was the norm. The Danish crown, like the Spanish in Naples with the Genoese, backed the foreign traders, not its own citizens, after the Bergen incident.[69] Long thought to have been exploitative of Norwegian fishermen, the cod trade is now considered beneficial to them, especially in the post-1400 context of rising prices. The relationship between Lubeck and its semi-colonies in both Norway and Sweden became quite intimate, like that of Istanbul and its circles of virtual hinterlands. Lubeck had little need for herds in its immediate hinterland because its overseas town supply districts delivered butter, hides, and wool. So Lubeck's immediate German hinterland turned to market gardens[70] and to hop production, with the hops exported to the overseas hinterlands to be used in their beer brewing.[71] Increasing absolute imports of this semi-luxury by plague-halved Scandinavian populations indicates against harsh economic exploitation by the Hanse, though no doubt the latter profited most. An element of cultural colonisation matched the economic, and can be traced archaeologically by the proliferation of quality German stoneware, even in non-elite homes. Lubeck exported other culture-carrying artefacts too, ranging from stoves to altars.[72] Swedish towns are said to have featured "a cosmopolitan Hanseatic signature".[73] How far acculturation went is hard to say, but it is likely to have smoothed the economic relationship. Bergen is said to have a taste for Lubeck-style beer to this day.[74]

To sum up, Lubeck's informal patchwork empire had multiple layers and components. One was membership of a wider organisation, the Hanseatic

League, which gave its partners a false but useful sense of parity with it. Another was its development of an urban hierarchy, with itself at the top, and some specialisation below: Luneberg in salt, Hamburg in beer, Gdansk in timber. Third was its leadership in the timber, herring, and cod trades. Fourth came its overseas semi-colonies: in and around Stora Kopparberget, the Swedish copper mining centre, the main Swedish ports of Stockholm, Malmo, and Kalmar, and Bergen in Norway. The economies of these and Lubeck's immediate hinterland adjusted to match each other. Finally, intertwined with the others, was Lubeck's post-plague systemisation of the transnational Eastern European pool of manpower and natural resources which, in the hands of others, literally enabled the global expansion of Western Europe.

Like Genoa's, Lubeck's camouflaged empire was as much a matter of condominium as sole rule, symbiosis as much as exploitation, and it was eventually muscled aside by nation-states, whose historians are sometimes overly eager in dating its demise and under-eager in recognising its contribution. From the early sixteenth century, in competition with the centralising monarchies of Denmark-Norway and Sweden, Lubeck introduced purpose-built warships, with broadsides of heavy cannon, culminating in the 2,000-ton *Adler* around 1570. By this time, Lubeck was losing out in the conflict, and its "role as a power on the same level as the two Nordic kingdoms, with ambitions to intervene in their domestic politics, was finished. . . . The ability of the centralised state to mobilise resources for war had been proved".[75] Yet a small city had managed to become a great power, despite/because of the Black Death, and to remain so for two centuries. By the late fifteenth century, its heirs in the cod trade were pushing further and further into the Northwest Atlantic in search of fresh fishing grounds. It was the city-state of Lubeck, not the nation-states of Denmark or Sweden, that energised this trade, pioneered urban colonialism in the north and mobilised the Eastern European transnational pool of raw materials and labour. These assets were taken over, lock, stock, and fish barrel, by the Dutch.

II Plague, Institutions, and the Rise of Holland

The ascent of the northern Netherlands from apparent backwater to global super-power in the century after 1568 is an astonishing tale, sometimes known as "the Dutch miracle". Led by the province of Holland, the Dutch shook off Spanish rule by 1580, defeated the Spanish and Portuguese empires by 1648, acquired a global empire of their own, achieved hegemony in world trade, and enjoyed a cultural florescence, all at the same time. Once associated with the sixteenth-century conversion to Protestantism and the Dutch Revolt, historians now look for deeper causes for this remarkable rise and spread. Benign institutions remain the favourite, but there have been commendable attempts to mix them with ecology. Much of Holland lay at or below sea level, and was reclaimed from the sea and from peat bogs in the eleventh to thirteenth centuries. The relatively few lords and prelates had to offer secure tenures to attract peasants to undertake this work, who developed collective organisations to maintain it against flooding with the famous dykes. This is thought, a trifle paradoxically, to have enhanced both individualism and collectivism. Though medieval Holland had some formidable sovereign counts, it does seem that lords, church, and urban guilds were comparatively weak. This may indeed have given Holland a flexibility that enabled it to cope with major change but more, I suspect, through the weakness of traditional institutions than their strength.

Medieval Holland had a surprising number of market towns, about two dozen, six of which were considered major. Its urbanisation rate is put at a high 23% in 1348. The institutional argument is that numerous competing towns combined with independent peasants and weak feudal institutions to give Holland unusually open markets, in labour and property as well as goods. The towns were accustomed to governing themselves, and to negotiating taxes with the count. From 1428, Burgundian (and, from 1482, Hapsburg) dynasts ruled Holland, along with the other 16 provinces of the Low Countries. Until the Hapsburgs adopted a repressive policy towards Protestants in the 1560s, their rule was quite benign. But they did need money to fight their wars, and the provincial "states" or assemblies (made up of the leading merchants of the main towns) became accustomed to negotiating and collecting taxes on a larger scale, developing a capacity for self-government and public debt. From the 1570s, this was one basis of Dutch success in their war against Spain. Environmental change has recently been added to the institutional argument. Land reclamation and peat mining for fuel sowed trouble for themselves by causing soil subsidence that, along with increasing flooding from the thirteenth century, reduced farmland. This combined with partible inheritance, which subdivided farms to below subsistence levels, to force people out of grain farming. "Instead of grain, farms started producing dairy, flax, and hemp, while surplus farm labor found work in fishing and transportation services".[76] Most transport had long involved water carriage, on the many inlets, rivers, and other waterways of the region. The extra hands freed by declining grain farming enabled Holland to develop its maritime capacity, which was another basis for the Dutch ascent.

This all seems plausible enough, but what of plague? The Second Pandemic was once thought to have largely bypassed the Low Countries. Wim Blockmans disproved this as long ago as 1980.[77] But Blockmans found that some strikes did not extend to Holland. Recent scholarship has found evidence of normally high plague mortalities in parts of the southern Low Countries, but not the north.[78] The activities of the flagellant movement, that strange self-sacrificial response to the first strike, permeated the south but reached only to Dordrecht in southernmost Holland.[79] What scholars have yet to explain is *why* plague in Holland might have been relatively mild. They acknowledge that the period 1350–1500 was prosperous in Holland, but not that this was also the case elsewhere. "Holland was an island of prosperity amid the general economic distress of Europe in the latter half of the fourteenth century".[80] Holland and its even smaller neighbour, Zeeland, "uniquely in Europe, experienced a continuous expansion of urban life throughout the long depression elsewhere".[81] Even a fine recent work which acknowledges that the "much-quoted late medieval crisis" is now contested, still concludes that "in the second half of the fourteenth century, Holland's economic development seems to have accelerated, . . . at a time when other countries were experiencing problems". It also claims that the "late fourteenth-century boom had [institutional] roots in the preceding period", namely the eleventh to thirteenth centuries, so discounting plague.[82] Explaining abnormally low plague mortality, and how it can be reconciled with a strong economic boom, is our first Dutch puzzle.

Did Holland escape the first strike? "The Holland narrative sources are silent about the Black Death",[83] but this was true of many places. Most medieval scribes saw no need to recount what was all too obvious to everyone, and Holland's paucity of lords and bishops might have reduced the record of replacement tenants and priests sometimes available elsewhere. Some Dutch economic historians suspect that the issue is absence of evidence, not absence of plague.[84] Predictably, Ole Benedictow has no doubt that the Black Death did hit the northern Netherlands. He cites a Deventer church register showing a 23-fold increase over average deaths in 1350; a reference to "enormous mortality" in Utrecht; and a sharp jump in income from intestate deaths.[85] Since Benedictow, a mid-fourteenth century undocumented mass grave with an estimated 800 burials and *Y. Pestis* DNA has been found at Bergen-op-Zoom.[86] None of these three towns are in Holland, but they are all close by and well connected to it. The Deventer evidence suggests 46% mortality if normal deaths were 2%. There are also strong indirect indications that the first strike hit Holland hard. Some are noted below, but one was a sharp rise in wages, which doubled in Leiden in the 1350s, while rye prices rose less than 50%.[87] On the whole it seems probable that Holland did suffer from the first strike, perhaps to much the same extent as other places. Holland certainly suffered from later strikes, at least four between 1360 and 1401. But, on Blockman's evidence, it missed two other strikes in this period, in 1363–64 and 1371–72. This trend became much stronger in the fifteenth century, when Holland missed, or was little affected by, seven of nine epidemics.[88] A recent study of a nunnery in Southeast Holland finds average death rates only half as high as those in England, 1412–1500.[89] After 1500, this nunnery's death rates return to the wider European pattern, as does Holland's epidemic history. It seems that Holland's plagues were not so much milder as fewer, especially in the fifteenth century. Drowned rats may explain this puzzle.

"Reclamation projects more or less came to an end" in Holland around 1350.[90] This is a further indication that the country was not spared the first strike: demand for land, and the labour to reclaim it, both suddenly fell away. But the inherited effects of reclamation in causing land to subside continued. Peat mining may even have increased, for export to the southern Netherlands whose peat supplies were depleting, and this too contributed to subsidence. On top of this, sea inundations increased markedly, from six major floods in the thirteenth century, to 12 in the fourteenth, and 17 in the fifteenth.[91] "All in all, the changes in Holland implied a substantial increase in the water surface area from 1350 onwards . . . easily covering more than 50 percent of the former land".[92] Shortages of labour worsened the situation around 1360 by reducing maintenance of dykes, dams, and drainage channels, yet another indicator of a first strike.[93] But it was the first quarter of the fifteenth century that was the worst period for floods. A particularly disastrous one in 1421 drowned 20 villages and 10,000 people around Dordrecht, leaving the town "isolated on a tiny island". "During the fifteenth century all the western coasts of the Netherlands were under attack by the waves".[94]

What these floods might have done is reduced rat populations in the countryside and created an unusual number of water barriers to their unassisted re-settlement. The northern Netherlands certainly had rats at various points in the early plague era. Peasant grain lofts had "owl holes" to encourage owls to hunt rats at night, and there are records of rat traps and payments to rat catchers.[95] But sudden floods, like plagues, would have wiped out rats in the affected districts. Navigable rivers and canals assisted rat re-colonisation by transporting the grain and other bulk cargoes in which they hitchhiked, but the increasing number of shallow lakes and peat bogs were not used for transport. All substantial bodies of water, navigable or not, blocked *unassisted* rat spread. Amphibian as West Eurasia was, few countries were quite so water-logged as the late medieval northern Netherlands. My theory is that rat saturation before the first strike, and near-extinction after it, was followed by incomplete resettlement by un-plagued rats, and the abnormally slow spread of unassisted plagued rats. A few other flood-prone parts of the Netherlands also have indications of more floods and less plague.[96]

So, while the Black Death itself around 1350 had the usual demographically negative and economically positive effects in Holland, some later epidemics missed parts of Holland's countryside, which was then able to repopulate plague-depleted towns. Fewer epidemics reduced Holland's human population decline by allowing post-plague baby booms to catch up faster than elsewhere. The best available statistics suggest a fall of only 20% between 1350 and 1400, from 260,000 to 209,000.[97] In the fifteenth century, unlike the rest of West Eurasia, the population rose, recovering the 1350 level around 1500 and reaching 275,000 in 1514. So Holland's plague experience was a game of two halves; a lethal one in the later fourteenth century, and a much less lethal one in the fifteenth. The pattern in real wage levels seems to support this. They are bewilderingly contested by the experts, but high wages in the later fourteenth century do appear to have been followed by lower ones in the fifteenth, making Dutch wages internationally competitive.[98] From 1400, the Dutch also had a higher and growing proportion of wage-earners. Here is another key to the Dutch puzzle. Holland became a precociously populous maritime "crew region." Unusually, it was able to employ its own crewmen, rather than export them—inside Europe as yet, but in distant waters and distant markets. The Dutch had their own post-plague economic boom, but it was briefer than most. After it, they serviced other peoples" continuing booms with their numerous crews, boats, and ships.

Contrary to the view of some scholars, Holland before 1350 does not look particularly prosperous, especially compared to Flanders, where Bruges and Ghent were already great cities. The high urbanisation figure in 1350, at 23%, is somewhat deceptive. No town reached the 10,000-person threshold, and only one exceeded 5,000—Dordrecht at 7,500. The towns doubled as farming villages, with dairy cattle inside the walls and townsfolk-tilled fields without, though they also had marketplaces and access to waterways.[99] Recent calculations of production per capita in 1348 put Holland behind Spain.[100] The evidence of urban and economic development tends to postdate 1350. Deep-sea herring fishing, the export of dairy products, and the importing of English wool for Holland weavers all surged in the 1350s, not before.[101] The towns of Leiden, Alkmaar, and Delft began investing in improved port and market facilities from that decade, and Enkhuizen built its first harbour.[102] The number of foreign merchants also increased from this time.[103] In Amsterdam they were brewers from Hamburg.

From 1353, Hamburg, partner of Lubeck and leading post-plague beer exporter, began using Amsterdam as the Low Countries distribution centre for its long-lasting hopped product.[104] As early as 1365, Amsterdam had 78 beer importers, 72 of them from Hamburg, and the former town took around half of the latter's exports, 13,000 tons in 1365–66.[105] There were only 3,000 or so Amsterdamers at this time, so however heroic their own consumption, most beer was re-exported to the rest of the Netherlands. This helped develop the town's fleet and distribution network, and prompted the Dutch to brew hopped beer themselves. They exported it to the southern Netherlands in great quantities until about 1500, when this region too began brewing its own. High beer consumption continued in the north into the sixteenth century and beyond, and taxes on it became a large part of town revenues, used to pay interest on public debt, which was held by the elite merchants doing the taxing. "Municipal finance . . . floated as a cork on a great pool of beer".[106] This is cited as an example of the importance of institutions in Holland's rise. But plague-boosted bulk trade and consumption were also required. In 1531, Holland's towns bribed the Hapsburg government into banning rural brewing[107]—not great evidence of a free market.

The northern Netherlands entered another, even greater, trade on Hanseatic coattails: the salt herring industry. Baltic and southern North Sea herring stocks were declining in the later fourteenth century. It was the Dutch who pushed further into the North Sea after herring, using new techniques: large drag nets, a gutting method that enhanced preservation, and specialised ships able to salt herring at sea. This "herring buss" was much larger than coastal fishing boats, with 14 to 20 crewmen, three masts (detachable to increase working space), and cargo capacities of 60–80 tons. "These methods won the Dutch access to larger, hitherto untouched, offshore North Sea stocks".[108] The busses stayed at sea from June to November (which meant that their crews missed the harvests) with the fish taken home by fast yachts, which also renewed salt supplies and provisions. This system did not fully click into place until the early fifteenth century, and some of it was borrowed from Lubeck.

Holland initially exported its herring through Lubeck's Scanian markets, beginning in the 1360s. By 1400, however, it was distributing herring from its own ports. Flanders and Zeeland were also active in the trade, but were overhauled by Holland. By 1562, Holland had 400 busses, Zeeland 200, and Flanders 100.[109] The total catch in 1550 was about 50,000 tons, a quarter eaten by the Dutch themselves, the rest exported. The catch peaked at between 80,000 and 100,000 tons in the early seventeenth century, when there were about a thousand Dutch busses at sea, most from Holland.[110] Again, an institutional gloss can be put on this great trade. Holland's herring ports were regulating it from 1424 at the latest,[111] and this was important for quality control. But burgeoning fifteenth-century consumer demand *outside* the Netherlands was more important still.

The herring fishery helped develop the most important Dutch industry of all—trade itself, in the capacious holds of full-rigged ships. The rigging and ship-building methods, a key feature of post-plague technology, may have come via the Basques, but the Dutch eventually added innovations of their own: wind-powered sawmills for ship-building and the famous *fluit*, a ship built of light timber, designed for big cargoes and small crews.[112] By the mid-seventeenth century, ship-building in Holland cost a third less than in England, and ships themselves were a major export.[113] Long before this, however, the Dutch had an edge over the competition in the number and efficiency of their ships, conceded by the Hanse itself in the mid-sixteenth century.[114] Technology was helped by the relatively large numbers and modest wages of fifteenth-century Dutch crews. The great expansion of the Dutch fleet began around 1400, matching the new supply of crew. By 1477, Holland had between 230 and 300 ocean-going ships excluding herring busses; and 400 in 1500, when it was building 40 full-rigged ships annually.[115] Its tonnage in 1477 of around 38,000 already made it one of Europe's leading maritime powers, long before Protestantism, Hapsburg tyranny, independence, or the full development of Dutch institutions. On the eve of the revolt, the Dutch fleet, still technically Hapsburg, had risen further, to 160,000 tons.

The herring trade required quality salt, and with Lubeck monopolising Luneberg this had to come from Bourgneuf in France or Setubal in Portugal. In 1400–1411, Hollanders and Zeelanders sold their beer and picked up their salt, and much else, at the Bruges outport of Sluis, where recent research shows they did almost a quarter of detected smuggling, much more than any other countries.[116] After this, they began sailing to Bourgneuf and Setubal themselves, picking up wine as well as salt. The herring trade also required markets, and timber and naval stores for the ships, and the Baltic delivered these.

Despite periodic clashes with Lubeck, Dutch Baltic trade reached dizzying heights—about 700 ship visits by 1497, 78% of them from Holland.[117] In 1475–85, the Dutch carried 39% of Gdansk's trade, compared to Lubeck's 50%, shipping in herring, wine, and cloth and shipping out timber and forest products—not much grain at this stage. By 1550–55, the Lubeck sorcerer had been outshone by its apprentice, with the Dutch now carrying 53% of the Polish trade. To add injury to insult, they provided three-quarters of the herring entering the Baltic.[118] By this time, grain featured large in the return cargoes.

Holland may have ceased growing enough grain to feed itself in the late fourteenth century, but early imports are likely to have come from the eastern Netherlands. We have seen that there was a turn to other types of farming; dairying and "industrial crops"—madder for dye, flax for linen, hemp for rope, and hops for beer. From 1400, most grain was imported, from northeastern France and perhaps northwest Germany. From the mid-fifteenth century, Holland added the Baltic to its grain sources, pushed by its growing population and a grain shortage in northwest Europe in 1437–39. In 1480–82, there was another dearth and Holland's Baltic imports took off, from 6,000 tons in 1460, to 20,000 tons in 1500, to well over 100,000 tons by 1560—around 90% of its grain consumption.[119] Holland was now completely dependent on distant Poland for grain and timber and remained so into the eighteenth century.

Lubeck sometimes cooperated with its Dutch rivals. The growing scale of the Baltic trades was more than even it could handle, and the Dutch initially accepted a subordinate position by selling through Hanseatic merchants. Several towns in the northern Netherlands were actually members of the Hanse. Holland's towns were not, but their beery relationship with Hamburg was close, and that with Lubeck was fairly good until the 1430s, and occasionally thereafter. In Amsterdam, its merchants stayed in a hotel called the Lubeck Arms.[120] But, from the 1430s, Lubeck sporadically tried to block Dutch entry to the Baltic by force, sometimes in alliance with other powers. In the war of 1437–41, Holland's fleet attacked Lubeck's several times, succeeded in forcing the Sounds into the Baltic in 1440, and secured free entry and peace in 1441.[121] In another war in 1509–12, Holland and its Danish ally were less successful, with the former losing 50 ships in one disastrous encounter in 1511, but again securing free entry in 1512. In 1523, Holland forced the Sound again, with 130 merchantmen and 12 warships. In 1533–35 there was another full-scale naval war in which Holland, with the help of both Sweden and Denmark, again defeated Lubeck.[122] A final Lubeck attempt to block the Sound in the 1540s also failed.

Clearly there was nothing peaceable about Holland's crews, and they were also well armed and financed. At sea, their approach in wartime was to select their biggest and sturdiest merchant ships, and equip them as "warships" with extra guns and men; they were not yet purpose-built for war. Dutch towns had good militias and a lot of cannon—anti-artillery measures in fortification appear from the early fifteenth century.[123] Holland's assembly usually voted a very modest tribute to its Hapsburg rulers, but these sums soared on the rare occasions that the latter seemed to be fighting in the former's interests, in 1521–23 for example, when East Friesland, a haven for pirates, was conquered.[124] The Baltic trade wars were entirely funded and organised by the Holland towns, with Burgundian and Hapsburg sovereigns at best cheering from the sidelines. Informally, Holland was a great naval power long before the successful Dutch revolt in 1572–1609. A key contributor to the success of the revolt was a piratical flotilla known as the Sea Beggars, who had not surrendered after the failure of an earlier revolt in the late 1560s. Said to be staunch Calvinists led by lesser nobles, they were prone to roistering, brutality, and plundering, of friends as well as foes—"violent carousers, indiscriminate plunderers, and coarse riffraff".[125] This looks more like plague-incubated crew culture than Protestant piety.

III Dutch Expansion

To argue that the "Dutch miracle" had a plague-influenced root is not to deny seventeenth-century Dutch dynamism in war, trade, and expansion. Between 1579 and 1586, Holland and its six smaller neighbours federated into the United Provinces of the (northern) Netherlands, which contained about 1.2 million people. A century later, the population had increased to 1.9 million, still a tiny demographic base for what was now a global superpower.[126] The United Provinces fought the Spanish most of the time between 1568 and 1648 ("The Eighty Years' War"); the French much of the time between 1672 and 1748; and occupied themselves in the intervals with two naval wars against the English, 1652–54 and 1665–67, with a third in 1672–74 when the English were allied to the French. All were formidable enemies, but the Dutch and their subsidised allies were usually a match for them.

These wars, particularly against the Spanish, were of the love-hate variety described in chapter 7: fighting with one hand and trading with the other. Despite relative decline and multiple conflicts, the Spanish recovered quickly from the failure of their Armada in 1588, aimed at knocking out the English ally of the Dutch rebels.[127] They then scored a number of successes on both land and sea, the latter particularly through privateers. Spain controlled Dunkirk between 1585 and 1646. This port was the Algiers of Europe, a flag-shifting nest of cosmopolitan corsairs who took thousands of Dutch ships during the Eighty Years' War, for the Spanish and, after 1662, for the French. The Dutch also lost some 2,000 ships to the English.[128] But the Dutch countered with privateering campaigns of their own, and with two great naval victories over Spain. They took the entire American silver fleet, worth 12 million florins, in 1628,[129] and they destroyed a "Second Spanish Armada" in 1639.[130] Yet the Dutch remained dependent on Iberian salt and silver, and the Iberians remained dependent on Dutch-transported Baltic goods. "Iberia could not survive without northern grain and naval stores".[131] "Despite the [Spanish] embargo, Dutch trade with Spain and Portugal continued unabated".[132] During the War of Spanish Succession, 1701–14, France too issued 4,000 trading licenses to its Dutch enemies.[133]

It was the Dutch who pioneered a practice that might be called "emergency outsourcing". By outsourcing in general I mean the acquisition outside Europe, not of exotic luxuries, but of mundane, ordinary goods traditionally produced inside Europe. This began on a large scale around 1500 with cod fishing in North America, on and around the Newfoundland Banks. The quantities of fish involved quickly became quite astonishing but seldom feature in analyses of the benefits for Europe of global expansion or in the measuring of transoceanic trade. Dutch, Spanish, and Portuguese were heavily involved at various times, but the long-term leaders were the French and English. These last two alone brought home 180,000 tons of cured cod, live-weight equivalent, in 1680 and "between 204,000 and 275,000 metric tons" a year, 1769–74.[134] But Dutch emergency outsourcing was a matter of salt for curing, not the fish itself. Rather like the Ming "trade bans", the Iberian embargo on Dutch traders was usually nominal, but had occasional brief spasms of genuine enforcement, one of them between 1599 and 1605. Cut off from Setubal salt, the Dutch turned to Caribbean natural salt sources, such as the island of Punta Araya on the Venezuelan coast. The Dutch sent more than 600 salt ships to the area in five years, by which time the embargo had become nominal again.[135] This trans-Atlantic emergency outsourcing enabled them to avoid Hapsburg strangulation of their crucial salt-fish trades. The British were to put the same technique to good use against Napoleon, this time in the form of Canadian timber.

Dutch expansion in Further Asia and the Atlantic took place at the very same time as the wars with Spain. "By 1648 the Dutch were indisputably the greatest trading nation in the world, with commercial outposts and fortified 'factories' scattered from Archangel to Recife and from New Amsterdam to Nagasaki."[136] Dutch empire was largely handled by two chartered joint-stock companies: in Asia, by the Dutch East Indies Company (*Vereigde Oost-Indische Compagnie*, or VOC), founded in 1602, and in the Atlantic, by the (first) West Indies Company (WIC, 1621). This corporate character is behind claims that the Dutch empire was one of commerce, not violence. In fact, both were Dutch stocks in trade. The companies were given monopolies on trade and colonisation in their respective zones by the state to compensate them for meeting the overheads on expansion, including gunships, forts, and soldiers. As one leading official of the VOC famously put it in 1614, "trade without war or war without trade cannot be maintained".[137]

The Dutch leapfrogged from latecomer to leader in East Indies trade in the 50 years after 1595, and held that lead for almost another century. They extended their trade tentacles to China and Japan by 1609. They were usually conciliatory towards these big powers, and to the Mughals in India, but used violence freely against European rivals and smaller Asian powers. They established their main base in Batavia, in Java, in 1619 and a much-needed halfway station at Cape Town, South Africa, in 1652. The neo-European Afrikaner (Boer) people were a side effect of this. The VOC seized most of the Portuguese bases in India and Southeast Asia, including Melaka. It conquered parts of Sri Lanka and Java and the whole of a half-dozen small but rich spice islands, and subordinated several Muslim sultanates. Selective violence correlated closely with monopoly profits. Like the Genoese with Mediterranean alum and mastic, the VOC tried to control production as well as distribution where possible, enabling them to rack up prices. The Banda Islands were the main producer of nutmeg and mace. After encountering fierce resistance, the Dutch conquered the islands with a force of 2,000 men in 1621, killed or expelled the 15,000 indigenes, and replaced them with slaves.[138] They then adjusted supply to increase prices—nutmeg sold in Europe for 4500% of its production cost. They were a little less successful with cloves from the Moluccas and cinnamon from Sri Lanka, in which the markup was "only" 1500%. Compare this to the 500% by now normal in the pepper trade, which the Dutch led but did not monopolise.[139] Despite strong surges by the British and French from the 1730s, they held the overall lead in European voyages to Further Asia between 1600 and 1800: 4,720 in all, compared to 2,676 British ships and 1,455 French.[140] As we saw in chapter 6, the VOC's ships carried almost a million men, half of them soldiers—interesting employees for an organisation "considered the epitome of capitalist enterprise".[141]

Dutch empire in the Atlantic was somewhat less successful, but it was not for want of trying. The Netherlands sent 200 ships to attack Portuguese posts and islands in western Africa between 1592 and 1607. One fleet in 1599 carried 8,000 soldiers and sailors.[142] On the Gold Coast, they built their own post, Fort Nassau, in 1612, took the main Portuguese base of El Mina in 1637, and acquired another dozen posts in the region.[143] "Between 1624–1636, the WIC equipped over eight hundred ships, with an average of 100 men on board, of which 40% were sailors and 60% soldiers".[144] By 1630, it was "the dominant European power on the Gold Coast".[145] It made wholehearted efforts to dislodge the Portuguese from Congo and Angola farther south, and from Brazil. These campaigns involved the largest troop transfers to the Americas up to that time—the Dutch repeatedly sent out armies of around 7,000 men. At peak in 1642, the WIC looked as though it would take over the whole Portuguese empire in the Atlantic. It held more than half of Brazil's sugar plantations, the main bases in Angola (Luanda and Benguela), and a lead in the slave trade, as well as the Guinea forts. All except the last had gone by 1661, and the WIC declined into insignificance. A promising settler and fur trading colony in North America, the New Netherlands (the New York region), established in 1621, lasted a little longer. It was taken by the English in 1664, recaptured in 1673, then finally swapped for Surinam in South America in 1674.

Surinam was a modest replacement for Brazil and New York, but its 50 sugar plantations of 1680 became 300 by 1800, at the expense of intensive fighting with the indigenous people, which lowered the settler population by two-thirds in the 1670s, and used up 13,000 Dutch troops between 1740 and 1794.[146] Apart from Surinam, the legend of a non-violent empire did become almost true in the Atlantic after 1674. Recent histories emphasise the role of the Dutch Caribbean islands of Curacao and St Eustatius as hubs of intercolonial and illicit trade. The British seized £7 million worth of goods when they sacked the latter in 1781.[147] They do not always note immense Dutch cod fishing and whaling activity in the North Atlantic. The former used 160 Dutch ships in 1768.[148] The latter involved 258 ships and up to 12,000 men at peak, and killed 80,000 whales between 1669 and 1768.[149]

These were indeed remarkable achievements for a people of two million: surviving endemic warfare with the two local superpowers; maintaining and expanding European trade despite this; hijacking most of the Portuguese empire in Asia and making a wholehearted attempt to do the same in the Atlantic. They required organisation as well as huge inflows of wealth, labour, and raw materials. Yet the formal institutions of the Dutch state hardly seem up to the task. There was not much central government; most administration was jealously divided between the seven provinces in a decentralised federal system. Naval administration was slightly better off—it was divided between only five admiralties. A prince of Orange, leader of the Dutch nobility, or a dominant official in Holland sometimes tried to supply centralisation, especially during crises in land warfare. But there were periods without dominant officials, and with powerless princes, and the influence of either on maritime affairs and the overseas empire seems limited. This is our second Dutch puzzle. Its solution, in a word, is Amsterdam.

IV Amsterdam's Empires

Holland, with 800,000 people in 1670, dominated the United Provinces, providing about 60% of its revenues.[150] Amsterdam, whose population rocketed from 30,000 to 200,000 people between 1570 and 1670, dominated Holland. Long before this, Amsterdam was developing an edge over rival towns. It sat at the centre of a web of canals, inland sea-lanes across the Zuider Zee, and even roads. Already in 1454 it was described as the first city in Holland.[151] Amsterdam itself did not escape plague. "Frequent epidemics . . . raged through the town".[152] But replacements flowed in from the countryside, which was less plagued than elsewhere. The town's households increased 35%, 1477–1514. But Amsterdam's leadership was not yet a matter of population, which at around 13,000 was no bigger than that of Leiden and Dordrecht.[153] Instead, it arose from a position at the apex of a "strikingly hierarchical" system of ports that had developed since 1350. "Amsterdam was the central importing and exporting centre for both the ports in northern Holland and for the whole wider Zuyder Zee area".[154] To suggest that mid-sixteenth century Amsterdam was "essentially a depot for Baltic grain and timber" is unduly dismissive.[155] As early as 1505, Amsterdam's merchants were markedly richer than those of rival towns.[156] In 1535, the fleet it dominated, of 400 ocean-going ships excluding herring busses, was said to be larger than the merchant fleets of France and England combined. In 1543–45, it exported three times as much as all other Holland towns combined, and its exports (and imports) covered the whole range, while other towns and ports tended to specialise. Amsterdam had overtaken Kampen's (in Overijssel) lead in shipping to the Baltic around 1400; it

owned five-sixths by value of the 50 Holland ships and cargoes taken by Lubeck in 1511; and by 1560 it and its immediate North Holland hinterland provided 80% of the thousand Dutch ships that visited that sea each year.[157] Like
Lubeck before it, Amsterdam converted its rivals into junior partners. By 1540,
Edam acknowledged it as "capital city" (*hoofstede*),[158] and the phrase "*Amsterdam cum sociis*", "Amsterdam and friends", was in use.[159]

Between 1500 and 1570, Amsterdam in its turn was junior partner to a much
larger rising city: Antwerp in Brabant. This city was taking over from Flemish
Bruges as the chief port of the southern Low Countries. "Antwerp's population
rose from about 40,000 around 1500 to over 90,000 by about 1560".[160] Neither
Antwerp nor Bruges hosted large fleets of their own. In the first stage of Amsterdam's partnership with Antwerp, the former provided shipping services
above all. Antwerp was the first capital of the Dutch revolt, but in 1585 it was
taken by the Spanish, and its assets were taken over by Amsterdam. This was
partly voluntary. Antwerp's Calvinists upped sticks for Amsterdam, with their
skills, connections, and money, halving the population of the former by 1589
and boosting the population of the latter.[161] "The immigration of Antwerp
merchants alone increased the city's capital stock by 50%".[162] Just to be sure,
the Hollanders blocked the Scheldt Estuary, ending Antwerp's easy access to
the sea, and diverting its trade to Amsterdam.

Antwerp was also a conduit for other urban legacies. The Jewish *converso*
network, which retained strong connections in Lisbon and the Hapsburg empires abroad, had its sixteenth-century northern base in Antwerp, where the
local authorities protected it from the Spanish Inquisition.[163] After 1585, it too
began shifting to Amsterdam, where it numbered 800 very well-connected
people by the 1620s.[164] Amsterdam was also just completing the process of
replacing Lubeck as chief hub of the North Sea and had good links with Hanseatic cities such as Hamburg and Gdansk. These transnational networks were
the keys to the Dutch ability to simultaneously trade and fight with the Hapsburgs and the French. They enabled the large-scale flag-shifting of Dutch ships,
to Portuguese or Hanse flags, noted in chapter 7. North Italian influences,
acquired via Antwerp, also contributed to a category of useful institutions
which did play a supporting role in the "Dutch miracle". They were not state
institutions, however, but provincial and civic ones, largely Amsterdam-based.
They included the founding of a stock exchange in 1603 (its building opened
in 1611), and of the *Wisselbank* (a bank of exchange) in 1609, as well as the
stabilisation of the currency in 1638—all initiatives of Amsterdam, not the
Dutch state.[165]

Amsterdam also led early Dutch expansion. Of the first 80 ships sent to Asia, 1595–1602, 50 were from Amsterdam,[166] and that city subsequently dominated the VOC. Provincial rivalries, and urban rivalry between towns in Holland meant this was not the formal situation. The Company had six chambers, five in Holland towns and one in Zeeland. But the Amsterdam chamber had five times the subscribers of the next largest chamber, and Amsterdam merchants invested in the other chambers as well. "Amsterdam was the principal market for all VOC shares".[167] Initially, the WIC was "also dominated by Amsterdam", and this was also true of second, less important, WIC, formed in 1675.[168] But, in the exception that proves the rule, the Dutch mega-city found the conquest of Brazil too expensive and unsuccessful by about 1648, and turned against the first WIC, which correlates with that company's decline. Those who ran the companies also ran Holland—Amsterdam had the swing vote in the provincial "States" (assembly)—in "a Holland-dominated United Provinces".[169] Amsterdam's admiralty provided more revenue than the other four admiralties combined.[170]

> Between them the Holland States and Amsterdam town council managed to monopolize the appointment and direction of the key personnel in matters of foreign policy, tax collection, the navy and the chartered companies. . . . Amsterdam itself controlled (and appointed and paid) many ambassadors, including those for Paris, the Scandinavian countries, and the Hanseatic cities.[171]

The Dutch chartered companies are key pillars of the view that modern European capitalism emerged in the seventeenth-century Netherlands, based on relatively open markets, widely accessible information, and the displacement of kin-based merchant networks by economically rational individualists freely trading with strangers. They may have marked a stage in a trend in this direction, but they did not spring from nowhere, or lack rivals or unwanted ancestors. Recent work suggests that it was an Amsterdam-based kinship network, or network of networks, that controlled the chartered companies as well as Holland and the Dutch "familial state". "The principles of "family government" reigned supreme in Batavia and the subordinate company settlements in Asia".[172]

Chapter 10 suggested that the chartered companies had a plague-incubated precedent in the Genoese *mahona* running Chios and Cyprus and other less formal syndicates of allied merchant families. A lineal connection is likely, via Antwerp. "The Genoese colony in Antwerp comprised almost half of all

Italians living in the city during the sixteenth century, and they were undoubt-edly the most visible of the various Italian merchant nations".[173] But a conver-gent response to similar situations might also have been at play. Genoa, Lu-beck, Amsterdam all experienced large-scale in-migrations, of outside merchants as well as labourers. In the two earlier cases, this was a matter of rapid repopulation after plague. In Amsterdam's case, post-plague repopula-tion was joined by the influx of merchants from Antwerp after 1585. "Virtual clans", like that in Rembrandt's "Nightwatch", emerged not only to reassemble plague-shattered families, but also to incorporate newcomers. Holland's net-works remained more kin-based than others perhaps because it suffered fewer plague deaths. We should not idealise these proto-capitalist "happy families". They derived their income from everyone else, often ruthlessly. But the idea of sociocultural strands in the origin of modern capitalism also derives support from the fact that Amsterdam's most fundamental "empire", underlying all the others, was largely institution-free.

Dutch power was underwritten by Lubeck's legacy: an informal patchwork empire in northeastern Europe. Led by Amsterdam, the Dutch took over, ex-tended, and sometimes intensified Lubeck's grip. In Sweden, merchants "from Amsterdam and the whole of Holland" were given the same trading rights as Hanseatics in 1487.[174] Sweden became fully independent of Denmark-Norway in 1523, established its own empire in what is now Finland and the Baltic states, and had its moment as a great land power in the seventeenth century under warrior kings. The Dutch blocked its attempts to control the Sounds entry to the Baltic with naval force in 1535, 1658–59, and 1676–78, but were normally on good terms with the Swedish state. Sweden had little access to the North Sea before its acquisition of Scania in 1658, and the Dutch helped establish its sole North Sea port of Goteborg in 1621. Goteborg was "a Dutch settlement on Swedish soil", its street plan similar to that of Batavia.[175] The Dutch helped further develop Sweden's iron and copper mines and took 53% of exports from the former in 1655.[176] They took 70–80% of exports, notably naval stores, from Swedish-controlled Riga and Reval in the late seventeenth century.[177] Sweden also held another important Baltic port, Narva, between 1581 and 1704, when it was retaken by Russia. Russian products continued to be exported through it in the interim—furs, hides, caviar, and more naval stores—mainly via the Dutch.

The Dutch also pioneered voyages to the alternative Russian port, Archan-gel, from the 1580s if not earlier, and helped develop Russia's exports, particu-larly high-quality hemp rope, of which sailing ships required huge quantities.

This was a useful alternative to the Baltic in emergencies. Amsterdam and the Polish grain trade grew together. Polish lords and their increasingly oppressed peasants specialised in rye for the market, and boated it down the Vistula to Gdansk, where there were 50 Dutch companies in 1650. A thousand Dutch ships then took it to Amsterdam and many other destinations. Grain exports doubled to more than 200,000 tons in the century after 1560.[178] In Amsterdam's contiguous Dutch hinterland, already-modest levels of arable farming halved over the same period, with farmers turning even more to dairying, market gardening, and industrial crops—a classic urban colonial shift.[179] This high level of mutual dependence *integrated* Amsterdam and the relevant Swedish and Polish, though perhaps not Russian, regions. The Dutch exercised "disproportionate influence" on Gdansk, and together with local merchants formed a "very close symbiotic relationship" with inland grain farmers.[180] Most grain came from the Vistula catchment areas of Prussia and Mazovia, where Dutch influence on farming techniques was noticeable from the 1560s—dairy farms were called "Dutch farms".[181] Grain price changes in Gdansk correlated more closely with those in Amsterdam than did those in nearby Liege, a stark example of how urban colonialism could trump distance.[182]

The Norwegian and Dutch timber industries also developed to fit each other. Norwegian pine had long supplemented Baltic timber, and in the seventeenth century the Dutch financed a southern Norwegian shift from hand-sawing to water-powered sawing, using single-blade saws. The semi-processed balks were carried to Amsterdam, and processing was completed with windmill-powered multi-bladed saws in the industrialising Zaan region just north of the city.[183] This single industry was half in Norway, half in Holland. It and its more Baltic-based sibling, plus the shipyards of the Zaan, enabled the Dutch to produce a staggering 500 ships a year, more than enough to make up for the depredations of the Dunkirkers and English.[184] Norway was subject to Denmark, and the Dutch kept the relationship tight by financing Denmark-Norway's public debt, of which it held 55% as late as the 1760s.[185] Economic historians are mystified by this low-profit investment by the canny Dutch, but in urban colonialism immediate profits are not everything. It also required the tailor-made and reliable production and processing of essential raw materials and city-sustaining foods. The profits could be made further down the line.

The water-powered timber industry was not hugely demanding of Norwegian labour, and Norway now imported its grain from Poland, via the Dutch. There was therefore a surplus of male labour, which went off to Amsterdam and its empire. Up to 30% of "Dutch" sailors were in fact Norwegian. Most came from very specific districts in Southern Norway, such as Mandal, Lister, and Agder. In these Norwegian crew regions, during their "Hollander period",[186] Dutch forenames and other cultural influences were common. "The Dutch influence was even said to have manifested itself in a concern about cleanliness".[187] More than half of "Dutch" seventeenth-century whaling crews came from the German and Danish Wadden Islands and the nearby coast of Oldenburg.[188] In the mid-eighteenth century, the Dutch and Swedish merchant fleets employed similar numbers of Swedes.[189] Foreigners—Swiss, English, and Scots as well as Germans and Scandinavians—comprised at least half of Dutch armies, inside and outside Europe. It was Amsterdam, not the Hague, that was the transnational/imperial capital. In 1650, foreigners made up 8% of the total population of the United Provinces, compared to 38% in Amsterdam.[190] By 1650, "Amsterdam and friends" was among Europe's biggest economies.

Amsterdam's final "empire" was an entwining with Britain. The relationship began promisingly, with English support for the Dutch rebellion, but soured for a time after 1604, when the former made peace with Spain. Indeed, the Dutch gave the English a dose of their own nineteenth-century medicine with a couple of ruthless exercises in "global policing". The better-known is the "Amboina massacre" of 1623 in the Moluccas, when the VOC executed 10 English merchants and 11 of their employees for an alleged plot to take over a fort.[191] A less well-known incident took place in 1614, when the Dutch attacked a pirate base in Ireland—at least nominally English territory—destroying ships and killing 30 men.[192] The Anglo-Dutch alliance was briefly renewed in the 1620s and featured a disastrous joint attack on Cadiz in 1625, and both sides sought Dutch help in Britain's great civil wars, 1642–51. But this was followed by the Anglo-Dutch Wars of 1652–74. In 1688, the Dutch famously invaded England and ejected the Catholic king, James II. Local support for this "Glorious Revolution" may have been less universal than is generally assumed. "The entire London area remained under Dutch military occupation until the spring of 1690. No English regiments were allowed within twenty miles of the city".[193] In fact, the Dutch need not have worried about London (see chapter 16). But there was heavy fighting in Scotland and Ireland—the Dutch Guards led the attack at the decisive Irish battle of the Boyne in 1690. The Dutch and English (British from 1707) remained closely allied until the 1740s, in successive wars against France. Between 1688 and the 1740s, "Britain . . . could be reasonably confident that the Dutch would come to their aid if needed" to secure the Protestant succession.[194]

The Anglo-Dutch entanglement went deeper than war and politics, as several historians have shown. In the early seventeenth century, Amsterdam sponsored the further development of England's important cast iron cannon industry.[195] England bought many of its ships, perhaps one-third, from the Dutch between the 1650s and 1670s, despite the wars.[196] "Economic historians are broadly agreed that after the Restoration [1660], England introduced financial systems and institutions in London modelled on the Dutch".[197] "That the Bank of England drew upon Dutch example (the Bank of Amsterdam, 'the great Sinews of Trade') is not in doubt. It also drew crucially upon Dutch finance".[198] In and around the 1750s, Dutch investors, mainly from Amsterdam, held 21.4% of the shares in the British East India Company, 19.2% of Bank of England stocks, and had 100 million guilders on loan to the British government, rising to well over 200 million by 1780.[199] "The two countries established a symbiotic relationship that finally fell into place from roughly 1723 to 1783",[200] when a fourth Anglo-Dutch war, 1780–84, damaged it. Initially the Dutch were the senior partner, but from about 1740 the balance shifted. Britain drew ahead of the Netherlands in the East Indies trade, the whaling industry, and the Baltic trade.[201] It had earlier acquired Dutch-founded New York and its fur trade, and later took over Dutch territories in Sri Lanka. Coupled with Dutch influences in industry, commercial practice, and investment, this made Britain the ultimate heir to Amsterdam's empires.

13

Muslim Colonial Empires

IN 1590, a small army of musket-armed conquistadors set out to invade a distant, gold-rich empire, and reached it after a five-week journey. Foreign guns trumped native numbers, with considerable help from collaborators and treachery. The emperor was invited to peace talks under promise of safe conduct, but was then taken prisoner and later killed. A puppet relative was appointed in his place. His capital proved easier for the conquistadors to enter than to hold, and urban rebellion had to be bloodily suppressed. Their numbers were small, 4,000 initially, but they kept coming: between 1591 and 1603, 23,000 reinforcements arrived, while a stream of gold went the other way. These conquistadors were Moroccan. They used caravans, not convoys, and the 1,700-kilometre space between metropolis and colony consisted of Saharan sands, not Atlantic water.[1]

In common usage, a "colonial empire" comprises a metropolitan country plus its far-flung colonies. The phrase is useful for distinguishing geographically fragmented empires like the British from contiguous empires like the Roman. We equate "colonial empires" with "overseas empires". This helps exclude Russian expansion from modern European imperialism, and does the same with the continental imperialism of the independent United States after 1783. Yet Russian colonies in Siberia (for centuries) and US colonies in what is now the American west (for decades) consisted of a few regions, usually rich in gold or furs, unreliably connected to their metropolis by a string of fortified posts, "island" bases in a much larger sea of independent native Siberian and American tribes. In this sense of being effectively non-contiguous before transcontinental railroads, Russia (to the 1880s) and the United States (to the 1860s) were colonial empires too. What we have hitherto failed to consider is whether this also applies to two Muslim West Eurasian expansions: the Moroccan conquest of the trans-Saharan Songhay Empire, referred to above, and the Mughal conquest of India from 1519. A third modern Muslim colonial empire, this time more conventionally maritime, was developed by Oman in the seventeenth to nineteenth centuries. This chapter tries to bring these imperial ventures into discussions of early modern colonialism and to confirm that you did not have to be white to use the plague-forged West Eurasian expansion kit.

I The Moroccan Colonial Empire

We left Morocco in chapter 10 with its western regions violently transformed by the Portuguese into a platform for further expansion down the West African coast and into the Atlantic. Moroccan horses and textiles bought West African gold and slaves, and Moroccan grain fed Portuguese crewmen. As we saw, Portuguese conquests in Morocco peaked in the period of their superiority in firearms, 1470–1515, after which the Moroccans began to catch up.[2] Their country remained fragmented. The Wattasid Dynasty had largely taken over from the Marinids, but some tribes and regions remained semi-independent. The Black Death had hit Morocco hard and later strikes were quite frequent, though I can pin down only three: in 1468, possibly 1578, and 1598–1603. As elsewhere in the Muslim South, the era witnessed "the popularity and spread of a growing number of powerful Sufi brotherhoods".[3] In the region of Sus, in southwestern Morocco, the Saʾids, a Sufi lineage claiming descent from the Prophet, gained support by resisting the Portuguese. They had little military success until 1515, but then began to acquire cannon and harquebuses in numbers. The Sus was the Moroccan region best able to grow sugar; it also had saltpetre deposits, and some West African gold was acquired overland.[4] Spanish, French, and English, desperate to breach Portugal's monopoly of the West African trade, exchanged guns for these goods at the few Atlantic harbours outside Portuguese control. Muslim and Morisco refugees from Spain brought knowledge of gun-making to regions farther north. From the 1540s if not earlier, the Ottoman Turks were also distributing gun technology in Morocco. The balance between indigenous Moroccan initiatives and plague adaptations and the various foreign inputs is not entirely clear. But in 1541, the Saʾids took the Portuguese fortress of Agadir using a large number of cannon.[5] By 1549, they controlled both Fez and Marrakesh and had reunited the country apart from a Wattasid remnant and the shrinking Portuguese domains.

Saʾid Moroccan relations with the Ottoman Turks began unpromisingly. The former took the latter's most westerly territory, Tlemcen in Algeria, in 1550. The Ottomans retook it in 1551 and went on to briefly occupy Fez in

1554–55, and to have the Saʾid sultan assassinated in 1557.[6] Thereafter they seem to have been more interested in keeping Morocco out of European hands than in conquering it themselves. Their main influence was indirect. While the first Moroccan adoption of guns may have had Iberian roots (from Muslim Granada as well as the Christian kingdoms), from the 1540s the Ottoman Turks became the main military influence. The process gathered pace from 1574–76, when the Ottomans helped a reformist Turcophile prince, Abd al-Malik, to become sultan. "The object of most of his reforming zeal was the army, which was reorganized along Turkish lines, even to the extent of applying Turkish terms to the ranking of officers".[7] Janissary-like musketeer units were recruited from outside Morocco, particularly from Iberian Moriscos, to balance local forces; and the full Ottoman range of cannon was produced, from big siege guns to field guns light enough to be carried on camels. Units of mounted musketeers who dismounted to fire may have been a Moroccan innovation—precursors of European dragoons. These military developments had economic and administrative foundations, including the developing sugar industry, scribes from all parts, and "an advanced treasury system".[8] In 1578, Portugal mounted a major effort to reboot its conquest of Morocco, and met the Saʾid army in decisive battle at Alcazar. The Portuguese were crushed, losing 15,000 men. Abd al-Malik died in the battle, as did the Portuguese king. The former's half-brother, Ahmad al-Malik, now known as al-Mansur, "the victorious", became sultan, and it was he who launched the Moroccan attempt at colonial empire in sub-Saharan Africa (see map 12).

Sub-Saharan West Africa, also known as the Western Sudan, had long been the seat of powerful Muslim cavalry empires, engaged in slave raiding and trading in slaves, gold, ivory, and salt. In the fifteenth century, the empire of Mali was replaced by that of Songhay, with its capital at Gao overseeing a dozen provinces.[9] Songhay may not have controlled the gold-producing regions, but did dominate the overland trade in alliance with the Tauregs, Berber nomads of the Sahara, and with various networks of traders. As previous chapters have noted, there was some disruption of the gold trade during the Mali-Songhay transition and intensive Moroccan civil warfare, 1390–1415. But Songhay soon had the system running again, and the overland trade continued strongly despite the siphoning off of some gold by the Portuguese on the coast from the 1440s. Songhay acquired Timbuktu in 1468, a renowned centre of trade and Islamic scholarship.[10]

Songhay remained rich and formidable in the late sixteenth century, and Al-Mansur prepared his attack with care and with clear colonising intent, also hoping to counter Portuguese access to West African gold. He seized the necessary bases in southern Morocco and sent intelligence-gathering patrols farther south in the 1580s. He assembled a small but balanced, well-equipped, and purpose-designed force: "experienced camel drivers, and sappers, . . . cannon pieces of all sizes and abundant supplies of gunpowder, lead and priming powder. The combatant forces consisted of a renegade group of 2,000 arquebusiers, 500 mounted gunmen, 70 former Christian war captives with blunderbusses, and only 1,500 Moroccan lancers".[11] The "renegades" seem to have been mostly Muslim and Morisco Iberians or their descendants, a fresh influx of whom had arrived in 1571 after a failed rebellion in Spain. The total, including noncombatants, was 5,000 men, with 2,000 horses and 10,000 camels.

The expedition set off in 1590 and seized the key cities of Timbuktu, Gao, and Jenne in 1591. The parallels with European overseas ventures, especially Cortes's conquest of central Mexico, really are striking. "In the desert, the army navigated with guides and compasses as if they were at sea". The "voyage" between metropolis and prospective colony lasted 35 days.[12] Even the commander, the able and ruthless ex-slave eunuch Judar Pasha, was Castilian. As noted at the beginning of this chapter, there was treachery, collaboration, and rebellion after initial conquest, in Timbuktu as in Tenochtitlan. In Songhay, as in Mexico and Peru, there was determined resistance, which continued after the initial conquest, and brutal repression was coupled with the building of administration and collaboration systems—some local notables were courted by the conquerors.[13] Here too, gunboats or "brigantines" were transported in pieces, in this case by camels, and assembled and deployed to good effect, in this case on the Middle Niger River.[14] For the Moroccan conquest of Songhay, however, no source that I have encountered, contemporary or historical—including Al-Mansur himself, or at least his hagiographer—denies that firearms were decisive.[15] The colonial garrison army in Songhay became known as "the *Arma*", "the Gunners."

Possession of Songhay and its gold, along with growing trades in sugar, slaves, and saltpetre, as well as the traditional cloth and horses, gave Al-Mansur "a truly massive amount of wealth"[16] in the 1590s. The European take of West African gold declined at this time, before recovering in the seventeenth century.[17] Archaeology suggests at least a dozen vast sugar plantations in the Sus, worked by up to 2,000 people each.[18] Morocco briefly became a major power, subsidising the king of France and seeking an alliance with the English against Spain—a joint attack on the Caribbean was proposed.[19] But Al-Mansur died of plague in 1603 before his reforms had taken root, and his dynasty declined and then collapsed in 1659. Faced with a declining metropolis, the Arma began electing their own pasha from 1613. One historian claims that they were soon overwhelmed by renewed Songhay (and Taureg and Fulani) resistance,[20] but others maintain that the Arma and their descendants retained control over a considerable area as an independent but colonial regime, claiming descent from, and vague allegiance to, Morocco into the eighteenth century.[21] There seems no good reason to continue their exclusion from the story of the early modern colonialisms built with the help of plague-forged expansion kits.

II The Omani Colonial Empire

As noted in chapter 9, Oman in Southeast Arabia, with a large shoreline on the Persian Gulf, was a region of considerable economic potential. It participated actively in the first pulse of post-plague West Eurasian expansion, the Arab-Persian mercantile push into the Indian Ocean in 1350–1500. During this era, much of Oman was controlled by the island city-state of Hormuz. The Portuguese established themselves in the Gulf soon after arriving in Asia, taking Hormuz in 1515, "after fighting a fierce naval battle against the island's navy".[22] They also acquired several other posts in the region, including Muscat. With the Ottoman counterattack to contend with, the Portuguese in this area strove mainly to profit from, not disrupt, the Muslim-run preexisting trades. They left local lords in place as vassals, cooperated with Muslim merchants, and tried to placate the powerful Safavids of Iran. They succeeded for a century, surviving Ottoman invasions in the 1550s and 1580s, with Hormuz customs duties providing a fifth of the revenues of their entire empire in Asia.[23] In the early seventeenth century, however, warfare with the Dutch and English, plus the desire of the formidable Safavid Shah Abbas to regain Persian territory, undermined the Portuguese position. The Iranians retook Bahrein in 1602, and Hormuz in 1622, the latter with English naval help. The Portuguese held on in Muscat until 1650, when it fell to the forces of a new Omani lineage of sultans and imams, the Ya'rubi. Unlike the Iranians, who (with one brief exception) did not try, and the Ottomans, who tried but failed, the Omanis succeeded in building an Indian Ocean fleet capable of challenging the Europeans, and used it to establish their own modern colonial overseas empire (see map 12).

Historians have long been aware of this empire,[24] but it is only recently that our attention has been drawn to the way it complicates the European-ness of modern imperialism.[25] Much remains obscure, but we do know that the

Omanis used artillery and muskets to snap up Portuguese forts and ports in the Gulf, beginning in 1624. Between 1650 and 1715, they pursued the Portuguese to India and Africa. They had up to two dozen European-style, sturdily built gun galleons in this period, including one of 80 guns, one of 74 guns, and two of 60 guns—genuine "ships of the line".[26] The most detailed study I can find is forced by its sources to take a Portuguese perspective, and so is stronger on Omani defeats than successes.[27] But the study does show that Portuguese maritime prowess was by no means moribund after naval reforms in the 1660s, and that the Omanis were a match for them at sea and more than a match on land. "Omani maritime power was shaped in the crucible of combat with Europeans in the Indian Ocean".[28] They sacked Diu, the second most important Portuguese base in India, in 1668, took Mombasa in 1698, and acquired the rest of Portugal's East African bases north of Mozambique soon afterwards. Omani imperialism experienced a hiatus between about 1720 and 1750, due to Persian invasions and civil wars, and some of its African viceroys declared independence. But it then entered a vigorous second phase. From 1750, a new dynasty, the Albusaidi, rebuilt the fleet, expanded trade, and revived the empire in Africa, which remained independent until 1890.

This bare-bones outline begs several questions. Did the Omanis depend on European alliances? How did they acquire their fleet? Just how substantive was their empire? They did buy firearms from Europeans—Dutch, English, and French, so that they were not dependent on any one source. They also probably made guns themselves, or acquired them from Iran—guns were among Oman's exports.[29] Suggestions that they operated as mere proxies for the Dutch or English East India companies seems doubtful. Close Omani relations with the Dutch were infrequent,[30] and the idea that an Anglo-Omani alliance, which did become important in the nineteenth and twentieth centuries, stretched back into the seventeenth or eighteenth seems mistaken. In 1694, the Omanis raided "Salsette, an island adjoining Bombay", which had been in English hands since 1661, and took 1,400 slaves.[31] They plundered EIC ships in 1705, around 1720, and perhaps more often. EIC officials noted that the Omanis had "become a Terror to all the trading people of India". A British agent concluded in 1721 that there was "no hope" of either they or the Dutch obtaining redress from Muscat for plundered ships.[32]

We are told that the Omani fleet was "comprised mainly of captured Portuguese ships". But how, then, did the Omanis capture the Portuguese ships in the first place? They must have had alternative access to ships.[33] Another source states that "Omani shipbuilders were able to replicate the larger, gun-bearing ships",[34] and indeed, at least smaller ships of up to 14 guns were built in Oman.[35] India was a likely source of their bigger ships, with or without European mediation. From the 1590s, Gujarat was producing gun galleons using local teak, for European and non-European buyers alike.[36] Royal Mughal purchasers never seem to have managed to man their galleons' guns very effectively; the Omanis did. While they had a fortified trading factory in Surat from the 1690s, just like the European colonial powers, the Omanis did not establish European-like fortified ports in western India, perhaps because they did not need to.[37] Their relations with Gujarati merchant networks were close. They took over the horse trade from the Portuguese after 1650, mixed trade with raid, had agents in Gujarat, and built up a close alliance with the rising Indian power of Mysore from 1760.[38] They had agents in other independent Indian states too, as well as in British Bombay.[39] Indian capital backed the Omani Empire in Africa, at least in its second phase, and Baluchi mercenaries helped too.

One expert has scoffed at this Omani "empire" in East Africa.

> there was no Ya'rubi nor indeed an Albusaidi "empire" with viable institutions enabling Omani rulers to exercise centralised authority in territories in East Africa, even in those areas where they exercised some degree of control. That control, motivated primarily by the desire to protect trade and to collect duties, was derived from tribal allegiances, political alliances with local rulers and long-established commercial relationships.[40]

This view stems from a reification of empire, drawing on idealised notions of modern European empires "exercising central authority" over entire countries. Such empires seldom existed before the nineteenth century, if then. Relying on "political alliances" and "commercial relationships", pinned together by fortified ports and backed by maritime force, was characteristic of the Portuguese Empire in East Africa too—and of the British in the region until the late nineteenth century. It is true that the Omani Empire in Africa, like the Portuguese, was restricted to a few major bases, and that an Omani clan, the Mazrui governors of Mombasa, declared independence and took over much of it in the later eighteenth century. But the Omanis proper recaptured Kilwa in 1785, Pemba Island in 1822, Pate in 1824, and Mombasa in 1837. From about 1800, they increasingly centred their operations on the island of Zanzibar, which they had controlled since 1698, moving their capital there from Muscat in 1840.[41]

It was not the extent of its territory that made Oman an important power, but the extent of its trade. Its fleet, martial and mercantile, is estimated at

40,000–50,000 tons in the later eighteenth century—hundreds of ships.[42] Omanis provided the 50 vessels of the annual "coffee fleet" from Yemen to the top of the Persian Gulf, from which point it was distributed to Iran and the Ottoman Empire. Omani ships carried about half of the trade between India and the Persian Gulf, and visited Batavia as well—and, in 1840, the United States.[43] From Zanzibar, they extended trade tentacles inland, using Swahili agents, and brought the regional slave and ivory trades to a peak. In 1848, Zanzibar re-exported 342 tons of ivory, representing 7,000 dead elephants.[44] Their slave trade is said to have reached 50,000 a year, supplying sugar plantations on the French islands of Mauritius until 1810, and they used many slaves themselves. There were 200,000 black African slaves in Zanzibar alone in 1857.[45] Here, they became a coerced part of a wider Omani exercise in reshuffling biota around the globe. Sugar was produced in Oman itself from at least 1650, on state-irrigated land, [46] and rice was introduced into Zanzibar to feed the slaves. But the main crop was cloves, transplanted from the Southeast Asian Maluku Islands, and worked by sub-Saharan slaves for immense profits.[47] Zanzibar and Pemba came close to monopolising world clove production in the later nineteenth century.[48] How much more European-like an imperialism can you get? From 1798, the British and Omani empires were in alliance, with the balance of benefits varying over time. Britain turned against the slave trade from 1807, but was hesitant in restraining its Omani ally. Treaties carved off inessential parts of the trade first, banning Omani slave exports to European colonies in 1822 and back to Oman in 1845, but leaving the core slave market, Zanzibar and Pemba themselves, alone until 1873.

Oman is an important example of why we need to globalise and deepen the history of colonialism. Its triangular form of maritime empire—Persian Gulf, western India, and East Africa—may date back to Sassanid Iran in pre-Islamic times. Omanis were active in Muslim mercantile settlement from its outset in the eighth century, notably in East Africa. They were believers in the Ibadi variant of Islam, and remained so, which may have given them extra cohesion. They were active in the new Arab-Persian mercantile push after 1350, driven by increased post-plague demand for Further Asian goods (chapter 9). The "soft" empire of Hormuz-Oman in the Indian Ocean was hijacked by the Portuguese between 1515 and 1650, then wrested back by the Omanis, whose adoption of the West Eurasian expansion kit was late but strong. Unlike the Ottomans, they managed to mesh this with Southern Arabian maritime expertise and Indian ship timber. During the later nineteenth century, like Portuguese, Dutch, and Moghul empires before them, the Omanis found themselves wrapped up in the British embrace. But in Zanzibar in 1850, as in Melaka

350 years earlier, it would have been difficult to argue that colonialism and globalisation were solely European-led.

III The Mughals: A West Eurasian Colonial Empire?

Chapter 8 made a case for including Turan (West Central Asia), along with its twin Iran, in Greater Persia and therefore in the West Eurasian world. In the sixteenth and seventeenth centuries, Turan was controlled by the Uzbeks and Iran by the Safavids. The Uzbeks were a neo-Mongol group like the Timurids, who first coalesced farther north, then mounted a "mass migration into Transoxiana and Balkh at the beginning of the sixteenth century".[49] The original number of Uzbeks migrants is put at 250,000, with as many as five million subjects by 1600, compared to six or seven million in Iran. The Uzbeks were usually a loose federation of nomad tribes, each with its own sedentary subjects. But they had spasms of unity which made them militarily formidable. The Turkic Safavids emerged before the Black Death as a Sufi religious movement, practicing their own form of Shi᾽ism. They were originally based in much-plagued Azerbaijan and eastern Anatolia. Though the full case cannot be made here, their history too shows signs of plague effects, beginning with ruthless skill at the great post-plague art of man-powering. Safavid Shi᾽ism was itself "an ideology with a capacity for mass mobilization".[50] Its ability to attract and energise formidable Turkic warriors known as Qizilbash (Red Heads, from their red turbans) was clear from around 1450, well before the dynasty took over Iran.[51] Once ensconced in Iran, the Safavids made great use of slave soldiers and officials, particularly Georgian Christians.[52]

Safavid warfare is said to have been less influenced by firearms than that of the Ottomans, especially before they were allegedly gifted gunnery by the English Shirley brothers in the seventeenth century. In fact, they used guns from about 1478, even before they recruited slave-soldier infantry and took over Iran.[53] Considerable use of gunpowder weapons during the takeover around 1500 appears in the oral tales of their veterans.[54] Even so, they were outgunned by the Ottomans at the battle of Chaldiran in 1514 and immediately engaged in a "crash program" to acquire more.[55] If they had a European fairy gunmother, it was Russia, from which they acquired 4,000 muskets and 30 cannon in 1569 alone.[56] The key to their firearms acquisition, and to their ability to pay for big cotton imports from India, was the increased sale of raw silk, abetted by a centralised mercantilist state.[57] Silk production grew from around 500 tons in the mid-sixteenth century to between two and three thousand tons in the seventeenth.[58] There were said to be no fewer than 1,000 caravanserais in the Iranian overland transport network by the 1670s, many established by the state.[59] Iran was the main provider of raw silk to the rest of the Middle East and to Europe, selling a surprising amount through an amphibian route across the Caspian to Russia in return for furs, guns, and silver.[60] More silver came from Western Europe via the Ottomans, with whom illegal trade did not stop even during wartime, though it was somewhat disrupted. War between Ottomans and Safavids was almost continuous between 1578 and 1639, and it may well have been this second front that prevented the former from overrunning Europe.

Safavid Iran is another example of the plague-sharpened Muslim talent for merging state, religious, and commercial development. Silk made it an important indirect player in global trade, operating through proxies. It used the services of numerous Indian merchants,[61] and of one of the greatest of Christian merchant networks: the Armenians. The Armenian diaspora dates from the 1360s, and had long specialised in trading Persian silk. Their early Iranian hub was Old Julfa, but this was too near the Ottoman border for the Safavids' liking and in 1605 they forcibly shifted the population to New Julfa, a suburb of the growing city of Isfahan. The Armenians made the best of their "symbiotic relationship" with the Safavids, and extruded a worldwide silk network from New Julfa in the seventeenth and eighteenth centuries, stretching to Moscow, London, Livorno, Surat, Manila, and Guangzhou.[62] From Iran's perspective, European and Omani merchants in the Persian Gulf provided useful alternative merchant networks, particularly when overland trade was diminished by hostilities with the Ottomans. The Portuguese in Hormuz cultivated friendly relations with the Safavids, mulcting their maritime trade with India, but not trying to stop it. The Safavids developed their own port at Bandar Abbas from about 1600, recapturing Hormuz as well in 1622. But Iran itself did not engage much in oceanic trade, and an attempt to borrow or buy an oceanic navy from Oman and the English East India Company, 1734–43, proved short-lived.[63] While coastal Persians had played a leading role alongside Arabs in early modern Muslim mercantile expansion, 1350–1500, the Safavids and Uzbeks of Iran and Turan were not directly involved in expansion outside West Eurasia. But they did have the mixed blessing of providing what might be called an "informal metropolis" for a group that did expand into another world: the Mughals.

———

The Moroccans of 1590 were not the only small army of Muslim conquistadors to leave West Eurasia in the sixteenth century. In 1525, a neo-Mongol group known as the Mughals, led by Babur, an obscure descendant of Timur, descended on India. Babur had his army counted as it crossed the Indus River—8,000 combatant troops and 4,000 camp followers. Babur's home was Fergana, a fertile region adjoining Transoxiana. He took Samarkand three times between 1497 and 1514, but was ejected each time by the Uzbeks, losing Fergana as well. He managed to establish himself at Kabul in the Hindu Kush Mountains, 800 kilometres from Samarkand, and this became the base from which he invaded India in 1525. The prosperous and cosmopolitan Indian world that the Mughals entered contained at least 100 million people.[64] Most were Hindu, in an infinite variety of polities, castes, and sub-castes. Since the early eighth century, successive waves of Muslims had superimposed themselves on parts of the subcontinent, arriving both by sea and by Babur's route. The Islamic Delhi sultanate emerged in 1175, and controlled much of India by the fourteenth century. In 1398, Timur sacked Delhi, and the sultanate declined. Imported Afghan warriors and Hindu Rajput warlords became semi-independent. The sultanate was still able to muster a much bigger army than the Mughals, but was heavily defeated by Babur at Panipat in 1526, a fate shared by a Rajput army in 1527. Babur died in 1530; his sons contested the succession; and Delhi's Afghan viceroy, Sher Shah, took power himself and was able to throw out the Mughals by 1540. But the Mughals mounted a reconquest from the 1540s, retook Delhi in 1555, and kept extending their conquests to 1687, when they controlled most of India.

The Mughals arrived in India only a couple of decades after the Portuguese and, like them, derived some advantage from gun technology. Yet the two incursions are seen as wholly separate, launched by sea and by land from the distinct subglobal worlds of Western Europe and Central Asia, and completely different in kind. This view needs questioning. We have seen that Turan had become more integrated than ever with Iran under the Timurids in the fifteenth century. The Mughals took pride in their Mongol heritage, but there is a strong case, recently endorsed by Richard Foltz, for seeing them as culturally Persianate. "The Mughal administrators were mainly ethnic Iranian immigrants or the children of Iranian mothers, and the elite culture was Persian".[65] In any case, Mughal power was forged in the post-plague late Timurid environment, and had to compete with, and coopt, plague-hardened technologies and techniques. Can the Mughals usefully be seen as another West Eurasian, early modern, colonial empire—the most populous of all? We can test the possibility by looking at their expansion kit, especially guns, statecraft, and economic management, and at the continuity and nature of their links with their distant "metropolis", Greater Persia.

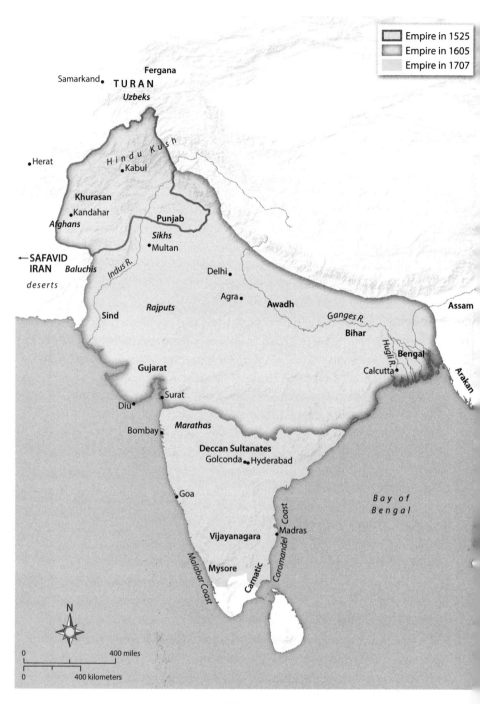

Samarkand • **TURAN**
Fergana
Uzbeks

• Herat

Hindu Kush

• Kabul

Khurasan

• Kandahar

Afghans

Punjab

Sikhs
• Multan

← **SAFAVID IRAN** *Baluchis*

deserts

Indus R.

Delhi •

Agra •

Awadh

Assam

Sind

Rajputs

Ganges R.

Bihar

Hugli R.

Bengal

Calcutta •

Arakan

Gujarat

• Surat

Diu •

Bombay •

Marathas

Deccan Sultanates
Golconda • • Hyderabad

• Goa

Bay of Bengal

Malabar Coast

Vijayanagara

Madras •

Coromandel Coast

Mysore

Carnatic

N

0 — 400 miles

0 — 400 kilometers

MAP 10. The Mughal Empire

Historians are sharply divided on the role of guns in Mughal success. Several scholars downplay their importance, on grounds that include the comments of Babur himself; the numerical predominance of cavalry in Mughal armies; and the fact that guns featured significantly in only a few major field battles.[66] It is true that Babur, in his memoirs *The Baburnama*, while noting his guns and gunners, is somewhat dismissive of their role in battle. Like other proud heirs of a cavalry ethos, he was prone to rhetorical gun denigration. The first guns he acquired derived from the Ming diffusion, but he made a deliberate decision to switch to the West Eurasian diffusion between 1514 and 1519, when there is a gap in *The Baburnama*.[67] The Safavids were making the same transition at the same time, and they were sometimes allies of the Mughals. But Babur also drew directly on the Ottomans, "There is evidence of actual physical presence of people in the army [of 1519] who had direct personal knowledge of the Ottomans". "Mustafa Rumi had made [the cannons] in the Anatolian fashion, so they were sleek and fast". Babur certainly knew all about Ottoman gunnery tactics. He wrote that in one 1526–27 engagement: "Master Ali Quli was told to tie [the cannons] together with ox-harness ropes instead of chains after the Rumi [Anatolian] fashion".[68] It is also true that Mughal field armies were mostly cavalry, but the whole point of guns was to multiply men by firepower. Firearms were prominent in only a few major battles, but there were few such battles for them to feature in, especially after 1600, when the Mughal's enemies avoided encounters in the field.

Babur had 700 gun carts or wagons at his first great victory, at Panipat in 1526. His tactics were those of the Ottomans, pivoting heavy cavalry and mounted archers on a solid base of infantry musketeers and field artillery, protected by laagered wagons.[69] It does seem that guns were the only category in which Babur had an advantage—his cavalry were very heavily outnumbered. He himself noted that some of his enemies had never seen muskets.[70] The gun wagons were a mobile field fortress. At his next victory in 1527, "The infantry, carts and light artillery continued to push forward, disrupting the Rajputs' formation. As the enemy began to lose cohesion, Babur finally released his cavalry to flank and encircle them".[71] Even if guns were not decisive in Babur's own campaigns, they seem crucial in the Mughal re-conquest of the 1540s and 1550s, and in at least some subsequent conquests. In a battle in 1540, the Mughal army deployed 5,000 musketeers, 21 heavy cannon, and 700 light cannon, known by their Ottoman name as *zarbans*. By 1545, they also had 4,000 pieces of very light artillery, weighing only 70 kilograms each, firing shot of around one kilogram, possibly camel-borne. By the 1560s, the Mughal siege train of very heavy cannon made many traditional Indian fortifications untenable.[72]

The Mughal main army was vast, with up to 100,000 cavalry, and in some pitched battles, these may have been decisive. But by 1595, the army also included 35,000 musketeers.[73] Outside the pitched battlefield, "the matchlock musket appears to have contributed from the very beginning significantly to the exercise of imperial control over disaffected localities".[74] Generally, the Mughal army was a typical West Eurasian hybrid, like those of the Ottomans and Russians, based on both guns and cavalry, and able to use gunboats as well. Muskets, cannon, and gunboats were certainly crucial in the long and difficult conquest of Bengal, which was among the Mughals' most important because it began a transformation of the whole Indian economy. It lasted from 1574 to 1612, and was then challenged by Arakanese, Assamese, and Portuguese renegades based on Sandwip Island, as well as by Bengali rebels. Much of the region was intersected by swamps, inlets, and rivers. The Mughals used a small, select, heavily gunned, and amphibious army, "averaging for each campaign 4,000 musketeers, 2100 mounted archers, and 300 war boats".[75] These boats carried men and supplies, but also mounted cannon, and were eventually a match for more than twice their number of local war boats.

The Mughals themselves had no experience with gunboats, and made use of captured local vessels, before beginning to systematically build their own from the mid-1590s. This, and the other information on which this paragraph draws, is from a fine 2019 study.[76] But signs that Mughal boats were better can elude scholars who do not distinguish between the West Eurasian and Ming Chinese diffusions of military technology. The Ming diffusion of firearms was strong in mainland Southeast Asia in the fifteenth century, and extended to the northernmost deltas of the Bay of Bengal. "Much before the arrival of the Mughals, intelligence about the manufacture and use of firearms had reached these eastern reaches of South Asia from China". Their guns were iron, perhaps wrought iron, not bronze. They were accompanied by "an abundance of fireworks", another tell-tale factor. "Imperial armies learnt how to mount cannons on big boats such as *ghurābs*, presumably from their local adversaries, their boatmen, or Portuguese mercenaries". The last are the most likely, and were in good supply. "In the course of the sixteenth century, Portuguese mercenaries and renegades fled the official control of Goa and gravitated towards the Bengal coast in large numbers". The Mughals employed many as mercenaries, and probably as boat-builders and cannon-makers. In the early 1660s, they also employed "at least one Englishman . . . in charge of building war-boats". A contemporary described him as "the master of the riverside, and employed in building boats and making ammunition for river fighting". As the next chapter will show, West Eurasian gunboats were built more sturdily than others, to brace for the recoil of their cannon and to provide some protection from enemy fire. This, plus better (cast bronze) cannon, gave them the kind of advantage the Mughals appear to have developed in amphibian warfare in Bengal between the 1590s and 1660s, though they never conquered Assam, which was outside their logistic limits. The Mughals took the best biotechnology from wherever they could get it—they used war elephants too—but especially from much-plagued West Eurasia.

Along the western coast of India, other powers had West Eurasian guns too. The technology was especially well developed in the Deccan. Here, western guns were first introduced about 1460, by the Mamluks.[77] A further surge in firearm introductions occurred from 1500, courtesy of the Portuguese and Ottomans. Guns featured prominently in a long contest, 1460s–1560s, between the Muslim sultanates of the Deccan and the Hindu kingdom of Vijayanagara which at peak controlled most of southern India.[78] The former had better access to guns and gunners. Indian artisans, among the best in the world, quickly proved adept at making guns of most types. But, for the first few decades, they needed guidance and prototypes from a regular inflow of West Eurasian experts. The Portuguese had a hand here too, but the Muslim sultanates drew mainly on Ottoman technology. Gunnery's "uptake and upkeep was dependent on immigrants from the larger Islamic world . . . a steady stream of skilled foreign manpower".[79] Their first datable cast-bronze guns, 1543–49, "were all made by a single gunfounder, Muhammad bin Husain Rumi, . . . an immigrant from Ottoman Turkey, where bronze gunfounding had achieved a high level of perfection". In a great battle in 1565, the Deccan sultanates finally overcame Vijayanagara through the "far more effective use of firepower".[80] As Mughal success and wealth grew in the late sixteenth century, the flow of Muslim guns and gun-makers from West Eurasia diverted to them, while that to the southern sultanates "became a trickle", which was presumably a factor in their eventual conquest by the Mughals in the 1680s.[81]

Guns and gunboats, of course, were only two elements of the expansion kit. The Mughal system of elite *mansabdars* holding land grants (*jagirs*) in return for military contingents was very like the Ottoman *timars*. One Mughal innovation may have been extending the Muslim synergy of state, military, commerce, and religion to non-Muslim creeds as well, at least until a downturn in their religious tolerance from 1658.[82] In 1579, Emperor Akbar abolished the traditional tax on non-Muslims and patronised Hindu temples as well as mosques. The Khatri caste of Hindu merchants had four representatives among senior Mughal notables, and worked with the state inside and outside their base in the Punjab, though some fell out with the regime as they increasingly entwined with the Sikhs after 1600.[83] Around a quarter of the high elite, top military officers and officials, were Hindu, notably Rajputs. Though considered noble, their mansabdar positions were not hereditary, at least in theory. It was the emperor, not their own heirs, that inherited even a mansabdar's personal property. As with Ottoman *timariots*, the muster of these troops was checked against the records by a small army of scribes, right down to the brand on each horse.[84] Scribes administered the twenty provinces of Mughal India, and conducted censuses of the growing amount of productive land. They oversaw local *zamindars* (landlords or gentry), who collected and shared the high taxes imposed on grain and rice.

This grain tax was one mainstay of Mughal revenues, and is traditionally thought to have been the only one. The Mughals were once said to have been uninterested in the sea, in commerce, and in anything but agrarian economic management. Historians have turned against this view, and a picture of light but deft state supervision is emerging. There remains an overlooked possibility that the Mughals were lucky enough to inherit a growing and changing economy. As discussed in chapter 9, the new Middle Eastern mercantile expansion combined with Ming outreach to increase India's trade in the fifteenth century. Indians responded by increasing production of pepper and cotton textiles, and by increasing inter-regional rice exports to allow more specialisation in both. Several historians also date the flowering of the *banjara* system of overland transport to the fifteenth century. The banjara were drovers who ran vast ox caravans, of up to 40,000 beasts, linking inland regions to each other and to the coast. They were slow-moving but low-cost. "Begun only in the later fifteenth century . . . [they] made a huge difference to economic possibilities. [It was] now possible to produce cotton in Gujarat, for ultimate sale and manufacture in Bengal".[85] Mughal and European stimulus to the economy takes the credit for this neglected earlier shift.

Mughal economic stimulus still seems real enough. They gave "great care and attention" to India's world-leading currency system—the silver rupee coinage was never debased between 1556 and 1707. "The mints were royal preserves, as was coinage, but access to minting was freely available to anyone with any bullion".[86] Their demand for taxes in cash enhanced monetisation and banking. We are told that "customs duties are estimated to have amounted to only 1 per cent of the total revenues of the Mughal empire".[87] But this refers to customs duties on foreign trade, not levies on internal trade, and in any case looks like a deliberate policy to encourage imports and exports. The Mughals cancelled duties at the key inland entry points of Kabul and Kandahar, and reduced them at the port of Cambay.[88] They sponsored the great free port of Surat in Gujarat from the 1570s, and encouraged cotton manufacturing for export. Mughal elite demand is now thought to have further stimulated Indian craft production.[89] No one could yet match the quality of Indian cottons, for which Indian merchants would take only silver,[90] like the Chinese for silks. Both countries therefore attracted a tide of foreign bullion. The best estimate for India seems to be an average of 140 tons a year, 1600–1800.[91] The inflow did not lead to the inflation apparent in West Eurasia, due to the sheer size of the Indian economy. [92] The Mughals also took great care of the infrastructure of overland trade, both themselves and by encouraging *vaqf* and their Sufi equivalent, the shrines of dead holy men or saints, which provided a "range of services . . . from housing travellers and stabling expensive horses to milling grain and providing water channels".[93] They expanded and maintained roads, caravanserai, and postal systems, reduced banditry, repaired old cities, and built new ones.[94]

The empire also developed East Bengal from 1580, encouraging settlement, founding towns, and clearing land.[95] Again, they had the help of energetic Sufis, who converted many peasants to Islam, as well as finance from the Khatris. The Mughal elite themselves also invested in "what was essentially their new colony".[96] The amount of revenue the Mughals derived from East Bengal doubled between 1595 and 1659. The newly cleared well-watered land was excellent for wet rice production, and rice exports increased, further stimulating specialisation in other regions, while cotton textile output increased too, with Bengal becoming the world's leading supplier by 1700. It was this global Bengal that the British inherited in the mid-eighteenth century, one already reconfigured by earlier West Eurasian expansions.

The Mughals took their cut of this burgeoning trade not at the ports, but at the mints and trade nodes further inland. A plausible recent argument is that gross income from various dues, gifts, tolls, and levies—mainly on goods assembled for trade, delivered just as much as the grain tax. It was "much easier to extort wealth once it had already been assembled and monetized by merchants rather than to seek to squeeze it out of thousands of small farmers scattered across an inaccessible landscape".[97] Various sub-elites took cuts, but the central state still received around half. This apparently gave it as much or more real income than the British Empire in India until the 1860s.[98] External trade was left to the many merchant networks available, both local and foreign: Hindu, Jain, Parsi, and Christian (both "St Thomas" Syrian and Armenian), as well as old and new Muslim networks. Northern Indian merchants known generically as "Multani" were leading agents in the overland trades with Iran and Turan, and established links to Russia.[99] One emperor instructed his officials to "especially see to it that merchants have a good opinion of you for their report carries far".[100] The Mughals usually saw Western Europeans as a useful addition to their collection of middlemen. They might be a threat to each other and to non-European networks. They were not a threat, on land, to the Mughals. As in China, adding Europeans to the network repertoire gave India good though indirect access to the biological bonanza of the Americas, acclimatising tobacco by 1600, and potatoes, tomatoes, chilies, peanuts, papaya, and pineapple over the next century. In Rajat Datta's recent assessment, the Mughal state was able to:

> create new synergies between itself and diverse agrarian regimes under its rule. This enabled it to manage and simultaneously reap benefits from expanding agrarian and maritime opportunities without having to control one or the other. This, in my view, explains the ability of the early modern state in India to both successfully extract high levels of agrarian surpluses and to ensure unprecedented degrees of political and social acceptability within diverse demographic and socio-cultural milieus.[101]

———

This rather rosy picture of Mughal modernity seems broadly accurate, but needs qualification. First, it is not clear that the mass of the people benefited from commercial prosperity, or from Mughal rule. Taxes on grain went as high as 50%, and there were some terrible regional famines. One study finds a decline in Indian GDP per capita from 1600, though others dispute this.[102] Second, the Mughal's empire was arguably of the now familiar "patchwork" variety, with difficult terrain excluding many regions from real control. The Emperor must "be regarded as ruling no more than half the dominions which he claims, since there are nearly as many rebels as subjects".[103] Third, there is some residual truth in the notion that the Mughals and other large Indian states kept maritime concerns at arm's length. The imperial family and leading officials had ocean-going ships built for them in Gujarat from the 1570s, and were very interested in annual voyages for the Hajj pilgrimage, which was a major exercise in overseas trade as well as religion.[104] But they seldom tried to fight Europeans or Omanis on the open ocean, and failed when they did. Between 1639 and 1698, the Mughals were sporadically at war with the tiniest of European lodgments in India, that of the Danes. The Danish "empire" in India was based at Tranquebar in the Coromandel and had a few unfortified factories as well. The Mughals could seize the factories, and probably Tranquebar too, but they kept losing ships to the Danes—two were blown up in the Hughli River, 35 kilometres north of Calcutta, in 1671.[105] This was no more than a pinprick to the Mughals, whose land power enabled them to hold European land possessions and trade networks hostage in a "balance of blackmail".[106] But the capacity to threaten Indian ships and the Hajj pilgrimage gave Europeans (and Omanis) more leverage than the other merchant networks. The final qualification is that Mughal "modernity" and success were not strictly Mughal, but rather a variant of West Eurasian expansion, Muslim style.

That the Mughals acquired and adapted a West Eurasian expansion kit, and used it for successful expansion, is only half of the argument here. Many experts would say that the expansion lapsed quickly into dispersal, losing strong connections to its homelands in Iran and Turan, with which relations were sometimes actively hostile. "For their own reasons, Indian historians working in the Orientalist, Marxist, nationalist, and other traditions have tended to minimize any connections that the Mughal nobility retained with their ancestral homeland".[107] The Mughals were just another wave of Muslim invaders, it is assumed, to be quickly domesticated by India except in religion. Yet Babur was not welcomed by the preexisting Muslim population. "Most Indian Muslims . . . regarded Babur as alien".[108] To a significant extent, the Mughal Empire remained rooted in Greater Persia until the beginning of its decline in 1707, without controlling the space between their "informal metropolis", to coin a term, and their great Indian "colony". Their continuing "obsession" with the homelands is sometimes dismissed as nostalgic and irrational.[109] "The thinly populated and barren lands of Central Asia could offer little in the way of added resources to the wealthy Mughal Empire".[110] Mughal India was indeed separated from Iran and Turan by formidable barriers, including the Hindu Kush mountains, up to 25,000 feet high, so named for causing the death of Hindus trying to cross them. Where the mountains petered out towards the ocean, the "desert marshes of Seistan squeezed between Registan (Land of Sand) and Dasht-i-Margo (Waterless Plain of Death)" took over.[111] There were human obstacles too. "All of the overland routes to Kabul, Iran and Turan ran through Afghan or Baluchi tribal territory, as did the Indus route to Thatta and the Arabian Sea. Ensuring safe passage through these regions was a consistent goal of Mughal policy".[112] Kabul and Kandahar, on the routes to Turan and Iran respectively, were halfway stations, fortified islands in a sea of mountain and desert. The Mughals usually held Kabul, but lost Kandahar to the Safavids, first in 1622 and then permanently in 1648. Both empires tried to fortify and improve roads and to buy off the brigands, with mixed success. From the northernmost Indian trading city of Multan to Kandahar was a journey of more than five weeks, "constantly threatened by Afghan tribesmen".[113] "The road from Lahore to Kabul is infested by Pathan brigands; and although the [Mughal] king has established 23 guard stations of troops at regular intervals, nonetheless travellers are frequently robbed by these brigands, who in the year 1611 actually attacked and looted the city of Kabul".[114] The Mughals did not have to completely control such routes, and probably could not, but they did have to be able to ensure fairly free passage—not just for trade, but also for the regular supply of fresh Mughals (and fresh horses) on whom their system depended. This, not nostalgia, was the basis of their consistent interest.

While the Mughals did briefly accept nominal vassalage to the Safavids in the mid-sixteenth century, to gain their support for the reconquest of Northern India, they were emphatically *not* a part of an informal empire run by the Safavids—or the Uzbeks, or the Ottomans, or anyone else. Instead, the relationship was inverted: Iran and Turan continued to be "informal metropolises" of the Mughal empire in India, whether Safavid or Uzbek states liked it or not. The Safavids made the best of necessity. "Safavid-Mughal relations were indeed cordial to the point of being affectionate. . . . Safavid aggression vis-à-vis Qandahar did little to alter that comity".[115] A key "building-block of the Mughal state was . . . the incorporation of migrant intermediaries, who flocked to their court from Iran and Central Asia. The latter, often generically designated 'Turanis', had been present under earlier rulers as well; it is the Iranian migration that increases dramatically in Mughal times".[116]

Early on, "*rumis*, or Anatolians, were particularly prized for their mastery of artillery".[117] In the decade 1565–1575, 40% of leading Mughal nobles were designated Iranian, another 40% were Turanian.[118] Between 1658 and 1678, among the 141 leading mansabdars (nominally owing 3,000 troops or more), 55 (39%) were Iranian, and 23 (16%) Turanian, together 55%.[119] These migrants, and the local mansabdars, took on an Ottoman-like "civic imperial" identity, as Mughals and "sons of the imperial household".[120] India, that is, was still led by a foreign colonial elite 160 years after Babur's first incursion. Between 1679 and 1707, the foreign percentage of high nobles declined, but only to 46.5%.[121] These were only the leaders; the immigration of Iranians and Turanians of lesser status was much greater. "In the sixteenth and seventeenth centuries Hindustan not only witnessed intensified commercial exchange, but also unprecedented high levels of migration into its territories".[122]

Military migrants served the purpose of a soldier-importing regime: ensuring the central state a core armed force without local roots and obligations. Not even nominal slavery was required because the Mughals paid so well— three or four times as much as the Safavids and Ottomans.[123] Consequently, these regimes could not stop the flow of their subjects to India. The Shahs may well have regretted that "Safavid elites . . . continued to flock to the Indian court"[124]—"a two-centuries long brain drain that depleted Iran, to the great benefit of India".[125] As the term "brain drain" suggests, warfare was not the only elite migrant talent. Poets, artists, scholars, Sufis, engineers, accountants, and administrators also came, transferring practices that Middle Eastern Muslims had developed in and after the early plague era, creating an ongoing "Mughal indebtedness to Iranian intellectual and managerial tools".[126] Migrants "brought with them Iranian traditions which readily combined in the practices of statecraft and commerce".[127] As we have seen with reference to Sufis, they also brought the practice of combining both with religion.

Elite human imports were joined by elite equine imports. Most of India was ecologically unsuitable for breeding heavy warhorses. In those regions that could breed them, quality was "dependent on regular crossbreeding with Central Eurasian horses".[128] Before the Mughals, coastal states imported them by sea from the Persian Gulf and the Red Sea, and this trade continued.[129] Northern states had imported them from Iran and Turan in difficult journeys across the Hindu Kush, and this was the Mughals' main source. What seems to have changed was the scale. Kabul, the key hub in this trade, sold 7,000–10,000 horses annually in the early sixteenth century. Under the Mughals, the number increased to between 20,000 and 100,000.[130] "It was the supply of strong warhorses that made the control of Kabul so crucial to the Mughals".[131] Even when Mughal control lapsed, "the rulers of both Kabul and Qandahar recognized the necessity of a policy of protection of the land-route, notwithstanding their political rivalries . . . rivalry between the Mughals and the Safavids over Qandahar, and the outbreak of wars with the Uzbeks around Kabul . . . (1626–1656) did not affect the traffic".[132] Turan may have been the biggest supplier of horses as against people, but enough of the former came from Iran for the Safavid Shahs to worry about "the apparently insatiable demand of the Mughals for horses".[133]

Mughal India has been described as "Islam's America", and its East Bengal settlement frontier has been compared to the American West. But it seems to me that this comparison yields most insight if we look at the British-US relationship in the nineteenth century. Like Mughal India, the United States was then a neo-colony that was enormous in comparison to its founder. For a century after political independence in 1783, it still needed imports of British migrants, skills, and biotechnology (including breeding stock to improve American horses, pigs, and cattle), as did Mughal India from Iran and Turan. Here too, the British could not stop the outflow even if they wanted to. There could be no question of political control by the informal metropolis over its giant semi-colony. Iran and Turan continued to function as Mughal homelands for almost two centuries after 1519, though the metropolitan states had little control over the process and may well have resented it. The metropolises were not contiguous with the giant colony; mountains and deserts, Baluchis and Afghans, lay between them, a bridge-barrier analogous to an ocean. This is the case for seeing Mughal India as another West Eurasian colonial empire, enabled by the plague-incubated expansion kit.

14

Plague and Russian Expansion

WE HAVE HITHERTO touched lightly on Europe's largest region, comprising today's European Russia, Ukraine, and Belarus. Before 1350, it was dominated by the Golden Horde, Turco-Mongols generically known as "Tartars". We have noted the plague-assisted breakup of the Horde, which despite the efforts of able leaders was dealt another blow by Timur in the 1390s. Its fragments claimed its mantle and some remained quite large and powerful. "By 1421 there were as many as six separate figures claiming to rule as khan of the Golden Horde".[1] The "Great Horde" held the lead until 1480. It was joined by the Khanates of Kazan, Astrakhan, and the Crimea. Each combined steppe regions of pastoral nomadism with sedentary agriculture and trading cities. More fully nomadic groups included the Nogai, the Uzbeks (discussed in the previous chapter), and the Kazakhs.

North of these Muslim Tartars lay the Orthodox Christian Russian or Rus' principalities, around a dozen in 1350. Some then fell under expansive Lithuania; most others continued paying sporadic tribute to the Tartars. In the 1350s, when Northern Russia was first hit by plague, Muscovy was only one of five leading principalities, the others being Novgorod in the far north, Suzdal and Tver in the centre, and Riazan in the south. By 1521, Muscovy had engulfed all of these. It also conquered Kazan and Astrakhan in the 1550s, though it was unable to overcome the Crimean Tartars for another two centuries. It's metamorphosis into Russia is traditionally dated to 1547, when Grand Prince Ivan IV "the Terrible" became tsar. Russia's extension into Siberia is usually dated to 1582; we have seen that it began earlier, by 1499. But the 1580s did mark the conquest of another Tartar Khanate, Sibir, itself a precocious expansionist. By 1639, Russian fur hunters had reached the Pacific, establishing a permanent presence there from 1648. Russia consolidated its hold on the southern steppes and Siberia in the eighteenth century, and in the nineteenth took possession of parts of Central Asia and the Caucasus. Around 1800, it claimed sovereignty of a million-square-mile chunk of North America—Alaska.

Despite this vast semi-global expansion, Russia is often excluded from the history of European imperialism, partly because its own European-ness was contested, but also because its expansion was mainly overland, which the previous chapter argued is flawed logic. To my knowledge, plague has rarely featured in explanations of Muscovy's early expansion. This chapter attempts to at least make a start on putting plague back into the history of Russian expansion, putting Russian expansion back into West Eurasian history, and testing our hypotheses about plague's effects using the Russian case. The attempt is complicated by conflicting sources, political dogma, retrospective nationalisms, Russo-philia and Russo-phobia. Soviet historians in particular promulgated a "white legend" of a non-racist, non-violent acquisition of Siberia. "From the late 1920s onwards historians denied or omitted to mention that Russians and native Siberians had ever fought at all".[2] Traces of a Western European assumption of Russia's "backwardness" remain. Until recently, it was often portrayed as "aggressive but illiterate, always bungling, ill equipped, impecunious, and late to the table of European civilization".[3] In the 2006 *Cambridge History of Russia*, we are told that smoky huts and vitamin deficiency "contributed mightily to making the Russian the short-lived, lethargic, marginally productive, minimally creative (original) person he was".[4] Such bias may lie behind a tendency to attribute any hint of Russian innovation to external influence: Scandinavian from the ninth century, Mongol from the thirteenth, and Western European, imported by Tsar Peter the Great, from the 1690s. These influences did have their significance, but none explains dynamic Russian expansion, 1360s–1650.

One thing Russian and Western European historiographies do have in common is a cleavage between pessimist and optimist views of the post-plague socioeconomy. A late convert to pessimism argued in 2015 that "Muscovy suffered a long period of economic stagnation and even depression, perhaps dating back to the second half of the fourteenth century".[5] More historians now acknowledge signs of prosperity, but seem mystified by it. "A surge of urban development beginning in the middle of the fourteenth century", mainly in the form of churches and fortifications, is well documented, especially for Novgorod and Moscow.[6] This boom "flies in the face of the well-known fact that the Black Death struck Russia during this period".[7] "Repeated epidemics of plague, had no measurably adverse effect on the building boom. . . . To explain this anomaly, historians have suggested that chroniclers exaggerated, that

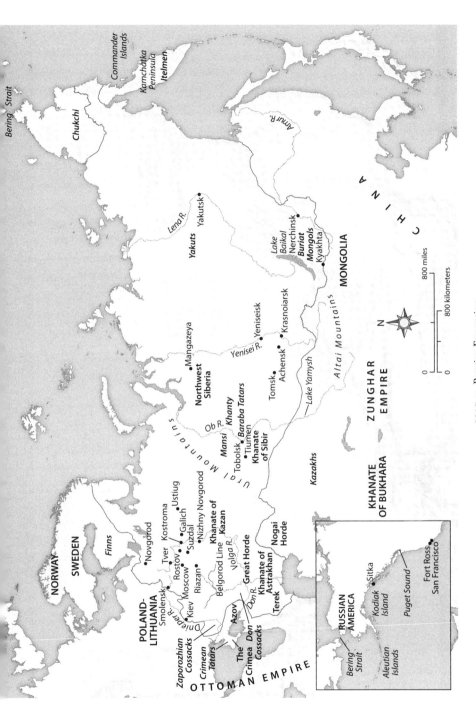

MAP 11. Russian Expansion

plague was less devastating in northern Rus'.[8] We now know that this was no anomaly. As elsewhere, plague roughly doubled the per capita availability of such resources as work animals and water-accessible building stone, boosted the incomes of elites at least, and encouraged them to look to their souls by endowing religious establishments.

There was also a rural building boom, in the form of monasteries. "By the end of the fourteenth century, forty-two new monasteries had been built in the northern and eastern peripheries of Rus. Fifty-seven more were built in the fifteenth century".[9] Other evidence also supports a picture of post-plague prosperity, although it is unclear how widely it was shared. Chapter 4 noted a massive upturn in Russian fur exports after 1350. "Most of the silver and money flowing into the heart of Russia during the fourteenth and fifteenth centuries came via Novgorod".[10] In fact, Novgorod was by no means the only player in the fur trade. Other Rus' principalities and several Tartar polities also extended their fur acquisition reaches to meet the new demand. The inflow of silver, of which Russia produced little itself, initially came in ingots, not coins—apparently there were no mints in Russia in 1350. By 1400, there were said to be 21 mints, suggesting a widespread increase in commerce. But it remains true that Novgorod was the early leader in economic growth—and in expansionism.[11]

I Novgorod: "Rome of the Waterways"

Novgorod's eminence and empire predated the Black Death.[12] In 1150, it was geographically "the largest state in all of medieval Europe".[13] Most of its domains were lightly held, consisting largely of fur acquisition networks, but its wealth and outreach were impressive. The city itself had at least 4,300 houses and 15 churches in 1211, when these were the numbers destroyed by a fire. Its citizens are said to have been rich enough to use sable blankets.[14] It had access to the Baltic via rivers and Lake Ladoga, and its own merchants once sailed that sea in Novgorod-built ships. But its trade to the west was increasingly handled by Lubeck-led Hanseatics, who had a large *kontor* in the city.[15] Novgorod's trade southwards was even more profitable and far-reaching. Archaeology has found an ornament with components from both Madagascar and the Maldive Islands, as well as the skull of an African macaque, presumably from a shivering pet.[16] Novogorod was hit by plague ten times between 1352 and 1478.[17] Its vast territory was already thinly populated, and it came under increasing pressure from rivals. Some historians see its post-plague history as one of decline, which is true from 1450. Yet in the preceding century, its responses to demographic catastrophe rank it among West Eurasia's great plague-managing city-states, along with Genoa, Lubeck, Dubrovnik, Aden, and Hormuz.

Novgorod was a merchant republic, like other European city-states, and some see in it an alternative path for Russian history, more capitalist and less autocratic. Recent revision claims that the city's republican antecedents are exaggerated, and that its famous assembly (*veche*) consisted only of around 300 boyars (nobles) and leading merchants.[18] Even more recent counter-revision claims that the veche accommodated several thousand, and other evidence, such as the fact that juries were half commoner, does suggest that at least middle-class men had some standing.[19] Novgorod was certainly more oligarchy than democracy, like most city-states, and it did have princes, brought in from outside like Italian *podesta*. But it changed them more often than its sable blankets, expelling one every two years in the twelfth century.[20] Even short-term princes lost power after reforms in the 1350s.[21] The local arch-bishops gained some, "but there is no indication that they attained the level of heads of state as some scholars contend".[22] Elected officials, *posadniki* and *tys-iatskie*, shared power with the archbishop. Foreign rulers thought it wise to cover all bases. "I, the illustrious King of Poland and Grand Prince of Lithua-nia, have concluded a treaty with the Archbishop-elect Feofil and with the *posadniki* of Novgorod, and with the *tysiatskie*, and with the boyars, and with the *zhitye liudi* [middling folk] and with the merchants, and with all Novgorod the Great".[23] So at least some of the lower ranks likely felt a degree of solidarity with the state. As with Genoa and Lubeck, this enhanced the city's military punch. As well as boyars and "boyars' sons" (the equivalent of knights), peas-ants and common townsfolk were important in Novgorod's armies.[24] More grain imports also enhanced available military manpower. "In the fourteenth and fifteenth centuries, Novgorod was becoming increasingly dependent on the supply of grain from the south-east".[25] It also drew grain from the Baltic littoral.[26] This would have increased the city-state's proportion of "disposable males", no longer needed for the grain harvest.

I can find no statistics for the population of Novgorod's whole territory before 1500, when it was around 400,000.[27] But it seems the city itself may actually have grown, like Lubeck, during the plague era, from 15,000 in 1350 to 22,000 or even 30,000 in the fifteenth century, repopulating itself through im-migration.[28] The economy certainly did grow, initially even more than that of rival states such as Muscovy. "We must wonder at Novgorod's wealth", writes one optimist, "the economic upturn came there first and most strongly". Of the 280 major building projects in all Rus' during 1413–37, 53% were under-taken by Novgorod.[29] Apart from furs and trade goods, Novgorod also ex-ported high-grade leather and up to 300 tons of wax per year, the former to the rest of Russia, the latter to Western Europe, providing candles for its scribes.[30] Other indicators of post-plague prosperity range from increased imports from Venice to increased consumption of veal.[31] There are also hints of both cultural renaissance—"a burst of cultural creativity"[32]—and religious reformation. The wealth meant that Novgorod was able to import and breed more and bigger horses than its Russian rivals, and more and better arms, armour, and merce-naries. It was able to muster surprisingly large armies in the plague con-text—8,000 men in 1398—including heavy cavalry, as well as riverine fleets of up to 150 boats.[33] In the century after 1352, Novgorod used these resources to undertake an astonishing series of aggressive initiatives.

These included a sequence of southwards raids, 1366–1409, by "the famous Novgorod *uzhkuyniki* ("marauding boatmen"). In 1366, "bandits from Novgorod . . . appeared on the middle Volga and massacred large numbers of Muslim and Armenian merchants". The raids were repeated in 1374 and 1375, when they penetrated as far as the outskirts of Bulgar, Sarai, and even Astra-khan.[34] Victims also included the Christian towns of Nizhny Novgorod, Us-tiug, and Kostroma. These campaigns aimed both at disrupting the fur net-works of rivals and at taking slaves. "It was not the Tartars and Moscow that were blocking the trade of Novgorod . . . it was the Novgorodians who were impeding the trade of the Tartars and Moscow".[35] Some slaves were sold, others were brought home, sometimes in direct response to a plague strike. In 1392, "Novgorod attacked Ustiug, killing many and taking many into captivity. This campaign followed the outbreak of a 'great plague', which occurred the year before in Novgorod".[36] Slave raiding also intensified in the north from 1375. "Novgorodians regularly took prisoners during raids into the areas of Finnic populations outside the Swedish, Novgorodian and Muscovite realms, and brought them to Novgorod. Transporting them was so difficult that the prisoners must have been valuable". One raid in 1398 took "countless prison-ers", and Novgorod slavers left a mark in Finnish folklore.[37]

Northward expansion was also aimed at colonisation of the White Sea coast, attempting to convert natives such as Karelians into subjects rather than slaves, but involving Novgorodian settlers as well, who became known as Pomors (coast-folk). In 1353, a year after its first plague, Novgorod founded the Northern Dvina River port of Kholmogory. Monasteries were usually the bases of northern colonisation, including Archangel Michael Monastery, in the later fourteenth century, which later gave its name to Archangel, and Solovetsky Monastery (1429), which became fabulously wealthy.[38] This "intense colonisation of the Russian North, which continued until the late fifteenth century",[39] is particularly remarkable in time of plague. Agriculture was very marginal this far north, so colonisation must have aimed at such maritime products as codfish and walrus, whose tusks, known as "fish teeth", were a source of ivory.

It has been claimed that "Novgorod's trade empire proved to be inflexible, for it remained based on squirrel fur when European demand shifted to luxury fur".[40] Novgorod did specialise in squirrel in its core territory, where they were taken by peasant trappers who left their fields for their hunting grounds in winter, when the pelts were prime. Each pair of trappers had their own hunting ground, one day's journey all round from a central base camp.[41] The re-use of these suggests to me a form of semi-farming, trapping only sustainable numbers. Some sources do suggest depletion, but others note that squirrel prices dropped from 1410, perhaps indicating over-supply, and that, as noted in chapter 4, "golden age" use of squirrel by common folk demoted it in the eyes of elite consumers.[42] But a market for prime squirrel continued, and Novgorod had long aimed at other luxury furs as well, hence the sable bedding.[43] Indeed, the city-state had developed a full package for the long-range extraction of luxury furs. Sable were trapped or tracked with dogs and shot with blunt arrows, to preserve the pelts, by river-borne crews of full-time trappers (*promyshlenniki*). They were also acquired through trade with various taiga forest peoples, or extorted from them as tribute. Trapping, trade, and tribute all utilised small fortified posts (*pogost*) in the far reaches of Novgorod's domains. The addition of Novgorodian methods and demand to local requirements increased the tendency towards depletion. From 1363 to 1445, furs were plundered or extorted from forest peoples beyond the Urals in Siberia, into which there were repeated Novgorodian incursions.[44]

Clearly, Novgorod was an acute case of the plague paradox—hectic expansionism despite halved population. Apart from the colonisation of the north, most initiatives seem aimed at getting people and furs rather than permanent land acquisition. Its gains proved fragile, however. Novgorod's economic success and man-powering raids made it more enemies. It fought Lithuania, the Teutonic Knights, the Hanseatic League, Norway, the Tartars, and at least two fellow Russian principalities, Tver and Muscovy, in the first half of the fifteenth century alone. Increasing demand led others to expand fur extraction too, and Novgorod's share diminished relatively. Muscovy in particular acquired

Rostov and its fur network in 1364, and sought to penetrate Novgorod's northern fur lands. Novgorod responded with a mix of retaliation, compromise, and resistance. We have noted the retaliations beginning in 1366. In the northern fur lands of Perm, it was defeated by Muscovy in 1383–85, and accepted some form of joint condominium—"patchwork empires" could overlay each other.[45] In the richer lands of the Dvina, it rolled back rebellion and Muscovite incursions in the 1390s.

> Novgorod recaptured its lost territories and meted out severe punishment to the most prominent of the rebels. Expecting no further help from Moscow, the rest of the population submitted. When Vasilii [Prince of Muscovy] made a second attempt to take over the area in 1401, his troops encountered bitter resistance and quickly abandoned the expedition.[46]

But, after Novgorod's final 1445 expedition to Siberia failed following initial success, Moscow took over its Siberian project. It also scored direct military successes against Novgorod from that time.[47] Novgorod's dependence on foreign grain fell short of urban colonisation, in which the dependence was mutual and the city controlled the trade routes. Enemies could cut the lifelines, and did so with blockades in the 1420s and 1440s, causing acute famines in Novgorod town, sometimes wrongly attributed to plague.[48] These combined with increasing monopoly of wealth by the elite plus religious dissension to reduce social cohesion. At least two Russian historians contend that this was a key factor in the Muscovite conquest in 1478.[49] Moscow took over not only Novgorod's empire, but also its methods of imperialism, added its own techniques, and gathered lands as well as people.

II Muscovite Expansion to 1500

Moscow was hit by almost as many plague strikes as Novgorod. Its standing before the Black Death is unclear. Some historians date the beginning of its rise to 1300. It did take the principality of Ustiug in 1328, and claim the title of grand prince for its ruler from 1331. But other princes made the same claim at various times. One suspects a situation like that of the Ottomans before 1350: that Muscovy's major rise postdates the Black Death, but was retrospectively backdated by its chroniclers to downplay the role of contingency. From 1359 to 1380, under the able military leadership of Prince Dimitri Donskoi and with an increasingly close alliance between church and state, Muscovy's achievements seem to dwarf those of the pre-1350 period. Among the Christian principalities, its slaving raids were second only to Novgorod in what was clearly a post-plague competition for scarce manpower. "The income gained from the slave trade or the ability to replenish depleted labour was sufficient incentive for the constant raids and wars among the Rus'". For instance, Muscovy devastated the outlands of rival Tver in 1370, "taking huge numbers captive".[50] From the outset it had its eye on lands and furs as well as people. It extended its holdings in Perm and other fur lands. "Between 1359 and 1379 Mari and Mordva lands fell into Muscovite hands. Some lands were taken by force, others simply bought".[51] As this suggests, Moscow was also second only to Novgorod in the availability of cash. It too experienced a building boom, 1363—1412. It replaced the Kremlin's wooden walls with stone in 1367–68, "on a scale unknown elsewhere in northern Rus".[52] This helped the city survive three Lithuanian invasions, 1368–72. Tartar attacks in the 1370s fell mostly on other principalities. In 1380, Donskoi led a Russian alliance against the Golden Horde and famously defeated it at the hard-fought Battle of Kulikovo. "By 1380, Moscow's victory was by no means complete, but its rulers had gathered some of the resources needed for the creation of a powerful kingdom".[53]

The next phase, to 1450, was more mixed. The Tartars struck back in 1382 and sacked Moscow despite its walls, and Muscovy continued sporadically to pay tribute to them. It subjected an important rival, Nizhny-Novgorod in 1392, consolidating its control by 1415. It burned the city of Galich in 1434, "when many captives were taken",[54] then conquered it in 1450. Tartar raids had devastated Moscow's hinterland again in 1408, but failed to take the city. Muscovy in its turn sacked the Muslim city of Bulgar in 1432. It was then afflicted by civil wars in the 1430s and 1440s, and also suffered heavy defeats at Tartar hands, 1439–45.[55] But in the 1450s, in an overlooked shift, the balance of military power turned in Muscovy's favour. The Tartars invaded yet again in 1451, but were unable to take the city and were "forced to abandon their captives". In 1455 and 1459, Muscovy inflicted further defeats on them.[56] The high phase of Muscovite expansion began in 1462, with the accession of Ivan III "The Great". Old rivals Novgorod, Tver, and Riazan were all acquired between 1478 and 1521, fur networks were extended in the north and in northwest Siberia, and Muscovy gained a large tract of eastern Lithuania, including Smolensk. In the 1550s, it conquered the formidable khanates of Kazan and Astrakhan. Muscovy's territory at least tripled between 1462 and 1556.[57]

Several factors lay behind Muscovy's expansive success, some its own, some adapted from other states, and most influenced by plague. They included various man-powering techniques, monastic colonisation, a scribal transition, the hijacking of other empires, the acquisition of crew and settler regions, and engagement with guns and long-range trade, the last two earlier than is generally thought. Once judged on untypical periods in the reign of Ivan IV, who was only spasmodically "Terrible", as irrational and tyrannical, historians are now portraying Muscovy's government as quite flexible, collective, and internally consent-seeking, though ruthlessly expansionist.[58] Contemporaries and historians noted that Muscovy was particularly good at what I call manpowering. Its princes "clearly outdistanced their rivals in obtaining peasants to settle on their lands, their energetic activities ranging from various inducements to free farms to the purchase of prisoners from the Mongols".[59] Peasants were reshuffled to more fertile regions or to populate frontiers. A Polish observer noted in 1517 that, in Muscovy, "people are thrown . . . from province to province for colonization".[60] "Forced migration was a well-established strategy of the Muscovite princes".[61] They were also "adept at getting Lithuanian princes and nobility and their attendant service people to come over into [Muscovite] service, and "equally adept if not more so" in recruiting Tartars. This last source of troops took off in the 1370s, involved 60 Tartar nobles and their retinues, and is said to have added 20% to Muscovite military manpower by 1500. Muscovy set up its own vassal khanate, Kasimov, in 1447.[62]

One might think that tightening serfdom was among Muscovy's manpowering measures, but this was not the case until deep into the sixteenth century. As we saw with Poland (chapter 12), intensifying serfdom correlated not with the early plague era, but with demographic recovery from it. Muscovite laws passed in 1455 and 1497 are deceptive. The first restricted peasant migration to a two-week period after the harvest, to ensure that they paid their debts, and applied only to a few monasteries. The second extended this moderate restriction to all peasants. Total bans on movement date to the 1550s and after, and were not consolidated until 1649. Even then, the government played a double game, tacitly allowing peasant migration to the frontiers.[63] What Muscovy did do was come up with a category of semi-slaves, known as *kholopy*, distinct from captive or debt slaves. This "limited-service contract slavery seems to have been a Muscovite innovation".[64] Kholopy indentured themselves for a period in return for a decent living—they escaped if it was not good enough. At most 10% of the Muscovite population, they were not used to work the land, but to provide artisans, officials, and soldiers—even informal lawyers—for boyar and princely households. Their importance seems to date from the 1350s. There were also genuine slaves, some of them Russian. Like other monotheisms, the Orthodox church disapproved of enslaving co-religionists, but was overridden by plague labour shortages until the six-teenth century.[65]

Another important man-powering innovation occurred from 1478, when Muscovy confiscated the lands of Novgorod's elite and forced them to migrate to other parts of its domains. It replaced them with a new class of military servitors, holding fiefs (*pomest'e*) on written contracts with strict conditions, and owing cavalry service directly to the Grand Prince without the traditional feudal intermediaries. In some other vassal states, local elites were left in place. But the pomest'e system was extended where possible, adapted to circum-stances, and carefully policed to ensure military service conditions were met. At least one historian has rightly noted the similarity to Ottoman *timariots*.[66] Muscovy had good connections and friendly relations with the Ottomans at the time it was established, and we have seen that the latter dominated West Eurasian military and man-powering best practice in the fifteenth and six-teenth centuries. In the 1540s, Moscow also established a corps of permanent waged musket-armed infantry (*streltsy*), emulating the Janissaries. Two other Ottoman-like developments may have emerged from similar responses to plague pressures rather than direct imitation: a rise of the scribe, and monastic colonisation.

It is easy to overlook the importance of literacy to expansion. It enables governments, elites, and networks to exert at least some long-range control and permits crews and proconsuls to report back, request support, and record payment and provisioning. You did not need mass literacy for these purposes, but you did need the literate minority to be quite substantial, extending be-yond the high elite. Novgorod was the early Russian leader here too, writing its letters on birch bark by the eleventh century. One scholar doubts that lit-eracy was at all widespread even in Novgorod, but the evidence is against him—the sheer number of birch bark letters found, now well into the thou-sands; the existence of graffiti and of teaching tablets.[67] In the sixteenth century, "functional literacy among the Muscovite elite compares fairly well with that of the contemporary French nobility or the aristocratic and urban elites of Tudor England".[68] In fact, a substantial minority of Muscovite com-moners are now thought to have been literate by this time—perhaps 10–15%. There are signs of a proliferation of professional scribes in the previous century.[69] The Muscovite state developed a nascent bureaucracy which of course was behind its capacity to maintain the effectiveness of its *timar*-like pomest'e troops from 1480. The role of scribes in expansion stretched well beyond the chancelleries in Moscow to the staffs of governors of distant provinces and the commanders of frontier forts, to the sophisticated postal system (a Mongol legacy), and even to various categories of crewmen. A surprising 11.2% of the garrison in one Siberian post in 1678 were literate, and a few soldiers "even moonlighted as public scribes".[70] As in Western Europe and the Muslim South, plague was likely a factor, increasing the disposable income per family that could be spent on education and leading to a proliferation of monasteries, which did the educating.

Monasteries sprouted around Moscow from 1363.[71] Like vakf in the Muslim South, they benefited from plague-prompted endowments and were used to resettle the best of plague-depopulated lands. Here, historians do make the plague connection. Monks and peasants were given tax immunity, which "generally ranged between five and ten years. . . . designed to replenish the peasant population in the abandoned fields and thereby restore agriculture along with a taxable income". In the case of the Simonov Monastery, "plague was an important catalyst for its acquisitions", not only in early strikes but after fifteenth-century strikes.[72] Kirillov Belozerskii monastery, founded in 1397, also "began to purchase waste lands (*pustoshi*) especially after the plague years of the 1420's". "Monastic colonisation is the defining type of settlement pattern of Muscovy's northern territory".[73] "Markets tended to emerge at the doors of monasteries", which also had bank-like functions, providing loans and mortgages.[74] As elsewhere in West Eurasia, more capital was invested in agriculture, and the diminished labour force was reshuffled to the most productive locations and activities. Monasteries also enhanced government control, collecting taxes and recording property transfers for example. The post-plague monastic foundations were less tied to local boyars than the old, and more to the centralising church and state, which themselves were becoming more tightly allied.[75] Again echoing the Muslim South, monastery-led recovery from plague morphed easily into monastic colonisation. Monasteries appeared early and in considerable numbers in newly conquered regions, in Kazan and Western Siberia as well as the north, "extending Muscovite influence, governance practices, and religious traditions farther into the territory".[76]

By about 1500, Muscovy was one of West Eurasia's leading expansionists, and its state at least was surprisingly rich. Figures given in rubles often seem deceptively low. The ruble was a unit of account and represented a substantial sum—two would buy a decent horse, five were an annual wage. It comprised 200 tiny silver denga coins.[77] Muscovy's annual revenue in 1486 was estimated at more than one million ducats—3.5 tons of gold, perhaps 450,000 rubles.[78] The figure is high, but plausible in the light of the acquisition of Novgorod's revenues from 1478. Muscovy fell out with Lubeck and the Hanse in the 1490s, irritated by such slights as the burning of a Russian by the Hanseatic town of Reval for sex with a horse (a mare), and the boiling of another Russian for the even worse crime of illegal coining, both in 1494.[79] But there were alternative outlets, overland, to such cities as Leipzig and Wroclaw, and through the Dutch, and the fur trade westward continued strongly, as did southwards commerce. Moscow itself grew to 100,000 people by 1500, now four times the size of Novgorod.

A rather sophisticated mercantile system, involving three guilds or corporations of state-registered big merchants (*gosti*), as well as many private merchants, first emerged in the early plague era. The *gosti-surozhane* were named for Sudak (Surozh in Russian) an outpost of Genoese Caffa in the Crimea, which indicates the importance of the southern trade. It appeared first in Moscow and Tver before, perhaps well before, 1450. *Gosti-sukonniki* also appeared, "trading primarily with Smolensk, Lithuania, and Novgorod".[80] A "Merchant Hundred", actually several hundred strong, may be a later development. "Among its tasks of expanding its tribute collections, establishing infrastructure, and suppressing opposition, the Russian state was keen to promote trade. Commerce played an important role in empire building as both method and incentive".[81] In peacetime, Tartar traders rode to Moscow to sell steppe horses in large numbers, to mount the Muscovite cavalry. In 1474, 4,000 of them brought 40,000 horses to the city.[82] Armenian, German, Polish, and Ottoman Greek traders were also frequent visitors, buying furs and slaves. Muscovy took over Tver's long-range trading network in 1485, which used amphibious routes involving the Don and Volga Rivers and the Black and Caspian Seas. One Tver merchant had reached India via these routes in the 1460s, and there were soon hundreds of Muscovite merchants involved, travelling in groups of between 45 and 120.[83] About 220 individuals are identified in documents relating to disasters such as death, raids, and accidents between 1488 and 1502 alone, presumably a fraction, though perhaps a large one, of the journeys that went well.[84] But for all this, Muscovy continued to leak manpower to Tartar raids and sporadically pay tribute to Tartar khans. As yet, it remained a victim as well as a perpetrator of expansionism.

III Hybridity and Empire on the Steppes

In the three centuries after 1450, Russia developed a two-pair hybrid empire on the Southern Steppes and in Siberia. While the former region was largely within Europe, it cannot easily be separated from empire in Siberia. The two expansions merged and blurred, and utilised similar techniques. One part of each pair involved Russian crewmen and settlers, in substantial numbers after 1580. The other was a strange love-hate co-venture with Muslim polities. On the Steppes, Muscovy acquired a military edge over the Tartars in the 1450s— earlier than is generally thought. It had usually been the other way around for the previous two centuries. This enabled Muscovy to reduce the net effect of Tartar raiding in its own territory, and to push south onto the steppes, some of which concealed fertile "Black Earth". Between 1451 and 1521, there were relatively few raids on Old Muscovy itself.[85] Behind the shift lay three hybrid developments: Muscovy's conversion of itself into a part-Tartar power, its adoption of a hybrid army, involving guns as well as cavalry, and the emergence of a hybrid crew culture: the Cossacks.

The last section noted Muscovite recruitment of Tartar nobles and their followings, which began as early as 1370. Until the 1450s, this usually involved Tartars coming to Muscovy, not the other way round. Tartars fleeing endemic conflict on the steppes sought refuge in Muscovy, and were given empty or thinly peopled lands, which were still abundant, in return for military service. From the 1450s, Muscovy began to conflict and collaborate with the big Tartar powers on equal terms or better, and this formed Plan A in its conquest of the Southern Steppes. The main polities were the khanates of Kazan, Astrakhan, and the Crimea, and the Great and Nogai Hordes. Muscovy was usually allied to one or more of these. It backed the Nogai and the Crimean Tartars against the Great Horde. The Crimeans destroyed or took over the Great Horde in 1502. Nogai power diminished from 1557, when that horde split into two, one usually a junior ally of the Crimean khanate, the other of Muscovy. Kazan was a rich state, ruling areas of sedentary farming, and at the centre of a fur acquisition network that stretched into Siberia.[86] It inflicted heavy defeats on Muscovy between 1439 and 1445, and again in the 1470s.[87] Between 1482 and 1535, however, Muscovy invaded Kazan on several occasions, and installed puppet rulers.[88] Kazan's resistance then hardened, and the Muscovites conquered it in 1552, after two unsuccessful attempts in the late 1540s. They added Astrakhan to their empire in 1556.

In contrast to Western European powers such as Portugal and Spain, Russia demonstrated a surprising talent for ruling Muslim vassals when it needed to. Tartar leaders were incorporated into the nobility, a degree of Tartar administration was left in place, and religious tolerance held sway. In Kazan, for example, there were still 536 mosques in 1744, when there was a sudden turn against toleration.[89] Until this time, Russian empire on the steppes—and, as we will soon see, in southern Siberia—was a joint venture with Muslim vassals, allies, and even enemies. Plan B of Russian expansionism on the Southern Steppes emerged from about 1580—settlement by Russian peasants. Between 1580 and 1600, the Russians built a string of fortified towns southward, reaching Belgorod in 1598. The process was slow until the development of a horizontal fortified line based on Belgorod in 1653, by which time there were only half a million settlers on the "Black Earth". Between then and 1710, however, the number quadrupled, to more than two million.

The first significant use of guns by the Russians is usually dated to the sixteenth century, a delay attributed first to Russian "backwardness" and then to the assumption that guns were of little use against light cavalry armies. But, as we have seen, they were of *some* use, notably in the attack and defense of fortifications and even, behind some sort of barricade, in field battles. Moscow used cannon in 1382 in defending the city from Tartars, and then in 1399 in a field battle against the Lithuanians—very soon after the first such use in Western Europe—but without much effect.[90] Guns, both cannon and harquebuses, do appear to have been significant in fending off another Tartar attack in 1451.[91] The latest bronze casting technology was imported to Moscow via an Italian expert in 1478.[92] Boat-borne cannon were used in Muscovite attacks on Novgorod in 1478, Kazan in 1482, and Tver in 1485.[93] From the 1450s, the Tartars were less able to take Muscovite forts and towns, and Muscovite armies won an increasing proportion of field battles—including three in the 1450s, noted above, and three more in the 1480s. Some experts feel that gunpowder weapons were not decisive even as late as the conquest of Kazan in 1552. Yet the Muscovites used a huge gunpowder mine to breach Kazan's main defenses.[94] They also brought along 150 heavy and medium cannon "in addition to an unknown number of light cannons".[95] It is not easy to think of another explanation for the upward shift in the Muscovite military success ratio against the Tartars from the 1450s, nor the restoration of parity after the 1550s, by which time some Tartars had acquired a decent number of guns too—from the Ottomans.

In 1475, the Ottomans conquered Genoese Caffa, and soon took over the rest of the coast of the Crimean Peninsula. They then installed the Tartar Girey Dynasty as rulers of the wider Crimean khanate. As we saw in chapter 11, a symbiosis developed between the two polities. The Ottomans supplied guns, money, and a janissary brigade. The Crimean Tartars supplied slaves, mainly Polish, Lithuanian, Circassian, and Russian. Despite this, relations with Muscovy were quite good until about 1520. In 1502, the Crimean Tartars "marched with a large force armed with cannons and long guns [harquebuses]" and put an end to the Great Horde. In 1521, they allied with Muscovy's surviving Slavic rival, Poland-Lithuania, and raided to the walls of Moscow, but were defeated in Astrakhan in 1523. They supplied that independent khanate with "cannons and muskets".[96] It was the Crimean Tartars who said that, while they had plenty of cavalry, "against the harquebuses also a 'harquebus army' is needed".[97] Their alliance with the Ottomans intensified, and sporadic slave raiding on Muscovy continued, driven by Istanbul demand. In 1569, the Ottomans themselves intervened on the steppes. This was potentially a dire moment for Muscovy. It was distracted by war against Poland and Sweden over Livonia and access to the Baltic, and by a series of self-inflicted internal wounds, beginning with an unfortunate experiment in reform, the *oprichnina* (1565–72), and ending with civil wars known as "the time of troubles" (1598–1613). Moscow's remaining ally on the steppes, the Nogai, repeatedly appealed for muskets, musketeers, and cannon "that could be used by nomadic people", but it appears they received few.[98] Instead, the Russians turned to a new player on the steppes, Plan C, the Cossacks.

The term "cossack" derives from the Turkic "qazak" meaning "outlaw" or "vagabond".[99] It was also used by the Kazakhs, yet another group stemming from the Golden Horde, and some hybridisation with the Tartars is obvious enough. Both Cossacks and Tartars lived a largely, but not completely, nomadic life on the Southern Steppes, hunting, herding, raiding, and fishing— the last an underestimated component of steppe diets. Up to a point they might be seen as an emulation of an Ottoman/Crimean Tartar innovation dating from about 1500—hybrid armies of nomad cavalry, plus guns. Yet there are also strong signs that the Cossacks were a European "crew culture", surprisingly similar to German and Swiss mercenaries and Dutch and English sailors. The two earliest "hosts" were the Don Cossacks, allies of Muscovy, and the Zaporozhian Cossacks, at first allies of Poland-Lithuania. Recent genetic research confirms the view that "ethnically, Slavs made up by far the largest group".[100] Don Cossacks were more closely related to the southern Rus principalities, such as Riazan, than to the central ones such as Muscovy. No Tartar group contributed very much, with the single exception of the Nogai, Muscovy's closest Tartar ally. The border principality of Riazan may be the actual place of origin. Riazan Cossacks in Muscovite service are first mentioned in 1444, and later "chronicles tell of massive migrations from Ryazan to the Upper Don".[101] Riazan "repeatedly suffered from Tartar predatory raids. It is not strange that sometimes Muscovite chroniclers portrayed Riazanians as wild and violent people, all but Tartars in their behavior".[102]

The Cossacks did share Tartar skill at violence, as light cavalry, but they were also good infantry and expert boatmen, on both river and sea, and had a taste for grain. Evidence of Cossacks living in any numbers south of Riazan dates to the early sixteenth century, when the Russian population began to grow again, and hardening serfdom first in Poland-Lithuania and then in Russia gave an extra incentive for flight. Unlike the Tartars or sedentary Russians, heredity was not important in the selection of leaders. Cossacks practiced a "cult of non-deference".[103] Atamen or Hetmen were elected, at first for each particular campaign. In 1638, the Russian government invited the Don Cossacks to send a delegation of the "best sort of people", eliciting the response, "we don't have best people on the Don".[104] "We are not robbers and we are not bandits", claimed their folktales, "we are all fine young lads. . . . good and bold young lads".[105] Like Western European crew, their meetings were held in circles, (*krug* or *kolo*), to avoid ringleaders, the hosts was made up of small crews, sworn "brotherhoods" of non-kin, and were good at incorporating newcomers.[106] Like Western European crew regions, their homelands were dependent on imports for grain. They were quick to guns, and mounted up to four cannon in each of their boats.[107] There was a crewlike transnational strand in their allegiances. The Zaporozhians of the eastern Ukraine switched en masse from Warsaw to Moscow in the later seventeenth century, and the Ottomans and Chinese also employed Cossack units. For all the transnationalism, however, it was Moscow that ultimately gained the allegiance of the great majority of Cossacks, underwriting the alliance with regular shipments of grain and gunpowder.[108]

Cossacks backed by Moscow built a fort at Terek in the 1560s, threatening Ottoman-Crimean control of the Northern Caucasus and the Black Sea littoral. The latter responded by invading Astrakhan in 1569, and planned to build a canal linking the Don and Volga Rivers. Both attempts proved too much even for Ottoman logistics, but the threat of full-scale war with them induced the Russians to hand back Terek.[109] The Ottomans too had distractions in the form of war with Iran, and the Russians used their hold on the Caspian port of Astrakhan to supply Iran with muskets and cannon, as mentioned in the previous chapter, and to increase their trade in silk.[110] The Cossacks replied to raids on Muscovy with raids on the Tartars beginning about 1538. After 1570, they also attacked Ottoman territory, raiding the key Ottoman fortress of Azov, near the mouth of the Don, in 1574 and 1593. From 1600, dozens of Cossack gunboats with crews of about 50 each would row down the Don to the Black Sea, erect masts, and raid the coasts. In 1620 and 1623, they raided to the gates of Istanbul itself, and sacked Trebizond and Sinope in 1625. That year, they were defeated in a fierce sea battle by the Ottoman Black Sea fleet.[111] But they recovered and managed to take Azov in 1637—without the help of Russian troops—and offered the fortress to the Tsar.[112]

Between the failure of the Ottoman invasion of Astrakhan, in 1570, and the fall of Azov in 1639, then, expanding Russia faced a vexed but tempting situation on the Southern Steppes. Ottoman backing had turned the Crimean Tartars into a formidable enemy, who continued to raid the outskirts of Moscow until 1633. But Cossack initiatives raised the attractive prospect of contesting the Black Sea with the Ottomans. Moscow, probably wisely, decided against this, abandoning Terek in 1570, and abandoning Azov in 1642. The Ottomans were too formidable an enemy—they had soundly defeated Poland-Lithuania in a war in 1621–23. Russia had the better of the Ottomans in a war in 1676–81, and did seize Azov in 1696, but these results were reversed by Ottoman victory in another war in 1711–13.[113] Azov was again returned, and the Russians destroyed their own Black Sea fleet as part of the peace agreement. Russia only developed a clear military edge over the Ottomans in the 1770s, and finally managed to conquer the Crimean Tartars soon after. For the preceding two centuries, they accepted a curious situation on the Southern Steppes: the coexistence of two empires in the same space—the Russian one gradually gathering lands, while the Crimean-Ottoman one continued to gather people. Early in this period, the Russians realised that expansion in Asian Siberia might be easier—here was the Ottoman "Great Diversion" at work.

IV Trade, Settlement, and Hunting in Siberia, 1390–1800

At five million square miles, Siberia accounts for about 40% of Asia's landmass, but was very thinly populated indeed. In 1662, when Russian forts already stretched to the Pacific, it contained am estimated 100,000 Russians and 250,000 other people. In this context, the distinction between overseas and overland colonial patchwork empires was largely meaningless. "Sites of Russian authority were tiny islands in a vast remoteness with thin tentacles stretching outward from those islands".[114] The Urals themselves were not difficult to cross in the south; the distance problem began thereafter.[115] Boat and sled travel, by river and portage, was the general rule. Three great river systems, the Ob, Yenisei, and Lena, were respectively the main highways of western, west central, and eastern Siberia. Each grew a Russian base in its southern reaches: Tobolsk, Yeniseisk, and Yakutsk. A boat journey from Moscow to Yakutsk took a year. "The round trip required anything from three to four years".[116] As late as 1711, 10–20% of travellers died on the way, and scurvy was a common problem due to lack of vegetables.[117] Horizontal bands of different terrain overlaid this pattern: tundra in the north, fur-producing taiga forest in the middle, and steppes in the south, where horses and camels could be used. Russian colonisation, which eventually produced the only neo-European society in Asia, now 30 million strong, also took threefold form: the hunt for furs, a striving for increased access to Chinese markets, and agricultural settlement, to provide a base for both.

The first post-plague expansionists in Siberia were Muslim, not Russian. This expansion began around 1390, possibly driven by plague-increased demand, like the Arab and Persian diaspora into the Indian Ocean around the same time (chapter 9). Here, the demand was for furs, not spices, and the role of Hormuz and Aden was played by Bukhara in Transoxiana. This city's recovery from sack by the Mongols in 1220 postdated the Black Death; it was still in ruins in the 1330s when visited by Ibn Battuta. By 1390, however, it had become so important a base for far-travelling camel caravans that "Bukharan" was a generic name for long-range Muslim merchants from Transoxiana, like "Sogdian" before it. Bukhara was also home to one of the most important post-plague Sufi movements, the Naqshbandi (also known as Khwajagani), who also became strong in Timurid Herat.[118]

> Bukhara was the cultural core from which numerous attempts to Islamize Western Siberia originated. The first Moslem missionaries in Siberia were the Naqshbandi sheiks sent from Bukhara . . . in the 1390s. . . . These original efforts at mass conversion were followed by a century's worth of missionaries accompanying Bukharan fur merchants.[119]

In contrast to the Indian Ocean, warfare against the locals accompanied commerce and conversion, and Muslim expansionists also fought among themselves. But a substantial fur trade, linked to that of Kazan, and competing with that of Muscovy in northwestern Siberia, emerged, along with several towns, notably Chimga-Tura, built in the late fourteenth century, "an attractive trade center for merchants".[120] Vying Tartar dynasties and polities eventually consolidated into the khanate of Sibir, which was the target of the Russian incursion in 1581–82. "The Siberian khanate continued to expand territorially from the middle of the fifteenth century to the late sixteenth century".[121] It inserted itself into a long-standing three-tiered system of fur extraction that stretched to Manchuria and had long supplied China and India. At the top were powerful nomad polities, including Sibir and the Buddhist Zhungar Mongols. In the middle were smaller groups of nomad warriors, such as the Kirgiz, the Baraba Tartars, and the Buriat Mongols. Their vassals, the Ugric-speaking peoples who actually caught the fur animals, were the bottom tier. The standard *iasak* tribute was five sables per man. In the 1550s, a new khan came to power in Bukhara "intent on gaining greater influence in Western Siberia in order to promote Bukharan trade".[122] In 1563 he backed a relative, Kuchum, in a successful attempt to take over and expand the khanate of Sibir. "Kuchum . . . was particularly successful against any still unsubjugated Ugrian tribes. He conquered the Ostiaks north of the Demianka river, outlying Vogul tribes to the north of the Tavda and eastward upstream on the Tura. The Baraba steppe Tartars were definitely under Kuchum's control".[123] Kuchum also competed for tribute payers with Kazan, which was now a Russian vassal.[124] It was this Muslim empire of Sibir that the Russians took over in the late sixteenth century, destroying the khanate, but taking over its towns, rebuilt as Tobolsk and Tiumen, its vassals, and its trade, as well as its symbiosis with the Bukharans.[125]

In what might be called Plan D of its expansion, the Russian state had contracted a rich merchant clan, the Stroganovs, to occupy and exploit the Kama River region in the Ural Mountains in 1558. They were allowed a private militia, and in 1574 were licensed to retaliate against raids from Sibir. It was the Stroganovs who hired Yermak Timofeyevich and 840 fellow Cossacks, with several cannon, to invade Sibir in 1581–82. Yermak scored a remarkable initial victory and became a Russian folk hero, but was in fact defeated and killed by Kuchum in 1584–85. Thereafter, the Russian state took over, and is generally said to have completed the conquest of Sibir by about 1600, though Kuchum's sons continued to resist until 1634.[126] Russia replaced Sibir as overlord of various nomad groups, some of whom simultaneously paid fur tributes to the Zungars. Like Sibir, it relied on Bukharan merchants to sell its furs to Central Asia, India, and China, taking silk, cottons, and eventually tea, in return. In the 1630s, 59 Bukharan merchants lived in the Russian base of Tobolsk. "By the end of the century, there were some 3,000 in Tiumen and Tobolsk".[127] Moscow insisted on good treatment of them until the intolerant 1740s, when they became more dispensable, and 75 mosques in the Tobolsk region were destroyed.[128] Until then, Russian patchwork expansion in southern Siberia entwined with a preexisting Muslim patchwork, the two cooperating rather more successfully than Muslims and Portuguese in the Indian Ocean.

The notion of an early Russian/Muslim co-venture in Siberia may solve an intriguing mystery which seems to have gone unnoticed in at least the English-language scholarship. Russian sources assert the state's share of Siberian furs was 200,000 sable and 500,000 squirrel furs in 1586—*before* any significant Russian conquests in southeast Siberia.[129] The figure seems incredibly high, but a massive gift of furs to the Holy Roman Emperor in 1595, to help him fight the Ottomans, supports it. The gift, including 40,000 sable and 337,000 squirrel furs, was worth 400,000 rubles in Prague, and naturally delighted the emperor.[130] The clear implication is that Russian penetration of western Siberia was very substantial *before* Yermak, with the hijacked Kazan Muslim network added to that of Novgorod. Muscovy had long-term fur tributaries in north-west Siberia from 1499 and its own fur stations from 1572 at the latest.[131] Indeed, Russian extraction, direct and indirect, may have been substantial enough to have already caused sable depletion in western Siberia by the early seventeenth century, which would help explain the astonishing pace of Russia's race to the Pacific thereafter.

———

The Russians reached Mangazeya and Tomsk, in west central Siberia, by 1604; Yakutsk by 1632; and the Pacific by 1639, establishing a post on the coast at Okhotsk in 1648. Scores of other forts and fortified settlements were established by this time, some in the taiga.[132] These frenetic forays resemble the Spanish entradas which crisscrossed Mexico in the sixteenth century, looking for loot. They were likely aimed at seizing the accumulated fur stores of indigenous groups, or buying them cheaply, and at creaming off sable in the places at which they were most accessible and abundant. Unlike Muslim fur-tribute takers, the Russians also hunted themselves, speeding up local depletion. They would use boats and portages to reach the prime spots, build a blockhouse, lay in fish and game for winter, when sable fur was at its best, then use baited traps or tracker dogs, blunt arrows, and nets to catch the animals, Novgorod-style.[133] The Russians also tried to force middle-level tribute-takers to give them a cut, or to bypass them and go direct to their fur-hunting tributaries in the taiga. Recent studies emphasise that tribute relations often fell well short of substantive empire, and there were some groups on which the Russians were unable to impose even these. But the fact remains that the Russians extracted millions of sables from indigenous Siberian and Turco-Mongol groups, as well as catching more millions themselves. One estimate of the total Russian take of sable in the 1640s is 120,000 a year, of which 70,000 were exported.[134] Between 1621 and 1690, the total is thought to be 7.2 million. This figure may be too high, but there were 3.5 million "at the very least", worth 5.5 million rubles.[135]

Russian fur hunting and extorting was carried out mainly by two groups of crewmen: hunters, mainly from the Novgorod region, and Cossacks from the Southern Steppes. Both operated in groups or "artels" as small as five to eight men, but often much larger, carrying guns and travelling in boats mounting cannon. Cossacks were a broadening category in Siberia. "Private fur hunters (*promyshlenniki*) often joined Cossacks or vice versa".[136] Other Russian soldiers called themselves "Cossacks", "possibly because of the freedom and prestige denoted by the appellation".[137] Some Siberian horse nomads were inducted as "half-Cossacks".[138] But "the essential backbone of the Cossack hosts consisted of Russians".[139] Certainly, crew culture flourished in Russian Asia, among both Cossacks and fur collectors. "Cossacks and *promyshlenniki* piled into town to blow off steam by drinking and brawling" in "sometimes murderous bacchanals".[140]

> Siberian units conspicuously manifested Cossack tendencies and traditions. Their command structure tended to be more egalitarian than in Europe and the promotion process often involved elections by the troops. They mutinied with great frequency, deserted in large numbers, and indiscriminately ravaged the encampments of the pacified as well as the hostile indigenes. [141]

Russian crew numbers may seem small, averaging about 20,000 in all Siberia over the seventeenth century, but they were ruthless and formidable foes. Like the crewmen of other European empires, they kept coming, at a rate of about 4,000 a year to 1700. The rate then declined to perhaps 2,000 in the eighteenth century, because an increasing number of crewmen in Siberia were locally born "neo-Russians". Russia soon realised that it needed peasant settlers as well as crewmen, to provide an agricultural base for hunting and trading. Both native-born crew and a settler population required either intermarriage with the natives by Russian men, whose offspring counted as "white" and Russian, or European settler foremothers. This matter falls afoul of controversy over the Russian "white legend". The notion that the Russian conquest of Siberia was somehow non-violent has been well and truly laid to rest, to the point where the persisting agency and autonomy of some indigenous peoples is underestimated. On the other hand, it is still sometimes suggested that

Russian racism was weaker than in the rest of Europe, at least in the seventeenth century, and that intermarriage was common.[142] Inter-racial sex certainly was common, but whether it often amounted to marriage, or whether the offspring counted as Russian and white, is not so clear. As elsewhere, long-term mixed partnerships, formal or informal, appeared at some times and places, but not in others, and the standing of mixed-race people also varied. The key factor may have been more the absence of Russian women than of Russian racism, which some see as little different from elsewhere in Europe.[143]

Muscovite elites had intermarried with Tartar nobility for centuries, but the Orthodox Church discouraged the practice from about 1450.[144] By 1622, the Patriarch was enraged by miscegenation beyond the Urals. Russian men "are mixing with foul Ostyak and Vogul women and doing filth with them, and some are living with unbaptized Tartar women as if with their wives and producing children with them". "The wealthier Slavs maintained the 'illusion of keeping their blood pure,' held the Khanty and their culture in contempt, but still carried on furtive liaisons with native women. Only poor peasant men officially married natives".[145] These comments applied to the early seventeenth century, and to western Siberia, and there were cases where the situation was different farther east. One was as far east as the Russians ever went, in Alaska, in the early nineteenth century, where there were virtually no Russian women and few Russian men—never more than one thousand. Here, the fur-seeking colony bred its own collaborators, known as Kreols, and treated them relatively well. They were educated and given "middling and at times high-level work within the colonial apparatus", in striking contrast to the earlier brutal treatment of native Aleuts.[146] The other case of large-scale intermarriage involved the Turkic-speaking Yakuts, who lived in Eastern Siberia at the base of the Lena River system. Yakutia was a region with particularly high-quality sable, and the Russian state banned peasant migration and restricted hunting to preserve them.[147] While there was conflict with some Yakut groups, the town of Yakutsk seems to have been a joint venture from the outset. Founded in 1632, it housed 280 Russian men and 123 Yakut men by 1641.[148] Both genetic and surname studies indicate a high level of intermarriage. But "the Yakuts are unique among Siberian populations in having a high number of haplotypes shared exclusively with Europeans".[149] When and where Russian women were available, they were the preferred partners for Russian men. By 1786, "careful perusal" of a sample of 406 marriages in Cossack settlements in the Altai region finds that only 2–3% were mixed.[150]

The largest of three injections of European female migrants to Siberia, 1593–1709, comprised Cossack women, perhaps 30,000 of whom migrated in the seventeenth century. Most were probably already married to senior Cossacks, who had obtained permission for their wives to join them, for which they received extra pay.[151] Back on the steppes, these women, like those of other crew regions, had a reputation for relative freedom and independence and, if early nineteenth-century rates held up earlier, extremely high illegitimacy.[152] But, in male folklore at least, "Cossack women did not want to marry any other Russian", let alone non-Russians.[153] In Krasnoiarsk in 1638, only 63 of 345 male Cossacks were married. Since the post was only ten years old, the 63 wives had probably migrated from the European Steppes.[154] The proportion of married Cossacks increased from 18% to around 40% over the seventeenth century.[155] Some of the later brides would have been Siberian-born Cossack women, and some would have been of mixed race. Others may have come from small and sporadic state attempts to send out single women as "domesticators", "who could offset and pacify the wild beast that was man".[156] More women came in families of exiles, who were expected to accompany their convict husbands and fathers. Some 10,000 female migrants, the second female injection, were among the 35,000 exiles that went to Siberia between 1649 and 1709.[157] These people were tasked with establishing farming settlements to provide hunting and trading with an agricultural base.

The final source of settler foremothers was a secondary settlement from Pomor'e on the Arctic coast, which Novgorod had settled in the early plague era. Like the Cossack steppes, this was both a crew region and a settling region. It too supports the thesis set out in chapter 6—that it was secondary settlement which cracked early modern European women's "do not emigrate long-range" principle. Pomors were seafarers, keeping "sea-books" (lotsiyas) of their travels to guide their descendants. They sought codfish, salmon, whales, and walrus, as well as fur animals, over a wide area of Arctic coasts and islands.[158] Whether they reached Svalbard/Spitzbergen before Western Europeans is a matter of controversy—probably not.[159] But their presence in Novaya Zemlya in the sixteenth century is well documented. By 1600, they were trading some of their catch with Dutch and English in and around Archangel. In 1601, the Pomors founded Mangazeya, between the Ob and Yenisei River systems. It boomed into Siberia's leading fur town in the middle quarters of the seventeenth century before fading from 1672.[160] Among the musketeers in Siberia, "many seem to have come from the northern region of European Russia bordering the Arctic Ocean",[161] and Pomors dominated "a mass movement of

peasants from the Russian North to Siberia in search of a better life".[162] Between 1629 and 1691, they made up 80% or more of migrants to the Yenisei
region. In the main town of Yeniseisk, 58% of male settlers were married in
1658, and 82% in 1691.[163] Predictably, in the settlements along the Yenisei, 90%
of marriages involved Russian women.[164] Novgorod's influence has been
traced in western Siberian women's crafts, such as the decoration of distaffs.[165]
One small group did make a mark on the record: 39 single women who came
voluntarily in 1631 for "marriage to Enisei [Yenisei] servitors [military service-
men] and ploughing peasants",[166] a bold move at the time, suggesting a strong
"folk filament". The total number of Russians of both sexes in Siberia was about
23,000 in 1622, 100,000 in 1662, 300,000 in 1709, and 900,000 in 1795, by which
time gender parity had been reached.[167]

———

Reinforced by settlers and locally born crewmen, Russian numbers were not
so small in comparison to what indigenous groups could muster. Historians
think that there were about 250,000 people in all Siberia in 1580, split into 30
ethnicities and as many as 500 tribal groups.[168] Disease, like racism, was part
of the Russian expansion kit too. Smallpox struck native Siberians from the
1630s, soon joined by measles, scarlet fever, and typhus, doing particular damage in central and eastern Siberia which had not encountered them before.[169]
Estimates of native Siberian seventeenth-century death tolls range up to 80%
for the worst hit, and 50% overall.[170] But we should bear in mind the caveats
noted in chapter 7. Some groups said to have been near-extinguished in the
seventeenth century were still actively resisting, or cooperating with, the Russians in the eighteenth. A more moderate general estimate of losses is 15%, but
the worst hit lost around 45% by 1700, after which a slow recovery began.[171]

Russian relations with non-Europeans in Siberia ranged across the spectra
of conflict and cooperation, victory and defeat, respect and contempt. At the
bottom end were the unfortunate Itelmen of the Kamchatka Peninsula in far
eastern Siberia. They first encountered the Russians in the 1690s, and resisted
them from 1709 to 1733, by which time Cossacks had "slaughtered a large part
of the population" of about 12,000. Subsequently at least two smallpox strikes
killed 45% of the survivors. A nearby group, the Chukchi, had an equally violent experience with a contrasting outcome. More dispersed than the Itelmen,
they had the better of their struggle with the Russians, defeating them several
times, 1720s–1740s. The Russians gave up trying in 1764.[172] In the middle of

the range of relationships were mid-level tribute-takers like the Kirgiz. The Kirgiz were mounted steppe people who drew fur tribute from a large region in and around the Yenisei, and were divided into several tribes. They sporadically fought the Russians with some success from 1604 to 1706, when the balance shifted. Some tribes paid iasak to the Russians some of the time, but all ceased doing so when they were united under a powerful leader, Erenak, between 1667 and 1687.[173] The Kirgiz continued the tradition of extracting furs from forest peoples further north and sharing them with high-level tributaries—not just the Russians but also the Zhungars. They sometimes paid sables to both at the same time, and even supported them in wars, but also managed to resist, divide, and avoid being ruled in a strange world of multiple overlapping patchwork empires. The claim that "in the course of their expansion in Siberia, the Russians encountered scattered and weak resistance", still being made in 2018, is not sustainable.[174]

The Zhungars were one of three partner-rivals at the top of the range of Russian relationships. They were a collection of Mongol tribes also known as Oirats and Kalmyks. One group came to Muscovite notice when they defeated the Kazakhs and Uzbeks in the mid-fifteenth century. They allied with the Russians in 1655 and fought for Peter the Great in his wars after 1700.[175] A larger group was expelled from Mongolia by a rival alliance, the Khalka, around 1600. Under able khans, the Zhungars created an empire in central Asia and avenged themselves on the Khalka over the course of the seventeenth century. "An increasingly confident Zunghar state dominated Central Asian political scene until 1755–7".[176] One of their khans, Galdan Tseren, was accompanied by his mobile library carried on a hundred camels, confounding any remaining assumptions about primitive nomads.[177] Zhungar relations with the Russians oscillated between warfare and cooperation, but the latter predominated, and there was an element of mutual respect. Both empires used the services of the Bukharans, the second of Russia's partner-rivals.

The main locus of interaction for all three was Yamysh, a salt lake near the Irtysh River, a tributary of the Ob. Salt was a crucial resource for Russia's Siberian enterprise, to preserve food and hides. Cossacks repeatedly tried to establish a post at Yamysh from 1613 and the Zungars kept expelling them. But a tentative understanding emerged from about 1635, and annual Russian expeditions of up to 600 men collected salt from Yamysh, while the Zungars did so too. By mid-century, both sides had established permanent settlements near the lake, and diplomatic relations were well established. Yamysh was the "largest trading center in Siberia for half a century".[178] A fur/silk trade with China was carried out on Russia's behalf by the Bukharans, who would use boats where navigable rivers were available, and buy or hire camels for the desert. The Zhungars taxed this trade, and could easily have put a stop to it. But the Russians made one thing they needed: guns. Through them, the Zhungars acquired "matchlocks, mortars, and cannons",[179] which helped them extend their empire. It also helped them secure early victories against their eventual nemesis, the Qing Chinese, in a long series of wars from the 1690s to the 1750s. The Qing were the third of Russian expansion's partner-rivals.

V   Russia, China, and Global Hunting

In the 1640s, in the frenetic phase of Russian expansion, Cossacks reached the relatively fertile Amur River region, and saw its potential as an agricultural base for their operations in eastern Siberia. Here, the Qing claimed suzerainty over the local Daur people. In 1651, a Cossack force of 200 men with a few large cannon sailed down the Amur and attacked a settlement containing 1,000 Daur and 50 Chinese troops. The cannon blasted down the walls, and the Cossacks took the place by assault. "Counting big and little we killed 661. Of the Russians only 4 lost their lives and 45 [were] temporarily disabled, a small price to pay for the plunder which included 243 women, 118 children, 237 horses, and 113 cattle".[180] The disparity between killed and wounded suggests that the Cossacks had some armour and/or that the opposition had few guns. The Cossacks built a fort at Achensk, which a Chinese force of 2,000 attacked the next year. It was repulsed with heavy losses. Hostilities continued in 1654, when a Russian river fleet with 400 men clashed with a Chinese one of 1,000, and won the naval battle. "The Russians held a distinct edge in shipbuilding technology", as a subsequent Chinese report confirmed. Their boats "had enormous bodies with a deck made out of thick planks and enclosed by layers of dense logwood . . . these vessels were so robust that they could not be penetrated even using 'Red Barbarian Cannon.'"[181]

The Qing (Manchu) were a Jurchen-descended group in Manchuria who had taken up both farming and the steppe nomad military arts. They consolidated into an empire in the early seventeenth century, and in the 1640s took over China, then suppressed subsequent rebellions by 1683. A remarkably adaptable people, they quickly adopted Ming diffusion firearms, but in the 1650s were still in the process of transition to the West Eurasian diffusion. The transition had already taken place in Japan, which invaded Korea in the 1590s, forcing that country too to adopt plague-incubated firearms. In 1654, faced with the Russian technical edge, the Qing called on their Korean vassals for musketeers, and were sent a couple of hundred. Together with rapid Qing upgrading of their own firearms and boats, these musketeers turned the tide against the Russians. In 1658, the Amur Cossacks and a Qing-Korean force, with an equal number of gunmen, clashed in a hard-fought engagement. The Russians lost, with 220 men killed to their opponents' 118. The Russians withdrew from the Lower Amur for a time, before making another attempt in the 1680s, with a similar result: early Russian success, because the Qing armies in the region had lost interest in musketeers,[182] then rapid Chinese catch-up and victory through equal technology and superior numbers. A peace treaty was signed in 1689 at Nerchinsk, where the Russians agreed to give up the Amur in return for improved access to Chinese trade.

In the end, war was far out-ranked by trade in Sino-Russian relations. Indirect trade in furs and silk, through the Bukharans, began in the sixteenth century and continued to the mid-eighteenth. The first official Russian mission, from Tomsk, was in 1618, but unofficial visits may have begun early, with Russians going along with the Bukharans.[183] The Chinese had a great appetite for sable and ermine, and techniques for giving squirrel and fox skins the feel and appearance of luxury furs, while Russia wanted silk either for itself, or to profitably on-sell to Western Europe. Between the conflicts of 1654–58 and 1685–87, Russian merchants and enterprising Cossacks cut themselves in on the China trade.[184] Volumes were modest, 13,000 sable in 1669, but the Chinese paid high prices. "Russia's traditional trade with the east was more profitable than European trade".[185] Commerce boomed after the treaty of 1689. Official caravans from Nerchinsk to Beijing numbered only 14 between 1689 and 1719; but Chinese records show there were another 36 unofficial ones in these years.[186] The return journey took 10–12 months, so usually there must have been two operating at any given time, like the Spanish silver flotillas in the Atlantic. Their size is indicated by that of their escorts, 400–500 Cossacks per caravan.[187] Bukharans took part, but Russian merchants, big and small, increasingly took the leading role. The number of such merchants in Nerchinsk increased from 172 in 1691 to 572 in 1697.[188]

Most histories still tell us that the Siberian fur trade declined sharply from the late seventeenth century, and this is true of the flow of furs to Western Europe. Nerchinsk was now the main exporter, and it sent 25,000 each of sable and ermine west to Moscow in 1691, plus 50,000 lesser furs (fox and squirrel). The number of sable was a half or a quarter that of earlier annual flows. The same year, 70,000 lesser furs, and only 638 sable, went south to Beijing. By

1696, the numbers were: Moscow, 6,300 sable and about 20,000 lesser furs; Beijing, 7,800 sable and 860,000 lesser furs.[189] It is not clear whether these numbers include the unofficial caravans. In 1727, a second inland Macao appeared by treaty at Kyakhta, near Lake Baikal, which like Nerchinsk was on the Sino-Russian border. The treaty required the Russians to stop supplying guns to the Zhungars, which may have been a factor in their defeat by the Chinese in 1757. Nominally, only one caravan from Kyakhta was allowed every three years, but if the Nerchinsk situation is any indication, there would have been unofficial ones too. Furthermore, Kyakhta was more of a place of exchange than a caravan base; 140 yards away, across its river, a matching Chinese trade-town sprouted. It was called Maimaicheng, a generic name for "fortress of commerce".

China was now Russian Siberia's main fur market, but according to one authority, this situation did not persist long.

> In summer 1719 the Chinese imperial government announced that trade with Russia was unnecessary. Chinese trappers in northern Manchuria and European ships at Canton satisfied Peking's needs for furs. Russian prices were too high . . . Thus, despite the Russo-Chinese treaty of 1727, Russo-Chinese trade via Siberia had already passed its best years. . . . But it was the rigid fiscal policy of Russia's own officials that dealt the coup-de-grace to Nerchinsk and Kiakhta, plunging "sandy Venice and Genoa" into oblivion.[190]

Either this is mistaken, or "oblivion" was temporary. A later study quotes early 1780s European and Chinese sources saying that Kyakhta and Maimaicheng were thriving. The former was "the general mart for all the commerce carried on by the Russians with China". In the latter, "stores are gathered together like clouds, the markets are loud and bustling, and the town has prospered greatly from the trade in the area north of the Gobi". In the 1790s, another commentator on the commerce of the two towns "declared that its annual value was around two million roubles".[191] An older work by an eminent scholar says that Maimaicheng was buying 7 million Russian squirrel pelts annually in this decade, plus another million assorted furs, and now selling tea and Chinese cotton, as well as silk, in return.[192]

Why did China's demand for furs increased so substantially? We should recall that 7 million squirrel might make only 50,000 coats, but this was still a half-million long-lasting coats per decade. The increasing wealth of the Chinese elite in the eighteenth century was surely a factor, with hints of top elites seeking rarer furs to keep their distance from aspiring sub-elites, as in Europe four centuries earlier. The Ming-Qing transition itself might be another factor. The Qing were culturally, if not economically, steppe horsemen, and they incorporated Han Chinese, as well as Mongols, into their military banners and practices. Furs were both practical and high-status for such people, including the Cossacks, who each received a sable hat on retirement. Whatever its explanation, Chinese demand drove global hunting well beyond Siberia.

––––––

As early as 1707, the Russians had an eye on the Americas, which could be reached from far eastern Siberia. "The benefit to be expected is that from the eastern side Russia will extend its possessions as far as California and Mexico".[193] Between 1719 and 1743, several expeditions explored the Bering Strait. But the immediate motive for expansion was depletive commercial hunting for the Chinese market. From 1750, Russian hunters sought fur-bearing marine mammals, which were particularly prone to depletion. The Chinese paid astonishing prices for fur seals and sea otter. Up to 60 rubles per sea-otter pelt were said to be offered at Kyakhta in the 1750s, and up to 140 rubles in the 1770s. "The Moscow Treasury paid only 14 to 15 rubles for sea-otter pelts, so nearly the entire catch was sold to the Chinese . . . In 1752, over 5,000 pelts entered the Chinese market, and though the figures varied from year to year, the sea otter trade was firmly established".[194] Between 1749 and 1754, the Russians depleted the sea otter of the Commander Islands and passed on to the Aleutians, then to Kodiak Island, then to Alaska, where they established several forts in the late 1790s. Huge island fur seal-breeding colonies were first encountered in 1786 and almost exterminated in the Bering Strait by 1805— 100,000 sealskins were taken by a single expedition.[195]

Expert Aleut and Kodiak hunters were coerced into assisting the Russians. Half the adult males of some communities went fur hunting, while the Russians held the rest, and the women and children, as hostages in effect. Not surprisingly, resistance was fierce, and was brutally repressed.[196] As noted earlier, mixed-blood Kreols were treated relatively well. They soon supplied the great majority of "Russian" manpower in Alaska, where 658 Russians lived with 1,902 Kreols in 1855.[197] The Tlingit of Alaska were treated with caution; they were armed with guns bought from British and American traders. In 1802, they attacked and destroyed the main Russian fort at Sitka, and Russian America had to start again from scratch.[198] Sea-otter and fur-seal ranged down the California coast. The Russians ranged after them, and were joined by British and American ships from the 1790s. Coastal California was weakly held by Spain, and a few Spanish ships also joined the hunt, so the western and eastern wings of European expansion met and merged after three centuries. Numerous sea otter were taken from California between 1786 and 1812, bringing them close to extinction, and the same thing happened to fur seals.[199] Despite the Spanish claim to California, the Russians established Fort Ross (Rus') in 1812, where their empire reached its furthest extent, 60 miles north of San Francisco.

The Russians had no monopoly on ruthless commercial hunting—it was a characteristic of all Northern European expansionists. But Russia was the pace-setter in the global hunt for furs. Even in North America, where the Russians had scarcely set foot before 1800, beaver pelts were packed and counted in forties in the tradition of medieval Novgorod.[200] For most of the seventeenth century, though their own beaver were now scarce, "the Russians had the most advanced technology" in the processing of this fur, so much so that the French in particular sent American beaver pelts to Russia to be turned into "*castor de Moscovie*" before being reimported.[201] The search for furs was inextricably linked with the drive for Further Asian trade, because furs were the main trade item. The global orientation of Russian expansion, like its similarity to that of other European efforts, has been underestimated.[202] It too was a major conduit for Chinese and Indian super-crafts. "Perhaps one-fifth of the silk reaching Europe was travelling through Russia".[203] It is no accident that the Russians joined the English as the first to addict themselves to Chinese tea. Surprisingly, sable sold well in India too, as did Indian cotton in Russia.[204] The Russian empire in Asia remained very much a patchwork in 1800, an archipelago of controlled places in a sea of indigenous autonomy, but it was a thickening archipelago. The empire was always amphibian, not land-bound, using the Arctic Ocean as well as rivers, and overflowing smoothly into North America. Like the other empires, it mixed violence with negotiation, trade with tribute and predation, and coupled its own dynamism and brutality with the motives and means bequeathed by the Black Death.

PART IV

Expansion, Industry, and Empire

EARLY MODERN GLOBAL expansion was undertaken by a wide range of West Eurasian powers, with no fewer than 11 major players. Four were Western European—Portugal, Spain, France, and Britain. One, the Netherlands, was itself located in Western Europe but had its resource base in Eastern Europe, while another (Russia) was unambiguously Eastern European. Then there were five Muslim expansionists (the Ottomans, Safavid Iran, Morocco, Oman, and Mughal India) which, like Russia, are usually excluded from the history of early modern colonialism. Most of these powers underwent decline in the eighteenth century, for reasons we can only touch on. Decline was often relative rather than absolute, and did not necessarily involve much loss of territory. Safavid Iran collapsed in 1722. The Ottomans were defeated in two wars by Russia in 1768–74 and 1787–92. Though there was still life left in them, they lost their standing as a great power. From 1707, the Mughal Empire also declined, fragmenting into autonomous parts. Among Muslim expansionists, only the Omanis retained dynamism, and that on a relatively small scale. As we have seen, Muslims were the grand masters of soldier-importing systems. These delivered world-class armies for a time, but within a century or two faced built-in obsolescence. The imported soldiers' offspring were not supposed to inherit, but they eventually did, and the lands, cash, and privileges which might have financed fresh recruits for the ruling dynasty were acquired by these illicit sub-dynasties. The problem was clearly at work in the Ottoman Empire in the eighteenth century, and was likely a factor in the decline of the Safavid and Mughal empires too.

Yet some reasons for decline crossed religious divides. Catholic Iberians, and even the Protestant Dutch, from 1740, underwent much the same fate as the Muslim empires. Some factors were ecological. Most plague effects pervaded West Eurasia, but preexisting ecological factors influenced adaptation to them. Waterpower, for example, was cheaper and more abundant in Northern Europe, while animal power was cheaper and more abundant in the Muslim South. Northern Europe had mixed natural endowment. As noted in chapter 4, it was colder and darker than both Southern Europe and the Muslim South. London had half the annual sunshine hours of Baghdad, and one-third less than Rome. This meant that the sun-deprived north was relatively more advantaged by the early plague era's "visual transition" (eyeglasses, window glass, whale oil lamps), allowing an element of cultural and technological catch-up with the south. It had better access to the prey of extractive hunting: fur animals, whales, seals, and codfish, and therefore was more inclined to pursue them globally as stocks depleted. Access to the Atlantic Ocean was another variable, obvious but important. Galleons were a difficult plague technology to adopt. They needed abundant accessible tall timber, and a physical and cultural infrastructure of shipyards, iron-making, naval stores, mast timber, ropewalks, and sailmakers, plus oceanic, not merely maritime, crew districts. Russia, Venice, and the Ottomans all came late to galleons. Atlantic Europe had somewhat better, or at least more direct, access to the globe than the rest of West Eurasia. If global ricochets back to sender were important to metropolitan dynamism, Atlantic Europe had more of them.

Ecology and possibly even plague may have been shared causes of Iberian and Ottoman decline. The Mediterranean littoral is thought to have suffered most from the "general crisis" and the Little Ice Age of the seventeenth century.[1] Deforestation was another shared problem among those powers with limited access to the Baltic. Spain was running short of prime timber for ships by the 1740s, Portugal long before, though both were able to build big ships in their colonies.[2] The Ottomans did not have this option, and grew short of ship timber from the mid-seventeenth century. Ongoing deforestation led to a tripling of timber prices in this empire between the 1740s and the 1760s, which might have been a factor in a disastrous naval defeat by Russia in 1770.[3] Between 1780 and 1810, Ottoman Egypt and surrounding regions were hit by a devastating series of animal murrains which cost it a major competitive advantage: cheaply maintained and abundant work animals.[4] Chapter 2 suggested that plague itself began to diverge regionally from 1500. Italy suffered more heavily than Northern Europe in the seventeenth century, and now the economic effects turned malign. Wages could not rise, nor tenures improve, without making production uncompetitive with less plagued nations. "The steady decline in inequality found after the Black Death did not occur after the

1630 epidemic".[5] Northern Italy was still much richer than England, though not Holland, in 1600, in terms of GDP per capita. But it fell behind by 1700—southern Italy was poorer still. Perhaps surprisingly, Spain too is thought to have been richer than England in 1600, but fell behind it in the following century.[6] Much of Italy was Spanish-controlled at the time, and the Iberian Peninsula may also have had more than its share of plagues, including severe strikes in 1595–1601, 1647–51, and 1678–80.[7] The same was even more true in the Muslim South, where the population growth of the sixteenth century was curbed or even reversed. Even at the lowest pre-plague estimate, Egypt had barely recovered its 1346 population in 1800, and the whole Ottoman Empire had much the same population in 1800 as in 1600, whereas Northern European population growth boomed again from 1720 after a fairly static seventeenth century. [8]

Thanks partly to immigrant Armenian artisans, the Ottomans led West Eurasia in the emulation of Indian cotton manufacturing in the seventeenth century,[9] but aside from this may have shared a case of "fiscal gout" ("Dutch disease") with Spain, Portugal, and the Dutch. As noted in chapter 10, it was tempting to use abundant bullion to buy in foreign manufactures, to the neglect of your own. The Dutch stock of bullion per capita in 1790 was 960 grams, compared to 550 in booming Britain, but Dutch capitalists now tended to invest in other peoples' industries.[10] Recent work has traced the way in which Spanish expansion evolved into a "stakeholder empire", with colonial elites gaining a large share of the profits of expansion, notably in bullion extraction, less and less of which made its way to Madrid.[11] Much the same happened to Lisbon and Istanbul. Portugal's eighteenth-century empire was in fact Portuguese-Brazilian in the Atlantic, and largely Asian in the Indian Ocean and Macao. Many have noted the rise of provincial notables, known as *ayans*, in the Ottoman Empire in the eighteenth century, who profited from tax farming in particular.[12] Such developments gave provincial and colonial elites a stake in an empire's survival, and so increased its durability, but they also reduced the central state's revenues and so sapped its power. In the eighteenth century, it was not so much the Ottoman economy which collapsed as the state's share of it. State revenues were on a par with those of Russia until 1751, but then suffered a very sharp decline to one-seventh of the Russian level by 1786.[13] Furthermore, Ottoman, Iberian, Mughal, and even Dutch empires increasingly entwined with other empires that were now more powerful and that extracted more benefits from the relationship. The next chapter assesses the state of Western European expansion and its impact on other peoples to 1800. The final chapter asks what difference a plagued and global perspective might make to our understanding of British maritime ascendancy and industrialisation.

15

Empire? What Empire?

EUROPEAN EXPANSION TO 1800

BY THE EIGHTEENTH CENTURY, with the modest exception of Oman, dynamic West Eurasian expansionism had retreated to Northern Europe: France, Britain, and Russia. In 1788, the British founded a penal settlement at Sydney, Australia. British and American whalers and sealers now had a potential base in the Pacific, and began using it almost immediately. As we saw in the last chapter, Russians entered the Pacific in force around the same time, with their empire closing in on San Francisco. France possessed the world's most profitable colony, Saint Domingue, claimed much of North America at various points in the century, and had the fastest-growing trade with India. In 1800, on the territorial measure mentioned in the introduction, Europeans controlled 35% of the planet, and claimed even more. But how much substance did European claims to empire in 1800 have? Did it really amount to global hegemony, and to whom, and from whom, did its benefits flow? In an attempt to find out, this chapter summarily surveys the state of West European expansion and empire in the late eighteenth century.

Here, we confront the vexed issue of defining "empire". The relevant literature is a maze in which some good historians have been lost. If we insist that empire means total control, it would be difficult to find anywhere before 1800. If we define it as any asymmetric relationship, it was widespread. "Empire" should imply some level of real control by one people over another—loose or tight, direct or indirect, formal or informal. Mere claims are not enough. But this still excludes many forms of violent and exploitative expansion, such as slaving systems and maritime protection rackets, as well as some in which predation was aimed more at animals than humans, such as whaling and fur extraction. Hence my preference for seeing empire as a subtype of expansion.

Greenland

Russian Alaska • Sitka Tlingit

Hudson Bay **BRITISH NORTH AMERICA**

French Canada (to Britain 1760)

Cree

Newfoundland

Denmark
Norwa
Dutch Republic
Britain

Plains Indians   Woodland Indians

• Acadia
• Halifax
New England
New York

France

• Fort Ross
• San Francisco
California (Spanish missions) *Apache*
Pennsylvania

THE 13 COLONIES (USA from 1783)
Chesapeake Bay

Portugal, **Spain**

French Louisiana

Carolinas

Fez
Morocco
Marrakesh •

Spanish Florida

Cuba (Spanish)

Mexico

St. Domingue (French)
Hispaniola (Spanish)

Moroccan-Songhay Empire (defunct by 1800)

The Sus

SA
DE

Mexico City •

Jamaica (English) *Caribbean Sea*

—*Guadalupe* (French)
—*Martinique* (French)
—*Barbados* (English)

Arguin

Goree

Rio Grande

Mosquito Coast

• Portobello
• Cartagena

Cacheu

Timbuktu
• Gao
Jenne

Niger R.

SPANISH AMERICA   Colombia

Dutch Guyana (Surinam)
French Guyana

Dahomey
Asante • Oyo
Elmina •
Whydah • *Gulf of Guinea*

Amazon R.

European Slave Trading Posts

• Palmares

Luar
Portuguese Ang
Bengu

Callao • Lima
Peru

Bahia • **Salvador**
Portuguese Brazil

Potosi •

Minas Gerais Rio de Janeiro
• Sao Paulo

Cape •
(Dutch, British from

Buenos • Aires *River Plate*

Araucanians

Mapuche

N

0 _____ 2,000 miles

0 _____ 2,000 kilometers

MAP 12. Empires in 1800

RUSSIAN EMPIRE

Chukchi

Aleutian
Islands
Russian
Alaska

Kazakhs

Zhungars

Mongolia

Manchuria

Uighurs

Beijing

QING EMPIRE

Korea

OMAN
MPIRE

IRANIAN
EMPIRE

Bukhara

Tibet

China

Shanghai

Persian
Gulf

Hormuz

Omani
Raids

Guangzhou
(Canton)

Fuzhou

Bahrein

Muscat

Diu
(Portuguese)

Bihar
Bengal

Taiwan
Macao (Portuguese)

Red Sea

Arabia

Oman

Bombay
(British)

Burma

BRITISH
INDIA

Siam

Vietnam

Manila (Spanish)

ghay
), before the
occan conquest

Omani Empire

Coromandel/
Carnatic

Philippines

Sri
Lanka

Aceh

Maluku Islands
(Dutch)

Pate

Sumatra

Mombasa
Pemba

Zanzibar

Makassar

Banda Islands
(Dutch)

Kilwa

Java
(Dutch)

Timor
(Portuguese)

Mozambique

Madagascar

Mauritius
(French)

Makassars
for trepang

Australia

Sydney
(British 1788)

Bass Strait

New Zealand

Foveaux
Strait

Contravening entrenched common usage, however, is often a lost cause. One cannot expect people to stop talking about early modern "colonial empires". "Patchwork empire" is an attempt at a compromise solution. Yet even this can obscure the autonomy and agency of local peoples, who could and did use the upheavals and biotechnologies of West European expansion to create "empires" of their own.

I Africans

There was very little European empire of any kind in sub-Saharan Africa in 1800, and for some decades thereafter. The two leading lodgements were small: Portuguese Angola and the Dutch Cape Colony, from 1805 in British hands. Each had a small kernel of empire around their coastal bases, and a little more in their hinterlands. The Cape had by far the most settlers, but even here we are only talking about 20,000 or so in 1800. The European population of Angola never exceeded 2,000, 1576–1800. What Europeans did have was a set of trading networks, dependent on African partners, suppling dozens of coastal trading posts with gold, ivory and, above all, slaves.

As we saw in chapter 4, Muslim North Africans had long dominated the trans-Saharan slave trade, in concert with allies farther south, and they did so until its demise in the nineteenth century. A vicious circle emerged, in which slaves were traded for horses, which enabled cavalry cultures to develop in the Sahel, which thereby created a military edge over unhorsed peoples, which was used to take more slaves.[1] The Portuguese inserted themselves by sea into the western flank of this system in the 1440s. Europeans did not invent the African slave trade, but they did boost it, in a series of steps. Plague revived slavery in Europe, and the number of slaves in some parts of southern Europe in 1500 was quite considerable, including the survivors of perhaps 150,000 imported black Africans.[2] The number inside Europe then diminished thereafter as free labour became cheaper. However, the "golden age" for common folk, 1350–1500, produced a deep cultural antagonism to "working like a slave", especially in hard, dangerous, and difficult occupations associated with coerced labour: deep mining, rowing war galleys and, perhaps, intensive plantation agriculture. "Some tasks . . . were so unpleasant and risky that free workers would shun them whatever the pay".[3] They would certainly not voluntarily migrate to take up such tasks. Christian doubts about hereditary chattel slavery revived with the easing of the early plague-era labour crisis from 1500, and these factors plus expansion motivated Europe to shift much of its slave work offshore, distancing itself from slavery while continuing to profit from it. In the Americas, Europeans at first took Amerindian slaves, in quite large numbers. This was quite distinct from forced labour under *repartimento, mita,* and *encomienda* systems. Overworked, and in close proximity to Europeans and their new diseases, Amerindian slaves died fast, and Spanish humanitarians, famously led by Bartolomé de las Casas, denounced the practice, encouraging an increase in imports of black African slaves.

At first, the Portuguese in West Africa traded horses for slaves just like their Muslim rivals, as well as copper and textiles. Portugal itself was not rich in such things, and as we saw in chapter 10, the horses and textiles came from its temporary imperial springboard in western Morocco. It was presumably Portuguese imports that halved horse prices in the sixteenth century.[4] Mounted slave raiding in inland Africa was difficult in densely forested areas, and impossible where tsetse flies spread diseases lethal to horses. But gun-toting pedestrians could penetrate such regions, where their guns substituted for horses in providing an advantage in violent slave-taking. Even before 1500, the Portuguese began injecting guns into the slaving system, usually in the hands of Afro-Portuguese.[5] A king of Benin acquired a cannon in 1516. But really large African imports of guns began only around 1650, when the British and French became heavily involved in slaving.[6] The number rose from a few thousand to an estimated 180,000 a year around 1730, reaching 300,000 by 1800, more than half of them British-made.[7] There were some low-quality "sham dam iron" muskets among them, but "the dangerous state of many of the guns imported into West Africa has been exaggerated". The African gun trade had the same suppliers as European armies, and while they did try to offload less well-tested and well-finished weapons in Africa, buyers there were usually discriminating.[8]

Scholars have had their doubts about the correlation of gun imports and slave-taking African warfare. It does seem that, with possible exceptions in Portuguese Angola, Europeans did not deliberately or directly foment wars to increase slave output. They did not have to. African polities did not typically enslave their own people, but took others or were taken by them. They had to take slaves to trade, first for horses and then for guns, to avoid being enslaved themselves. This involved more than the one-off purchase of a gun. They needed ongoing supplies of replacements, ammunition and flints, in effect addicting to the trade. While Africans could and did make some of their own gunpowder, the Dutch alone sold 20,000 tons in West Africa in 1700.[9] Recent research has documented this vicious circle in the eighteenth century, when the British took the lead in the gun and slave trades. They "locked the slave trade into a self-perpetuating gun-slave cycle, a cycle that generated explosive growth in both slave exports and conflict among Africans".[10]

Yet another disturbing cycle was interlinked with this: high slave mortality underwrote continuing demand. Perhaps 20% of slaves died during the process of enslavement, the overland journey to the coast, and in the terrible barracoons while waiting for ships. Another 10–15% died during the dreaded "middle passage". But perhaps the most lethal component of the slaving system was work on sugar plantations. The United States often patted itself on the back for the relatively low mortality and high reproduction of its slaves compared to those in Brazil and the Caribbean. But this was because the United States grew little sugar. Where it did, in Louisiana, its slaves failed to reproduce too.[11] It was not that high death rates were inherent in sugar production; there are many cases, with free labour, in which it was not lethal. But big planters found it more profitable to work a limited number of slaves, including children and pregnant women, very hard, and then replace them with fresh purchases when they died.[12] The sugar masters did sometimes express concern about the failure of their slaves to reproduce, but were usually unable or unwilling to do anything effective about it. This conclusion is neither recent nor radical, but has been widely accepted among historians for at least 50 years. "Much has been written on the planter's need to conserve the slaves . . . but the facts say that he worked them to an early death".[13]

European slave trading on the African coast intensified fairly steadily from the late fifteenth century, but was regionally selective. There was little slave exporting from the Gold Coast until gold began to run short around 1700. Senegambia to the north was the main sixteenth-century trade location, though not necessarily of the homes of the slaves themselves, who might come from far inland. The net spread wider in the seventeenth century, taking in Angola and the Bights of Benin and Biafra, and wider still in the eighteenth, backfilling in Sierra Leone and the Gold and Windward Coasts, and stretching around the Cape to Mozambique and Madagascar. No fewer than 43 major European slaving forts have been documented on the western coast of Africa,[14] and there were many other lesser posts. The Danes alone, minor players in the trade, had had 30 posts of some sort at some point in time.[15] All worked with African partner polities—a main partner or two on the coast itself, and an inland network or two of traders and raiders.[16] Heavy mortality from disease meant that there were a thousand Europeans at most in all these forts at any one time, excluding Angola. African elite slaves did the work and manned the guns.[17] Some of the larger gun forts were capable of repelling surprise attacks, but none could afford to cross their main local ally in the long term. Any European illusions of control were quickly deflated. As a British official noted in 1752, "in Africa we were only tenants of the soil which we held at the goodwill of the natives".[18] Seventy years earlier, two chief factors of the Royal Africa Company successively were deported after offending the local African ruler. Some African states grew powerful by manipulating multiple partners, European and African: first cavalry states like Songhay and Bornu, then coastal states like Benin and Whydah; then the gunpowder empires of Asante and Dahomey.[19]

Remarkably, tiny Portugal maintained the overall lead in the European-African slave trade, despite being expelled from most of their Gulf of Guinea posts by the Dutch in the seventeenth century, and despite being unable to match the inflow of British and French guns in the eighteenth. Their most interesting technique, touched on in chapter 6, was breeding or fully coopting their own collaborators—the latter was unusual for a European power. In 1462, with Genoese assistance, the Portuguese settled the Cape Verde Islands 300 miles off the coast of West Africa, but were unable to attract European women there because they were less healthy for Europeans than the Madeira and Azores Islands further north. So they took black African wives, with later generations counting locally as free Portuguese first-class citizens—*vizinhos* or "honourable men". In 1513, on the main island of Santiago, there were 58 "white" vizinhos and 16 black—the first known instance of "black Europeans". By 1600, there were 600 vizinhos, now of mostly African descent, but considering themselves Portuguese and in practice if not principle recognised as such by other Portuguese. The Cape Verdes became a crucial hub of the trans-Atlantic slave trade, with links to another set of Afro-Portuguese communities on the mainland initiated by Portuguese men who had "gone native" from the 1490s, known as *lancados*. They in turn linked up with the African coastal polities who actually acquired the slaves. "Wherever the Lancados settled . . . the export of slaves soon followed".[20] Like the Cape Verdeans, lancado and their descendants self-defined as Portuguese.[21] One of their communities was Cacheu, "the largest European settlement in sixteenth century West Africa." It gained official city status from the Portuguese crown in 1605.[22] A system similar to Cape Verde, based on the Sao Tome Islands, later developed farther south. This diverse Afro-Portuguese broker culture seems strikingly similar to the Swahili on the opposite coast. It was well armed with guns, and was distinct from, though intertwined with, the more formal system based on the

Portuguese coastal forts, which were also dependent on African allies. It was probably lancados who enabled Portugal to continue to draw slaves from the Guinea coast, from such places as Bissau, even after the takeover of their forts by the Dutch.

Farther south, the Portuguese arrived in West Central Africa (Angola and the western Congo) in 1483, but had little success in extracting slaves until they set up a base at Luanda in 1576, followed by another at Benguela in 1617.[23] Exceptionally, they acquired the whip hand over their immediate African neighbours, and repeatedly intervened in the wars of larger African powers further inland with forces of a few hundred Portuguese or *casta* musketeers and a few thousand African allies or slave soldiers. The Portuguese may have aspired to a large empire in Angola. They did not get it, but they did get an increasing flow of slaves. Helping African powers defeat their enemies and suppress rebellions yielded prisoners. In Angola too, the children of Portuguese men and African women were "classified as white and Portuguese."[24] One such child, Joao Vieira, became governor in 1658.[25] A somewhat different system emerged in Mozambique from the seventeenth century, with mixed-race independent-minded *prazeiros* in charge of inland operations and slave soldiers doing the slave-taking. A formidable military culture, the Chikunda, descended from the latter, developed in the eighteenth century.[26] There was plenty of African agency in Portugal's operations in the continent, but much of it was employed in acquiring other Africans as slaves. Another unusual feature of Portugal's patchwork empire in Africa was the extent to which it was co-owned by Brazil. Brazilian settler and casta troops and ships helped reconquer Angola from the Dutch in the mid-seventeenth century. Brazil was not only the dominant market for slaves, but also the leading shipper, and increasingly the producer of the goods used in exchange: tobacco and rum. "Brazilian rum purchased 25 percent of the slaves exported from Central Africa to Portuguese America" in 1710–1830, and tobacco bought a similar proportion.[27] Most was produced by slaves, thus making the system pay for itself.

Portugal alone took 5.84 million African slaves over the four centuries of its trade. In the last 20 years, historians David Eltis, Stephen Behrendt, and their colleagues have created a vast database on the trans-Atlantic slave trade. No doubt it has its flaws, but it is about as good as pre-modern numbers get.[28] The database shows that a total of 12.5 million African slaves embarked, mostly for the Americas, 1501–1875, of whom 11 million arrived. About 8.5 million embarked between 1500 and 1800.[29] Not even this terrible toll was the whole story, though we must rely on guesses for the rest. Allowing 20% for deaths on the way to the ships, the total involved in the Afro-European trade, 1500–1875, comes to 15 million. At an average of 5,000 people per year, the overland trans-Saharan trade would have added another 1.875 million—indeed, one recent estimate is twice as high.[30] Omani- and Ottoman-connected slavers took perhaps another 2 million from East Africa. Allowing for 20% deaths en route, non-European slaving added some 4.6 million to the toll, bringing the grand total close to 20 million.

The fiercely contested question of the effects of this mass extraction of human beings on the European economies they were forced to serve is discussed in the next chapter. The effects on Africa are also debated. Even 20 million averages out at 50,000 a year over four centuries, from a population estimated at about 40 million. It is not clear that some major developments, such as the rise of the Sokoto caliphate from around 1800, had much to do with external influences at all. But some scholars argue that the corrosive effects of slave trades and slaving wars on the "social capital" of African polities are still with us, and help explain the state of the continent today.[31] Pre-modern sub-Saharan Africa had unrecognised similarities to the other great long-term slaving ground: the Caucasus, the alleged heartland of Aryan whiteness. Both had a high degree of linguistic, religious, and political fragmentation; small but resilient kin-based groups existing cheek-by-jowl with larger polities, and with competing predatory agents of still larger powers with hungry slave markets.[32] This should always have made nonsense of racist claims that black Africans were somehow "natural slaves". Europe's role in the slave trade did not involve much empire—that came to Africa later and lasted barely a century. But it did permit the involuntary transfer of millions of people to Amerindian lands where they were massively exploited in European interests. Between 1750 and 1800, Britain temporarily took over the lead in the trade, extracting 1.58 million slaves compared to Portugal's 1.2 million.

II The Americas

European expansion in the Americas before 1800 took three main forms: plantation, extraction, and settlement. Plantation colonies produced exotic products, new and old, for export. American tobacco and cacao added to a list of addictive trades, which also included coffee, sugar, and alcohol. Perhaps fortunately, early Spanish plans to market coca leaves came to nothing.[33] Addictive trades reduced the lead time for the mass uptake of a product and made it less sensitive to price increases; this became a significant "drug-dealing" component in the West European expansion kit. There are said to have been tobacco addicts in Poland and Russia by 1529, 37 years after it was first offered to Columbus. Tobacco became a global "commodity of mass consumption" within a century.[34] Portuguese Brazil and English Virginia were key producers, and the Dutch were important middlemen. Old World exotics transplanted to the Americas included coffee and species of cotton more productive and marketable than the American variety. These products were produced mainly by slave labour. The leading plantation product was always slave-produced sugar. Northeast Brazil led production from 1570 until about 1650, when its sugar exports were worth £3.75 million a year. When prices were high, as in 1627, sugar taxes provide 40% of the revenues of the Portuguese state.[35] The average volume was around 20,000 tons a year, and Brazilian sugar exports continued at around this level. From about 1775, coffee and cotton were added to its plantation exports. Caribbean islands took the lead in sugar after 1650, particularly those of the French and British, which exported a staggering ten million tons of sugar between them, 1698–1791.[36] The French had an edge over the British in sugar production, due to their great sugar mine of St Domingue. I would trace the exponential rise of European sugar consumption back to the Black Death: perhaps 1,000 tons a year in 1300, around 10,000 tons in 1500, and in excess of 100,000 in 1800. Thanks to the post-plague consumption boom, the rate of growth in the first two centuries, 1300–1500, was even greater than in the next three, 1500–1800.

The main extractives from the Americas were codfish, bullion, and "soft gold" in the form of furs, especially beaver. Dutch New York was essentially a beaver extraction base, using the Hudson River for inland access, but the French were again the leading European player. Quebec was established in 1608 as the base for their fur trading network. Britain acquired the Dutch and French fur networks in 1664 and 1759 respectively, and developed its own vast network from 1672, accessed by sea via Hudson Bay.[37] The fur was used mainly for hats, considered a marker of gentility in Western Europe and European America, where they were "*de rigeur* for the well-dressed man". From the 1720s, mercury was used in their processing and sometimes inhaled by the hat maker, giving rise to the term "mad hatter". France and Britain between them exported more than 40 million beaver hats between 1700 and 1770, costing around £2 each, in addition to a similar domestic consumption.[38] Beavers are quite substantial animals, about 40 pounds in weight as adults, and other materials were also used in beaver hats, so several hats could be made from one pelt. Being herbivores, beavers were more abundant and were depleted less rapidly than sable. But mass extraction still took its toll. Britain's Hudson Bay Company alone acquired 2.75 million beaver pelts between 1700 and 1763, and French networks took even more. From 1741 to 1758, "France imported more than twice as many beaver pelts as England".[39] Counting earlier and later periods and including the Dutch, 20 million pelts worth about £10 million seems a reasonable estimate, 1608–1800. Disease aside, in terms of the area influenced, this beaver trade was the most extensive European impact on the Americas before 1800, but it scarcely amounted to empire. "The Indians never considered themselves to be French subjects, and the French were never able to treat them as such", and the same is true of other European fur networks.[40]

Squeezing bullion out of Native Americans and their land began at first contact in 1492, as we saw in chapter 10. Production at the Spanish Bolivian "silver mountain" of Potosi declined after 1650, and even the introduction of gunpowder blasting to excavate additional mine shafts in the 1670s failed to revive it. It still produced something like 4,000 tons of silver between 1650 and 1800,[41] bringing its total output to 20,000 tons. From 1700, Mexico increasingly took the lead in Spanish silver production, in 450 mining settlements containing about 5,000 mines. By 1800, it had produced at least 50,000 tons of silver, about two-thirds of the world's supply, plus 800 tons of gold. The Portuguese too became heavily engaged in New World bullion extraction. About 1695, *bandeirante* expeditions found alluvial gold inland and north of São Paulo. A series of substantial gold rushes followed, first in Minas Gerais—the "General Mines"—and then farther west in Goias and Matto Grosso. Output peaked at 17 tons a year in the 1740s, and the main rush phase ceased around 1760, but Brazil's estimated gold production was close to 1,000 tons, 1695–1800, excluding substantial smuggling, the equivalent of about 12,000 tons of silver.[42] Just who benefited from these outflows is another story, but there is no doubt about the importance of European global bullion extraction, which began in Northwest Africa in 1415 and mushroomed in the Americas less than a century later.

The fur trade was geographically the widest European trade in the Americas, and bullion was by far the most valuable, but the biggest in volume was something more prosaic: codfish. Cod fishing in North American waters was, as we have seen, a clear offshoot of the post-plague surge in North Atlantic fishing. It is not always listed among Europe's imports, and its scale is surprising. As early as 1578, 380 European ships were fishing around Newfoundland, numbers doubted by some but confirmed by French archives—again, the French were the leading participants.[43] By the seventeenth century, some

50,000 tons of cured cod were being sent to Europe annually, and this increased throughout the eighteenth century. The volume of sugar reached even greater heights, but the cured cod represented five times their weight of live fish, and so substituted for a quarter-million to a half-million tons of fish from European waters.[44] Cod stocks overall may have held up until the nineteenth century, but real or apparent local depletion drove extensions from the Newfoundland Banks to the Gulf of St Lawrence and Labrador and Greenland waters. A similar tale could be told for whaling, and we should also note one other hunt trade: wild cattle hides. As early as the 1550s, feral cattle abounded in the interiors of the big Caribbean islands, and they were soon even more numerous in the grasslands around the River Plate. Cured hides were exported to Europe from the seventeenth century, and they became significant by the 1780s, when the Plata region dispatched 1.5 million hides a year.[45]

The third form of European expansion in the Americas, the establishment of settler colonies, looms largest in retrospect. It founded great nations, and is generally cast as an inexorable process beginning in 1492 for Spain, 1532 for Portugal, 1607 for England—and 1608 for France, whose few but prolific Acadian, Quebecois, and Louisiana settlers fell under other flags from 1755. Neither the preeminence nor the inevitability were so clear in the late eighteenth century. A few settler colonies, like New England and Pennsylvania, were founded by cohesive private migrations. A few more were established by states to support strategic bases, like Salvador in Brazil in 1549 and Halifax in Nova Scotia in 1749. Most grew incrementally as supports for plantations or extractive trades. The key function of Spanish settlement in northern Argentina from 1580 was to supply Potosi with horses and mules. Lima was the administrative capital of the Potosi system, with Lima's port of Callao as its outlet. Acapulco in Mexico and Portabello in Panama, the latter reached by mule train across the Isthmus, were its outposts, shipping its silver to Manila and to Seville or Cadiz. French Quebec and Dutch New York were essentially bases for far-flung fur trade networks. "Poor white" settlements, often of Ulster Scots in what became the US Old South, were auxiliaries of coastal plantations, supplying cheap pork and corn, and tough militias useful against Indians, rebel slaves, and European rivals alike. New England and the Middle Colonies' leading export destination was the Caribbean, supplying slaves with food and other goods.[46] Unlike fur trading, settlement did not coexist easily with indigenous peoples.

Settlement was to grow and spread explosively in the nineteenth century, and the slower and smaller settlement of previous centuries was the crucial base for this. But this future was not obvious in the late eighteenth century, when it might well have seemed that European empire in the Americas had reached its limits. The neo-British of the United States threw off London's rule in the 1780s, and the neo-Africans of St Domingue did the same to that of Paris in the 1790s. Alongside this was a less recognised development: the constraints placed on empire by Native American resilience and resistance, alliance, and adaptation. In both British North America and Portuguese Brazil, bitter warfare and easy access to introduced diseases overcame coastal Indians in the first century of settlement. Further inland, the frontier hardened as Indians learned to cope with European expansion, and to acquire and use its horses and weapons. To some extent, they also became immunised to, or remained distanced from, introduced diseases. As noted in chapter 7, newer findings undermine the received picture of wave-like "Fatal Impact". "This research argues that infectious disease diffusion ahead of its introduction at a frontier cannot be assumed to have been a uniform, wave-like-process. Instead, diffusion probably took an idiosyncratic path that followed the kinds of interaction that best promoted transmission".[47]

As also noted in chapter 7, the big selective killers, smallpox, measles, and the relevant type of typhus, conferred immunity on survivors, and the same was true of yellow fever and *falciparum* malaria, to which Europeans were as vulnerable as Amerindians. About a century after the first epidemics, some Indian populations began to grow again—perhaps as early as 1620 in central Mexico, and 1680 elsewhere.[48] Native Mexican numbers are much contested, but the more reasonable suggest about 8 million at contact, falling to 2.4 million in 1595, and perhaps further to 1.5 million by 1620. Numbers recovered to about 2.5 million by 1700, and 4 million by 1800, now including many *castas* of mainly Indian descent.[49] The Viceregality of Peru had a similar pattern. This suggests that diseases like smallpox had become *endemic*, killing a relatively small number of children annually, but not enough to prevent population growth. Epidemiologists tell us that interactive populations of at least 250,000 are required for such diseases to become endemic, and sometimes imply that these must live in a single big city. Mexico City reached 100,000 only around 1780, with Potosi declining from 160,000 after 1611. But research on the Guarani in 98 Jesuit mission towns in Paraguay, which was part of Potosi's support system, seems to suggest that locations in regular interaction with such cities could contribute to the endemism threshold. In Paraguay, six strikes of smallpox, 1653–1765, killed many Guarani, but not enough to prevent population growth.[50] Farther north, some "woodland Indian" populations—Choctaw, Chickasaw, and Creek—also grew modestly from 1715 to 1790.[51]

Many, perhaps most, Indians in the former Aztec and Inca empires, did come under Spanish control, in varying degrees.[52] Some were forced to pay regular tribute and provide periodic labour services. But Spain took over these empires, rather than dismantled them, and local administration at first stayed largely in the hands of native caciques. Over time, the introduction of Spanish co-administrators (*corregidors*) and the establishment of private Spanish mines, agricultural estates, and ranches, all eager for Indian labour, complicated the picture, and mission towns, arguably a form of "monastic colonisation", also proliferated. But some room remained for Indian agency. In corregidor-administered regions, "resistance to foreign masters tended to be passive but effective".[53] While Potosi initially depended on coerced Indian labour, free labour came to predominate, and it was the norm in eighteenth-century Mexican mines.[54] Often, Spanish-administered Indians had autonomous kin nearby, flight to whom was always an option, and being "reduced" to mission towns had its benefits. "In converting to Christianity and accepting resident Franciscan friars, chiefs gained not only the largesse of Catholic church and Spanish crown, but also a resident cultural broker and advocate to act on their behalf to Spanish military government".[55] This refers to Spanish Florida, where the "largesse of the crown" was considerable—55,000 pesos in 1794—due to fears that the British or their rebel American offspring might suborn the Indians.[56] In this and many other regions featuring rival European powers, Indian groups, sometimes in new alliances woven together by religious prophets, divided and avoided being ruled.

Spanish silver extraction depended on Indian labour, and the first planters hoped to do so too. A million or more Indian slaves were captured, or traded from other Indians, mainly before 1700, and especially in Brazil, but also in the Caribbean and what is now the United States. The fur trade too depended on Indians, but here coercion simply did not work. The numerous forts set up by fur traders across North America were not symbols of empire, but markets in Indian territory at which beaver pelts were exchanged for European goods, notably guns. Reliance on guns did addict Indians to European trade. As in Africa, you needed not just the one-off purchase of a gun, but also ongoing supplies of replacements and ammunition. But guns also inoculated Indians against European empire. The Iroquois of New York and New England, a famous case, used guns acquired by the fur trade to create their own empire during the seventeenth century. First the Dutch and then the English were their eager allies, and they retained their independence until at least 1794.[57] Armed by the fur trade, able to play off European powers against each other, and forming fresh alliances, the "Woodland Indians" in and around the Appalachians were able to pen Europeans in to the Atlantic coast until 1795.[58] Similar strategies allowed native Central Americans to do even better against the Spanish in Darien and the Mosquito Coast.[59] Muzzle-loading guns were of limited use for fighting on horseback; bows, lances, and bolas were at least as useful. In the many vast grasslands of the Americas, it was self-reproducing horses more than guns that underwrote persistent Indian independence. As late as 1870, let alone 1800, the mounted nomad "empires" of the Lakota Sioux and the Comanche controlled about a quarter of the United States. Like the Mongols, Comanche warriors each had multiple horses, as well as guns, and terrorised Anglo-Americans, Spanish Americans, and other Indians alike.[60] Mounted Mapuche, in Chile, and Araucanians, in Argentina, controlled huge parts of their countries at the same late date.[61]

How much of Brazil was genuinely under Portuguese control in 1800 is hard to measure. Until 1690, it was probably not much more than Salvador and Bahia provinces in the northeast, and Rio de Janiero and São Paulo in the southeast. The white population was still only around 100,000, and the number of subject Indians was probably fewer than the 50,000 missionised in 1601.[62] The numerous slaving expeditions into the interior, almost by definition, did not indicate ongoing control. The existence of more than a hundred communities of escaped slaves in the interior, known as *quilombos*, often in alliance with local Indians, does not indicate much control either. The largest, Palmares, had 20,000 people and repelled Portuguese and Dutch attacks for most of the seventeenth century—"an 'African Kingdom' in Brazil".[63] The gold rushes changed things somewhat in the eighteenth century, but the persistence of both slave raids and quilombos suggests that control of inland regions remained very partial. The goldfields provided opportunities for black slaves to escape or buy freedom.[64] The formidable Botocudo Indians continued to control a large swathe of even the most heavily settled mining province, Minas Gerais, at least until 1808, and Portuguese penetration of Amazonia remained very modest. In Brazil's far south, the mounted Kadieweu of the Chaco signed a treaty in in 1791, usually an indicator of nominal submission and actual autonomy in Iberian America at the time.[65]

When recognised, the persistence of Indian independence in most of Spanish America is sometimes attributed to Spanish disinterest in their regions because of the apparent absence of gold or silver. Actually, Spanish California had plenty of gold, but there were never enough Spanish on the ground to find it. Spain preferred to rule its dominions in fact as well as in name, recognising that "only occupancy buttressed territorial claims".[66] Fearing rival Europeans, it repeatedly tried to impose some real control over its frontiers. It developed a sophisticated system of collaboration with white colonial elites to incentivise them to help it do so—"stakeholder empire". It also relied on Indian allies from the outset, who typically paid no tribute and retained their autonomy. The Tlaxcalans, co-conquerors of the Aztecs in the 1520s, retained privileges as military settlers in the thinly held north and west of New Spain as late as the 1760s.[67] Powerful local groups in this vast region, the Yacqui and the Apache, retained independence through a mix of trade, alliance, and effective resistance.[68] Spain's efforts to turn nominal empire into real empire climaxed with a major military effort in the second half of the eighteenth century, but "attempts to beat these Indians into submission generally failed".[69] As in Chile and Argentina, mounted tribes on the grasslands of Colombia and Venezuela retained independence until 1800 and beyond.[70]

In 1800, then, European empire in the Americas was a stalled project, which would require fresh developments in the nineteenth century to restart. It was largely restricted to a "European pale", like that of the English in Ireland centuries earlier. Some imperial borders were long-standing. In Argentina, "by the 1820s the frontier of settlement had scarcely advanced beyond that of 1580".[71] "Effective territorial occupation of the *campaña* never extended beyond ten miles from the River Plate".[72] The newly independent United States controlled about half its nominal 900,000 square miles, which in turn was only 15% of what became the 48 states. On average, this proportion might hold for all the Americas—more in Spanish South America, but hardly anything at all in the entire midwest and west of North America. While African slaves continued to flow in, and bullion, beaver, codfish, and sugar continued to flow out, the prime benefits did not necessarily accrue to the European powers that had established the exchange. The French fur trade fell to the British in 1763. The Spanish and Portuguese empires stayed afloat, but sprang more leaks, through which their bullion flowed out to others.

III India

After the death of Emperor Aurangzeb in 1707, the Mughal Empire began to disintegrate. Provincial viceroys became independent in practice, though the emperors retained moral authority and residual spasms of regional power. While there is continuing debate about the cause of Mughal decline, most agree that European pressure was not among them.[73] Substantial successor states included Awadh, Bengal, and Hyderabad, various Rajput lordships, and the rising powers of Mysore in the south and the Sikhs in the Punjab (see map 10). The Marathas continued to dominate central India. Some of these "fragments" still had the wealth and population of the biggest European states; there was no free-for-all for intruders. But European-held factories and port cities increased their business. A residue of Portuguese influence remained at Goa, Diu, and Daman on the western coast, its resilience largely due to "Black Portuguese" converts and mixed-race "White Portuguese", who also went freelance elsewhere. Until the 1730s, the Dutch VOC retained its lead in India, and also continued to dominate long-range trade in Southeast Asia, now helped by 10,000 Asian soldiers as well as Chinese settlers.[74] In India, the British EIC was in second place, with a revived French East India Company closing in rapidly on it. In the 1740s, the Dutch sent on average 31 ships a year to Further Asia, the British and French about 18 each.[75] All three powers had ports and/ or factories in each of India's four major sea-trading regions, Gujarat and Malabar in the west, and Bengal and Coromandel in the east. Some contend that, due to the low price of rice, Indian average living standards were still on par with those of Western Europe in the eighteenth century. A growing number of studies assert that this was no longer the case.[76] But Indian commerce remained strong and Europeans still conceded the superiority of Indian manufacturing by shipping in large quantities of bullion in exchange for cotton cloth. Change to this picture was initiated by two sets of developments over the first half of the eighteenth century, one economic and one military.

As we saw in chapter 13, the Mughal Empire, contrary to some legends, was a merchant-friendly regime, so its decline raised issues for Indian inter-regional and maritime trade. Non-European merchant networks had long entwined with European ones, and the trend intensified after 1707. Local mercantile migration to the European ports increased and found a ready welcome. Christian Armenians, who could be considered "white", were favourites. The British offered local citizenship to the males "as if they were Englishmen born"; the Dutch offered marriage to the females.[77] But Hindu, Parsi, Jain, Indo-Portuguese, and even Muslim merchants were also sought after.[78] Recent work stresses "partnership and reciprocity", "interdependence and mutual benefit".[79] Such partnerships deepened and strengthened the European reach into inland India for prime cloth, and into the "country trades" with East Africa, the Persian Gulf, and Southeast Asia, and they made quick loans available from Indian bankers. From the Indian perspective, while the Europeans before 1740 had little land power, their fortified ports and warships offered some security for Indian merchant families and for their own ocean trades. This was a commercial symbiosis, not a step up in European empire, which still scarcely existed in India. One scholar puts it in the context of an old struggle between the Indian coast, with small states, where merchants had great influence, and the interior, with big states, where merchants had less leverage.[80]

This general shift was coupled with a regional one, whereby European and non-European merchants alike increasingly looked to Bengal. As chapter 13 noted, the Mughals had colonised East Bengal and enhanced its wet rice production, which became the cheapest and most abundant in India by the late seventeenth century. Bengal also produced surpluses of indigo dye and raw silk. Cheap rice lowered costs for craft production, including silks but particularly cotton cloth. Bengal grew a lot of cotton, but its lead in manufacturing grew so marked that it came to import a lot more from other Indian regions. The population of 20 million or so produced state revenues of £2.5 million from taxes on farming, not commerce. Merchants were drawn in like moths to a flame.[81] India's leading Jain banking family, the Jagat Seths, were among them, along with thousands of Armenians. European trading posts had long existed in Bengal, but their number surged in 1690–92, when the British acquired Calcutta, and the French Chandernagore. Both, like the Dutch trading settlements of Pipeli and Chinsura, were on the Hugli River, an offshoot of the Ganges, which allowed access to inland Bengal. Bengal's own Nawabs remained in control, but by mid-century the VOC drew almost half its Indian goods from Bengal, the EIC, three-quarters.[82] Bengal had become the heartland of India's European-mediated global commerce.

Turning to military changes, Iranian and Turanian cavalrymen and horses "vanished from the Indian order of battle" in the early eighteenth century.[83] From 1739, they came as invaders instead. In 1709, some Afghan tribes united and successfully rebelled against Iranian control. In 1722, they invaded Iran itself. Iranian resistance consolidated under an able officer, Nader Shah, who threw out the Afghans and usurped the Safavid throne in 1736. Two years later, he conquered Afghanistan in its turn, and went on to invade India. In 1739, he sacked the Mughal capital of Delhi and returned home with immense plunder. Nader was assassinated in 1747, and his short-lived empire fell apart. But the Afghans repeatedly invaded northern India, seeking plunder not conquest. They sacked Delhi again in 1757, and inflicted a terrible defeat on the Marathas in 1761. Nader Shah and the Afghan Ahmad Shah were able leaders, but they were helped by a biotechnical advantage: swivel guns (*zamburaks*) firing one- or two-pound shot long range, and mounted on fast camels trained to kneel as the gun was loaded, and the shot aimed and fired.[84] The resilient Marathas recovered within ten years, and re-established their protectorate over Delhi and its poor emperor. Cavalry, though with fewer good horses, continued to play an important role in Indian armies. Infantry were hired as needed from a "military market" of part-time peasant matchlock musketeers. These could be very effective in some conditions, but could not withstand cavalry charges on open ground.[85]

Also around 1740, another military innovation arrived in India from the other end of West Eurasia. The new import was a bayonet-led synergy developed in Europe around 1700, the big exception to the rule of stable military technology, 1500–1850. Flintlock muskets replaced matchlocks; they were not more powerful or longer-range but they did permit a higher rate of fire. Ring bayonets did away with the need for pikemen, so doubling the firepower of a given number of infantry. Standardised drill was a third element, enabling infantry formations to change fluidly from column to line to square, and making the process of reloading semi-automatic, useful in the heat of battle. This required constant training, but allowed regular infantry to repel cavalry. The transfer to India took place in the early 1740s, and it was found that Indians, peasants, and higher castes alike could pick up the bayonet synergy just as readily as Europeans, as long as they were employed full-time, in all seasons, for years on end, which in turn required their being paid regularly. The emergence of these "sepoy" armies in the 1740s was a game-changer, but not necessarily a harbinger of doom for Indian independence. Indian states—Mysore, the Marathas, the Sikhs—eventually produced bayonet infantry as good as any. While European reports sometimes exaggerated the size of Indian armies by counting its camp followers, but not their own, the locals still had the advantage in numbers. Moreover, the Europeans were at first more concerned about fighting each other, with as much Indian help as possible.

Between 1744 and 1761, the French and British fought almost constantly, despite peace in Europe 1748–56, directly and through Indian proxies, backing different sides in local succession struggles, particularly in the Carnatic, an extension of the Coromandel coast. The French, who pioneered sepoys, had the initial advantage, and they took Madras in 1746. But, in 1757–61, the British turned the tide against them. The Dutch were also defeated in a last attempt to assert themselves in Bengal, despite peace at home, against the British in 1759. The French did not give up. They backed Indian powers against the British into the 1790s. Mysore defeated the EIC in one war, 1766–69, and held them to a draw in the next, 1780–84.[86] As late as 1780–82, a Maratha victory on land and French successes at sea left "the British Empire in India . . . tottering to its foundation".[87] It recovered, and the British had a modest advantage from 1757, and a greater one after 1782, but they still controlled less than 10% of India ten years later.[88]

In traditional accounts, the limits on British success went unnoticed, and it was attributed to exceptional leaders like Stringer Lawrence, Eyre Coote, and of course Robert Clive, the British Cortes. I do not discount this entirely. The period 1740–80 was the opening phase of British conquests in India and, like the early Portuguese and Spanish campaigns in the Indian Ocean and the Americas, it had a rapacious, frenzied character, when huge private fortunes seemed available for the taking. Europeans in India had a low life expectancy, and they knew it. About one-quarter of Europeans in India died each year, a plague-like toll.[89] They wanted to "shake the pagoda tree" as quickly as possible and head home with their takings. High risk this year was better than lower risk next year, and risk-taking was Clive's stock in trade, along with military brilliance and lack of scruple. But the French also had able leaders willing to chance their arms, and in the end the British beat them too, as well as more cautious and more numerous Indian enemies with good sepoy armies. The same applies to support for the French and British companies from their metropolitan states, particularly naval support. This was significant from 1744 to 1782 but, with one or two exceptions, Paris and London tended to cancel each other out. The EIC's decisive advantage over European and Indian foes alike was its control of Bengal.

In 1717, the EIC acquired, partly through bribery, special privileges in Bengal from the Mughal emperor, consolidating its already promising position in that province, and then linked up with the Jagat Seth bankers.[90] From about 1725, it bought and exported more cotton cloth from Bengal than from the Bombay and Madras Presidencies combined, and more from Bengal than the Dutch VOC did from the whole of India.[91] By 1755, before the EIC acquired political control, Bengal contributed 2.5 times as much to EIC exports as the rest of India combined.[92] Exasperated by the company's profiteering, a new Nawab of Bengal seized Calcutta in 1756. Clive recaptured it in 1757 and went on to win the Battle of Plassey the same year. Further battles, 1761–64, secured the EIC hold on Bengal, and the Nawab became its puppet, with the Company collecting all tax revenue from 1765. Clive later claimed to be "astounded" by his own "moderation", but he and his colleagues' rapacity knew few bounds. Between 1757 and 1765, company officials acquired personal fortunes of about £6 million.[93] In 1770, their plundering threatened not so much to kill the goose that laid the golden egg, but to let it die of hunger. Rice shortages led to famine which killed perhaps a fifth of Bengal's population. Famine could have been alleviated by rice imports, but the company chose to concentrate instead on exporting cottons, acquiring monopolies of other goods such as salt, and collecting 40–45% of rice production in taxes to resell to the starving at high prices.[94] Bengal recovered, and the depredations of the Company and its associates calmed down from about 1780. But, from about 1750 to 1800 and beyond, Bengal provided the British with a larger and more reliable surplus revenue than any other power in India. The French "never ensured that their agents in India had enough money to pay their troops on time and so keep up their morale and commitment, which turned out to be the key requirement in ensuring their military superiority; it was this that ultimately led to their downfall".[95] By contrast, the EIC was able to pay its men regularly and relatively well, and "spared no expense to ensure that their sepoys were issued with the same weapons and trained in the same way as the Company's European troops".[96] In 1748, the EIC employed at most 2,000–3,000 troops, 90% Indian. By 1763, it had 11,500 troops in Bengal alone and was using Bengal revenues to help out the other presidencies, Madras and Bombay. By 1773, the EIC"s regular army had 54,000 men, growing to 115,000 by 1782, and 155,000 by 1805, the great majority of them well-drilled, well-armed, Bengal-paid sepoys.[97]

We are accustomed to equating the British presence in eighteenth-century India solely with the East India Company, but research is now suggesting that the company was only half the picture. The British state took a hand from 1748 and, in an exception to the rule that it was usually matched by Paris, bailed the company out of a financial crisis after the famine of 1770 with loans that exceeded £5 million—equivalent to about two-thirds of British government tax revenue at the time.[98] It also provided a naval squadron and a few thousand royal troops. But the company paid for the latter, gave the state £400,000 a year from its Bengal profits, and made several loans to it in turn. The state also did well from duties on the East Indies trade, which provided "24 per cent of net customs and excise revenues on worldwide imports", 1765–1812.[99] A more shadowy new player was "a tangled web of private interests": company servants in private trade, British "interlopers" officially unconnected to the company (and so useful for dubious trades like opium), Indian partners, and non-British European networks cooperating with the British.[100] This informal doppelganger of the EIC had interests that sometimes differed from those of the company but were often compatible with them. The coupling of formal and informal systems was practiced by the Portuguese in West Africa, and may have been pioneered by them in India as well. It permitted a Genoese-like flexibility, allowing the EIC to break its own rules if it so chose.

The EIC had long been willing to allow its servants to engage in private trade within Asia, and its ship captains and crews had allowances of cargo space for trade between Asia and Europe. One study suggests that this encouraged "horizontal networking" which enhanced British licit and illicit trades alike.[101] British "interlopers" were allowed an increasing role in the intra-Asian trades, running 40 ships out of Calcutta by 1730.[102] Also in Bengal, an intensified intertwining with non-European merchant networks is apparent from the 1740s, with company servants "closely bound up with Asian merchant capital" in both their official and unofficial capacities.[103] The number of Armenians in Bengal reached three or four thousand in 1774.[104] A 2019 study of the Ostend East Indies Company reveals the role of non-British Europeans. This company, chartered by the Austrian rulers of Belgium in 1722, had only a few years of official existence, but "was a much more resilient organization than has previously been understood". It had its own trading post on the Hugli, just north of Calcutta, where it kept trading until at least 1745. Linked to Portuguese and Swedish trading interests allied to Britain, it also "forged connections with French and Danish merchants who clandestinely traded with them and worked together with English country traders".[105] Dutch, Danish, and finally American traders took over this role in the second half of the century. "This 'clandestine' trade at times exceeded the English Company's".[106]

The British capacity to extract benefits from Bengal was considerably enhanced by this informal shadow self, and extract they did. Until the 1750s, the British were sending about £1 million a year out to India in bullion, most of it to Bengal to buy cotton cloth. Around 1760, this flow suddenly reversed, inverting a millennia-old flow—a major watershed in global history, though it did not yet apply to China. Bengal began sending silver back to Britain or on to China for the British to use to buy tea. Along with raw Bengali cotton and processed Bengali opium, this lifted the profitable tea trade to a new order of magnitude.[107] Private traders, company servants on their own account, and the company itself all repatriated their fortunes by using money made in Bengal to buy Bengali or Chinese goods which they then sold in Britain at a high profit—two bites of the apple, or even three. In one year, the company proposed using the £1.3 million surplus on its Bengal tax revenues to buy commodities expected to fetch £2.4 million in London.[108] The total drain from Bengal to Britain between 1757 and 1780 has been put as high as £38 million; about half this amount would be the minimum.[109] The EIC also spent Bengal's money within India. In the decade after 1773, the company doubled its tax take in Bengal to £5 million, of which £2.5 million was surplus.[110] Much of this went on the sepoy army, which was used to improve the British position in India outside Bengal. Military expenses burgeoned out of control, as they tend to do, and from 1792, it had to resume modest imports of British bullion into India.[111] But, between 1798 and 1805, a fresh round of conquests took Britain's empire in India from 10% to 30% of the subcontinent's territory. Empire in India, huge inflows of money, and a greatly enhanced China tea trade were not Bengal's only gifts to Britain. Others are discussed in the next chapter, in the context of British industrialisation.

IV China's World

The Qing/Manchu Empire was founded beyond China's borders, in Manchuria in the 1580s. As chapter 14 noted, the Manchu were formidable and adaptable soldiers. They began as steppe-style cavalry with powerful compound bows and three horses each, organised in "banner" units. They added European-style cannon by 1631 and musket-armed infantry soon afterwards. They conquered and incorporated Korea and some eastern Mongol tribes by 1637, before they took on the Ming, adding Mongols as well as renegade Han Chinese to their banners.[112] The Qing took over China by 1662 and overcame rebellion in the south by 1683. Experts debate whether they are best seen as another Chinese dynasty or an "East Eurasian" Manchurian empire of which China was part.[113] The Qing certainly tried to partner up with the Han Chinese elite, and made some effort to conciliate peasants. They ran a slim state in comparison to Western Europe, with about half its per capita tax rate. They retained and improved the examination system, which recruited officials and, along with wealth and refinement, conferred genteel status. But they sold some nominal positions and reserved half of the most important for Manchu candidates, who were at most 2% of the Chinese population.[114] Until the 1770s at least, no Manchu was officially supposed to serve under a Han in the bureaucracy.[115]

Whether the Qing can be seen as another "gunpowder empire", like those of West Eurasia, consistently pursuing expansion, is also debatable. Their main conquest apart from China was the western Mongol Zunghar empire, including its Tibetan ally. They organised Zhungaria and the lands of their own Uighur allies into Xinjiang, "the New Dominion", in 1768.[116] Both the Qing and the Zunghars used guns but look as much like steppe empires as West Eurasian colonial ones. It is actually the most stubborn of the Qing's enemies, the Ming loyalist Koxinga clan, that seems most like an incipient colonial empire, and a European-style maritime one at that. The clan was based on the Fujian coast and on Taiwan 200 kilometres offshore, from which it ejected the Dutch in 1662. The Qing went to great efforts to close the mainland coast against them for 20 years thereafter, but the Koxinga plied the China Sea, outcompeting the Dutch and the Portuguese in trade with Japan and threatening Spanish Manila. Their income was comparable to that of a respectable state, at least 50 tons of silver a year, and their cannon, musket infantry, and perhaps even warships were in the European style. They built bigger, sturdier ships with two rein-forced gun decks and up to 36 cannon each, though it is not clear that they mastered full-rigged sail plans. Taiwan might have become the base of a European-like maritime colonial empire, foreshadowing the Japanese two cen-turies later. But the Koxinga made the mistake of joining the "Three Feudato-ries" mainland rebellion against the Qing in 1675, and lost much of their army by 1680. The Qing then induced a Koxinga admiral to defect, and with his help set about "adopting Dutch military technology on navy vessels". They defeated the Koxinga fleet and occupied Taiwan in 1683.[117] Like the two Qing clashes with the Russians in the same period, the Koxinga case provides further sup-port for the point made in chapter 7: that the Chinese could emulate pre-industrial European military technology when they needed to, but let it lapse when the need ceased.

The Qing re-opened the coast to foreign trade in 1684, through a network of licensed ports, of which Guangzhou (Canton) became the biggest, but at-tempted no further big naval ventures. A century-long boom followed, which doubled the size of the economy. This built on a similar earlier boom under the Ming, interrupted by the bloody transition from one dynasty to another. The two booms together have been described as a Chinese "commercial revo-lution"[118] and featured a huge increase in coastal and inland water transport, which encouraged regional specialisation, rural crafts, and near-universal en-gagement with the market. Within China, connectivity increased to the point of bulk circulation, with Beijing importing 280,000 tons of rice a year. The Yangtze Delta went from China's rice basket to a mixed urban/rural handicraft region, growing the likes of silk and sugarcane and importing its rice from farther up the river system. Around 1800, the coastal trade of its port of Shang-hai totalled 500,000 tons, while river and canal trade added another 300,000.[119] Rice cultivation was extended into terraced upland regions, and to frontiers in

and around Yunnan, while new crops—maize, peanuts, and sweet potatoes—
filled niches unsuitable for rice.

The hitch was that China's population also doubled over the eighteenth
century, to at least 300 million.[120] Whether economic growth fell behind
population growth is contested in "the" Great Divergence debate about precisely when the Western European economy overtook the rest of the world.
The case for Asian parity looks stronger here than for India. "By many standards the economic well-being of China's population in the eighteenth century
was unsurpassed by any other contemporary society.".[121] Demand for foreign
imports clearly grew, not just for luxuries like furs and exotic foodstuffs, but
also for raw cotton, which had a mass market and could be grown in China.
Demand for cotton clothing, that is, outpaced the very considerable extension
of China's own cotton lands. But the main point for us is that, to 1800, China
remained the magnetic hub of the global economy. Silver and extractive goods
like furs flowed in; manufactured silks and porcelain flowed out. The latter
were joined by tea, whose export to Europe was booming in the eighteenth
century. Tea was "much more of a processed good than many people might
think. It required highly varied, complex procedures to convert the raw vege-
table matter of the leaves into a consumable commodity".[122] While overseas
trade was small compared to domestic commerce, it was not insignificant, and
was mostly carried in Chinese ships as far as Japan and Southeast Asia.

As we saw in chapter 9, however, the Chinese also used foreign middlemen
or agents to bring goods to them, prompting an extension of globalisation if
the relevant goods were a depleting natural resource. An example is the trade
in cured trepang or sea cucumber, considered a delicacy. China's own stocks,
and those of much of Southeast Asia, were depleted by the late seventeenth
century, and its merchants reached further afield. The Ainu of Hokkaido, in the
process of being colonised by Japan, turned to trepang gathering, and in 1764,
Japan's own fisherfolk were instructed to learn "how to prepare them in ac-
cordance with the needs of the Chinese".[123] Chinese merchants also enlisted
Makassar fishers to hunt trepang on the northeast Australian coast by 1750 at
the latest, bringing the last habitable continent into the old worlds' system well
before the British established Sydney in 1788. The Qing/Manchu themselves
could be counted among the agents of Chinese consumers. The founder himself, Nurhaci, made seven trade-tribute visits to Ming Beijing between 1589
and 1611.[124] The Manchu exported horses and furs, and obtained a near-
monopoly of the supply of ginseng, a valued medicinal root thought to be an

aphrodisiac, and gave the Han Chinese a taste of their own medicine by making them pay in silver. One source suggests as much as a quarter of Ming China's silver imports in the early seventeenth century went north to the Manchu, which "very largely financed the conquest".[125] If there was a lesson here for the Qing, they did not learn it, and continued the Ming tradition of relying on Europeans for their long-range trades, supplemented by medium-range Chinese shipping and overseas Chinese communities in Southeast Asia. They too considered such communities to be disposable. In 1742, when the Dutch apologised for a massacre of Chinese in Batavia, they were allegedly told: "those who leave their ancestors' tombs to make profits overseas are outcasts of China, and no longer have anything to do with the Court, no matter what happens to them".[126]

We saw in chapter 14 that the Russians were scouring Siberia for furs for the Chinese market from 1689, taking over from the Manchu who now had more profitable things to do. By the 1790s, the Russians were sending as many as eight million pelts a year. They also pioneered the sea otter trade, and were soon joined by the British and Americans, who also took sealing to the Southern Hemisphere in this decade. They delivered 3.5 million fur seal skins to Guangzhou in 1795–97.[127] From end to end of the vast Pacific, from the Bering Strait to the Bass and Foveaux Straits south of Australia and New Zealand, Europeans hunted furs for China. This was a new round in an old game, which had long delivered American biota and American silver to China. The Portuguese brought peanuts and maize by the 1530s and sweet potatoes by 1568, when all three were growing in southern China.[128] As noted earlier, these plants supplemented rice production and helped feed China's growing population. The scale and effect of European-mediated silver inflows into China are contested. Recently, the inflow has been conservatively estimated at 70 tons a year on average, 1571–1821, half from Europe, the other half from Japan or direct from America via Manila, implying that the effect on the vast Chinese economy was not great.[129] Given that a Manila galleon would carry at least 35 tons of silver, that there were sometimes two,[130] and that Japan supplied an average of 30 tons a year, 1560–1640, (much of it in Dutch and Portuguese ships), this looks low, and other estimates are much higher. Spanish American silver exports, which were about 80% of the world supply, had two cycles, one from Potosi, ending about 1650, and another from Mexico, starting a little later and ending in 1808. A recent thesis cites Spanish officials reporting that annual exports to Manila in the first cycle peaked at 300 tons in 1597. An accurate-looking study of imports late in the second cycle puts the annual average for Guangzhou at 87.5 tons in the 1780s, 102.5 tons in 1796–1806, and 200 tons at peak.[131]

Guangzhou was the main port for the European trade from 1757, but not the only one. Macao and Fuzhou were also important,[132] and the "outports" of Manila and Batavia, mainly accessed by Chinese ships, were even more so. Consequently, inflows through Guangzhou may not tell the whole story. European-borne gifts of silver were not big enough to afflict the Qing economy with "Dutch disease", but they were probably of significant if not vital help to it. Certainly, Europeans did everything they could to find things other than silver that the Chinese would accept. In 1659, the Dutch began selling opium grown and processed in Bengal to Chinese in Southeast Asia. Chinese shippers took it home from Batavia. The British took over this trade when they took over Bengal. Opium smoking was first banned in China in 1729, with the prohibition reiterated in 1799, but the trade grew under British management. The EIC claimed a monopoly over sales in Bengal in 1773, auctioning the product to private traders for shipment to Guangzhou. Chinese demand grew even faster than supply, and prices rocketed from the 1780s. But opium did not become Britain's leading export to China until the 1820s, when the flow of silver finally reversed. Raw Indian cotton was more important until then.[133] Tea was now the big return trade, and the British were still paying for half of it in silver in 1786.[134] Much was Bengali silver, but that did not bother the Chinese. They still sat at the centre of the global economy, with Europeans increasingly the chief agents in bringing them what they wanted. Before 1800, China was not a victim of European expansion but a silent partner in it.

V Entwined Empires

If we could suspend retrospect, it might have looked as if European imperialism, Bengal aside, had shot its bolt in the late eighteenth century. Many peoples had taken its measure. In India, the Marathas, Mysore, and the Sikhs, all with sepoy armies, plus most of the rest of the country, remained independent in 1798. The Chinese had twice slapped the Russians on the snout in the seventeenth century, and controlled growing trade with them through Nerchinsk and Kiakhta in 1800. Similarly, they controlled their interaction with seaborne Europeans through Guangzhou, Fuzhou, and Macao, the "outports" of Manila and Batavia, and their old filtration system of small islands. Elsewhere, many resilient indigenous resisters were no more under Europe's thumb than they had been a century earlier, such as the Chukchi in Siberia (chapter 14). As noted earlier in this chapter, many Amerindian groups had managed to pen empire inside a set of "European Pales". Valuable bits of empire, like St Domingue, had even begun to drop off, arguably a sign of imperial overstretch. Before the British acquisition of Bengal in 1760, and with Siberia excepted, the Dutch had the biggest European empire in Asia, and they too found that local resilience constricted them. They got the better of some major Southeast Asian trading states, Makassar in 1669 and Banten in 1682, but in the 1720s their share of "Makassar's traffic" was only 25%, increasing to 45% 50 years later.[135] They were unable to overcome the Sultanate of Aceh in Sumatra, a leading pepper trader, until 1904.[136] "In terms of surface area, Java and Ceylon were the main VOC conquests".[137] Yet the Dutch did not complete the conquest of Java until 1830, and never managed that of Ceylon. There, the inland kingdom of Kandy repelled Dutch invasions just as they had Portuguese until the Dutch were expelled by the British in 1795–96.[138] The standard estimate of European empires' grip on the world—35%—looks exaggerated, perhaps twofold. But this picture needs two qualifications. Empire might have stalled, but expansion had not, and its prime benefits were increasingly funnelling towards a narrowing number of powers.

While Southern Arabian pioneering of post-plague West Eurasian mercantile expansion into Asian seas remains under-recognised, many historians have noted that Asian maritime traders long competed successfully with Europeans. The sixteenth-century European pioneer, Portugal, was merely "part of a vast world of Asia trading in which Portuguese played a secondary role to Gujaratis, Chinese, Javanese, and Japanese".[139] This remained mostly true of European traders in general until the later eighteenth century. But European powers were the silver medallists in multiple trade races, not just one or two. Portugal's second place to all four of "Gujaratis, Chinese, Javanese, and Japanese" means first on points, overall. Taking goods from Nagasaki to Amsterdam cut out whole sequences of middlemen, so multiplying profits, and enabling lucrative "country trades" on the side, in Japanese copper and silver to China for example, or Indian cottons to Southeast Asia. Further, European powers added the Atlantic and eventually the Pacific to their ocean-crossing portfolios, while Asians did not. India and China acquired silver and useful new biota but, with the exception of Omani Zanzibar, were less able to reshuffle such things, plus slave labour and conquered land, around the globe. The classic example is sugar, an Asian crop grown on seized Amerindian land by enslaved African labour for European consumption—and profit. Such reshuffling was not one-off, but a continuing dynamic. Arabian coffee was

transplanted to Java, Brazil, and the Caribbean, and the Caribbean sugar industry was reinforced around 1790 by the introduction of superior Tahitian
cane, said to increase productivity by 60%.[140] Whatever the case with empire,
expansion and its global reshufflings delivered net profits.

Expansion could extend not just beyond empire, but also beyond commerce. It could even be exempt from empire's contractions. The British–
United States relationship after 1783 illustrates both features. American settlers
retained British language, tastes, and connections. Indeed, as I and others have
argued, its economic and cultural connections with Britain actually increased
after independence. "America's commercial relations with England remained
largely unscathed by independence".[141] The Thirteen Colonies took 22% of
Britain's domestic exports in 1772–74. Imports recovered this level as early as
1784–86, grew to 27% in 1794–96, and kept growing. After 1800, slave-produced
raw cotton exports from the US South became vital to British manufacturing.
To be sure, there were periodic tensions, and another war in 1812–14. But during that time some trade continued, the British bank Barings continued to finance the US government, and American "victory furniture" was made in
Birmingham.[142] The United States ceased to be part of the British empire in
1783. But, because strong connections persisted, it did not cease to part of
British, now perhaps "Anglophone", expansion, just as independent Carthage
continued to be part of Phoenician expansion 2,500 years earlier.

The expansion and entwining of Anglo-American whaling, a matter of depletive hunting rather than trade, shows how the relationship worked in practice. British demand for whale oil increased greatly between the 1760s and the
1820s, not just for crinolines and London street lamps (of which 5,000 were
using whale oil around 1800), but also for machine oil—it was by far the best
machine lubricant. Dutch and French whaling declined sharply in the second
half of the eighteenth century, in the face of British competition and diminishing numbers of Atlantic whales—122,000 whales are estimated to have been
killed in that ocean between 1650 and 1800. New England was the British Empire's whaling capital; its island of Nantucket was a specialist whaling crew
district. New England provided 90% of Britain's whale oil around 1775. After
American independence, the British slapped prohibitive duties on American
whale products, and grew their own fleet from 83 to 250 whalers, 1783–88. But,
with their merchant marine burgeoning, the British could not find the necessary 10,000 men, or the expertise, and had to turn to New Englanders, now
technically foreigners. Atlantic depletion pushed whale hunting on to the
Pacific from 1788. Most ships there were British, but most captains were

American—two-thirds between 1788 and 1812. Americans ship numbers grew after 1815, and British whaling peaked in the 1820s, after which the Americans took the lead in their own right. Whaling spread right across the Pacific, providing many Pacific peoples with their first encounter with European expansion, but not empire.[143]

During the long eighteenth century, there were some similarities among the big expansionists that had retained dynamism: Russia, France, and Britain. The population, foreign trade, and state revenues of all three grew substantially. Russia became a major military power *in* Western Europe, if not *of* it, fighting both Prussia and France with some success—it briefly occupied Berlin in 1762 and Paris in 1814. It also fought Poland, Persia, Sweden, and the Ottomans, with consistent success. But war expenditure and population growth overstretched the economy, taxes doubled, and standards of living fell. Serfs, on average, shrank four centimetres in height during the eighteenth century.[144] France and Britain were also economically challenged by population growth and massive war spending, but proved better than Russia at entwining with other empires. The French specialised in the Ottoman and Spanish. They pulled ahead of the Dutch and British in trade with the former during the eighteenth century, controlling about half the total.[145] Their symbiosis with the Spanish Empire preceded its official birthday, in 1702, when a Bourbon prince inherited the Spanish throne. French manufactures comprised 40% of Spain's official exports to its American colonies in 1686.[146] But French penetration of the Spanish imperial economy increased after 1702, stretching almost immediately to its Pacific possessions.[147] France's trade with its own colonies increased tenfold, and this boosted associated industries. "Analysts of the eighteenth-century French economy insist on the dynamism of its industry and trade".[148] Some have noted that in manufactures such as silk, in the growth of foreign trade and merchant fleets, state revenues and even, sometimes, in naval construction the French matched or outmatched the British.[149] This is somewhat deceptive—there were three times as many French as British—but it does help explain why France remained a contender for maritime as well as military leadership of Western Europe and its expansions.

The "second hundred years' war" between Britain and France is an oft-told tale, and needs only brief recounting here. The two countries fought seven wars between 1689 and 1815: the Nine Years' War, 1689–97, the Wars of Spanish and Austrian Succession, 1702–13 and 1742–48 (the British were already at war with Spain from 1739), the Seven Years' War, 1756–63, the War of American Independence (1775–83), and the two "French Wars" (1793–1802 and 1803–1815).

Britain was allied to the Dutch in the first three conflicts, but the Dutch pulled out of great power rivalry after 1748, with a brief and ill-fated exception in 1780–83. After 1702, Spain was usually allied to France, and the British normally had continental allies too. Britain's only defeat, in the American War, was the exception to the rule—the French were for once able to focus on naval warfare. It remains true that the British were consistently able to extract proportionately more tax from their economy than the French, and that this usually gave them an edge in sea power. From about 1710, they had Europe's largest fleet; their precedence verged on dominance from 1760; faltered in the American war around 1780; then consolidated from the 1790s.

British expansion was not just a matter of the British Empire. We have already noted several of Britain's profitable foreign entanglements: with the Dutch, 1740–80; with the Mughal Empire, whose viceroy in Bengal the EIC became, and with the United States, even after independence. The British also competed with the French in accessing Spanish American products and markets. This trade is difficult to measure because much was contraband, but is thought to have grown strongly after 1763.[150] Britain's entwining with the Portuguese Empire was stronger still. England had joined the Dutch in attacking Portugal's shipping when it was under the Spanish crown, but even before the end of the Iberian union in 1640 it had turned to friendly relations with the Portuguese in India, and in Brazil from 1649.[151] The relationship intensified after the Methuen Treaty in 1703. In 1710, Britain shipped in three-quarters of Lisbon's wheat, and all of its dyed cloth. By 1716, its trade with Portugal exceeded that of the Dutch and French combined. By 1732, there were 2,000 British merchants in Lisbon, as well as up to a hundred ships.[152] In the 1750s, the British exported £1.3 million worth of goods to Portugal, much of which went on to Brazil, importing £250,000 worth of goods in return, mainly port wine.[153] The balance, and more, was made up by Brazilian gold, about half of Lisbon receipts of which made their way to London. "So great was British involvement in the Portugal trade that by the mid-eighteenth century the small Iberian country and its rich overseas empire had become virtual economic vassals of Britain".[154] "Portugal transferred the advantages of its colonial assets to England".[155] By the 1790s, Britain had by far the world's largest navy and the largest merchant fleet, and to some extent American, Portuguese, and other foreign merchant shipping acted as its auxiliaries. Not all transoceanic routes led to Britain, but most did.

16

Plaguing Britain

THE FOURTH, plague-triggered, Great Divergence had an hourglass shape. Its broad top, fourteenth to seventeenth centuries, involved most of West Eurasia. Its broad bottom, nineteenth and twentieth centuries, impacted most of the world. Between the two, in the long eighteenth century, was the narrowing waist of the hourglass. In the process sometimes known as "The Little Divergence", the beneficiaries of plague's most dynamic after-effects on economic growth and geographic expansion declined in number, from a dozen powers, to two or three, and then to one: Britain. It was Britain alone which hosted two unprecedented developments: a single nation's ascent to global maritime hegemony, 1702–1815, and the Industrial Revolution, 1740–1840. The former was sketched in the last chapter. The latter also needs a quick outline.

Like plague itself, "250 years after its first appearance the Industrial Revolution remains one of the great puzzles of human history". Unlike plague, this is definitely not a consequence of evasion: one search finds 824,000 books and articles with "Industrial Revolution" in the title.[1] While we may no longer share the confidence of previous centuries in the permanence or universal benevolence of ongoing industrialisation, there is still no doubt of its massive importance. There is in fact some consensus on the revolution's basics. It took place first in Britain, though some argue that the country was merely the first cab of the Western European rank. We can dicker about decades, but there is broad agreement on time as well as place: roughly the century before 1840, with takeoff in the 1760s. Perhaps surprisingly, there is also some consensus that science, for all its eventual importance, was *not* a key cause. The sixteenth-seventeenth century Scientific Revolution of Galileo, Copernicus, and Newton was interested in knowledge for its own sake. It was not until the later nineteenth century that science was systematically harnessed to economics and technology. Most would also accept that the Industrial Revolution's key technological changes involved coal and cotton. The part-mechanised manufacture of all-cotton cloth took off in Lancashire from the 1760s and stimulated the development of the factory, a large, mechanised, and tightly controlled workhouse. The key cotton spinning technologies came on-stream between 1765 and 1779.

Coal had a threefold utility. It powered stationary steam engines, available from 1712 but generally uneconomic until the 1760s.[2] They mainly pumped water from mines in their early years, but eventually allowed industry to put powered factories where it wanted them, rather than always beside sources of waterpower. Effective mobile steam engines, coal's second great contribution, powered viable steamboats from 1810 and railway engines from 1830. Coal's final contribution was to Britain's iron industry, which was stuttering in the eighteenth century due to shortages of charcoal. From 1709, coal was converted to coke, which could be used to produce pig iron. Coke-smelted iron was initially inferior to charcoal-smelted iron, however, and it was not until about 1770 that the output of the former outpaced the latter. This, plus improved techniques for making wrought iron from 1784, enabled British iron production to quadruple in the later eighteenth century.[3] Like previous spasms of divergence, industrialisation was quickly emulated, going global in the nineteenth century.

Locating the roots of eighteenth-century British globalisation and industrialisation in the plague era four centuries earlier may seem to draw a very long bow indeed. I do not suggest that plague was their sole cause—only their biggest under-recognised cause. It is not completely unrecognised. It is some comfort to note that several British economic historians now see its role as seminal for their subject. "The origins of the Little Divergence are to be found in the age of plague". It was in the early plague era that "the foundations for England's later industrial rise were laid".[4] But they focus on only a few of plague's effects. They do not see them as initially European-wide, including Eastern Europe, let alone West Eurasian wide, nor that they delivered means and the motives for global expansion. If the fruits of expansion influenced industrialisation—we will see that the matter is controversial—then they too were indirect effects of plague. Britain's peculiarities, such as a vast natural endowment of coal, were important, as was its own particular history of plague influence. But so were factors forged by plague elsewhere, which then filtered and funnelled back to Britain in adapted form. They include some old suspects, like capitalist-friendly institutions and large-scale commercial farming, and some familiar but underestimated factors like plague-improved guns, galleons, and glasses, as well as plague-forged printing. There were also what I label "recurrent dynamics", which could emerge and develop with or without plague, but whose full resonance is only apparent with a plagued and globalised perspective. Among these were transnational resource pools, outsourcing—including its emergency variant, crew cultures, entwined empires, and urban colonialism.

I England's Plague Era

English history fits a schematic plague chronology rather well. Its early plague era ended around 1520 with the beginnings of demographic upturn. It featured a "golden age" for common folk which peasant rebellions between 1381 and 1549 sought to defend or restore. England's late plague era, in which Scotland and Ireland became increasingly entwined, ended around 1650—bracketed by 1642, when the great civil wars broke out, and 1665, when the last big plague strike took place. The post-plague era, 1650–1800, corresponds with the emergence of Britain as a great industrial power. Indeed, each period marked an economic step up: from "a laggard by European standards"[5] before the Black Death to the middle ranks by 1500; the higher ranks by 1650, able to compete with the Dutch and French, and the top rank by 1800. But, contrary to "Whig" histories of inexorable Progress, there was nothing inevitable about this ascent. There were many choke points where it could easily have been stymied. Four factors are widely recognised as foundations of England's ascent and as necessary though not sufficient conditions for industrialisation: commercial farming, manufactured exports, maritime enterprise, and the dominance of London. What is not always recognised is that these developments were rooted in the early plague era and owed a lot to plague's traumatic pressure-cooking.

The early plague era was the period in which English commercial farming overtook feudal and subsistence agriculture. Serfdom was dealt its mortal wound between 1380 and 1420. As we saw in chapter 3, peasants increasingly bought their cloth and paid to have their grain milled, rather than spinning and hand-grinding themselves. They bought and sold food in the market more often. Vacant land was widely available, but many peasants kept their holdings small—14 acres might be typical—to allow time for wage work which was now well paid. A substantial minority, however, acquired multiple peasant holdings, or all or part of a manorial demesne—these averaged 165 acres. They usually leased rather than bought. Lords kept the landownership and took the rents, leaving this new class of commercial farmers, known as "yeomen," to take the risks. Whether or not these farms were literally "enclosed" by fences, rough stone walls, or hedges, they were distinguished from commons and open field farming by being consolidated and having a single authorised user. The term "yeomen" is sometimes restricted to freeholders, but historians now include substantial leaseholders too. Yeomen did not experience their own "golden age" until after 1550, but they were creatures of plague. The first known use of the word in our sense, and the point where they were "clearly identifiable as a social group", both date to 1410–11.[6] The notion that peasant farming using shares of open fields was primitive and inefficient in comparison to enclosed farming has long been dismissed. But the latter did have a small edge in arable output, around 15%, due to advantages of scale and greater access to capital. In the long term, the rise of the yeoman corresponded with a modest upturn in English farm output—not in itself enough to revolutionise agriculture. Enclosure was seldom coercive before 1520, but once demographic recovery began it showed its teeth in dispossessing peasants, usually with some tincture of legality. Some 45% of English farmland was already enclosed in 1500, and the proportion reached 70% by 1700, when less than half the workforce was still employed in farming.[7]

Much has been claimed for the significance and exceptionality of these developments. They have been seen as an agrarian origin for English capitalism, indeed for global capitalism. Some still claim that "capitalism originated in the English countryside" between 1400 and 1600, displacing the "'bourgeois revolution' of the mid- and late seventeenth century", once preferred by Marxist scholars.[8] Both views have lost traction, and the uniqueness of English yeomen is also contested. "Over the last two centuries of the Middle Ages, rural elites flourished throughout Europe", producing "European yeomanries".[9] Many of the improvements in English farming were imported from the Low Countries. Yet plague's effects on English agriculture were quite important, and perhaps a little different from elsewhere in West Eurasia, socially if not economically. Peasants not only suffered a decline in living standards, they also ceased to be peasants, to a greater degree than in most places on the continent. A curious social alchemy occurred further up the class structure. Merchants merged with nobles, emulating each others' manners and customs—this also occurred in Northern Italy and the Low Countries. What may have been more unusual was that the English merger extended to the upper levels of the yeomanry, producing the country gentry, an untitled semi-aristocracy. One reason may be that the lordly demesnes which these folk acquired were two or three times the size of those in the other fertile parts of Western Europe. All this broadened the English elite, tightened its grip on the countryside, rendered it more commerce-friendly, and provided it with cheap labour after 1500.

In the early fourteenth century, England had no significant manufactured exports. Its main export was raw wool. In 1338, the crown put a substantial tax on this trade to raise money for the Hundred Years' War, which had the side effect of advantaging wool cloth exports over raw wool. This triggered a small manufactured export industry—1734 "cloths" (24×1.75 yard lengths of fabric) in 1348–49. The real boom followed. As noted in chapter 3, new figures suggest that sheep numbers fell only slightly, 1350–1400, then grew as arable land was turned to pasture, so more than doubling per human capita.[10] Raw wool exports fell, but both domestic and export wool cloth-making boomed as plague boosted disposable incomes. Annual cloth exports reached 33,000 in 1400; 81,000 in 1500; and 150,000 in 1553.[11] English production specialised in broadcloth, and at first merely supplemented Flanders, the lead producer. But it soon found new markets of its own, notably in Eastern Europe. The broadcloth boom ended in the mid-sixteenth century, but more modest ongoing exports of that product were joined by English entry into the making of the cheaper and lighter wool cloths known as the "new draperies", another post-plague shift pioneered in northern Italy and Flanders. Immigrant Flemish artisans, fleeces with longer fibres, water-powered fulling, and cheaper labour after 1500, along with growing overseas demand, all contributed to the continued growth of the English woollens industry. In 1700, wool cloth comprised 69% of English exports.[12]

Before 1350, England's trade, including raw wool, was mainly carried in foreign ships: Genoese, Venetian, Hanseatic, and Gascon. The biggest English maritime activity was commercial fishing for herring off the east coast. In 1359, the average size of English vessels large enough to be at all useful in war was only 36 tons—scarcely ships at all.[13] As noted in chapter 4, the increased number of ships per capita met plague-boosted demand for fish until about 1380. After that, new fisheries developed based on the West Country, in the Bay of Biscay and the waters off western Ireland. Exeter's fishing trade increased sixfold in value between 1383 and 1498.[14] From 1412, east coast fishers went to Iceland for cod, in "doggers" of 30–100 tons with crews of 20–40 men.[15] A company of "Merchant Adventurers" was chartered in 1407, a sign of English entry into longer-range merchant shipping. By 1450, the average tonnage of all English ships had increased to 100 tons—almost three times the size of a century before.[16] England's imports of Baltic timber shot up after the Black Death, possibly doubling between 1350 and 1400, and England was second only to the Dutch in foreign voyages to that sea by the 1490s.[17] Fishers or merchants, English crews shared the general taste for violent predation. English merchant crews plundered Genoese vessels on their way to Lubeck in 1422 and took a Hanseatic fleet in 1449. English cod fishers in Iceland kidnapped one governor and murdered another.[18] The cod-fishing fleet, which reached 150 ships in 1528, began visiting the Newfoundland Banks from 1502.[19] English merchant ships handled more and more of the country's trade—woollens out, wine and wood in. England did not reach Dutch levels of shipping tonnage until the mid-seventeenth century, but between 1380 and 1500 we see the plague-incubated emergence of English sea power.

Before the Black Death, London contained 1.5% of the population of England and Wales and 2% of national wealth, five times that of its nearest competitor, Bristol. By the 1520s, its share of the diminished population had only increased to around 2.5%, but its wealth was now 17 times greater than Bristol's. "London was much smaller than before but, on account of its close engagement with Continental markets, sharply increased its share of English wealth".[20] "Between the tax assessments of 1334 and 1515 London's share had increased from 2 per cent to 9 per cent of the country's assessable wealth".[21] As early as 1400, the capital exported half of all English cloth and handled almost half of all imports. "It is clear that the port of London was already moving towards the commanding position, indeed perhaps stranglehold, that it was to achieve in the course of the next century".[22] By 1553, London's share of wool exports had reached 90%.[23] Its growing centrality in the English economy can also be measured by such things as its share of trials for debt, which increased by 150% between 1424 and 1570. [24]

This first stage of London's growth was marked more by greater wealth and economic centrality than by population increase. Around 1500, at 50,000 people, London was still substantially smaller than before the Black Death. Amsterdam and Lubeck had shared this experience (chapter 12), growing richer as leading hubs of plague boosted trade, and more influential at the apex of an urban hierarchy, but not much more populous because urban migration barely kept pace with continued high plague mortality. Lubeck never went beyond this stage, but from 1550, as general population growth gained pace, London, like Amsterdam, grew in size as well as wealth. Over the sixteenth century, London's population quadrupled to 200,000. King James I remarked in 1616 that if this continued, "England will only be London".[25] During the seventeenth century, "the bulk of urban growth in the country as a whole took place in the capital alone", whose population was closing on half a million by 1700.[26]

II Peculiar Institutions?

Before re-joining the London escalator, we need to consider the role of institutions. As earlier chapters have noted, the most common scholarly explanation for Western Europe's rise, culminating in British maritime hegemony and industrialisation, is institutional. I confess to a long-standing irritation at ritual genuflections to, and universalist definitions of, institutions by economic historians. If one defines them, with leading thinker Douglass North, as "informal norms of behavior, and shared beliefs about the world",[27] then of course they were fundamental. But most would consider such things to be customs and ideologies. The Northodox definition is so broad as to deprive institutions of real explanatory power. I do not for one moment deny that formal institutions, including centralised states, representative assemblies, legal systems, and religious establishments could be decisive in historical change and continuity. But their influence can be exaggerated through their dominance of archives. It should be demonstrated, not assumed, and compared to that of other factors. Yet I am also aware of the danger of exasperated over-reaction to institutional determinism.

One "institutional" explanation is the (western) "European Marriage Pattern" of late marriage, less marriage, and fewer births. I am drawn to a recent iteration of this thesis, *Capital Women*.[28] It plausibly emphasises the pattern's association with women's agency and empowerment. It also takes the Black Death seriously, giving it a major role in boosting, if not creating, the marriage pattern. But, as noted in chapter 1, most evidence does not support a plagued origin in this case. Plague strikes were followed by wedding booms and baby booms; it was plague, not choice, that kept families small. But it it may still be possible that the pattern accompanied the upturn in population after 1500, with people seeking to retain the benefits of smaller families through deliberate action rather than plague mortality. Whether this can really be considered an institutional change, rather than a shift in popular breeding practices, is a matter of opinion. A comparably resonant shift, a great Mother's Mutiny in several Anglophone countries between about 1880 and 1945 that halved the size of families, has never been considered to be institutional. Whatever one labels it, a new European marriage pattern, from 1500, might have reduced the pressure of population on resources, led to higher average incomes, and so to increased "human capital" as parents spent more money on the education and training of fewer children. *Capital Women* shows brilliantly that economic history can provide new insight into the fate of the female half of humanity. But whether the marriage pattern can help explain industrialisation and divergence, great or little, is another matter.

For one thing, another impressive team of economic historians remain adamant that the pattern did not have the positive effects claimed for it on economies and innovation.[29] For another, *Capital Women* finds the pattern to be most marked in both Britain, which did experience an Industrial Revolution, and the Dutch Republic, which did not. Finally, Britain took a very long time out from the pattern in the very period of industrialisation. The average age of women at marriage fell from about 1650, human capital as measured by literacy and education actually declined in the eighteenth century, and the population grew—from 1750 at a higher rate than at any time before or since. "The 'baby boom' that took place during the second half of the eighteenth century was quite exceptional: demographic growth in England was much faster than elsewhere". *Capital Women* concedes all this, but dismisses it as a "Malthusian intermezzo" which, regrettably, will not do.[30] Industrialising Britain *inverted* the European Marriage Pattern.

A more traditional, but perhaps also more plausible, institutional argument for Britain's success in the long eighteenth century, if not for industrialisation itself, is John Brewer's "peculiarly British version of the fiscal-military state".[31] We saw in chapter 7 that European proto-nations struggled to disentangle themselves from transnational networks until after 1600, when West Eurasia's most efficient large state was the Ottoman Empire. Thereafter, however, relatively powerful and centralised "fiscal-military states" did emerge, mostly in autocratic monarchies—France, Prussia, Austria, Russia—but also in the Dutch Republic and the constitutional monarchy of Britain. The British version's key quartet included a rambunctious but often effective parliament; high but sustainable public debt managed by a central bank; spasmodically efficient government; and Europe's largest navy. Private but state-chartered joint-stock companies were also important, but were also used successfully by the absolutist French and Portuguese. The Whig tradition portrays the British package as having emerged fully fledged with the "Glorious Revolution" of 1688, which expelled the Catholic king, James II, and permanently installed constitutional monarchy and the "Protestant Succession". Brewer's formulation is more nuanced. He allows for somewhat older origins, with Oliver Cromwell's regime in the 1650s, and for Dutch precedents. He constantly reminds us that there was nothing inevitable about the emergence or survival of the British warfare state, and aims more at explaining the advent of British maritime power than of industrialisation. Others are less cautious, but do neatly summarise the orthodoxy. "It was in the eighteenth century that the British state developed the peculiar institutional combination of bureaucracy, parliament, debt and bank that enabled Britain at once to empire-build and to industrialize".[32]

Around 1500, most European states, including Russia and Poland, had something like parliaments, but outside Britain they were sidelined over time by centralising monarchies. The Civil Wars of the 1640s prevented this in Britain. Whatever the British parliament's virtues, democracy was not among them before 1867. In 1800, about 3% of British men had the vote, rising to 20% with reforms in 1832.[33] Earlier, the proportion of Scots voters (whose assembly was merged with the English in 1707) was even lower. "Scotland's forty-five representatives in the Commons in 1774 were returned by a grand total of 428 voters", an average of less than ten each.[34] What parliament did do was represent local, regional, and national landed elites, and deliver their (often grudging) consent to increasing taxes, some of which they themselves collected. It also proved able to incorporate new elites: the upper ranks of the yeomen, leading merchants, and privileged Scots.

English long-term public debt had its origins in the 1650s, but moved up a major step in 1694 in partnership with the Bank of England established in that year. The Bank was a privately owned chartered company, like the East India Company, but its state-delegated monopoly was joint-stock banking, not Asian trade and empire. Various forms of short-term public debt continued to be used, but were periodically consolidated into long-term debt. Particular loans were secured by particular taxes, and were increasingly seen as reliable. By about 1730, shares of the public debt were easily saleable on the stock market, in effect meaning that the principal need never be repaid. The constraint was the proportion of government revenue needed to pay interest, which after 1707 was never less than 30%.[35] The system had its crises, but it consistently enabled Britain to heavily outspend its French rivals in war on a per capita basis. France still had an absolute edge due to its greater size, but this was usually balanced by its higher continental military commitments. Britain's public debt grew from £16.7 million in 1697 to £745 million in 1815,[36] while its government revenues, corrected for inflation, increased ninefold between 1680 and 1815.[37] More than 80% of this money was spent on war, preparation for war, or the payment of interest on war debt.[38]

British bureaucracy in the eighteenth century was therefore mainly focused on financing, recruiting, and supplying the armed forces, and on managing the interference of party politics, interest groups, and still-influential sovereigns—a warfare state. It was actually a mixed bag in terms of efficiency, as Brewer and others acknowledge. "Eighteenth-century administration was 'an extraordinary patchwork—of old and new, useless and efficient, corrupt and honest—mixed in together'."[39] The excise service, which collected indirect internal taxes on such items as salt and alcohol, is widely seen as very effective. By contrast, the customs service, which collected indirect external taxes on the likes of tea and tobacco, is widely seen as corrupt and inefficient, though that may be because many people considered smuggling a socially acceptable crime. In any case, Britain's fiscal-military state leaked like a sieve at the borders.[40] Sources from the diaries of Samuel Pepys to the magisterial histories of Nicholas Rodger suggest that the Royal Navy had almost as many problems with its own warfare state as with its enemies at sea. The early eighteenth-century Admiralty was "in the business of getting higher real expenditure for the Navy by exploiting the ignorance of Parliament and the Treasury".[41] Rodger and Brewer both remind us that the effectiveness of British statesmen, admirals, and generals fluctuated, and that Britain's rise, 1688–1815, was something of a rollercoaster. In the 1690s, "close as the English came to disaster, they succeeded in averting catastrophe".[42] "A dispassionate analysis of the British war effort in the wars of 1739 to 1748 would have to report a large measure of weakness . . . In the aftermath of the Seven Years' War [1756–63], fumbling British governments had rapidly dissipated what seemed an unassailable position of power and prestige".[43] As late as 1783, after the loss of 13 of its American colonies, Britain's rivals rubbed their hands with glee at "the end of Britain's brief and precarious period as a major power".[44] But rising taxes, rising public debt, grudging elite support, and spasms of good management delivered by fiscal-military institutions was indeed a necessary condition of Britain's rise to European—and global—maritime preeminence. It was far from the only cause of economic and military ascent, however, and it is by no means clear that it was a major direct cause of industrialisation itself.

Just how "peculiar" was Britain's fiscal military state? British historians are now acknowledging that central banking and long-term public debt were derived from the Dutch, and that the early breakthroughs in public debt and naval power date to Cromwell's military dictatorship in the 1650s, and not to the "Glorious Revolution" of 1688. But where did the Dutch, or Cromwell, get these ideas and, crucially, the evidence that they could actually work? Northern Italian city-states was chapter 10's emphatic answer. The key "peculiar" institutions, plus joint-stock chartered companies and the patenting of inventions, were plague-refined products of Catholic urban clannishness, not enlightened, rational, Protestant individualism.[45] The analogies with Genoese experience go deeper than a shared liking for St George. As with the Genoese public debt in the fourteenth and fifteenth centuries, a large range of people bought into British debt, in the eighteenth century, increasing the number of people with a stake in the system in both cases. As in Genoa, British elites preferred to make the lower orders pay the taxes where possible, but came to the party with their own money in an existential crisis. There just might have been a direct north Italian link. Even a cursory search turns up a dozen Genoese prominent in sixteenth-century English finance, particularly from the great Vivaldi syndicate, and two comparable north Italian financiers in the early seventeenth century. One of the latter, Philip Burlamachi, was reputedly the first, in 1636, to suggest an English central bank managing public debt. He was descended from Calvinist refugees who had fled Lucca around 1560, and had remained a part of their network. He financed England's disastrous war with Spain in 1624–29 to the tune of £150,000. The second was Horatio Palavicino, scion of a wealthy Genoese clan—his mother was a Spinola. He too was a leading English financier and was knighted by Elizabeth I in 1587. But it is his family's entwining with the Cromwell clan that is most intriguing. Sir Oliver Cromwell of Hinchinbrook, "uncle and godfather of the future lord protector", married Palavicino's widow in 1601. He then arranged the marriages of three of his own children to three of his Palavicino stepchildren, "so that there was no way in which the Palavicino fortune could not fall into the Cromwell family's hands".[46] As it happens, an earlier Cromwell—Thomas—Henry VIII's ill-fated chief adviser, had bought the Vivaldi's London mansion in 1534.[47]

Uncle Oliver may not have had much influence on his nephew, and these connections may not be very significant in themselves. But they seem scarcely noticeable in the Whig tradition, and even in more recent and convincing formulations of the "peculiar" British fiscal-military state. They do suggest that the seventeenth-century English were well aware of north Italian precedents, and not solely through Dutch intermediaries. Central banks, long-term public debts, elite representative government, chartered companies, and powerful navies were all stock-standard Genoese institutions. The truly unusual magic trick performed by the British (and by the Dutch, as we saw in chapter 12) was the hybridising of plague-tempered city-state characteristics, institutional or not, with those of a nation-state. Amsterdam and London were the magicians.

III London's Empires

One could almost see the British civil wars beginning in 1642 as a rebellion by King and Countryside against London's growing hegemony. The monarchy was restored in 1660, but London continued to hold much of the country in either a friendly embrace or an armlock. Economic historians now acknowledge that it was not agricultural revolution, or evolution, that induced London's growth, but the reverse. While three-field rotations, turnips, clover, seed drills, and enclosure had their roles, "agriculture was an early beneficiary of the capital's growing appetite for provisions and organic raw materials, as is now acknowledged in accounts which stress the drawn-out character of English agricultural progress".[48] Between 1550 and 1800, the urban giant gradually integrated and transformed the rest of the country, select parts first. Initially, it was London's contiguous hinterland that was transformed by commercial farming and regional specialisation. Kent supplied most of London's wheat in the early seventeenth century, and Sussex and Suffolk, most dairy products.[49] The intimacy of the relationship is illustrated by the way in which changes in Kentish farming corresponded with the surge in London's growth that so alarmed King James I. Between 1580 and the 1630s, the amount of Kentish grain sent to London increased fivefold, and the number of large yeomen farms (over 100 acres) at least tripled.[50]

What I can add to the story is urban colonisation. As with Istanbul earlier, a fast-growing, high-paying, but demanding urban market plus reliable coastal shipping soon brought into being "virtual" London hinterlands some distance way: in Cheshire for example. By 1750, London's wholesale cheese-mongers monopolised the trade in Cheshire cheese. "In 1766, Daniel Defoe noted that Cheshire 'though remote from London is one of those [counties] which contributes most to its support'".[51] London kept growing. The city doubled in size during the eighteenth century, to about one million, dwarfing Paris and Istanbul, let alone Amsterdam. Increases in farming productivity continued, and more land was brought into production through such means as draining wetlands and re-converting pasture to grain fields. London's immediate hinterland came to specialise in market gardens, milk, hay for horses, and fattening pastures for livestock, now driven from as far away as Wales and Scotland.[52] But burgeoning population growth, now England-wide, began to overhaul food production around 1760. The initial solution was Ireland. Until 1758, Irish food imports were banned to protect British farmers, except for provisions such as salt pork and beef for colonial plantations, fleets, and armies. From then, Ireland met most of Britain's food deficit until the 1840s. This required transforming its economy to specialise in large-scale wheat and pastoral farming, marginalising Catholic peasants, eventually with disastrous results in the form of famine in the 1840s.[53]

Specialised foreign outsources, some verging on "virtual hinterlands" or semi-colonies, were also emerging, though they came to full fruition only in the nineteenth century. After the advent of recurrent warfare with France in 1689, French wine and brandy were usually banned. Despite substantial smuggling, Portuguese wine regions near Oporto and on the island of Madeira developed specifically to supply London and its network with fortified, and therefore well-travelling, wine. The trade was run by resident British merchants. Some 70% of Portugal's port wine production went to Britain in the eighteenth century; the Oporto region was dependent on the British market. Perhaps Britain's ascent could have done without the port and madeira, but it could not have done without wood products and other naval stores from the Baltic resource region. Britain's dependence on the Baltic (and Norway and Russia) for naval stores increased steadily, though the intimacy of the relationship with particular ports and regions may not have reached Lubeckian or Dutch levels. Like the Dutch, British fleets repeatedly visited the Baltic to keep it open to their merchant shipping—20 times between 1658 and 1814.[54] From 1630, docksides piled with timber and naval stores are thought to have made London more vulnerable to great fires. By 1750, half of Britain's overseas trade by volume consisted of Baltic wood products, plus naval stores like flax for sails and hemp for rope. In 1787, 850 British ships a year went to the Baltic, compared to 350 Dutch.[55]

An expansion of London's domestic empire, similar to that in agriculture, occurred in manufacturing, shipping, and fuel supply. Until 1650, London did much of its own manufacturing, including ship-building, which it dominated.[56] More proto-industry, notably ironworking, took place nearby, drawing on the diminishing forests of the Weald of Kent and Sussex for fuel.[57] An ever-growing London then developed other "virtual hinterlands" far from the capital, including industrial auxiliaries and outports. These regions did rather better than Ireland from their intensifying links with London. Outports like Liverpool and Glasgow burgeoned in size and wealth. Shipbuilding was increasingly delegated to other ports. Industrial auxiliaries also appeared, including Manchester and Birmingham, which had waterpower, cheaper wages, and sea access to London through Liverpool and its River Mersey. Birmingham's tool-making career dates back to the early plague era, when it "developed a niche in the production of scythe-blades".[58] Regional historians may not like the terms "outports" and "auxiliaries", but the fact is that no other city in Britain was even a tenth of London's size in 1800.[59] London's "growth as a centre of concentrated demand and conspicuous consumption . . . boosted production of a host of industrial manufactures at many remoter locations, with Londoners providing much of the capital".[60]

After 1550, London's population growth outpaced all available wood fuel supplies, and it began shipping in coal from Newcastle to heat its houses, cook its food, and fuel the many industries requiring heat, such as glass-making and sugar-refining. Under this stimulus, and with other regions also running short of fuel, British coal output increased 66-fold between 1560 and 1800. Coal deposits in other regions served the rest of the country, but Newcastle remained London's main supplier because of ease of sea transport and the quality of its coal. The Tyne-side mines were forced to go deeper and became damper, and so needed pumping out. Horsepower was used at first, but by the late seventeenth century the scale, depth, and flooding of mines had exceeded its capacity. Various steam contrivances had been developed in France and elsewhere, notably by Denis Papin, a Huguenot refugee who spent some years in England and invented the pressure-cooker in 1679. He produced a design for an atmospheric steam engine around 1690. In England in 1698, Thomas Savery adapted such ideas and built an engine which he hoped could be used for draining mines. It did not work, but in 1712, Thomas Newcomen developed another engine, adapting Savery's work in turn, for the same purpose. It "could do little more than pump water and was grossly inefficient by later standards".[61] It used so much coal that it was only really viable on top of a coal mine, where its fuel was virtually free. It was used for this from 1715, and by the 1740s was common in Tyneside but not yet elsewhere.[62] From 1765, James Watt improved on the Newcomen steam engine with a model that used much less fuel. It became commercially available in 1776, powered its first cotton factory in 1785, and spread nationwide. From 1810, the Newcastle artisan George Stephenson, among others, developed high-pressure engines, compact enough to power boats and railway locomotives, and the steam power revolution was fully under way.

Clearly, there were multiple factors behind this, not least the impressive ingenuity and determination of the key inventors. The sheer size of Britain's natural endowment of coal deposits was unusual, if not unique—a few other regions in Europe and China matched it. Britain's profligacy with its forests was perhaps another factor. But careful coppicing was practiced, and it seems forest management was simply ambushed by London's growth. While aspects of this growth had post-plague precedents elsewhere in West Eurasia, its intensive use of coal did not. If there was one unique thing about eighteenth-century Britain, it was its massive employment of coal. As early as 1700, the country produced 80% of Europe's coal.[63] This must have been a factor behind the re-invention (there was an unconnected medieval Song Chinese precedent) of coked coal in 1709. But the blowtorch of London demand was also crucial for developing steam engines, creating a long lineage of accumulating invention. Early Newcomen engines used up to 45 pounds of coal to produce one horsepower for an hour, as much weight as a horse itself over the course of a day.[64] So expensive a technology is unlikely to have progressed without London's need for more and more coal, specifically from Newcastle's deep, wet, sea-accessed mines.

The last two paragraphs mostly follow Robert Allen's incisive 2009 study of the Industrial Revolution. Allen also posits another factor, which may be more problematic. England's exceptionally high wages, he argues, made labour-saving through steam engines and mechanised cotton spinning more important than elsewhere. He considered this a long-standing difference, dating back to an unusually slow and slight fall in real wages after 1500, shared only by the Netherlands. More recent work suggests that English real wages too fell "dramatically" from the later fifteenth century until 1650.[65] Household incomes, measured by average GDP per capita, fell less sharply, due to a further increase in "industriousness"—more hours worked by men, and more women and children's wage work. Other recent research suggests that real wages did increase from 1650, but that this was true of many regions in Europe, not just England. "As late as in the mid-1720s the real wages of labourers in southern England, Spain, Portugal, Italy, Sweden, and Germany were on a very similar level. Only after the 1720s did a wedge develop between England and the rest of Europe".[66] Allen's "high wage thesis" has also fallen foul of those who insist that, at least until 1850, the Industrial Revolution had few if any benefits for workers. Together with evidence of static working-class heights, indicating no improvement in nutrition, they make a convincing case for the persistence of widespread poverty, which high wages should have alleviated. That average GDP per capita was slowly creeping up in the eighteenth century does not necessarily disprove this, because averages are not medians—the income levels around which most people cluster.[67]

Most evidence for real wages relates to urban male wages, especially London wages in the case of England. The recent research supports the view that real wages in London were higher much earlier than in the rest of the country—they had to be to keep attracting in-migration to a destination known to have higher mortality and higher costs. But, on a country-to-country comparison, "it appears that real wages of agricultural and building laborers in England were not higher than the levels prevailing in France before 1750", due largely to grain being cheaper in France.[68] London's real wages were an exception. They were higher than those in Paris, as well as those in the rest of France and England. By 1750, however, both high wages and new spending habits were spreading from London to the regions and industries whose connections with it were strongest, the virtual hinterlands. Between 1750 and 1790, wages for male labourers in Lancashire grew by 64%, compared to 20% in Kent.[69] By the 1780s and 1790s, while agricultural labourers country-wide spent 75% of their incomes on food, mining and industrial workers spent "only" 58% and 60% respectively.[70]

The consumption patterns of English workers were changing in the eighteenth century, more so than in France or elsewhere. The post-plague "golden age", 1350–1500, had addicted the English to sugar and strong drink. Clinging on to these new consumption patterns led to the first great rise in "industriousness" in the sixteenth century. In the eighteenth century, "another industrious revolution was in progress",[71] to permit consumption of tobacco, gin, tea, and more sugar to go with it. Diverting spending to these addictives, as people do even in the present, may help explain the lack of improvement in nutrition as measured by height. In any case, the new consumption was most marked first in London, and then in its satellites, beginning with Newcastle and its region.

> According to Lorna Weatherill's national survey of inventories 1675 and 1725, North-East England led the way in chinaware ownership in urban areas, with 15 per cent of urban household recording chinaware in their inventories, compared with 13 per cent in the urban areas of London, 4 per cent in East Kent and 2 per cent in Cambridgeshire . . . Newcastle's close relations with London were an important accelerator in the transfer of the latest metropolitan fashions in dress, furniture and china to Newcastle, together with the latest books, plays and ideas.[72]

This was urban colonisation at work—coal out from Newcastle, culture back from London, the latter subsidised by the former. "Rising demand for coal in the capital created a near-umbilical economic and cultural fusion between Newcastle and London, the consumption habits of the former being moulded by its relationship with the latter".[73]

London continued to dominate England's growing internal and external trade, "combining the interests of multiple regional trades alongside international commercial networks".[74] "In 1700, London alone accounted for 69 percent of all inland trade, with the majority of this figure being provided by coastal shipping, especially in coal and grains".[75] London also dominated overseas trade, with Europe and, even more, with the wider world. Like Amsterdam, London had led its country's transoceanic trade from the outset. All of the first 20 English ships that went to West Africa for slaves and gold in 1553–65 came from London, while the Royal Africa Company charted in 1660 was London-funded.[76] Other ports, notably Bristol, had a share in the Atlantic trades, but the East India Company was "birthed by London merchants and investors".[77] "Trade with Asia was managed exclusively from London and overwhelmingly financed by the investments of the London merchant community".[78] By 1686, "colonial trade had become by far the largest consumer of London's overseas trading tonnage".[79] In 1700, it "handled 80% of all exports to Africa, the West Indies, and American colonies".[80] London was never a city-state, but it had become an empire-city.

IV Peripheral Peripheries?

Why did London grow so big? Robert Allen thinks that the fruits of overseas expansion were the leading stimulus, but his is a minority position—let us call it "externalist" in that it allows for global inputs. Most experts are "internalist", claiming that colonies were "neither a necessary or a sufficient condition for the industrial revolution; it is likely that the latter would have started even without colonial exploitation . . . On the whole, the role of the 'periphery' was 'peripheral.'"[81] This last phrase was coined by leading economic historian Patrick O'Brien in 1982. He himself now sees it as overstatement, but it is still often quoted, and it remains the majority view.[82]

> Economic historians are . . . in broad agreement that the colonial trades were not consistently profitable enough to account for any significant share of the capital accumulation required to fuel the industrial revolution. O'Brien estimates that under the most generous of assumptions, the colonial trades accounted for no more than 1 per cent of aggregate GNP for western Europe, and not more than 10 per cent of gross investment.[83]

Even without political control and without the support of the British navy, Britain would have been able to secure what it needed from the rest of the world as long as it could pay. The Industrial Revolution did not require the creation of British India or the control of Canada, nor did it depend on the cheap sugar from the Caribbean.[84]

One usefully blunt scholar, Peer Vries, claimed in 2015 that "among economic historians one can hardly find anyone still defending" the externalist position— that British industrialisation required non-European inputs.[85] In fact, the debate is still very much alive. It has developed a polemical edge, particularly with regard to the profits from Atlantic slavery. Any implication that internalists are defending the slave trade is unfair. Whether or not it was a significant contributor to industrialisation, it remains a crime against humanity. But it is equally unfair to imply that externalists are driven by "political correctness" rather than by evidence. After all, the beginnings of British maritime hegemony were quickly followed by the beginnings of industrialisation, a rather curious coincidence.

The debate dates back to 1944, when the Trinidadian historian (and prime minister) Eric Williams published *Capitalism and Slavery*.[86] He argued that the British abolition of the slave trade (1807) and of slavery itself (1833) owed more to the declining profitability of slave-worked Caribbean plantations than to British humanitarianism. This is unconvincing, because Britain's sugar plantations were booming right up to 1807.[87] But Williams also suggested that, earlier, the British exploitation of slaves had provided profits that laid the basis for the Industrial Revolution. Other scholars emphatically rejected this. But since 1997 several historians have revived and developed William's second argument, including Robin Blackburn and Joseph Inikori.[88] Most recently, Sven Beckert posited the eighteenth- century emergence of a British-led system of "war capitalism"—violent, exploitative, and now land-hungry too. "The beating heart of this new system was slavery." War capitalism was "the precondition for the Industrial Revolution".[89] Beckert puts his emphasis on slave-produced cotton, not sugar. He is quite right that a rising tide of slave-produced raw cotton from the southern United States was crucial in fuelling the massive expansion of the British cotton industry after 1800. It is also true that the much smaller quantities of raw cotton required by Britain between 1774 and 1800 were supplied by slaves too, working in Brazil and the Caribbean.[90] But sufficient raw cotton was arguably readily available elsewhere. If the sweat, blood, and shortened lives of slaves were vital to the Industrial Revolution before 1800, sugar seems a more promising candidate.

It has long been argued that sugar literally powered industrialisation by giving British workers consuming it, usually with tea, shots of cheap energy.[91] I have been sceptical about this notion because, while sugar provides energy, it does not provide nutrition, only "empty calories". But English sugar consumption did reach 10.5 kilograms per capita in the 1770s, by far the highest in Europe. Sugar intakes were higher still in London and its satellites.[92] I have since found that slave workers in the Americas, notoriously including women and children, were themselves big consumers of sugar, in the form of chewed raw cane or cane juice, when working around the clock during the harvest season. Early Japanese industrialisation in the later nineteenth century was also marked by a big rise in sugar consumption.[93] Acquiring addictive sugar and tea are generally seen as key motives for the second surge in British "industriousness" in the eighteenth century. As noted in chapter 3, "industriousness" could be redefined as "overwork", reducing adult leisure time to the point of "wage-slavery" and involving child wage workers. There might after all be a correlation between this and sugared energy. A less speculative possibility is the stimulus sugar trades gave to the growth of the British economy. We need to consider this as part of the broader question of the contribution of "the periphery"—never a happy term—either to eighteenth-century British economic growth in general, or to industrialisation directly.

Many scholars, externalist as well as internalist, are prone to myopia when considering global inputs into eighteenth-century Britain. They consider only a part of the picture: just cotton, just sugar, just British colonies, just colonies. A 2018 study of the whole British slave plantation complex in the Americas broadens the picture somewhat, suggesting it contributed around 11% of GDP in 1800, much higher than earlier estimates.[94] Taking into account all British colonial trades is another improvement. As quoted above, estimates of the colonial contribution to Western European GDP overall go as low as 1%. But the figure is much higher for the most successful expansionists. A recent estimate for the contribution of colonial trades overall to British GDP is 8.5% in 1720, 10% in 1755, and 12% in 1790.[95] This predates the new research on the higher contribution of the slave complex, so the figure may creep up a little further. Other scholars have tried to calculate the colonial contribution to capital formation—the fraction of a country's income productively re-invested in the economy. They too come up with figures ranging from 8% to 12%.[96] This may still seem small. Similar figures for British investment in the United States in the nineteenth century have also been dismissed as trivial. But both eighteenth-century Britain and the nineteenth-century United States had fast-growing populations, with which housing, infrastructure, and existing industries had to keep up. Most capital formation was already spoken for, as it were. Capital from outside the domestic economy might therefore have been disproportionately significant for new industries.

This depends partly on how much expansionist profiteers, such as big merchants, West Indian sugar planters, and "nabobs" from India, invested productively, rather than spent on such things as country mansions and London townhouses—the building of which still contributed to overall economic activity. When planters and nabobs did invest rather than consume, it was mostly in agricultural estates and stocks and bonds, not coke-fuelled iron foundries or cotton mills. The latter are thought to have been funded from loans from friends and family, and from ploughed-back profits, and to have avoided loans from banks or big merchants. Their capital requirements are said to have been modest in any case. There are some problems with this received picture. Mill owners bought their raw cotton from merchants in transoceanic trades and, at least until 1774, sold their product to the same people. Substantial commercial credit, supplied by merchants who sourced their profits from outside Europe, must surely have been involved.[97] Cotton mills might not require a lot of capital, but cotton printing works did. "The average manufacturing business in England in the 1780s was insured for a value between £300 and £500 . . . Yet just among the London calico printers 1755–1790, ten businesses had insurances at a value more than £5,000"—one approached £10,000.[98] It seems unlikely that ploughed-back profits and small family loans could have met this level of investment. Expansionist profiteers did keep some of their money in banks, which made some loans to industry.

Global inputs were never distributed equally throughout the British economy, but were biased towards particular activities and places. European expansion had created settler societies in the Americas accustomed to buying its manufactures, and also addicted West African slave trading societies to some of them. Though growing fast, Britain's domestic market remained limited; its extra-continental markets grew faster. "In 1726–30, colonial markets accounted for 16.2 percent of British exports; by 1781–85, this proportion had increased to 39.4 percent, but at least half of that went to what was just about to become the United States".[99] One issue with this is that, as the last chapter noted, the United States had left the British Empire, but not the global British economy. Another issue is that the figure must exclude exports to non-European markets that were *not* either British colonies or the United States. In 1784–86, years of peace, 56%, not 39%, of British domestic exports had destinations outside

Europe.[100] Legally or illegally, Iberian America was an increasingly important market for British goods in the late eighteenth century. Some were smuggled in from the West Indies; others sent via Lisbon and Cadiz, where British shipping was dominant. Trade with Spanish America grew in wartime, with Spanish, Dutch, and French exports being much more disrupted than British ones. During the French Wars, "British textile manufactures achieved a virtual monopoly in [all] American markets".[101] Finally, while exports to the Americas included long-standing trades in provisions, tools, woollens, and linens, they were particularly crucial for fast growth in new industries: coke-smelted iron wares and all-cotton cloth. The Americas took at least a third of the *increase* in British iron production in the 1750s and 1760s, as the new coke-fuelled industry found its feet.[102] Africa and America took most of Lancashire's infant cotton industry's output between 1721 and 1774, and a fluctuating but substantial amount thereafter. "Between 1780 and 1801 the Americas accounted for roughly 60 percent of additional British exports. British innovators were largely dependent on overseas markets as their industries expanded".[103]

Global inputs were also regionally selective. London itself was not quite so dominant in British intercontinental trade in 1800 as it had been in 1700. Some trade had been delegated to outports like Liverpool, which had rocketed in population from 5,000 to 90,000 over the course of the century.[104] But profits and economic activity generated by expansion were still overwhelmingly concentrated in London and its urban satellites. On his modelling, writes Allen, in the seventeenth and eighteenth centuries "over half of England's urban expansion is attributed to empire".[105] This should now seem very plausible. London's hyper-growth in turn was the main engine behind Britain's agricultural and industrial transformation. In particular, its demand for ever-increasing amounts of coal from deep, wet, mines pressure-cooked—a nod to Denis Papin—the development of steam engines, seeing them through their experimental phase, 1710s–1760s, when they were too fuel-intensive to be economically viable. Plague prompted London's early growth and that of the maritime power necessary for overseas expansion. Returns to Britain from overseas expansion prompted more London growth, which in turn helped incubate industrialisation. On this basis alone, both plague and "peripheries" begin to look less peripheral.

Some key questions remain. Does "colonial trade" or the benefits "attributed to empire" capture the whole of Britain's eighteenth-century dividend on West Eurasian global expansion? Is the dividend measurable solely by its monetary value, or are there other measures? What remained of the dividend once costs, most notably expensive warfare, were deducted? We have already seen that colonial markets for British exports extended beyond its own colonies to those of other powers, to its ungrateful US offspring, and to West Africa. We have also seen that Britain was not just an empire in itself, but an empire-broker, replacing Genoa as the master of entwining with other empires: Dutch, Portuguese, Spanish, and Mughal. In the mid-eighteenth century, Dutch investors held about a fifth each of Bank of England and British East India company stock, plus about a sixth of Britain's national debt. Much of this money came from Dutch expansion—the VOC had averaged a profit of 22.5% over the previous 120 years.[106] About half of the Brazilian gold reaching Portugal between 1700 and 1760 ended up in Britain—perhaps a million sterling a year. Is it counted in estimates of colonial contributions? The evidence "does reveal a genuine dependence of the London mint house on the supply of Portuguese gold".[107] "Brazilian gold stimulated British textile exports, increased British coinage, and permissively infiltrated the British economy".[108] While inflows declined after the 1760s, some do think that they "helped lay the basis for the Industrial Revolution".[109]

This is only part of a bigger problem with the internalist position, which seems strangely immune to the general acceptance of American bullion's substantial impact. It "accelerated the development of the European economy".[110] "Had it not been for a 33-fold increase in the silver coinage in the Old World between 1500 and 1800, centralization of European fiscal systems might not have occurred".[111] "In western Europe Spanish American bullion was a major factor in the commercializing process and the development of domestic markets".[112] Between 1550 and 1750, the Americas supplied 80% of world production of silver, and 70% of gold, the great bulk of which went initially to Europe, where at least half of it stayed. This damaged the Iberian economies, but boosted others, including those of France, the Netherlands, and Britain as noted in chapter 10. It caused inflation, but less so as economies grew, and more in farm products than in manufactures, whose export it encouraged. "Bullion became a 'harvested exportable' that lubricated European economies and made the Atlantic a marketplace".[113] In the eighteenth century, it lubricated the British economy most. True, much bullion was re-exported to China and India, but there it purchased goods that were sold for big profits. Gross profits on Britain's tea trade were around 110%.[114]

Vital global inputs were not always a matter of cash value. Britain in 1800 was already beginning to outgrow its capacity to feed itself, and it had long been short of other essentials. Unlike spices, sugar, cotton, and silk, these were not very profitable or prominent. They included such mundane things as hides for leather, an often forgotten necessity.[115] A world with no rubber or plastic needed a lot of it. Domestic leather output was one of the few things not increasing in eighteenth-century Britain.[116] Imports of "red Russian hides" helped,[117] but demand began to exceed even this supply in the earlier decades of the century. Britain turned to Spanish American cattle regions, such as Argentina, which was exporting 1.5 million hides a year by the 1780s.[118] Imports supplied only 5% of Britain's leather in 1750, but 20% in 1800.[119] A similar tale can be told for ships. "By 1760 probably one English ship in four was of American origin, and for Scotland the figures were even higher". Other ships were built in India. Most ships were still British made, but colonial sources added some 50% to British output by 1775.[120]

An intriguing case of the long-range "outsourcing" of things traditionally produced at home was saltpetre, an essential ingredient of gunpowder. As mentioned in chapter 5, it could be produced artificially, but the "ballistic power of saltpetre depends on strength of original chemical bonds broken during detonation, usually stronger in natural saltpetre than in artificial".[121] India had the world's best and largest natural deposits, especially in Bihar, a province adjacent to, and often included in, Bengal. From the mid-sixteenth century, most Western European expansionist powers came to rely on Indian saltpetre, downgrading and even suspending their own production. "English domestic production of saltpetre ended in 1667, and was only used as a last resort thereafter".[122] An attempt to peacefully allocate Bihari supplies between the French, Dutch, and British East India Companies in 1736 soon broke down, and the Dutch briefly dominated the source in the 1740s. But, like so many others, this global input began to funnel towards Britain from 1757, after which "almost all saltpetre shipped from India to Europe . . . was carried in British ships".[123] This was a major problem for the French. Even in peacetime, they struggled for means of "delivering us from the tribute paid to England for the saltpetre of Asia". They did increase their domestic production from 1784, but Britain's Bihari supply remained superior in quality and quantity, and in wartime they kept it for themselves and their allies. Although absent in Britain's traditional military history, this is now thought to have given it an advantage in the French Wars. Between 1793 and 1809, the EIC took home at least 50,000 tons of saltpetre, and were made by the state "to sell this saltpetre at less than a third of the cost of shipping it".[124] Unlike the French, the British army and navy had enough gunpowder to fire live rounds in training, and to use high-firepower line infantry formations against low-firepower column formations in battle. It was also "the superior grade of saltpetre that gave British cannon an edge".[125]

Outsourcing from other continents only supplemented Britain's supplies of hides and ships, but it dominated supplies of saltpetre, the first of many traditionally domestic products for which Britain was to become dependent on the "periphery". The second was prime timber. From 1806, and more effectively from 1808, Napoleon famously attempted to impose a blockade on Britain's trade with continental Europe. It is generally seen as a failure, and indeed did not greatly affect most elements of the British economy—except prime timber. "In 1808 the virtual closing off of the Baltic forced British importers to shift rapidly to the American sources of supply," just as the Dutch had done for salt in the early seventeenth century (chapter 12).[126] In fact the Americas did not yet have a large or widespread timber export industry (except in the form of ships) to which one could easily turn for 100,000 tons of prime timber. The main new supplier was a small new British colony, New Brunswick, carved out of Nova Scotia in 1784 to accommodate refugee loyalists from the United States, whose forestry industry had hitherto been focused on busily building itself. Between 1806 and 1812, its timber exports rocketed from 5,000 to 100,000 tons. Exports from a nearby water-accessible part of Quebec increased 13-fold, 1808–1812.[127] Between 1803 and 1807, Britain had drawn only 6% of its timber imports from Canada, the rest from the Baltic. Between 1808 and 1812, the Canadian periphery provided 62%. Could Britain's expanding fleets, industries, and infrastructure have survived without this emergency outsource?[128]

Expansion did have its price, of course. Some feel that military and naval costs are likely to have outweighed, or almost outweighed, the benefits of empire.[129] Others wonder whether expensive conflict "crowded out" investment in British industrialisation, so delaying its full advent until after 1815 or, by contrast, that it was actually the stimulus of warfare that brought the Industrial Revolution to fruition. Recently, Priya Satia has argued precisely this: "war made the industrial revolution".[130] She makes a fascinating case for a fruitful interaction between the Birmingham musket-making industry and the Ordnance Board, the government department in charge of supplying weapons to both army and navy. She argues that the Board deliberately sponsored Birmingham gun-makers from 1692 to avoid over-reliance on the London gun-makers who had hitherto monopolised supply. She also shows that various firms in various separate subcategories of the trade, makers of gun locks, stocks, and barrels, were encouraged to cooperate to the point that the

Birmingham industry became integrated, a "virtual factory". Earlier, Philip Hoffman argued similarly but more broadly that "price data carry the startling implication that Europe's military sector could maintain productivity growth for centuries, a feat virtually unknown elsewhere in pre-industrial economies".[131] Hoffman ranked France with Britain in musket production, but Satia shows that, helped by burgeoning Birmingham production, Britain pulled ahead of France by 1803—in absolute, not just per capita, terms. Others suggest that it was naval construction that stimulated industrialisation: dockyards were Britain's biggest workplaces, and ships of the line, of 74 guns and more, its biggest capital investments. Around 1800, the dockyards began using advanced machinery to mass-produce tackle blocks, and steam power to pump out dry docks.[132] There is no doubt that war was among eighteenth-century Britain's biggest industries, but such arguments seem to put the cart before the horse. During the climactic conflict of 1803–1815, war industries began applying industrial techniques, but this does not explain the earlier emergence of those techniques. Moreover, war industries did not produce new technology comparable to the steam engine or the cotton spinning mule. Muskets were much the same in 1850 as in 1700, despite Birmingham's "virtual factory". The same is largely true of warships. While successful British warfare may have sheltered, supplied, and boosted the Industrial Revolution, and while it had significant indirect effects, it did not contribute directly to its causes.

On the other hand, opinion has now turned against the view that, in 1793–1815, the costs of war "crowded out" other investments. For one thing, fear of the French "crowded in" continental elites from Amsterdam, Hamburg, and elsewhere, who fled to Britain with their money, skills, and connections—the Rothschilds are only the best known example.[133] Total real GDP increased despite inflation, camouflaged somewhat by high population growth.[134] British exports grew 92% in value.[135] Between 1792 and 1815, alongside a huge navy, British merchant marine tonnage more than doubled, from 1.2 million to 2.6 million tons, despite heavy losses to privateers, more than the rest of Europe combined.[136] The increase was not just in long-range shipping, but also in coastal vessels, which confirms continued domestic economic growth. "The French Wars period seems to be associated with a tremendous increase in coastal tonnage".[137] There were periodic crises, but the general impression is of a bustling economy, rather like that of the United States in World War II. It was the *end* of the war, in 1815, that produced recession.[138] Somehow, the British had found a way of combining intensive warfare with continued economic growth. It remains true that Britain's rise faced a number of wartime crises, or choke points, 1689–1815. Some are well-known: the financial crisis of 1696–97, which forced Britain out of its first French war; the Jacobite invasion of England in 1745, which reached to within 130 miles of London; the multiple crises of 1797–99, when French landings, naval mutinies, Irish rebellion, and another fiscal crisis forced the Bank of England to suspend the convertibility of its paper money into gold and eventually forced the government into the unfavourable Peace of Amiens in 1802. One less recognised "choke point" was the timber crisis of 1806–15. Another was a crisis in maritime manpower in the later eighteenth century.

Earlier chapters have noted that European powers had many transnational tricks up their sleeves to ease the impact of war on sea trade, such as flag-shifting, smuggling, and licensed exemptions from trade embargoes, which were often halfhearted in any case. Normally, however, these were palliatives rather than solutions—the War of Spanish Succession, for example, halved both French and British cod fishing.[139] The capture of merchantmen by naval ships and privateers was the obvious part of the problem, but beneath this lurked the issue of maritime manpower. Western European states simply did not have enough sailors to crew both an increasing number of merchantmen *and* an increasing number of warships: they could increase their navy or their sea trade, but not both at the same time. For a trading nation, the biggest potential cost of warfare was that it could cripple maritime commerce in this way. Landsmen could be trained but this took time, and efficient ships required a quorum of able seamen. Merchant seamen moved into warships and privateers on the outbreak of each conflict. Sea trade therefore declined for most powers in most wars. In 1750, a peacetime year, there were perhaps 65,000 British merchant sailors, similar to the number available to the French or Spanish. By 1792, before the war, the number had increased to 101,000, far more than France or Spain.[140] During the war years 1793–1802, merchant seamen increased further, to 138,000, *despite* there being another 129,000 men in the Royal Navy.[141] More landsmen and more marines (shipboard soldiers) would account for part of the naval number, but clearly Britain's professional sailors increased far faster than its own population growth or the numbers available to its continental rivals. While the American War may be an exception, during the Seven Years' War, 1756–63, and the French Wars, 1793–1815, the British were able to *both* fight more and trade more.

The British manned these vast fleets partly by drawing on the old North Sea labour pool, particularly Scandinavia, as the Dutch had done before them.[142] The maximum of one-quarter foreigners in any ship's company imposed by the Navigation Acts was relaxed in wartime.[143] But this pool had its limits and was also supplying the growing merchant fleets of Sweden and

Denmark-Norway. "Neo-European" crew regions, such as Bermuda and Nantucket, were also beginning to contribute to Britain's maritime crew. Even after the United States became independent, several thousand American sailors were to be found in the British navy, and even more, as we have seen, in the British whaling fleet.[144] There was also an increasing use of Scots and Irish sailors.[145] At least the former may have been influenced by the embryonic sense of British nationalism identified by Linda Colley. The images, tracts, ballads, books, and newspapers behind this emanated from London, a cultural dimension mirroring its integrative effect on the British economy. It was not that economics determined culture, but that both used the same transport. Just as Istanbul's urban colonisation encouraged Ottomanism, so London's did Britonism. This was only one of a number of ways, on which I cannot dwell, in which Scots gingered-up British expansion. Still more manpower came from a "crew culture" effect. London's influence on the British economy increased the size and productivity of farms, which caused them to use less labour. Grain-growing concentrated increasingly in the most fertile parts of the country, while others became, in effect, crew regions. The share of men working in agriculture fell from 44% to 35% between 1755 and about 1813, releasing 9% for work as merchant and naval sailors and in the army, as well as in embryonic industry.[146] To some extent, restructuring Britain was becoming a "crew country", a step up on a crew region. A huge rise in illegitimacy, a characteristic of crew culture, over the eighteenth century supports this impression.[147]

Non-European outsources of hides, ships, and saltpetre, traditionally produced at home, enabled Britain to begin to escape its own, and indeed Europe's, ecological limits, as did massive emergency supplies of Canadian timber. Resort to transnational manpower pools, some now outside Europe, plus growing crew regions, allowed it to overcome the normal economic constraint on maritime trading nations at war. All this suggests a cause-effect spiral between "peripheral" inputs and Britain's economic and military ascent. But, leaving aside London's impact on steam technology, it might still be argued that such developments were not direct causes of the Industrial Revolution. This brings us to cotton.

V Transposing Lancashire and Bengal

Until 1750, Britain produced little in the way of all-cotton textiles. Like many other West Eurasian countries, it had a small fustian industry, producing mixed cotton and linen cloth, plus a modest textile-printing industry whose main business was colouring plain Indian cottons, imported undyed, for re-export. Fustian manufacture was concentrated in Lancashire, which already produced linen cloth. Its "humid micro-climate" suited the processing of cotton and linen fibres.[148] The printing was mostly done in London. Average annual imports of raw cotton for cloth production in Britain crept up slowly from 1.1 million pounds a year in the 1700s decade to 2.1 million in the 1740s. At midcentury they were still under 3 million pounds, less than French imports, and "dwarfed by Bengal, which produced about 85 million pounds per year".[149] The small amounts of coarse British cloth produced, around 50,000 pieces, went, not to the domestic market, but to West Africa and North America, and even here Indian cloth was preferred when available. "Britain's cotton producers were still not able to compete seriously on world markets".[150] As late as 1774, Lancashire had only eight cotton factories. From that year, however, the industry took off in no uncertain terms, with annual exports valued at £2.6 million by the 1790s, around a million pieces, and with Lancashire cottons now dominating some segments of the British domestic market for cotton cloth.[151] Cotton still only contributed 3.4% of total British exports in 1800, which has deceived some (including myself in earlier work) into discounting cotton's role in early industrialisation.[152] But by 1801–1802 it already contributed 17%—more than one-sixth—of all value added by British industry, and its exports "had surpassed those of woollens" in value.[153] Cotton manufacturing continued to grow exponentially. By 1830, it accounted for half of all exports, and it was Britain, not India, that was clothing the world.[154]

Standard explanations for the sudden emergence of Britain's world leading cotton industry are not wholly convincing. The idea that it arose from a "push-me pull-you" competition between weaving and spinning technology is plausible at first sight. The invention of the flying shuttle (1733) increased the productivity of handloom weavers, creating a bottleneck in spinning, which was overcome by the spinning jenny (1765), the spinning frame (1769), and the spinning mule (1779). There was now a bottleneck in weaving, which in turn was overcome by the invention of the power loom (1785). We have seen that similar ratcheting competitions occurred after the Black Death, between wrought and cast cannon, and gun galleys and gun galleons. But if Britain had a special propensity to such inventive ratcheting, or indeed a special incentive for it in the form of exceptionally high wages, then it should have appeared first in the wool industry, which was very much larger.[155] Another point is that the power loom "did not make meaningful inroads into the cotton weaving trade before 1810" when the exponential growth of cotton manufacturing was already 30 years old. Indeed, the number of handloom weavers kept growing until 1825.[156]

A second explanation is the shelter provided by the "Calico Acts" of 1701 and 1721, designed to stem the flood of Indian cottons into Britain after high tariffs had failed to do so. The first Act banned Indian cottons for domestic consumption except for undyed cloth to be printed locally for re-export. The second tightened the ban, which was not lifted until 1774. These Acts prohibited domestic cotton manufactures too, except for export, and were intended to protect manufacturers of wool and linen, not cotton. Wool interests in particular had strong political leverage because much of the rental income of the landed gentry derived from sheep farming. Much of the work in the new cotton industry was done by women and children at low rates of pay. An interesting exception is the spinning mule itself, which required considerable upper body strength to operate before it was connected to water or steam power, and so employed, perhaps for the first time in British history, male spinners. These men were highly paid, but this was compensated for by a shift to female handloom weavers with lower wages.[157]

Others have noticed flaws in our understanding of the birth of British cotton manufacturing, one of the two great engines of industrialisation, and that it might be filled by considering India. "This dramatic change in international competitive advantage, which must surely rank as one of the most important developments of the industrial revolution period, is often described entirely in terms of developments within Britain, without any reference to India".[158] As chapters 13 and 15 indicated, Bengal became the world's leading cotton manufacturer under the Mughals by the mid-seventeenth century. Its exports were dominated by the British by the 1730s, who acquired full control by 1765. At first, Britain's involvement expanded Bengal's cotton export industry, though this was not necessarily good for the workforce. "The cotton export trade from Bengal increased by about 200 per cent during the period 1720–95, from 780,000 pieces to 2.3 million pieces".[159] Exports declined from 1803, as Lancashire cottons took over. They began selling in India from 1820, like coal to Newcastle, and they dominated the Indian domestic market within a few decades.[160] In a nutshell, Britain seems to have picked up the world-leading Bengali cotton export industry and transferred it to Lancashire during its first half-century in control of Bengal.

Attempting to emulate India cottons—and Chinese silks and porcelain—was of course a very old game in West Eurasia. Emulation normally involved diffusion from one intermediary region to the next by migrant artisans. This was the case with the transfer of cotton colouring techniques to Western Europe, as against spinning and weaving. Armenians transferred Indian block printing and dyeing methods in the seventeenth and early eighteenth centuries, coming via Iran and the Ottoman Empire. The latter, and some European countries—the Dutch Republic, to 1750, and a French-financed industry in Catalonia, to 1780—held the lead over England in cotton printing.[161] Here was a typical, slow, and broad diffusion of partial emulation, centuries old and West Eurasian-wide. But artisanal transfer did not work for the other segments of the industry: spinning and weaving. The French made a gallant attempt in 1785, when they brought in 50 skilled Indian spinners to teach French apprentices, but the "results were disastrous, to say the least", and the Indians went home in 1787.[162] This was an era in which the last thing an Indian artisan wanted to do was live in Europe. There were two alternative avenues of transfer. One was the close investigation of Indian techniques on the spot by Europeans, who could then write and tell about them. The other was the cumulatively increasing mass and range of examples of Indian cottons available to even the lowliest craftsmen in Britain, enabling them to "unpick", as it were, the production process.

From 1757, an increasing flow of "journeymen-consultants were sent from Europe to Bengal to observe production and to advise regarding potential improvements in technique and the production of patterns, cuts, and weaves suitable to prevailing European tastes".[163] No doubt they did, and they may also have transferred crucial knowledge back to Europe. Yet attempts to pin down particular transmissions have so far proved frustrating.

> The East India companies were indeed keen to find out how exactly production worked The companies did their best to acquire knowledge of the processes of bowing, [carding, or aligning the cotton fibres in preparation for spinning, with a bow-like instrument] spinning and weaving—shown in the many 18th century prints and drawings of textile manufacturing in India. However, with the exception of textile printing and painting, there is no clear understanding of how much this acquired knowledge of production processes in India informed the development of a European industry.[164]

Nevertheless, it seems reasonable to assume that British control of Bengal gave it broader and deeper penetration into cotton's secrets than mere mercantile access had done. Britain also took the lead in access to Chinese porcelains in the 1760s. Emulation in Britain's top pottery region, Staffordshire, suddenly improved in the same decade, notably in the hands of Josiah

Wedgwood. Improvement continued, alongside growing imports of genuine china, totaling perhaps 215 million pieces by 1791, after which Staffordshire china began displacing Chinese china in the British domestic market. [165] But this British product never had the global edge that Lancashire developed in cotton cloth—Delftware and Dresden china were up there with it. The difference might be that Britain physically controlled the leading Indian cotton textile region, Bengal, but not a leading Chinese one.

Still, the sheer mass of imports as models and rivals mattered in cotton too. Apart from the flying shuttle (1733), the key early innovations came in spinning rather than weaving, in three steps: early spinning machines (around 1740), the spinning jenny and the spinning frame (1765–69) and, most important, 1774–79, when the hybrid spinning mule was developed. Despite the Calico Acts, Indian cottons continued to find their way into the British domestic market through smuggling.[166] The EIC itself was not the villain. Between 1701 and 1774, the cottons it imported into Britain were kept in sealed warehouses and sold to other merchants, who exported them to overseas markets in the Americas, West Africa, and continental Europe. The rough parity of imports and re-exports throughout this period suggest that the company largely kept to the rules.[167] It was in any case not keen on promoting rivals to its own Bengali producers.[168] But the EIC's "doppelganger", the private British traders and their transnational partners discussed in the last chapter, had no such scruples. It was behind the smuggling of Indian cotton cloth, particularly the higher grades which carried illicit costs better than low. "Very large quantities of goods, especially tea and textiles, were often run ashore in Ireland, the south of England, and the continent", from which they often crossed the Channel.[169] If the ebb and flow of illegal cotton textile imports tracked that of legal ones (for re-export), which seems likely, then the modest technical advances in Britain around 1740 and in the 1760s matched modest surges in Indian cloth imports—they declined between the two periods.[170] But it was not until after the lifting of the Calico Acts in 1774 that the key technology, Crompton's mule, emerged, perhaps in response to a really big surge in Indian imports, now legal.[171]

The challenge British inventors set themselves was to replicate Bengal's finest "high count" cotton yarn, such as muslin. In the case of John Wyatt, an inventor of spinning machines in 1739–43, "it is clear that the prospect of producing finer yarn was firmly in mind, and in the minds of the other famous innovators," namely Arkwright and Crompton. Wyatt managed a 15-count yarn in 1743, Arkwright and his spinning frame up to an 80-count, in or soon after 1769, and Crompton and his spinning mule even more from 1779.[172] "The effective imitation of Indian goods in England was made possible by the invention in 1779 of the muslin wheel or mule".[173] Cost reductions were initially much greater in fine cloth than in middle-grade and coarse cloth. The first plummeted in price 15% a year between 1785 and 1800; the second only 4%; while the third, the "mainstay of pre-invention industry", scarcely changed at all.[174] These inventors did not imitate Indian skills—they could not—but *substituted* for them to make the same article. It was not just that multiple spindles saved labour costs. It was also that inventors could disaggregate and re-aggregate the manual spinning process, merging, leap-frogging, shortcutting, and mechanising particular parts of it through trial and error, so substituting for Bengali artisan skill inculcated from childhood.

British innovation in spinning, then, correlates with periods of high Indian imports into the country. By 1784–86, annual Indian cotton cloth imports into Britain were worth £1,344,000, while re-exports were worth only £395,000.[175] The difference, of almost a million pounds sterling, may indicate the level of legal British domestic consumption of Indian textiles after 1780. In response, raw cotton imports also rose—almost fourfold, 1781–1786.[176] Weavers were drawn from the county's linen industry, which therefore almost disappeared by 1788. "Within about fifteen years of its introduction, the mule had come to dominate spinning" in Lancashire.[177] "Cotton textile production increased tenfold between 1770 and 1790 and tenfold again in the following dozen years".[178] By 1794–96, legal Indian imports consumed in Britain (i.e., the difference between imports and re-exports) had almost halved compared to ten years earlier, suggesting that British-made cottons were now competing effectively, in at least parts of the market.[179]

Why would the East India Company have acquiesced in this? Revelations about its corruption in India, and its involving of the government in expensive warfare, reduced its leverage with the state in the 1770s and 1780s. It tried to strike back, first by sending its Indian raw cotton to China rather than Europe, leaving Lancashire to rely on slave-produced Caribbean and Brazilian cotton. It then reduced prices of cotton textiles by screwing down the wages of Indian artisans, helped by the acquisition of French and Dutch production networks, which gave it a near-monopoly of Indian export production.[180] Now state action did come to the rescue. British cotton producers, who had now gained some political clout, responded in turn by pressing for tariff increases on Indian cloth for British domestic consumption, succeeding in 1797. Between that year and 1819, "under pressure from textile interests", tariffs were increased a dozen times, to the point where they exceeded 85%.[181] To top things off, British domestic exports of cotton cloth were given a substantial state bounty between 1783 and 1812.[182] Furthermore, the EIC now had plenty of other business. Its exports of Indian cotton textiles to other markets continued to grow until 1803—indeed, they doubled over the previous decade. The EIC was also becoming a major military power, and perhaps the conquest of Mysore took precedence over dealing with emerging competition in Lancashire.[183] Further, its China trade was burgeoning, now shipping in Bengali raw cotton and opium as well as bullion in return for silk, porcelain, and tea. Britain's "brilliant tinkerers" in cottons were certainly determined and ingenious. But they were striving to make an old Indian product in a new way, not something new. Some mystery remains, but the increasing availability of Bengal cotton textiles, as models and rivals, coupled with the deeper penetration into Bengali crafts enabled by conquest, may have played a key role. Bengal turned out to be Britain's Potosi in other ways too, supplying the silver, raw cotton, and opium that turned the China trade in its favour, and the cash, saltpetre, and sepoys that helped it win its wars in India and elsewhere.

To bring the strands of this chapter together, Bengali factors joined many other so-called peripheral inputs into British maritime hegemony, economic growth, and industrialisation. These included profits and economic stimulus from slave plantations and settler markets, and from the China trade and the hunt trades for codfish, beaver, seals, and whales. Iberian American bullion; outsources of hides, ships, and prime timber also seem crucial. These were fruits of expansion—not just Britain's, but also that of the other West Eurasian empires that it managed to partially cannibalise. In turn, the motives and the means for expansion were forged in the hellish furnace of plague, so expansion's ricochets back home were indirect plague effects. The Black Death also had direct effects on Britain. It incubated commercial farming, manufactured exports, maritime enterprise, and London's centrality even before 1500. Other influences included plague-refined city-state institutions, more crew regions, and recurrent but plague-boosted dynamics such as larger and more fluid transnational resource pools and intensified urban colonialism. Other West Eurasian powers shared these effects, and had growing "empire cities" too. But, compared to London, these either had less access to global inputs (Moscow, Istanbul), or smaller national bases (Amsterdam, Lisbon). All were less well-endowed with accessible coal, and none grew as fast or as far as London, much of whose growth came from global trade. Local factors, in the industrial hearths of Lancashire, Staffordshire, and Tyneside, were also important. But it was the London magnifying glass that concentrated plagued and global rays on these hearths until they burst into industrial flame.

Conclusion

SOME 5,500 YEARS ago our series of great divergences began. Ecology was implicated in the birth of all four, entwining with human agency. These divergences were not just one-off events, but continued in spurts, like new volcanoes given to spells of dormancy. They were "great" not because of their great men, great triumphs, or great art, but because they affected great numbers of people, sub-globally, semi-globally, and globally. The first, horse nomad, great divergence was triggered by people of Central Eurasia being blessed or cursed with unusually complete economic dependence on horse-hunting, which pressured them into domesticating horses and learning to ride them. As we saw, this tripled human power, speed, and range. But it was a thousand years before steppe riders erupted into semi-global expansion. This eruption stemmed from the invention of the war chariot 4,000 years ago, a complex machine. It is echoed in the "sulky" still used in harness racing. The war chariot weighed only 34 kilograms and could travel 33 kilometres an hour. It required several kinds of wood, found in regions far apart, as well as specialised crafts in metal and leatherwork, such as three-layered leather tyres. Its horses needed seven months to train.[1] The biggest eruption from the steppes was the Mongol Empire of the thirteenth century, possibly influenced by climate change and based on five or ten horses per man as well as the genius of Chinggis Khan. The time-scale of the Fourth Divergence was somewhat shorter, 1350–1800. It was launched by the Plague Revolution, 1350–1500, continued with Europe's expansion to chief globaliser if not hegemon, and culminated in the Industrial Revolution, 1760–1840. As on the steppes, the people in the lead changed repeatedly. The space affected grew over time, while the space to which prime benefits accrued narrowed, from the whole Steppes to the Mongolians, and from all West Eurasia to the British—apologies to both peoples for the analogy.

This book has argued that plague's dire crucible triggered the Fourth Divergence. This is not to deny that there were pre-requisites and co-requisites unrelated to plague, some stemming from earlier divergences. West Eurasian expansion is hard to imagine without horses, or without the incentive of acquiring Further Asian super-crafts. The Muslim South's burst of expansion after 1350 utilised existing Islamic pathways; Christian Europe sought to emulate them, or substitute for them. Monotheism might have been an unplagued component of the Terrible Twin's expansion kit, contributing cohesion and perhaps aggression.[2] Monotheists did not just have their own single god, but dismissed all others, as lesser prophets, demons, or delusions, rendering unbelievers fair prey for conquest and conversion. This may help explain the third *and* fourth divergences, but not the latter alone. Much the same applies to the great Graeco-Roman legacy, which was shared by Islam.

Since Machiavelli, scholars of Western Europe have wondered whether its stable yet competitive state system gave it an edge. A powerful recent iteration of this thesis, by Walter Scheidel, argues that it dates from the "escape from Rome" in the fifth century CE.[3] Yet there is little sign of an edge between 400 and 1400, or indeed of a stable competitive state system. Once it arrived, it was indeed important. As both Scheidel and I have pointed out, Columbus could shift his project to Spain once Portugal had turned him down, while there was nowhere else for Zheng He to go. Furthermore, while interstate competition did not improve military technology between 1500 and 1800, it did keep it up to its plague-forged level, whereas China could abandon its emulations when no longer needed.

City-states too have been suggested as the key cause of a Western European path to capitalism and world empire that began around 1100—too early for plague.[4] That states ruled by traders should be the most trade-friendly is surely no surprise. It did not surprise one Englishman in the 1650s. "It is no wonder that these Dutchmen should thrive before us. Their statesmen are all merchants".[5] Mercantile city-states had long featured all over the old worlds, cropping up at the hubs of trade: in Sogdiana and Phoenicia as well as Greater Greece, in the Inner Asian oases of the Silk routes, in East Africa, and in Southeast Asia. Western Europe did have more city-states than most subcontinents, but it was plague that picked and boosted the winners among them. One winner, Genoa, proceeded to midwife Iberian expansion, from 1415. Another, Lubeck, created an informal patchwork empire that mobilised the resources of northeastern Europe, only to see it taken over by Amsterdam. Amsterdam and London were not city-states, but rather mega-cities in wider domains, booming at least partly because of global trade. They meshed their nations with plague-sharpened characteristics of city-states, some of them institutional.

This book has identified several "recurrent dynamics" in global history, which could and did operate independently of plague pressures. One, depletion-driven expansion, was possibly the engine behind the great dispersals of the Thule Inuit and the Polynesians. Like the latter, Vikings too may have been drawn on from island to island by the rapid depletion of abundant and helpless sea mammals and breeding seabirds. Some Norsemen at least preferred the flesh-mines of Iceland and Greenland to the fleshpots of Paris in the ninth and tenth centuries. But the renewal of depletion-driven expansion by North Europeans from 1350 was a product of the Black Death and its paradoxical boosting of demand for furs, fish, and whale products. When Europeans began to find furs less fashionable around 1700, Qing Chinese demand took up the slack, helping to prompt the great European hunt trades to go fully global, and bringing some prey animals to the verge of extinction.

We have seen how plague provided means as well as motives for geographic expansion—and for economic growth. Labour shortages put a premium on non-human sources of energy: waterpower, wind power, gunpowder, as well as work animals, which instantly doubled in number per human capita after the Black Death. More and better water-powered fulling mills, silk twisting machines, metal refining hammers, and blast furnaces quickly emerged. Farm labour gained an iron edge, among other plague boosts. Scribal and artistic labour was enhanced by better light: more eyeglasses, window glass, whale oil lamps, wax candles. Military labour was enhanced by steel armour and all-steel swords as well as many more guns, now including handguns. Some technologies were boosted by plague pressures, a few were given birth by them. Mechanised printing was one, topping off a sequence of plague-pressured labour-saving improvements in book production, tracked in chapter 5. Big three-masted, full-rigged ships, galleons for short, were another. They too emerged in traceable plague-pressured steps. These developments did not create an inexorable trajectory towards industrialisation. Most technologies, not just the military and the maritime, remained stable between 1500 and 1800. But they did create an expansion kit which gave West Eurasia enhanced access to the resources and manufactures of the rest of the world.

Having an Atlantic coast helped when it came to galleons, and galleons in turn helped Europe to eventually overhaul the Muslim South, by giving it still better access to global inputs. Crews and settlers also help explain this "Little

Divergence". Chapter 6 noted that "disposable males", a second recurrent dynamic, were the cutting edge of great expansions, Arab, Viking, and Mongol, and that pre-plague Europe was short of them. Plague's brutal solution was the regional specialisation of grain farming, which mass death concentrated on the most fertile regions, leaving others to become "crew regions". Crew culture flourished afresh in the nineteenth century. It was less family farmers than single crewmen that staffed the growth industries of booming settler frontiers, living in camps, but building towns, as well as canals, harbour works, and eventually railways. It was they who crewed ships and riverboats, and staffed lumber and mining camps, giving early booming settler societies a much higher crime rate than later ones, whose growth was slower and whose genders were more balanced. The late heyday of Anglophone crews came in the gold rush era of mid-century, in California, Victoria, and Otago, to which they moved independently, free of employers and state help, in masses of a hundred thousand.

Crew cultures may also have existed in non-European, non-Islamic societies, perhaps in Fujian or South-Central Africa. Overseas settlement certainly did—Chinese in Taiwan, Japanese in Hokkaido. Here too were "settler societies". But there were not many of them. Long-range settlement does seem to be something of a European specialty, and this was important for both early modern expansion and its durability in the present, in the form of the many countries still dominated by "Neo-Europeans". But it was not "driven on by an innate restless energy"[6] as an eminent prehistorian recently claimed. Vikings apart, Europeans stuck largely to their own continent until 1400. Before that, they were usually the invaded, not the invaders. Afterwards, only a few European nations produced settlers in any numbers before 1800: Russia, Britain, Iberia. The reasons were convergent, but contingent—previous experience of short-range settlement; distant possessions and a "folk filament" to convincingly communicate its merits; and, perhaps, the more widely shared memory of the post-plague "golden age". These factors continued to apply in the nineteenth century, though a "settler revolution" moved migration up a whole order of magnitude.[7] As chapter 6 argued, racism seems inescapable in explaining the unusual success of European settler societies. It does not feature in lists of "Killer Apps" or tools of empire.

The Ottomans were great users of crew cultures, but mostly of European ones—Albanian, Vlach, and Greek. They were not great commercial hunters, though they were avid consumers, nor great users of print, galleons, or long-range settlement. But they were quick to take up guns and gunpowder, gun galleys, and gunboats. They were the first big modern state in West Eurasia because they were the best large-scale plague managers. It was the Ottomans who were the first, since the Romans, to have a regular army and navy, notions of a "civic imperial" collective identity that transcended ethnicity (though not religion), plus a meritocratic bureaucracy. The last was behind the hybrid Ottoman timariot system, a curiously modern feudalism in which a large army of fief-holders was rendered durable and reliable by a small army of scribes, some wearing eyeglasses. Scribes also helped with sophisticated Ottoman re-covery/colonisation techniques, including "monastic" Sufi-led colonisation, and their various man-powering gambits, ranging from the attraction of vol-untary Christian renegades to the systematic extraction of slaves from outside regions, mostly by auxiliaries. Ottoman influence filtered west and north, a process camouflaged by Eurocentrism. The Ottoman raising of the bar for Europe in war and statecraft, and their diversion of European expansion away from the south, is more easily traceable. But their leading early emulators were the Iranian and Turanian conquistadores who founded and maintained the Mughal Empire, and restructured the Bengal economy, to Britain's ultimate benefit.

The Ottomans were also great practioners of "urban colonialism", our third plague-boosted recurrent dynamic. Istanbul's unusually strong growth eco-nomically transformed select real and virtual hinterlands, otherwise known as contiguous and distant town supply districts. This was easiest when the dis-tricts were worked by Ottoman settlers, as in Deliorman in Thrace, but there were few cases of this. Urban colonisation could be good or bad for those in the countryside. Bursa, Edirne, and the Crimean cities became Istanbul's urban auxiliaries. A strikingly similar process emanated from London after about 1650, where it was good for Lancashire, Cheshire, and Tyneside but not for Ireland. It was the London effect in the nineteenth and early twentieth centuries that sparked my notion of "urban colonisation". In earlier work, I called it "recolonisation" because most of the transformed economies had pre-viously been settled by Britain.[8] London's tentacles reached all the way to the US West and to Canada, then still further to Australia and New Zealand, and to "adopted dominions" like Argentina. This did not cause British industriali-sation, but it did sustain it, with flows of cotton, timber, wool, and food, as well as gold-rush bullion. Even if reliable surpluses of goods had been available elsewhere, they would not have come in forms so well-adapted to Britain's needs. Only a global perspective lets you usefully compare the histories of London and Istanbul, and of Thracian and New Zealand fat-lamb farming.

———

This book is an experiment in intensive global history, bringing global perspectives to bear on a particular historical problem. In this case the problem is "Why Europe", but the approach might also work for "Why China", "Why Islam", or even "Why not Africa". It requires crossing, but not ignoring, conventional boundaries of time, space, and discipline. In theory, all of history's subdisciplines and sister disciplines should be involved. In practice, one picks those that seem most useful, or least used, and tries to force them into conversation with each other, however much their dialects differ. Economic history features large in my own toolkit, which is a little chastening because I have been critical of the subject as currently practiced, and because many interested in mainstream history are not great fans of it. But in the end I make no apology for its prominence. Economics is not some arcane semi-science but the very guts of history. Whether they had food in their bellies, clothes on their backs, and roofs over their heads mattered to people in the past, and it should matter to us. My other tools include the "recurrent dynamics" noted above, plus one that this study forced on my attention: hybridity. In history, one and one do sometimes equal three.

The prologue mentioned the classic hybrid, bronze, and noted several other pre-plague examples. The plague era itself produced more cases of resonant hybridity, such as the way in which Amsterdam and London hybridised city-state and nation-state. The Second Plague Pandemic was itself a hybrid, of a kind all too familiar to us in the present, a co-venture between a terrible disease and human connectivity. Despite the best efforts of Kazakh great gerbils, the Black Death could not have made it from the Tien Shan to Kazan without caravans, if not Mongols. The economic enterprise of the neo-Mongol Golden Horde helped plague sweep downriver to the Black Sea with the grain trade, where Genoese shipping took it on to the Mediterranean—thanks again, Genoa. Most if not all of the subsequent widespread strikes also relied on bulk trade for rat re-settlement. By the late fifteenth century, increasing trade connectivity spread those non-plague killers, smallpox, influenza, and typhus, to the Atlantic shore, where they sometimes found their way into European expansion kits. In the Americas, they demonstrated the contrast between differential and non-differential epidemics. Europeans were largely immune to smallpox, and may have had greater resistance to influenza and typhus than Amerindians. These infectious diseases were therefore a relative advantage to them. As other historians have noted, if the Mongols had brought plague to

Europe, and if they had benefited from a nomad exemption, our books might have been written in Mongolian, or Chinese if that had become the language of the Khans' scribes.

No study of the spread and rise of Europe can wholly avoid Eurocentrism. The term actually conflates two different things: Euro-bias and Euro-focus. Euro-bias is a not-uncommon form of collective subjectivity. Most civilisations preferred to emphasise their own virtues in explaining their success, rather than their vices, the accident of their "natural endowment" of resources, or "mere" contingency. But it is Europe's particular auto-hagiography that happens to be our own problem, and some less blatant elements of it still permeate our thinking. When, not long ago, I first wrote the words "modern Asian imperialism in Europe", meaning the Ottomans, my computer software gave them green underlining, indicating dodgy prose. Asians did not do modern empires, it seemed to Microsoft, least of all *inside* Europe. The very conception of Europe as a continent separate from Asia is contestable. The dividing Urals are about the same modest height as the Appalachians. There is no point in trying to redefine continents. What we can do is question the role of innate culture traits and of peculiar institutions, testing them against explanations that demonstrate a causal sequence of intersecting contingencies. You have to have some Euro-focus in addressing the "Why Europe" question. But I have tried to re-contextualise and cross-germinate it by positing the earlier great divergences, by insisting on the crucial roles of Eastern Europe and and the Muslim South, by reconsidering the ricochet effects of global expansion back to Europe, by taking ecology as seriously as any other historical variable, and by reminding us that China featured prominently as a magnet for, and silent partner of, European expansion.

Though it might sometimes seem so, this book does not argue that plague was the dominant piece, the master variable, in the three-dimensional jigsaw of global history after 1350. Cultures, institutions, and individuals all had their roles in West Eurasian economic development and geographic expansion, which in any case was by no means the only game in town. The book does argue that plague was the biggest *missing* piece. It is not completely missing, and several important exceptions to plague evasion have been noted, especially among economic historians. Yet few scholars see it as a major long-term determinant of Europe's own history, let alone of its global expansion. A surprising number avoid it like the elephant in the room or, indeed, "avoid it like the plague". More allow it a tragic and evocative vignette, as a terrible but ephemeral natural catastrophe, but do not allow it the potential for revolutionary effects. One or two other historians have noticed this. "A certain historiographical consensus . . . has tended to minimise the effects of the Black Death."[9] "Ambivalence or caution prevails in the historiography of the Black Death."[10]

Historians rightly suspect master variables or single-factor determinisms. They are also suspicious of exogenous (external) variables, particularly curveballs from nature. Humans are supposed to make their own history. "We historians are extremely uncomfortable with the idea that natural forces in some way circumscribe human agency."[11] Most major historical phenomena do have multiple causes, and natural disasters or sudden climate change can easily become simplistic silver-bullet solutions to complex problems. Yet the Black Death not only halved populations, but also doubled the average amount per person of *everything*. In this it differed from other catastrophes. Flood, fire, earthquake, and war destroy buildings, crops, tools, and animals as well as kill people. Famine leads starving people to eat their breed stock and seed corn. Plague inverted the balance not just between labour and capital, but also between people and all kinds of goods and resources, and gave common folk among the survivors a taste of a materially better life—one they did not forget. "Revolution" may be an over-used term, but if the sudden halving of people and the doubling of everything else is not potentially revolutionary, what is?

ACKNOWLEDGMENTS

FIRST, LET ME THANK New Zealand's Marsden Fund for generous support in 2010–12, which enabled me to embark on this project. Its willingness to devote some of its limited humanities research funding to an ambitious global history seems to me greatly to its credit. I am delighted to, at last, deliver on its investment. During this period, I was based at the Stout Research Centre, Victoria University of Wellington, where I received important help and support from Richard Hill, Joe Lawson, Neil Quigley, Franchesca Walker, and, above all, Charlotte Bennett.

At Oxford, from 2012, many colleagues, visitors, and students helped in various ways, and I thank them all. The following deserve special acknowledgement: Cheryl Birdseye, Erica Charters, Claire Phillips, and Chris Wickham. From those further afield, I would particularly like to acknowledge Felicity Barnes, the late Chris Bayly, Rob Bell, John L. Brooke, Linda Colley, Michael Kelly, Joachim Muller, Neil Pearce, James Pullen, Bob Tristram, and Leslie Young. Quite a number of listeners to my G. M. Trevelyan Lectures at Cambridge in 2014 surprised me with their generous encouragement of a generalist blundering into their fields of expertise. I hope they will accept a generic but heartfelt "thank you". The same applies to the many specialists on whose work I have drawn—and sometimes questioned or redeployed—particularly to the authors of digitally acessible graduate theses.

I also owe thanks to Ben Tate, Josh Drake, Karen Carter, and Dimitri Karetnikov of Princeton University Press; to copyeditor Karen Verde; and to cartographer Rob McCaleb.

Finally, six heroic individuals read and commented usefully on the whole manuscript: Margaret Belich, Pekka Hämäläinen, Robert Hymes, John Darwin, David Scott, and Andrew Thompson. I am immensely grateful for their advice but did not always take it. I, of course, am responsible for remaining errors and misapprehensions.

NOTES

Introduction

1. Petrarch, "Letters on Familiar Matters", in Rosemary Horrox, *The Black Death*, Manchester University Press, 1994, 248.

2. S. Broadberry et al., *British Economic Growth, 1270–1870*, Cambridge University Press, 2015, 32.

3. Philip T. Hoffman, *Why Did Europe Conquer the World?* Princeton University Press, 2015, 18, notes 4 and 5, confirming the estimate made by D. K. Fieldhouse in 1973.

4. Peter Munz, *The Shapes of Time. A New Look at the Philosophy of History*, Wesleyan University Press, 1977, 16–17.

5. E.g., Jacob Burckhardt, *Civilization of the Renaissance in Italy*, Batoche Books edn, 2001 (orig. 1860); A. R. Bridbury, *Economic Growth. England in the Later Middle Ages*, Routledge Revivals, 2016 (orig. 1962), 84–91, and "The Black Death", *Economic History Review*, 26, 1973, 393–410; David Herlihy, *The Black Death and the Transformation of the West*, Samuel K. Cohn (ed.), Harvard University Press, 1997, 51–57, 81.

6. Mark Bailey, *After the Black Death: Economy, Society, and the Law in Fourteenth-Century England*, Oxford University Press, 2021, Conclusion.

7. Richard C. Hoffman, *An Environmental History of Medieval Europe*, Cambridge University Press, 2014, 350.

8. Gregory Clark, "Microbes and Markets: Was the Black Death an Economic Revolution? *Journal of Demographic Economics*, 82, 2016, 139–165.

9. Joel Mokyr, *The Enlightened Economy*, Penguin, 2009; Deirdre N. McCloskey, *Bourgeois Dignity. Why Economics Can't Explain the Modern World*, University of Chicago Press, 2010.

10. Jonathan Daly, *Historians Debate the Rise of the West*, Routledge, 2015, 31.

Prologue

1. Earlier versions of a few elements of the following two sections first appeared in my section of the introduction in James Belich et al. (eds.), *The Prospect of Global History*, Oxford University Press, 2016.

2. Johan Ling and Zofia Stos-Gale, "Representations of Oxhide Ingots in Scandinavian Rock Art: The Sketchbook of a Bronze Age Traveller?" *Antiquity*, 89, 2015, 191–209.

3. Haripriya Rangan, Judith Carney, and Tim Denham, "Environmental History of Botanical Exchanges in the Indian Ocean World", *Environment and History*, 18, 2012, 311–342; N. Boivin

and D.Q. Fuller, "Shell Middens, Ships and Seeds: Exploring Coastal Subsistence, Maritime Trade and the Dispersal of Domesticates in and Around the Ancient Arabian Peninsula", *Journal of World Prehistory*, 22, 2009, 113–180; Daniel Zohary, Maria Hopf, and Ehud Weiss, *Domestication of Plants in the Old World: The Origin and Spread of Domesticated Plants in Southwest Asia, Europe, and the Mediterranean Basin*, Oxford University Press, 2015, ch. 1; Nicole Boivin et al., "East Africa and Madagascar in the Indian Ocean World", *Journal of World Prehistory*, 26, 2013, 213–281.

4. Michael Whitby, "The Grain Trade of Athens in the Fourth Century BC", in Helen Parkins and Christopher Smith (eds.), *Trade, Traders and the Ancient City*, Routledge, 1998.

5. Kenneth Pomeranz, *The Great Divergence: China, Europe, and the Making of the Modern World Economy*, Princeton University Press, 2000. This was preceded by the similar views of R. Bin Wong, *China Transformed: Historical Change and the Limits of European Experience*, Cornell University Press, 1997, and Andre Gundar Frank, *Re-Orient: Global Economy in the Asian Age*, University of California Press, 1998. A still earlier precursor was Jack Goody in various works.

6. Until recently, the notion of the steppe origins of proto-Indo-European languages was contested by the hypothesis that they first emerged in Anatolia and spread from there with farmer migrations. (e.g., R. Bouckaert et al., "Mapping the Origins and Expansion of the Indo-European Language Family", *Science*, 337:6097, 2012). But the balance of evidence now favours the steppe hypothesis, long preferred by leading scholars such as David Anthony and Barry Cunliffe (e.g., Will Chang et al., "Ancestry-Constrained Phylogenetic Analysis Supports the Indo-European Steppe Hypothesis", *Language*, 91:1, 2015; Wolfgang Haak et al., "Massive Migration from the Steppe is a Source for Indo-European Languages in Europe", *Nature*, 2015 (doi:10.1038/nature14317).

7. J. P. Mallory and Victor H. Mair, *The Tarim Mummies: Ancient China and the Mystery of the Earliest Peoples from the West*, Thames & Hudson, 2008; Tomas Larsen Høisæter, "Polities and Nomads: The Emergence of the Silk Road Exchange in the Tarim Basin Region During Late Prehistory (2000–400 BCE)", *Bulletin of SOAS*, 80:2, 2017, 339–363.

8. Ricardo Duchesne, "Indo-Europeans Were the Most Historically Significant Nomads of the Steppes", *Cliodynamics*, 4:1, 2013.

9. Charleen Gaunitz et al., "Ancient Genomes Revisit the Ancestry of Domestic and Przewalski's Horses", *Science*, 360:6384, 2018, 111–114; Peter de Barros Damgaard et al., "The First Horse Herders and the Impact of Early Bronze Age Steppe Expansions into Asia", *Science*, 360:1422, 2018; Alan K. Outram et al., "The Earliest Horse Harnessing and Milking", *Science*, 323, 2009. Also see David W. Anthony, *The Horse, the Wheel and Language: How Bronze-Age Riders from the Eurasian Steppes Shaped the Modern World*, Princeton University Press, 2007; Robin Bendrey, "From Wild Horses to Domestic Horses: A European Perspective", *World Archaeology*, 44:1, 2012, 135–157; Alessandro Achilli et al., "Mitochondrial Genomes from Modern Horses Reveal the Major Haplogroups that Underwent Domestication", *Proceedings of the National Academy of Science, USA*, 14.109(7), 2012, 2449–2454; Michael Cieslak et al., "Origin and History of Mitochondrial DNA Lineages in Domestic Horses", *PLoS one*, 5:12, 2010; A. Outram and A. Bogaard, " Horse Domestication and the Origins of Pastoralism in Central Asia", in *Subsistence and Society in Prehistory: New Directions in Economic Archaeology*, Cambridge University Press, 2019.

10. Asko Parpola, "The Problem of Samoyed Origins in the Light of Archaeology: On the Formation and Dispersal of East Uralic (Proto-Ugro-Samoyed)", in *Per Urales ad Orientem. Iter*

polyphonicum multilingue. Festskrift tillägnad Juha Janhunen. Mémoires de la Société Finno-Ougrienne 264, 2012, 287–298; Damgaard et al., "The First Horse Herders"; Michael D. Frachetti, *Pastoralist Landscapes and Social Interaction in Bronze Age Eurasia*, University of California Press, 2008, 45–46.

11. Gaunitz et al., "Ancient Genomes"; Saskia Wutke et al., "Decline of Genetic Diversity in Ancient Domestic Stallions in Europe", *Scientific Advances*, 4:4, 2018.

12. Pablo Librado et al., "Ancient Genomic Changes Associated with Domestication of the Horse", *Science*, 356, 2017, 442–445; W.T.T. Taylor et al., "A Bayesian Chronology for Early Domestic Horse Use in the Eastern Steppe", *Journal of Archaeological Science*, 81, 2017, 49–58; M. F. Unterländer et al., "Ancestry and Demography and Descendants of Iron Age Nomads of the Eurasian Steppe", *Nature Communications*, 8:14615, 2017; Barry Cunliffe, *By Steppe, Desert, and Ocean: The Birth of Eurasia*, Oxford University Press, 2015, 188, 197.

13. Hayashi Toshio, "The Beginning and the Maturity of Nomadic Powers in the Eurasian Steppes: Growing and Downsizing of Elite Tumuli", *Ancient Civilizations from Scythia to Siberia*, 19, 2013, 105–141; Librado et al., "Ancient Genomic Changes"; Barry Cunliffe, *The Scythians: Nomad Warriors of the Steppe*, Oxford University Press, 2019.

14. Only two of 600 horses in Coronado's 1540s expedition into what is now the southern United States were mares. Peter Mitchell, *Horse Nations. The Worldwide Impact of the Horse on Indigenous Societies Post-1492*. Oxford University Press, 2015, 79.

15. Joel A. Tarr, "A Note on the Horse as an Urban Power Source", *Journal of Urban History*, 25:3, 1999, 434–448.

16. Robert Finlay, "The Pilgrim Art: The Culture of Porcelain in World History", *Journal of World History*, 9:2, 1998, 141–187.

17. Pita Kelekna, *The Horse in Human History*, Cambridge University Press, 2009, 161; David Christian, "Silk Roads or Steppe Roads? The Silk Roads in World History", *Journal of World History*, 11:1, 2000, 1–26; Xiaoyan Wang and Jinsuo Zhao, "The Cultural Exchange between Sino-Western: Silk Trade in Han Dynasty", *Asian Culture and History*, 4:1, 2012.

18. Eliso Kvavadze et al., "Fibres of Linum (Flax), Gossypium (Cotton) and Animal Wool as Non-Pollen Palynomorphs in the Late Bronze Age Burials of Saphar-Kharaba, Southern Georgia", *Vegetation History and Archaeobotany*, 19:5–6, 2010, 479–494; Richard L. Smith, *Premodern Trade in World History*, Routledge, 2009, 94.

19. Giorgio Riello and Tirthankar Roy (eds.), *How India Clothed the World: The World of South Asian Textiles, 1500–1850*, Brill, 2009; David Washbrook, "India in the Early Modern World Economy: Modes of Production, Reproduction and Exchange", *Journal of World History*, 2:1, 2007; Scott C. Levi, "Commercial Structures", in David O. Morgan and Anthony Reid (eds.), *The New Cambridge History of Islam*, Vol. 3. , Cambridge University Press, 2010.

20. Matthew P. Fitzpatrick, "Provincializing Rome: The Indian Ocean Trade Network and Roman Imperialism", *Journal of World History*, 22.1, 2011, 27–54; Dick Whittaker, "Conjunctures and Conjectures: Kerala and Roman Trade", *South Asian Studies*, 25:1, 2009, 1–9; Ece Gülsüm Turnator, "Turning the Economic Tables in the Medieval Mediterranean: The Latin Crusader Empire and the Transformation of the Byzantine Economy, ca. 1100–1400", PhD dissertation, Harvard University, 2013, 11.

21. Olivia Remie Constable, *Trade and Traders in Muslim Spain: The Commercial Realignment of the Iberian Peninsula, 900–1500*, Cambridge University Press, 1994, 167.

22. Alan Williams, *The Sword and the Crucible: A History of the Metallurgy of European Swords Up to the 16th Century*, Brill, 2012; Tirthankar Roy, "Knowledge and Divergence from the Perspective of Early Modern India," *Journal of World History*, 3, 2008, 361–387.

23. William Schell Jr., "Silver Symbiosis: Re-Orienting Mexican Economic History", *Hispanic American Historical Review*, 81:1, 2001; Heidi Michelle Sherman, "Barbarians Come to Market: The Emporia of Western Eurasia from 500 BC to AD 1000", PhD dissertation, University of Minnesota, 2008, 70.

24. Y. Subbarayalu, *South India under the Cholas*, Oxford University Press, 2012, and see chapter 9 this volume.

25. Hyunhee Park, *Mapping the Chinese and Islamic Worlds: Cross-Cultural Exchange in Premodern Asia*, Cambridge University Press, 2012; Derek Heng Thiam Soon, "Structures, Networks and Commercial Practices of Private Chinese Maritime Traders in Island Southeast Asia in the Early Second Millennium AD", *International Journal of Maritime History*, 20:2, 2008, 27–54; Hugh R. Clark, "Frontier Discourse and China's Maritime Frontier: China's Frontiers and the Encounter with the Sea through Early Imperial History", *Journal of World History*, 20:1, 2009, 1–33.

26. Quoted by Tonio Andrade, *The Gunpowder Age. China, Military Innovation, and the Rise of the West in World History*, Princeton University Press, 2016, 21.

27. Robert Bedrosian, "China and the Chinese According to 5th–13th Century Classical Armenian Sources", *Armenian Review*, 34, 1981, 17–24.

28. Smith, *Premodern Trade*, 97–8; Bedrosian, "China and the Chinese"; Amita Satyal, "The Mughal Empire, Overland Trade, and Merchants of Northern India, 1526–1707," PhD thesis, UC Berkeley, 2008.

29. Quoted in Satyal, "The Mughal Empire", 216.

30. Anya H. King, "The Musk Trade and the Near East in the Early Medieval Period", PhD thesis, Indiana University, 2007; C. Patterson Giersch, "Across Zomia with Merchants, Monks, and Musk: Process Geographies, Trade Networks, and the Inner-East–Southeast Asian Borderlands", *JWH*, 5, 2010, 215–239.

31. Silk weight calculated from figures in Etienne de la Vaissiere in "Trans-Asian Trade, or the Silk Road Deconstructed (Antiquity, Middle Ages)", in *The Cambridge History of Capitalism. Vol 1*. For cotton, see Prasannan Parthasarathi, *Why Europe Grew Rich and Asia Did Not: Global Economic Divergence, 1600–1850*, Cambridge University Press, 2011, 33.

32. Xinru Liu, *The Silk Road in World History*, Oxford University Press, 2010.

33. Washbrook, "India in the Early Modern World Economy"; Thomas Ertl, "Silkworms, Capital and Merchant Ships: European Silk Industry in the Medieval World Economy", *Mediterranean Historical Review*, 9:2, 2006.

34. Ali Bahrani Pour, "The Trade in Horses Across the Silk Road between Khorasan and India in the 13th–17th Centuries", *The Silk Road*, 11, 2013, 123–138.

35. Valerie Hansen, *The Silk Road: A New History*, Oxford University Press, 2012, 238. Also see Khodadad Rezakhani, "The Road That Never Was: The Silk Road and Trans-Eurasian Exchange", *Comparative Studies of South Asia, Africa and the Middle East*, 30:3, 2010.

36. Christopher I. Beckwith, "The Impact of the Horse and Silk Trade on the Economies of Tang China and the Uighur Empire: On the Importance of International Commerce in the Early Middle Ages", *Journal of the Economic and Social History of the Orient*, 34, 1991, 183–198.

37. Quoted in Christian, "Silk Roads or Steppe Roads?"

38. David F. Graf, "The Silk Road between Syria and China", in Andrew Wilson and Alan Bowman (eds.), *Trade, Commerce, and the State in the Roman World*, Oxford University Press, 2017.

39. Hansen, *The Silk Road*, 5.

40. Immanuel Wallerstein, *The Modern World-System*, 3 vols., University of California Press, Berkeley, 2011 (orig. 1974–89); Manuel Castells, *The Information Age: Economy, Society, and Culture*, 3 vols., Blackwell, 1996–1998.

41. Fernand Braudel, *The Mediterranean and the Mediterranean World in the Age of Philip II*, 3 vols., trans. Siân Reynolds, University of California Press, Berkeley, 1995; Peregrine Horden and Nicholas Purcell, *The Corrupting Sea: A Study of Mediterranean History*, Blackwell, 2000; David Abulafia, *The Great Sea: A Human History of the Mediterranean*, Oxford University Press, 2011.

42. R. Helen Farr, "Island Colonisation and Trade in the Mediterranean", in Anderson, Atholl et al. (eds.), *The Global Origins and Development of Seafaring*, McDonald Institute for Archaeological Research, 2010; A. Bernard Knapp, "Cyprus's Earliest Prehistory: Seafarers, Foragers and Settlers", *Journal of World Prehistory*, 23, 2010, 79–120.

43. Zohary et al., *Domestication of Plants in the Old World*, ch. 1; Shahal Abbo, Simcha Lev-Yadun, and Avi Gopher, "Plant Domestication and Crop Evolution in the Near East: On Events and Processes," *Critical Reviews in Plant Sciences*, 31, 2012, 241–257; Dorian Q. Fuller, George Willcox, and Robin G. Allaby, "Early Agricultural Pathways: Moving Outside the 'Core Area' Hypothesis in Southwest Asia", *Journal of Experimental Botany*, 63:2, 2012, 617–633; Bleda S. During, "Breaking the Bond: Investigating the Neolithic Expansion in Asia Minor in the Seventh Millennium BC", *Journal of World Prehistory*, 26, 2013, 75–100.

44. Pita Kelekna, "The Politico-Economic Impact of the Horse on Old World Cultures: An Overview", *Sino-Platonic Papers*, 190, 2009. Also see Agnieszka Czekaj-Zastawny et al., "Long Distance Exchange in the Central European Neolithic: Hungary to the Baltic", *Antiquity*, 85, 2011, 43–58; L. B. Kirtcho, "The Earliest Wheeled Transport in Southwestern Central Asia: New Finds from Altyn-Depe", *Archaeology Ethnology & Anthropology of Eurasia*, 37:1, 2009, 25–33.

45. Kelekna, *The Horse in Human History*, 118; Michael Axworthy, *A History of Iran: Empire of the Mind*, Basic Books, 2008, 5–7, 28, 30, 49.

46. Eivind Heldaas Seland, "Trade and Christianity in the Indian Ocean during Late Antiquity", *Journal of Late Antiquity*, 5:1, 2012, 72–86.

47. F. Almathen et al., "Ancient and Modern DNA Reveal Dynamics of Domestication and Cross-Continental Dispersal of the Dromedary", *Proceedings of the National Academy of Science, USA*, 113:24, 2016, 6707–6712.

48. Manfred W. Wenner, "The Arab/Muslim Presence in Medieval Central Europe", *International Journal of Middle East Studies*, 12:1, 1980, 59–79.

49. Hugh Kennedy, *The Great Arab Conquests: How the Spread of Islam Changed The World We Live In*, Weidenfeld and Nicolson, 2007.

50. Peter Sarris, *Empires of Faith: The Fall of Rome to the Rise of Islam, 500–700*, Oxford University Press, 2011, ch. 7.

51. Kennedy, *The Great Arab Conquests*, 370; G. W. Bowersock, *Empires in Collision in Late Antiquity*. Brandeis University Press, 2012, ch. 3.

52. Michael W. Dols, "Plague in Early Islamic History", *Journal of the American Oriental Society*, 94.3, 1974.

53. Ole Benedictow, "The Justinianic Plague Pandemic: Progress and Problems", *Early Science and Medicine*, 14, 2009, 543–548. Also see Dionysios Stathakopoulos, "The Justinianic Plague Revisited", *Byzantine and Modern Greek Studies*, 24, 2000, 256–276; McCormick, *Origins of the European Economy*, 41.

54. Paul Yule, "A Late Antique Christian King from Zafār, Southern Arabia", *Antiquity*, 87, 2013, 1124–1135.

55. Martin Sicker, *Islamic World in Ascendency*, Greenwood Press, 2000.

56. Gene W. Heck, "Gold Mining in Arabia and the Rise of the Islamic State", *Journal of the Economic and Social History of the Orient*, 42:3, 1999, 364–395; Greg Fisher, "Kingdoms or Dynasties? Arabs, History, and Identity before Islam", *Journal of Late Antiquity*, 4:2, 2011, 245–267; Tim Mackintosh-Smith, *Arabs. A 3,000-Year History of Peoples, Tribes and Empires*, Yale University Press, 2019, Loc. 1262; Michael Morony, "The Early Islamic Mining Boom", *Journal of the Economic and Social History of the Orient*, 62:1, 2019, 166–221.

57. Bernard Lewis, *The Middle East: 2000 Years of History from the Rise of Christianity to the Present Day*, Phoenix, 1996 (orig. 1995), 63.

58. Michael C. A. Macdonald, "Was There a 'Bedouinization of Arabia'?", *Der Islam*, 92:1, 2015, 42–84.

59. John W. Jandora, "Archers of Islam: A Search for 'Lost' History", *Mediterranean Historical Review*, 13.1, 2010, 97–114; Eduard Alofs, "Studies on Mounted Warfare in Asia I: Continuity and Change in Middle Eastern Warfare, c. CE 550–1350—What Happened to the Horse Archer?", *War in History*, 21:4, 2014, 423–444.

60. Reuven Amitai, "The Mamlūk Institution, or One Thousand Years of Military Slavery in the Islamic World", in Christopher Leslie Brown and Philip D. Morgan (eds.), *Arming Slaves: From Classical Times to the Modern Age*, Yale University Press, 2006, 40–78. Also see Albrecht Fuess, "Taxation and Armies", in *The New Cambridge History of Islam*, Vol. 2; Edmund Bosworth, "The Steppe Peoples in the Islamic World", *New Cambridge History of Islam*, Vol. 3.

61. Heck, "Gold Mining in Arabia". Also see Michael N. Pearson, "Creating a Littoral Community: Muslim Reformers in the Early Modern Indian Ocean World", in Charles H. Parker and Jerry H. Bentley (eds.), *Between the Middle Ages and Modernity: Individual and Community in the Early Modern World*, Rowman & Littlefield, 2007, 157; Kenneth J. Hall, "Local and International Trade and Traders in the Straits of Melaka Region, 600–1500", *Journal of the Economic and Social History of the Orient*, 47:2, 2004.

62. André Wink, "The Early Expansion of Islam in India", in *The New Cambridge History of Islam*, Vol. 3.

63. Lewis, *The Middle East*, 88; Erika Monahan, *The Merchants of Siberia. Trade in Early Modern Eurasia*, Cornell University Press, 2016, 73; Katarina Stulrajterova, "Convivenza, Convenienza, and Conversion to Islam in Medieval Hungary", *Journal of Islamic Studies*, 24:2, 2013, 175–198; Sonja Magnavita, "Sahara and West Africa", in Erik Hermans (ed.), *A Companion to the Early Global Middle Ages*, Arc Humanities, 2020.

64. Kennedy, *The Great Arab Conquests*, 374–375.

65. See chapter 6 in this volume.

66. Mackintosh-Smith, *Arabs*, loc. 3573. Also see Sarris, *Empires of Faith*, ch. 7; Jack Tannous, *The Making of the Medieval Middle East*, Princeton University Press, 2019.

67. Kennedy, *The Great Arab Conquests*, 271.

Part I: A Plague of Mysteries

1. Heidi Michelle Sherman, "Barbarians Come to Market: The Emporia of Western Eurasia from 500 BC to AD 1000", PhD dissertation, University of Minnesota, 2008.

2. Walter Scheidel, *Escape from Rome: The Failure of Empire and the Road to Prosperity*, Princeton University Press, 2019.

3. Edward James, *Europe's Barbarians, AD 200–600*, Pearson Longman, 2009, 32; Peter Sarris, *Empires of Faith: The Fall of Rome to the Rise of Islam, 500–700*, Oxford University Press, 2011, 47.

4. Rebała Krzysztof et al., "Y-STR Variation Among Slavs: Evidence for the Slavic Homeland in the Middle Dnieper Basin", *Journal of Human Genetics*, 52, 2007, 406–414; P. M. Barford, *The Early Slavs: Culture and Society in Early Medieval Eastern Europe*, Cornell University Press, 2001.

5. Edmund Bosworth, "The Steppe Peoples in the Islamic World," in David O. Morgan and Anthony Reid (eds.), *The New Cambridge History of Islam*, Vol. 3, Cambridge University Press, 2010.

6. David Christian, *A History of Russia, Central Asia and Mongolia. Volume I, Inner Eurasia from Prehistory to the Mongol Empire*, Blackwell, 1998, 363.

7. Christian Raffensperger, *Reimagining Europe: Kievan Rus' in the Medieval World*, Harvard University Press, 2012; Charles J. Halperin, *Russia and the Golden Horde: The Mongol Impact on Medieval Russia*, Indiana University Press, 1987.

8. Peter Jackson, *The Mongols and the West, 1221–1410*, Pearson Longman, 2005; Norman Davies, *God's Playground. A History of Poland, Vol. 1*, Clarendon Press, 1981, 77, 87; John Giebfried, "The Mongol Invasions and the Aegean World (1241–61)", *Mediterranean Historical Review*, 28:2, 2013, 129–139.

9. Christian, *Inner Eurasia*, 411. Charles Halperin disagreed in *Russia and the Golden Horde*, 47–48.

10. Ramzi Rouighi, *The Making of a Mediterranean Emirate: Ifrīqiyā and Its Andalusis, 1200–1400*, University of Pennsylvania Press, 2011; Allen Fromherz, *The Near West: Medieval North Africa, Latin Europe and the Mediterranean in the Second Axial Age*, Edinburgh University Press, 2016.

11. Stephan Barisitz, *Central Asia and the Silk Road. Economic Rise and Decline over Several Millennia*, Springer Cham, 2017, ch. 3.

12. Thomas F. Madden, "Outside and Inside the Fourth Crusade", *International History Review*, 17:4, 1995.

13. For a recent assessment of the evidence, see Peter Jackson, *The Mongols and the Islamic World: From Conquest to Conversion*, Yale University Press, 2017, ch. 6.

14. Jiger Janabel, "From Mongol Empire to Qazaq Juzder: Studies on the Steppe Political Cycle (13th–18th Centuries)", PhD thesis, Harvard University, 1997, 20; Miklos Molnar, *A Concise History of Hungary*, trans. Anna Magyar, Cambridge University Press, 2001 (orig. 1996), 34; John Watts, *The Making of Polities: Europe, 1300–1500* Cambridge University Press, 2009, 80.

15. Daniel C. Waugh, "The 'Owl of Misfortune' or the 'Phoenix of Prosperity'? Rethinking the Impact of the Mongols", *Journal of Eurasian Studies*, 8, 2017, 10–21.

16. Marie Favereau, "The Golden Horde and the Mamluks", *Golden Horde Review*, 5:1, 2017; Thomas T. Allsen, "Mongols as Vectors for Cultural Transmission', in Nicola Di Cosmo, Allen J. Frank, and Peter B. Golden (eds.), *The Cambridge History of Inner Asia: The Chinggisid Age*, Cambridge University Press, 2009.

17. Michael Mitterauer, *Why Europe? The Medieval Origins of its Special Path*, trans. Gerald Chapple, University of Chicago Press, 2010 (German orig. 2003), 1.

18. R. I. Moore, Review of Thomas Bisson, *The Crisis of the Twelfth Century: Power, Lordship, and the Origins of European Government* (2009), *American Historical Review*, 115:1, 2010, 172–174. Also see R. I. Moore, *The First European Revolution, c.970–1215*, Blackwell, 2000. Others who date Europe's divergence to around 1000 AD include Jonathan Daly, *The Rise of Western Power. A Comparative History of Western Civilization*, Bloomsbury, 2014; Michael McCormick, *Origins of the European Economy: Communications and Commerce, A.D. 300–900*, Cambridge University Press, 2001, 777, 794; David Landes, *The Wealth and Poverty of Nations: Why Some Are So Rich and Some So Poor*, W.W. Norton, 1998; Eric Mielants, *The Origins of Capitalism and the "Rise of the West"*, Temple University Press; Jan Luiten van Zanden, "The Road to the Industrial Revolution: Hypotheses and Conjectures about the Medieval Origins of the "European Miracle", *Journal of World History*, 3, 2008, 337–359.

19. Robert Bartlett, *The Making of Europe. Conquest, Colonization, and Cultural Change, 950–1350*, Princeton University Press, 1993, 292.

20. Christian, *Inner Eurasia*, 264, 293; Christopher I. Beckwith, *Empires of the Silk Road: A History of Central Eurasia from the Bronze Age to the Present*, Princeton University Press, 2009, 148–149.

21. Aleksander Pluskowski, *The Archaeology of the Prussian Crusade. Holy War and Colonisation*, Routledge, 2013, 5; N.J.G. Pounds, *An Historical Geography of Europe, 450 BC–AD 1330*, Cambridge University Press, 1973, 341; Bartlett, *The Making of Europe*, 144; Charles W. Ingrao and Franz A. J. Szabo (eds.), *The Germans and the East*, Purdue University Press, 2008.

22. Alex Brown and Aleks Pluskowski, "Detecting the Environmental Impact of the Baltic Crusades on a Late-Medieval (13th–15th Century) Frontier Landscape: Palynological Analysis from Malbork Castle and Hinterland, Northern Poland", *Journal of Archaeological Science*, 38 (2011) 1957–1966.

23. Examples of a vast literature include: John France, *The Crusades and the Expansion of Catholic Christendom, 1000–1714*, Routledge, 2005; Andrew Jotischky, *Crusading and the Crusader States*, Pearson Longman, 2004; James Powell, "The Crusades in Recent Research", *Catholic Historical Review*, 95:2, 2009, 313–319, and the various works of Christopher Tyerman.

24. Bernard S. Bachrach and David S. Bachrach, *Warfare in Medieval Europe c.400–c.1453*, Routledge, 2017. Also see the works of Susan Reynolds.

25. Dominique Valérian, "Ifrîqiyan Muslim Merchants in the Mediterranean at the End of the Middle Ages", *Mediterranean Historical Review*, 14:2, 1999, 47–66; Olivia R. Constable, "Muslim Trade in the Late Medieval Mediterranean World", in Maribel Fierro (ed.), *The New Cambridge History of Islam*, Vol. 2, Cambridge University Press, 2010; Susan Rose, "Islam Versus Christendom: The Naval Dimension, 1000–1600", *Journal of Military History*, 63:3, 1999, 561–578; Travis Bruce, "The Politics of Violence and Trade: Denia and Pisa in the Eleventh Century", *Journal of Medieval History*, 32, 2006, 127–142.

26. John L. Brooke, *Climate Change and the Course of Global History. A Rough Journey*, Cambridge University Press, 2014, 373.

27. William Jordan, "The Great Famine 1315–1322 Revisited", in Scott G. Bruce, (ed.), *Ecologies and Economies in Medieval and Early Modern Europe: Studies in Environmental History for Richard C. Hoffmann*, Brill, 2010; Anne E.C. McCants, "Historical Demography", in Hamish Scott (ed.), *The Oxford Handbook of Early Modern European History, 1350–1750: Vol. 1*, Oxford University Press, 2015; Andrew Noymer, "Contesting the Cause and Severity of the Black Death: A Review Essay", *Population and Development Review*, 33:3, 2007, 616–627; Christopher Dyer, "The Material World of English Peasants, 1200–1540: Archaeological Perspectives on Rural Economy and Welfare", *Agricultural History Review*, 62:1, 2014, 1–22; Thomas B. van Hoof et al., "Forest Re-Growth on Medieval Farmland after the Black Death Pandemic—Implications for Atmospheric CO_2 Levels", *Palaeogeography, Palaeoclimatology, Palaeoecology*, 237:2–4, 4, 2006, 396–409; Pavel Murdzhev, "The Medieval Town in Bulgaria", PhD dissertation, University of Florida, 2008, 56.

28. Bruce M. S. Campbell, *The Great Transition. Climate, Disease, and Society in the Late-Medieval World*, Cambridge University Press, 2016, 36, 19.

29. Benjamin Lieberman and Elizabeth Gordon, *Climate Change in Human History: Prehistory to the Present*, Bloomsbury Academic, 2018, Location 2538.

30. William C. Jordan, *The Great Famine: Northern Europe in the Early Fourteenth Century*, Princeton University Press, 1996, and "The Great Famine Revisited". In the later article, Jordan wisely revises the suggestion of a Malthusian crisis contributing to the Black Death made in his earlier book. Also see Philip Slavin, "Market Failure during the Great Famine in England and Wales (1315–1317)", *Past & Present*, 222, 2014.

31. S. Broadberry et al., *British Economic Growth, 1270–1870*, Cambridge University Press, 2015, 20, 106.

32. J. C. Hubby, "Lordship and Rural Society in Medieval Bavaria: The Estates of the Abbey of Tergernsee, c.979–1450", PhD dissertation, Columbia University, 2000, 357.

33. Richard C. Hoffman, *An Environmental History of Medieval Europe*, Cambridge University Press, 2014, 202.

34. Campbell, *The Great Transition*, 171. Also see Guido Alfani, "The Rich in Historical Perspective: Evidence for Preindustrial Europe (ca. 1300–1800)", *Cliometrica*, 2016.

35. Chris Wickham, *The Inheritance of Rome: A History of Europe from 400 to 1000*, Allen Lane, 2009, ch. 22; Bartlett, *The Making of Europe*, 155.

Chapter 1: The Black Death and the Plague Era

1. Kenneth L. Gage, "Factors Affecting the Spread and Maintenance of Plague", in A.M.P. de Almeida and N. C. Leal (eds.), *Advances in Yersinia Research*, Springer, 2012; Idir Bitam et al., "New Rural Focus of Plague, Algeria", *Emerging Infectious Diseases*,16:10, 2010, 1639–1640.

2. Louis Heyligen, in Rosemary Horrox, *The Black Death*, Manchester University Press, 1994, 41–45.

3. Susan Scott and Christopher J. Duncan, *Biology of Plagues; Evidence from Historical Populations*, Cambridge University Press, 2001, 101.

4. Samuel K. Cohn Jr., *The Black Death Transformed. Disease and Culture in Early Renaissance Europe*, Arnold, 2002, 1.

5. J. W. Wood et al., "The Temporal Dynamics of the Fourteenth-Century Black Death: New Evidence from English Ecclesiastical Records", *Human Biology*, 75:4, 2003, 427–448. Also see

George Christakos and Ricardo A. Olea, "New Space-Time Perspectives on the Propagation Characteristics of the Black Death Epidemic and Its Relation to Bubonic Plague", *Stochastic Environmental Research and Risk Assessment*, 19, 2005, 307–314; Brian H. Bossak and Mark R. Welford, "Did Medieval Trade Activity and a Viral Etiology Control the Spatial Extent and Seasonal Distribution of Black Death Mortality?" *Medical Hypotheses*, 72:6, 2009, 749–752.

6. Gerald Harriss, *Shaping the Nation. England, 1360–1461*, Clarendon Press, 2005. Also see A. R. Disney, *A History of Portugal and the Portuguese Empire*, 2 Vols, Cambridge University Press, 2009, I. 107–8. Guido Ruggiero, *The Renaissance. A Social and Cultural History of the Rinascimento*, Cambridge University Press, 2015, ch. 3; Steven A. Epstein, *An Economic and Social History of Later Medieval Europe, 1000–1500*, Cambridge University Press, 2009, 173–174.

7. Benedict Gummer in *The Scourging Angel: The Black Death in the British Isles*, Bodley Head, 2009, 419.

8. Ole J. Benedictow, *The Black Death 1346–1353: The Complete History*, Boydell Press, 2004, and *What Disease Was Plague? On the Controversy Over the Microbiological Identity of Plague Epidemics of the Past*, Brill, 2010.

9. William Naphy and Andrew Spicer, *The Black Death. A History of Plagues, 1345–1730*, Tempus, 2000, 56.

10. S. Haensch et al., "Distinct Clones of *Yersinia pestis* Caused the Black Death", *PLoS Pathogens* 6:10, 2010. Also see Sacha Kacki et al., "Black Death in the Rural Cemetery of Saint-Laurent-de-la-Cabrerisse Aude-Languedoc, Southern France, 14th Century: Immunological Evidence", *Journal of Archaeological Science*, 38, 2011, 581–587, and K. Bos et al., "A Draft Genome of *Yersinia pestis* from Victims of the Black Death", *Nature*, 478, 2011, 506–510.

11. E.g., Cohn, *The Black Death Transformed*, 248; Epstein, *An Economic and Social History*, 173–174.

12. E.g., Verena Schuenemann et al., "Targeted Enrichment of Ancient Pathogens Yielding the pPCP1 Plasmid of *Yersinia pestis* from Victims of the Black Death", *Proceedings of the National Academy of Science, USA*, 108:38, 2011; Ingrid Wiechmann et al., "Definite *Y Pestis* Finds from Mass Grave in Bavaria, 1348–1500", *Emerging Infectious Diseases*, 16:11, 2010.

13. Thi-nguyen-ny Tran et al., "High Throughput, Multiplexed Pathogen Detection Authenticates Plague Waves in Medieval Venice, Italy", *PLoS one*, 6:3, 2011.

14. Dr. Johannes Krause, quoted in "Black Death Bacterium Identified: Genetic Analysis of Medieval Plague Skeletons Shows Presence of *Yersinia pestis* Bacteria", *Science Daily*, August 29, 2011. Also see M. Drancourt, "Finally, Plague Is Plague", *Clinical Microbiology and Infection*, 18:2, 2012, 105–106.

15. Henry C. Dick et al., "Detection and Characterisation of Black Death Burials by Multi-Proxy Geophysical Methods", *Journal of Archaeological Science*, 59, 2015, 132–141.

16. Lisa Seifert et al., "Genotyping *Yersinia pestis* in Historical Plague: Evidence for Long-Term Persistence of *Y. pestis* in Europe from the 14th to the 17th Century", *PLoS one*, 13 January, 2016; Monica Green (ed.), *Pandemic Disease in the Medieval World: Rethinking the Black Death*, ARC Medieval Press, 2014; Nükhet Varlık, *Plague and Empire in the Early Modern Mediterranean World: The Ottoman Experience, 1347–1600*, Cambridge University Press, 2015; A. Namouchi et al., "Integrative Approach Using *Yersinia pestis* Genomes to Revisit the Historical Landscape of Plague during the Medieval Period", *Proceedings of the National Academy of Science, USA*, 115: E11790–E11797, 2018; A. Spyrou et al., "A Phylogeography of the Second Plague Pandemic

Revealed through the Analysis of Historical *Y. Pestis* Genomes," *Nature Communications*, 10, 2019; Hugh Willmott et al., "Black Death Mass Grave at Thornton Abbey: The Discovery and Examination of a Fourteenth-Century Rural Catastrophe", *Antiquity*, 94 (373), 2020; I. Morozova et al., "New Ancient Eastern European *Yersinia pestis* Genomes Illuminate the Dispersal of Plague in Europe", *Philosophical Transactions of the Royal Society.B*, 375: 20190569, 2020.

17. "McCormick, "Rats, Communications, and Plague".

18. Lars Börner and Battista Severgnini, "Epidemic Trade", Free University Berlin, School of Business & Economics Discussion Paper: No. 2011/12, http://hdl.handle.net/10419/49294; Benedictow, *Complete History*, 102 and note 20.

19. Hannah Barker, "Laying the Corpses to Rest: Grain, Embargoes, and *Yersinia pestis* in the Black Sea, 1346–48", *Speculum* 96:1, 2021. Also see Hans Ditrich, "The Transmission of the Black Death to Western Europe: A Critical Review of the Existing Evidence", *Mediterranean Historical Review*, 32:1, 2017, 25–39.

20. Barker, "Laying the Corpses to Rest".

21. Uli Schamiloglu, "The Impact of the Black Death on the Golden Horde: Politics, Economy, Society, Civilization", *Golden Horde Review*, 5:2, 2017.

22. Alisher Ilkhamov, "Archaeology of Uzbek Identity", *Central Asian Survey*, 23:3, 2004, 289–326.

23. Stephan Barisitz, *Central Asia and the Silk Road. Economic Rise and Decline over Several Millennia*, Springer Cham, 2017, ch. 3.

24. A. Spyrou et al., "A Phylogeography of the Second Plague Pandemic Revealed through the Analysis of Historical *Y. Pestis* Genomes". *Nature Communications*, 10, 2019; Namouchi et al., "Integrative Approach Using *Yersinia pestis* Genomes"; Monica H. Greene, 'The Four Black Deaths', *AHR*, 125:5, 2020, 1601–1631.

25. For the low estimate, see J.F. . Shrewsbury, *A History of Bubonic Plague in the British Isles*, Cambridge University Press, 1970. The higher estimates are documented below.

26. Benedictow, *Complete History*. Also see his *What Disease Was Plague?* and Ole Benedictow, Raffaella Bianucci, Sacha Kacki, and Ingrid Wiechmann, "History of the Plague", in Michaela Harbeck, Kristin von Heyking, and Heiner Schwarzberg (eds.), *Sickness, Hunger, War, and Religion: Multidisciplinary Perspectives*, Rachel Carson Center Perspectives, 3, 2012.

27. Andrew Noymer, "Contesting the Cause and Severity of the Black Death: A Review Essay", *Population and Development Review* 33:3, 2007, 616–627.

28. Barney Sloane, *The Black Death in London*, History Press, 2011, 153.

29. John Hatcher, *The Black Death. An Intimate History*, Weidenfeld and Nicolson, 2008, 152.

30. Willmott et al., "Black Death Mass Grave at Thornton Abbey".

31. Mark Bailey, *Medieval Suffolk: An Economic and Social History, 1200–1500*, Boydell Press, 2007, 176–177.

32. Peter Larson, "Rural Transformation in Northern England: Village Communities of Durham, 1340–1400", in Ben Dodds and Richard Britnell (eds.), *Agriculture and Rural Society after the Black Death: Common Themes and Regional Variations*, Hertfordshire University Press, 2008, 199–214, and "Conflict and Compromise in the Late Medieval Countryside: Lords and Peasants in Durham, 1349–1430", PhD dissertation, Rutgers University, 2004.

33. Adam Lucas, *Ecclesiastical Lordship, Seigneurial Power, and the Commercialization of Milling in Medieval England*, Ashgate, 2014, 41.

34. Sharon N. DeWitte, "The Anthropology of Plague: Insights from Bioarcheological Analyses of Epidemic Cemeteries", Green (ed.), *Pandemic Disease in the Medieval World*, 2014.

35. Carenza Lewis, "Disaster Recovery: New Archaeological Evidence for the Long-Term Impact of the 'Calamitous' Fourteenth Century", *Antiquity*, 90 351 (2016): 777–797. Also see *Guardian*, May 23, 2016.

36. Stephen Broadberry, Bruce M. S. Campbell, and Bas van Leeuwen, "English Medieval Population: Reconciling Times Series and Cross-Sectional Evidence", University of Warwick Working Paper, July 27, 2010 and Broadberry et al., *British Economic Growth*, 183,

37. Bailey, *Medieval Suffolk*, 183; Isla Fay, *Health and the City. Disease, Environment, and Government in Norwich, 1200–1575*, York Medieval Press, 2015.

38. George Grantham, "France", in Harry Kitsikopoulos (ed.), *Agrarian Change and Crisis in Europe, 1200–1500*, Routledge, 2012, 57–92.

39. Graeme Small, *Late Medieval France*, Palgrave Macmillan, 2009, 56, 174.

40. Mark A. Aloisio, "Economy, Society, and Institutions in Late Medieval Sicily: Sciacca and Its Hinterland in the Fifteenth Century", PhD thesis, University of Minnesota, 2008, ch. 2; Daniel R. Curtis, "Florence and Its Hinterlands in the Late Middle Ages: Contrasting Fortunes in the Tuscan Countryside, 1300–1500", *Journal of Medieval History*, 38:4, 2012, 472–499; M. E. Bratchel, *Medieval Lucca and the Evolution of the Renaissance State*, Oxford University Press, 2008; Karen Anne Frank, "Jewish Women and Their Community in Late Medieval and Renaissance Perugia", PhD dissertation, UC Santa Barbara, 2012, 89.

41. William J. Connell and Andrea Zorzi (eds.), *Florentine Tuscany: Structures and Practices of Power*, Cambridge University Press 2000, Editor's Intro.

42. Toubert, Pierre, "La Peste Noire dans les Abruzzes (1348–1350)", *Le Moyen Age*, 1, 2014, 11–26.

43. D. Cesana, O. J. Benedictow, and R. Bianucci, "The Origin and Early Spread of the Black Death in Italy: First Evidence of Plague Victims from 14th-Century Liguria (northern Italy)", *Anthropological Science*, 125:1, 2017, 15–24.

44. Guido Alfani, *Calamities and the Economy in Renaissance Italy: The Grand Tour of the Horsemen of the Apocalypse*, trans. Christine Calvert, Palgrave Macmillan, 2013, 165.

45. John Aberth, *From the Brink of the Apocalypse: Confronting Famine, War, Plague and Death in the Later Middle Ages*, 2nd edn, Routledge, 2010, 92–4.

46. Per Lagerås et al., "Abandonment, Agricultural Change and Ecology", in Lagerås (ed.), *Environment, Society and the Black Death: An Interdisciplinary Approach to the Late-Medieval Crisis in Sweden*, Casemate Publishers, 2015.

47. John Ragnar Myking, "Reviews" [of Kåre Lunden, *Frå svartedauen til 17. mai: 1350–1814* [*From the Black Death to the 17th of May 1350–1814*], *Scandinavian Journal of History*, 28: 3–4, 2002, 286–288; Massimo Livi Bacci, *The Population of Europe*, Blackwell, 2000, 111.

48. Hans Antonson, "The Extent of Farm Desertion in Central Sweden During the Late Medieval Agrarian Crisis: Landscape as a Source", *Journal of Historical Geography*, 35:4, 2009, 619–641; Lars Skog and Hans Hauska, "Spatial Modeling of the Black Death in Sweden", *Transactions in GIS*, 17:4, 2013, 589–611; Gustaf Svedjemo et al., *Landscape Dynamics: Spatial Analyses of Villages and Farms on Gotland AD 200–1700*, Uppsala Universitet, 2014; Eva Sköld, "Temporal Cultural Landscape Dynamics in a Marginal Upland Area: Agricultural Expansions and Contractions Inferred from Palynological Evidence at Yttra Berg, Southern Sweden", *Vegetation*

History and Archaeobotany, 19:2, 2010, 121–136. Also see Janken Myrdal and Mats Morell (eds.), *Agrarian History of Sweden: From 4000 BC to AD 2000*, Nordic Academic Press, 2011, 77.

49. Cassady J. Yoder, "The Late Medieval Agrarian Crisis and Black Death Plague Epidemic in Medieval Denmark: A Paleopathological and Paleodietary Perspective", PhD thesis, Texas A&M University, 2006, esp. 151; Sharon N. DeWitte, "The Paleodemography of the Black Death 1347–1351", PhD thesis in Anthropology, Pennsylvania State University, 2006.

50. Janken Myrdal, "The Black Death in the North: 1349–1350", in Lars Bisgaard and Leif Søndergaard (eds.), *Living with The Black Death*, University Press of Southern Denmark, 2009, 63–84.

51. Mika Kallioinen, "Plagues and Governments", *Scandinavian Journal of History*, 31:1, 2006, 35–51.

52. David C. Mengel, "A Plague in Bohemia? Mapping the Black Death", *Past & Present*, 211, 2011, 3–34.

53. *Prague Daily Monitor/CTK*, November 10, 2017.

54. Mengel, "A Plague on Bohemia?"; Manfred Vasold, "The Diffusion of the Black Death 1348–1350 in Central Europe", in Bisgaard and Søndergaard (eds.), *Living with The Black Death*, 47–61; Kay Peter Jankrift, "The Language of Plague and Its Regional Perspectives: The Case of Medieval Germany", *Medical History*, 52, 2008, 53–58; Shami Ghosh, "Rural Economies and Transitions to Capitalism: Germany and England Compared (c.1200–c.1800)", *Journal of Agrarian Change*, 16:2, 255–290, 2016.

55. J. C. Hubby, "Lordship and Rural Society in Medieval Bavaria: The Estates of the Abbey of Tergernsee, c. 979–1450", PhD dissertation, Columbia University, 2000.

56. Hubby, "Lordship and Rural Society", 380; Dan Yeloff and Bas van Geel, "Abandonment of Farmland and Vegetation Succession Following the Eurasian Plague Pandemic of AD 1347–52", *Journal of Biogeography*, 34, 2007, 575–582; Ingrid Wiechmann, Michaela Harbeck, and Gisela Grupe, "*Yersinia pestis* DNA Sequences in Late Medieval Skeletal Finds, Bavaria", *Emerging Infectious Diseases*, 16:11, 2010; Mark Haberlin, *The Fuggers of Augsburg. Pursuing Wealth and Honor in Renaissance Germany*, University of Virginia Press, 2012, 22.

57. Yeloff and van Geel, "Abandonment of Farmland"; Thomas B. van Hoof et al., "Forest Re-Growth on Medieval Farmland After the Black Death Pandemic—Implications for Atmospheric CO_2 Levels", *Palaeogeography, Palaeoclimatology, Palaeoecology*, 237:2–4, 2006, 396–409.

58. Stephan A. Lutgert, "Victims of the Great Famine and the Black Death? The Archaeology of the Mass Graves Found in the Former Graveyard of Holy Ghost Hospital, Lubeck (N. Germany), in the European Context", *Hikuin*, 27, 2000, 255–264; J. Gaudart et al., "Demographic and Spatial Factors as Causes of an Epidemic Spread, the Copule Approach: Application to the Retro-prediction of the Black Death Epidemy of 1346", 2010, 24th International Conference on Advanced Information Networking and Applications Workshops, April 2010, 751–758; George Christakos, Ricardo A. Olea, Ma-rc L. Serre, Hwa-Lung Yu, and Lin-Lin Wang, "Black Death: The Background", in *Interdisciplinary Public Health Reasoning and Epidemic Modelling: The Case of Black Death*, Springer-Verlag, 2005.

59. Samuel K. Cohn, "The Black Death and the Burning of Jews", *Past & Present*, 196, 2007, 3–36; Nico Voigtlaender and Hans-Joachim Voth, "Persecution Perpetuated: The Medieval Origins of Anti-Semitic Violence in Nazi Germany", NBER Working Paper, no. 17113. 201;

Theresa S. Finley, "Essays on Religion and Institutions in European Economic History", PhD Economics Dissertation, George Mason University, 2017, 48.

60. Christakos et al., "Black Death: The Background".

61. Anne Müller, "Managing Crises: Institutional Re-stabilisation of the Religious Orders in England after the Black Death (1347–1350)", Revue Mabillon, 16, 2005, 205–219.

62. Carlos Alvarez-Nogal and Leandro Prados de la Escosura, "The Rise and Fall of Spain (1270–1850)", Economic History Review, 66:1, 2013, 1–37.

63. Benedictow, Complete History, 278; Randal Paul Garza, Understanding Plague: The Medical and Imaginative Texts of Medieval Spain, Peter Lang, 2008, 60.

64. Thomas N. Bisson, Medieval Crown of Aragon: A Short History, Clarendon Press, 2000, 165.

65. Antoni Riera, "Crises and Changes in the Late Middle Ages", in Flocel Sabaté (ed.), The Crown of Aragon: A Singular Mediterranean Empire, Brill, 2017.

66. Teofilo F. Ruiz, Crisis and Continuity: Land and Town in Late Medieval Castile, University of Pennsylvania Press, 1994.

67. Ana Rodriguez, "Spain", in Kitsikopoulos (ed.), Agrarian Change.

68. Joseph P. Byrne, Encyclopedia of the Black Death, ABC-CLIO, 2012, 238; Janet Martin, Medieval Russia 980–1584, 2nd edn, Cambridge University Press, 2007, 223; John T. Alexander, Bubonic Plague in Early Modern Russia. Public Health and Urban Discourse, Oxford University Press, 2003 (orig. 1980).

69. Uli Schamiloglu, "Preliminary Remarks on the Role of Disease in the History of the Golden Horde", Central Asian Survey, 12:4, 1993, 447–457.

70. Schamiloglu, "The Impact of the Black Death on the Golden Horde".

71. Varlık, Plague and Empire, 118.

72. Idir Bitam et al., "New Rural Focus of Plague, Algeria", Emerging Infectious Diseases, 16:10, 2010, 1639–1640; Nicolas Cabanel et al., "Plague Outbreak in Libya, 2009, Unrelated to Plague in Algeria", Emerging Infectious Diseases, 19:2, 2013.

73. Jean-Claude Garcin, "The Regime of the Circassian Mamlūks", in Carl F. Petry (ed.), The Cambridge History of Egypt, Volume I. Islamic Egypt, 640–1517, Cambridge University Press, 1998; Stuart J. Borsch, "Nile Floods and the Irrigation System in Fifteenth-Century Egypt", Mamluk Studies Review, 4, 2000, 133; Karen Barkey, Empire of Difference. The Ottomans in Comparative Perspective, Cambridge University Press, 2008, 38; Russell Hopley, "Contagion in Islamic Lands Responses from Medieval Andalusia and North Africa", Journal for Early Modern Cultural Studies, 10:2, 2010, 45–64; Schamiloglu, "The Impact of the Black Death on the Golden Horde".

74. N. Voigtländer and H-J. Voth, "How the West 'Invented' Fertility Restriction", NBER Working Paper 17314, 2011.

75. Robert Bideleux and Ian Jeffries, A History of Eastern Europe: Crisis and Change, 2nd edn., Routledge, 2007. Also see Norman Davies, God's Playground. A History of Poland, Vol. I, Clarendon Press, 1981, 96.

76. Aleksander Pluskowski, The Archaeology of the Prussian Crusade. Holy War and Colonisation, Routledge, 2013, 308.

77. Daniel Panzac, "Plague and Seafaring in the Ottoman Mediterranean in the Eighteenth Century", in Maria Fusaro, Colin Heywood, and Mohamed-Salah Omri (eds.), Trade and Cultural Exchange in the Early Modern Mediterranean: Braudel's Maritime Legacy, I.B. Tauris, 2010.

Also see I Morozova et al., "New Ancient Eastern European *Yersinia Pestis* Genomes Illuminate the Dispersal of Plague in Europe", *Philosophical Transactions of the Royal Society B*, 375: 20190569, 2020.

78. Pal Engel, *Realm of St. Stephen: A History of Medieval Hungary, 895–1526*. I.B. Tauris, 2001, 169.

79. Jean W. Sedlar, *History of East Central Europe, Volume 3: East Central Europe in the Middle Ages, 1000–1500*, Washington University Press, 2011, 139.

80. David B. Miller, "Monumental Building as an Indicator of Economic Trends in Northern Rus' in the Late Kievan and Mongol Periods, 1138–1462", *American Historical Review*, 94:2, 1989, 360–390.

81. Lawrence N. Langer, "Plague and the Russian Countryside: Monastic Estates in the Late Fourteenth and Fifteenth Centuries", *Canadian-American Slavic Studies*, 10:3, 1973, 351–68.

82. Alexander, *Bubonic Plague in Early Modern Russia*.

83. Lawrence N. Langer, "The Black Death in Russia: Its Effects Upon Urban Labor", *Russian History*, 2.1, 1975, 53–67.

84. J.V.A. Fine, *The Late Medieval Balkans. A Critical Survey from the Late 12th Century to the Ottoman Conquest*, University of Michigan Press, 1987, 320–321.

85. Robin Harris, *Dubrovnik. A History*, SAQI, 2003, 210–211.

86. Zlata Blazina Tomic and Vesna Blazina, *Expelling the Plague: The Health Office and the Implementation of Quarantine in Dubrovnik, 1377–1533*. McGill-Queens University Press, 2015, 278 n.31.

87. Effie F. Athanassopoulos, "Landscape Archaeology and the Medieval Countryside: Settlement and Abandonment in the Nemea Region", *International Journal of Historical Archaeology*, 14:2, 2010, 255–270; David Jacoby, "Rural Exploitation and Market Economy in the Late Medieval Peloponnese", in Sharon E. J. Gerstel (ed.), *Viewing the Morea: Land and People in the Late Medieval Peloponnese*, Dumbarton Oaks Research Library, 2013, 213–275; Marian Malowist, *Western Europe, Eastern Europe and World Development 13th–18th Centuries: Essays of Marian Małowist*, J. Batou and H. Szlajfer (eds.), Brill, 2009, ch. 1; Heath W. Lowry, "Pushing the Stone Uphill: The Impact of Bubonic Plague on Ottoman Urban Society in the Fifteenth and Sixteenth Centuries", *Journal of Ottoman Studies*, 23, 2003, 93–132; Nukhet Varlik, "Disease and Empire: A History of Plague Epidemics in the Early Modern Ottoman Empire (1453–1600)", PhD thesis, University of Chicago, 2008, 100; Jonathan Shea, "The Late Byzantine City: Social, Economic and Institutional Profile", University of Birmingham PhD thesis, 2010.

88. Varlık, *Plague and Empire*, 124.

89. Pavel Murdzhev, "The Medieval Town in Bulgaria", PhD Dissertation, University of Florida, 2008.

90. Byrne, *Encyclopedia of the Black Death*, 87; Varlık, "Disease and Empire"; Gisele Marien, "The Black Death in Early Ottoman Territories: 1347–1550", MA thesis, Bilkent University, 2009.

91. Byrne, *Encyclopedia of the Black Death*; Varlık, *Plague and Empire*.

92. Russell Hopley, "Plague, Demographic Upheaval and Civilisational Decline: Ibn Khaldūn and Muḥammad al-Shaqūrī on the Black Death in North Africa and Islamic Spain", *Landscapes*, 17:2, 2016, 171–184.

93. Varlık, *Plague and Empire*, 138.

94. Marien, "The Black Death in Early Ottoman Territories", 89.

95. Uli Schamiloglu, "The Rise of the Ottoman Empire: The Black Death in Medieval Anatolia and Its Impact on Turkish Civilization", Neguin Yavari, Lawrence G. Potter, and Jean-Marc Ran Oppenheim (eds.), *Views from the Edge: Essays in Honor of Richard W. Bulliet*, Columbia University Press, 2004, 270; Also see Varlik, *Plague and Empire*, ch. 3–6; Barkey, *Empire of Difference*, 38; Şevket Pamuk, "The Black Death and the Origins of the 'Great Divergence' across Europe, 1300–1600", *European Review of Economic History*, 11 (2007), 289–317 (Pamuk actually focuses on the "Little Divergence"); Angeliki E. Laiou, "The Palaiologoi and the World Around Them (1261–1400)", *The Cambridge History of the Byzantine Empire c.500–1492*, Cambridge University Press, 2009, 803–833.

96. David Ayalon, "Regarding Population Estimates in the Countries of Medieval Islam", *Journal of the Economic and Social History of the Orient*, 28:1, 1985, 1–19.

97. E.g., Michael W. Dols, *The Black Death in the Middle East*, Princeton University Press, 1977, 204 n33.

98. Eliyahu Ashtor, "The Economic Decline of the Middle East during the Later Middle Ages: An Outline", in B. Z. Kedar (ed.), *Technology, Industry and Trade: The Levant versus Europe, 1250–1500*, Variorum, 1992.

99. Varlık, *Plague and Empire*, 194.

100. Bethany J. Walker, "From Ceramics to Social Theory: Reflections on Mamluk Archaeology Today", *Mamlūk Studies Review*, 14, 2010, 109–157.

101. Ashtor, "The Economic Decline of the Middle East"; Dols, *The Black Death in the Middle East*, 38–40, 45–6; Benedictow, *Complete History*, 61–62.

102. Michael W. Dols, "The Second Plague Pandemic and Its Recurrences in the Middle East: 1347–1894", *Journal of the Economic and Social History of the Orient*, 22:1, 1979, 162–189.

103. Albrecht Fuess, "Taxation and Armies" in Maribel Fierro (ed.), *The New Cambridge History of Islam*, Vol. 2, Cambridge University Press, 2010.

104. Stuart J. Borsch, *The Black Death in Egypt and England: A Comparative Study*, University of Texas Press, 2005, 24–25. Also see Yossef Rapoport, "Marriage and Divorce in the Muslim Near East, 1250–1517", PhD dissertation, Princeton University, 2002; Jean-Claude Garcin, "The Regime of the Circassian Mamlūks", in Carl F. Petry (ed.), *The Cambridge History of Egypt, Vol. 1*, Cambridge University Press, 1998; Melanie Koskella, "A Universal Approach to Plague Epidemics in Fifteenth Century Mamluk Egypt and Syria: Contemporary Bias, Classical Islamic Medicine and the Voices of the Ulama", PhD dissertation, University of Utah, 2014.

105. Stuart Borsch, "Plague Depopulation and Irrigation Decay in Medieval Egypt", in Green (ed.), *Pandemic Disease in the Medieval World*.

106. Stuart Borsch and Tarek Sabraa, "Plague Mortality in Late Medieval Cairo: Quantifying the Plague Outbreaks of 833/1430 and 864/1460", *Mamlūk Studies Review*, 19, 2016, 115–148.

107. Patricia Kozlik Kabra, "Patterns of Economic Continuity and Change in Early Hafsid Ifriqiya", PhD thesis, University of California, Los Angeles, 1994; Ramzi Rouighi, *The Making of a Mediterranean Emirate: Ifrīqiyā and Its Andalusis, 1200–1400*, University of Pennsylvania Press, 2011.

108. Said Ennahid, "Political Economy and Settlement Systems of Medieval Northern Morocco: An Archaeological-Historical Approach", PhD dissertation, Arizona State University, 2001, 125. Also see 115.

109. Byrne, *Encyclopedia of the Black Death*, 51; Benedictow, *Complete History*, 61–62 and passim.

110. Patrick Wing, *The Jalayirids: Dynastic State Formation in the Mongol Middle East*, Edinburgh University Press, 2016, ch. 5, 6. Also see Peter Jackson, "Jalayerids", *Encyclopedia Iranica*, available online.

111. Dols, *The Black Death in the Middle East*, 168, 215.

112. Ahmad Fazlinejad and Farajollah Ahmadi, "The Black Death in Iran, According to Iranian Historical Accounts from the Fourteenth through Fifteenth Centuries", *Journal of Persianate Studies*, 11.1, 56–71, 2018.

113. Jackson, "Jalayerids", Charles Melville and ʿAbbas Zaryab, "Chobanids", ʿAbbas Zaryab, "Iraq: From the Mongols to the Safavids", all in *Encyclopaedia Iranica*.

114. H. Algar, "Astarabadi, Fazlallah (d. 796/1394), Founder of the Ḥorūfī Religion", *Encyclopaedia Iranica*.

115. Maria Subtelny, *Timurids in Transition: Turko-Persian Politics and Acculturation in Medieval Iran*, Brill, 2007, 121n.

116. H. R. Roemer, "The Successors of Timur", in Peter Jackson and Lawrence Lockhart (eds.), *The Cambridge History of Iran Vol. 6*, Cambridge University Press, 1986.

117. Fazlinejad and Ahmadi, "The Black Death in Iran"; Maria Subtelny, *Timurids in Transition*, 120–121.

118. David J. Roxburg, *The Persian Album, 1400–1600*, Yale University Press, 2005, ch. 3.

119. *Encyclopedia Islamica*.

120. James L. Webb, "Globalization of Disease, 1300–1900", and Robert B. Marks, "Exhausting the Earth: Environment and History in the Early Modern World", both in J. H. Bentley, S. Subrahmanyam, and M. Wiesner-Hanks (eds.), *The Cambridge World History, Vol. 6*, Cambridge University Press, 2015.

121. Stephan Barisitz, *Central Asia and the Silk Road. Economic Rise and Decline over Several Millennia*, Springer Cham, 2017, ch. 3.

122. Justin B. Black, "Population Genetic Analysis of Invasive Rattus: Implications for Evolutionary Biology, Disease Ecology and Invasion Biology", PhD dissertation, Oklahoma State University, 2012, 25.

123. Carla Rahn Phillips, *Six Galleons for the King of Spain. Imperial Defense in the Early 17th Century*, Johns Hopkins University Press, 1986, 157.

124. Jeremy Baskes, "Risky Ventures: Reconsidering Mexico's Colonial Trade System", *Colonial Latin American Review*, 14:1, 2005, 27–54.

125. Tomic and Blazina, *Expelling the Plague*.

126. Byrne, *Encyclopedia of the Black Death*, 305–306; Bossak and Welford, "Medieval Trade Activity and a Viral Etiology".

127. Ibid.; Lars Walloe, "Medieval and Modern Bubonic Plague; Some Clinical Continuities", in Vivian Nutton (ed.), *Pestilential Complexities: Understanding Medieval Plague*, Wellcome Trust Centre for the History of Medicine at UCL, 2008.

128. Benedictow, *What Disease Was Plague?*, 6, and *The Complete History*, 58–59; Roberto Rebeil, "Induction of the *Yersinia pestis* PhoP-PhoQ Regulatory System in the Flea and Its Role in Producing a Transmissible Infection", *Journal of Bacteriology*, 195.9, 2013, 1920–1930; Walloe, "Medieval and Modern Bubonic Plague".

129. Panzac, "Plague and Seafaring".

130. Gérard Chouin, "Reflections on Plague in African History (14th–19th c), *Afriques*, 9, 2018. Also see Daphne E. Gallagher and Stephen A. Dueppen, "Recognizing Plague Epidemics in the Archaeological Record of West Africa", in the same publication.

131. *The Travels of Ibn Battuta, AD 1325–1354. Volume IV*, H.A.R. Gibb and C. F. Beckingham (eds.), Routledge, 2016 edn. Also see Ulrich Rebstock, "West Africa and Its Early Empires", in Maribel Fierro (ed.), *The New Cambridge History of Islam*, Vol. 2, Cambridge University Press, 2010.

132. Marie-Laure Derat, "Du lexique aux talismans: occurrences de la peste dans la Corne de l'Afrique du XIIIe au XVe siècle", and Monica H. Green, "Putting Africa on the Black Death Map: Narratives from Genetics and History", both in *Afriques*, 9, 2018.

133. Green, "Putting Africa on the Black Death Map."

134. Mary E. Prendergast et al., "Reconstructing Asian Faunal Introductions to Eastern Africa from Multi-Proxy Biomolecular and Archaeological Datasets", *PLoS one*, 12.8, 2017.

135. Barry Cunliffe, *By Steppe, Desert, and Ocean: The Birth of Eurasia*, Oxford University Press, 2015, 24; Shireen Moosvi, *People, Taxation, and Trade in Mughal India*, Oxford University Press, 2008, 248; Christoph Marcinowski, "The Safavid Presence in the Indian Ocean: A Reappraisal of the *Ship of Solayman*, a Seventeenth-Century Travel Account to Siam", in Willem Floor and Edmund Herzig (eds.), *Iran and the World in the Safavid Age*, , I.B. Tauris, 2012.

136. E.g., Andelko Vlasic, "Georgius Huszthius, a Traveler from Croatia and His Account of the Ottoman Naval Campaign in India (1538–9)", *Acta Orientalia Academiae Scientiarum Hung.*, 68.3 (3), 2015, 349–362; Sanjay Subrahmanyam, "A Note on the Rise of Surat in the Sixteenth Century", *Journal of the Economic and Social History of the Orient*, 43.1, 2000, 23–33.

137. Dols, *The Black Death in the Middle East*, 43.

138. Victor Lieberman, "Charter State Collapse in Southeast Asia, ca. 1250–1400, as a Problem in Regional and World History", *American Historical Review*, 116.4, 2011, 937–963.

139. B. M. Ansari, "An Account of Bubonic Plague in Seventeenth Century India in an Autobiography of a Mughal Emperor", *Journal of Infection*, 29, 1994, 351–352.

140. Tim Dyson, *A Population History of India: From the First Modern People to the Present Day*, Oxford University Press, 2018.

141. Nükhet Varlık, "Conquest, Urbanization and Plague Networks in the Ottoman Empire, 1453–1600", in Christine Woodhead (ed.), *The Ottoman World*, Taylor & Francis, 2011.

142. Paul Slack, *The Impact of Plague in Tudor and Stuart England*, Clarendon Press, 1985, 108.

143. Dols, "The Second Plague Pandemic".

144. Geoffrey Parker, *Global Crisis: War, Climate Change and Catastrophe in the Seventeenth Century*, Yale University Press, 2013, ch. 4; E. A. Ekert, "The Retreat of Plague from Central Europe, 1640–1720: A Geomedical Approach", *Bulletin of the History of Medicine*, 2000 (74), 1–28; Erika Monahan, *The Merchants of Siberia. Trade in Early Modern Eurasia*, Cornell University Press, 2016, 219; Katharine R. Dean et al., "Human Ectoparasites and the Spread of Plague in Europe during the Second Pandemic", *Proceedings of the National Academy of Science, USA* Early Edition, January 2018; www.pnas.org/cgi/doi/10.1073/pnas.1715640115; Varlık, *Plague and Empire*, 194.

145. Sharon DeWitte and Philip Slavin, "Between Famine and Death: England on the Eve of the Black Death—Evidence from Paleoepidemiology and Manorial Accounts", *Journal of*

Interdisciplinary History, 44:1, 2013, 37–60; Sharon N. DeWitte, "Archaeological Evidence of Epidemics Can Inform Future Epidemics", *Annual Review of Anthropology*, 45, 2016, 63–77.

146. William Jordan, "The Great Famine 1315–1322 Revisited", in Scott G. Bruce (ed.), *Ecologies and Economies in Medieval and Early Modern Europe: Studies in Environmental History for Richard C. Hoffmann*, Brill, 2010, 45.

147. E.g., Paul Slack, *Plague. A Very Short Introduction*, Oxford University Press, 2012, 23; C. M. Woolgar, T. Waldron, and D. Serjeantson (eds.), *Food in Medieval England: Diet and Nutrition*, Oxford University Press, 2006; Morgan Kelly and Cormac O'Grada, "Living Standards and Mortality Since the Middle Ages", *Economic History Review*, 67:2, 2014, 358–381.

148. Neil Cummins, "Lifespans of the European Elite, 800–1800", *Journal of Economic History*, 77:2, 2017, 406–439.

149. Bruce M. S. Campbell, *The Great Transition. Climate, Disease, and Society in the Late-Medieval World*, Cambridge University Press, 2016, 308, 316.

150. Guido Alfani, "Plague in Seventeenth-Century Europe and the Decline of Italy: An Epidemiological Hypothesis", *European Review of Economic History*, 17, 2013, 408–430; Cohn, *The Black Death Transformed*, 229; Christakos and Olea, "New Space-Time Perspectives"; Willian Rees, "The Black Death in Wales", *Transactions of the Royal Historical Society*, Fourth Series, 3, 1920, 115–135; Small, *Late Medieval France*, 55.

151. Chris Given-Wilson, *The English Nobility in the Late Middle Ages: The Fourteenth-Century Political Community*, Routledge, 1996, 114.

152. Karl-Erik Frandsen, *The Last Plague in the Baltic Region 1709–1713*, Copenhagen University Press, 2010; Byrne, *Encyclopedia of the Black Death*; Ekert, "The Retreat of Plague from Central Europe".

153. Paul Lendvai, *The Hungarians. A Thousand Years of Victory in Defeat*, C. Hurst, 2003 (orig. 1999), 153.

154. Roger Scholfield, "The Last Visitation of the Plague in Sweden: The Case of Bräkne-Hoby in 1710–11", *Economic History Review*, 69:2, 2016, 600–626.

155. Jean-Noël Biraben, "Certain Demographic Characteristics of the Plague Epidemic in France, 1720–22", *Daedalus*, 97:2, 1968, 536–545; Michel Signoli et al., "Paleodemography and Historical Demography in the Context of an Epidemic: Plague in Provence in the Eighteenth Century", *Population*, 57:6, 2002; Christian A. Devaux, "Small Oversights that Led to the Great Plague of Marseille (1720–1723): Lessons from the Past", *Infection, Genetics and Evolution*, 14, 2013, 169–185.

156. Alfani, *Calamities and the Economy in Renaissance Italy*, 46.

157. Alexander, *Bubonic Plague in Early Modern Russia*, ch. 10, and "Reconsiderations on Plague in Early Modern Russia", *Jahrbücher für Geschichte Osteuropas*, 34.2, 1986.

158. Hans Heilbronner, "The Russian Plague of 1878–79", *Slavic Review*, 21.1, 1962, 89–112.

159. Varlık, *Plague and Empire*.

160. Nükhet Varlık, "Why the Ottoman Experience of Plague Matters", in Green (ed.), *Pandemic Disease in the Medieval World*.

161. Panzac, "Plague and Seafaring".

162. Alan Mikhail, "Plague and Environment in Late Ottoman Egypt", in Alan Mikhail (ed.), *Water on Sand: Environmental Histories of the Middle East and North Africa*, Oxford University Press, 2013.

163. Houari Touatiin, "Ottoman Maghrib", *The New Cambridge History of Islam*, Vol. 2.

164. David Herlihy, *The Black Death and the Transformation of the West*, Samuel K. Cohn (ed.), Harvard University Press, 1997, 57; Voigtländer and Voth, "How the West 'Invented' Fertility Restriction"; Jan Luiten van Zanden, Sarah Carmichael, and Tine De Moor, *Capital Women: The European Marriage Pattern, Female Empowerment and Economic Development in Western Europe 1300–1800*, Oxford University Press, 2019.

165. T. De Moor and J. L. Van Zanden, "Girl Power: The European Marriage Pattern and Labour Markets in the North Sea Region in the Late Medieval and Early Modern Period", *Economic History Review*, 63:1, 2010, 1–33.

166. Tracy Dennison and Sheilagh Ogilvie, "Does the European Marriage Pattern Explain Economic Growth?", *Journal of Economic History*, 74:3, 2014; Jeremy Edwards and Sheilagh Ogilvie, "Did the Black Death Cause Economic Development by 'Inventing' Fertility Restriction?", CESIFO Working Papers, No. 7016, 2018.

167. Christiane Klapisch-Zuber, "Plague and Family Life", in Michael Jones (ed.), *The New Cambridge Medieval History, Vol. 6*, Cambridge University Press, 2000, 40; Cohn, *The Black Death Transformed*, 199n. Also see Alfani, "Plague in Seventeenth-Century Europe and the Decline of Italy", 408–430; Sloane, *The Black Death in London*, 76; Hatcher, *The Black Death. An Intimate History*; Scott and Duncan, *Biology of Plagues*.

168. Byrne, *Encyclopedia of the Black Death*, 312–313.

169. Benedictow, *Complete History*, 271.

170. Peter R. Larson, "Conflict and Compromise in the Late Medieval Countryside: Lords and Peasants in Durham, 1349–1430", PhD dissertation, Rutgers University, 2004, 124.

171. Benedictow, "New Perspectives in Medieval Demography: The Medieval Demographic System"; also see Hatcher, *The Black Death. An Intimate History*; Scott and Duncan, *Biology of Plagues*; Sloane, *The Black Death in London*, 76; Maryanne Kowaleski, "Gendering Demographic Change in the Middle Ages", in Judith Bennett and Ruth Karras (eds.), *The Oxford Handbook of Women and Gender in Medieval Europe*, , 2013; D. L. Smail, "Mapping Networks and Knowledge in Medieval Marseille, 13377–1362", PhD dissertation, University of Michigan, 1994, 70–74.

172. *Cronaca aquilana rimata di Buccio di Ranallo*, reproduced in Trevor Dean (ed.), *The Towns of Italy in the Later Middle Ages*, Manchester University Press, 2000, 185–186. Punctuation adjusted.

173. Paolo Malanima, "Energy and Population Growth in Europe: The Medieval Growth: (10th–14th Centuries)", Institute of Studies on Mediterranean Societies, National Research Council, 2010.

174. Paolo Malanima, *Pre-Modern European Economy: One Thousand Years (10th–19th Centuries)*, Brill, 2009, 2–9. Also see Anne E. C. McCants, "Historical Demography", in Hamish Scott (ed.), *The Oxford Handbook of Early Modern European History, 1350–1750: Vol I*, 2015; Richard C. Hoffman, *An Environmental History of Medieval Europe*, Cambridge University Press, 2014, 293; For older estimates, see Josiah C. Russell, "Population in Europe", in Carlo M. Cipolla (ed.), *The Fontana Economic History of Europe, Vol. I*, Collins/Fontana, 1972, 25–71; Paul Bairoch, *Cities and Economic Development. From the Dawn of History to the Present*, Chicago University Press, 1988, 128; Livi Bacci, *The Population of Europe*.

175. McCants, "Historical Demography"; Geoffrey, *Global Crisis*; Jan de Vries, "The Economic Crisis of the Seventeenth Century after Fifty Years", *Journal of Interdisciplinary History*, 40:2, 2009, 151–194.

Chapter 2: The Origins and Dynamics of the Black Death

1. Giovanna Morelli et al., "*Yersinia pestis* Genome Sequencing Identifies Patterns of Global Phylogenetic Diversity", *Nature Genetics*, 42.12, 2010–12, 1140–1143; Cui Y. and Song Y., "Genome and Evolution of *Yersinia pestis*", in R. Yang and A. Anisimov (eds.), *Yersinia pestis: Retrospective and Perspective*, Springer, 2016; C. Demeure et al., "*Yersinia pestis* and Plague: An Updated View on Evolution, Virulence Determinants, Immune Subversion, Vaccination, and Diagnostics", *Genes and Immunity*, 20:5, 2019, 357–370; B. J. Hinnebusch, C. O. Jarrett, and D. M. Bland, "Molecular and Genetic Mechanisms That Mediate Transmission of *Yersinia pestis* by Fleas", *Biomolecules*, 2021, 11, 210; R. Barbieri et al., "*Yersinia pestis*: The Natural History of Plague", *Clinical Microbiology Reviews*, 34:1, 2020.

2. Nicolas Rascovan et al., "Emergence and Spread of Basal Lineages of *Yersinia pestis* during the Neolithic Decline", *Cell*, 176, 2019, 295–305.

3. S. Rasmussen et al., "Early Divergent Strains of *Yersinia pestis* in Eurasia 5,000 Years Ago", *Cell* 163, 2015, 571–582; Daniel L. Zimbler et al., "Early Emergence of *Yersinia pestis* as a Severe Respiratory Pathogen", *Nature Communications*, 6:7487, 2015.

4. Maria A. Spyrou et al., "Analysis of 3800-Year-Old *Yersinia pestis* Genomes Suggests Bronze Age Origin for Bubonic Plague", *Nature Communications*, 9:2234, 2018.

5. Amy J. Vogler , Paul Keim, and David M.Wagner, "A Review of Methods for Subtyping *Yersinia pestis*: From Phenotypes to Whole Genome Sequencing", *Infection, Genetics and Evolution*, 37, 2016, 21–36; Also see Z. Qi, Y. Cui, Q. Zhang, and R. Yang, "Taxonomy of *Yersinia pestis*", in Yang and Anisimov (eds.), *Yersinia pestis*.

6. Kirsten I. Bos et al., "A Draft Genome of *Yersinia Pestis* from Victims of the Black Death," *Nature*, 478:12, 2011; Monica H. Green, "Taking 'Pandemic' Seriously: Making the Black Death Global", and Ann G. Carmichael, "Plague Persistence in Western Europe: A Hypothesis", both in Green (ed.), *Pandemic Disease in the Medieval World: Rethinking the Black Death*, ARC Medieval Press, 2014; K. I. Bos et al., "Eighteenth Century *Yersinia pestis* Genomes Reveal the Long-Term Persistence of an Historical Plague Focus", *eLife*, 5, 2016; David M. Wagner et al., "*Yersinia pestis* and the Plague of Justinian 541–543 AD: A Genomic Analysis", the *lancet.com/infection*, 14, 2014.

7. Qi et al., "Taxonomy of *Yersinia pestis*".

8. V. V Kutyrev et al., "Phylogeny and Classification of *Yersinia pestis* through the Lens of Strains from the Plague Foci of Commonwealth of Independent States", *Frontiers in Microbiology*, 9:1106, 2018; Barbieri et al., "Natural History of Plague"; Marcel Keller et al., "Ancient *Yersinia pestis* Genomes from across Western Europe Reveal Early Diversification during the First Pandemic (541–750)", *PNAS Evolution*, 116 (25):12363–12372, 2019.

9. Yujun Cui et al., "Historical Variations in Mutation Rate in an Epidemic Pathogen, *Yersinia pestis*", *Proceedings of the National Academy of Science, USA*, 110:2, 2013, 577–582. Also see Xiaoqing Xu et al., "Genetic Diversity and Spatial-Temporal Distribution of *Yersinia pestis* in Qinghai Plateau, China", *PLOS Neglected Tropical Diseases*, 12:6, 2018.

10. Galina A. Eroshenko et al., "*Yersinia pestis* Strains of Ancient Phylogenetic Branch 0.ANT Are Widely Spread in the High Mountain Plague Foci of Kyrgyzstan", *PLoS one*, 12:10, 2017; Kutyrev et al., "Phylogeny and Classification of *Yersinia pestis*". I am indebted to John L. Brooke for first drawing my attention to this research.

11. Gulmira Sariyeva et al., "Marmots and *Yersinia pestis* Strains in Two Plague Endemic Areas of Tien Shan Mountains", *Frontiers in Veterinary Science*, 6:207, 2019, and "Current Status of the

Sari-Dzhas Natural Focus of Plague, Kyrgyzstan: Epizootic Activity and Marmot Population", *Vector-Borne Zoonotic Diseases*, 18:10, 2018, 524–532; J. Batbold, N. Batsaikhan, and S. Shar, *Marmota baibacina* (errata version published in 2017). *The IUCN Red List of Threatened Species* 2016: https://dx.doi.org/10.2305/IUCN.UK.2016-3.RLTS.T12829A22258206.en.

12. The fullest recent study is P. W. Markman, "Candidate Reservoir Underlying Re-emergent Plague Outbreaks", PhD dissertation, Colorado State University, 2019.

13. Kenneth B. Armitage, *Marmot Biology. Sociality, Individual Fitness, and Population Dynamics*, Cambridge University Press, 2014, ch. 17; Philip Slavin, "Death by the Lake: Mortality Crisis in Early Fourteenth-Century Central Asia", *Journal of Interdisciplinary History*, L.1, 2019, 59–90; Markman, "Re-emergent Plague Outbreaks", ch. 3.

14. Barbieri et al., "Natural History of Plague".

15. G. Sariyeva et al., "Marmots and *Yersinia pestis* Strains in Two Plague Endemic Areas of Tien Shan Mountains", *Frontiers in Veterinary Science*, 6:207, 2019. doi: 10.3389/fvets.2019.00207.

16. George D. Sussman, "Was the Black Death in India and China?", *Bulletin of the History of Medicine*, 85.3, 2011, 319–355. Also see Wilhelm Baum and Dietmar W. Winkler, *The Church of the East: A Concise History*, Routledge, 2003, 77–78.

17. Elizabeth Brite et al., "Kara-tepe, Karakalpakstan: Agropastoralism in a Central Eurasian Oasis in the 4th/5th century A.D. Transition", *Journal of Field Archaeology*, 42:6, 2017, 514–529.

18. Slavin, "Death by the Lake".

19. Uli Schamiloglu, "The Impact of the Black Death on the Golden Horde: Politics, Economy, Society, Civilization", *Golden Horde Review*, 5:2, 2017.

20. Michael Dols, "Geographical Origins of the Black Death. Comment", *Bulletin of the History of Medicine*, 52:1, 1978, 112–120.

21. Sussman, "Was the Black Death in India and China?".

22. Richard Von Glahn, *The Economic History of China*, Cambridge University Press, 2015, ch. 2 and 4.

23. Slavin, "Death by the Lake".

24. Robert Hymes, "Epilogue: A Hypothesis on the East Asian Beginnings of the *Yersinia pestis* Polytomy", in Green (ed.), *Pandemic Disease in the Medieval World*.

25. Robert Hymes, "*Yersinia pestis* in Thirteenth-Century China? Evidence from Chinese Medical Writings", Columbia University, 2020. Copy kindly provided by the author.

26. Monica H. Greene, "The Four Black Deaths'," *American Historical Review*, 125:5, 2020, 1601–1631.

27. Sussman, "Was the Black Death in India and China?"

28. Quoted in ibid.

29. Monica Green, Review of *The Great Transition* by Bruce Campbell, *Inference*, 4:1, 2018.

30. Demeure et al.,"*Yersinia pestis* and Plague"; Keller et al., "Ancient *Yersinia pestis* genomes"; Eroshenko et al., "Evolution and Circulation of *Yersinia pestis* in the Northern Caspian and Northern Aral Sea Regions in the 20th–21st Centuries", *PLoS one*, 16(2): e0244615, 2021.

31. Kenneth B. Armitage, *Marmot Biology. Sociality, Individual Fitness, & Population Dynamics*, Cambridge University Press, 2014, ch. 2.

32. Liesbeth I. Wilschut, "Remote Sensing for Landscape Epidemiology: Spatial Analysis of Plague Hosts in Kazakhstan", PhD dissertation, Universiteit Utrecht, 2015, and see section III of this chapter.

33. Slavin, "Death by the Lake".

34. Thomas T. Allsen, "Mongols as Vectors for Cultural Transmission", in Nicola Di Cosmo, Allen J. Frank, and Peter B. Golden (eds.), *The Cambridge History of Inner Asia: The Chinggisid Age*, Cambridge University Press, 2009.

35. Hymes, "A Hypothesis on the East Asian Beginnings of the *Yersinia pestis* Polytomy".

36. Sussman, "Was the Black Death in India and China?"; Ole Benedictow et al., "History of the Plague", in Michaela Harbeck, Kristin von Heyking, and Heiner Schwarzberg (eds.), *Sickness, Hunger, War, and Religion. Multidisciplinary Perspectives*, Rachel Carson Center, 2012.

37. Yujiang Zhang et al., "Dynamics of *Yersinia pestis* and Its Antibody Response in Great Gerbils (*Rhombomys opimus*) by Subcutaneous Infection", *PLoS one*, 7(10), 2012, 46820. Also see B. V. Schmid et al., "Local Persistence and Extinction of Plague in a Metapopulation of Great Gerbil Burrows, Kazakhstan", *Epidemics*, 4, 2012, 211–218; Lise Heier et al., "Persistence of Plague Outbreaks Among Great Gerbils in Kazakhstan: Effects of Host Population Dynamics", *Population Ecology*, 57, 2015, 473–484; J. Reijniers et al., "Plague Epizootic Cycles in Central Asia", *Biology Letters*, 10, 2014, 0302; Gage, "Factors Affecting the Spread and Maintenance of Plague"; Stephen Davis et al., "Predictive Thresholds for Plague in Kazakhstan", *Science*, 304.5671, 2004, 736–738.

38. Zhang et al., "Dynamics of *Yersinia pestis* and Its Antibody Response in Great Gerbils".

39. Susan D. Jones et al., "Living with Plague: Lessons from the Soviet Union's Anti-Plague System", *Proceedings of the National Academy of Science*, 116:19, 2019, 9155–9163.

40. V. M. Dubyanskiy and A. B. Yeshanov, "Ecology of *Yersinia pestis* and the Epidemiology of Plague", in Yang and Anisimov (eds.), *Yersinia pestis*.

41. Zhang et al., "Dynamics of *Yersinia pestis* and Its Antibody Response in Great Gerbils".

42. Dubyanskiy and Yeshanov, "Ecology of *Yersinia pestis*".

43. Ibid.

44. Eroshenko et al., "Evolution and Circulation of *Yersinia pestis*".

45. Surong Sun et al., "Draft Genome Sequence of *Yersinia pestis* Strain 2501, an Isolate from the Great Gerbil Plague Focus in Xinjiang, China", *Journal of Bacteriology*, 194:19, 2012, 5447–5448.

46. Alim Aikimbajev et al., "Plague Peculiarities in Kazakhstan at the Present Time", *Przeglad Epidemiologiczny*, 57, 2003, 593–598.

47. Liesbeth I. Wilschut, "Remote Sensing for Landscape Epidemiology", section 3.2.3.

48. Aikimbajev et al., "Plague Peculiarities in Kazakhstan"; B. V. Schmid et al., "Local Persistence and Extinction of Plague in a Metapopulation of Great Gerbil Burrows, Kazakhstan", *Epidemics*, 4, 2012, 211–218.

49. D. T. Potts, "Camel Hybridization and the Role of *Camelus bactrianus* in the Ancient Near East", *Journal of the Economic and Social History of the Orient*, 47:2, 2004, 143–165.

50. V. N. Fedorov, "Plague in Camels and Its Prevention in the USSR", *Bulletin of the World Health Organization*, 23, 1960, 275–281.

51. Aikimbajev et al., "Plague Peculiarities in Kazakhstan".

52. Wilschut, "Remote Sensing for Landscape Epidemiology".

53. Fedorov, "Plague in Camels and Its Prevention in the USSR".

54. Maliya Alia Malek, Idir Bitam, and Michel Drancourt, "Plague in Arab Maghreb, 1940–2015: A Review", *Frontiers in Public Health*, 4:112, 2016.

55. Stephan Barisitz, *Central Asia and the Silk Road. Economic Rise and Decline over Several Millennia*, Springer Cham, 2017, ch. 2.

56. Slavin, "Death by the Lake".

57. Manuel Berdoy and Lee C. Drickamer, "Comparative Social Organization and Life History of *Rattus* and *Mus*", in Jerry O. Wolff and Paul W. Sherman (eds.), *Rodent Societies: An Ecological and Evolutionary Perspective*, University of Chicago Press, 2008.

58. Ken P. Aplin et al., "Multiple Geographic Origins of Commensalism and Complex Dispersal History of Black Rats (Commensalism and Dispersal History of Black Rats)", *PLoS one*, 2011, 6:11, 26357; Mumtaz Baig et al., "Phylogeography of the Black Rat *Rattus rattus* in India and the Implications for Its Dispersal History in Eurasia", *Biological Invasions*, 21:2, 2019, 417–433.

59. P. Armitage, "Unwelcome Companions: Ancient Rats Reviewed", *Antiquity*, 68, 1994, 231–240; Z. S. Kovacs, "Dispersal History of an Invasive Rodent in Hungary—Subfossil Finds of *rattus rattus*", *Acta Zoologica Academiae Scientiarum Hungaricae*, 58:4, 379–394, 2012.

60. Armitage, "Unwelcome Companions".

61. Lars Walloe, "Medieval and Modern Bubonic Plague; Some Clinical Continuities", in Vivian Nutton (ed.), *Pestilential Complexities: Understanding Medieval Plague*, Wellcome Trust Centre for the History of Medicine at UCL, 2008; Daniel Panzac, "Plague and Seafaring in the Ottoman Mediterranean in the Eighteenth Century", in Maria Fusaro, Colin Heywood, and Mohamed-Salah Omri (eds.), *Trade and Cultural Exchange in the Early Modern Mediterranean: Braudel's Maritime Legacy*, I.B. Tauris, 2010, 54; Christakos and Olea, "New Space-Time Perspectives".

62. Cohn, *Black Death Transformed*, 9.

63. Gillespie, "*Rattus rattus*"; "Rattus rattus", Animal Diversity Web, University of Michigan.

64. Joseph P. Byrne, *Encyclopedia of the Black Death*, ABC-CLIO, 2012, p. 308; Voahangy Andrianaivoarimanana et al., "Immune Responses to Plague Infection in Wild *Rattus rattus*, in Madagascar: A Role in Foci Persistence?", *PLoS one*, 7:6, 2012.

65. Philip Armitage, Barbara West, and Ken Steedman, "New Evidence of Black Rat in Roman London", *London Archaeologist*, 4, 1984, 381.

66. David Durham and Elizabeth R. Casman, "Threshold Conditions for the Persistence of Plague Transmission in Urban Rats", *Risk Analysis*, 29:12, 2009, 1655–1663.

67. David E. Davis, "The Scarcity of Rats and the Black Death: An Ecological History", *Journal of Interdisciplinary History*, 16:3, 1986, 455–470.

68. A. B. Savinetsky and O. A. Krylovich, "On the History of the Spread of the Black Rat (*Rattus rattus*) in Northwestern Russia", *Biology Bulletin*, 38:2, 2011, 203–207.

69. Maev Kennedy, "Black Death Study Lets Rats Off the Hook", *Guardian*, August 17, 2011, reporting interview with archaeologist Barney Sloane.

70. Anne Hufthammer and Lars Walloe, "Rats Cannot Have Been Intermediate Hosts for *Yersinia pestis* during Medieval Plague Epidemics in Northern Europe", *Journal of Archaeological Science*, 40:4, 2013, 1752–1759.

71. Daniel Antoine, "The Archaeology of 'Plague'," in Nutton (ed.), *Pestilential Complexities*.

72. Savinetsky and Krylovich, "On the History of the Spread of the Black Rat (*Rattus rattus* L., 1758) in Northwestern Russia".

73. Eva Panagiotakopulu, "Pharaonic Egypt and the Origins of Plague", *Journal of Biogeography*, 31:2, 2004, 269–275.

74. Michael McCormick, "Rats, Communications, and Plague: Toward an Ecological History", *Journal of Interdisciplinary History*, 34:1, 2003, 1–25.

75. Ole Georg Moseng, "Climate, Ecology and Plague: The Second and the Third Pandemic Reconsidered", in Lars Bisgaard and Leif Søndergaard (eds.), *Living with The Black Death*, Southern Denmark University Press, 2009, 23–45.

76. Michael Kosoy et al., "Aboriginal and Invasive Rats of Genus Rattus as Hosts of Infectious Agents", *Vector-borne and Zoonotic Diseases*, 15:1, 2015; Barbieri et al., "Natural History of Plague".

77. C. Tollenaere et al., "AFLP Genome Scan in the Black Rat (*Rattus rattus*) from Madagascar: Detecting Genetic Markers Undergoing Plague-Mediated Selection", *Molecular Ecology*, 20, 2011, 1026–1038; Stuart Borsch and Tarek Sabraa, "Plague Mortality in Late Medieval Cairo: Quantifying the Plague Outbreaks of 833/1430 and 864/1460", *Mamluk Studies Review*, 19, 2016, 115–148.

78. Kevin Reilly, "The Black Rat", in Terry O'Connor and Naomi Sykes (eds.), *Extinctions and Invasions. A Social History of British Fauna*, Windgather, 2010.

79. Terry O'Connor, "The House Mouse", in ibid.

80. Armitage, "Unwelcome Companions"; Kovacs, "Dispersal History"; E. E. Puckett et al., "Commensal Rats and Humans: Integrating Rodent Phylogeography and Zooarchaeology to Highlight Connections between Human Societies", *BioEssays: News and Reviews in Molecular, Cellular and Developmental Biology*, 42:5, 2020, e1900160.

81. Barney Sloane interviewed by Maev Kennedy in "Black Death Study Lets Rats Off the Hook"; Barney Sloane, *The Black Death in London*, History Press, 2011.

82. Sloane, *The Black Death in London*, 184.

83. Dionysios Ch. Stathakopoulos, *Famine and Pestilence in the Late Roman and Early Byzantine Empire: A Systematic Survey of Subsistence Crises and Epidemics*, Ashgate, 2004.

84. R. D. Perry and J. D. Fetherston, "*Yersinia pestis*—Etiologic Agent of Plague", *Clinical Microbiology Reviews*, 10:1, 1997, 35–66.

85. Kosoy et al., "Aboriginal and Invasive Rats of Genus *Rattus*"; Barbara Bramanti et al., "The Third Plague Pandemic in Europe", *Proceedings of the Royal Society B*, 286: 2018242, 2019.

86. R. A. McDonald, M. R. Hutchings, and J.G.M. Keeling, "The Status of Ship Rats *Rattus rattus* on the Shiant Islands, Outer Hebrides, Scotland", *Biological Conservation*, 82:1, 1997, 113–117.

87. Savinetsky and Krylovich, "On the History of the Spread of the Black Rat (*Rattus rattus* L., 1758) in Northwestern Russia".

88. I. Morozova et al., "New Ancient Eastern European *Yersinia pestis* Genomes Illuminate the Dispersal of Plague in Europe", *Philosophical Transactions of the Royal Society B*, 375, 2020, 20190569.

89. Michael Winter, "The Ottoman Occupation", in Carl F. Petry (ed.), *The Cambridge History of Egypt, Vol. I*, Cambridge University Press, 1998, 509.

90. B. Joseph Hinnebusch, Clayton O. Jarrett, and David M. Bland, "'Fleaing' the Plague: Adaptations of *Yersinia pestis* to Its Insect Vector That Lead to Transmission", *Annual Review of Microbiology*, 71, 2017, 215–232.

91. Nicole Boivin et al., "East Africa and Madagascar in the Indian Ocean World", *Journal of World Prehistory*, 26, 2013, 213–281; Russell E. Enscore et al., "The Changing Triad of Plague in Uganda: Invasive Black Rats (*Rattus Rattus*), Indigenous Small Mammals, and Their Fleas", *Journal of Vector Ecology*, 45:2, 2020, 333–355.

92. Katharine R. Dean et al., "Human Ectoparasites and the Spread of Plague in Europe during the Second Pandemic", *Proceedings of the National Academy of Science, USA*, 115:6, 2018, 1304–1309; Rémi Barbieri et al., "Plague, Camels, and Lice", *PNAS Microbiology*, 16, 2019, 7620–7621; S. Badiaga and P. Brouqui, "Human Louse-Transmitted Infectious Diseases", *Clinical Microbiology and Infection*, 18, 2012, 332–337; S. W. Park et al., "Human Ectoparasite Transmission of the Plague During the Second Pandemic Is Only Weakly Supported by Proposed Mathematical Models", *Proceedings of the National Academy of Science, USA*, 115:34, 2018, E7892–E7893; K. R. Dean et al., "Reply to Park et al.: Human Ectoparasite Transmission of Plague During the Second Pandemic Is Still Plausible", *Proceedings of the National Academy of Science, USA*, 115:34, 2018, E7894–E7895.

93. Badiaga and Brouqui, "Human Louse-Transmitted Infectious Diseases".

94. Bitam et al., "Fleas and Flea-Borne Diseases".

95. Dean et al., "Human Ectoparasites and the Spread of Plague in Europe during the Second Pandemic".

96. Rebecca Eisen, David Dennis, and Kenneth Gage, "The Role of Early-Phase Transmission in the Spread of *Yersinia pestis*", *Journal of Medical Entomology*, 52:6, 2015.

97. D. M. Bland et al., "Infectious Blood Source Alters Early Foregut Infection and Regurgitative Transmission of *Yersinia pestis* by Rodent Fleas", *PLoS Pathogens*, 14:1, 2018; Hinnebusch et al., "'Fleaing' the Plague".

98. Joseph Hinnebusch, "The Evolution of Flea-borne Transmission in *Yersinia pestis*", *Current Issues in Molecular Biology*, 7, 2005, 197–212. Also Hinnebusch et al., "'Fleaing' the Plague".

99. Barbieri et al., "Natural History of Plague".

100. Kenneth Gage and Michael Y. Kosoy, "Natural History of Plague: Perspectives from More Than a Century of Research", *Annual Review of Entomology*, 50, 2005, 505–528. Also see J. Trivedi, "Xenopsylla cheopis", Animal Diversity Web 2003, at http://animaldiversity.ummz .umich.edu/accounts/Xenopsylla_cheopis; Gage, "Factors Affecting the Spread and Maintenance of Plague"; Gage and Kosoy, "Natural History of Plague".

101. Eisen et al., "The Role of Early-Phase Transmission".

102. Ole J. Benedictow, *The Black Death 1346–1353: The Complete History*, Boydell Press, 2004, 20, and *What Disease Was Plague? On the Controversy Over the Microbiological Identity of Plague Epidemics of the Past*, Brill, 2010, 6, 279–283; Trivedi, "Xenopsylla cheopis"; Bitam et al., "Fleas and flea-borne diseases".

103. Schmid et al., "Local Persistence and Extinction of Plague". An older source suggests a maximum survival time of one month. See Panagiotakopulu, "Pharaonic Egypt and the Origins of Plague".

104. Durham and Casman, "Threshold Conditions for the Persistence of Plague Transmission in Urban Rats". Also see Hinnebusch, "The Evolution of Flea-borne Transmission".

105. S. Mears et al., "Host Location, Survival and Fecundity of the Oriental Rat Flea *Xenopsylla cheopis* (Siphonaptera: Pulicidae) in Relation to Black Rat *Rattus rattus* (Rodentia: Muridae) Host Age and Sex", *Bulletin of Entomological Research*, 2002, 92:5, 375–384; Bitam et al., "Fleas and Flea-Borne Diseases".

106. Hinnebusch et al., " 'Fleaing' the Plague, 215–232.

107. Gage, "Factors Affecting the Spread and Maintenance of Plague"; Perry and Fetherston, "*Yersinia pestis*—Etiologic Agent of Plague", 50.

108. James W. Wood, Rebecca J. Ferrell, and Sharon N. Dewitte-Avina, "The Temporal Dynamics of the Fourteenth-Century Black Death: New Evidence from English Ecclesiastical Records", *Human Biology*, 75:4, 2003, 427–448.

109. Fabian Crespo and Matthew B. Lawrenz, "Heterogenous Immunological Landscapes and Medieval Plague: An Invitation to a New Dialogue between Historians and Immunologists", in Green (ed.), *Pandemic Disease in the Medieval World*; Rindra Randremanana et al., 'Epidemiological Characteristics of an Urban Plague Epidemic in Madagascar, August–November, 2017: An Outbreak Report', *Lancet Infectious Diseases*, 19:5, 2019, 537–545.

110. John Theilmann and Frances Cate, "A Plague of Plagues: The Problem of Plague Diagnosis in Medieval England", *Journal of Interdisciplinary History*, 37:3, 2007, 371–393; Sloane, *Black Death in London*, 174.

111. Berdoy and Drickamer, "Comparative Social Organization and Life History".

112. X. Didelot, L. K. Whittles, and I. Hall, "Model-Based Analysis of an Outbreak of Bubonic Plague in Cairo in 1801", *Journal of the Royal Society Interface*, 14, 2017, 20170160.

113. Green, "The Four Black Deaths"; Benedictow, *Complete History*, 28.

114. A. F. Hinkley et al., "Transmission Rates of Primary Pneumonic Plague in the USA", *Epidemiology and Infection*, 140:3, 2012, 554.

115. Samuel K. Cohn Jr., "Epidemiology of the Black Death and Successive Waves of Plague", in Nutton (ed.), *Pestilential Complexities*, 93; Scott and Duncan, *Biology of Plagues*, 67–69; Wood et al., "Temporal Dynamics of the Fourteenth-Century Black Death"; Lars Skog and Hans Hauska, "Spatial Modeling of the Black Death in Sweden", *Transactions in GIS*, 17:4, 2013, 589–611; Welford and Bossak, "Validation of Inverse Seasonal Peak Mortality in Medieval Plagues"; Benedictow, *What Disease Was Plague?*; Myron J. Echenberg, *Plague Ports: The Global Urban Impact of Bubonic Plague,1894–1901*, New York University Press, 2007, 8.

116. Christos Lynteris, "Skilled Natives, Inept Coolies: Marmot Hunting and the Great Manchurian Pneumonic Plague (1910–1911)", *History and Anthropology*, 24:3, 2013, 303–321; Gage and Kosoy, "Natural History of Plague"; Theilmann and Cate, "A Plague of Plagues"; John Kelly, *The Great Mortality: An Intimate History of the Black Death*, Fourth Estate, 2005, 38.

117. H. Gillespie, "Rattus rattus", 2004, *Animal Diversity Web*, at http://animaldiversity.ummz.umich.edu/accounts/Rattus_rattus/; Lyudmila Khlyap, Gregory Glass, and Michael Kosoy, "Rodents in Urban Ecosystems of Russia and the USA", in Alfeo Triunveri and Desi Scalise (eds.), *Rodents: Habitat, Pathology and Environmental Impact*, Nova Science, 2012, 1–21.

118. Alice Y. T. Feng and Chelsea G. Himsworth, "The Secret Life of the City Rat: A Review of the Ecology of Urban Norway and Black Rats (*Rattus norvegicus* and *Rattus rattus*)", *Urban Ecosystems*, 17, 2014, 149–162.

119. Berdoy and Drickamer, "Comparative Social Organization and Life History"; Durham and Casman, "Threshold Conditions for the Persistence of Plague Transmission".

120. John T. Alexander, *Bubonic Plague in Early Modern Russia. Public Health and Urban Discourse*, Oxford University Press 2003 (orig. 1980), 6.

121. Edwin S. Hunt, *The Medieval Super-Companies: A Study of the Peruzzi of Florence*, Cambridge University Press, 1994, 48. On the grain trade, also see Marie D'Aguanno Ito, "Orsanmichele—The Florentine Grain Market: Trade and Worship in the Later Middle Ages",

PhD dissertation, Catholic University, 2014; Johan Söderberg, "Grain Prices in Cairo and Europe in the Middle Ages", *Research in Economic History*, 24, 2007, 189–216; Jessica Dijkman, *Shaping Medieval Markets: The Organisation of Commodity Markets in Holland, c. 1200–c. 1450*, Brill, 2011.

122. Nils Hybel, "The Grain Trade in Northern Europe before 1350", *Economic History Review*, 40:2, 2002, 219–247.

123. William C. Jordan, *Great Famine: Northern Europe in the Early Fourteenth Century*, Princeton University Press, 1996, 48.

124. Hybel, "The Grain Trade in Northern Europe". Also see Nils Hybel, "Early Commercial Contacts between England, Prussia, and Poland", in Richard W. Unger and Jakub Basista (eds.), *Britain and Poland-Lithuania: Contact and Comparison from the Middle Ages to 1795*, Brill, 2008; Söderberg, "Grain Prices in Cairo and Europe".

125. N.J.G. Pounds, *A Historical Geography of Europe, 450 BC–AD 1330*, Cambridge University Press, 1973, 428.

126. John H. Munro, "Medieval Woollens: The Western European Woollen Industries and Their Struggles for International Markets, c. 1000–1500", in David Jenkins (ed.), *The Cambridge History of Western Textiles, Vol. I*, Cambridge University Press, 2003, 236; Michel Balard, "Latins in the Aegean and the Balkans in the Fourteenth Century", in Michael Jones (ed.), *The New Cambridge Medieval History, Volume 6*, Cambridge University Press, 2000.

127. Gunnar Karlsson, "Plague without Rats: The Case of Fifteenth Century Iceland", *Journal of Medieval History*, 22:3, 1996, 263–284.

128. Ragnar Edvardsson, "The Role of Marine Resources in the Medieval Economy of Vestfirðir, Iceland", Anthropology PhD thesis, City University of New York, 2010.

129. Bruce E. Gelsinger, *Icelandic Enterprise: Commerce and Economy in the Middle Ages*, University of South Carolina Press, 1981; Viola Giulia Miglio, "'Go shag a horse!': The 17th–18th Century Basque-Icelandic Glossaries Revisited", *Journal of the North Atlantic*, 1:1, 2008, 25–36; Brian Fagan, *Fish on Friday: Feasting, Fasting and the Discovery of the New World*, Basic Books, 2006, 179; David C. Orton et al., "Fish for the City: Meta-Analysis of Archaeological Cod Remains and the Growth of London's Northern Trade", *Antiquity*, 88, 2014, 516–530; Baldur Thórhallsson and Thorsteinn Kristinsson, "Iceland's External Affairs from 1400 to the Reformation: Anglo-German Economic and Societal Shelter in a Danish Political Vacuum", *Icelandic Review of Politics and Administration*, 9:1, 2013, 113–137; Evan T. Jones, "Charting the World of English Fishermen in Early Modern Iceland", *The Mariner's Mirror*, 90:4, 2004, 398–409.

130. Chris Callow and Charles Evans, "The Mystery of Plague in Medieval Iceland", *Journal of Medieval History*, 42:2, 2016, 254–284.

131. Edvardsson, "The Role of Marine Resources", ch. 4.

132. Christakos and Olea, "New Space-Time Perspectives".

133. Benedictow, *Complete History*, 218.

134. Ole Benedictow, "Plague", in Phillip Pulsiano and Kirsten Wolf (eds.), *Medieval Scandinavia: An Encyclopedia*, Garland, 1993, 508. Also see Walloe, "Medieval and Modern Bubonic Plague".

135. Cohn, "Epidemiology of the Black Death"; Benedictow in the various works cited above.

136. Byrne, *Encyclopedia of the Black Death*, 61–62, 111–112; Paul Slack, *The Impact of Plague in Tudor and Stuart England*, Clarendon Press, 1985, ch. 6.

137. John T. Alexander, *Bubonic Plague in Early Modern Russia: Public Health and Urban Discourse*, Oxford University Press, 2003 (orig. 1980), 61.

138. Cohn, "Epidemiology of the Black Death".

139. Cohn, ibid., and *Black Death Transformed*.

140. Richard C. Hoffman, *An Environmental History of Medieval Europe*, Cambridge University Press, 2014, 293.

141. Byrne, *Encyclopedia of the Black Death*, 73–74.

142. Naphy and Spicer, *Black Death*, 56.

143. Stefan Monecke, Hannelore Monecke, and Jochen Monecke, "Modelling the Black Death. A Historical Case Study and Implications for the Epidemiology of Bubonic Plague", *International Journal of Medical Microbiology*, 299, 2009, 582–593.

144. Joseph A. Lewnard and Jeffrey P. Townsend, "Climatic and Evolutionary Drivers of Phase Shifts in the Plague Epidemics of Colonial India", *Proceedings of the National Academy of Science, USA*, 113.51, 2016, 14601–14608.

145. Aplin et al., "Multiple Geographic Origins".

146. Jean Duplantier et al., "Systematics of the Black Rat in Madagascar: Consequences for the Transmission and Distribution Of Plague", *Biological Journal of the Linnean Society*, 78:3, 2003, 335–341.

147. C. Andrianaivoarimanana et al., "Plague Circulation and Population Genetics of the Reservoir *Rattus rattus*: The Influence of Topographic Relief on the Distribution of the Disease within the Madagascan Focus", *PLoS Neglected Tropical Diseases*, 7:6, e2266; Vogler et al., "A Decade of Plague in Mahajanga"; C. Tollenaere et al., "AFLP Genome Scan in the Black Rat (*Rattus rattus*) from Madagascar: Detecting Genetic Markers Undergoing Plague-Mediated Selection", *Molecular Ecology*, 20.5, 2011, 1026–3108; Christine Graham et al., "Evaluation of the Effect of Host Immune Status on Short-Term *Yersinia Pestis* Infection in Fleas with Implications for the Enzootic Host Model for Maintenance of Y. Pestis During Interepizootic Periods", *Journal of Medical Entomology*, 51:5, 2014, 1079–86; Adélaïde Miarinjara et al., "*Xenopsylla brasiliensis* Fleas in Plague Focus Areas, Madagascar", *Emerging Infectious Diseases*, 22:12, 2016; A. J. Vogler et al., "Temporal Phylogeography of *Yersinia Pestis* in Madagascar: Insights into the Long-Term Maintenance of Plague", *PLoS Neglected Tropical Diseases*, 11:9, 2017.

148. Vogler et al., "A Decade of Plague in Mahajanga".

149. Tollenaere et al., "AFLP Genome Scan in the Black Rat"; Fanny Gascuel et al., "Host Resistance, Population Structure and the Long-Term Persistence of Bubonic Plague: Contributions of a Modelling Approach in the Malagasy Focus", *PLoS Computational Biology*, 9:5, 2013; Andrianaivoarimanana et al., "Immune Responses to Plague Infection".

150. Panzac, "Plague and Seafaring". Joseph Byrne gives somewhat different, but broadly compatible, dates and details. Byrne, *Encyclopedia*, 31.

151. Slack, *The Impact of Plague*, ch. 6.

152. Panzac, "Plague and Seafaring". Also see Nükhet Varlık, "Why the Ottoman Experience of Plague Matters", in Green (ed.), *Pandemic Disease in the Medieval World*.

153. Keith Wrightson, *Ralph Tailor's Summer: A Scrivener, His City, and the Plague*, Yale University Press, 2011.

154. Slack, *The Impact of Plague*, ch. 6.

155. Panzac, "Plague and Seafaring".

156. E. A. Eckert, "The Retreat of Plague from Central Europe, 1640–1720: A Geomedical Approach", *Bulletin of the History of Medicine*, 74:1, 2000, 1–28; Kari Konkola, "More than a Co-Incidence? The Arrival of Arsenic and Disappearance of Plague in Early Modern Europe", *Journal of the History of Medicine and Allied Sciences*, 47, 1992, 186–209; Neil Cummins, Morgan Kelly, and Cormac Ó Gráda, "Living Standards and Plague in London, 1560–1665", *Economic History Review*, 69:1, 2016, 3–34.

157. Guido Alfani, "Plague in Seventeenth-Century Europe and the Decline of Italy: An Epidemiological Hypothesis", *European Review of Economic History*, 17, 2013, 408–430.

158. Panzac, "Plague and Seafaring".

159. Sam White, "Ecology, Climate, and Crisis in the Ottoman Near East", PhD dissertation, Columbia University, 2008, 125–127; Nükhet Varlık, *Plague and Empire in the Early Modern Mediterranean World: The Ottoman Experience, 1347–1600*, Cambridge University Press, 2015, 26, 278–279.

160. Carmichael, "Plague Persistence in Western Europe"; K. Pribyl, *Farming, Famine and Plague*, Springer AG, 2017, 216.

161. A. Namouchi et al., "Integrative Approach Using *Yersinia pestis* Genomes to Revisit the Historical Landscape of Plague during the Medieval Period", *Proceedings of the National Academy of Science, USA*, 115, 2018, E11790–E11797.

162. E. E. Puckett et al., "Global Population Divergence and Admixture of the Brown Rat (*Rattus norvegicus*)". *Proceedings of the Royal Society B*, 283, 2016, 1762; Lin Zeng et al., "Out of Southern East Asia of the Brown Rat Revealed by Large-Scale Genome Sequencing", *Molecular Biology and Evolution*, 35:1, 2018, 149–158.

163. Mark A. Suckow et al., *The Laboratory Rat*, 2nd edn, Elsevier Academic Press, 2006, 74; Berdoy and Drickamer, "Comparative Social Organization and Life History".

164. Gillespie, "*Rattus rattus*".

165. Feng and Himsworth, "The Secret Life of the City Rat".

166. Khlyap, Glass, and Kosoy, "Rodents in Urban Ecosystems Off Russia and the USA"; Bitam et al., "Fleas and Flea-Borne Diseases"; Gage and Kosoy, "Natural History of Plague".

167. Sohail Soliman, "Seasonal Studies on Commensal Rats and Their Ectoparasites in a Rural Area of Egypt: The Relationship of Ectoparasites to the Species, Locality, and Relative Abundance of the Host", *Journal of Parasitology*, 87:3, 2001, 545–553; Malek, Bitam, and Drancourt, "Plague in Arab Maghreb, 1940–2015"; Seyedeh Maryam Ghafari et al., "Morphologic, Morphometric and Molecular Comparison of Two Sister Species of Rodents as Potential Reservoir Hosts of Zoonotic Cutaneous Leishmaniasis in the Southwest of Iran", *Journal of Medical Microbiology and Infectious Diseases*, 7:3, 2019, 79–84.

Part II: Plague and Expansionism in Western Europe

1. István Zimonyi, "The Nomadic Factor in Mediaeval European History", *Acta Orientalia Academiae Scientiarum Hungaricae*, 58.1, 2005, 33–40; Jiger Janabel, "From Mongol Empire to Qazaq Juzder: Studies on the Steppe Political Cycle (13th–18th Centuries)", PhD thesis, Harvard University, 1997; Uli Schamiloglu, "Preliminary Remarks on the Role of Disease in the History of the Golden Horde", *Central Asian Survey*, 12:4, 1993, 447–457.

2. Nükhet Varlık, *Plague and Empire in the Early Modern Mediterranean World: The Ottoman Experience, 1347–1600*, Cambridge University Press, 2015, 4.

3. Uli Schamiloglu, "The Rise of the Ottoman Empire: The Black Death in Medieval Anatolia and Its Impact on Turkish Civilization", in Neguin Yavari, Lawrence G. Potter, and Jean-Marc Ran Oppenheim (eds.), *Views from the Edge: Essays in Honor of Richard W. Bulliet*, Columbia University Press, 2004, 270. Also see I. Metin Kunt, "The Rise of the Ottomans", in Michael Jones (ed.), *The New Cambridge Medieval History, Volume VI, c. 1300–c. 1415*, Cambridge University Press, 2000, 862; Gisele Marien, "The Black Death in Early Ottoman Territories: 1347–1550", MA thesis, Bilkent University, 2009, 94–96.

4. Stephen Dale, *The Muslim Empires of the Ottomans, Safavids, and Mughals*, Cambridge University Press, 2010, 62.

5. William Urban, *Medieval Mercenaries. The Business of War*, Greenhill Books, 2006, 226.

6. Mark Bailey, *Medieval Suffolk: An Economic and Social History, 1200–1500*, Boydell Press, 2007, 180. Also see Daniel Lord Smail, "Mapping Networks and Knowledge in Medieval Marseille, 1337–1362", PhD dissertation, University of Michigan, 1994, 36–37, 80; Richard W. Emery, "The Black Death of 1348 in Perpignan", *Speculum*, 42: 4, 1967, 611–623; James L. Goldsmith, "The Crisis of the Late Middle Ages. The Case of France", *French History*, 9:4, 1995, 417–450; Kelly Wray, *Communities and Crisis: Bologna During the Black Death*, Brill, 2009.

7. Samuel K. Cohn Jr., *The Black Death Transformed. Disease and Culture in Early Renaissance Europe*, Arnold, 2002, 224.

Chapter 3: A Golden Age?

1. On the historiography of the debate, see John Hatcher, 'England in the Aftermath of the Black Death', *Past & Present*, 144, 1994, 3–35.

2. Robert S. Lopez, "The Trade of Medieval Europe: The South", in M. M. Postan, Edward Miller, and Cynthia Postan (eds.), *The Cambridge Economic History of Europe, Vol. 2*, Cambridge University Press, 1987.

3. John Munro, "'Money Matters': A Critique of the Postan Thesis on Medieval Population, Prices, and Wages", in John Drendel (ed.), *Crisis in the Later Middle Ages: Beyond the Postan-Duby Paradigm*, Brepols, 2015, 127–194.

4. Jerry Brotton, *Renaissance Bazaar: From the Silk Road to Michelangelo*, Oxford University Press, 2002, 40.

5. Charles F. Briggs, *The Body Broken. Medieval Europe 1300–1520*, Routledge, 2011, 266.

6. Paolo Malanima, "Italy in the Renaissance: A Leading Economy in the European Context, 1350–1550", *Economic History Review*, 71:1, 2018, 3–30.

7. Bruce M. S. Campbell, *The Great Transition. Climate, Disease, and Society in the Late-Medieval World*, Cambridge University Press, 2016, 355.

8. S. Broadberry et al., *British Economic Growth, 1270–1870*, Cambridge University Press, 2015, 271.

9. Sarah Rees Jones, *York: The Making of a City 1068–1350*, Oxford University Press, 2014.

10. Bruce M. S. Campbell, "Grain Yields on English Demesnes after the Black Death", in Mark Bailey and Stephen Rigby (eds.), *Town and Countryside in the Age of the Black Death. Essays in Honour of John Hatcher*, Turnhout Brepols, 2011, and "Nature as Historical Protagonist: Environment and Society in Pre-Industrial England", *Economic History Review*, 63:2, 2010, 281–314.

11. Campbell, *The Great Transition. Climate*, 287 n73. Also see Broadberry et al., *British Economic Growth*, 98.

12. Stephen Broadberry et al., "British Economic Growth, 1270–1870", Working Paper, 2011, http://www.lse.ac.uk/economicHistory/seminars/ModernAndComparative/papers2011-12/Papers/Broadberry.pdf

13. B.J.P. van Bavel, *Manors and Markets: Economy and Society in the Low Countries, 500–1600*, Oxford University Press, 2010, ch. 6; Rosemary L. Hopcroft, "Local Institutions and Rural Development in European History", *Social Science History*, 27:1, 2003, 25–74.

14. Janken Myrdal and Alexandra Sapoznik, "Technology, Labour, and Productivity Potential in Peasant Agriculture: England, c.1000 to 1348", *Agricultural History Review*, 65.2, 2017, 194–212.

15. Broadberry et al., *British Economic Growth*, 77.

16. E.g., Finbar Mccormick and Emily Murray, "The Zooarchaeology of Medieval Ireland", and Terry O'Connor, "Animals in Urban Life in Medieval to Early Modern England", both in Umberto Albarella et al. (eds.), *The Oxford Handbook of Zooarchaeology*, Oxford University Press, 2017; Antoni Riera, "Crises and Changes in the Late Middle Ages", in Flocel Sabaté (ed.), *The Crown of Aragon: A Singular Mediterranean Empire*, Brill, 2017.

17. David Nicholas, *Medieval Flanders*, Longman, 1992, 359.

18. Richard C. Hoffman, *An Environmental History of Medieval Europe*, Cambridge University Press, 2014, 215.

19. Janken Myrdal and Mats Morell (eds.), *Agrarian History of Sweden: From 4000 BC to AD 2000*, Nordic Academic Press, 2011, 83.

20. David Stone, *Decision-Making in Medieval Agriculture*, Oxford University Press, 2005, 249–250; Mark Bailey, *Medieval Suffolk: An Economic and Social History, 1200–1500*, Boydell Press, 2007, 205–206; W. R. Mead, *An Historical Geography of Scandinavia*, Academic Press, 1981; Michael Toch, "Agricultural Progress and Agricultural Technology in Medieval Germany; An Alternative Model", in Elizabeth Bradford Smith and Michael Wolfe (eds.), *Technology and Resource Use in Medieval Europe: Cathedrals, Mills, and Mines*, Ashgate, 1997.

21. Christopher Dyer, "Peasant Farming in Late Medieval England: Evidence from the Tithe Estimations by Worcester Cathedral Priory", in Maryanne Kowaleski, John Langdon, and Phillipp R. Schofield (eds.), *Peasants and Lords in the Medieval English Economy: Essays in Honour of Bruce M. S. Campbell*, Brepols, 2015.

22. Michael Toch, "Agricultural Progress and Agricultural Technology".

23. Audrey M. Lambert, *The Making of the Dutch Landscape: An Historical Geography of the Netherlands*, Seminar Press, 1971, 159.

24. Paolo Malanima, *Pre-Modern European Economy: One Thousand Years (10th–19th Centuries)*, Brill, 2009, 149,155, 279; Samuel K. Cohn Jr., "Rich and Poor in Western Europe, c. 1375–1475: The Political Paradox of Material Well-Being", in Sharon Farmer (ed.), *Approaches to Poverty in Medieval Europe: Complexities, Contradictions, Transformations, c. 1100–1500*, Brepols, 2016; Broadberry et al., *British Economic Growth*, ch. 9, 10.

25. Marie D'Aguanno Ito, "Orsanmichele—The Florentine Grain Market: Trade and Worship in the Later Middle Ages", PhD dissertation, Catholic University, 2014; Edwin S. Hunt and James M. Murray, *A History of Business in Medieval Europe, 1200–1550*, Cambridge University Press, 1999, 120.

26. Peter Spufford, *Power and Profit: The Merchant in Medieval Europe*, Thames and Hudson, 2005 (orig. 2002), 48, 104; Hoffman, *Environmental History*, 236.

27. Faruk Tabak, *The Waning of the Mediterranean, 1550–1870: A Geohistorical Approach*, Johns Hopkins University Press, 2010, 43; Stephan R. Epstein, *An Island for Itself: Economic Development and Social Change in Late Medieval Sicily*, Cambridge University Press, 1992, ch. 6.

28. Bailey, *Medieval Suffolk*, 205.

29. J. C. Hubby, "Lordship and Rural Society in Medieval Bavaria: The Estates of the Abbey of Tergernsee, c979–1450", PhD dissertation, Columbia University, 2000, esp. 211–212.

30. Michael Blatter, "The Transformation of the Alpine Economy in the 14th to 18th Centuries: Harvesting 'Wild Hay' in the High Mountains", *Nomadic Peoples*, 13.2, 2009, 146–159.

31. Julien Demade, "The Medieval Countryside in German-Language Historiography since the 1930s", in Isabel Alfonso (ed.), *The Rural History of Medieval European Societies: Trends and Perspectives*, Brepols, 2007. Also see Tom Scott, "Liberty and Community in Medieval Switzerland", *German History*, 13:1, 1995.

32. Dan Yeloff and Bas van Geel, "Abandonment of Farmland and Vegetation Succession Following the Eurasian Plague Pandemic of AD 1347–52", *Journal of Biogeography*, 34, 2007, 575–582.

33. Simon J. M. Davis, "Zooarchaeological Evidence for Moslem and Christian Improvements of Sheep and Cattle in Portugal", *Journal of Archaeological Science*, 35, 2008, 991–1010.

34. R. Thomas, *Animals, Economy and Status: The Integration of Zooarchaeological and Historical Evidence in the Study of Dudley Castle, West Midlands (c.1100–1750)*, Archaeopress, 2005.

35. Davis, "Zooarchaeological Evidence for Moslem and Christian Improvements of Sheep and Cattle in Portugal".

36. Derrick Rixson, *The History of Meat Trading*, Nottingham University Press, 2000, 94.

37. John Casparis, "The Swiss Mercenary System: Labor Emigration from the Semiperiphery", *Review (Fernand Braudel Center)*, 5:4, 1982, 593–642; Ian Blanchard, "The Continental European Cattle Trades, 1400–1600", *Economic History Review*, 39:3, 1986, 427–460.

38. Bruce M. S. Campbell, "Matching Supply to Demand: Crop Production and Disposal by English Demesnes in the Century of the Black Death", *Journal of Economic History*, 57.4, 1997, 827–858; Ben Dodds, "Output and Productivity: Common Themes and Regional Variations", in Ben Dodds and Richard Britnell (eds.), *Agriculture and Rural Society after the Black Death: Common Themes and Regional Variations*, Hertfordshire University Press, 2008.

39. Hans Antonson, "The Extent of Farm Desertion in Central Sweden During the Late Medieval Agrarian Crisis: Landscape as a Source", *Journal of Historical Geography*, 35, 2009, 619–641.

40. Johan Soderberg, "Prices and Economic Change in Medieval Sweden", *Scandinavian Economic History Review*, 55:2 2007, 128–152. For Denmark, see Bjørn Poulsen, "Trade and Consumption among Late Medieval and Early Modern Danish Peasants", *Scandinavian Economic History Review*, 52:1, 2004, 52–68.

41. Riera, "Crises and Changes in the Late Middle Ages".

42. R. C. Hoffman, "Frontier Foods for Late Medieval Consumers: Culture, Economy, Ecology", *Environment and History*, 7:2, 2001, 131–167.

43. For the latest discussion of this issue, see Mark Bailey, *After the Black Death: Economy, Society, and the Law in Fourteenth-Century England*, Oxford University Press, 2021.

44. Hubby, "Lordship and Rural Society in Medieval Bavaria", 211–212.

45. Paul Warde, *Ecology, Economy and State Formation in Early Modern Germany*, Cambridge University Press, 2005. Also see Robert Paul Dees, "Economies and Politics of Peasant

Production in South Germany, 1450–1650", PhD dissertation, University of California, Los Angeles, 2007.

46. Hans-Peter Baum, "Annuities in Late Medieval Hanse Towns", *Business History Review*, 59.1, 1985.

47. Franz Irsigier, "Industrial Production, International Trade and Public Finance in Cologne XIVth and XVth Centuries, *Journal of European Economic History*, 6, 1977, 269–306.

48. Campbell, *Great Transition*, 313.

49. Antonio Henriques, "Plenty of Land, Land of Plenty: The Agrarian Output of Portugal (1311–20)", *European Review of Economic History*, 19:2, 2015, 149–170.

50. Carlos Alvarez-Nobal and Leandro Prados De La Escosura, "The Rise and Fall of Spain (1270–1850)", *Economic History Review*, 66: 1, 2013, 1–37.

51. Ana Rodriguez, "Spain", in Harry Kitsikopoulos (ed.), *Agrarian Change and Crisis in Europe, 1200–1500*, Routledge, 2012.

52. Robert O. Crummey, *The Formation of Muscovy, 1304–1613*, 1987, Longman, 15.

53. Quoted by Malanima, "Premodern European Economy", 132n. Also see Carla Rahn Phillips and William D. Phillips Jr., *Spain's Golden Fleece. Wool Production and the Wool Trade from the Middle Ages to the Nineteenth Century*, Johns Hopkins University Press, 1997; John Munro, "Spanish Merino Wools and the Nouvelles Draperies: An Industrial Transformation in the Late Medieval Low Countries", *Economic History Review*, 58:3, 2005, 431–484.

54. Gloria Cristina Florez, "Vicissitudes of Commercial Trading: Castile and Flanders at the End of the Fifteenth Century (1474–94)", *Medieval History Journal*, 6.1 2003. Also see Hoffman, *Environmental History*, 178; Rodriguez, "Spain".

55. John Edwards, "Development" and 'Underdevelopment' in the Western Mediterranean: The Case of Córdoba and Its Region in the Late Fifteenth and Early Sixteenth Centuries", *Mediterranean Historical Review*, 2:1, 1987, 3–45; Rowena Hernández-Múzquiz, "Economy and Society in Medieval and Early Modern Seville (1391–1506): A Study of the Abastecimiento [Provisioning] of an Iberian Urban Center", Columbia University PhD dissertation, 2005. See chapter 10 for Valencia.

56. Adam J. Franklin-Lyons, "Famine—Preparation and Response in Catalonia after the Black Death", PhD dissertation, Yale University, 2009; Maria Teresa Ferrer, "Catalan Commerce in the Late Middle Ages", *Catalan Historical Review*, 5: 29–65, 2012; Thomas Bisson, *Medieval Crown of Aragon: A Short History*, Oxford: Clarendon Press, 2000, ch. 7; Stephen P. Bensch, "Catalonia", in E. Michael Gerli (ed.), *Medieval Iberia: An Encyclopedia*, Taylor & Francis, 2013.

57. Morgan Kelly and Cormac Ó Gráda, "Living Standards and Mortality since the Middle Ages", *Economic History Review*, 67:2, 2014; Hoffman, *Environmental History*, 320.

58. Campbell, *Great Transition*, 340.

59. Cohn, "Rich and Poor in Western Europe".

60. Paolo Malanima, *Pre-Modern European Economy: One Thousand Years (10th–19th Centuries)*, Brill, 2009, 246–249.

61. Paolo Malanima, "Italy in the Renaissance: A Leading Economy in the European Context, 1350–1550", *Economic History Review*, 71:1, 2018, 3–30.

62. Tom Scott, *Society and Economy in Germany, 1300–1600*, Palgrave, 2002. Also see Keith D. Lilley, "Urban Planning after the Black Death: Townscape Transformation in Later Medieval England (1350–1530)", *Urban History*, 42, 2015, 22–42.

63. Malanima, "Italy in the Renaissance".

64. Malanima, *Pre-Modern European Economy*, 247.

65. Samuel K. Cohn Jr., *The Black Death Transformed: Disease and Culture in Early Renaissance Europe*, Arnold, 2002, 199. Also see B. Van Bavel, "Markets for Land, Labor, and Capital in Northern Italy and the Low Countries, Twelfth to Seventeenth Centuries", *Journal of Interdisciplinary History*, 41:4, 2011, 503–531; Maarten Bosker et al., "Ports, Plagues and Politics: Explaining Italian City Growth 1300–1861", *European Review of Economic History*, 12, 97–131, 2008; Samuel Cohn, "After the Black Death: Labour Legislation and Attitudes towards Labour in Late-Medieval Western Europe", *Economic History Review*, 60:3, 2007, 457–485.

66. Cohn, "After the Black Death".

67. William P. Caferro, "Warfare and Economy in Renaissance Italy, 1350–1450", *Journal of Interdisciplinary History*, 39:2, 2008, 167–209.

68. E.g., Benjamin G. Kohl, *Padua under the Carrara, 1318–1405*, Johns Hopkins University Press, 1998, 141–142; Nicholas, *Medieval Flanders*, 310.

69. Frederik Buylaert, "Lordship, Urbanization and Social Change in Late Medieval Flanders", *Past &d Present*, 227, May 2015; Tom Beaumont James and Edward Roberts, "Winchester and Late Medieval Urban Development: From Palace to Pentice", *Medieval Archaeology*, 44:1, 2000, 181–200.

70. Bosker et al., "Ports, Plagues and Politics".

71. Michael North, *The Expansion of Europe, 1250–1500*, Manchester University Press, 2012 (German original 2007), 94; Charlotte Masemann, "Cultivation and Consumption: Medieval Lübeck's Gardens", in Lawrin Armstrong, Ivana Elbl, and Martin M. Elbl (eds.), *Late Medieval Europe: Essays in Honour of John H. A. Munro*, Brill, 2007; Stephen H. Rigby, "Urban Population in Late Medieval England: The Evidence of the Lay Subsidies", *Economic History Review*, 63:2, 2010, 393–417.

72. Campbell, *Great Transition*, 334.

73. Alan M. Stahl, *Zecca: The Mint of Venice in the Middle Ages*, Johns Hopkins University Press, 2001, ch. 4.

74. Reinhold C. Mueller, *The Venetian Money Market: Banks, Panics, and the Public Debt, 1200–1500*, Johns Hopkins University Press, 1997.

75. Hunt and Murray, *A History of Business in Medieval Europe*, 140.

76. Nathan Sussman, "The Late Medieval Bullion Famine Reconsidered", *Journal of Economic History*, 58.1, 1998, 126–154.

77. J. L. Bolton, *Money in the Medieval English Economy, 973–1489*, Manchester University Press, 2012, 293.

78. Martin Allen, "The Volume of the English Currency, 1158–1470", *Economic History Review*, 54.4, 2001, 595–611, and "Silver Production and the Money Supply in England and Wales, 1086–c.1500", *Economic History Review*, 64:1, 2011, 114–131.

79. Bolton, *Money in the Medieval English Economy*, 284. Also see Pamela Nightingale, "Gold, Credit, and Mortality: Distinguishing Deflationary Pressures on the Late Medieval English Economy", *Economic History Review*, 63:4, 2010, 1081–1104.

80. Ian Blanchard, "Egyptian Specie Markets and the International Gold Crisis of the Early Fifteenth Century", in Armstrong, Elbl, and Elbl (eds.), *Money, Markets and Trade*.

81. On rents, see John Langdon, *Mills in the Medieval Economy. England 1300–1540*, Oxford University Press, 2004, 302; on interest, see Şevket Pamuk, "The Black Death and the Origins

of the 'Great Divergence' across Europe, 1300–1600", *European Review of Economic History*, 11.3, 2007, 289–317; S. R. Epstein, *Freedom and Growth: The Rise of States and Markets in Europe, 1300–1750*, Routledge, 2000.

82. John Munro, "Bullion Flows and Monetary Contraction in Late-Medieval England and the Low Countries", in John Richards (ed.), *Precious Metals in the Later Medieval and Early Modern Worlds*, Carolina Academic Press, 1983, citing Eliyahu Ashtor.

83. John Hatcher, quoted in Adam Lucas, *Ecclesiastical Lordship, Seigneurial Power, and the Commercialization of Milling in Medieval England*, Ashgate, 2014. Also see Ole Benedictow, "New Perspectives in Medieval Demography: The Medieval Demographic System", in Bailey and Rigby (eds.), *Town and Countryside*.

84. Mary Lindemann, "Plague, Disease, and Hunger", in Guido Ruggiero (ed.), *A Companion to the Worlds of the Renaissance*, Blackwell, 2002, 427–443.

85. J. R. Maddicott, "Plague in Seventh-Century England", *Past & Present*, 156, 1997.

86. John L. Flood, "'Safer on the Battlefield than in the City': England, The 'Sweating Sickness', and the Continent", *Renaissance Studies*, 17.2, 2003; Ynez Viole O'Neil, "Diseases of the Middle Ages", in Kenneth Kiple (ed.), *The Cambridge World History of Human Disease*, Cambridge University Press, 1993.

87. Massimo Livi Bacci, *Conquest: The Destruction of the American Indios*, Polity Press, 2008 (orig. 2005), 63.

88. Mark Bailey, "Demographic Decline in Late Medieval England: Some Thoughts on Recent Research", *Economic History Review*, 49, 1996, 1–19.

89. Judith M. Bennett, "Compulsory Service in Late Medieval England", *Past & Present*, 209, 2010. Also see Joanne Filippone Overty, "The Cost of Doing Scribal Business: Prices of Manuscript Books in England, 1300–1483", *Book History*, 11, 2008, 1–32.

90. Mosher Stuard, *Gilding the Market*, 132; Jeffery Fynn-Paul, "Civic Debt, Civic Taxes, and Urban Unrest: A Catalan Key to Interpreting the Late Fourteenth-Century European Crisis", in Armstrong, Elbl, and Elbl (eds.), *Money, Markets and Trade*; Daniel Lord Smail, "Mapping Networks and Knowledge in Medieval Marseille, 13377–1362", PhD thesis, University of Michigan, 1994, 68.

91. Epstein, *An Island for Itself*, 56.

92. J. L. Van Zanden, "A Third Road to Capitalism? Proto-Industrialisation and the Moderate Nature of the Late Medieval Crisis in Flanders and Holland, 1350–1550", in P.C.M. Hoppenbrouwers and J. L. van Zanden (eds.), *Peasants into Farmers?: The Transformation of Rural Economy and Society in the Low Countries (Middle Ages–19th Century) in Light of the Brenner Debate*, Brepols, 2001; Graeme Small, *Late Medieval France*, Palgrave Macmillan, 2009, 64; Cohn, "After the Black Death"; Caroline Arcini et al., "Living Conditions in Time of Plague", in Per Lagerås (ed.), *Environment, Society and the Black Death: An Interdisciplinary Approach to the Late-Medieval Crisis in Sweden*, Casemate, 2015.

93. Gerald Harriss, *Shaping the Nation. England, 1360–1461*, Clarendon Press, 2005, 227; Gregory Clark, *A Farewell to Alms: A Brief Economic History of the World*, Princeton University Press, 2007, 99. Also see his "The Condition of the Working-Class in England, 1209–2004", *Journal of Political Economy*, 113.6 (2005), 1307–1340.

94. Mark Bailey, "The Transformation of Customary Tenures in Southern England, c.1350 to c.1500", *Agricultural History Review*, 62:2, 2014, 210–230.

95. Martin Stephenson, "Risk and Capital Formation: Seigneurial Investment in an Age of Adversity", in Bailey and Rigby (eds.), *Town and Countryside*.

96. George Grantham, "France" in Kitsikopoulos (ed.), *Agrarian Change and Crisis*; Rodriguez, "Spain"; Antoni Riera, "Crises and Changes in the Late Middle Ages"; Antoni Furió and Ferran Garcia-Oliver, "Household, Peasant Holding and Labour Relations in a Mediterranean Rural Society. The Valencian Country in the Late Middle Ages", in Erich Landsteiner and Ernst Langthaler (eds.), *Agrosystems and Labour Relations in European Rural Societies*, Brepols, 2010; Jeppe Büchert Netterstrøm, "Feud, Protection, and Serfdom in Late Medieval and Early Modern Denmark (c. 1400–1600)", in Paul Freedman and Monique Bourin (eds.), *Forms of Servitude in Northern and Central Europe: Decline, Resistance, and Expansion*, Brepols, 2005, 369–384; David Gaunt, "The Peasants of Scandinavia, 1300–1700", in Tom Scott (ed.), *The Peasantries of Europe: From the Fourteenth to the Eighteenth Centuries*, Longman, 1998, 313–337; Dees, "Economies and Politics of Peasant Production"; Hubby, "Lordship and Rural Society in Medieval Bavaria", 336–337; Tim Soens, "The Origins of the Western Scheldt. Environmental Transformation, Storm Surges and Human Agency in the Flemish Coastal Plain (1250–1600)", in E. Thoen et al. (eds.), *Landscapes or Seascapes? The History of the Coastal Environment in the North Sea Area Reconsidered*, Brepols, 2013.

97. Daniel R. Curtis, "Florence and Its Hinterlands in the Late Middle Ages: Contrasting Fortunes in the Tuscan Countryside, 1300–1500, *Journal of Medieval History*, 38:4, 2012, 472–499.

98. Rebecca Jean Emigh, *The Undevelopment of Capitalism: Sectors and Markets in Fifteenth-Century Tuscany*, Temple University Press, 2009.

99. Curtis, "Florence and Its Hinterlands".

100. George Grantham, "France"; Hubby, "Lordship and Rural Society in Medieval Bavaria".

101. Frederic Aparisi, "Village Entrepreneurs: The Economic Foundations of Valencian Rural Elites in the Fifteenth Century", *Agricultural History*, 89:3, 2015, 336–357; Small, *Late Medieval France*, 67; William W. Hagen, "European Yeomanries: A Non-Immiseration Model of Agrarian Social History, 1350–1800", *Agricultural History Review*, 59:2, 2011, 259–265.

102. Tom Scott, "Historiographical Review: Medieval Viticulture in the German-speaking Lands", *German History*, 20:1, 2002.

103. Tim Unwin, *Wine and the Vine; An Historical Geography of Viticulture and the Wine Trade*, Routledge, 1991, 203.

104. Christopher Dyer, "Villeins, Bondsmen, Neifs, and Serfs: New Serfdom in England, c. 1200–1600", in Freedman and Bourin (eds.), *Forms of Servitude in Northern and Central Europe*. Also see Philippa Maddern, "Moving Households: Geographical Mobility and Serial Monogamy in England, 1350–1500", *Parergon*, 24:2, 2007, 69–92; Ian D. Whyte, *Migration and Society in Britain, 1550–1830*, Macmillan, 2000, 26.

105. Richard Britnell, "Land and Lordship: Common Themes and Regional Variations", in Dodds and Britnell (eds.), *Agriculture and Rural Society after the Black Death*, 161. Also see Harald Kleinschmidt, *People on the Move: Attitudes toward and Perceptions of Migration in Medieval and Modern Europe*, Praeger, 2003; Cohn, *The Black Death Transformed*, 199; Small, *Late Medieval France*, 175–176; Guy Lurie, "Citizenship in Later Medieval France, c.1370—c.1480", PhD dissertation, Georgetown University, 2012; M. E. Bratchel, *Medieval Lucca and the Evolution of the Renaissance State*, Oxford University Press, 2009.

106. M.H.D Larmuseau et al., "High Y-Chromosomal Diversity and Low Relatedness Between Paternal Lineages on a Communal Scale in the Western European Low Countries During the Surname Establishment", *Heredity*, Advance online publication, April 15, 2015; Stephen Wilson, *The Means of Naming: A Social and Cultural History of Personal Naming in Western Europe*, UCL Press, 1998.

107. Constance H. Berman, "Women's Work in Family, Village, and Town after 1000 CE: Contributions to Economic Growth?", *Journal of Women's History*, 19:3, 2007, 10–32.

108. John Hatcher, "Women's Work Reconsidered: Gender and Wage Differentiation in Late Medieval England", *Past & Present*, 173, 2001, 191–198; T. De Moor and J. L. Van Zanden, "Girl Power: The European Marriage Pattern and Labour Markets in the North Sea Region in the Late Medieval and Early Modern Period", *Economic History Review*, 63:1, 2010, 1–33. Other examples of a large literature include Maryanne Kowaleski, "Gendering Demographic Change in the Middle Ages", and Jane Whittle, "Rural Economies", both in Judith Bennett and Ruth Karras (eds.), *Oxford Handbook of Women and Gender in Medieval Europe*, Oxford University Press, 2013; Jan Luiten van Zanden, Sarah Carmichael, and Tine De Moor, *Capital Women: The European Marriage Pattern, Female Empowerment and Economic Development in Western Europe 1300–1800*, Oxford University Press, 2019.

109. Arcini et al., "Living Conditions in Time of Plague".

110. Jane Humphries and Jacob Weisdorf, "The Wages of Women in England, 1260–1850", *Journal of Economic History*, 2015, 75:2, 405–447.

111. Richard A. Goldthwaite, *The Economy of Renaissance Florence*, Johns Hopkins University Press, 2009, 324–325.

112. Judith M. Bennett, *Ale, Beer and Brewsters in England: Women's Work in a Changing World, 1300–1600*, Oxford University Press, 1996; B. Ann Tlusty, "Water of Life, Water of Death. The Controversy Over Brandy and Gin in Early Modern Augsburg", *Central European History*, 31:1–2, 1998, 1–30.

113. Samuel Cohn, "After the Black Death: Labour Legislation and Attitudes towards Labour in Late-Medieval Western Europe", *Economic History Review*, 60:3, 2007, 457–485.

114. Bennett, "Compulsory Service in Late Medieval England".

115. Samuel K. Cohn, *Lust for Liberty. The Politics of Social Revolt in Medieval Europe, 1200–1425, Italy, France, and Flanders*, Harvard University Press, 2006, esp. 228.

116. Small, *Late Medieval France*, 73.

117. Margaret L. Kekewich and Susan Rose, *Britain, France and the Empire, 1350–1500*, Palgrave Macmillan, 2005.

118. Bennett, "Compulsory Service in Late Medieval England".

119. Harriss, *Shaping the Nation*, 234.

120. Quoted in Annemarieke Willemsen, "'Man is a sack of muck girded with silver': Metal Decoration on Late-Medieval Leather Belts and Purses from the Netherlands", *Medieval Archaeology*, 56, 2012.

121. Quoted in Trevor Dean (ed.), *The Towns of Italy in the Later Middle Ages*, Manchester University Press, 2000, 79.

122. C. M. Woolgar, "Meat and Dairy Products in Late Medieval England", in C. M. Woolgar, T. Waldron, and D. Serjeantson (eds.), *Food in Medieval England: Diet and Nutrition*, Oxford University Press, 2006.

123. James Graham-Campbell and Magdalena Valor (eds.), *The Archaeology of Medieval Europe*, 2007, Aarhus University Press, vol. 2, 88; Aleks Pluskowski, "The Medieval Wild," in Christopher Gerrard and Alejandra Gutiérrez (eds.), *The Oxford Handbook of Later Medieval Archaeology in Britain*, , 2018; D. Serjeantson, "Birds: Food as a Mark of Status", and D. J. Stone, "The Consumption and Supply of Birds in Late Medieval England", both in Woolgar et al. (eds.), *Food in Medieval England*.

124. Mosher Stuard, *Gilding the Market*, 224.

125. Quoted in Colin Platt, *King Death: The Black Death and Its Aftermath in Late-Medieval England*, UCL Press, 1996, 127–128.

126. Alan Hunt, *Governance of the Passions. A History of Sumptuary Law*, Macmillan, 1996, 37.

127. Frances Pritchard, "The Uses of Textiles, c. 1000–1500", in David Jenkins (ed.), *The Cambridge History of Western Textiles, Vol. I*, Cambridge University Press, 2003, 369.

128. Carlo Marco Belfanti, "The Civilization of Fashion: At the Origins of a Western Social Institution", *Journal of Social History*, 43, 2009, 261–283; Aileen Ribeiro, "Dress in the Early Modern Period, c.1500–1780", in Jenkins (ed.), *The Cambridge History of Western Textiles*.

129. Laurel Ann Wilson, "*De novo modo*: The Birth of Fashion in the Middle Ages", PhD dissertation, Fordham University, 2011.

130. Isis Sturtewagen, "Unveiling Social Fashion Patterns: A Case Study of Frilled Veils in the Low Countries (1200–1500)", in Robin Netherton and Gale R. Owen-Crocker (eds.), *Medieval Clothing and Textiles, Vol. 7*, Boydell & Brewer, 2011, 33. Also see Evelyn Welch, *Shopping in the Renaissance. Consumer Cultures in Italy, 1400–1600*, Yale University Press, 2005.

131. S. R. Epstein, "The Late Medieval Crisis as an 'Integration Crisis,'" in Maarten Prak (ed.), *Early Modern Capitalism: Economic and Social Change in Europe, 1400–1800*, Routledge, 2001, 25–50. Also see his *Freedom and Growth*, 55–57.

132. Mosher Stuard, *Gilding the Market*, 183.

133. Samuel K. Cohn Jr., "Demography and the Politics of Fiscality", in William J. Connell and Andrea Zorzi (eds.), *Florentine Tuscany: Structures and Practices of Power*, Cambridge University Press, 2000.

134. Dries Tys and Marnix Pieters, "Understanding a Medieval Fishing Settlement Along the Southern North Sea, Walraversijde, c.1200–1630", in Louis Sicking and Darlene Abreu-Ferreira (eds.), *Beyond the Catch: Fisheries of the North Atlantic, the North Sea and the Baltic, 900–1850*, Brill, 2008.

135. Richard Britnell, "Urban Demand in the English Economy, 1300–1600", in James Galloway (ed.), *Trade, Urban Hinterlands and Market Integration, c.1300–1600*, Centre for Metropolitan History, 2000, 1–2; David Alban Hinton, *Gold and Gilt, Pots and Pins: Possessions and People in Medieval Britain*, Oxford University Press, 2005.

136. Jaco Zuijderduijn and Roos van Oosten, "Breaking the Piggy Bank. What Can Historical and Archaeological Sources Tell Us About Late-Medieval Saving Behaviour?", CGEH Working Paper Series 65, Utrecht University, 2015.

137. *Agrarian History of Sweden: From 4000 BC to AD 2000*, Janken Myrdal, and Mats Morell (eds.), Nordic Academic Press, 2011, 81; Arcini et al., "Living Conditions in Time of Plague".

138. Sverre Bagge, *Cross and Scepter: The Rise of the Scandinavian Kingdoms from the Vikings to the Reformation*, Princeton University Press, 2014, 132.

139. Konrad Smiarowski et al., "Zooarchaeology of the Scandinavian Settlements in Iceland and Greenland: Diverging Pathways", in Umberto Albarella et al. (eds.), *The Oxford Handbook of Zooarchaeology*, Oxford University Press, 2017.

140. Baldur Thórhallsson and Thorsteinn Kristinsson, "Iceland's External Affairs from 1400 to the Reformation: Anglo-German Economic and Societal Shelter in a Danish Political Vacuum", *Icelandic Review of Politics and Administration*, 9:1, 2013, 113–137.

141. Bjørn Poulsen, "Trade and Consumption Among Late Medieval and Early Modern Danish Peasants", *Scandinavian Economic History Review*, 52:1, 2004, 52–68.

142. Quoted in Mark Haberlin, *The Fuggers of Augsburg. Pursuing Wealth and Honor in Renaissance Germany*, University of Virginia Press, 2012, 22.

143. Maureen Fennell Mazzaoui, "The Cotton Industry of Northern Italy in the Late Middle Ages: 1150–1450", *Journal of Economic History*, 32.1 (1972), 262–286; North, *The Expansion of Europe*, 174.

144. Calculated from figures in Franz Irsigier, "Industrial Production, International Trade and Public Finance in Cologne XIVth and XVth Centuries," *Journal of European Economic History*, 6, 1977, 269–306.

145. Haberlin, *The Fuggers of Augsburg*, 22; Kilian Baur, "The Trade with Fustian from Germany to Denmark in the Late Middle Ages", in Angela Ling Huang and Carsten Jahnke (eds.), *Textiles and the Medieval Economy: Production, Trade, and Consumption of Textiles, 8th–16th Centuries*, Oxbow, 2015.

146. John Munro, "The Symbiosis of Towns and Textiles: Urban Institutions and the Changing Fortunes of Cloth Manufacturing in the Low Countries and England, 1270–1570", *Journal of Early Modern History*, 3:1, 1999, 1–74; "Medieval Woollens: Textiles, Textile Technology, and Industrial Organization, c. 800–1500", in Jenkins (ed.), *The Cambridge History of Western Textiles*; "The Late Medieval Decline of English Demesne Agriculture: Demographic, Monetary, and Political-Fiscal Factors", in Bailey and Rigby (eds.), *Town and Countryside*.

147. John Oldland, "Wool and Cloth Production in Late Medieval and Early Tudor England", *Economic History Review*, 67:1, 2014, 125–147.

148. Robin Ward, *The World of the Medieval Shipmaster. Law, Business, and the Sea, c.1350–1450*, Boydell Press, 2009.

149. Oldland, "Wool and Cloth Production"; Pamela Nightingale, "The Rise and Decline of Medieval York: A Reassessment", *Past & Present*, 206, 2010; J. N. Hare, "Growth and Recession in the Fifteenth-Century Economy: The Wiltshire Textile Industry and the Countryside", *Economic History Review*, 52:1, 1999, 1–26; Herman Van Der Wee, "The Western European Woollen Industries, 1500–1750", in Jenkins (ed.), *The Cambridge History of Western Textiles*.

150. Bart Lambert and Milan Pajic, "Drapery in Exile: Edward III, Colchester and the Flemings, 1351–1367", *History*, 99, 2014, 733–753.

151. Quote from Bailey, *Medieval Suffolk*, 269. Also see Eleanor Quinton and John Oldland, "London Merchant's Cloth Exports, 1350–1500", in Netherton and Owen-Crocker (eds.), *Medieval Clothing and Textiles*; Brenda Collins and Philip Ollerenshaw, *The European Linen Industry in Historical Perspective*, Oxford University Press, Pasold Research Fund, 2003.

152. Epstein, *Freedom and Growth*, 65.

153. Carsten Jahnke, "The Baltic Trade", in Donald J. Harreld (ed.), *A Companion to the Hanseatic League*, Brill, 2015.

154. Broadberry et al., *British Economic Growth*, 281.

155. Bennett, *Ale, Beer and Brewsters in England*, 43.

156. Richard W. Unger, "English Energy Consumption and the Impact of the Black Death", *European Review of Economic History*, 24.1, 2020, 134–156.

157. Briggs, *The Body Broken*, 70; Mack P. Holt, "Wine, Life, and Death in Early Modern Burgundy", *Food and Foodways*, 8:2, 1999, 73–98; Unwin, *Wine and the Vine*; Tom Scott, "Historiographical Review: Medieval Viticulture".

158. Rodriguez, "Spain".

159. Susan Rose, *The Wine Trade in Medieval Europe 1000–1500*, Continuum, 2011, ch. 4.

160. Warde, *Ecology, Economy and State Formation in Early Modern Germany*, 86.

161. Woolgar et al. (eds.), *Food in Medieval England*; Blanchard, "The Continental European Cattle Trades"; R. C. Hoffman, "Frontier Foods".

162. G. Muldner and M. P. Richards, "Diet in Medieval England: The Evidence from Stable Isotopes", in Woolgar et al. (eds.), *Food in Medieval England*; Graham-Campbell and Valor (eds.), *The Archaeology of Medieval Europe*, vol. 2, 141–142.

163. Woolgar, "Meat and Dairy Products in Late Medieval England".

164. Hoffman, "Frontier Foods". Also see Blanchard, "The Continental European Cattle Trades".

165. Jacob Burckhardt, *Civilization of the Renaissance in Italy*, Batoche Books edn, 2001, 67.

166. C. M. Woolgar, "Gifts of Food in Late Medieval England", *Journal of Medieval History*, 37, 2011, 6–18, and *The Culture of Food in England, 1200–1500*, Yale University Press, 2016, 232; Goldthwaite, *The Economy of Renaissance Florence*, 373.

167. Christopher Dyer, "Rural Living 1100–1540", in *The Oxford Handbook of Later Medieval Archaeology in Britain*, 20; Stephen Mileson, "Openness and Closure in the Later Medieval Village", *Past & Present*, 234:1, 2017, 3–37; Hubby, "Lordship and Rural Society in Medieval Bavaria", 192; Hipólito Rafae andl Oliva Herrer, "The Peasant Domus and Material Culture in Northern Castile in the Later Middle Ages", in Cordelia Beattie, Anna Maslakovic, and Sarah Rees Jones (eds.), *The Medieval Household in Christian Europe, c. 850–c. 1550: Managing Power, Wealth, and the Body*, Brepols, 2003.

168. Arcini et al., "Living Conditions in Time of Plague"; John L. Brooke, *Climate Change and the Course of Global History. A Rough Journey*, Cambridge University Press, 2014, 255 (graph); Hans de Beer, "Observations on the History of Dutch Physical Stature from the Late-Middle Ages to the Present", *Economics and Human Biology*, 2, 2004, 45–55.

169. Cohn, "After the Black Death". Also see Chris Given-Wilson, *The English Nobility in the Late Middle Ages: The Fourteenth-Century Political Community*, Routledge, 1996.

170. Robin J. Burls, "Society, Economy and Lordship in Devon in the Age of the First Two Courtenay Earls, c. 1297–1377", PhD thesis, University of Oxford, 2002, 108.

171. Hunt and Murray, *A History of Business in Medieval Europe*, 229.

172. Markus Cerman, *Villagers and Lords in Eastern Europe, 1300–1800*, Palgrave Macmillan, 2012, 121.

173. de Beer, "Observations on the History of Dutch Physical Stature"; Giovanni Federico, "Heights, Calories and Welfare: A New Perspective on Italian Industrialization, 1854–1913", *Economics & Human Biology*, 1:3, 2003, 289–308.

174. Jord Hanus, "Real Inequality in the Early Modern Low Countries: The City of 's-Hertogenbosch, 1500–1660", *Economic History Review*, 66:3, 2013, 733–756.

175. R. C. Allen and J. L. Weisdorf, "Was There an 'Industrious Revolution' before the Industrial Revolution? An Empirical Exercise for England, c. 1300–1830", *Economic History Review*, 64:3, 2011, 715–729.

176. Jan De Vries, *The Industrious Revolution. Consumer Behavior and the Household Economy, 1650 to the Present*, Cambridge University Press, 2008, 87.

177. Malanima, *Premodern European Economy*, 143.

178. Broadberry et al., *British Economic Growth*, 250–252, 259, 277.

179. Craig Muldrew, *Food, Energy and the Creation of Industriousness: Work and Material Culture in Agrarian England, 1550–1780*, Cambridge University Press, 2011.

Chapter 4: Expansive Trades

1. Richard A. Goldthwaite, *The Economy of Renaissance Florence*, Johns Hopkins University Press, 2009, 350.

2. Margaret F. Rosenthal, "Cultures of Clothing in Later Medieval and Early Modern Europe, *Journal of Medieval and Early Modern Studies*, 39:3, 2009.

3. Damien Coulon, "The Commercial Influence of the Crown of Aragon in the Eastern Mediterranean (Thirteenth–Fifteenth Centuries)", in Flocel Sabaté (ed.), *The Crown of Aragon: A Singular Mediterranean Empire*, Brill, 2017.

4. Wim Blockmans and Walter Prevenier, *The Promised Lands: The Low Countries Under Burgundian Rule, 1369–1530*, University of Pennsylvania Press, 2003, 67.

5. H. Kitsikopoulos, "The Impact of the Black Death on Peasant Economy in England, 1350–1500", *Journal of Peasant Studies*, 29:2, 2002, 71–90.

6. Guido Alfani, "The Rich in Historical Perspective: Evidence for Preindustrial Europe (ca. 1300–1800)", *Cliometrica*, 2016.

7. D. W. Prowse, *A History of Newfoundland from the English, Colonial and Foreign Records*, Heritage Books, orig. 1895, reprint 2003, 49.

8. Vicki Ellen Szabo, *Monstrous Fishes and the Mead-Dark Sea: Whaling in the Medieval North Atlantic*, Brill, 2008; Jean-Pierre Proulx, *Whaling in the North Atlantic: From Earliest Times to the Mid-19th Century*, Parks Canada, 1986; W.M.A. de Smet, "Evidence of Whaling in the North Sea and English Channel during the Middle Ages", in *Mammals in the Seas: General Papers and Large Cetaceans, FAO Fisheries Series, No. 5, Volume III*, 1981; Ole Lindquist, *Peasant Fisherman Whaling in the Northeast Atlantic Area, ca. 900–1900 AD*, University of Akureyri, 1997; Julian de Zuleta, "Basque Whalers; The Source of Their Success", *Mariner's Mirror*, 86:3, 2000; Robert C. Allen and Ian Keay, "Saving the Whales: Lessons from the Extinction of the Eastern Arctic Bowhead", *Journal of Economic History*, 64:2, 2004.

9. Allen and Keay, "Saving the Whales", and Marloes Rijkelijkhuizen, "Whales, Walruses, and Elephants: Artisans in Ivory, Baleen, and Other Skeletal Materials in Seventeenth- and Eighteenth-Century Amsterdam", *International Journal of Historical Archaeology*, 13:4, 2009, 409–429; Selma Huxley Barkham, "The Basque Whaling Establishments in Labrador 1536–1632—A Summary", *Arctic*, 37:4, 1984, 515–519; Chesley W. Sanger, "'Oil Is an Indispensable Necessity of Life': The Impact of Oscillating Oil and Baleen (Bone) Prices on Cyclical Variations in the Scale and Scope of Northern Commercial Whaling, 1600–1900", *International Journal of Maritime History*, 15:2, 2003, 147–157.

10. Barkham, "The Basque Whaling Establishments in Labrador".

11. Viola Giulia Miglio, "'Go Shag a Horse!': The 17th–18th Century Basque-Icelandic Glossaries Revisited", *Journal of the North Atlantic*, 1:1, 2008, 25–36.

12. Andreas Hess, "'Working the Waves': The Plebeian Culture and Moral Economy of Traditional Basque Fishing Brotherhoods", *Journal of Interdisciplinary History*, 40:4, 2010, 551–578.

13. Lindquist, *Peasant Fisherman Whaling*, 38.

14. Ibid.; William A. Douglass and Jon Bilbao, *Amerikanuak: Basques in the New World*, University of Nevada Press, 1975, 52; Inês Amorim, "The Evolution of Portuguese Fisheries in the Medieval and Early Modern Period. A Fiscal Approach", in Louis Sicking and Darlene Abreu-Ferreira (eds.), *Beyond the Catch: Fisheries of the North Atlantic, the North Sea and the Baltic, 900–1850*, Brill, 2009.

15. Michael M. Barkham, "The Spanish Basque Irish Fishery & Trade in the Sixteenth-Century", *History Ireland*, 9:3, 2001, 12–15.

16. Miglio, "'Go shag a horse!'"

17. Richard Hoffman, "Medieval Fishing", in Paolo Squatriti (ed.), *Working with Water in Medieval Europe: Technology and Resource-Use*, 2, Brill, 2000; Chloé Deligne, "Carp in the City. Fish-Farming Ponds and Urban Dynamics in Brabant and Hainaut, 1100–1500", in Sicking and Abreu-Ferreira (eds.), *Beyond the Catch*.

18. Richard C. Hoffmann, "Economic Development and Aquatic Ecosystems in Medieval Europe", *American Historical Review*, 101.3, 1996, 631–669. Also see Petra J.E.M. van Dam, "Fish for Feast and Fast. Fish Consumption in the Netherlands in the Late Middle Ages", in Sicking and Abreu-Ferreira (eds.), *Beyond the Catch*.

19. David Abulafia, *The Great Sea: A Human History of the Mediterranean*, Oxford University Press, 2011, 396.

20. Stephan R. Epstein, *An Island for Itself: Economic Development and Social Change in Late Medieval Sicily*, Cambridge University Press, 1992, ch. 6.

21. Maryanne Kowaleski, "The Commercialization of the Sea Fisheries in Medieval England and Wales", *International Journal of Maritime History*, 15:2, 2003, 177–231, and "The Seasonality of Fishing in Medieval Britain", in Scott G. Bruce (ed.), *Ecologies and Economies in Medieval and Early Modern Europe: Studies in Environmental History for Richard C. Hoffmann*, Brill, 2010.

22. Mette Svart Kristiansen, "Fish for Peasants and Kings—a Danish Perspective", in Jan Klápště and Petr Sommer (eds.), *Processing, Storage, Distribution of Food. Food in the Medieval Rural Environment*, Turnhout Brepols, 2011; Klaus Friedland, "The Hanseatic League and Hanse Towns in the Early Penetration of the North", *Arctic*, 37:4, 1984, 538–543; Carsten Jahnke, "The Medieval Herring Industry in the Western Baltic", in Sicking and Abreu-Ferreira (eds.), *Beyond the Catch*.

23. Peter E. Pope, *Fish into Wine: The Newfoundland Plantation in the Seventeenth Century*, University of North Carolina Press, 2003, 11.

24. Michael McCormick, "History's Changing Climate: Climate Science, Genomics, and the Emerging Consilient Approach to Interdisciplinary History", *Journal of Interdisciplinary History*, 42:2, 2011, 251–223.

25. R. C. Hoffman, "Frontier Foods for Late Medieval Consumers: Culture, Economy, Ecology", *Environment and History*, 7:2, 2001, 131–167.

26. Kristiansen, "Fish for Peasants and Kings—a Danish Perspective".

27. Kowaleski, "The Commercialization of the Sea Fisheries".

28. Justyna Wubs-Mrozewicz, "Fish, Stock, and Barrel. Changes in the Stockfish Trade in Northern Europe, c.1360–1560", in Sicking and Abreu-Ferreira (eds.), *Beyond the Catch*, 188.

29. Kowaleski, "The Seasonality of Fishing".

30. Konrad Smiarowski et al., "Zooarchaeology of the Scandinavian Settlements in Iceland and Greenland: Diverging Pathways", in Umberto Albarella et al. (eds.), *The Oxford Handbook of Zooarchaeology*, Oxford University Press, 2017.

31. Evan T. Jones, "Charting the World of English Fishermen in Early Modern Iceland", *The Mariner's Mirror*, 90:4, 2004, 398–409; Brian Fagan, *Fish on Friday. Feasting, Fasting and the Discovery of the New World*, Basic Books, 2006.

32. Bruce E. Gelsinger, *Icelandic Enterprise: Commerce and Economy in the Middle Ages*, University of South Carolina Press, 1981, 187–189.

33. David C. Orton et al., "Fish for the City: Meta-Analysis of Archaeological Cod Remains and the Growth of London's Northern Trade", *Antiquity*, 88:340, 2014, 516–530.

34. Sophia P. Perdikaris, "From Chiefly Provisioning to State Capital Ventures: The Transition from Natural to Market Economy and the Commercialization of Cod Fisheries in Medieval Arctic Norway", PhD dissertation, City University of New York, 1998.

35. Wubs-Mrozewicz, "Fish, Stock, and Barrel".

36. Friedland, "The Hanseatic League and Hanse Towns".

37. Alan Hunt, *Governance of the Passions. A History of Sumptuary Law*, Macmillan, 1996, 126; Elizabeth Veale, *The English Fur Trade in the Later Middle Ages*, Clarendon Press, 1966, 6–7.

38. Susan Mosher Stuard, *Gilding the Market: Luxury and Fashion in Fourteenth-Century Italy*, University of Pennsylvania Press, 2006, 63.

39. Hoffmann, "Economic Development and Aquatic Ecosystems". Also see Lee Rayea, "The Early Extinction Date of the Beaver (*Castor fiber*) in Britain", *Historical Biology*, 27:8, 2015, 1029–1041.

40. Sakari Mykr, Timo Vuorisalo, and Mari Pohja-mykr, "A History of Organized Persecution and Conservation of Wildlife: Species Categorizations in Finnish Legislation from Medieval Times to 1923", *Oryx*, 39:3, 2005, 275–283.

41. Carsten Jahnke, "The Baltic Trade", in Donald J. Harreld (ed.), *A Companion to the Hanseatic League*, Brill, Leiden, 2015.

42. Veale, *The English Fur Trade*, 29.

43. Ibid., 67; Franz Irsigier, "Industrial Production, International Trade and Public Finance in Cologne XIVth and XVth Centuries", *Journal of European Economic History*, 6, 1977, 269–306.

44. Janet Martin, *Treasure of the Land of Darkness: The Fur Trade and Its Significance for Medieval Russia*, Cambridge University Press, 1986, 82; Andrew Gentes, *Exile to Siberia, 1590–1822*, Palgrave Macmillan, 2008, 19.

45. C. Raymond Beazley, "The Russian Expansion Towards Asia and the Arctic in the Middle Ages (to 1500)", *American Historical Review*, 13:4, 1908, 731–741. Also see Raymond H. Fisher, *The Russian Fur Trade, 1550–1700*, University of California Press, Berkeley, 1943; Michael Rywkin, "Russian Colonial Expansion before Ivan the Dread: A Survey of Basic Trends", *Russian Review*, 32:3, 1973, 286–293; Richard Vaughan, "The Arctic in the Middle Ages", *Journal of Medieval History*, 8, 1982, 313–342; Martin, *Treasure of the Land of Darkness*, 80.

46. Robert S. Lopez, "The Trade of Medieval Europe: The South", in M. M. Postan, Edward Miller, and Cynthia Postan (eds.), *Trade and Industry in the Middle Ages, The Cambridge Economic History of Europe, Vol. 2*, Cambridge University Press, 1987.

47. Thomas Ertl, "Silkworms, Capital and Merchant Ships: European Silk Industry in the Medieval World Economy", *Medieval History Journal*, 9:2, 2006; Goldthwaite, *The Economy of Renaissance Florence*, 282–284.

48. Maureen Fennell Mazzaoui, "The Cotton Industry of Northern Italy in the Late Middle Ages: 1150–1450", *Journal of Economic History*, 32:1, 1972, 262–286.

49. Anna Muthesius, "Silk in the Medieval World", in David Jenkins (ed.), *The Cambridge History of Western Textiles, Vol. I*, Cambridge University Press, 2003, 341.

50. Carole Collier Frick, "Dressing a Renaissance City: Society, Economics, and Gender in the Clothing of Fifteenth-Century Florence", PhD dissertation, University of California, Los Angeles, 1995, 256–262.

51. Judith C. Brown, "Economies", in Michael Wyatt (ed.), *The Cambridge Companion to the Italian Renaissance*, Cambridge University Press, 2014.

52. Ertl, "Silkworms, Capital and Merchant Ships"; Luca Molà, *Silk Industry of Renaissance Venice*, Johns Hopkins University Press, 2000; Edmund M. Herzig, "The Volume of Iranian Raw Silk Exports in the Safavid Period", *Iranian Studies*, 25:1–2, 1992, 61–79; Edoardo Demo, "New Products and Technological Innovation in the Silk Industry of Vicenza in the Fifteenth and Sixteenth Centuries", in Karel Davids and Bert De Munck (eds.), *Innovation and Creativity in Late Medieval and Early Modern European Cities*, Routledge, 2014.

53. Ertl, "Silkworms, Capital and Merchant Ships". Also see Anon., "Silk and the European Economy", *Journal of European Economic History*, 36:2–3, 2007, 367–380, and Fabio Giusberti and Francesca Roversi Monaco, "Economy and Demography", in Sarah Blanshei (ed.), *A Companion to Medieval and Renaissance Bologna*, Brill, 2017.

54. Fernando de Sousa, "The Silk Industry in Tras-os-Montes", *E-Journal of Portuguese History*, 3:2, 2005.

55. Eliyahu Ashtor, "The Economic Decline of the Middle East During the Later Middle Ages: An Outline", in B. Z. Kedar (ed.), *Technology, Industry and Trade: The Levant versus Europe, 1250–1500*, Variorum, 1992. Also see David Jacoby, *Trade, Commodities and Shipping in the Medieval Mediterranean*, Ashgate, 1997; Muthesius, "Silk in the Medieval World"; Willem Floor and Patrick Clawson, "Safavid Iran's Search for Silver and Gold", *International Journal of Middle East Studies*, 32:3, 2000, 345–368.

56. Li Bozhong, *Fazhan yu zhiyue: Ming Qing JIangnan shengchanli yanjiu* (Development and Constraint: Productivity in Jiangnan in the Ming and Qing Dynasties) Lianjing, 2002, 379–380 (translated by Dr Joe Lawson); Herzig, "The Volume of Iranian Raw Silk Exports"; Rudi Mathee, "The Safavid Economy as Part of the World Economy", in Willem M. Floor and Edmund Herzig (eds.), *Iran and the World in the Safavid Age*, I.B. Tauris, 2012.

57. Jong-Kuk Nam, *Le commerce du coton en Méditerranée a la fin du Moyen Age*, Brill, 2007.

58. David Jacoby, "Rural Exploitation and Market Economy in the Late Medieval Peloponnese", in Sharon E. J. Gerstel (ed.), *Viewing the Morea: Land and People in the Late Medieval Peloponnese*, Dumbarton Oaks, 2013, 213–275.

59. Ayşe Devrim Atauz, *Eight Thousand Years of Maltese Maritime History: Trade, Piracy, and Naval Warfare in the Central Mediterranean*, Florida Scholarship Online, 2011, ch. 2.

60. David Brewer, *Greece, the Hidden Centuries: Turkish Rule from the Fall of Constantinople to Greek Independence*, I.B. Tauris, 2010; G. D. Pagratis, "Trade and Shipping in Corfu, 1496–1538", *International Journal of Maritime History*, 16:2, 2004, 169–220; Anthony T. Luttrell, "The Latins and Life on the Smaller Aegean Islands: 1204–1453", in Benjamin Arbel, Bernard Hamilton, and David Jacoby (eds.), *Latins and Greeks in the Eastern Mediterranean after 1204*, Frank Cass, 1989, 46–157.

61. Kenneth R. Hall, "Local and International Trade and Traders in the Straits of Melaka Region, 600–1500", *Journal of the Economic and Social History of the Orient*, 47:2, 2004.

62. Lawrence N. Langer, "Slavery in the Appanage Era: Rus' and the Mongols", in Christoph Witzenrath (ed.), *Eurasian Slavery, Ransom and Abolition in World History, 1200–1860*, Taylor & Francis, 2015; Valeria Fiorani Piacentini, "The Golden Age of Genoa's Eastwards Trade (13th–15th Centuries)", *Journal of Central Asian Studies*, 19:1, 2010, 25–40; Clements R. Markham (ed.), *Narrative of the Embassy of Ruy Gonzalez de Clavijo to the Court of Timour, at Samarcand, A.D. 1403–6*, Hakluyt Society, 1859, 89–90.

63. Charles Verlinden, "Medieval Slavers", *Explorations in Economic History*, 7:1, 1969, 1–14.

64. Sanjay Subrahmanyam, "The Birth-Pangs of Portuguese Asia: Revisiting the Fateful 'Long Decade' 1498–1509", *Journal of World History*, 2, 2007, 261–280; Richard Eaton and Philip Wagoner, "Warfare on the Deccan Plateau, 1450–1600: A Military Revolution in Early Modern India?", *Journal of World History*, 25:1, 2014.

65. Paul Freedman, *Out of the East. Spices and the Medieval Imagination*, Yale University Press, 2008, 115.

66. Eliyahu Ashtor, *Levant Trade in the Later Middle Ages*, Princeton University Press, 1983; Kevin H. O'Rourke and Jeffrey G. Williamson, "After Columbus: Explaining Europe's Overseas Trade Boom, 1500–1800", *Journal of Economic History*, 62:2, 2002, 417–456.

67. Ashtor, *Levant Trade*, 183.

68. Anthony Reid, "An 'Age of Commerce' in Southeast Asian History", *Modern Asian Studies*, 24:1, 1990, 1–30.

69. Francisco Apellániz, "Venetian Trading Networks in the Medieval Mediterranean", *Journal of Interdisciplinary History*, 44:2, 2013, 157–179.

70. Kevin H. O'Rourke and Jeffrey G. Williamson, "Did Vasco da Gama Matter for European Markets?", *Economic History Review*, 62:3, 2009, 655–684.

71. C.H.H. Wake, "The Volume of European Spice Imports at the Beginning and End of the Fifteenth Century", *Journal of European Economic History*, 15:3, 1986.

72. O'Rourke and Williamson, "Did Vasco da Gama Matter".

73. Paul Freedman, "Spices and Late-Medieval European Ideas of Scarcity and Value", *Speculum*, 80:4, 2005, 1209–1227.

74. C.H.H. Wake, "The Changing Pattern of Europe's Pepper and Spice Imports, ca. 1400–1700", *Journal of European Economic History*, 3, 1979, 361–403, reprinted in M. N. Pearson (ed.), *Spices in the Indian Ocean World*, Variorum, 1996.

75. C. M. Woolgar, *The Culture of Food in England, 1200–1500*, Yale University Press, 2016, 85; Paul Freedman, "The Medieval Spice Trade", in J. M. Pilcher (ed.), *The Oxford Handbook of Food History*, 2012; Stefan Halikoswki Smith, "Demystifying a Change in Taste: Spices, Space, and Social Hierarchy in Europe, 1380–1750", *International History Review*, 29:2, 2007, 237–257.

76. Freedman, *Out of the East*, 24, 117.

77. O'Rourke and Williamson, "Did Vasco da Gama Matter".

78. Daniel R. Curtis, "Florence and Its Hinterlands in the Late Middle Ages: Contrasting Fortunes in the Tuscan Countryside, 1300–1500", *Journal of Medieval History*, 38:4, 2012, 472–499.

79. Woolgar, *The Culture of Food*, 85.

80. Freedman, "The Medieval Spice Trade".

81. Timothy F. Garrard, "Myth and Metrology: The Early Trans-Saharan Gold Trade", *Journal of African History*, 23, 1982, 443–461.

82. John L. Vogt, "Crusading and Commercial Elements in the Portuguese Capture of Ceuta", *Muslim World*, 59:3–4, 1969, 287–299.

83. Toby Green, *The Rise of the Trans-Atlantic Slave Trade in Western Africa, 1300–1589*, Cambridge University Press, 2012, 74; Ousmane Traoré, "State Control and Regulation of Commerce on the Waterways and Coast of Senegambia, ca. 1500–1800", in Carina E. Ray and Jeremy Rich (eds.), *Navigating African Maritime History*, Liverpool University Press, 2009.

84. Marian Małowist, *Western Europe, Eastern Europe and World Development 13th–18th Centuries: Essays of Marian Małowist*, J. Batou and H. Szlajfer (eds.), Brill, 2009, ch. 5.

85. Toby Green, *A Fistful of Shells: West Africa from the Rise of the Slave Trade to the Age of Revolution*, Allen Lane, 2019, 160. Also see Thomas D. Boston, "Sixteenth-Century European Expansion and the Economic Decline of Africa", *Review of Black Political Economy*, 20:4, 1992, 5–38.

86. Alice Louise Willard, "Rivers of Gold, Oceans of Sand: The Songhay in the West African World-System", PhD dissertation, Johns Hopkins University, 1999, ch. 7; James Miller, "Trading through Islam: The Interconnections of Sijilmasa, Ghana and the Almoravid Movement", *Journal of North African Studies*, 6:1, 2001, 29–58.

87. Abdallah Laroui, *The History of the Maghrib. An Interpretive Essay*, Princeton University Press, 1977, 217; Vincent J. Cornell, "Socio-economic Dimensions of Reconquista and Jihad in Morocco: Portuguese Dukkala and the Said Sus, 1450–1557", *International Journal of Middle East Studies*, 22, 1990, 379–418.

88. Dale R. Lightfoot and James A. Miller, "Sijilmassa: The Rise and Fall of a Walled Oasis in Medieval Morocco", *Annals of the Association of American Geographers*, 86:1, 1996, 78–81; Willard, "Rivers of Gold".

89. H. V. Livermore, "On the Conquest of Ceuta", *Luso-Brazilian Review*, 2:1, 1965, 3–13. Also see Ian Blanchard, "Egyptian Specie Markets and the International Gold Crisis of the Early Fifteenth Century", in Lawrin Armstrong, Evana Elbl, and Martin M. Elbl (eds.), *Money, Markets and Trade in Late Medieval Europe: Essays in Honour of John H.A. Munro*, Brill, 2007, 383–410.

90. Steven A. Epstein, *Genoa and the Genoese, 958–1528*, University of North Carolina Press, 1996, 122.

91. David Abulafia, "Sugar in Spain", *European Review*, 16:2, 2009, 191–210. Also see J. H. Galloway, *The Sugar Cane Industry: An Historical Geography from Its Origins to 1914*, Cambridge University Press, 1989; Ashtor, *Levant Trade*; Małowist, *Western Europe, Eastern Europe*, ch. 4.

92. Abulafia, "Sugar in Spain".

93. Peter Edbury, "The State of Research: Cyprus under the Lusignans and Venetians, 1991–1998", *Journal of Medieval History*, 25.1, 1999, 57–65; Thomas Devaney, "Spectacle, Community

and Holy War in Fourteenth-Century Cyprus", *Medieval Encounters*, 19, 2013, 300–341; Laura Balletto, "Ethnic Groups, Cross-Social and Cross-Cultural Contacts on Fifteenth-Century Cyprus", *Mediterranean Historical Review*, 10:1–2, 1995, 35–48; G. V. Scammell, *The World Encompassed: The First European Maritime Empires c.800–1650*, Methuen, 1981, 187–188.

94. Ouerfelli, *Le sucre*, 158, 160.

95. Alberto García Porras and Adela Fábregas García, "Genoese Trade Networks in the Southern Iberian Peninsula: Trade, Transmission of Technical Knowledge and Economic Interactions", *Mediterranean Historical Review*, 25:1, 2010, 35–51.

96. Woolgar, *The Culture of Food*, 98.

97. Filipe Themudo Barata, "Portugal and the Mediterranean Trade: A Prelude to the Discovery of the 'New World'," *Al-Masaq: Islam and the Medieval Mediterranean*, 17:2, 2005, 205–219; Smith, "Demystifying a Change in Taste".

98. Jason W. Moore, "Madeira, Sugar, and the Conquest of Nature, in the 'First' Sixteenth Century; Part One: From 'Island of Timber' to Sugar Revolution, 1420–1506", *Review—Fernand Braudel Center*, 32:4, 2009, 345–390. Also see Bethany J. Walker, "Sowing the Seeds of Rural Decline? Agriculture as an Economic Barometer for Late Mamluk Jordan", *Mamluk Studies Review*, 11:1, 2007.

99. Mosher Stuard, *Gilding the Market*, 138; Mikhail B. Kizilov, "The Black Sea and the Slave Trade: The Role of Crimean Maritime Towns in the Trade in Slaves and Captives in the Fifteenth to Eighteenth Centuries", *International Journal of Maritime History*, 17:1, 2005, 211–235; James Waterson, *The Knights of Islam: The Wars of the Mamluks*, Greenhill, 2007, 223.

100. Ramzi Rouighi, *The Making of a Mediterranean Emirate: Ifrīqiyā and Its Andalusis, 1200–1400*, University of Pennsylvania Press, 2011, 51, 91.

101. Peregrine Horden and Nicholas Purcell, *The Corrupting Sea. A Study of Mediterranean History*, Blackwell, 200, 380.

102. Robert C. Davis, *Christian Slaves, Muslim Masters: White Slavery in the Mediterranean, the Barbary Coast, and Italy, 1500–1800*, Palgrave Macmillan, 2004, 8–9, 23; Jan and Leo Lucassen, "The Mobility Transition Revisited, 1500–1900: What the Case of Europe Can Offer to Global History," *Journal of World History*, 4, 2009, 347–377.

103. Molly Greene, *Catholic Pirates and Greek Merchants: A Maritime History of the Mediterranean*, Princeton University Press, 2010, 93, 95; Henry Kamen, *Empire. How Spain Became a World Power, 1492–1763*, Harper Collins, 2003, 72.

104. Hannah Barker, *That Most Precious Merchandise: The Mediterranean Trade in Black Sea Slaves, 1260–1500*, University of Pennsylvania Press, 2019, ch. 4.

105. Jeffrey Fynn-Paul, "Tartars in Spain: Renaissance Slavery in the Catalan City of Manresa, c.1408", *Journal of Medieval History*, 34, 2008, 347–359. Also see Fynn-Paul, "Empire, Monotheism and Slavery in the Greater Mediterranean Region from Antiquity to the Early Modern Era", *Past & Present*, 205:1, 2009, 3–40; Debra Blumenthal, *Enemies and Familiars: Slavery and Mastery in Fifteenth-Century Valencia*, Cornell University Press, 2009; Paola Pinelli, "From Dubrovnik (Ragusa) to Florence: Observations on the Recruiting of Domestic Servants in the 15th Century", *Dubrovnik Annals*, 12, 2008, 57–71.

106. Arsenio Peter Martinez, "Institutional Development, Revenues and Trade", in Nicola Di Cosmo, Allen J. Frank, and Peter B. Golden (eds.), *The Cambridge History of Inner Asia: The Chinggisid Age*, Cambridge University Press, 2009.

107. John Wright, *The Trans-Saharan Slave Trade*, Routledge, 2007, 30, 39.

108. S. Tognetti, "The Trade in Black African Slaves in Fifteenth-Century Florence", in T. F. Earle and K.J.P. Lowe (eds.), *Black Africans in Renaissance Europe*, Cambridge University Press, 2005; John Bryan Williams, "From the Commercial Revolution to the Slave Revolution: The Development of Slavery in Medieval Genoa", PhD dissertation, University of Chicago, 1995; Barker, *That Most Precious Merchandise*, 65; Núria Silleras-Fernández, "*Nigra Sum Sed Formosa*: Black Slaves and Exotica in the Court of a Fourteenth-Century Aragonese Queen", *Medieval Encounters*, 13, 2007, 546–565.

109. P. E. Russell, *A Social History of Black Slaves and Freedmen in Portugal, 1441–1555*, Cambridge University Press, 1982, 55–57.

110. Debra Blumenthal, *Enemies and Familiars: Slavery and Mastery in Fifteenth-Century Valencia*, Cornell University Press, 2009, 9; Fynn-Paul, "Tartars in Spain"; Scammell, *The World Encompassed*, 174.

111. Green, *The Rise of the Trans-Atlantic Save Trade*, 81.

112. William D. Phillips Jr., *Slavery in Medieval and Early Modern Iberia*, University of Pennsylvania Press, 2013, 10; Thomas N. Bisson, *Medieval Crown of Aragon: A Short History*, Clarendon Press, 2000, 165.

113. Alejandra C. Ordonez et al., "Genetic Studies on the Prehispanic Population Buried in Punta Azulcave (El Hierro, Canary Islands)", *Journal of Archaeological Science*, 78, 2017, 20–28.

114. Joseph F. O'Callaghan, "Castile, Portugal and the Canary Islands. Claims and Counterclaims, 1344–1479", *Viator*, 24, 1993, 287–310; Alfred W. Crosby, "An Ecohistory of the Canary Islands", *Environmental Review*, 8:3, 1984, 214–235; William D. Phillips Jr., "Slavery in the Atlantic Islands and the Early Modern Spanish Atlantic World", in David Eltis and Stanley L. Engerman (eds.), *The Cambridge World History of Slavery Volume 3: AD 1420–AD 1804*, Cambridge University Press, 2011; Carlos-Alberto Campos, "The Atlantic Islands and the Development of Southern Castile at the Turn of the Fifteenth Century", *International History Review*, 9:2, 1987, 173–194; Anthony M. Stevens-Arroyo, "The Inter-Atlantic Paradigm: The Failure of Spanish Medieval Colonisation of the Canary and Caribbean Islands", *Comparative Studies in Society and History*, 35:3, 1993, 515–543; Mohamed Adhikari, "Europe's First Settler Colonial Incursion into Africa: The Genocide of Aboriginal Canary Islanders", *African Historical Review*, 49:1, 2017, 1–26; John Mercer, *The Canary Islands. Their Prehistory, Conquest, and Survival*, Collings, 1980; Felipe Fernandez-Armesto, *The Canary Islands After the Conquest: The Making of a Colonial Society*, Oxford University Press, 1982.

115. Charles F. Briggs, *The Body Broken. Medieval Europe 1300–1520*, Routledge, 2011, 77; P. E. Russell, "Castilian Documentary Sources for the History of the Portuguese Expansion in Guinea, in the Last Years of the Reign of Dom Alfonso V", in P. E. Russell (ed.), *Portugal, Spain and the African Atlantic, 1343–1940: Chivalry and Crusade from John of Gaunt to Henry the Navigator*, Ashgate, 1995; Trevor P. Hall, "The Role of Cape Verde Islanders in Organizing and Operating Maritime Trade Between West Africa and Iberian Territories, 1441–1616", PhD dissertation, Johns Hopkins University, 1993, 470–495; Stefan Halikowski Smith, "The Mid-Atlantic Islands: A Theatre of Early Modern Ecocide?", *International Review of Social History*, 55, 2010, 51–77.

116. Malyn Newitt, *A History of Portuguese Overseas Expansion, 1400–1668*, Routledge, 2005, 15.

117. A. R. Disney, *A History of Portugal and the Portuguese Empire: From Beginnings to 1807. Volume II: The Portuguese Empire*, Cambridge University Press, 2009, 46.

118. Roger C. Smith, *Vanguard of Empire: Ships of Exploration in the Age of Columbus*, Oxford University Press, 1993, 40. Also see Felipe Fernandez-Armesto, *Pathfinders. A Global History of Exploration*, W.W. Norton, 2006, 135–143.

119. O'Rourke and Williamson, "After Columbus".

Chapter 5: Plague Revolutions?

1. See, for example, E. M. Carus-Wilson, "An Industrial Revolution of the Thirteenth Century", *Economic History Review*, 11, 1941, 182–210, and A. R. Lucas, "Industrial Milling in the Ancient and Medieval Worlds: A Survey of the Evidence for an Industrial Revolution in Medieval Europe", *Technology and Culture*, 46:1, 2005.

2. Geoffrey Parker, *The Military Revolution: Military Innovation and the Rise of the West 1500–1800*, Cambridge University Press, 1988.

3. John Langdon, *Mills in the Medieval Economy. England 1300–1540*, Oxford University Press, 2004, 39–40.

4. Ibid., 46.

5. H.J.R. Lenders et al., "Historical Rise of Waterpower Initiated the Collapse of Salmon Stocks", *Scientific Reports*, 6, no. 29269, 2016.

6. Lucas, "Industrial Milling in the Ancient and Medieval Worlds"; Paul Benoit and Josephine Rouillard, "Medieval Hydraulics in France", in Paolo Squatriti (ed.), *Working with Water in Medieval Europe: Technology and Resource-Use*, Brill, 2000; Mathieu Arnoux, "Technical Innovation and the Genesis of Enterprise: Some Reflections on the Example of the European Metallurgical Industry, 13th–16th Centuries", *Histoire, Économie et Société*, 20:4, 2001, 447–454.

7. Lucas, "Industrial Milling in the Ancient and Medieval Worlds".

8. John Munro, "The Symbiosis of Towns and Textiles: Urban Institutions and the Changing Fortunes of Cloth Manufacturing in the Low Countries and England, 1270–1570", *Journal of Early Modern History*, 3:1, 1999, 1–74, and "Medieval Woollens: Textiles, Textile Technology, and Industrial Organization, c. 800–1500", in David Jenkins (ed.), *The Cambridge History of Western Textiles, Volume I*, Cambridge University Press, 2003, 204; Benjamin Braude, "The Rise and Fall of Salonica Woollens, 1500–1650: Technology Transfer and Western Competition", *Mediterranean Historical Review*, 6:2, 1991, 216–236.

9. Fabio Giusberti and Francesca Roversi Monaco, "Economy and Demography", in Sarah Blanshei (ed.), *A Companion to Medieval and Renaissance Bologna*, Brill, 2017. All quotations in this paragraph are from this source.

10. David Gaunt, "The Peasants of Scandinavia, 1300–1700", in Tom Scott (ed.), *The Peasantries of Europe: From the Fourteenth to the Eighteenth Centuries*, Longman, 1998, 313–337.

11. Richard Hayman, *Ironmaking: The History and Archaeology of the Iron Industry*, Tempus, 2005, 18. Also see David Killick and Thomas Fenn, "Archaeometallurgy: The Study of Preindustrial Mining and Metallurgy", *Annual Review of Anthropology*, 41, 2012, 559–575; John U. Nef, "Mining and Metallurgy in Medieval Civilisation", in M. M. Postan, Edward Miller, and Cynthia Postan (eds.), *Trade and Industry in the Middle Ages. The Cambridge Economic History of Europe, Vol. 2*, Cambridge University Press, 1987; Tom Scott, *Society and Economy in Germany, 1300–1600*, Palgrave, 2002, 107.

12. Brian G. Awty, "The Development and Dissemination of the Walloon Method of Iron-working", *Technology and Culture*, 48:4, 2007, 783–803.

13. Paolo Malanima, *Pre-Modern European Economy: One Thousand Years (10th–19th Centuries)*, Brill, 2009, 234.

14. Johan Söderberg, "Prices and Economic Change in Medieval Sweden", *Scandinavian Economic History Review*, 55:2, 2007, 128–152.

15. Awty, "The Development and Dissemination of the Walloon Method".

16. E.g., Nef, "Mining and Metallurgy".

17. Söderberg, "Prices and Economic Change".

18. Rodney Edvinsson and Johan Söderberg, "Prices and the Growth of the Knowledge Economy in Sweden and Western Europe Before the Industrial Revolution", *Scandinavian Economic History Review*, 59:3, 2011, 250–272.

19. Alan Williams, *The Sword and the Crucible: A History of the Metallurgy of European Swords Up to the 16th Century*, Brill, 2012, 95, and "A Note on Liquid Iron in Medieval Europe", *Ambix*, 56:1, 2009, 68–75.

20. F. Grazzi et al., "Ancient and Historic Steel in Japan, India and Europe, A Non-Invasive Comparative Study Using Thermal Neutron Diffraction", *Analytical and Bioanalytical Chemistry*, 400:5, 2011, 1493–1500.

21. Sean McGrail, *Boats of the World: From the Stone Age to Medieval Times*, Oxford University Press, 2001, 93, 141.

22. Ian Friel, "The Carrack: The Advent of the Full Rigged Ship", in Robert Gardiner and Richard W. Unger (eds.), *Cogs, Caravels and Galleons: The Sailing Ship 1000–1650*, Conway Maritime Press, 1994, 77–90.

23. Jeffrey Miner and Stefan Stantchev, "The Genoese Economy", in Carrie E. Benes (ed.), *A Companion to Medieval Genoa*, Brill, 2018.

24. Eliyahu Ashtor, *Levant Trade in the Later Middle Ages*, Princeton University Press, 1983, 384.

25. Thomas Kirk, "Mediterranean Rivalries", in *A Companion to Medieval Genoa*; Daniel Zwick, "Bayonese Cogs, Genoese Carracks, English Dromons and Breton Carvels—Late Medieval Technology Transfer in Northern and Southern European Shipbuilding", Author's blog, 2011; Filipe Castro, "In Search of Unique Iberian Ship Design Concepts", *Historical Archaeology*, 42:2, 2008, 63–87, and "Shipbuilding in Portugal in the Middle Age", in Michel Balard (ed.), *The Sea in History. The Medieval World/La mer dans l'histoire. Le moyen age*, Boydell Press, 2017.

26. Robin Ward, *The World of the Medieval Shipmaster: Law, Business, and the Sea, c.1350–1450*, Boydell Press, 2009, 4.

27. Richard W. Unger, *The Ship in the Medieval Economy, 600–1600*, Croom Helm, 1980, 169; Natascha Mehler and Mark Gardiner, "English and Hanseatic Trading and Fishing Sites in Medieval Iceland: Report on Initial Fieldwork", *Germania*, 85:2, 2007, 385–427; Friel, "The Carrack"; Detlev Ellmers, "The Cog as Cargo Carrier", in Gardiner and Unger (eds.), *Cogs, Caravels and Galleons*; Jan Glete, *Warfare at Sea, 1500–1650: Maritime Conflicts and the Transformation of Europe*, Routledge, 2000, 29.

28. Saturnino Monteiro, *Portuguese Sea Battles 1139–1975*, Oeiras, 2010, Vol. I, 237.

29. Peter Spufford, "Trade in Fourteenth-Century Europe", in Michael Jones (ed.), *The New Cambridge Medieval History, Volume VI c. 1300–c. 1415*, Cambridge University Press, 2000, 185.

Also see Edvinsson and Söderberg, "Prices and the Growth of the European Knowledge Economy"; Söderberg, "Prices and Economic Change".

30. Richard W. Unger, "Shipping and Western European Economic Growth in the Later Renaissance: Potential Connections", *International Journal of Maritime History*, 18:2, 2006, 85–104.

31. McGrail, *Boats of the World*, 93, 171.

32. James Raven, "Printing and Printedness", in Hamish Scott (ed.), *The Oxford Handbook of Early Modern European History, 1350–1750: Volume I: Peoples and Place*, Oxford University Press, 2015. Also see Adrian Johns, "The Coming of Print to Europe", in Leslie Howsam (ed.), *The Cambridge Companion to the History of the Book*, Cambridge University Press, 2015.

33. David Herlihy, in Samuel K. Cohn (ed.), *The Black Death and the Transformation of the West*, Harvard University Press, 1997, 69.

34. Eltjo Buringh and Jan Luiten Van Zanden, "Charting the 'Rise of the West': Manuscripts and Printed Books in Europe, A Long-Term Perspective from the Sixth through Eighteenth Centuries", *Journal of Economic History*, 69:2, 2009, 409–445.

35. Eltjo Buringh, "Books Do Not Die: The Price of Information, Human Capital and the Black Death in the Long Fourteenth Century", Working Paper 55, Utrecht University, Centre for Global Economic History, 2014. Also see Joanne Filippone Overty, "The Cost of Doing Scribal Business: Prices of Manuscript Books in England, 1300–1483", *Book History*, 11, 2008, 1–32.

36. Raven, "Printing and Printedness".

37. David Sheffler, "Late Medieval Education: Continuity and Change", *History Compass*, 8/9, 2010, 1067–1082.

38. M. T. Clanchy, "Parchment and Paper: Manuscript Culture 1100–1500", in Simon Eliot and Jonathan Rose (eds.), *A Companion to the History of the Book*, Blackwell, 2007.

39. Lotte Hellinga, "The Gutenberg Revolutions", in Eliot and Rose (eds.), *A Companion to the History of the Book*.

40. Benoit and Rouillard, "Medieval Hydraulics in France"; Michael Mitterauer, *Why Europe. The Medieval Origins of Its Special Path*, University of Chicago Press, 2010 (German orig. 2003), 255–256.

41. Edvinsson and Söderberg, "Prices and the Growth of the Knowledge Economy".

42. Overty, "The Cost of Doing Scribal Business".

43. Robert Black, "Education and the Emergence of a Literate Society", in John M. Najemy (ed.), *Italy in the Age of the Renaissance, 1300–1550*, Oxford University Press, 2004.

44. Buringh, "Books do not die". Also see J. L. Van Zanden, "The Skill Premium and the 'Great Divergence'." *European Review of Economic History*, 13, 2009, 121–153; John Hatcher, "Women's Work Reconsidered: Gender and Wage Differentiation in Late Medieval England", *Past & Present*, 173, 2001, 191–198; S. Broadberry et al., *British Economic Growth, 1270–1870*, Cambridge University Press, 2015, 314.

45. Brian A'Hearn et al., "Quantifying Quantitative Literacy: Age Heaping and the History of Human Capital", *Journal of Economic History*, 69:3, 2009, 783–808.

46. Alexandra Sapoznik, "Bees in the Medieval Economy: Religious Observance and the Production, Trade, and Consumption of Wax in England, c. 1300–1555", *Economic History Review*, 72:4, 2019, 1152–1174.

47. Carsten Jahnke, "The Baltic Trade", in Donald J. Harreld (ed.), *A Companion to the Hanseatic League*, Brill, 2015. Also see Söderberg, "Prices and Economic Change"; Dorothy Galton, *Survey of a Thousand Years of Beekeeping in Russia*, Bee Research Association, London, 1971.

48. Rossica Panova, "The Black Sea Coastal Cities in the Economic and Political Interrelations among Medieval Bulgaria, Venice and Genoa", *Etudes Balkaniques* 1–2, 1999, 52–58; Pavel Murdzhev, "The Medieval Town in Bulgaria", PhD dissertation, University of Florida, 2008, 204–205.

49. Chiara Frugoni, *Inventions of the Middle Ages*, trans. William McCuaig, Folio Society, 2007 (orig. 2001), 27.

50. David Jacoby, *Trade, Commodities and Shipping in the Medieval Mediterranean*, Ashgate, 1997, ch. 9.

51. Liliane Hilaire-Pérez and Catherine Verna, "Dissemination of Technical Knowledge in the Middle Ages and the Early Modern Era: New Approaches and Methodological Issues", *Technology and Culture*, 47.3, 2006.

52. Dries Tys and Marnix Pieters, "Understanding a Medieval Fishing Settlement Along the Southern North Sea, Walraversijde, c.1200–1630", in Louis Sicking and Darlene Abreu-Ferreira (eds.), *Beyond the Catch: Fisheries of the North Atlantic, the North Sea and the Baltic, 900–1850*, Brill, 2008.

53. David Scheffler, *Schools and Schooling in Late Medieval Germany: Regensburg, 1250–1500*, Brill, 2008, 8–9.

54. Am de Pleijt, "Human Capital Formation in the Long Run: Evidence from Average Years of Schooling in England, 1300–1900", *Cliometrica*, 12:1, 2018. 99–126.

55. Sheffler, "Late Medieval Education"; Black, "Education and the Emergence of a Literate Society".

56. Oscar Gelderblom, *Cities of Commerce: The Institutional Foundations of International Trade in the Low Countries, 1250–1650*, Princeton University Press, 2013, 90.

57. Michael North, *The Expansion of Europe, 1250–1500*, Manchester University Press, 2012 (German original 2007), 167; Alessandro Silvestri, "Ruling from Afar: Government and Information Management iln Late Medieval Sicily", *Journal of Medieval History*, 42:3, 2016, 357–381.

58. João Gouveia Monteiro et al., "Another 1415: Portugal's Military Landscape at the Time of Agincourt", *Journal of Medieval History*, 43:1, 2017, 118–135.

59. Camilla Townsend, "Burying the White Gods: New Perspectives on the Conquest of Mexico", *American Historical Review*, 108:3, 2003, 659–687.

60. S. G. Haw, "The Mongol Empire—the First 'Gunpowder Empire'?" *Journal of the Royal Asiatic Society*, 23, 2013, 441–469.

61. Thomas T. Allsen, "Mongols as Vectors for Cultural Transmission", in Nicola Di Cosmo, Allen J. Frank, and Peter B. Golden (eds.), *The Cambridge History of Inner Asia: The Chinggisid Age*, Cambridge University Press, 2009.

62. Williams, *The Sword and the Crucible*, 45.

63. Haw, "The Mongol Empire—the First 'Gunpowder Empire'?"

64. Sun Laichen, "Military Technology Transfers from Ming China and the Emergence of Northern Mainland Southeast Asia (c. 1390–1527)", *Journal of Southeast Asian Studies*, 34:3, 2003, 495–517; Iqtidar Alam Khan, *Gunpowder and Firearms: Warfare in Medieval India*. Oxford

University Press, 2004, 22–31; Ravi Palat, *The Making of an Indian Ocean World-Economy, 1250–1650. Princes, Paddy Fields, and Bazaars*, Palgrave Macmillan, 2015, 84.

65. Williams, *The Sword and the Crucible*, 106.

66. Carmel Ferragud and Juan Vicente Garcia Marsilla, "The Great Fire of Medieval Valencia (1447)", *Urban History*, 43.4 (2016); Tonio Andrade, *The Gunpowder Age. China, Military Innovation, and the Rise of the West in World History*, Princeton University Press, 2016, 76; Bernard S. Bachrach and David S. Bachrach, *Warfare in Medieval Europe c.400–c.1453*, Routledge, 2017, 240; E. Michael Gerli (ed.), *Medieval Iberia: An Encyclopedia*, Taylor & Francis, 2013, 119, 742.

67. Bert S. Hall, *Weapons and Warfare in Renaissance Europe. Gunpowder, Technology, and Tactics*, Johns Hopkins University Press, 1997, 51; Kelly DeVries, *Guns and Men in Medieval Europe, 1200–1500: Studies in Military History and Technology*, Ashgate/Variorium, 2002, ch. 8.

68. Andrade, *The Gunpowder Age*, 90.

69. DeVries, *Guns and Men in Medieval Europe*, ch. 12.

70. Dan Spencer, "'The Scourge of the Stones': English Gunpowder Artillery at the Siege of Harfleur", *Journal of Medieval History*, 43:1, 2017, 59–73.

71. David Cressy, *Saltpeter: The Mother of Gunpowder*, Oxford University Press, 2013; Kenneth Chase, *Firearms. A Global History to 1700*, Cambridge University Press, 2003; Hall, *Weapons and Warfare*; Kelly DeVries, "Catapults Are Not Atomic Bombs: Towards a Redefinition of 'Effectiveness' in Premodern Military Technology", *War in History*, 4:4, 1997, 454–470; Clifford J. Rogers, "The Military Revolutions of the Hundred Years' War", *Journal of Military History*, 57:2, 1993, 241–278.

72. Spencer "'The Scourge of the Stones'."

73. Andrew de la Garza, "Mughals at War: Babur, Akbar, and the Indian Military Revolution, 1500–1605", PhD dissertation, Ohio State University, 2010, 120.

74. John Francis Guilmartin, "The Earliest Shipboard Gunpowder Ordnance: An Analysis of Its Technical Parameters and Tactical Capabilities", *Journal of Military History*, 71:3, 2007, 649–669.

75. Fabrizio Ansani, "The Life of a Renaissance Gunmaker: Bonaccorso Ghiberti and the Development of Florentine Artillery in the Late Fifteenth Century", *Technology and Culture*, 58:3, 2017, 749–789.

76. Jeffrey G. Royal and John M. McManamon, "Three Renaissance Wrecks from Turkey and Their Implications for Maritime History in the Eastern Mediterranean", *Journal of Maritime Archaeology*, 4:2, 2009, 103–129.

77. DeVries, *Guns and Men in Medieval Europe*, ch. 12.

78. DeVries, "Catapults Are Not Atomic Bombs".

79. John Landers, *The Field and the Forge: Population, Production, and Power in the Pre-Industrial West*, Oxford University Press, 2005, 182.

80. Malyn Newitt, *A History of Portuguese Overseas Expansion, 1400–1668*, Routledge, 2005, 99; Pedro de Brito, "Knights, Squires and Foot Soldiers in Portugal during the Sixteenth Century Military Revolution", *Mediterranean Studies*, 17:1, 2008, 118–147; Geoffrey Parker, "The Artillery Fortress as an Engine of European Overseas Expansion, 1480–1750", in James D. Tracy (ed.), *City Walls: The Urban Enceinte in Global Perspective*, Cambridge University Press, 2000, 386–416.

81. Friel, "The Carrack"; Dan Spencer, *Royal and Urban Gunpowder Weapons in Late Medieval England*, Boydell Press, 2019, ch. 3.

82. John F. Guilmartin, "Guns and Gunnery", in Gardiner and Unger (eds.), *Cogs, Caravels and Galleons*.

83. Louis Sicking, "Naval Warfare in Europe, c. 1330–c. 1680", in Frank Tallett and D.J.B. Trim (eds.), *European Warfare, 1350–1750*, Cambridge University Press, 2010.

84. E. Galili and B. Rosen, "A 15th-Century Wreck of an Ordnance-Carrying Ship from Atlit North Bay, Israel", *International Journal of Nautical Archaeology*, 43:1, 2014, 115–127.

85. Roger C. Smith, *Vanguard of Empire: Ships of Exploration in the Age of Columbus*, Oxford University Press, 1993, 165.

86. Philip T. Hoffman, *Why Did Europe Conquer the World?* Princeton University Press, 2015, fig. 2.3.

87. Joseph Eliav, "Tactics of Sixteenth-century Galley Artillery", *The Mariner's Mirror*, 99:4, 2013, 398–409.

88. DeVries, "Catapults Are Not Atomic Bombs"; Sicking, "Naval Warfare in Europe"; Guilmartin, "The Earliest Shipboard Gunpowder Ordnance"; N.A.M. Rodger, "The New Atlantic: Naval Warfare in the Sixteenth Century", in John B. Hattendorf and Richard W. Unger (eds.), *War at Sea in the Middle Ages and Renaissance*, Boydell Press, 2003, 233–247.

89. John F. Guilmartin, "The Military Revolution in Warfare at Sea during the Early Modern Era: Technological Origins, Operational Outcomes and Strategic Consequences", *Journal for Maritime Research*, 13:2, 2011, 129–137.

90. F. Castro et al., "A Quantitative Look at Mediterranean Lateen- and Square-Rigged Ships (Part 1)", *International Journal of Nautical Archaeology*, 3:2, 2008, 347–359.

91. Leonor Freire Costa, Pedro Lains, and Susana Munch Miranda, *An Economic History of Portugal, 1143–2010*, Cambridge University Press, 2016, 36.

92. Guilmartin, "The Military Revolution in Warfare at Sea".

93. Monteiro, *Portuguese Sea Battles*, Vol. I, 107–128; Carla Rahn Phillips, "The Caravel and the Galleon", in Gardiner and Unger (eds.), *Cogs, Caravels and Galleons*; Guilmartin, "The Earliest Shipboard Gunpowder Ordnance".

94. Lawrence V. Mott, "Iberian Naval Power, 1000–1650", in Hattendorf and Unger (eds.), *War At Sea*.

95. Guilmartin, "The Military Revolution in Warfare at Sea".

96. Ian Friel, "Oars, Sails and Guns: The English and War at Sea, *c.*1200–*c.*1500", in Hattendorf and Unger (eds.), *War at Sea*, 72.

97. Glete, *Warfare at Sea*, 34.

98. Kelly De Vries, "The Effectiveness of Fifteenth-Century Shipboard Artillery", *The Mariner's Mirror*, 84:4, 1998, 389–399; Ellmers, "The Cog as Cargo Carrier"; Smith, *Vanguard of Empire*, 164; Guilmartin, "The Earliest Shipboard Gunpowder Ordnance"; DeVries, *Guns and Men*, ch. 14; Rodger, *Safeguard of the Sea*, 163.

99. Monteiro, *Portuguese Sea Battles*, Vol. I, 237.

100. David L. Mearns, David Parham, and Bruno Frohlich, "A Portuguese East Indiaman from the 1502–1503 Fleet of Vasco da Gama Off Al Hallaniyah Island, Oman: An Interim Report", *International Journal of Nautical Archaeology*, 45:2, 2016, 1–21.

101. Jeremy Black, "Naval Capability in the Early Modern Period: An Introduction", *Mariner's Mirror*, 97:2, 2011.

102. Friel, "Oars, Sails and Guns".

103. Michael G. Vickers, "The Structure of Military Revolutions", PhD dissertation, Johns Hopkins University, 2010, 215.

104. Jim Bradbury, *The Routledge Companion to Medieval Warfare*, Routledge, 2004, 243.

105. Hall, *Weapons and Warfare*, 17.

106. Hall, *Weapons and Warfare*; Clifford J. Rogers, "Tactics and the Face of Battle", in Tallett and Trim (eds.), *European Warfare*.

107. Susan Mosher Stuard, *Gilding the Market. Luxury and Fashion in Fourteenth-century Italy*, University of Pennsylvania Press, 2006, 7.

108. Rogers, "Tactics and the Face of Battle".

109. Thom Richardson, "Armour in England, 1325–99", *Journal of Medieval History*, 37 (2011), 304–320.

110. Williams, *The Sword and the Crucible*, ch. 10.

111. Helen Nicholson, *Medieval Warfare: Theory and Practice of War in Europe, 300–1500*, Palgrave Macmillan, 2004, 88.

112. Bert Hall, "Weapons of War and Late Medieval Cities; Technological Innovation and Tactical Changes", in Elizabeth Bradford Smith and Michael Wolfe (eds.), *Technology and Resource Use in Medieval Europe: Cathedrals, Mills, and Mines*, Ashgate, 1997.

113. Nicholson, *Medieval Warfare*, 89; Stephen E. Lahey, *The Hussites (Past Imperfect)*, Arc Humanities Press, 2019, ch. 2; John J. Jefferson, "The Ottoman-Hungarian Campaigns of 1442", *Journal of Medieval Military History*, 10, 2012.

114. Khan, *Gunpowder and Firearms*, 129.

115. Hall, "Weapons of War", 182.

116. Andrade, *The Gunpowder Age*, 167.

117. Landers, *The Field and the Forge*, 69.

118. Herman Van Der Wee, "The Western European Woollen Industries, 1500–1750", in Jenkins (ed.), *The Cambridge History of Western Textiles*, 412.

119. Malanima, *Pre-Modern European Economy*, 234.

120. Luis Angeles, "The Great Divergence and the Economics of Printing", *Economic History Review*, 70:1, 2017, 30–51.

121. Raven, "Printing and Printedness".

122. Richard W. Unger, "Ship Design and Energy Use 1350–1875", in Richard W. Unger (ed.), *Shipping and Economic Growth 1350–1850*, Brill, 2011, 252. Also see Cláudia Rei, "The organization of merchant empires", PhD dissertation, Boston University, 2009.

123. Gervase Phillips, "Longbow and Hackbutt: Weapons Technology and Technology Transfer in Early Modern England", *Technology and Culture*, 40:3, 1999, 576–579.

124. Rhoads Murphey, *Ottoman Warfare, 1500–1700*, Rutgers University Press, 1999, 107–108. Also see Vickers, "The Structure of Military Revolutions", 202–203; Andrade, *The Gunpowder Age*, 102–107; Hall, *Weapons and Warfare*, 156, 216; Landers, *The Field and the Forge*, 152.

Chapter 6: Expansive Labour

1. J. Belich, "Race", in David Armitage and Alison Bashford (eds.), *Pacific Histories. Ocean, Land, People*, Palgrave Macmillan, 2014.

2. Mark Larrimore, "Antinomies of Race: Diversity and Destiny in Kant", *Patterns of Prejudice*, 42:4–5, 2008, 341–363.

3. Robert Bartlett, *The Making of Europe: Conquest, Colonization, and Cultural Change, 950–1350*, Princeton University Press, 1993, 13; B. Isaac, J. Ziegler, and M. Eliav-Feldon (eds.), *The Origins of Racism in the West*, Cambridge University Press, 2009; James M. Thomas, "The Racial Formation of Medieval Jews: A Challenge to the Field", *Ethnic and Racial Studies*, 33:10, 2010, 1737–1755.

4. R. I. Moore, *The Formation of a Persecuting Society: Power and Deviance in Western Europe, 950–1250*, Blackwell, 1987.

5. Randal Paul Garza, *Understanding Plague: The Medical and Imaginative Texts of Medieval Spain*, Peter Lang, 2008.

6. David Nirenberg, *Communities of Violence: Persecution of Minorities in the Middle Ages*, Princeton University Press, 1996, 231.

7. Jean-Paul Zúñiga, "Visible Signs of Belonging. The Spanish Empire and the Rise of Racial Logics in the Early Modern Period", in Pedro Cardim et al. (eds.), *Polycentric Monarchies: How Did Early Modern Spain and Portugal Achieve and Maintain a Global Hegemony?* Sussex Academic Press, 2012.

8. María Elena Martínez, "The Black Blood of New Spain: Limpieza de Sangre, Racial Violence, and Gendered Power in Early Colonial Mexico," *William and Mary Quarterly*, 61:3, 2004, 479–520.

9. David M. Goldenberg, *The Curse of Ham: Race and Slavery in Early Judaism, Christianity, and Islam*, Princeton University Press, 2005.

10. Kristen Black and Jenny Shaw, "Subjects without an Empire: The Irish in the Early Modern Caribbean", *Past & Present*, 210:1, 2011.

11. Trevor Burnard, *Mastery, Tyranny, and Desire: Thomas Thistlewood and His Slaves in the Anglo-Jamaican World*, University of North Carolina Press, 2004, 21.

12. Russell R. Menard, *Sweet Negotiations: Sugar, Slavery, and Plantation Agriculture in Early Barbados*, University of Virginia Press, 2006, 119.

13. Joanne Rappaport, "'Asi lo paresçe por su aspeto'. Physiognomy and the Construction of Difference in Colonial Bogotá", *Hispanic American Historical Review*, 91:4, 2011, citing María Elena Martínez, *Genealogical Fictions: Limpieza de Sangre, Religion, and Gender in Colonial Mexico*, Stanford University Press, 2008. Also see Peter B. Villella, "'Pure and Noble Indians, Untainted by Inferior Idolatrous Races': Native Elites and the Discourse of Blood Purity in Late Colonial Mexico", *Hispanic American Historical Review*, 91:4, 2011, 633–663; David Nirenberg, "Was There Race Before Modernity? The Example of 'Jewish' Blood in Late Medieval Spain", in Isaac, Ziegler, and Eliav-Feldon (eds.), *The Origins of Racism*.

14. Philippe-Andre Rodriguez, "Colonial Ricochet: Human Nature, Racism and *Hispanidad* in the Early Spanish Empire, 1492–1552", D Phil thesis, Oxford University, 2019.

15. Ibid.

16. Quoted in Gabriel Paquette, *The European Seaborne Empires: From the Thirty Years' War to the Age of Revolutions*, Yale University Press, 2019, 166. Also see Anthony Pagden, "The Peopling of the New World: Ethnos, Race and Empire in the Early-Modern World", in Isaac, Ziegler, and Eliav-Feldon (eds.), *Origins of Racism*; Carville Earle, "Pioneers of Providence: The Anglo-American Experience, 1492–1792", *Annals of the Association of American Geographers*, 82:3, 1992,

478–499; C. J. Jaenen and D. Standen, "Regeneration or Degeneration? Some French Views of the Effects of Colonization", *Proceedings of the Annual Meeting of the French Colonial Historical Society*, 20, 1994, 1–10; Zúñiga, "Visible Signs of Belonging"; Joyce E. Chaplin, "The British Atlantic", in *The Oxford Handbook of the Atlantic World: 1450–1850*, Nicholas Canny and Philip Morgan (eds.), Oxford University Press, 2011; J. H. Elliott, *Empires of the Atlantic World. Britain and Spain in Am 1492–1830*, Yale University Press, 2006, 235–236.

17. Quoted by Steven Martinot, "Motherhood and the Invention of Race", *Hypatia*, 22:2, 2007, 79–97.

18. Martínez, "The Black Blood of New Spain".

19. Sylvia van Kirk, "From 'Marrying-In' to 'Marrying-Out'. Changing Patterns of Aboriginal/Non-Aboriginal Marriage in Colonial Canada", *Frontiers*, 2002, 23:3.

20. Francisco Bethencourt, *Racisms. From the Crusades to the Twentieth Century*, Princeton University Press, 2013, 167. Also see Zúñiga, "Visible Signs of Belonging".

21. Heinrich Harke, "Anglo-Saxon Immigration and Ethnogenesis", *Medieval Archaeology*, 55, 2011.

22. Bethencourt, *Racisms*, 47.

23. Michael Balard, "The Genoese in the Aegean (1204–1566)", *Mediterranean Historical Review*, 4:1, 1989, 158–174.

24. Sally McKee, "Inherited Status and Slavery in Late Medieval Italy and Venetian Crete", *Past & Present*, 182, 2004, 31–53.

25. Ibid. Also see Laura Balletto, "Ethnic Groups, Cross-Social and Cross-Cultural Contacts on Fifteenth-Century Cyprus", *Mediterranean Historical Review*, 10:1–2, 1995, 35–48.

26. Luiz Vélez de Guevar, "The King Counts More Than Blood", in Ann Twinam (ed.), *Purchasing Whiteness: Pardos, Mulattos, and the Quest for Social Mobility in the Spanish Indies*, Stanford University Press, 2015.

27. Stuart B. Schwartz, "The Iberian Atlantic to 1650", in Canny and Morgan (eds.), *The Oxford Handbook of the Atlantic World*.

28. Nicole Macameyer, "Mitochondrial DNA Diversity in 17th–18th Century Remains from Tenerife (Canary Islands)", *American Journal of Physical Anthropology*, 127, 2005, 418–426; Manuel Hernández González, "Canary Island Immigration to the Hispanic Caribbean", *Oxford Research Encyclopedia of Latin American History*, 2017.

29. Massimo Livi Bacci, *Conquest: The Destruction of the American Indios*, Polity Press, 2008 (orig. 2005), 17.

30. Ida Altman, "Spanish Women in the Caribbean, 1493–1540", in Sarah E. Owens and Jane E. Mangan (eds.), *Women of the Iberian Atlantic*, Louisiana University Press, 2012.

31. Ida Altman, "Spanish Women in the Caribbean, 1493–1540".

32. Susan D. de France, "Diet and Provisioning in the High Andes: A Spanish Colonial Settlement on the Outskirts of Potosí, Bolivia", *International Journal of Historical Archaeology*, 7:2, 2003, 99–125.

33. Henry Kamen, *Empire. How Spain Became a World Power, 1492–1763*, Harper Collins, 2003 (orig. 2002), 354. Also see 266.

34. Rappaport, "'Asi lo paresçe por su aspeto'".

35. James Horn, quoted in Nuran Cinlar, "Marriage in the Colonial Chesapeake, 1607–1770: A Study in Cultural Adaptation and Reformulation", PhD dissertation, Johns Hopkins University, 2001, 34.

36. Guillaume Aubert, "'The Blood of France': Race and Purity of Blood in the French Atlantic", *William and Mary Quarterly*, 61.3, 2004, 439–478. Also see Claude Bherer et al., "Admixed Ancestry and Stratification of Quebec Regional Populations", *American Journal of Physical Anthropology*, 144. 2011, 432–441; David N. Collins, "Sexual Imbalance in Frontier Communities: Siberia and New France to 1760", *Sibirica*, 4:2, 2004, 162–185.

37. Ken Coates, "Western Manitoba and the 1885 Rebellion", *Manitoba History*, 20, 1990, 32–41; Desmond Morton, *The Last War Drum. The Northwest Campaign of 1885*, Hakkert, 1970; D. N. Sprague, *Canada and the Metis, 1869–185*, Wilfrid Laurier University Press, 1988.

38. Richard W. Slatta, *Gauchos and the Vanishing Frontier*, Nebraska University Press, 1992 (orig. 1983).

39. Hal Langfur, "Colonial Brazil (1500–1622)", in Thomas H. Holloway (ed.), *A Companion to Latin American History*, Wiley-Blackwell, 2011.

40. Angelo Alves Carrara, "The Population of Brazil, 1570–1700: A Historiographical Review", *Revista Tempo*, 20, 2015; Vitorino Magalhães Godinho, "Portuguese Emigration from the Fifteenth to the Twentieth Century: Constants and Changes", in P. C. Emmer and M. Mörner (eds.), *European Expansion and Migration: Essays on the Intercontinental Migration from Africa, Asia, and Europe*, Berg, 1992; Alida C. Metcalf, *Go-Betweens and the Colonization of Brazil: 1500–1600*, University of Texas Press, 2005.

41. Erik Lars Myrup, "To Rule from Afar: The Overseas Council and the making of the Brazilian West, 1642–1807", PhD dissertation, Yale University, 2006, 148.

42. B. G. Adriana et al., "Mitochondrial DNA Control Region Polymorphism in the Population of Alagoas State, North-Eastern Brazil", *Journal of Forensic Sciences*, 53:1, 2008, 142–146; Laura Valverde et al., "Segments HVS-I and HVS-II of Mitochondrial DNA in a Population from Santa Catarina (Brazil): Predominance of European Lineages", *Forensic Science International: Genetics Supplement Series*, 2, 2009, 338–339; Isabela Brunelli Ambrosio et al., "Mitochondrial DNA 30-SNP Data Confirm High Prevalence of African Lineages in the Population of Espirito Santo, Brazil", *Forensic Science International: Genetics Supplement Series 5*, 2015, 346–347. For Y DNA, see note 22 above.

43. Metcalf, *Go-Betweens and the Colonization of Brazil*, 96–97; Thomas M. Cohen, "Racial and Ethnic Minorities in the Society of Jesus", in *The Cambridge Companion to the Jesuits*, Cambridge University Press, 2008.

44. Richard Gott, "Latin America as a White Settler Society", *Bulletin of Latin American Research*, 26, 2007, 269–289.

45. Luiz Vélez de Guevar, "The King Counts More Than Blood".

46. George M. Fredrickson, "Mulattoes and Metis. Attitudes toward Miscegenation in the United States and France since the Seventeenth Century", *International Social Science Journal*, 57:183, 2005, 103–112.

47. Martínez, "The Black Blood of New Spain".

48. de Guevar, "The King Counts More Than Blood".

49. Daniel Livesay, "The Decline of Jamaica's Interracial Households and the Fall of the Planter Class, 1733–1823", *Atlantic Studies*, 9:1, 2012, 107–123.

50. Lower figures are sometimes given, but often because they are estimates for 1760 or 1780, not 1800. The figures for Brazil's white population vary wildly—I have gone with the figure of one million suggested by Dauril Alden. ("The Population of Brazil in the Late Eighteenth Century: A Preliminary Study", *Hispanic American Historical Review*, 43, 1963, 173–205.) Three

million for Spanish America is a little higher than some estimates, but I allow for 200,000 "whites" in Santo Domingo, Puerto Rico, and Cuba. The United States' white population in 1800 was 3.5 million according to the census of that year. I have allowed 500,000 for British North America, including French Canadians, and for the British Caribbean. These figures converge with those of leading population historian Massimo Livi Bacci (*The Population of Europe. A History*, trans. Cynthia De Nardi Ipsen and Carl Ipsen, Blackwell, 2000, 119–21, and *Conquest*, 7). The numbers for 1760 are from Olivier Pétré-Grenouilleau, "Maritime Powers, Colonial Powers; The Role of Migration (c. 1492–1792)", in Wim Klooster (ed.), *Migration, Trade, and Slavery in an Expanding World*, Brill, 2009, citing the research of Bouda Etehad. Also see Stanley Engerman, "War, Colonization and Migration over Five Centuries", in Klooster (ed.), *Migration, Trade, and Slavery*, 193; Nicholas P. Canny (ed.), *Europeans on the Move: Studies on European Migration, 1500–1800*, Clarendon Press, 1994.

51. James L. Webb, "Globalization of Disease, 1300–1900", in J. H. Bentley, S. Subrahmanyam, and M. Wiesner-Hanks (eds.), *The Cambridge World History, Volume VI: The Construction of a Global World, 1400–1800, Part I: Foundations*. Cambridge University Press, 2015, 54–75; Hugh Cagle, "Beyond the Senegal: Inventing the Tropics in the Late Middle Ages", *Journal of Medieval Iberian Studies*, 7:2, 2015, 197–217; Alvaro Molina-Cruz et al., "Mosquito Vectors and the Globalization of *Plasmodium falciparum* Malaria", *Annual Review of Genetics*, 50, 2016, 447–465; Erica Charters, *Disease, War, and the Imperial State: The Welfare of British Forces during the Seven Years' War, 1756–63*, University of Chicago Press, 2014, esp. 60; K. F. Kiple, "Biology and African Slavery", in R. L. Paquette and M. M. Smith (eds.), *The Oxford Handbook of Slavery in the Americas*, Oxford University Press, 2010; John McNeill, *Mosquito Empires. Ecology and War in the Greater Caribbean, 1620–1914*, Cambridge University Press, 2010, 95.

52. Peter Boyd-Bowman, "Patterns of Spanish Emigration to the Indies until 1600", *Hispanic American Historical Review*, 56:4, 1976, 580–604. Boyd-Bowman thinks his sample of 55,000 represents between a fifth and a quarter of the whole. I use a multiplier of 4.5. Also see Magnus Mörner, "Spanish Historians on Spanish Migration to America During the Colonial Period", *Latin American Research Review*, 30:2, 1995; Karl W. Butzer, "Spanish Colonization of the New World: Cultural Continuity and Change in Mexico", *Erdkunde*, 45:3, 1991, 205–219.

53. Virginia Dejohn Anderson, "New England in the Seventeenth Century", in Nicholas Canny (ed.), *The Oxford History of the British Empire, Vol I, The Origins of Empire: British Overseas Enterprise to the Close of the Seventeenth Century*, Oxford University Press, 1998. Also see Anderson, "Migrants and Motives: Religion and the Settlement of New England, 1630–1640", *New England Quarterly*, 58:3, 1985, 339–383; Nicholas Canny, "English Migration into and across the Atlantic during the Seventeenth and Eighteenth Centuries", in Canny (ed.), *Europeans on the Move*; David W. Galenson, "The Settlement and Growth of the Colonies: Population, Labour, and Economic Development", in Stanley L Engerman and Robert E. Gallman (eds.), *The Cambridge Economic History of the United States, Vol. I: The Colonial Era*, Cambridge University Press, 1996.

54. David Hackett Fischer, *Albion's Seed. Four British Folkways in America*, Oxford University Press, 1989, 17.

55. Nuala Zahedieh, "Trade, Plunder and Economic Development in Early English Jamaica", *Economic History Review*, 39:2, 1986, 205–222.

56. Similar calculations seem to work very roughly for San Domingue in 1683, using figures from James Pritchard, *In Search of Empire: The French in the Americas, 1670–1730*, Cambridge University Press, 2004, 61–66; for a Dutch settlement at Recife in the 1640s, using figures from Wim Klooster, *The Dutch Moment. War, Trade and Settlement in the Seventeenth-Century Atlantic World*, Cornell University Press, 2016, 192; and for the founding British settlement in Nova Scotia in 1749, from figures in "Censuses of Canada 1665 to 1871", Statistics Canada, www .statcan.gc.

57. Mörner, "Spanish Historians on Spanish Migration".

58. Quoted in Megan Vaughan, *Creating the Creole Island: Slavery in Eighteenth-century Mauritius*, Duke University Press, 2005, 39.

59. Pétré-Grenouilleau, "The Role of Migration" and "The Northern European Atlantic World", in Canny and Morgan (eds.), *The Oxford Handbook of the Atlantic World: 1450–1850*.

60. David Eltis, "The English, the Dutch, and Transoceanic Migration", in Eltis, *The Rise of African Slavery in the Americas*, Cambridge University Press, 2000.

61. Anderson, "New England in the Seventeenth Century", 211.

62. Elliott, *Empires of the Atlantic World*, xiii.

63. A.J.R. Russell-Wood, *The Portuguese Empire, 1415–1808: A World on the Move*, Johns Hopkins University Press, 1998 (orig. 1992), 109.

64. Hilary McD. Beckles, "The 'Hub of Empire': The Caribbean and Britain in the Seventeenth Century", in Canny (ed.), *The Oxford History of the British Empire*, Vol. I; Aaron S. Fogleman, "From Slaves, Convicts, and Servants to Free Passengers: The Transformation of Immigration in the Era of the American Revolution", *Journal of American History*, 85:1, 1998; David W. Galenson, "The Settlement and Growth of the Colonies: Population, Labour, and Economic Development", in Engerman and Gallman (eds.), *The Cambridge Economic History of the United States*, vol. I.

65. Boyd-Bowman, "Patterns of Spanish Emigration to the Indies until 1600".

66. J. Belich, *Replenishing the Earth. The Settler Revolution and the Rise of the Anglo-world, 1780s–1920s*, Oxford University Press, 2009, and "Settler Utopianism? English Ideologies of Emigration, 1815–1880", in John Morrow and Jonathan Scott (eds.), *Liberty, Authority, Formality: Political Ideas and Culture, 1600–1900*, Imprint Academic, 2008.

67. Stephen Fender, *Sea Changes. British Emigration and American Literature*, Cambridge University Press, 1992, 63.

68. Jon Gjerde, *The Minds of the West. Ethnocultural Evolution in the Rural Middle West, 1830–1917*, University of North Carolina Press, 1997, 28–31; Alan Taylor, *American Colonies*, Penguin, 2001, 371–374; Merle Curti and Kendall Birr, "The Immigrant and the American Image in Europe, 1860–1914", *Mississippi Valley Historical Review*, 37, 1950, 203–230; Willard Sunderland, "Peasant Pioneering: Russian Peasant Settlers Describe Colonization and the Eastern Frontier, 1880s–1910s", *Journal of Social History*, 34, 2001, 895–922.

69. David C. Gentilcore, "The Subcultures of the Renaissance World", in Guido Ruggiero (ed.), *A Companion to the Worlds of the Renaissance*, Blackwell, 2002, 299–315.

70. Richard C. Hoffman, *An Environmental History of Medieval Europe*, Cambridge University Press, 2014, 192; Michael North, *The Expansion of Europe, 1250–1500*, Manchester University Press, 2012 (German original 2007), 396; Mirian Muller, "Conflict and Revolt: The Bishop of Ely and His Peasants at the Manor of Brandon in Suffolk c. 1300–81", *Rural History*, 23:1, 2012,

and "A Divided Class? Peasants and Peasant Communities in Later Medieval England", *Past & Present*, 196, 2007, Supplement 2.

71. Timothy D. Walker, "The Medicines Trade in the Portuguese Atlantic World: Acquisition and Dissemination of Healing Knowledge from Brazil (c. 1580–1800)", *Social History of Medicine*, 26:3, 2013, 403–431.

72. Henry A. Gemery, "The White Population of the Colonial US", in Michael R. Haines and Richard H. Steckel (eds.), *A Population History of North America*, Cambridge University Press, 2000, 174–175.

73. Ida Altman, *Emigrants and Society. Extremadura and America in the Sixteenth Century*, University of California Press, 1989, 204.

74. Anthony M. Stevens-Arroyo, "The Inter-Atlantic Paradigm: The Failure of Spanish Medieval Colonization of the Canary and Caribbean Islands", *Comparative Studies in Society and History*, 35:3, 1993, 515–543.

75. Andrew Hess, *The Forgotten Frontier; A History of the Sixteenth-century Ibero-African Frontier*, University of Chicago Press, 1978, 134. Also see Olivia Remie Hamilton, *Trade and Traders in Muslim Spain. The Commercial Realignment of the Iberian Peninsula, 900–1500*, Cambridge University Press, 1994.

76. David Coleman, *Creating Christian Granada: Society and Religious Culture in an Old-World Frontier City, 1492–1600*, Cornell University Press, 2003, 31.

77. Peter Boyd-Bowman, "Patterns of Spanish Emigration to the Indies".

78. Mörner, "Spanish Historians on Spanish Migration".

79. E.g., A.H.R. Russell-Wood, "Patterns of Settlement in the Portuguese Empire, 1400–1800", in Francisco Bethencourt and Diogo Ramada Curto (eds.), *Portuguese Oceanic Expansion, 1400–1800*, Cambridge University Press, 2007, 161–196.

80. Malyn Newitt, *Emigration and the Sea*, Oxford University Press, 2015, ch. 2.

81. Donald Ramos, "From Minho to Minas: The Portuguese Roots of the Mineiro Family", *Hispanic American Historical Review*, 73:4, 1993, 639–662.

82. Malyn Newitt, *A History of Portuguese Overseas Expansion, 1400–1668*, Routledge, 2005, 43.

83. A. R. Disney, *A History of Portugal and the Portuguese Empire*, 2 vols., Cambridge University Press, 2009, Vol. 2, 89–90.

84. Bill M. Donovan, "The Politics of Immigration to 18th Century Brazil: Azorean Migrants to Santa Caterina", *Itinerario*, 16:1, 1992, 35–56.

85. Russell-Wood, "Patterns of Settlement in the Portuguese Empire".

86. Ian D. Whyte, *Migration and Society in Britain: 1550–1830*, Macmillan, 2000, 124–125, 183–184.

87. Kenneth W. Keller, "From the Rhineland to the Virginia Frontier. Flax Production as a Commercial Enterprise", *Virginia Magazine of History and Biography*, 98:3, 1990.

88. Thomas M. Truxes, *Irish-American Trade, 1660–1783*, Cambridge University Press, 1988; Keller, "From the Rhineland to the Virginia Frontier"; Marianne S. Wokeck, *Trade in Strangers: The Beginnings of Mass Migration to North America*, Pennsylvania State University Press, 1999, and "Irish and German Migration to Eighteenth-Century North America", in David Eltis (ed.), *Coerced and Free Migration: Global Perspectives*, Stanford University Press, 2002; Graeme Kirkham, "Ulster Emigration to North America, 1680–1720", and Trevor Parkhill, "Philadelphia

Here I Come: A Study of the Letters of Ulster Immigrants in Pennsylvania, 1750–1875", both in Tyler Blethen and Curtis Wood (eds.), *Ulster and North America: Transatlantic Perspectives on the Scotch-Irish*, University of Alabama Press, 1997; Patrick Griffin, "The People with No Name: Ulster's Migrants and Identity Formation in Eighteenth-Century Pennsylvania", *William and Mary Quarterly*, 58:3, 2001; David W. Miller, "Searching for a New World: The Background and Baggage of Scots-Irish Immigrants", in Warren R. Hofstra (ed.), *Ulster to America: The Scots-Irish Migration Experience, 1680–1830*, University of Tennessee Press, 2011; Graeme Kirkham, "Ulster Emigration to North America", in Blethen and Woods (eds.), *Ulster and North America: Transatlantic Perspectives on the Scotch-Irish*, University of Alabama Press, 1997; Bryan C. Rindfleisch, "Family, Linen, and Emigration in Ulster, 1700–1740: The Galphin Family in Two Worlds", *New Hibernia Review / Iris Éireannach Nua*, 20:4, 2016, 128–143.

89. Georg Fertig, "Transatlantic Migration from the German-Speaking Parts of Central Europe, 1600–1800: Proportions, Structures, and Explanations", in Canny (ed.), *Europeans on the Move*.

90. Emma Rothschild, "A Horrible Tragedy in the French Atlantic", *Past & Present*, 192, 2006, 67–108.

91. Pritchard, *In Search of Empire*, 300.

92. Alan Forrest, *The Death of the French Atlantic. Trade, War, and Slavery in the Age of Revolution*, Oxford University Press, 2020, 92.

93. Tim Mackintosh-Smith, *Arabs. A 3,000-Year History of Peoples, Tribes and Empires*, Yale University Press, Loc. 3876–3877.

94. E.g., Rebecca Jones et al., "Y-Chromosome Haplotypes Reveal Relationships Between Populations of the Arabian Peninsula, North Africa and South Asia", *Annals of Human Biology*, 44:8, 2017, 738–746.

95. Andre Wink, *Al-Hind, the Making of the Indo-Islamic World. Volume 3, Indo-Islamic Society, 14th–15th Centuries*, Brill, 2004, 183.

96. Engseng Ho, *The Graves of Tarim: Genealogy and Mobility Across the Indian Ocean*, University of California Press, 2006, 68, 72.

97. Abdelhafidh Hajjeja et al., "Anthropological Analysis of Tunisian Populations as Inferred from HLA Class I and Class II Genetic Diversity: A Meta-Analysis", *Immunology Letters* 185, 2017, 12–26.

98. Ben Raffield, Neil Price, and Mark Collard, "Male-biased Operational Sex Ratios and the Viking Phenomenon: An Evolutionary Anthropological Perspective on Late Iron Age Scandinavian Raiding", *Evolution and Human Behavior*, 38, 2017, 315–324.

99. Anne-Lise Head-König, "Migration in the Swiss Alps and Swiss Jura from the Middle Ages to the Mid-20th Century: A Brief Review", *Revue de géographie alpine*, 99, 2011; Jon Mathieu, *History of the Alps, 1500–1900: Environment, Development, and Society*, University of West Virginia Press, 2011, 61–62; Tom Scott, "Liberty and Community in Medieval Switzerland", *German History*, 13:1, 1995, 98.

100. John Casparis, "The Swiss Mercenary System: Labor Emigration from the Semiperiphery", *Fernand Braudel Center Review*, 5:4, 1982, 593–642.

101. Ibid.

102. Michael Blatter, "The Transformation of the Alpine Economy in the 14th And 15th Centuries. Harvesting 'Wild Hay' in the High Mountains", *Nomadic Peoples*, 13:2, 2009, 146–159.

103. Clifford J. Rogers, "The Military Revolutions of the Hundred Years' War", *Journal of Military History*, 57:2, 1993, 241–278.

104. Michael Prestwich, *Armies and Warfare in the Middle Ages: The English Experience*, Yale University Press, 1996, 127. Also see Jonathan Sumption, *The Hundred Years' War, Volume III: Divided Houses*, Faber and Faber, 2009, 776.

105. Bert S. Hall, *Weapons and Warfare in Renaissance Europe. Gunpowder, Technology, and Tactics*, Johns Hopkins University Press, 1997, 225.

106. John McManamon, "Maltese Seafaring in Mediaeval and Post-Mediaeval Times", *Mediterranean Historical Review*, 18:1, 2003, 32–58.

107. Ayşe Devrim Atauz, *Eight Thousand Years of Maltese Maritime History: Trade, Piracy, and Naval Warfare in the Central Mediterranean*, University of Florida Press, 2011, ch. 2.

108. Ibid., ch. 6.

109. Rosemary L. Hopcroft, "Local Institutions and Rural Development in European History", *Social Science History*, 27:1, 2003, 25–74.

110. Sven Ekdahl, "The Teutonic Order's Mercenaries during the 'Great War' with Poland-Lithuania (1409–11)", in John France (ed.), *Mercenaries and Paid Men: The Mercenary Identity in the Middle Ages*, Brill, 2008, 345–362. Also see Juhan Kreem, "The Business of War: Mercenary Market and Organisation in Reval in the Fifteenth and Early Sixteenth Centuries", *Scandinavian Economic History Review*, 49:2, 2001, 26–42.

111. Martin Rheinheimer, "Biographical Research and Maritime History", *International Journal of Maritime History*, 14:2, 2002, 249–264.

112. Jaap R. Bruijn and Els S. van Eyck van Heslinga, "Seamen's Employment in the Netherlands (c.1600–c.1800)", *Mariner's Mirror*, 70:1, 1984.

113. Michael Jones, "Breton Soldiers from the Battle of the Thirty (26 March 1351) to Nicopolis (25 September 1396)", in Adrian R. Bell (ed.), *The Soldier Experience in the Fourteenth Century*, 2011, Boydell & Brewer; Graeme Small, *Late Medieval France*, Palgrave Macmillan, 2009, 126, 128.

114. Ph. Haudrere, "The 'Compagnie Des Indes' and Maritime Matters, 1725–70", in Jaap R. Bruijn and Femme S. Gaastra (eds.), *Ships, Sailors and Spices: East India Companies and Their Shipping in the 16th, 17th and 18th Centuries*, NEHA, 1993.

115. Pritchard, *In Search of Empire*, 31–32.

116. Gerard Le Bouedec, "Small Ports from the Sixteenth to the Early Twentieth Century and the Local Economy of the French Atlantic Coast", *International Journal of Maritime History*, 21:2, 2009, 103–126.

117. David Parrott, "From Military Enterprise to Standing Armies: War, State, and Society in Western Europe, 1600–1700", in Frank Tallett and D.J.B. Trim (eds.), *European Warfare, 1350–1750*, Cambridge University Press, 2010, 74–95.

118. J. Belich, *Making Peoples. A History of the New Zealanders, from Polynesian Settlement to the End of the 19th Century*, Allen Lane, 1996, ch.16.

119. Kevin P. McDonal, *Pirates, Merchants, Settlers, and Slaves: Colonial America and the Indo-Atlantic World*, University of California Press, 2015, ch. 1. Also see David J. Starkey, "Voluntaries and Sea Robbers: A Review of the Academic Literature on Privateering, Corsairing, Buccaneering and Piracy", *Mariner's Mirror*, 2011, 97:1, 127–147; Timothy Lee Sullivan, "The Devil's Brethren: Origins and Nature of Pirate Counterculture, 1600–1730", PhD dissertation, University of Texas at Arlington, 2003.

120. Marcus Rediker, *Villains of All Nations: Atlantic Pirates in the Golden Age*, Verso, 2004, 26.

121. Nigel Worden, "'Below the Line the Devil Reigns': Death and Dissent Aboard a VOC Vessel", *South African Historical Journal*, 61:4, 2009, 702–730.

122. *OED* and Pablo E. Perez-Mallaina, *Spain's Men of the Sea: Daily Life on the Indies Fleets in the Sixteenth Century*, trans. Carla Rahn Phillips, Johns Hopkins University Press, 1998, 203.

123. Ibid., 228.

124. Benerson Little, *The Buccaneer's Realm: Pirate Life on the Spanish Main, 1674–1688*, Potomac Books, 2007, 31.

125. Brian J. Rouleau, "Dead Men Do Tell Tales: Folklore, Fraternity, and the Forecastle", *Early American Studies*, 5:1, 2007, 30–62.

126. J. Rodrigues, "A New World in the Atlantic: Sailors and Rites of Passage Cross the Equator, from the 15th to the 20th Centuries", *Revista brasileira de história*, 33:65, 2013, 235–276.

127. Little, *The Buccaneer's Realm*, 133.

128. David Parrott, *The Business of War. Military Enterprise and Military Revolution in Early Modern Europe*, Cambridge University Press, 2012, 62–63.

129. Erik Swart, "From '*Landsknecht*' to 'Soldier': The Low German Foot Soldiers of the Low Countries in the Second Half of the Sixteenth Century", *International Review of Social History*, 51:1, 2006, 79.

130. Carla Rahn Phillips and William D. Phillips Jr., *Spain's Golden Fleece. Wool Production and the Wool Trade from the Middle Ages to the Nineteenth Century*, Johns Hopkins University Press, 1997, 21.

131. Hermann Rebel, "Peasantries under the Austrian Empire, 1300–1800", in Tom Scott (ed.), *The Peasantries of Europe: From the Fourteenth to the Eighteenth Centuries*, Longman, 1998.

132. Jan Lucassen, "The Other Proletarians: Seasonal Labourers, Mercenaries and Miners", *International Review of Social History*, 39: 2, 1994, 171–194.

133. Peter Earle, *Sailors: English Merchant Seamen 1650–1775*, Methuen, 1998, 177, citing Alain Caboutous.

134. Peter Earle, *The Pirate Wars*, 2nd edn, Methuen, 2004, 25.

135. Perez-Mallaina, *Spain's Men of the Sea*, 74. Also see Worden, "Below the Line the Devil Reigns".

136. J. Thierry du Pasquier, "The Whalers of Honfleur in the Seventeenth Century", *Arctic*, 37:4, 1984, 533–538.

137. Heide Gerstenberger, "On Maritime Labour and Maritime Labour Markets in Germany, 1700–1900", in Richard Gorski (ed.), *Maritime Labour: Contributions to the History of Work at Sea, 1500–2000*, Aksant, 2007; Emily Erickson, *Between Monopoly and Free Trade. The English East India Company, 1600–1757*, Princeton University Press, 2014, 58, 72; Klooster, *The Dutch Moment*, 125.

138. Cinlar, "Marriage in the Colonial Chesapeake", 26.

139. Matthew Restall, *Seven Myths of the Spanish Conquest*, Oxford University Press, 2003, 36–37; Clay Mathers, "Contest and Violence on the Northern Borderlands Frontier Patterns of Native–European Conflict in the Sixteenth-Century Southwest", in Mathers, Mitchem, and Haecker (eds.), *Native and Spanish New Worlds: Sixteenth-Century Entradas in the American Southwest and Southeast*, University of Arizona Press, 2013.

140. John E. Worth, "Inventing Florida. Constructing a Colonial Society in an Indigenous Landscape", in Mathers, Mitchem, and Haecker (eds.), *Native and Spanish New Worlds*; "European Fort Discovered in the Appalachian Mountains", Red Orbit website, July 24, 2013.

141. Kamen, *Empire*, 125.

142. Harry E. Cross, "South American Bullion and Export, 1550–1750", in John Richards (ed.), *Precious Metals in the Later Medieval and Early Modern Worlds*, Carolina Academic Press, 1983; Caroline A. Williams, "Resistance and Rebellion on the Spanish Frontier: Native Responses to Colonization in the Colombian Chocó, 1670–1690", *Hispanic American Historical Review*, 79:3, 1999, 397–424.

143. McDonal, *Pirates, Merchants, Settlers, and Slaves*.

144. Manon van der Heijden and Danielle van den Heuvel, "Sailors' Families and the Urban Institutional Framework in Early Modern Holland", *History of the Family*, 12, 2007, 296–309.

145. Perez-Mallaina, *Spain's Men of the Sea*, 18; Olwen Hufton, "Widowhood", in *The Prospect Before Her: A History of Women in Western Europe, Volume One 1500–1800*, Harper-Collins, 1995; David Coleman, *Creating Christian Granada*; Maryanne Kowaleski, "Medieval People in Town and Country: New Perspectives from Demography and Bioarchaeology", *Speculum*, 89:3, 2014, 573–600.

146. Maryanne Kowaleski, "The Demography of Maritime Communities in Late Medieval England", in Mark Bailey and Stephen Rigby (eds.), *Town and Countryside in the Age of the Black Death*, Brepols, 2012.

147. Annette de Wit, "Women in Dutch Fishing Communities: The Cases of Ter Heijde and Maassluis, c. 1600–1700", in Louis Sicking and Darlene Abreu-Ferreira (eds.), *Beyond the Catch: Fisheries of the North Atlantic, the North Sea and the Baltic, 900–1850*, Brill, 2009.

148. Pier Paolo Viazzo, "Mortality, Fertility, and Family", in David I. Kertzer and Marzio Barbagli (eds.), *The History of the European Family—Volume One: Family Life in Early Modern Times, 1500–1789*, Yale University Press, 2001, 157–190; Julien Demade, "The Medieval Countryside in German-language Historiography since the 1930s", in Isabel Alfonso (ed.), *The Rural History of Medieval European Societies: Trends and Perspectives*, Brepols, 2007.

149. Carla Rahn Phillips, *Six Galleons for the King of Spain. Imperial Defense in the Early 17th Century*, Johns Hopkins University Press, 1986, 99.

150. Hufton, "Widowhood".

151. Darlene Abreu-Ferreira, "The Cod Trade in Early-Modern Portugal: Deregulation, English Domination, and the Decline of Female Cod Merchants", PhD thesis, Memorial University of Newfoundland, 1995.

152. M. Newitt, "Formal and Informal Empire in the History of Portuguese Expansion", *Portuguese Studies*, 17, 2001, 2–21.

153. Ramos, "From Minho to Minas".

154. Darlene Abreu-Ferreira, "Fishmongers and Shipowners: Women in Maritime Communities of Early Modern Portugal", *The Sixteenth Century Journal*, 31:1, 2000, 7–23.

155. Amelia Polonia, "Global Interactions; Representations of the East and Far East in Sixteenth Century Portugal", in Rila Mukherjee (ed.), *Networks in the First Global Age, 1400–1800*, Primus Books, 2011.

156. Abreu-Ferreira, "Fishmongers and Shipowners".

157. Allyson M. Poska, *Women and Authority in Early Modern Spain: The Peasants of Galicia*, Oxford University Press, 2005, ch. 1.

158. Barbara J. Logue, "The Whaling Industry and Fertility Decline: Nantucket, Massachusetts 1660–1850", *Social Science History*, 7:4, 1983, 427–456.

159. Louwrens Hacquebord and Dag Avango, "Settlements in an Arctic Resource Frontier Region", *Arctic Anthropology*, 46:1–2, 2009, 25–39; Robert C. Allen and Ian Keay, "Saving the Whales: Lessons from the Extinction of the Eastern Arctic Bowhead", *Journal of Economic History*, 64:2, 2004; Jean-Pierre Proulx, *Whaling in the North Atlantic: From Earliest Times to the Mid-19th Century*, Parks Canada, 1986, 54.

160. Victor Enthoven, "Dutch Crossings. Migration between the Netherlands and the New World, 1600–1800", *Atlantic Studies*, 2:2, 2005.

161. Kamen, *Empire*, 118.

162. Ernst van Veen, *Decay or Defeat? An Inquiry into the Portuguese Decline in Asia 1580–1645*, Leiden University Press, 2000.

163. Femme De Gaastra, "Soldiers and Merchants; Aspects of Migration From Europe to Asia in the Dutch East India Company in the Eighteenth Century", in Klooster (ed.), *Migration, Trade, and Slavery*.

164. McNeill, *Mosquito Empires*, 99.

165. Michael Duffy, *Soldiers, Sugar and Seapower. The British Expeditions to the West Indies and the War against Revolutionary France*, Clarendon Press, 1987.

166. Paul van Royen, Jaap Bruijn, and Jan Lucassen (eds.), *"Those Emblems of Hell"? European Sailors and the Maritime Labour Market, 1570–1870*, International Maritime Economic History Association, 1997. Also see Jan Glete, *Warfare at Sea, 1500–1650: Maritime Conflicts and the Transformation of Europe*, Routledge, 2000, 57; John Landers, *The Field and the Forge: Population, Production, and Power in the Pre-industrial West*, Oxford University Press, 2005, 304–305.

167. Kamen, *Empire*, 393; Ida Altman, *Emigrants and Society*, 94; Carla Rahn Phillips, "Maritime Labour in Early Modern Spain", in Lewis R. Fischer (ed.), *The Market for Seamen in the Age of Sail*, International Maritime Economic History Association, 1994.

168. Denver Brunsman, "Men of War: British Sailors and the Impressment Paradox", *Journal of Early Modern History*, 14:1–22, 2010, 9–44; J. R. Dancy, *The Myth of the Press Gang: Volunteers, Impressment and the Naval Manpower Problem in the Late Eighteenth Century*, Boydell Press, 2015.

169. Sullivan, "The Devil's Brethren", 149, 259.

170. Earle, *Sailors*, 189.

171. Quoted in Rouleau, "Dead Men Do Tell Tales".

172. Quoted in Rediker, *Between the Devil and the Deep Blue Sea*, 250.

173. Raphael B. Folsom, *Yaquis and the Empire: Violence, Spanish Imperial Power, and Native Resilience in Colonial Mexico*, Yale University Press, 2015.

174. Toby Green, *The Rise of the Trans-Atlantic Slave Trade in Western Africa, 1300–1589*, Cambridge University Press, 2012, 124; António dos Santos Pereira, "The Urgent Empire Portugal Between 1475 and 1525", *e-Journal of Portuguese History*, 4:2, 2006.

175. Geoffrey Parker, *Emperor. A New Life of Charles V*, Yale University Press, 2019, Loc.2326.

176. Paul Slack, *The Impact of Plague in Tudor and Stuart England*, Clarendon Press, 1985.

177. Disney, *A History of Portugal*, I, 176.

178. Mark Greengrass, *Christendom Destroyed. Europe 1617–1648*, Allen Lane, 2014, 58.

Chapter 7: States, Interstates, and the European Expansion Kit

1. Charles Tilly, *The Formation of National States in Western Europe*, Princeton University Press, 1975, 42.

2. J. C. Sharman, "Myths of Military Revolution: European Expansion and Eurocentrism", *European Journal of International Relations*, 24:3, 2018, 491–513.

3. John Brewer, *The Sinews of Power: War and the English State, 1688–1783*, Unwin Hyman, 1989.

4. Philip T. Hoffman, *Why Did Europe Conquer the World?* Princeton University Press, 2015.

5. Douglass C. North, "Institutions, Transaction Costs, and the Rise of Merchant Empires", in James D. Tracy (ed.), *The Political Economy of Merchant Empires. State Power and World Trade 1350–1750*, Cambridge University Press, 1991, and see chapter 16 below.

6. Albert Rigaudière, "The Theory and Practice of Government in Western Europe in the Fourteenth Century", in Michael Jones (ed.), *The New Cambridge Medieval History, Volume VI, c. 1300–c. 1415*, Cambridge University Press, 2000, 25, 17.

7. Harry F. Lee et al., "Positive Correlation between the North Atlantic Oscillation and Violent Conflicts in Europe", *Climate Research*, 56:1, 2013.

8. John Bell Henneman, *Royal Taxation in Fourteenth-Century France: The Development of War Financing, 1322–1359*, Princeton University Press, 1972, 249.

9. Graeme Small, *Late Medieval France*, Palgrave Macmillan, 2009, ch. 3, 89.

10. Jonathan Sumption, *The Hundred Years' War, Volume II: Trial by Fire*, University of Pennsylvania Press, 1999, 158.

11. Bruce M. S. Campbell, *The Great Transition. Climate, Disease, and Society in the Late-Medieval World*, Cambridge University Press, 2016, 170.

12. Ole J. Benedictow, *The Black Death 1346–1353: The Complete History*, Boydell Press, 2004, 260. Also see B. Van Bavel, "Markets for Land, Labor, and Capital in Northern Italy and the Low Countries, Twelfth to Seventeenth Centuries", *Journal of Interdisciplinary History*, 41:4, 2011, 503–531.

13. Justine Firnhaber-Baker, "Seigneural War and Royal Power in Late Medieval Southern France", *Past & Present*, 208, 2010, 37–76.

14. Gerald Harriss, *Shaping the Nation: England, 1360–1461*, Clarendon Press, 2005, 52–53.

15. Kelly DeVries, "Gunpowder Weaponry and the Rise of the Early Modern State", *War in History*, 5, 1998, 127–145.

16. John Francis Guilmartin, "The Earliest Shipboard Gunpowder Ordnance: An Analysis of Its Technical Parameters and Tactical Capabilities", *Journal of Military History*, 71:3, 2007, 649–669. Also see DeVries, "Gunpowder Weaponry".

17. Gábor Ágoston, *Guns for the Sultan: Military Power and the Weapons Industry in the Ottoman Empire*, Cambridge University Press, 2005, 17.

18. Željko Peković and Nikolina Topić, "A Late-Medieval and Post-Medieval Foundry in the Historic Centre of Dubrovnik", *Post-Medieval Archaeology*, 45:2, 2011, 266–290.

19. Lazlo Veszpremy, "The State and Military Affairs in East-Central Europe, 1380–c1520s", in Frank Tallett and D.J.B. Trim (eds.), *European Warfare, 1350–1750*, Cambridge University Press, 2010.

20. Small, *Late Medieval France*, 201.

21. David Parrott, *The Business of War: Military Enterprise and Military Revolution in Early Modern Europe*, Cambridge University Press, 2012; John Watts, *The Making of Polities: Europe, 1300–1500*, Cambridge University Press, 2009, introduction; Steven Gunn, David Grummitt, and Hans Cools, "War and the State in Early Modern Europe: Widening the Debate", *War in History*, 15:4, 2008, 371–388.

22. Daviken Studnicki-Gizbert, *A Nation upon the Ocean Sea: Portugal's Atlantic Diaspora and the Crisis of the Spanish Empire, 1492–1640*, Oxford University Press, 2007, 5, 72. Also see Richard L. Kagan and Philip D. Morgan (eds.), *Atlantic Diasporas: Jews, Conversos, and Crypto-Jews in the Age of Mercantilism, 1500–1800*, Johns Hopkins University Press, 2009.

23. Christopher Ebert, *Between Empires: Brazilian Sugar in the Early Atlantic Economy, 1550–1630*, Brill, 2008, 7.

24. Daviken Studnicki-Gizbert, "*La Nación* among the Nations: Portuguese and Other Maritime Trading Diasporas in the Atlantic, Sixteenth to Eighteenth Centuries", in Kagan and Morgan (eds.), *Atlantic Diasporas*; Ned C. Landsman, "National Migration and the Province in the First British Empire; Scotland and the Americas, 1600–1800", *American Historical Review*, 104:2, 1999, 463–475.

25. Kathryn L. Reyerson, "The Transitional Role of Jacques Coeur in the Fifteenth Century", in Charles H. Parker and Jerry H. Bentley (eds.), *Between the Middle Ages and Modernity: Individual and Community in the Early Modern World*, Rowman & Littlefield, 2007, 253–269.

26. Natalie Rothman, *Brokering Empire: Trans-Imperial Subjects between Venice and Istanbul*, Cornell University Press, 2011.

27. Cátia Antunes and Amélia Polónia, "Introduction", in Antunes and Polónia (eds.), *Beyond Empires: Global, Self-Organizing, Cross-Imperial Networks, 1500–1800*, Brill, 2016.

28. Bernard Doumerc, "Cosmopolitanism on Board Venetian Ships (Fourteenth-Fifteenth Centuries)", *Medieval Encounters*, 13:1, 2007, 78–95; Jan Glete, *Warfare at Sea, 1500–1650: Maritime Conflicts and the Transformation of Europe*, Routledge, 2000, 66.

29. Parrott, *The Business of War*, 27–28.

30. Mark Greengrass, *Christendom Destroyed Europe 1617–1648*, Allen Lane, 2014, 419.

31. Parrott, *The Business of War*, 82.

32. Parrott, *The Business of War*, 320.

33. Guido Alfani and Francesco Ammannati, "Economic Inequality and Poverty in the Very Long Run: The Case of the Florentine State (Late Thirteenth–Early Nineteenth Centuries)", Working Paper No. 70, Carlo F. Dondena Centre for Research on Social Dynamics, 2014.

34. William Caferro, "Petrarch's War: Florentine Wages and the Black Death", *Speculum*, 88.1, 2013, 144–165.

35. Monique O'Connell, *Men of Empire: Power and Negotiation in Venice's Maritime State*, Johns Hopkins University Press, 2009, 22.

36. Frederic C. Lane, *Venice, A Maritime Republic*, Johns Hopkins University Press, 1973, 337; M. E. Mallet and J. R. Hale, *The Military Organization of a Renaissance State: Venice c.1400 to 1617*, Cambridge University Press, 1984, 34.

37. Robin Harris, *Dubrovnik: A History*, Saqi Books, 2003, 122.

38. Zlata Blazina Tomic and Vesna Blazina, *Expelling the Plague: The Health Office and the Implementation of Quarantine in Dubrovnik, 1377–1533*, McGill-Queens University Press, 2015, 272, n.117; Anon., "Mediterranean Ports and Trade in the XVth and XVIth Centuries", *Journal of*

European Economic History, 36:2–3, 2007, 351–365; Susan Mosher Stuard, *A State of Deference: Ragusa/Dubrovnik in the Medieval Centuries*, University of Pennsylvania Press, 1992, 203–204; Thomas Allison Kirk, *Genoa and the Sea: Policy and Power in an Early Modern Maritime Republic, 1559–1684*, Johns Hopkins University Press, 2005, 35; Harris, *Dubrovnik*, 170.

39. Kirk, *Genoa and the Sea*, 37.

40. Pauline Croft, "Trading with the Enemy 1585–1604", *Historical Journal*, 32:2, 1989, 281–302.

41. Ebert, *Between Empires*, 47.

42. Christopher Ebert, "Early Modern Atlantic Trade and the Development of Maritime Insurance to 1630", *Past & Present*, 213, 2011; Croft, "Trading with the Enemy".

43. Ebert, *Between Empires*; Wim Klooster, "The Northern European Atlantic World", in Nicholas Canny and Philip Morgan (eds.), *The Oxford Handbook of the Atlantic World: 1450–1850*, Oxford University Press, 2011.

44. Justyna Wubs-Mrozewicz, *Traders, Ties and Tensions: The Interactions of Lübeckers, Overijsslers and Hollanders in Late Medieval Bergen*, Uitgeverij Verloren, 2008, 23.

45. Here I disagree with Walter Scheidel's *Escape from Rome: The Failure of Empire and the Road to Prosperity*, Princeton University Press, 2019.

46. William R. Thompson, "The Military Superiority Thesis and the Ascendancy of Western Eurasia in the World System", *Journal of World History*, 10:1, 1999, 143–178. For other examples, see George Raudzens, "So Why Were the Aztecs Conquered, and What Were the Wider Implications? Testing Military Superiority as a Cause of Europe's Pre-industrial Colonial Conquests", *War in History*, 1995, 2:1, 87–104, and Sharman, "Myths of Military Revolution".

47. Raudzens, "So Why Were the Aztecs Conquered?"

48. Wayne E. Lee, *Waging War. Conflict, Culture, and Innovation in World History*, Oxford University Press, 2016, 254.

49. Sharman, "Myths of Military Revolution".

50. Ibid.

51. J. Belich, *The New Zealand Wars and the Victorian Interpretation of Racial Conflict*, Auckland University Press, 1986 (Penguin, 1988); "The Victorian Interpretation of Racial Conflict and the New Zealand Wars: An Approach to the Problem of One-Sided Evidence", *Journal of Imperial and Commonwealth History*, 15:2, 1987, 123–147; and "The New Zealand Wars and the Myth of Conquest", in Robert Borofsky (ed.), *Remembrance of Pacific Pasts: An Invitation to Remake History*, Hawai'i University Press, 2000.

52. Tonio Andrade, *The Gunpowder Age. China, Military Innovation, and the Rise of the West in World History*, Princeton University Press, 2016, 171–173.

53. Hyeok Hweon Kang, "Big Heads and Buddhist Demons: The Korean Musketry Revolution and the Northern Expeditions of 1654 and 1658", *Journal of Chinese Military History*, 2, 2013, 127–189.

54. Clifford J. Rogers, "Tactics and the Face of Battle", in Tallett and Trim (eds.), *European Warfare*.

55. Ibid.

56. Tonio Andrade, "Cannibals with Cannons: The Sino-Portuguese Clashes of 1521–1522 and the Early Chinese Adoption of Western Guns", *Journal of Early Modern History*, 19, 2015, 311–335. Also see James Fujitani, "The Ming Rejection of the Portuguese Embassy of 1517: A Re-assessment", *Journal of World History*, 27:1, 2016, 87–102.

57. Victor Ostapchuk, "The Ottoman Black Sea Frontier and the Relations of the Porte with the Polish-Lithuanian Commonwealth d Muscovy, 1622–1628", PhD dissertation, Harvard University, 1989, 83.

58. Andrey V. Ivanov, "Conflicting Loyalties: Fugitives and 'Traitors' in the Russo-Manchurian Frontier, 1651–1689", *Journal of Early Modern History*, 13, 2009, 333–358.

59. Andrade, "Cannibals with Cannons".

60. Tonio Andrade, *Lost Colony: The Untold Story of China's First Great Victory over the West*, Princeton University Press, 2011.

61. Quoted in Tonio Andrade, "Was the European Sailing Ship a Key Technology of European Expansion? Evidence from East Asia", *International Journal of Maritime History*, 23:2, 2011, 17–40.

62. Norbert Finzsch, "'Extirpate or Remove That Vermine': Genocide, Biological Warfare, and Settler Imperialism in the Eighteenth and Early Nineteenth Century", *Journal of Genocide Research*, 10:2, 2008, 215–232.

63. Massimo Livi Bacci, *Conquest: The Destruction of the American Indios*, Polity Press, 2008 (orig. 2005), 17; Chantal Cramaussel, "Population and Epidemics North of Zacatecas", in Danna A. Levin Rojo and Cynthia Radding (eds.), *The Handbook of Borderlands of the Iberian World*, Oxford University Press, 2019.

64. Sandra M. Tomkins, "The Influenza Epidemic of 1918–9 in Western Samoa", *Journal of Pacific History*, 27:2, 1992, 181–197.

65. Alfred W. Crosby, "Influenza", in Kiple, Kenneth F. et al. (eds.), *The Cambridge World History of Human Disease*, Cambridge University Press, 1993; David M. Morens and Jeffery K. Taubenberger, "Historical Thoughts on Influenza Viral Ecosystems, or Behold a Pale Horse, Dead Dogs, Failing Fowl, and Sick Swine", *Influenza and Other Respiratory Viruses*, 4:6, 2010, 327–337; H. B. Pryor, "Influenza: That Extraordinary Malady. Notes on Its History and Epidemiology", *Clinical Pediatrics*, 3, 1964, 19–24.

66. V. A. Harden, "Typhus", and R. J. Kim-Farley, "Measles", both in Kiple et al. (eds.), *The Cambridge World History of Human Disease*; Livi Bacci, *Conquest*, 49, 55–57, 63; S. Badiaga and P. Brouqui, "Human Louse-Transmitted Infectious Diseases", *Clinical Microbiology and Infection*, 18, 2012, 332–337; James C. Riley, "Smallpox and American Indians Revisited", *Journal of the History of Medicine and Allied Sciences*, 65:4, 2010, 445–477.

67. Kathryn Magee Labelle, "'They Only Spoke in Sighs': The Loss of Leaders and Life in Wendake, 1633–1639", *Journal of Historical Biography*, 6, 2009, 1–33.

68. Ann M. Carlos and Frank D. Lewis, "Smallpox and Native American Mortality: The 1780s Epidemic in the Hudson Bay Region", *Explorations in Economic History*, 49, 2012, 277–290; Erica Charters, *Disease, War, and the Imperial State: The Welfare of British Forces during the Seven Years War, 1756–63*, University of Chicago Press, 2014, 45.

69. Robert McCaa, "Spanish and Nahuatl Views on Smallpox and Demographic Catastrophe in Mexico", *Journal of Interdisciplinary History*, 25:3, 1995, 397–431.

70. Riley, "Smallpox and American Indians Revisited".

71. Livi Bacci, *Conquest*, 63.

72. Anthony M. Stevens-Arroyo, "The Inter-Atlantic paradigm: The Failure of Spanish Medieval Colonization of the Canary and Caribbean Islands", *Comparative Studies in Society and History*, 35:3, 1993, 515–543, 527.

73. Felipe Fernandez-Armesto, *Pathfinders. A Global History of Exploration*, W.W. Norton, 2006, 133; John Mercer, *The Canary Islands. Their Prehistory, Conquest, and Survival*, London, 1980; Alfred W. Crosby, "An Ecohistory of the Canary Islands", *Environmental Review*, 8:3, 1984, 214–235; Mohamed Adhikari, "Europe's First Settler Colonial Incursion into Africa: The Genocide of Aboriginal Canary Islanders", *African Historical Review*, 49:1, 2017, 1–26.

74. Adhikari, "Europe's First Settler Colonial Incursion into Africa".

75. Barbara E. Mundy, "Aztec Geography and Spatial Imagination", in Kurt A. Raaflaub and Richard J. A. Talbert (eds.), *Geography and Ethnography: Perceptions of the World in Pre-Modern Societies*, Wiley-Blackwell, 2010.

76. E.g., Matthew Restall, *Seven Myths of the Spanish Conquest*, Oxford University Press, 2003; D. K. Abbass, "Horses and Heroes. The Myth of the Importance of the Horse to the Conquest of the Indies", *Terrae Incognitae*, 18, 1986, 21–41; Michel R. Oudijk, "The Conquest of Mexico", in Deborah L. Nichols (ed.), *The Oxford Handbook of Mesoamerican Archaeology*, Oxford University Press, 2012.

77. Hugh Thomas, *The Conquest of Mexico*, Pimlico, 1993, 512.

78. Arlen F. Chase, Diane Z. Chase, and Michael E. Smith, "States and Empires in Ancient Mesoamerica", *Ancient Mesoamerica*, 20, 2009, 175–182.

79. Miguel Leon-Portilla, *The Broken Spears. The Aztec Account of the Conquest of Mexico*, Beacon Press, 1990 (orig. 1962); Camilla Townsend, "Burying the White Gods: New Perspectives on the Conquest of Mexico", *American Historical Review*, 108:3, 2003, 659–687.

80. Bernal Diaz, *The Conquest of New Spain*, trans. J. M. Cohen, Penguin, 1963, 150, 75–77.

81. John Hemming, *The Conquest of the Incas*, Macmillan, 1993 (orig. 1970), 136.

82. E.g., by Leon-Portilla, *The Broken Spears*, xliii.

83. Saturnino Monteiro, *Portuguese Sea Battles 1139–1975*, 2010, Oeiras, Vol. I, 258, 198–199.

84. Andrew de la Garza, "Mughals at War: Babur, Akbar, and the Indian Military Revolution, 1500–1605", PhD dissertation, Ohio State University, 2010, 113.

85. S. Schroeder, and D. E. Tavarez (eds.), *Chimalpahin's Conquest: A Nahua Historian's Rewriting of Francisco Lopez de Gomara's la Conquista de Mexico*, Stanford University Press, 2010, 65–67.

86. Diaz, *The Conquest of New Spain*, 284.

87. Schroeder and Tavarez (eds.), *Chimalpahin's Conquest*, 365.

88. Thomas, *The Conquest of Mexico*, 357. Also see 274, 469–470, and 473. Another source notes that the Cortes family had friends and relatives in Naples, which was becoming a Genoese semi-colony. *Chimalpahin's Conquest*, 52 ,and see chapter 10 below.

89. Weston F. Cook, *The Hundred Years' War for Morocco: Gunpowder and the Military Revolution in the Early Modern Muslim World*, Westview Press, 1994, 157, n.11.

90. Francis J. Brooks doubts that the disease was smallpox or that it killed many people ("Revising the Conquest of Mexico: Smallpox, Sources, and Populations", *Journal of Interdisciplinary History*, 24.1, 1993, 1–29). But the Spanish, who were familiar with the disease, considered it to be smallpox and noted pockmarks on some of the survivors (Leon-Portilla, *The Broken Spears*, 93). This is also the judgment of leading historical demographer Massimo Livi Bacci (*Conquest* and "The Depopulation of Hispanic America after the Conquest", *Population and Development Review*, 32:2, 2006, 199–232). Also see McCaa, "Spanish and Nahuatl Views on Smallpox".

91. Tonio Andrade, "An Accelerating Divergence? The Revisionist Model of World History and the Question of Eurasian Military Parity: Data from East Asian Source", *Canadian Journal of Sociology*, 36:2, 2011.

92. John Vogt, "Saint Barbara's Legion: Portuguese Artillery in the Struggle for Morocco, 1415–1578", *Military Affairs*, 41:4, 1977, 176–82.

Chapter 8: Plague's Impact in the Muslim South

1. Justin McCarthy, *The Ottoman Turks. An Introductory History*, Longman, 1997, 199.

2. Amina Elbendary, *Crowds and Sultans: Urban Protest in Late Medieval Egypt and Syria*, American University in Cairo Press, 2015, 22.

3. Eliyahu Ashtor, "The Economic Decline of the Middle East During the Later Middle Ages: An Outline", in B. Z. Kedar (ed.), *Technology, Industry and Trade: The Levant versus Europe, 1250–1500*, Variorum, 1992.

4. Ronald Findlay and Kevin H. O'Rourke, *Power and Plenty: Trade, War, and the World Economy in the Second Millennium*, Princeton University Press, 2007, 129.

5. Timur Kuran, "Why the Middle East Is Economically Underdeveloped: Historical Mechanisms of Institutional Stagnation", *Journal of Economic Perspectives*, 18:3, 2004, 71–90. The "vehicle" quote is from Marshall Hodgson (1974), whose work is a turning point in the reconsideration of early modern Islam. Also see Kuran, *The Long Divergence: How Islamic Law Held Back the Middle East*, Princeton University Press, 2010; Mohamed Saleh, "A 'New' Economic History of the Middle East and North Africa (MENA) Region", *Economics of Transition*, 25:2, 2017, 149–163.

6. E.g., Timur Kuran and Jared Rubin, "The Financial Power of the Powerless: Socioeconomic Status and Interest Rates under Partial Rule of Law", *Economic Journal*, 128:609, 2018, 758–796.

7. Taha Tarawneh, "The Province of Damascus during the Second Mamluk Period (784/1382–922/1516)", PhD dissertation, Indiana University, 1987, 132.

8. Michael W. Dols, *The Black Death in the Middle East*, Princeton University Press, 1977, 282.

9. Şevket Pamuk, "The Black Death and the Origins of the 'Great Divergence' across Europe, 1300–1600", *European Review of Economic History*, 11, 2007, 289–317.

10. Dols, *The Black Death in the Middle East*, 270; Joseph P. Byrne, *Encyclopedia of the Black Death*, ABC-CLIO, 2012, 66.

11. Yossef Rapoport, "Marriage and Divorce in the Muslim Near East, 1250–1517", PhD dissertation, Princeton University, 2002.

12. Doris Behrens-Abouseif, "Craftsmen, Upstarts, and Sufis in the Late Mamluk Period", *Bulletin of the School of Oriental and African Studies*, 74:3, 2011, 375–395; Pamuk, "Black Death and the Origins of the 'Great Divergence'"; Şevket Pamuk and Maya Shatzmiller, "Plagues, Wages, and Economic Change in the Islamic Middle East, 700–1500", *Journal of Economic History*, 74:1, 2014, 196–229; Robert Irwin, *The Middle East in the Middle Ages: The Early Mamluk Sultanate, 1250–1382*, Southern Illinois University Press, 1986; Elbendary, *Crowds and Sultans*, 47–48, 59; Bethany J. Walker, "The Ceramic Correlates of Decline in the Mamluk Sultanate: An Analysis of Late Medieval Sgraffito Wares", PhD thesis, University of Toronto, 1998, 225.

13. Quoted in "Mamluk Cairo", *Encyclopedia Islamica*, Brill, 2008; available online.

14. Stuart Borsch and Tarek Sabraa, "Plague Mortality in Late Medieval Cairo: Quantifying the Plague Outbreaks of 833/1430 and 864/1460", *Mamluk Studies Review*, 19, 2016, 115–148.

15. Bethany J. Walker, "Sowing the Seeds of Rural Decline? Agriculture as an Economic Barometer for Late Mamluk Jordan", *Mamluk Studies Review*, 11:1, 2007.

16. Dols, *The Black Death in the Middle East*, 262.

17. Stuard J. Borsch, "Nile Floods and the Irrigation System in Fifteenth-Century Egypt", *Mamluk Studies Review*, 4, 2000, 133; Alan Mikhail, *Nature and Empire in Ottoman Egypt: An Environmental History*, Cambridge University Press, 2011, and *Under Osman's Tree: The Ottoman Empire, Egypt, and Environmental History*, University of Chicago Press, 2017.

18. Jean-Claude Garcin, "The Regime of the Circassian Mamlūks", in Carl F. Petry (ed.), *The Cambridge History of Egypt, Volume I Islamic Egypt, 640–1517*, Cambridge University Press, 1998, 290–317.

19. See three works by Stuart Borsch: "Plague Depopulation and Irrigation Decay in Medieval Egypt", in Monica Green (ed.), *Pandemic Disease in the Medieval World: Rethinking the Black Death*, ARC Medieval Press, 2014; "Nile Floods"; and *The Black Death in Egypt and England: A Comparative Study*, University of Texas Press–Austin, 2005.

20. Boaz Shoshan, "Money Supply and Grain Prices in Fifteenth-Century Egypt", *Economic History Review*, 36:1, 1983, 47–67.

21. Nicholas Coureas, "Cyprus and Ragusa (Dubrovnik) 1280–1450", *Mediterranean Historical Review*, 17:2, 2002, 1–13.

22. Wan Kamal Mujani, "European Technological Innovation That Surpassed Muslim Technology in the Middle Ages: An Example During the Circassian Mamluk Period", *Acta Orientalia Academiae Scientiarum Hung.*, 65:1, 2012, 39–54.

23. Eliyahu Ashtor, *Levant Trade in the Later Middle Ages*, Princeton University Press, 1983, 206–208.

24. John Lash Meloy, "Mamluk Authority, Meccan Autonomy, and Red Sea Trade, 797–859/1359–1455", PhD dissertation, University of Chicago, 1998, 191–193; Sato Tsugitaka, "Slave Traders and Karimi Merchants during the Mamluk Period: A Comparative Study", *Mamluk Studies Review*, 10:1, 2006.

25. James Waterson, *The Knights of Islam: The Wars of the Mamluks*, Greenhill, 2007, 223.

26. Byrne, *Encyclopedia of the Black Death*, 66.

27. Elbendary, *Crowds and Sultans*; Borsch, "Nile Floods".

28. Francisco Apellaniz, "Judging the Franks: Proof, Justice, and Diversity in Late Medieval Alexandria and Damascus", *Comparative Studies in Society and History*, 58:2, 2016, 350–378.

29. Meloy, "Mamluk Authority, Meccan Autonomy", ch. 4; Igarashi Daisuke, "The Evolution of the Sultanic Fisc and *al-Dhakhīrah* during the Circassian Mamluk Period", *Mamlūk Studies Review*, 14, 2010, 85–108; "Pepper Prices in Mamluk Egypt, 1303–1516", Global Price and Income History Group database.

30. Yehoshua Frenkel, "Alexandria in the Ninth/Fifteenth Century: A Mediterranean Port City and a Mamlūk Prison City", *Al-Masaq: Journal of the Medieval Mediterranean*, 26:1, 2014, 78–92.

31. Molly Greene, *Catholic Pirates and Greek Merchants: A Maritime History of the Mediterranean*, Princeton University Press, 2010, 117.

32. Georg Christ, "The Venetian Consul and the Cosmopolitan Mercantile Community of Alexandria at the Beginning of the Ninth/Fifteenth Century", and Niall Christie,

"Cosmopolitan Trade Centre or Bone of Contention? Alexandria and the Crusades, 487–857/1095–1453", both in *Al-Masaq: Journal of the Medieval Mediterranean*, 26:1 2014, 62–77 and 49–61.

33. Cited in John Munro, "Bullion Flows and Monetary Contraction in Late-Medieval England and the Low Countries", in John Richards (ed.), *Precious Metals in the Later Medieval and Early Modern Worlds*, Carolina Academic Press, 1983.

34. Daniel Mahoney, "The Political Landscape of the Dhamar Plain in the Central Highlands of Yemen During the Late Medieval and Early Ottoman Periods", PhD dissertation, University of Chicago, 2014; Malika Dekkiche, "New Source, New Debate: Re-evaluation of the Mamluk-Timurid Struggle for Religious Supremacy in the Hijaz", *Mamluk Studies Review*, 18, 2014–15.

35. Sanjay Subrahmanyam, "Of Imarat and Tijarat: Asian Merchants and State Power in the Western Indian Ocean, 1400 to 1750", *Comparative Studies in Society and History*, 37:4, 1995, 750–780; Tsugitaka, "Slave Traders and Karimi Merchants"; Michael Chamberlain, "The Crusader Era and the Ayyūbid Dynasty", in Petry (ed.), *The Cambridge History of Egypt*.

36. Meloy, "Mamluk Authority, Meccan Autonomy".

37. Patrick Wing, "Indian Ocean Trade and Sultanic Authority: The Nāẓir of Jedda and the Mamluk Political Economy", *Journal of the Economic and Social History of the Orient*, 57:1, 2014, 55–75.

38. Tsugitaka, "Slave Traders and Karimi Merchants".

39. Meloy, "Mamluk Authority, Meccan Autonomy", ch. 4; Pius Malekandathil, "Winds of Change and Links of Continuity: A Study on the Merchant Groups of Kerala and the Channels of Their Trade, 1000–1800", *Journal of the Economic and Social History of the Orient*, 50:2–3, 2007.

40. Tarawneh, "The Province of Damascus", 156.

41. E.g., Ross Burns, *Damascus: A History*, Taylor & Francis, 2005, 217.

42. Paul Freedman, "Mastic: A Mediterranean Luxury Product", *Mediterranean Historical Review*, 26:1, 2011, 99–113.

43. T. A. Sinclair, *Eastern Trade and the Mediterranean in the Middle Ages: Pegolotti's Ayas-Tabriz Itinerary and Its Commercial Context*, Routledge, 2019, 131–132.

44. Tarawneh, "The Province of Damascus", 132, 167.

45. Sinclair, *Eastern Trade and the Mediterranean*, 131–132.

46. Tarawneh, "The Province of Damascus", 191.

47. Amita Satyal, "The Mughal Empire, Overland Trade, and Merchants of Northern India, 1526–1707", PhD dissertation, University of California, Berkeley, 2008.

48. Charles L. Wilkins, "A Demographic Profile of Slaves in Early Ottoman Aleppo", in Christoph Witzenrath (ed.), *Eurasian Slavery, Ransom and Abolition in World History, 1200–1860*, Taylor & Francis, 2015.

49. Benjamin Arbel, "The Last Decades of Venice's Trade with the Mamluks: Importations into Egypt and Syria", *Mamluk Studies Review*, 8:2, 2004.

50. Ayşe Devrim Atauz, *Eight Thousand Years of Maltese Maritime History: Trade, Piracy, and Naval Warfare in the Central Mediterranean*, University of Florida Press, 2011, ch. 2.

51. Jong-Kuk Nam, *Le commerce du coton en Méditerranée a la fin du Moyen Age*, Brill, 2007.

52. Peter Burke, Luke Clossey, and Felipe Fernández-Armesto, "The Global Renaissance", *Journal of World History*, 28:1, 2017, 1–30.

53. Walker, "Sowing the Seeds of Rural Decline?"

54. Nelly Hanna, *Artisan Entrepreneurs in Cairo and Early Modern Capitalism (1600–1800)*, Syracuse University Press, 2011; Iklil Oya Selcuk, "State and Society in the Marketplace: A Study of Late Fifteenth-Century Bursa", PhD dissertation, Harvard University, 2009, ch. 4; Nikolay Antov, "Imperial Expansion, Colonization, and Conversion to Islam in the Islamic World's 'Wild West': The Formation of the Muslim Community in Ottoman Deliorman (N.E. Balkans), 15th–16th cc", PhD dissertation, University of Chicago, 2011; Maria Subtelny, "Socioeconomic Bases of Cultural Patronage Under the Later Timurids", *International Journal of Middle East Studies*, 20, 1988, 479–505, and *Timurids in Transition: Turko-Persian Politics and Acculturation in Medieval Iran*, Brill, 2007, 156; Şevket Pamuk, "Institutional Change and Economic Development in the Middle East, 700–1800", in Larry Neal and Jeffrey G. Williamson (eds.), *The Cambridge History of Capitalism. Volume 1, The Rise of Capitalism: From Ancient Origins to 1848*, Cambridge University Press, 2014.

55. E.g., Igarashi Daisuke, "The Financial Reforms of Sultan Qāytbāy", *Mamlūk Studies Review*, 13:1, 2009, 27–52.

56. Michael Winter, "The Ottoman Occupation", in Petry (ed.), *The Cambridge History of Egypt*.

57. Emire Cihan Muslu, "Ottoman-Mamluk Relations: Diplomacy and Perceptions", PhD dissertation, Harvard University, 2007.

58. Mesut Uyar and Edward J. Erickson, *A Military History of the Ottomans. From Osman to Ataturk*, Praeger Security International, 2009, 69.

59. Elbendary, *Crowds and Sultans*, 24.

60. Stephen Dale, *The Muslim Empires of the Ottomans, Safavids, and Mughals*, Cambridge University Press, 2010, 114.

61. Mikhail, *Nature and Empire in Ottoman Egypt*, 38.

62. Alberto García Porras and Adela Fábregas García, "Genoese Trade Networks in the Southern Iberian Peninsula: Trade, Transmission of Technical Knowledge and Economic Interactions", *Mediterranean Historical Review*, 25:1, 2010, 35–51; Ádela Fábregas García, "Other Markets: Complementary Commercial Zones in the Naṣrid World of the Western Mediterranean (Seventh/Thirteenth to Ninth/ Fifteenth Centuries)", *Al-Masaq: Journal of the Medieval Mediterranean*, 25:1, 2013, 135–153; Anastasia G. Yangaki, "A First Overview of Late Medieval Pottery from the Iberian Peninsula in Greece", *Viator*, 44:1 , 2013; Enrique Rodríguez-Picavea, "The Military Orders and the War of Granada (1350–1492)", *Mediterranean Studies*, 19, 2010, 14–42.

63. Elizabeth D. Henman, "Urban Formation and Landscape: Symbol and Agent of Social, Political and Environmental Change in Fourteenth Century Nasrid Granada", PhD dissertation, Harvard University, 1996; E. Michael Gerli (ed.), *Medieval Iberia: An Encyclopedia*, Taylor & Francis, 2003; García, "Other Markets: Complementary Commercial Zones in the Naṣrid World"; David Coleman, *Creating Christian Granada: Society and Religious Culture in an Old-World Frontier City, 1492–1600*, Cornell University Press, 2003.

64. Rodríguez-Picavea, "The Military Orders".

65. Ibn al-Katib, quoted by Henman, "Urban Formation and Landscape", 53.

66. Ibid., 219.

67. Bas van Bavel, Eltjo Buringh, and Jessica Dijkman, "Immovable Capital Goods in Medieval Muslim Lands: Why Water-Mills and Building Cranes Went Missing", CGEH Working Paper Series, No. 69, 2015.

68. Leo Africanus, *A Geographical Historie of Africa* ... Translated and collected by John Pory, 1600, 163–167. Online access through *The Making of the Modern World* database.

69. Ramzi Rouighi, *The Making of a Mediterranean Emirate: Ifrīqiyā and Its Andalusis, 1200–1400*, University of Pennsylvania Press, 2011, ch. 1; Abdallah Laroui, *The History of the Maghrib: An Interpretive Essay*, Princeton University Press, 1977, 236–237.

70. Leo Africanus, *The History and Description of Africa and of the Notable Things Therein Contained*, Vol. III, Robert Brown (ed.), Ashgate, 2010, 722.

71. Allen Fromherz, *The Near West: Medieval North Africa, Latin Europe and the Mediterranean in the Second Axial Age*, 2016, Edinburgh University Press, 110, 117–118.

72. Fromherz, *The Near West*, 117; Dominique Valérian, "Ifriqiyan Muslim Merchants in the Mediterranean at the End of the Middle Ages", *Mediterranean Historical Review*, 14:2, 1999, 47–66.

73. Roland Oliver and Anthony Atmore, *Medieval Africa, 1250–1800*, revised edn, Cambridge University Press, 2001, 35.

74. Patricia Kozlik Kabra, "Patterns of Economic Continuity and Change in Early Hafsid Ifriqiya", PhD thesis, University of California, Los Angeles, 1994, 18.

75. Kabra, "Patterns of Economic Continuity and Change in Early Hafsid Ifriqiya", 197.

76. Africanus, *The History and Description of Africa*, Vol. III, 700–701.

77. Olivia Remie Constable, "Muslim Trade in the Late Medieval Mediterranean World", in Maribel Fierrom (ed.), *The New Cambridge History of Islam* ,Vol. 2, Cambridge University Press, 2010.

78. Africanus, *The History and Description of Africa*, Vol. III, 734–735.

79. Valérian, "Ifriqiyan muslim merchants".

80. Rouighi, *Making of a Mediterranean Emirate*, 91–92; Susan Rose, "Islam Versus Christendom: The Naval Dimension, 1000–1600", *Journal of Military History*, 63:3, 1999, 561–578; John McManamon, "Maltese Seafaring in Mediaeval and Post-Mediaeval Times", *Mediterranean Historical Review*, 18:1, 2003, 32–58.

81. Jacob Abadi, *Tunisia since the Arab Conquest: The Saga of a Westernized Muslim State*, Garnet, 2013, 171. Also see Laroui, *The History of the Maghrib*; Kabra, "Patterns of Economic Continuity and Change in Early Hafsid Ifriqiya".

82. Robert Bideleux and Ian Jeffries, *A History of Eastern Europe: Crisis and Change*, 2nd edn, Routledge, 2007, 73.

83. Rhoads Murhpy, "The Ottoman Economy in the Early Imperial Age," in Christine Woodhead (ed.), *The Ottoman World*, Taylor & Francis, 2011.

84. Pavel Murdzhev, "The Medieval Town in Bulgaria", PhD dissertation, University of Florida, 2008, 109–110.

85. Zlata Blazina Tomic and Vesna Blazina, *Expelling the Plague: The Health Office and the Implementation of Quarantine in Dubrovnik, 1377–1533*, McGill-Queens University Press, 2015, ch. 1; David Turnock, *The Making of Eastern Europe: From the Earliest Times to 1815*, Routledge, 1988, 194.

86. Susan Mosher Stuard, "Dowry Increase and Increment in Wealth in Medieval Ragusa (Dubrovnik)", *Journal of Economic History*, 41:4, 1981, 795–811.

87. Susan Mosher Stuard, *A State of Deference: Ragusa/Dubrovnik in the Medieval Centuries*, University of Pennsylvania Press, 1992, 75–78.

88. Robin Harris, *Dubrovnik: A History*, Saqi Books, 2003, 260–261.

89. Tomic and Blazina, *Expelling the Plague*, 47; Stuard, *State of Deference*, 118.

90. Paola Pinelli, "From Dubrovnik (Ragusa) to Florence: Observations on the Recruiting of Domestic Servants in the 15th Century", *Dubrovnik Annals*, 12, 2008, 57–71.

91. Tomic and Blazina, *Expelling the Plague*, 65, n.52.

92. Nenad Vekaric, "The Population of the Dubrovnik Republic in the 15th, 16th, and 17th Centuries", *Dubrovnik Annals*, 2, 1998, 7–28.

93. Elisaveta Todorova, "River Trade in the Balkans during the Middle Ages", *Études balkaniques*, 20:4, 1984, 38–50; Stuard, *A State of Deference*, 183–184.

94. Maren Frejdenberg, "The Birth of the Ragusan Republic", *Mediterranean Historical Review*, 7:2, 1992, 201–207.

95. Tomic and Blazina, *Expelling the Plague*, ch. 1.

96. Jonathan Shea, "The Late Byzantine City: Social, Economic and Institutional Profile", PhD thesis, University of Birmingham, 2010, ch. 3.

97. Anon., "Mediterranean Ports and Trade in the XVth and XVIth Centuries", *Journal of European Economic History*, 36:2–3, 2007, 351–365; Tomic and Blazina, *Expelling the Plague*, 272 n.117; Stuard, *State of Deference*, 203–204; Thomas Allison Kirk, *Genoa and the Sea: Policy and Power in an Early Modern Maritime Republic, 1559–1684*, Johns Hopkins University Press, 2005, 35; Harris, *Dubrovnik*, 170.

98. Daniel Goffman, *The Ottoman Empire and Early Modern Europe*, Cambridge University Press, 2002, 178.

99. Ian Blanchard, "The Continental European Cattle Trades, 1400–1600", *Economic History Review*, 39:3, 1986, 427–460; Michael North, *The Expansion of Europe, 1250–1500*, Manchester University Press, 2012 (German original 2007), 248.

100. Edit Sárosi, "The Development of a Market Town and Its Market Places in the Hungarian Great Plain. Kecskemét, a Case Study". *Historia Urbana*, 21, 2013, 139–161.

101. Bruno Škreblin, "Ethnic Groups in Zagreb's Gradec in the Late Middle Ages", *Review of Croatian History*, 1, 2013, 2559.

102. Pal Engel, *Realm of St. Stephen: A History of Medieval Hungary, 895–1526*, I.B. Tauris, 2001, 186–7.

103. Jean W. Sedlar, *East Central Europe in the Middle Ages, 1000–1500*, Washington University Press, 1994, 102.

104. J. M. Bak, "Servitude in the Medieval Kingdom of Hungary (A Sketchy Outline)", in Paul Freedman and Monique Bourin (eds.), *Forms of Servitude in Northern and Central Europe: Decline, Resistance, and Expansion*, Brepols, 2005, 387–400.

105. J.V.A. Fine, *The Late Medieval Balkans. A Critical Survey from the Late 12th Century to the Ottoman Conquest*, Michigan University Press, 1987, 358.

106. Kenneth Morrison and Elizabeth Roberts, *The Sandžak: A History*, Oxford University Press, 2013, 24.

107. Antov, "Imperial Expansion, Colonization, and Conversion", ch. 3.

108. Viorel Panaite, "From Allegiance to Conquest. Ottomans and Moldo-Wallachians from the Late Fourteenth to Mid-Sixteenth Centuries", *Revue Etudes Sud-Est Europe*, 48, 2010, 211–231; Sedlar, *East Central Europe in the Middle Ages*, ch. 5; Panova Rossica, "The Black Sea Coastal Cities in the Economic and Political Interrelations among Medieval Bulgaria, Venice and Genoa", *Etudes Balkaniques*, 1–2, 1999, 52–58; Laurenţiu Rădvan, "On Urban Economy in

Medieval Moldavia (the End of the 14th Century–the Former Half of the 16th Century)", *Historia Urbana*, 17, 2009, 323–338.

109. Daniel Chirot, *Social Change in a Peripheral Society: The Creation of a Balkan Colony*, Academic Press, 1976, ch. 3.

110. Irina Petroviciua et al., "Identification of Natural Dyes in Historical Textiles from Romanian Collections By LC-DAD and LC-MS (Single Stage and Tandem MS)", *Journal of Cultural Heritage*, 13:1, 2012, 89–97.

111. George C. Soulis, "The Gypsies in the Byzantine Empire and the Balkans in the Late Middle Ages", *Dumbarton Oaks Papers*, 15, 1961, 141–165; Rachel V. Lawrence, "Mastered Men. The Medieval Origins of Romani Persecution", MA thesis, Illinois State University, 2016.

112. David M. Crowe, *A History of the Gypsies of Eastern Europe and Russia*, St Martin's Press, 1995, ch. 4. Also see Elena Marushiakova and Vesselin Popov, "Gypsy Slavery in Wallachia and Moldavia", in Tomasz Kamusella, and Krzysztof Jaskulowski (eds.), *Nationalisms Today*, Peter Lang, 2009, 89–124.

113. Angeliki E. Laiou, "The Palaiologoi and the World Around Them (1261–1400)", *The Cambridge History of the Byzantine Empire c.500–1492*, Cambridge University Press, 2009, 803–833.

114. Pamuk, "The Black Death and the Origins of the 'Great Divergence.'"

115. Nükhet Varlık, *Plague and Empire in the Early Modern Mediterranean World: The Ottoman Experience, 1347–1600*, Cambridge University Press, 2015, 155. Also see Panagiotis Kontolaimos, "The Transformation of Late Byzantine Adrianople to Early Ottoman Edirne", *Journal of the Ottoman and Turkish Studies Association*, 3:1, 2016, 7–27; Amy Singer, "Enter, Riding on an Elephant: How to Approach Early Ottoman Edirne", *Journal of the Ottoman and Turkish Studies Association*, 3:1, 2016, 89–109; Grigor Boykov, "The T-shaped Zaviye/İmarets of Edirne: A Key Mechanism for Ottoman Urban Morphological Transformation", *Journal of the Ottoman and Turkish Studies Association*, 3:1, 2016, 29–48.

116. Fikret Adanır, "The Ottoman Peasantries, *c.*1360-*c.*1860", in Tom Scott (ed.), *The Peasantries of Europe: From the Fourteenth to the Eighteenth Centuries*, Longman, 1998, 269–310.

117. Murdzhev, "The Medieval Town in Bulgaria", and "The Rise of Towns in The Byzantine and Bulgarian Lands, Thirteenth to Fourteenth Century", *Historia Urbana*, 19, 2011, 55–83.

118. Shea, "The Late Byzantine City".

119. Benjamin Braude, "The Rise and Fall of Salonica Woollens, 1500–1650: Technology Transfer and Western Competition", *Mediterranean Historical Review*, 6:2, 1991, 216–236.

120. Charalambos Bakirtzis, "The Urban Continuity and Size of Late Byzantine Thessalonike", *Dumbarton Oaks Papers*, 57, 2003, 35–64.

121. Shea, "The Late Byzantine City", ch. 1.

122. David Jacoby, "Rural Exploitation and Market Economy in the Late Medieval Peloponnese", in Sharon E. J. Gerstel (ed.), *Viewing the Morea: Land and People in the Late Medieval Peloponnese*, Dumbarton Oaks Research Library, 2013, 213–275.

123. Athanasios K. Vionis, *Crusader, Ottoman, and Early Modern Aegean Archaeology: Built Environment and Domestic Material Culture in the Medieval and Post-Medieval Cyclades, Greece (13th–20th Centuries AD)*, Leiden University Press, 2008.

124. David Brewer, *Greece, the Hidden Centuries: Turkish Rule from the Fall of Constantinople to Greek Independence*, I.B. Tauris, 2010; G. D. Pagratis, "Trade and Shipping in Corfu,

1496–1538", *International Journal of Maritime History*, 16:2, 2004, 169–220; Anthony T. Luttrell, "The Latins and Life on the Smaller Aegean Islands: 1204–1453", in Benjamin Arbel, Bernard Hamilton, and David Jacoby (eds.), *Latins and Greeks in the Eastern Mediterranean after 1204*, Frank Cass, 1989, 146–157; Murdzhev, "The Medieval Town in Bulgaria", 104.

125. Marian Małowist, *Western Europe, Eastern Europe and World Development 13th–18th Centuries: Essays of Marian Małowist*, J. Batou and H. Szlajfer (eds.), Brill, 2009, ch. 1.

126. Pagratis, "Trade and Shipping in Corfu".

127. Kate Fleet, "The Turkish Economy 1071–1453", in Kate Fleet (ed.), *The Cambridge History of Turkey. Vol. 1*, Cambridge University Press, 2009.

128. Nicolas Trepanier, "Food as a Window into Daily Life in Fourteenth Century Anatolia", PhD dissertation, Harvard University, 2008.

129. Rudi Paul Lindner, "Anatolia, 1300–1451", in Fleet (ed.) *Cambridge History of Turkey Vol 1*; Suraiya N. Faroqhi, "Declines and Revivals in Textile Production", in Faroqhi (ed.), *The Cambridge History of Turkey, Vol 3, The Later Ottoman Empire, 1603–1839*, Cambridge University Press, 2006; Kate Fleet, *European and Islamic Trade in the Early Ottoman State: The Merchants of Genoa and Turkey*, Cambridge University Press, 1999, 106.

130. Mehmet Bulut, "The Role of the Ottomans and Dutch in the Commercial Integration between the Levant and Atlantic in the Seventeenth Century", *Journal of the Economic and Social History of the Orient*, 45:2, 2002, 197–230.

131. Sam White, "Ecology, Climate, and Crisis in the Ottoman Near East", PhD dissertation, Columbia University, 2008.

132. Resat Kasaba, "Nomads and Ottoman Tribes in the Ottoman Empire", in Christine Woodhead (ed.), *The Ottoman World*, Taylor & Francis, 2011.

133. Nükhet, *Plague and Empire*, 155.

134. Selcuk, "State and Society in the Marketplace".

135. Halil Inalcik, "Bursa and the Commerce of the Levant", *Journal of the Economic and Social History of the Orient*, 3:2, 1960, 131–147.

136. Willem Floor and Patrick Clawson, "Safavid Iran's Search for Silver and Gold", *International Journal of Middle East Studies*, 32:3, 2000, 345–368.

137. Inalcik, "Bursa and the Commerce of the Levant".

138. Selcuk, "State and Society in the Marketplace", 29 citing Inalcik. Another estimate, which refers to silk alone, gives 120,000 ducats. Murat Çizakça, "A Short History of the Bursa Silk Industry (1500–1900)", *Journal of the Economic and Social History of the Orient*, 23:1–2, 1980, 142–152.

139. Nükhet Varlık, "Conquest, Urbanization and Plague Networks in the Ottoman Empire, 1453–1600", in Woodhead (ed.), *The Ottoman World*.

140. White, "Ecology, Climate, and Crisis".

141. Hitomi Hongo, "Patterns of Animal Husbandry in Central Anatolia from the Second Millennium BC Through the Middle Ages. Faunal Remains from Kaman-Kalehoyuk, Turkey", PhD dissertation, Harvard University, 1996, 152–60.

142. White, "Ecology, Climate, and Crisis", 51–4.

143. Heath W. Lowry, *The Nature of the Early Ottoman State*, State University of New York Press, 2003, 1–9.

144. Pamuk and Shatzmiller, "Plagues, Wages, and Economic Change".

145. Maria Subtelny, *Timurids in Transition: Turko-Persian Politics and Acculturation in Medieval Iran*, Brill, 2007.

146. Ronald Ferrier, "Trade from the Mid-14th Century to the End of the Safavid Period", in Peter Jackson and Laurence Lockhart (eds.), *Cambridge History of Iran*, Cambridge University Press, 1986.

147. Patrick Wing, "'Rich in Goods and Abounding in Wealth': The Ilkhanid and Post-Ilkhanid Ruling Elite and the Politics of Commercial Life at Tabriz, 1250–1400", in Judith Pfeiffer (ed.), *Iran Studies: Politics, Patronage and the Transmission of Knowledge in 13th–15th Century Tabriz*, Brill, 2013.

148. Clements R. Markham (ed.), *Narrative of the Embassy of Ruy Gonzalez de Clavijo to the Court of Timour, at Samarcand, A.D. 1403–6*, Hakluyt Society, 1859, 185.

149. Clavijo, *Narrative*, 93–95.

150. David Durand-Guédy, "Isfahan during the Turko-Mongol Period (11th–15th Centuries)", in David Durand-Guédy, Roy Mottahedeh, and Jürgen Paul (eds.), *Medieval Iran*, Brill, 2020.

151. "Isfahan", *Encyclopedia Iranica*; Subtelny, *Timurids in Transition*, 121, n.78; H. R. Roemer, "The Successors of Timur", in *Cambridge History of Iran Volume 6*.

152. Ute Franke, "Ancient Herat Revisited. Recent Archaeological New Data from Fieldwork", in Rocco Rante (ed.), *Greater Khorasan: History, Geography, Archaeology and Material Culture*, De Gruyter, 2015.

153. Jürgen Paul, "The Histories of Herat", *Iranian Studies*, 33:1–2, 2000, 93–115.

154. Subtelny, *Timurids in Transition*, and "Tamerlane and His Descendants: From Paladins to Patrons", in David O. Morgan and Anthony Reid (eds.), *The New Cambridge History of Islam Vol. 3*, Cambridge University Press, 2010.

155. Subtelny, *Timurids in Transition*, 228; V.V. Barthold, *An Historical Geography of Iran*, Princeton University Press, 2014 (orig. 1903), 51.

156. "Herat", *Encyclopedia Iranica*.

157. Subtelny, *Timurids in Transition*, 156, 199.

158. Roemer, "The Successors of Timur".

159. Ahmad Fazlinejad and Farajollah Ahmadi, "The Impact of the Black Death on Iranian Trade (1340s–1450s A.D.)", *Iran and the Caucasus*, 23, 2019, 221–232.

160. Archibald Lewis, "Maritime Skills in the Indian Ocean 1368–1500", *Journal of the Economic and Social History of the Orient*, 16:2–3, 1973.

161. Sebastian R. Prange, "'Measuring by the Bushel': Reweighing the Indian Ocean Pepper Trade", *Historical Research*, 84:224, 2011.

162. Janet Martin, "Muscovite Travelling Merchants: The Trade with the Muslim East (15th and 16th Centuries)", *Central Asian Survey*, 4:3, 1985, 21–38; Edhem Eldem, "Capitulations and Western Trade", in Faroqhi (ed.), *The Cambridge History of Turkey, Volume 3*, 302; Ferrier, "Trade from the Mid-14th Century".

163. Richard Bulliet, *Cotton, Climate, and Camels in Early Islamic Iran*, Columbia University Press, 2009.

164. Quoted in Stephen Dale, *Indian Merchants and Eurasian Trade, 1600–1750*, Cambridge University Press, 1994, 23.

165. Scott C. Levi, "Commercial Structures", in *The New Cambridge History of Islam, Volume 3*.

166. Zsombor Rajkai, "Japanese and Chinese Research on the Timurid-Ming Chinese Contacts", *Acta orientalia Academiae Scientiarum Hung*, 63:1 2010, 63–103.

167. John Miksic, "Chinese Ceramic Production and Trade", *Oxford Research Encyclopedia of Asian History*, 2017; William S. Atwell, "Time, Money, and the Weather: Ming China and the 'Great Depression' of the Mid-Fifteenth Century", 61:1, 2002, 83–113. Also see Kwangmin Kim, "Saintly Brokers: Uyghur Muslims, Trade, and the Making of Qing Central Asia, 1696–1814", PhD dissertation, University of California, Berkeley, 2008; Yolande Crowe, "The Safavid Potter at the Crossroad of Styles", in Floor and Herzig (eds.), *Iran and the World in the Safavid Age*; Robert Finlay, "The Pilgrim Art: The Culture of Porcelain in World History", *Journal of World History*, 9:2, 1998, 141–187; Stacey Pierson, "The Movement of Chinese Ceramics: Appropriation in Global History", *Journal of World History*, 23:1, 2012, 9–39.

168. Lin Meicun and Ran Zhang, "Zheng He's Voyages to Hormuz: The Archaeological Evidence", *Antiquity*, 89, 2015, 417–432.

169. Subtelny, "Tamerlane and His Descendants".

170. Linda T. Darling, "The Renaissance and the Middle East", in Guido Ruggiero (ed.), *A Companion to the Worlds of the Renaissance*, Blackwell, 2002, 55–69; Stephen Dale, "The Later Timurids c. 1450–1526", in Nicola Di Cosmo, Allen J. Frank, and Peter B. Golden (eds.), *The Cambridge History of Inner Asia: The Chinggisid Age*, Cambridge University Press, 2009.

171. Atwell, "Time, Money, and the Weather".

172. Oktay Özel, "Population Changes in Ottoman Anatolia during the 16th and 17th Centuries: The "Demographic Crisis" Reconsidered", *International Journal of Middle East Studies*, 36:2, 2004, 183–205.

173. Bas van Bavel, Eltjo Buringh, and Jessica Dijkman, "Immovable Capital Goods in Medieval Muslim Lands: Why Water-Mills and Building Cranes Went Missing", CGEH Working Paper Series, No. 69, 2015.

174. Bernard Lewis and Amnon Cohen, *Population and Revenue in the Towns of Palestine in the Sixteenth Century*, Princeton University Press, 2015 (orig. 1978).

175. Nicolas Trepanier, "Food as a Window", 138; Stephen McPhillips, "Harnessing Hydraulic Power in Ottoman Syria Water Mills and the Rural Economy of the Upper Orontes Valley", in Stephen McPhillips and Paul D. Wordsworth (eds.), *Landscapes of the Islamic World: Archaeology, History, and Ethnography*, University of Pennsylvania Press, 2016; Miquel Barceló, "The Missing Water-Mill: A Question of Technological Diffusion in the High Middle Ages", in Miquel Barceló and Francois Sigaut (eds.), *Making of Feudal Agricultures?*, Brill, 2004.

176. Mujani, "European Technological Innovation".

177. Helena Kirchner, "Watermills in the Balearic Islands during the Muslim Period", in Jan Klápště and Petr Sommer (eds.), *Processing, Storage, Distribution of Food. Food in the Medieval Rural Environment*, Brepols, 2011, 45–55.

178. Richard W. Bulliet, "History and Animal Energy in the Arid Zone", in Alan Mikhail (ed.), *Water on Sand: Environmental Histories of the Middle East and North Africa*, Oxford University Press, 2013.

179. Bulliet, "History and Animal Energy in the Arid Zone".

180. van Bavel, Buringh, and Dijkman, "Immovable Capital Goods".

181. Joseph F. O'Callaghan, *Gibraltar Crusade: Castile and the Battle for the Strait*, University of Pennsylvania Press, 2011.

182. Kenneth Chase, *Firearms: A Global History to 1700*, Cambridge University Press, 2003, 97–98.

183. Abbès Zouache, "Western vs. Eastern Way of War in the Late Medieval Near East: An Unsuitable Paradigm", *Mamlūk Studies Review*, 18, 2014–5, 302–325.

184. Robert Irwin (ed.), *A Mission to the Medieval Middle East: The Travels of Bertrandon de la Brocquière to Jerusalem and Constantinople*, I.B. Tauris, 2019.

185. Waterson, *The Knights of Islam*, 276.

186. Richard Eaton and Philip Wagoner, "Warfare on the Deccan Plateau, 1450–1600: A Military Revolution in Early Modern India?", *Journal of World History*, 25:1, 2014.

187. Daisuke, "The Financial Reforms of Sultan Qāytbāy" ; Albrecht Fuess, "Les janissaires, les mamelouks et les armes à feu; Une comparaison des systèmes militaires ottoman et mamelouk à partir du milieu du XVe siècle", *Turcica*, 41, 2009, 209–227.

188. Uyar and Erickson, *A Military History of the Ottomans*, 72

189. Reuven Amitai, "Armies and Their Economic Basis in Iran and the Surrounding Lands, c. 1000–1500", in *The New Cambridge History of Islam, Vol. 3*.

190. Roger Savory, *Iran under the Safavids*, Cambridge University Press, 1980, 43–44. Also see Ali Anooshahr, "The Rise of the Safavids According to Their Old Veterans: Amini Haravi's Futuhat-e Shahi", *Iranian Studies*, 48:2, 2015, 249–267.

191. H. Burcu Ozguven, "Early Modern Military Architecture in the Ottoman Empire", *Nexus Network Journal*, 16:3, 2014, 737–749; Andrew de la Garza, "Mughals at War: Babur, Akbar, and the Indian Military Revolution, 1500–1605", Ph.D. dissertation, Ohio State University, 2010, 45.

192. Palmira Johnson Brummett, *Ottoman Seapower and Levantine Diplomacy in the Age of Discovery*, State University of New York Press, 1994, 173, quoting John Guilmartin.

193. Amir Mazor and Keren Abbou Hershkovits, "Spectacles in the Muslim World: New Evidence from the Mid-Fourteenth Century", *Early Science and Medicine*, 18:3, 2013, 291–305.

194. Ibid. Also see Vincent Ilardi, *Renaissance Vision from Spectacles to Telescopes*, American Philosophical Society, 2007.

195. Maya Shatzmiller, "An Early Knowledge Economy: The Adoption of Paper, Human Capital and Economic Change in the Medieval Islamic Middle East, 700–1300 AD", CGEH Working Paper Series, No. 64, 2015.

196. Toby E. Huff, *The Rise of Early Modern Science. Islam, China and the West*, 3rd edn, Cambridge University Press, 2017, 148. Also see 143.

197. Svatopluk Soucek, *A History of Inner Asia*, Cambridge University Press, 2000.

198. Nelly Hanna, "Literacy and the 'Great Divide' in the Islamic World, 1300–1800", *Journal of World History*, 2 (2007) 175–193.

199. Edmund Burke III, "Islam at the Center: Technological Complexes and the Roots of Modernity", *Journal of World History*, 20:2, 2009, 165–186.

200. Hanna, "Literacy and the 'Great Divide.'"

201. Subtelny, *Timurids in Transition*.

202. Wing, "Indian Ocean Trade".

203. Philip Mansel, *Constantinople. City of the World's Desire, 1453–1924*, Penguin, 1997, 135. Also see K. K. Karaman and S. Pamuk, "Ottoman State Finances in European Perspective, 1500–1914", *Journal of Economic History*, 70.3 (2010); Selcuk, "State and Society in the Marketplace", 220; Mikhail, *Under Osman's Tree*, 20.

204. Victor Ostapchuk, "The Ottoman Black Sea Frontier and the Relations of the Porte with the Polish-Lithuanian Commonwealth d Muscovy, 1622–1628", PhD thesis, Harvard University, 1989, 181–182.

205. Colin Imber, "The Ottoman Empire (Tenth/Sixteenth Century)", in Maribel Fierro (ed.), *The New Cambridge History of Islam Vol. 2*, Cambridge University Press, 2010. Also see Gabor Agoston, "Military Transformation in the Ottoman Empire and Russia, 1500–1800", *Kritika: Explorations in Russian and Eurasian History*, 12:2, 2011, 281–319; Rossitsa Gradeva, "Between the Hinterland and the Frontier: Ottoman Vidin, 15th to 18th centuries" in A.C.S. Peacock (ed.), *The Frontiers of the Ottoman World*, Oxford University Press, 2009.

206. Houari Touatiin, "Ottoman Maghrib", in *The New Cambridge History of Islam, Vol 2*.

207. Richard Bulliet, "Conversion to Islam", in *The New Cambridge History of Islam, Vol. 3*.

208. Resul Ay, "Sufi Shaykhs and Society in Thirteenth and Fifteenth Century Anatolia: Spiritual Influence and Rivalry", *Journal of Islamic Studies*, 24:1, 2013, 1–24.

209. Adam Sabra, "From Artisan to Courtier: Sufism and Social Mobility in 15th Century Egypt", in Margariti Roxani, Adam Sabra, and Petra Sijpesteijn (eds.), *Islamic History and Civilization: Histories of the Middle East: Studies in Middle Eastern Society, Economy and Law*, Brill, 2010.

210. Paul Jürgen, "The Rise of the Khwajagan-Naqshbandiyya Sufi Order in Timurid Herat", in Nile Green (ed.), *Afghanistan's Islam: From Conversion to the Taliban*, University of California Press, 2016; Bethany J. Walker, "The Globalizing Effects of 'Hajj' in the Medieval and Modern Eras", in Øystein Sakala LaBianca and Sandra Arnold Scham (eds.), *Connectivity in Antiquity: Globalization as a Long Term Historical Process*, Equinox, 2006.

211. Turkish scholar Ömer Lütfi Barkan first developed the thesis. See Antov, "Imperial Expansion, Colonization, and Conversion", ch. 5.

212. Iklil Oya Selcuk, "State and Society in the Marketplace", 157–158.

213. Nile Green, *Making Space: Sufis and Settlers in Early Modern India*, Oxford University Press, 2012, Intro. Also see ch. 5.

214. Paul, "The Rise of the Khwajagan-Naqshbandiyya".

215. Ali Anooshahr, "Timurids and Turcomans: Transition and Flowering in the Fifteenth Century", in Touraj Daryaee (ed.), *The Oxford Handbook of Iranian History*, Oxford University Press, 2012.

216. Selcuk, "State and Society in the Marketplace", 163.

217. Singer, "Enter, Riding on an Elephant".

218. Ay, "Sufi Shaykhs and Society".

219. William Caferro, *Contesting the Renaissance*, Wiley Blackwell, 2011, 22–23.

220. Peter Burke, Luke Clossey, and Felipe Fernández-Armesto, "The Global Renaissance", *Journal of World History*, 28:1, 2017, 1–30.

221. Caferro, *Contesting the Renaissance*, 16.

222. Bideleux and Jeffries, *A History of Eastern Europe*, 141, 155; Norman Davies, *God's Playground. A History of Poland, Vol. 1—The Origins to 1795*, Clarendon Press, 1981, 148–150; Agnieszka Bartoszewicz, *Urban Literacy in Late Medieval Poland*, Brepols, 2017; Robert O. Crummey, *The Formation of Muscovy, 1304–1613*, 1987, Longman, 57, and ch. 7.

223. Jerry Brotton, *Renaissance Bazaar: from the Silk Road to Michelangelo*, Oxford University Press, 2002; Jack Goody, *Renaissances. The One or the Many?* Cambridge University Press, 2010.

224. Stephen Dale, "The Legacy of the Timurids", *Journal of the Royal Asiatic Society*, 8:1. 1998, 43–58; Dominic Parviz Brookshaw, *Hafiz and His Contemporaries. Poetry, Performance and Patronage in Fourteenth-century Iran*, I.B. Tauris, 2019; Corinne Lefèvre, "Messianism, Rationalism and Inter-Asian Connections: The Majalis-i Jahangiri (1608–11) and the Socio-intellectual History of the Mughal 'ulama,'" *Indian Economic and Social History Review*, 54:3, 2017, 317–338. Also see note 174 above.

225. Burke et al., "The Global Renaissance".

226. Sheryl E. Reiss, "A Taxonomy of Art Patronage in Renaissance Italy", in Babette Bohn and James M. Saslow (eds.), *A Companion to Renaissance and Baroque Art*, Wiley, 2013.

227. James S. Amelang, "Social Hierarchies: The Lower Classes", in Guido Ruggiero (ed.), *A Companion to the Worlds of the Renaissance*, Blackwell, 2002; Virginia Cox, *A Short History of the Italian Renaissance*, I.B. Tauris, 2015, 39; Millard Meiss, *Painting in Florence and Siena After the Black Death: The Arts, Religion, and Society in the Mid-Fourteenth Century*, Princeton University Press, 1978, 69.

228. Editor's intro, in William J. Connell and Andrea Zorzi (eds.), *Florentine Tuscany: Structures and Practices of Power*, Cambridge University Press, 2000; Samuel K. Cohn Jr., *The Black Death Transformed. Disease and Culture in Early Renaissance Europe*, Arnold, 2002; Mary Lindemann, "Plague, Disease, and Hunger", in Ruggiero (ed.), *A Companion to the Worlds of the Renaissance*.

229. Gene Brucker, "The Italian Renaissance", in Ruggiero (ed.), *A Companion to the Worlds of the Renaissance*; Amelang, "Social Hierarchies: The Lower Classes"; Cox, *The Italian Renaissance*, 41.

230. R. Po-chia Hsia, "Religious Cultures (Spirituality, Reform, High and Low)", in Ruggiero (ed.), *A Companion to the Worlds of the Renaissance*.

231. Marcela Klicova Perett, "Battle for the Public Mind: John Hus and Hussite Movement", PhD dissertation, University of Notre Dame, 2009, 143–144; Stephen E. Lahey, *The Hussites (Past Imperfect)*, Arc Humanities Press, 2019; Howard Louthan, "The Bohemian Reformations", in Ulinka Rublack (ed.), *The Oxford Handbook of the Protestant Reformations*, Oxford University Press, 2016.

232. Charles Freeman, *Holy Bones, Holy Dust. How Relics Shaped the History of Medieval Europe*, Yale University Press, 2011, 103.

233. Diarmaid MacCulloch, *Reformation: Europe's House Divided, 1490–1700*, Penguin, 2004, 13.

234. Lawrence N. Langer, "The Black Death in Russia: Its Effects Upon Urban Labor", *Russian History*, 1975, 2:1, 53–67; Henrik Birnbaum, *Novgorod in Focus: Sselected Essays*, Slavica, 1996, 34–35. Also see Teresa Pac, "Churches at the Edge: A Comparative Study of Christianization Processes along the Baltic Sea in the Middle Ages: Gdańsk and Novgorod", PhD dissertation, State University of New York at Binghamton, 2005.

235. Lovorka Čoralić, "Relations between Croatia and England in the late Middle Ages", *Balkan Studies (Etudes balkaniques)*, 4, 2010, 196–211.

236. István Keul, *Early Modern Religious Communities in East-Central Europe: Ethnic Diversity, Denominational Plurality, and Corporative Politics in the Principality of Transylvania (1526–1691)*, Brill, 2009, ch. 4 (quote p. 48).

237. On Luther, see Lyndal Roper, *Martin Luther: Renegade and Prophet*, Bodley Head, 2016.

Chapter 9: Early Modern Ming-Muslim Globalisation

1. Timothy Brook, *The Troubled Empire: China in the Ming and Yuan Dynasties*, Belknap Press, 2010, 90–111; Wang Yuquan 王毓铨, Liu Zhongri 刘重日, and Zhang Xianqing 张显清. *Zhongguo jingji tongshi (xia)* 中国经济通史. 明代经济卷 （上 *General History of the Chinese Economy. The Ming Dynasty I.* Zhongguo shehui kexue yuan, 2007. The relevant parts of this work, and of the other Chinese language works cited, were translated for me by Dr. Joe Lawson.

2. Deng Huia and Li Xina, "The Asian Monsoons and Zheng He's Voyages to the Western Ocean," *Journal of Navigation*, 64:2, 2011, 207–218; Tonio Andrade, "An Accelerating Divergence? The Revisionist Model of World History and the Question of Eurasian Military Parity: Data from East Asian Source", *Canadian Journal of Sociology*, 36:2, 2011, 185.

3. Tim Mackintosh-Smith, *Arabs. A 3,000-Year History of Peoples, Tribes and Empires*, Yale University Press, 2019, Loc. 1208.

4. N. Boivin and D. Q. Fuller, "Shell Middens, Ships and Seeds: Exploring Coastal Subsistence, Maritime Trade and the Dispersal of Domesticates in and Around the Ancient Arabian Peninsula", *Journal of World Prehistory*, 22, 2009, 113–80.

5. Sean McGrail, "The Global Origins of Seagoing Water Transport", in Atholl Anderson, James H. Barrett, and Katherine V. Boyle (eds.), *The Global Origins and Development of Seafaring*, McDonald Institute for Archaeological Research, 2010.

6. Engseng Ho, *The Graves of Tarim: Genealogy and Mobility Across the Indian Ocean*, California University Press, 2006, 49 n.15.

7. Andre Wink, *Al-Hind, the Making of the Indo-Islamic World. Vol 3, Indo-Islamic Society, 14th–15th Centuries*, Brill, 2004, 225.

8. Sanjay Subrahmanyam, *Portuguese Empire in Asia, 1500–1700*, Wiley, 2012, 38.

9. Beatrice Forbes Manz, "Temür and the Early Timurids to c. 1450", in Nicola Di Cosmo, Allen J. Frank, and Peter B. Golden (eds.), *The Cambridge History of Inner Asia: The Chinggisid Age*, Cambridge University Press, 2009; Ralph Kauz and Roderich Ptak, "Hormuz in Yuan and Ming Sources", *Bulletin de l'Ecole française d'Extrême-Orient*, 88, 2001, 27–75.

10. P. Colangelo et al., "Mitochondrial Phylogeography of the Black Rat Supports a Single Invasion of the Western Mediterranean Basin", *Biol Invasions*, 17, 2015; Hervé Monchot and Claude Guintard, "Chronic Diseases in Cats from the Medieval Site of Qalhât (Oman)", *International Journal of Paleopathology*, 17, 2017, 1–9.

11. Chinese source quoted by Wink, *Al-Hind*, 192.

12. Lin Meicun and Ran Zhang, "Zheng He's Voyages to Hormuz: The Archaeological Evidence", *Antiquity*, 89, 2015, 417–432; "Hormuz", *Encyclopedia Iranica*; Valeria Piacentini Fiorani, "The Gulf: A Cosmopolitan Mobile Society—Hormuz, 1475–1515 CE", in Allen James Fromherz (ed.), *The Gulf in World History: Arabian, Persian and Global Connections*, Edinburgh University Press, 2018.

13. Andre Wink, *Al-Hind*, 193–194.

14. Donald Ferguson, "A Short Narrative of the Origin of the Kingdom of Harmuz, and of Its Kings, Down to Its Conquest by the Portuguese; Extracted from Its History, Written by Torunxa, King of the Same", in William F. Sinclair (ed.), *The Travels of Pedro Teixeira; with His "Kings of Harmuz", and Extracts from His "Kings of Persia"*, Hakluyt Society edn, 2010.

15. Wink, *Al-Hind*, 194–6; Rudi Mathee, "The Safavid Economy as Part of the World Economy", in Floor, Willem M., and Herzig, Edmund (eds.), *Iran and the World in the Safavid Age*, I.B. Tauris, 2012.

16. Beatrice Cardi, "Trucial Oman in the Sixteenth and Seventeenth Centuries", *Antiquity*, 44, 1970, 288–295; J. C. Wilkinson, "A Sketch of the Historical Geography of the Trucial Oman Down to the Beginning of the Sixteenth Century", *Geographical Journal*, 130:3, 1964, 337–349; Kauz and Ptak, "Hormuz in Yuan and Ming Sources".

17. Robert Carter, "The History and Prehistory of Pearling in the Persian Gulf", *Journal of the Economic and Social History of the Orient*, 48.2, 2005, 139–209; Juan Cole, "Rival Empires of Trade and Imami Shi'ism in Eastern Arabia, 1300–1800", *International Journal of Middle East Studies*, 19:2, 1987, 177–204; Torunxa, "A Short Narrative".

18. S. Digby, "The Maritime Trade of India", in T. Raychaudhuri and I. Habib (eds.), *The Cambridge Economic History of India, Vol. 1, c.1200–c.1750*, Oxford University Press, 1982, 125–159; Donald Hawley, "Some Surprising Aspects of Omani History", *Asian Affairs*, 13:1, 1982, 28–39.

19. John Lash Meloy, "Mamluk Authority, Meccan Autonomy, and Red Sea Trade, 797–859/1359–1455", PhD dissertation, University of Chicago, 1998, ch. 2; Digby, "Maritime Trade of India".

20. Ho, *Graves of Tarim*, 47–48. Also see Roxani Margariti, "Like the Place Of Congregation on Judgement Day: Maritime Trade and Urban Organization in Medieval Aden (ca. 1083–1229)", PhD dissertation, Princeton University, 2002; Daniel Mahoney, "The Political Landscape of the Dhamar Plain in the Central Highlands of Yemen During the Late Medieval and Early Ottoman Periods", PhD dissertation, University of Chicago, 2014.

21. Subrahmanyam, *Portuguese Empire in Asia*, 16.

22. Daniel Mahoney, "The Role of Horses in the Politics of Late Medieval South Arabia", *Arabian Humanities*, 8, 2017.

23. It may have had ship timber in ancient times. Boivin and Fuller, "Shell Middens, Ships and Seeds".

24. Roxani Margariti, "Mercantile Networks, Port Cities, and 'Pirate' States: Conflict and Competition in the Indian Ocean World of Trade before the Sixteenth Century", *Journal of the Economic and Social History of the Orient*, 51, 2008, 543–577.

25. Ho, *The Graves of Tarim*.

26. Jane Hathaway, *Arab Lands under Ottoman Rule, 1516–1800*, Pearson Longman, 2008, 162.

27. Cheryl Ward and Uzi Baram, "Global Markets, Local Practice: Ottoman-period Clay Pipes and Smoking Paraphernalia from the Red Sea Shipwreck at Sadana Island, Egypt", *International Journal of Historical Archaeology*, 10:2, 2006, 135–158.

28. Ho, *The Graves of Tarim*, 61–62. Also see 38.

29. Jeyamalar Kathirithamby-Wells, "Hadhrami Mediators of Ottoman Influence in Southeast Asia", in ACS Peacock and Annabel Teh Gallop (eds.), *From Anatolia to Aceh. Ottomans, Turks and Southeast Asia*, Oxford University Press, 2015; R. Michael Feener and Michael F. Laffan, "Sufi Scents across the Indian Ocean: Yemeni Hagiography as a Source for the Earliest History of Southeast Asian Islam", *Archipel*, 70, 2005, 185–208; Luís Filipe Thomaz, "Iranian Diaspora in Maritime Asia: A Study of Sixteenth Century Portuguese Sources", *Studies in History*, 31:1, 2015.

30. M. H. Ilias, "Mappila Muslims and the Cultural Content of Trading Arab Diaspora on the Malabar Coast", *Asian Journal of Social Science*, 35, 2007, 434–456.

31. George Hatke, 'Northeast Africa', in Erik Hermans (ed.), *A Companion to the Early Global Middle Ages*, Arc Humanities, 2020.

32. Abdul Sheriff, "The Swahili in the African and Indian Ocean Worlds to c. 1500", *Oxford Research Encyclopedia of African History*; Molly B. Patterson, "South Arabian Maritime Expansion and the Origins of East African Islam", PhD dissertation, University of Wisconsin–Madison, 2009.

33. This is not an original analogy, but I have forgotten my source.

34. Patterson, "South Arabian Maritime Expansion".

35. Edward Pollard, Jeffrey Fleisher, and Stephanie Wynne-Jones, "Beyond the Stone Town: Maritime Architecture at Fourteenth–Fifteenth Century Songo Mnara, Tanzania", *Journal of Maritime Archaeology*, 7, 2012, 43–62.

36. Philippe Beaujard, "East Africa, the Comoros Islands and Madagascar before the Sixteenth Century", *Azania: Archaeological Research in Africa*, 42:1, 15–35.

37. Andrea Seligman, "Encircling Value: Inland Trade in the Precolonial East African-Indian Ocean World, ca. 1st–17th Centuries", PhD dissertation, Northwestern University, 2014, 200.

38. N. Thomas Håkansson, "The Human Ecology of World Systems in East Africa: The Impact of the Ivory Trade", *Human Ecology*, 32:5, 2004, 561–591.

39. Rahul Oka, "Resilience and Adaptation of Trade Networks in East African and South Asian Port Polities, 1500–1800 C.E", PhD dissertation in Anthropology, University of Chicago, 2008, 297.

40. Patterson, "South Arabian Maritime Expansion", 210.

41. Abdul Sheriff, "The Swahili in the African and Indian Ocean Worlds to c. 1500", *Oxford Research Encyclopedia of African History*; Patterson, "South Arabian Maritime Expansion", 212.

42. Robert M. Maxon, *East Africa: An Introductory History*, 3rd edn, West Virginia University Press, 2009, 43.

43. Beaujard, "East Africa, the Comoros Islands and Madagascar". Also see Paterson, "South Arabian Maritime Expansion", 121; Nicole Boivin et al., "East Africa and Madagascar in the Indian Ocean World", *Journal of World Prehistory*, 26, 2013, 213–281; Abdul Sheriff, "The Swahili in the African and Indian Ocean Worlds to c. 1500", *Oxford Research Encyclopedia of African History*, Oxford University Press, 2015; Richard B. Allen, "Satisfying the 'Want for Labouring People': European Slave Trading in the Indian Ocean, 1500–1850", *Journal of World History*, 21:1, 2010, 45–73.

44. Samira Sheikh, *Forging a Region: Sultans, Traders, and Pilgrims in Gujarat, 1200–1500*, Oxford University Press, 2012 (orig. 2009), 64.

45. Ibid., 78.

46. Jyoti Gulati Balachandran, "Texts, Tombs and Memory: The Migration, Settlement, and Formation of a Learned Muslim Community in Fifteenth-Century Gujarat", PhD dissertation, UCLA, 2012, 49.

47. Pius Malekandathil, "Winds of Change and Links of Continuity: A Study on the Merchant Groups of Kerala and the Channels of Their Trade, 1000–1800", *Journal of the Economic and Social History of the Orient*, 50:2–3, 2007.

48. Etienne de la Vaissiere, "Trans-Asian Trade, or the Silk Road Deconstructed (Antiquity, Middle Ages)", in Larry Neal and Jeffrey G. Williamson (eds.), *The Cambridge History of*

Capitalism. Volume 1, The Rise of Capitalism: From Ancient Origins to 1848, Cambridge University Press, 2014.

49. Malekandathil, "Winds of Change"; Ilias, "Mappila Muslims".

50. Ho, *The Graves of Tarim*, 100.

51. Thomaz, "Iranian Diaspora in Maritime Asia".

52. Quoted in Archibald Lewis, "Maritime Skills in the Indian Ocean 1368–1500", *Journal of the Economic and Social History of the Orient*, 16.2–3, 1973.

53. Kenneth R. Hall, "Ports-of-Trade, Maritime Diasporas, and Networks of Trade and Cultural Integration in the Bay of Bengal Region of the Indian Ocean: c. 1300–1500", *Journal of the Economic and Social History of the Orient*, 53, 2010, 109–145.

54. Kenneth R. Hall, *A History of Early Southeast Asia: Maritime Trade and Societal Development, 100–1500*, Rowman & Littlefield, 2010, ch. 9.

55. Sheikh, *Forging a Region*, 186.

56. Wink, *Al-Hind*, 99.

57. B. Arunachalam, "Technology of Indian Sea Navigation (c. 1200–c. 1800)", *Medieval History Journal*, 11.2, 2008, 187–227; Michael Flecker, "The South-China-Sea Tradition: The Hybrid Hulls of South-East Asia", *International Journal of Nautical Archaeology*, 36:1, 2007; Pierre-Yves Manguin, "Ships and Shipping in Southeast Asia", *Oxford Research Encyclopedia of Asian History*, 2017.

58. Brook, *The Troubled Empire*, 91; Wang Gungwu, "Ming Foreign Relations: Southeast Asia", in Denis C. Twitchett and Frederick W. Mote (eds.), *The Cambridge History of China, Vol. 8*, Cambridge University Press, 1998.

59. Geoff Wade, "The Zheng He Voyages, a Reassessment,", *Journal of the Malaysian Branch of the Royal Asiatic Society*, 78:1, 2005. Also see Zachary Reddick, "The Zheng He Voyages Reconsidered: A Means of Imperial Power Projection", *Quarterly Journal of Chinese Studies*, 3:1, 2014, 55–65.

60. Sen Tansen, "The Impact of Zheng He's Expeditions on Indian Ocean Interactions", *Bulletin of SOAS*, 79:3, 2016, 609–636; Hall, *A History of Early Southeast Asia*, ch. 8.

61. Quote in Sen, "The Impact of Zheng He's Expeditions".

62. Kenneth R. Hall, "Multi-Dimensional Networking: Fifteenth-Century Indian Ocean Maritime Diaspora in Southeast Asian Perspective", *Journal of the Economic and Social History of the Orient*, 49:4, 2006, 454–481, citing the work of Wang Ming in particular.

63. William S. Atwell, "Time, Money, and the Weather: Ming China and the 'Great Depression'of the Mid-Fifteenth Century", *Journal of Asian Studies*, 61:1, 2002, 83–113, quoting Haraprasad Ray.

64. Craig Clunas, "Things in Between: Splendour and Excess in Ming China", in Frank Trentmann (ed.), *The Oxford Handbook of the History of Consumption*, Oxford University Press, 2012.

65. Geoff Wade, "Engaging the South: Ming China and Southeast Asia in the Fifteenth Century", *Journal of the Economic and Social History of the Orient*, 51, 2008, 578–638.

66. Timothy Brook, *The Confusions of Pleasure: Commerce and Culture in Ming China*, University of California Press, 1998, 119.

67. Huang Li-sheng, "'lhe Issues of Islands Governing in Early Ming Dynasty", *Journal of Marine and Island Cultures*, 5, 2016, 5–10; John W. Dardess, *Ming China, 1368–1644: A Concise History of a Resilient Empire*, Rowman & Littlefield, 2011, ch.1.

68. Ouyang Zongshu 欧阳宗书. *Haishang renjia: haiyang yuye jingji yu yumin shehui* 海上人家：海洋渔业经济与渔民社会 (Ocean people: The Maritime Fishing Economy and Fishing Communities). Nanchang: Jiangxi gaoxiao chubanshe, 1998, 48.

69. James Kai-Sing Kung and Cicheng Ma, "Autarky and the Rise and Fall of Piracy in Ming China", *Journal of Economic History*, 74.2, 2014.

70. Quoted in Dahpon David Ho, "Sealords Live in Vain: Fujian and the Making of a Maritime Frontier in Seventeenth-Century China", PhD thesis, University of California, San Diego, 2011, 76.

71. Harriet Zurndorfer, "Oceans of History, Seas of Change: Recent Revisionist Writing in Western Languages About China and East Asian Maritime History During the Period 1500–1630", *International Journal of Asian Studies*, 13:1, 2016, 61–94; Angela Schottenhammer, "The East Asian Maritime World, c. 1400–1800: Its Fabrics of Power and Dynamics of Exchanges—China and Her Neighbours", in Schottenhammer (ed.), *The East Asian Maritime World 1400–1800: Its Fabrics of Power and Dynamics of Exchanges*, Otto Harrassowitz, 2007, 1–86; Richard von Glahn, "Chinese Coin and Changes in Monetary Preferences in Maritime East Asia in the Fifteenth–Seventeenth Centuries", *Journal of the Economic and Social History of the Orient*, 57, 2014, 629–668.

72. Huang Li-sheng, "The Issues of Islands Governing".

73. James Fujitani, "The Ming Rejection of the Portuguese Embassy of 1517: A Reassessment", *Journal of World History*, 27:1, 2016, 87–102.

74. Lin Ming 林明, and Xiang Guangyu 向广宇. "Mingdai haijin zhengce xia de Hainan jingji shehui bianhua 明代海禁政策下的海禁经济社会变化", *Xin Dongfang* 新东方 no. 1 (2010).

75. Akira Matsuura 松浦章. *Ming Qing shidai dongya haiyu de wenhua jiaoliu* 明清时代东亚海域的文化交流 (Cultural Exchange in Maritime East Asia in the Ming and Qing Dynasties). Translated by Zheng Jiexi 郑洁西. Nanjing: Jiangsu renmin chubanshe, 2009.

76. Brook, *The Troubled Empire*, 221.

77. ShawnaKim Lowey-Ball, "Liquid Market, Solid State: The Rise and Demise of the Great Global Emporium at Malacca, 1400–1641", PhD dissertation, Yale University, 2015, 34.

78. John Chaffee, "Diasporic Identities in the Historical Development of the Maritime Muslim Communities of Song-Yuan China", *Journal of the Economic and Social History of the Orient*, 49:4, 2006, 395–420.

79. Geoff Wade, "Early Muslim Expansion in South-East Asia, Eighth to Fifteenth Centuries", in David O. Morgan and Anthony Reid (eds.), *The New Cambridge History of Islam, Vol. 3*, Cambridge University Press, 2010; Chaffee, "Diasporic Identities".

80. Ho, "Sealords Live in Vain", 56.

81. Sen, "The Impact of Zheng He's Expeditions".

82. Reddick, "The Zheng He Voyages Reconsidered"; Lowey-Ball, "Liquid Market, Solid State", 88.

83. Ranabir Chakravarti, "Early Medieval Bengal and the Trade in Horses: A Note", *Journal of the Economic and Social History of the Orient*, 42:2, 1999, 194–211.

84. Jennifer L. Gaynor, "Ages of Sail, Ocean Basins, and Southeast Asia", *Journal of World History*, 24:2, 2013, 309–333; Naomi Standen (ed.), *Demystifying China: New Understandings of Chinese History*, Rowman & Littlefield, 2012, 109.

85. Zsombor Rajkai, "Japanese and Chinese Research on the Timurid-Ming Chinese Contacts", *Acta orientalia Academiae Scientiarum Hung*, 63:1 2010, 63–103.

86. Kwangmin Kim, "Saintly Brokers: Uyghur Muslims, Trade, and the Making of Qing Central Asia, 1696–1814", PhD dissertation, University of California, Berkeley, 2008, 74.

87. Dardess, *Ming China*, ch. 1.

88. Wade, "Engaging the South"; Hall, "Multi-Dimensional Networking"; Sen, "The Impact of Zheng He's Expeditions".

89. Wang, Liu, and Zhang, *General History of the Chinese Economy*, 253–255.

90. Kenneth R. Hall, "Revisionist Study of Cross-Cultural Commercial Competition on the Vietnam Coastline in the Fourteenth and Fifteenth Centuries and Its Wider Implications", *Journal of World History*, 24:1, 2013.

91. Atwell, "Time, Money, and the Weather".

92. Jiang Jianxin of the Ceramic Archaeology Institute of Jingdezhen, quoted in *Archaeology News*, 23 April 2019.

93. Ho, "Sealords Live in Vain".

94. Nanny Kim, "Silver Mines and Mobile Miners in the Southwestern Borderlands of the Qing Empire", *Journal of the Economic and Social History of the Orient*, 63:1, 2019.

95. John E. Herman, *Amid the Clouds and Mist: China's Colonization of Guizhou, 1200–1700*, Harvard University Press, 2007.

96. Glahn, "Chinese Coin".

97. Brook, *The Troubled Empire*, 121; Ho, "Sealords Live in Vain", 77.

98. John E. Wills, Jr. (ed.), *China and Maritime Europe, 1500–1800: Trade, Settlement, Diplomacy, and Missions*, Cambridge University Press, 2011, Editor's intro.

99. Victor Lieberman, *Strange Parallels: Southeast Asia in Global Context, c. 800–1830*. 2 vols., Cambridge University Press, 2003–2009.

100. James C. Scott, *The Art of Not Being Governed: An Anarchist History of Upland Southeast Asia*, Yale University Press, 2009.

101. Quoted in Wade, "Early Muslim Expansion in South-East Asia".

102. Ibid.; Hall, *A History of Early Southeast Asia*, ch. 8.

103. Hall, *A History of Early Southeast Asia*, ch. 9.

104. Anthony Reid, "An 'Age of Commerce' in Southeast Asian History", *Modern Asian Studies*, 24:1, 1990, 1–30.

105. Peter V. Lape, "Contact and Conflict in the Banda Islands, Eastern Indonesia 11th–17th Centuries", PhD thesis, Brown University, 2000, ch. 2.

106. Lape, "Contact and Conflict in the Banda Islands", 19.

107. Reid, "An 'Age of Commerce'"; David Bulbeck, Anthony Reid, Lay Cheng Tan, and Yigi Wu, *Southeast Asian Exports since the 14th Century: Cloves, Pepper, Coffee and Sugar*, Institute of Southeast Asian Studies, 1998, 62; Sebastian R. Prange, "'Measuring by the Bushel': Reweighing the Indian Ocean Pepper Trade", *Historical Research*, 84:224, 2011; Sen, "The Impact of Zheng He's Expeditions".

108. Sanjay Subrahmanyam, "The Birth-Pangs of Portuguese Asia: Revisiting the Fateful "Long Decade"1498–1509", *Journal of World History*, 2, 2007, 261–280; Prange, "'Measuring by the bushel.'"

109. Prange, "'Measuring by the Bushel.'"

110. Hall, *A History of Early Southeast Asia*, ch. 9.

111. Wade, "Early Muslim Expansion in South-East Asia"; Hall, "Ports-of-Trade".

112. Elizabeth Lambourn, "From Cambay to Samudera-Pasai and Gresik—the Export of Gujarati Grave Memorials to Sumatra and Java in the Fifteenth Century C.E.", *Indonesia and the Malay World*, 31:90, 2003, 221–284.

113. Hall, *A History of Early Southeast Asia*, ch. 9, and "Local and International Trade and Traders in the Straits of Melaka Region, 600–1500", *Journal of the Economic and Social History of the Orient*, 47:2, 2004; Donald B. Freeman, *The Straits of Malacca: Gateway or Gauntlet?* McGill-Queen's University Press, 2003, 84–85.

114. Craig A. Lockard, "'The Sea Common to All': Maritime Frontiers, Port Cities, and Chinese Traders in the Southeast Asian Age of Commerce, ca. 1400–1750", *Journal of World History*, 21:2, 2010, 219–247.

115. Reid, "An 'Age of Commerce.'"

116. Lowey-Ball, "Liquid Market, Solid State", 87.

117. Ibid., 208, 237.

118. Manguin, "Ships and Shipping in Southeast Asia".

119. Michael Pearson, "Islamic Trade, Shipping, Port-States and Merchant Communities in the Indian Ocean, Seventh to Sixteenth Centuries", in *The New Cambridge History of Islam*, Vol. 3.

120. Michael Pearson, "Creating a Littoral Community: Muslim Reformers in the Early Modern Indian Ocean World", in Charles H. Parker and Jerry H. Bentley (eds.), *Between the Middle Ages and Modernity: Individual and Community in the Early Modern World*, Rowman & Littlefield, 2007, 160.

121. Richard Eaton and Philip Wagoner, "Warfare on the Deccan Plateau, 1450–1600: A Military Revolution in Early Modern India?", *Journal of World History*, 25:1, 2014; Subrahmanyam, "The Birth-Pangs of Portuguese Asia".

122. Quoted in Lowey-Ball, "Liquid Market, Solid State", 257.

123. Margariti, "Mercantile Networks, Port Cities, and 'Pirate' States"; Prange, "A Trade of No Dishonor; Sheikh, *Forging a Region*, 88; Sinnappah Arasaratnam, *Maritime India in the Seventeenth Century*, Oxford University Press, 1994, 149.

124. Lowey-Ball, "Liquid Market, Solid State", 231–2. For Gujarat, see Sheikh, *Forging a Region*.

125. Adam Clulow, "European Maritime Violence and Territorial States in Early Modern Asia, 1600–1650", *Itinerario*, 33:3, 2009.

126. Malyn Newitt, *A History of Portuguese Overseas Expansion, 1400–1668*, Routledge, 2005, 82; Malekandathil, "Winds of Change".

127. Palmira Johnson Brummett, *Ottoman Seapower and Levantine Diplomacy in the Age of Discovery*, State University of New York Press, 1994, 171; Om Prakash, *The New Cambridge History of India: European Commercial Enterprise in Pre-Colonial India*, Cambridge University Press, 1998, 45.

128. Newitt, *A History of Portuguese Overseas Expansion*, 181.

129. Victor Enthoven, "Dutch Crossings. Migration between the Netherlands and the New World, 1600–1800", *Atlantic Studies*, 2:2, 2005.

130. Subrahmanyam, *Portuguese Empire in Asia*, 60.

131. Thomaz, "Iranian Diaspora in Maritime Asia".

132. Ho, "Sealords Live in Vain".

133. Lockard, "The Sea Common to All".

134. Luke Clossey, "Merchants, Migrants, Missionaries, and Globalization in the Early-Modern Pacific", *Journal of World History*, 1:1, 2006, 41–58.

135. Stephanie Mawson, "Rebellion and Mutiny in the Mariana Islands, 1680–1690", *Journal of Pacific History*, 50:2, 2015, 128–148; Ethan P. Hawkley, "Reviving the Reconquista in Southeast Asia: Moros and the Making of the Philippines, 1565–1662", *Journal of World History*, 25:2–3, 2014, 285–310.

136. Jonathan Gebhardt, "Microhistory and Microcosm: Chinese Migrants, Spanish Empire, and Globalization in Early Modern Manila", *Journal of Medieval and Early Modern Studies*, 47:1, 2017.

137. Lucille Chia, "The Butcher, the Baker, and the Carpenter: Chinese Sojourners in the Spanish Philippines and Their Impact on Southern Fujian (Sixteenth–Eighteenth Centuries)", *Journal of the Economic and Social History of the Orient*, 49:4, 2006, 509–534.

138. Chia, "The Butcher, the Baker, and the Carpenter".

139. John E. Wills, Jr., "Maritime Europe and the Ming", in Wills (ed.), *China and Maritime Europe*, 77.

140. Kwee Hui Kian, "The Expansion of Chinese Inter-Insular and Hinterland Trade in Southeast Asia, c. 1400–1850", in David Henley and Henk Schulte Nordholt (eds.), *Environment, Trade and Society in Southeast Asia*, Brill, 2015.

Chapter 10: Entwined Empires

1. Bruce M. S. Campbell, *The Great Transition. Climate, Disease, and Society in the Late-Medieval World*, Cambridge University Press, 2016, 275, agreeing with B. Z. Kedar, *Merchants in Crisis: Genoese and Venetian Men of Affairs and the Fourteenth-Century Depression*, Yale University Press, 1976.

2. Seth Parry, "'Fifty Years of failed plans'": Venice, Humanism, and the Turks (1453–1503)", PhD dissertation, City University of New York, 2008, 64.

3. Ian Blanchard, "Egyptian Specie Markets and the International Gold Crisis of the Early Fifteenth Century", in Lawrin Armstrong, Evana Elbl, and Martin M. Elbl (eds.), *Money, Markets and Trade in Late Medieval Europe: Essays in Honour of John H.A. Munro*, Brill, 2007.

4. Jeffrey D. Miner, "Lest We Break Faith with Our Creditors: Public Debt and Civic Culture in Fourteenth Century Genoa", PhD dissertation, Stanford University, 2011, 9.

5. Céline Dauverd, *Imperial Ambition in the Early Modern Mediterranean: Genoese Merchants and the Spanish Crown*, Cambridge University Press, 2015, 11. Also see Antonio Musarra, "Political Alliance and Conflict", in Carrie E. Benes (ed.), *A Companion to Medieval Genoa*, Brill, 2018.

6. Steven A. Epstein, *Genoa and the Genoese, 958–1528*, University of North Carolina Press, 1996, 325–327; Brian Nathaniel Becker, "Life and Local Administration on Fifteenth Century Genoese Chios", PhD dissertation, Western Michigan University, 2010.

7. Epstein, *Genoa and the Genoese*, 320.

8. Benjamin G. Kohl, *Padua under the Carrara, 1318–1405*, Johns Hopkins University Press, 1998, 219; John Dotson, "Venice, Genoa and Control of the Seas in the Thirteenth and Fourteen

Centuries", in John B. Hattendorf and Richard W. Unger (eds.), *War at Sea in the Middle Ages and Renaissance*, Boydell Press, 2003; David Abulafia, *The Great Sea: A Human History of the Mediterranean*, Oxford University Press, 2011, 377; Ruthy Gertwagen, "Venice's Policy Towards the Ionian and Aegean Islands, c. 1204–1423", *International Journal of Maritime History*, 2014, 26, 529–548; Thomas Kirk, "Mediterranean Rivalries", in Benes (ed.), *Companion to Medieval Genoa*.

9. Dauverd, *Imperial Ambition*, 2, 10; David Alonso Garcia, "Between Three Continents: The Fornari Networks and their Business at the Beginning of the First Global Age," in Rila Mukherjee (ed.), *Networks in the First Global Age, 1400–1800*, Primus Books, 2011; Thomas Kirk, "The Apogee of the Hispano-Genoese Bond, 1576–1627", *Hispania: Revista Espanola de Historia*, 65:1, 2005, 45–65.

10. Jeffrey Miner and Stefan Stantchev, "The Genoese Economy", in Benes (ed.), *Companion to Medieval Genoa*.

11. Peter Stabel et al., 'Production, Markets and Socio-economic Structures II: c.1320–c.1500', in Andrew Brown and Jan Dumolyn (eds.), *Medieval Bruges, c. 850–1550*, Cambridge University Press, 2018; Donald J. Harreld, *High Germans in the Low Countries: German Merchants and Commerce in Gold Age Antwerp*, Brill, 2004, 54.

12. Richard A. Goldthwaite, *The Economy of Renaissance Florence*, Johns Hopkins University Press, 2009, 128.

13. John Francis Guilmartin, "The Earliest Shipboard Gunpowder Ordnance: An Analysis of Its Technical Parameters and Tactical Capabilities", *Journal of Military History*, 71:3, 2007, 649–669; Susan Rose, *Medieval Naval Warfare, 1000–1500*, Routledge, 2002.

14. Tasha Vorderstrasse, "Trade and Textiles from Medieval Antioch", *Al-Masaq: Islam and the Medieval Mediterranean*, 22:2, 2010, 151–171, 168–169.

15. George Ramsay, "Thomas More, Joint Keeper of the Exchange: A Forgotten Episode in the History of Exchange Control in England", *Historical Research*, 84:226, 2011; Joseph L. Grossi, Jr., "Imaging Genoa in Late Medieval England", *Viator*, 25, 2004, 387–434; "Palavicino, Horatio", *New Dictionary of National Biography*, Oxford University Press, 2004.

16. Francesco Guidi-Bruscoli, "John Cabot and His Italian Financiers", *Historical Research*, 85.229, 2012.

17. Peter J. Perry, "L'arbre à pain: le châtaignier en Corse", *Annales du Midi*, 96:165, 1984, 71–84; George Bruce Malleson, *Studies from Genoese History*, Longman, Green and Co., 1875, 77–92.

18. O. J. Margolis, "Cipriano de' Mari's Lucianic Speech for Rene of Anjou (St-Die, MS 37): Humanism and Diplomacy in Genoa and Beyond", *Renaissance Studies*, 27:2, 2013, 219–235.

19. Leo Africanus, in Robert Brown (ed.), *The History and Description of Africa and of the Notable Things Therein Contained*, Ashgate, 2010, Vol. III, 769 (editor's note).

20. J. H. Galloway, *The Sugar Cane Industry: An Historical Geography from Its Origins to 1914*, Cambridge University Press, 1989, 45; Vincent J. Cornell, "Socio-economic Dimensions of Reconquista and Jihad in Morocco: Portuguese Dukkala and the Said Sus, 1450–1557", *International Journal of Middle East Studies*, 22, 1990, 379–418.

21. Louis Mitler, "The Genoese in Galata: 1453–1682," *International Journal of Middle East Studies*, 10:1, 1979, 71–91; Geo Pistarino, "The Genoese in Pera–Turkish Galata, *Mediterranean Historical Review*, 1:1, 1986, 63–85; G. V. Scammell, *The world Encompassed: The First European*

Maritime Empires c.800–1650, Methuen, 1981, 185; Robert Bideleux and Ian Jeffries, *A History of Eastern Europe: Crisis and Change*, 2nd edn, Routledge, 2007, 63.

22. Christopher Wright, "Florentine Alum Mining in the Hospitaller Islands: The Appalto of 1442", *Journal of Medieval History*, 36, 2010, 175–191; Kate Fleet, *European and Islamic Trade in the Early Ottoman State. The Merchants of Genoa and Turkey*, Cambridge University Press, 1999, Ch. 7.

23. Mike Carr, "Trade or Crusade? The Zaccaria of Chios and Crusades against the Turks", in Mike Carr et al (eds.), *Crusades—Subsidia: Contact and Conflict in Frankish Greece and the Aegean, 1204–1453*, Ashgate, 2014; Michael Balard, "The Genoese in the Aegean (1204–1566)", *Mediterranean Historical Review*, 4:1, 1989, 158–174.

24. Becker, "Life and Local Administration on Fifteenth Century Genoese Chios".

25. Paul Freedman, "Mastic: A Mediterranean Luxury Product", *Mediterranean Historical Review*, 26:1, 2011, 99–113.

26. Lorenzo Pubblici, "Some Remarks on the Slave Trade in the Heart of the Golden Horde (14th century) in the Wake of C. Verlinden's Research", *Zolotoordynskoe Obozrenie*, 5:3, 2017, 566–576.

27. Charles King, *The Black Sea. A History*, Oxford University Press, 2004, 84. Also see E. Slater, "Caffa. Early Western Expansion in the Late Medieval World, 1261–1475", *Review, Fernand Braudel Center*, 29:3, 2006, 271–283; Evgeny Khvalkov, "A Regionalisation or Long-Distance Trade? Transformations and Shifts in the Role of Tana in the Black Sea Trade in the First Half of the Fifteenth Century", *European Review of History: Revue européenne d'histoire*, 23:3, 2016, 508–525; Peter Jackson, *The Mongols and the West, 1221–1410*, Pearson Longman, 2005, 307.

28. Marie Favereau, "The Golden Horde and the Mamluks", *Golden Horde Review*, 5:1, 2017.

29. Zsigmond Pál Pach, "Hungary and the Levantine Trade in the 14th–17th Centuries", *Acta Orientalia Academiae Scientiarum Hungaricae*, 60:1, 2007, 9–31.

30. "Anonimo genovese", "Account of Genoa c. 1300", reproduced in Trevor Dean (ed.), *The Towns of Italy in the Later Middle Ages*, Manchester University Press, 2000.

31. Marian Małowist, *Western Europe, Eastern Europe and World Development 13th–18th Centuries: Essays of Marian Małowist*, J. Batou and H. Szlajfer (eds.), Brill, 2009, ch. 4; Michel Balard, "The Greeks of Crimea under Genoese Rule in the XIVth and XVth Centuries", *Dumbarton Oaks Papers*, 49, 1995, 23–32; Hannah Barker, *That Most Precious Merchandise: The Mediterranean Trade in Black Sea Slaves, 1260–1500*, University of Pennsylvania Press, 2019, ch. 6; J.R.S. Phillips, *The Medieval Expansion of Europe*, Oxford University Press, 2011 (orig. 1998), ch. 6; Rossica Panova, "The Black Sea Coastal Cities in the Economic and Political Interrelations among Medieval Bulgaria, Venice and Genoa", *Etudes Balkaniques*, 1–2, 1999, 52–58.

32. Christopher Wright, *Gattilusio Lordships and the Aegean World, 1355–1462*, Brill, 2014.

33. Michel Balard, "Latins in the Aegean and the Balkans in the Fourteenth Century", in Michael Jones (ed.), *The New Cambridge Medieval History, Vol. 6, c.1300–c.1415*, Cambridge University Press, 2000, 825–838; Carr, "Trade or Crusade?"

34. Kate Fleet, "The Rise of the Ottomans", in Maribel Fierro (ed.), *The New Cambridge History of Islam Vol. 2*, Cambridge University Press, 2010; Cristian Caselli, "Genoa, Genoese Merchants and the Ottoman Empire in the First Half of the Fifteenth Century: Rumours and Reality", *Al-Masaq: Journal of the Medieval Mediterranean*, 25:2, 2013, 252–263.

35. Kate Fleet, "The Treaty of 1387 between Murād I and the Genoese", *Bulletin of the School of Oriental and African Studies*, 56:1, 1993.

36. Simon Alexandru, "Lasting Falls and Wishful Recoveries: Crusading in the Black Sea Region after the Fall of Constantinople", *Imago TemporIs. medIum aevum*, 6, 2012, 299–313.

37. Stefan Stantchev, "Devedo: The Venetian Response to the Sultan Mehmed II in the Venetian-Ottoman Conflict of 1462–79", *Mediterranean Studies*, 19, 2010, 43–66 .

38. Jamie Adelia Smith, "Navigating Absence: Law and the Family in Genoa, 1380—1420, PhD thesis, University of Toronto, 2007, 60; John Law, "The Italian North", in Jones (ed.), *The New Cambridge Medieval History, Vol. 6*, 461–462.

39. Jessica L. Goldberg, "Choosing and Enforcing Business Relationships in the Eleventh-Century Mediterranean: Reassessing the 'Maghribī Traders'", *Past & Present*, 216, 2012, 3–40.

40. Wright, *Gattilusio Lordships*, 242.

41. Epstein, *Genoa and the Genoese*, 287; Abulafia, *The Great Sea*, 396; Maria Fusaro, *Political Economies of Empire in the Early Modern Mediterranean: The Decline of Venice and the Rise of England, 1450–1700*, Cambridge University Press, 2015, 30–31.

42. John Bryan Williams, "From the Commercial Revolution to the Slave Revolution: The Development of Slavery in Medieval Genoa", PhD thesis, University of Chicago, 1995, 157.

43. Paul F. Grendler, *Schooling in Renaissance Italy: Literacy and Learning 1300–1600*, Johns Hopkins University Press, 1989, 10–11.

44. Mitler, "The Genoese in Galata"; Pistarino, "The Genoese in Pera".

45. Edwin S. Hunt and James M. Murray, *A History of Business in Medieval Europe, 1200–1550*, Cambridge University Press, 1999, 181; Pubblici, "Some Remarks on the Slave Trade".

46. Miner, "Lest We Break Faith", 1.

47. Stantchev, "The Venetian Response"; Charles Verlinden, "Medieval 'Slavers'", *Explorations in Economic History*, 7:1, 1969, 1–14.

48. Quentin Van Doosselaere, *Commercial Agreements and Social Dynamics in Medieval Genoa*, Cambridge University Press, 2009, 89.

49. Susan Mosher Stuard, *Gilding the Market. Luxury and Fashion in Fourteenth-Century Italy*, University of Pennsylvania Press, 2006, 5; Epstein, *Genoa and the Genoese*, xiii; Maureen Fennell Mazzaoui, "The Cotton Industry of Northern Italy in the Late Middle Ages: 1150–1450", *Journal of Economic History*, 32:1, 1972, 262–286.

50. Scammell, *The World Encompassed*, 166. Also see Robert S. Lopez, "The Trade of Medieval Europe: The South," in M. M. Postan, Edward Miller, and Cynthia Postan (eds.), *The Cambridge Economic History of Europe, Vol. 2*, Cambridge University Press, 1987; Caselli, "Genoa, Genoese Merchants and the Ottoman Empire".

51. Luciano Pezzolo, "The *via italiana* to Capitalism", in Larry Neal and Jeffrey G. Williamson (eds.), *The Cambridge History of Capitalism. Vol. 1, The Rise of Capitalism: From Ancient Origins to 1848*, Cambridge University Press, 2014.

52. Smith, "Navigating Absence", 192, n.9; Epstein, *Genoa and the Genoese*, 213, 52, 320 ; E. P. Wardi , "Rank and File Participation in Politics in Late-Medieval Genoa: The Commune's Submission to the French in 1396", *Journal of Medieval History*, 28, 2002, 373–399; Thomas Kirk, "A Little Country in a World of Empires: Genoese Attempts to Penetrate the Maritime Trading Empires of the Seventeenth Century", *Journal of European Economic History*, 25:2, 1996, 407–421; Guido Alfani, "Plague in Seventeenth-century Europe and the Decline of Italy: An Epidemiological Hypothesis", *European Review of Economic History*, 17, 2013, 408–430.

53. Miner, "Lest we break faith", 106.

54. Balard, "The Genoese in the Aegean"; Becker, "Life and Local Administration", ch. 3.

55. Becker, "Life and Local Administration", 330--331; Susan Mosher Stuard, "Dowry Increase and Increment in Wealth in Medieval Ragusa (Dubrovnik)", *Journal of Economic History*, 41:4, 1981, 795–811; Denise Bezzina, "Social Landscapes", in Benes (ed.), *Companion to Medieval Genoa*.

56. Scammell, *The World Encompassed*, 187; Williams, "From the Commercial Revolution to the Slave Revolution", 95.

57. Scammell, *The World Encompassed*, 197–198; William Caferro, "Petrarch's War: Florentine Wages and the Black Death", *Speculum*, 88:1, 2013, 144–165.

58. Laura Balletto, "Ethnic Groups, Cross-Social and Cross-Cultural Contacts on Fifteenth-Century Cyprus", *Mediterranean Historical Review*, 10:1–2, 1995, 35–48; Luca Codignola and M. Elisabetta Tonizzi, "The Swiss Community in Genoa from the Old Regime to the Late Nineteenth Century", *Journal of Modern Italian Studies*, 13:2, 2008, 152–170; Panova, "The Black Sea Coastal Cities"; Georges Jehel, "Jews and Muslims in Medieval Genoa: From the Twelfth to the Fourteenth Century", *Mediterranean Historical Review*, 10:1–2, 1995, 120–132, 120–121.

59. Luciano Pezzolo, "The Venetian Government Debt 1350–1650", in Marc Boone, C. A. Davids, and Paul Janssens (eds.), *Urban Public Debts: Urban Governments and the Market for Annuities in Western Europe (14th–18th Centuries)*, Brepols, 2003.

60. Miner, "Lest we break faith", 7, 25, 6.

61. Smith, "Navigating Absence", 52–56.

62. Musarra, "Political Alliance and Conflict".

63. Wardi, "Rank and File Participation".

64. Christine Shaw, "Counsel and Consent in Fifteenth-Century Genoa", *English Historical Review*, 116:468, 2001, 834–862.

65. Carrie E. Beneš, "Civic Identity", in Benes (ed.), *Companion to Medieval Genoa*.

66. Malleson, *Studies from Genoese History*, ch. 7.

67. Kirk, "Mediterranean Rivalries".

68. Van Doosselaere, *Commercial Agreements and Social Dynamics*, 121.

69. Wardi, "Rank and File Participation".

70. Dauverd, *Imperial Ambition*, 37, 42 n.80.

71. Thomas Allison Kirk, *Genoa and the Sea: Policy and Power in an Early Modern Maritime Republic, 1559–1684*, Johns Hopkins University Press, 2005, 30.

72. Pezzolo, "The Venetian Government Debt".

73. Michele Fratianni and Franco Spinelli, "Italian City-States and Financial Evolution", *European Review of Economic History*, 10:3, 2006, 257–278.

74. W. Behringer, "Communications Revolutions: A Historiographical Concept", *German History*, 24.3, 2006, 333–374.

75. Jong Kuk Nam, "The *scarsella* between the Mediterranean and the Atlantic in the 1400s", *Mediterranean Review*, 9:1, 2016, 53–75.

76. Claudio Marsilio, "The Genoese Exchange Fairs and the Bank of Amsterdam: Comparing Two Financial Institutions of the 17th Century", 1958, https://www.aehe.es/wp-content/uploads/2008/09/the-genoese-exchange.pdf

77. Fratianni and Spinelli, "Italian City-States and Financial Evolution".

78. Oscar Gelderblom, *Cities of Commerce: The Institutional Foundations of International Trade in the Low Countries, 1250–1650*, Princeton University Press, 2013, 191.

79. Van Doosselaere, *Commercial Agreements and Social Dynamics*, 186–187.

80. Gelderblom, *Cities of Commerce*, 191–194; Christopher Kingston, "Governance and Institutional Change in Marine Insurance, 1350–1850", *European Review of Economic History*, 18, 2013, 1–18.

81. Christopher Ebert, "Early Modern Atlantic Trade and the Development of Maritime Insurance to 1630", *Past & Present*, 213, 2011.

82. Annne Goldgar, *Tulipmania. Money, Honor and Knowledge in the Dutch Golden Age*, University of Chicago Press, 2007, 223.

83. Chiara Frugoni, *Inventions of the Middle Ages*, trans. William McCuaig, Folio Society, 2007 (orig. 2001), 74; E. Michael Gerli (ed.), *Medieval Iberia: An Encyclopedia*, Taylor & Francis, 2013, 353.

84. Evelyn Welch, "Lotteries in Early Modern Italy", *Past & Present*, 199, 2008, 71–111.

85. Van Doosselaere, *Commercial Agreements and Social Dynamics*, 182–183, 191.

86. Gerald Harriss, *Shaping the Nation. England, 1360–1461*, Clarendon Press, 2005, 360.

87. Celine Dauverd, "Mediterranean Symbiotic Empire: The Genoese Trade Diaspora of Spanish Naples, 1460–1640", PhD dissertation, University of California, 2007, 263; Graeme Small, *Late Medieval France*, Palgrave Macmillan, 2009, 183. Also see Judith Potter, "Social Networks in Late Medieval Lubeck", PhD dissertation, New York University, 2001.

88. Smith, "Navigating Absence".

89. Bezzina, "Social Landscapes".

90. Garcia, "Between Three Continents: The Fornari Networks".

91. Kirk, *Genoa and the Sea*, 25.

92. Stephen Wilson, *The Means of Naming: A Social and Cultural History of Personal Naming in Western Europe*, UCL Press, 1998, 168–169.

93. Ibid.; Guido Alfani, *Fathers and Godfathers: Spiritual Kinship in Early-Modern Italy*, Ashgate, 2009, ch. 1–2; Miner, "Lest we break faith".

94. Becker, "Life and Local Administration", esp. ch. 4; William Miller, "The Genoese in Chios, 1346–1566", *English Historical Review*, 30:119, 1915, 418–432.

95. Van Doosselaere, *Commercial Agreements and Social Dynamics*; Kirk, *Genoa and the Sea*; Avner Greif, *Institutions and the Path to the Modern Economy: Lessons from Medieval Trade*, Cambridge University Press, 2006; Joanne M. Ferraro, "Family and Clan in the Renaissance World", in Guido Ruggiero (ed.), *A Companion to the Worlds of the Renaissance*, Blackwell, 2002, 173–187.

96. Wilson, *The Means of Naming*, 169.

97. Pezzolo, "The *via italiana* to Capitalism".

98. Musarra, "Political Alliance and Conflict".

99. Pezzolo "The *via italiana* to Capitalism".

100. Mark Haberlin, *The Fuggers of Augsburg. Pursuing Wealth and Honor in Renaissance Germany*, University of Virginia Press, 2012, e.g., 44, 55, 62–64, 146.

101. Darlene Abreu-Ferreira, "The Cod Trade in Early-Modern Portugal: Deregulation, English Domination, and the Decline of Female Cod Merchants", PhD thesis, Memorial University of Newfoundland, 1995; Carla Rahn Phillips, "The Caravel and the Galleon", in Robert Gardiner and Richard W. Unger (eds.), *Cogs, Caravels and Galleons: The Sailing Ship 1000–1650*, Conway Maritime Press, 1994, 2000, 91–114.

102. E.g., Felipe Fernandez-Armesto, "Portuguese Expansion in a Global Context", in Francisco Bethencourt and Diogo Ramada Curto (eds.), *Portuguese Oceanic Expansion, 1400–1800*, Cambridge University Press, 2007.

103. Miranda Flávio, "Before the Empire: Portugal and the Atlantic Trade in the late Middle Ages", *Journal of Medieval Iberian Studies*, 5:1, 2013, 69–85.

104. Filipe Themudo Barata, "Portugal and the Mediterranean trade: A Prelude to the Discovery of the 'New World'", *Al-Masaq: Islam and the Medieval Mediterranean*, 17:2, 2005, 205–219.

105. A. R. Disney, *A History of Portugal and the Portuguese Empire: From Beginnings to 1807. Volume I: Portugal*, Cambridge University Press, 2009, 101.

106. Miranda, "Before the Empire".

107. Andrew Hess, *The Forgotten Frontier; A History of the Sixteenth-Century Ibero-African Frontier*, University of Chicago Press, 1978, 29; John L. Vogt, "Crusading and Commercial Elements in the Portuguese Capture of Ceuta", *Muslim World*, 59:3–4, 1969, 287–299.

108. Cornell, "Socio-economic Dimensions of Reconquista".

109. Catherine Kovesi Killerby, *Sumptuary Law in Italy 1200–1500*, Oxford University Press, 2002, ch. 3. Also see Ian Blanchard, *Mining, Metallurgy and Minting in the Middle Ages. Vol II, Afro-European Supremacy, 1125–1225*, Steiner, 2001, 747.

110. John Vogt, "Notes on the Portuguese Cloth Trade in West Africa, 1480–1540", *International Journal of African Historical Studies*, 8.4 (1975), 623–651; Earnest W. Porta, "Morocco in the Early Atlantic World, 1415–1603", PhD dissertation, Georgetown University, 2018, 201.

111. Cornell, "Socio-economic Dimensions of Reconquista".

112. Porta, "Morocco in the Early Atlantic World", 64.

113. Porta, "Morocco in the Early Atlantic World", 159.

114. Cornell, "Socio-economic Dimensions of Reconquista".

115. Malyn Newitt, *A History of Portuguese Overseas Expansion, 1400–1668*, Routledge, 2005, 7.

116. Andreas Massing, "Mapping the Malagueta Coast: A History of the Lower Guinea Coast, 1460–1510 through Portuguese Maps and Accounts", *History in Africa*, 36, 2009, 331–365.

117. Newitt, *Portuguese Overseas Expansion*, 37–38.

118. Toby Green, *The Rise of the Trans-Atlantic Slave Trade in Western Africa, 1300–1589*, Cambridge University Press, 2012, 98–99.

119. Trevor Paul Hall, "The Role of Cape Verde Islanders in organizing and Operating Maritime Trade Between West Africa and Iberian Territories, 1441–1616", PhD dissertation, Johns Hopkins University, 1993, 470–88; Massing, "Mapping the Malagueta Coast".

120. Hall, "The Role of Cape Verde Islanders", 495.

121. Robin Blackburn, *The Making of New World Slavery. From the Baroque to the Modern, 1492–1800*, Verso, 2010 (orig. 1997), 108; Jason w. Moore, "Madeira, Sugar, and the Conquest of Nature, in the 'First' Sixteenth Century; Part One: From 'Island of Timber' to Sugar Revolution, 1420–1506", *Review–Fernand Braudel Center*, 32:4, 2009, 345–390.

122. A. R. Disney, *A History of Portugal and the Portuguese Empire: From Beginnings to 1807. Volume II: The Portuguese Empire*, Cambridge University Press, 2009, 110 -112; Van Doosselaere, *Commercial Agreements and Social*, 174n; Leonor Freire Costa, Pedro Lains, and Susana Munch Miranda, *An Economic History of Portugal, 1143–2010*, Cambridge University Press, 2016, 68.

123. Moore, "Madeira, Sugar, and the Conquest of Nature".

124. Hall, "The Role of Cape Verde Islanders", 469.

125. Massing, "Mapping the Malagueta Coast".

126. Henry Kamen, *Empire. How Spain Became a World Power, 1492–1763*, Harper Collins, 2003 (orig. 2002), 200.

127. Ernst van Veen, *Decay or Defeat? An Inquiry into the Portuguese Decline in Asia 1580–1645*, Leiden University Press, 2000.

128. Antonio Henriques, "Plenty of Land, Land of Plenty: The Agrarian Output of Portugal (1311–20)", *European Review of Economic History*, 19, 2015, 149–170.

129. Barata, "Portugal and the Mediterranean Trade"; Miranda, "Before the Empire".

130. António Henriques, "The Rise of a Tax State: Portugal, 1371–1401", *e-Journal of Portuguese History*, 12:1, 2014; Costa et al., *An Economic History of Portugal*, 41.

131. Catia Antunes, "The Commercial Relationship between Amsterdam and the Portuguese Salt-Exporting Ports: Aveiro and Setubal, 1580–1715", *Journal of Early Modern History*, 12:1, 2008, 25–53.

132. Sanjay Subrahmanyam, *Portuguese Empire in Asia, 1500–1700*, Wiley, 2012, 42; Daviken Studnicki-Gizbert, *A Nation upon the Ocean Sea: Portugal's Atlantic Diaspora and the Crisis of the Spanish Empire, 1492–1640*, Oxford University Press, 2007, 20.

133. Costa et al., *An Economic History of Portugal*, 67.

134. Simon J. M. Davis, "Zooarchaeological Evidence for Moslem and Christian Improvements of Sheep and Cattle in Portugal", *Journal of Archaeological Science*, 35, 2008, 991–1010.

135. Costa et al., *An Economic History of Portugal*, 66, 70–71.

136. Miguel Bandeira Jerónimo, "Portuguese Colonialism in Africa", *Oxford Research Encyclopedia of African History*, Oxford University Press, 2018.

137. João Gouveia Monteiro, Miguel Gomes Martins, and Tiago Viúla de Faria, "Another 1415: Portugal's Military Landscape at the Time of Agincourt", *Journal of Medieval History*, 43:1, 2017, 118–135; Disney, *A History of Portugal Vol. I*, 40.

138. Saturnino Monteiro, *Portuguese Sea Battles 1139–1975*, Vol. I, 2010, Oeiras, 100.

139. Porta, "Morocco in the Early Atlantic World", 150–151.

140. António dos Santos Pereira, "The Urgent Empire Portugal Between 1475 and 1525", *e-Journal of Portuguese History*, 4:2, 2006.

141. Palmira Johnson Brummett, *Ottoman Seapower and Levantine Diplomacy in the Age of Discovery*, State University of New York Press, 1994, 173, quoting John Guilmartin.

142. John Vogt, "Saint Barbara's Legion: Portuguese Artillery in the Struggle for Morocco, 1415–1578", *Military Affairs*, 41:4, 1977, 176–182.

143. Channa Wickremesekera, *Kandy at War: Indigenous Military Resistance to European Expansion in Sri Lanka 1594–1818*, Manohar, 2004.

144. Pius Malekandathil, "Indian Ocean in the Shaping of Late Medieval India", *Studies in History*, 30:2, 2014.

145. Toby Green, *A Fistful of Shells: West Africa from the Rise of the Slave Trade to the Age of Revolution*, Allen Lane, 2019, ch. 3.

146. Thomas D. Boston, "Sixteenth-Century European Expansion and the Economic Decline of Africa", *Review of Black Political Economy*, 20:4, 1992, 5–38.

147. Christopher Ebert, *Between Empires. Brazilian Sugar in the Early Atlantic Economy 1550–1630*, Brill, 2008, 170–171 and "Early Modern Atlantic Trade".

148. Mark Greengrass, *Christendom Destroyed. Europe 1517–1648*, Allen Lane, 2014, 282.

149. Louis Sicking, *Neptune and the Netherlands: State, Economy, and War at Sea in the Renaissance*, Brill, 2004, ch. 4.

150. Hess, *The Forgotten Frontier*; Barbara Fuchs and Yuen-Gen Liang (eds.), "A Forgotten Empire; The Spanish-North African Borderlands", *Journal of Spanish Cultural Studies Special Issue*, 12:3, 2011; Abdallah Laroui, *The History of the Maghrib: An Interpretive Essay*, Princeton University Press, 1977; Amira Bennison, "Liminal States: Morocco and the Iberian Frontier between the Twelfth and Nineteenth Centuries", *Journal of North African Studies*, 6:1, 2001, 11–28.

151. Greengrass, *Christendom Destroyed*, 13.

152. S. P. Karpov, "The Grain Trade in the Southern Black Sea Region: The Thirteenth to the Fifteenth Century", *Mediterranean Historical Review*, 8:1, 1993, 55–73.

153. Adela Fábregas García, "Other Markets: Complementary Commercial Zones in the Naṣrid World of the Western Mediterranean (Seventh/Thirteenth to Ninth/ Fifteenth Centuries)", *Al-Masaq: Islam and the Medieval Mediterranean*, 25:1, 2013, 135–153; Rowena Hernández-Múzquiz, "Economy and Society in Medieval and Early Modern Seville (1391–1506): A Study of the *Abastecimiento* [provisioning] of an Iberian Urban Center", PhD dissertation, Columbia University, 2005, 135.

154. García, "Other Markets".

155. John Edwards, "'Development' and 'underdevelopment' in the Western Mediterranean: The Case of Córdoba and Its Region in the Late Fifteenth and Early Sixteenth Centuries", *Mediterranean Historical Review*, 2:1, 1987, 3–45; "Valencia", in Gerli (ed.), *Medieval Iberia: An Encyclopedia*.

156. Edwards, "'Development' and 'underdevelopment'".

157. Alberto García Porras, and Adela Fábregas García, "Genoese Trade Networks in the Southern Iberian Peninsula: Trade, Transmission of Technical Knowledge and Economic Interactions", *Mediterranean Historical Review*, 25:1, 2010, 35–51; García, "Other Markets".

158. Kamen, *Empire*, 40; Ruth Pike, *Enterprise and Adventure. The Genoese in Seville and the Opening of the New World*, Cornell University Press, 1966, 1–2.

159. Pike, *Enterprise and Adventure*, 77.

160. Vicent Baydal, "Political Power in the Kingdom of Valencia during the 14th Century. Breakdown or Development?", *Catalan Historical Review*, 10, 2017, 27–41.

161. Antoni Riera, "Crises and Changes in the Late Middle Ages", in Flocel Sabaté (ed.), *The Crown of Aragon: A Singular Mediterranean Empire*, Brill, 2017; David Igual Luis, "Great and Small Trade in the Crown of Aragon. The Example of Valencia in the Late Middle Ages", *Imago Temporis. Medium Aevum*, 3, 2009, 231–248.

162. Michael North, *The Expansion of Europe, 1250–1500*, Manchester University Press, 2012 (German original 2007), n.94; Carmel Ferragud and Juan Vicente Garcia Marsilla, "The Great Fire of Medieval Valencia (1447), *Urban History*, 43:4, 2016.

163. Porras and García, "Genoese Trade Networks".

164. García, "Other Markets"; Stephan R. Epstein, *An Island for Itself: Economic Development and Social Change in Late Medieval Sicily*, Cambridge University Press, 1992.

165. Dauverd, "Mediterranean Symbiotic Empire", 60, 91.

166. Luca Molà, *Silk Industry of Renaissance Venice*, Johns Hopkins University Press, 2000, 16–18.

167. Kirk, "The Apogee of the Hispano-Genoese Bond" and *Genoa and the Sea*, 85.

168. Carla Rahn Phillips and William D. Phillips Jr., *Spain's Golden Fleece. Wool Production and the Wool Trade from the Middle Ages to the Nineteenth Century*, Johns Hopkins University Press, 1997, 256.

169. Pike, *Enterprise and Adventure*, 144, 8.

170. Miguel Ángel Ladero Quesada, "The Military Resources of the Kings of Castile around 1500", in P.C.M. Hoppenbrouwers, Antheun Janse, and Robert Stein (eds.), *Power and Persuasion. Essays on the Art of State Building in Honour of W.P. Blockmans*, Brepols, 2010; Studnicki-Gizbert, *A Nation upon the Ocean Sea*, 27.

171. Dauverd, *Imperial Ambition*, 15–16, and "Mediterranean Symbiotic Empire", 76. Also see Mark A. Aloisio, "Economy, Society, and Institutions in Late Medieval Sicily: Sciacca and Its Hinterland in the Fifteenth Century", PhD thesis, University of Minnesota, 2008.

172. Dauverd, "Mediterranean Symbiotic Empire, 136–137.

173. Aurelio Espinosa, "The Grand Strategy of Charles V (1500–1558): Castile, War, and Dynastic Priority in the Mediterranean", *Journal of Early Modern History*, 9:3, 2005, 239–283; Touati, "The Ottoman Maghrib"; Porta, "Morocco in the Early Atlantic World"; Hess, *The Forgotten Frontier*.

174. Kirk, *Genoa and the Sea*, 76.

175. Geoffrey Parker, *Emperor. A New Life of Charles V*, Yale University Press, 2019, Locs. 3782–3783.

176. Kamen, *Empire*, 13.

177. Pike, *Enterprise and Adventure*, 159.

178. Goldthwaite, *The Economy of Renaissance Florence*, 160.

179. Kamen, *Empire*, 69.

180. Boston, "Sixteenth-century European Expansion".

181. William D. Phillips, "Slavery in the Atlantic Islands and the Early Modern Spanish Atlantic World", in David Eltis and Stanley L. Engerman (eds.), *The Cambridge World History of Slavery, Vol. 3: AD 1420–AD 1804*, Cambridge University Press, 2011; Pike, *Enterprise and Adventure*.

182. John R. Fisher, *The Economic Aspects of Spanish Imperialism in America, 1492–1810*, Liverpool University Press, 1997, 27.

183. John TePaske, *A New World of Gold And Silver*, Kendall W. Brown (ed.), Brill, 2010, 27–32.

184. Harry E. Cross, "South American Bullion and Export, 1550–1750", in John Richards (ed.), *Precious Metals in the Later Medieval and Early Modern Worlds*, Carolina Academic Press, 1983; Caroline A. Williams, "Resistance and Rebellion on the Spanish Frontier: Native Responses to Colonization in the Colombian Chocó, 1670–1690", *Hispanic American Historical Review*, 79.3, 1999, 397–424.

185. Mary Van Buren and Ana Maria Presta, "The Organization of Inka Silver Production in Porco, Bolivia" in Michael A. Malpass and Sonia Alconini (eds.), *Distant Provinces in the Inka Empire: Toward a Deeper Understanding of Inka Imperialism*, University of Iowa Press, 2010.

186. Stanley J. Stein and Barbara H. Stein, *Silver, Trade, and War: Spain and America in the Making of Early Modern Europe*, Johns Hopkins University Press, 2000, 21.

187. Kris Lane, "Potosí Mines", in *Oxford Research Encyclopedia of Latin American History*.

188. Henry Kamen, *Empire*, 286.

189. Susan D. deFrance, "Diet and Provisioning in the High Andes: A Spanish Colonial Settlement on the Outskirts of Potosí, Bolivia", *International Journal of Historical Archaeology*, 7:2, 2003, 99–125.

190. Stein and Stein, *Silver, Trade, and War*, 46.

191. Fratianni and Spinelli, "Italian City-States and Financial Evolution", 274.

192. Stein and Stein, *Silver, Trade, and War*, 43.

193. Haberlin, *The Fuggers of Augsburg*, 76.

194. Mauricio Drelichman and Hans-Joachim Voth, "Lending to the Borrower from Hell: Debt and Default in the Age of Philip II", *Economic Journal*, 121:557, 2011, 1205–1227.

195. Carlos Álvarez-Nogal and Christophe Chamley, "Debt Policy under Constraints between Philip II, the Cortes and Genoese Bankers", *Working Papers in Economic History*, 11–06, 2011.

196. Luciano Pezzolo and Giuseppe Tattara, "'Una fiera senza luogo': Was Bisenzone an International Capital Market in Sixteenth-Century Italy?" *Journal of Economic History*, 68:4, 2008.

197. Stein and Stein, *Silver, Trade, and War*, 42.

198. Kirk, "The Apogee of the Hispano-Genoese Bond".

199. Mauricio Drelichman, "The Curse of Moctezuma: American Silver and the Dutch Disease", *Explorations in Economic History*, 42:3, 2005, 349–380.

200. Jean W. Sedlar, *History of East Central Europe, Vol. 3: East Central Europe in the Middle Ages, 1000–1500*, Washington University Press, 2011, 348.

201. Claudio Veliz, *The New World of the Gothic Fox. Culture and Economy in English and Spanish America*, University of California Press, 1994, 206.

Chapter 11: The Ottomans and the Great Diversion

1. John Stoye, *The Siege of Vienna*, Collins, 1964, 139.

2. Justin McCarthy, *The Ottoman Turks. An Introductory History*, Longman, 1997, 199.

3. Nükhet Varlık, *Plague and Empire in the Early Modern Mediterranean World: The Ottoman Experience, 1347–1600*, Cambridge University Press, 2015, 122.

4. Ibid., 127.

5. Rhoads Murphey, *Ottoman Warfare, 1500–1700*, Rutgers University Press, 1999, 171; Rudi Paul Lindner, "Anatolia, 1300–1451", in Kate Fleet (ed.), *The Cambridge History of Turkey, Vol. 1*, Cambridge University Press, 2009; Caroline Finkel, *Osman's Dream. The Story of the Ottoman Empire*, 1300–1923, John Murray, 2005, 13–19.

6. John Fine, *The Late Medieval Balkans: A Critical Survey from the Late 12th Century to the Ottoman Conquest*, University of Michigan Press, 1987.

7. Nikolay Antov, "Imperial Expansion, Colonization, And Conversion to Islam in the Islamic World's "Wild West": The Formation of the Muslim Community in Ottoman Deliorman (N.E. Balkans), 15th–16th cc", PhD dissertation, University of Chicago, 2011, ch. 3; Jan Dumolyn and Hilmi Kaçar, "The Battle of Nicopolis (1396), Burgundian Catastrophe and Ottoman Fait Divers", *Revue belge de Philologie et d'Histoire*, 91:4, 2013, 905–934.

8. Gabor Agoston, "Military Transformation in the Ottoman Empire and Russia, 1500–1800", *Kritika: Explorations in Russian and Eurasian History*, 12:2, 2011, 281–319; Kate Fleet, "Tax

Farming in the Early Ottoman State", *Medieval History Journal*, 6:2 2003; Jonathan Grant, "Rethinking the Ottoman 'Decline': Military Technology Diffusion in the Ottoman Empire, Fifteenth to Eighteenth Centuries", *Journal of World History*, 10:1, 1999, 179–201.

9. Stephen Frederic Dale, *The Muslim Empires of the Ottomans, Safavids, and Mughals*, Cambridge University Press, 2010, 60.

10. I. Metin Kunt, "The Rise of the Ottomans", in Michael Jones (ed.), *The New Cambridge Medieval History, Volume VI, c.1300–c.1415*, Cambridge University Press, 2000, 846.

11. Heath W. Lowry, *The Nature of the Early Ottoman State*, State University of New York Press, 2003, 65.

12. Mesut Uyar and Edward J. Erickson, *A Military History of the Ottomans. From Osman to Ataturk*, Praeger, 2009, 24–29.

13. Finkel, *Osman's Dream*, 41.

14. Uyar and Erickson, *A Military History of the Ottomans*, ch. 2.

15. Agoston, "Military Transformation".

16. Mark Stein, "Military Service and Material Gain on the Ottoman-Hapsburg Frontier", in A.C.S. Peacock (ed.), *The Frontiers of the Ottoman World*, Oxford University Press, 2009; Rossitsa Gradeva, "Between the Hinterland and the Frontier: Ottoman Vidin, 15th to 18th Centuries", in Peacock (ed.), *The Frontiers of the Ottoman World*.

17. Sam White, "Ecology, Climate, and Crisis in the Ottoman Near East", PhD dissertation, Columbia University, 2008, 84.

18. Jane Hathaway, *Arab Lands under Ottoman rule, 1516–1800*, Pearson Longman, 2008, 51.

19. Murphey, *Ottoman Warfare*, 10, 32–33, 42.

20. Quoted in Grant, "Rethinking the Ottoman 'Decline'". Also see Palmira Johnson Brummett, *Ottoman Seapower and Levantine Diplomacy in the Age of Discovery*, State University of New York Press, 1994, ch. 4; Jan Glete, *Warfare at Sea, 1500–1650: Maritime Conflicts and the Transformation of Europe*, Routledge, 2000, ch. 6.

21. Tuncay Zorlu, *Innovation and Empire in Turkey: Sultan Selim III and the Modernisation of the Ottoman Navy*, Tauris, 2008; Guido Candiani, "A New Battle Fleet: The Evolution of the Ottoman Sailing Navy, 1650–1718, Revealed through Venetian Sources", *The Mariner's Mirror*, 104:1, 2018, 18–26.

22. Miri Shefer Mossensohn, "Medical Treatment in the Ottoman Navy in the Early Modern Period", *Journal of the Economic and Social History of the Orient*, 50:4, 2007.

23. David O. Morgan, "The Mongols and the Eastern Mediterranean", in Benjamin Arbel, Bernard Hamilton, and David Jacoby (eds.), *Latins and Greeks in the Eastern Mediterranean after 1204*, Frank Cass, 1989, 198–211.

24. Anthony T. Luttrell, "The Latins and Life on the Smaller Aegean Islands, 1204–1453", *Mediterranean Historical Review*, 4:1, 1989, 146–157. For grain imports, see Morgan, "The Mongols and the Eastern Mediterranean".

25. Christian Luca, "The Rise of the Greek 'Conquering Merchant' in the Trade between the Eastern Mediterranean and the Romanian Principalities in the Sixteenth and Seventeenth Centuries", *Journal of Mediterranean Studies*, 19:2, 2010, 311–334; Gerassimos D. Pagratis, "Shipping Enterprise in the Eighteenth Century: The Case of the Greek Subjects of Venice", *Mediterranean Historical Review*, 25:1, 2010, 67–81; Olga Katsiardi-Hering, "City-ports in the Eastern and Central Mediterranean from the Mid-sixteenth to the Nineteenth Century: Urban and Social

Aspects", *Mediterranean Historical Review*, 26:2, 2011, 151–170; Molly Greene, "Beyond the Northern Invasion. The Mediterranean in the Seventeenth Century", *Past & Present*, 174, 2002, and *Catholic Pirates and Greek Merchants: A Maritime History of the Mediterranean*, Princeton University Press, 2010.

26. Faruk Tabak, *The Waning of the Mediterranean, 1550–1870: A Geohistorical Approach*, Johns Hopkins University Press, 2010 .

27. Eric R. Dursteler, *Venetians in Constantinople: Nation, Identity, and Coexistence in the Early Modern Mediterranean*, Johns Hopkins University Press, 2006, 169; Kate Fleet, *European and Islamic Trade in the Early Ottoman State: The Merchants of Genoa and Turkey*, Cambridge University Press, 1999, 19; Olivia Remie Constable, "Muslim Trade in the Late Medieval Mediterranean World", in Maribel Fierro (ed.), *The New Cambridge History of Islam Volume 2*, Cambridge University Press, 2010.

28. Eric Dursteler, "Commerce and Coexistence: Veneto-Ottoman Trade in the Early Modern Era", *Turcica*, 34, 2002, 105–133.

29. E. Natalie Rothman, *Brokering Empire: Trans-Imperial Subjects between Venice and Istanbul*, Cornell University Press, 2011.

30. Faisal H. Husain, *Rivers of the Sultan: The Tigris and Euphrates in the Ottoman Empire*, Oxford University Press 2021, ch. 3.

31. Douglas E. Streusand, *Islamic Gunpowder Empires: Ottomans, Safavids, and Mughals*, Westview Press, 2010, 107–108.

32. Mehmet Bulut, "The Role of the Ottomans and Dutch in the Commercial Integration between the Levant and Atlantic in the Seventeenth Century", *Journal of the Economic and Social History of the Orient*, 45:2, 2002, 197–230.

33. Gábor Ágoston, *Guns for the Sultan: Military Power and the Weapons Industry in the Ottoman Empire*, Cambridge University Press, 2005, 167. Also see Pavel Murdzhev, "The Medieval Town in Bulgaria", PhD dissertation, University of Florida, 2008, 212–214.

34. K. K. Karaman and S. Pamuk, "Ottoman State Finances in European Perspective, 1500–1914", *Journal of Economic History*, 70:3, 2010.

35. Streusand, *Islamic Gunpowder Empires*, 126.

36. Uyar and Erickson, *A Military History of the Ottomans*, ch. 2; Gülay Yılmaz, "The Economic and Social Roles of Janissaries in a 17th Century Ottoman City: The Case of Istanbul", PhD dissertation, McGill University, 2011.

37. Robert Bideleux and Ian Jeffries, *A History of Eastern Europe: Crisis and Change*, 2nd edn, Routledge, 2007, 80.

38. Andrew Baruch Wachtel, *The Balkans in World History*, Oxford University Press, 2008, 57.

39. Evgeni Radushev, "'Peasant' Janissaries?", *Journal of Social History*, 42:2, 2008, 447–467.

40. Maternal communication.

41. Martin Rheinheimer, "Biographical Research and Maritime History", *International Journal of Maritime History*, 14:2, 2002, 249–264.

42. Borsteinn Helgason, "Historical Narrative as Collective Therapy: The Case of the Turkish Raid in Iceland", *Scandinavian Journal of History*, 22:4, 1997, 275–289.

43. Glen O'Hara, *Britain and the Sea. Since 1600*, Palgrave Macmillan, 2010, 47; Nabil Matar, "The Barbary Corsairs, King Charles I and the Civil War", *Seventeenth Century*, 16:2, 2001, 252; Robert C. Davis, *Christian Slaves, Muslim Masters: White Slavery in the Mediterranean, the*

Barbary Coast, and Italy, 1500–1800, Palgrave Macmillan, 2004, 3–5. On the raids in general, see Alan G. Jamieson, *Lords of the Sea. A History of the Barbary Corsairs*, Reaktion Books, 2012.

44. Dursteler, *Venetians in Constantinople*, 112–113.

45. Glete, *Warfare at Sea*, 104–106; Daniel Goffman, *The Ottoman Empire and Early Modern Europe*, Cambridge University Press, 2002, 159; Niccolò Capponi, *Victory of the West: The Story of the Battle of Lepanto*, Pan Macmillan, 2006.

46. Kelly DeVries, "Warfare and the International State System", in Frank Tallett and D.J.B. Trim (eds.), *European Warfare, 1350–1750*, Cambridge University Press, 2010, 41n.

47. Sam White, "Ecology, Climate, and Crisis in the Ottoman Near East", PhD dissertation, Columbia University, 2008, 148.

48. Ibid., 361–363.

49. Sanjay Subrahmanyam, "A Tale of Three Empires: Mughals, Ottomans, and Habsburgs in a Comparative Context", *Common Knowledge*, 12:1, 2006, 66–92.

50. Quoted in Rhoads Murphey, "The Ottoman Economy in the Early Imperial Age", in Christine Woodhead (ed.), *The Ottoman World*, Taylor & Francis, 2011. Also see Suphan Kirmizialtin, "Conversion in Ottoman Balkans: A Historiographical Survey", *History Compass*, 5:2, 2007, 646–657; Lindner, "Anatolia, 1300–1451".

51. Suraiya N. Faroqhi, "Ottoman Population", in Faroqhi and Kate Fleet (eds.), *The Cambridge History of Turkey, Vol. 2*, 2012.

52. Nükhet Varlık, "Conquest, Urbanization and Plague Networks in the Ottoman Empire, 1453–1600", in Woodhead (ed.), *The Ottoman World*.

53. Most of these estimates are from Varlık, *Plague and Empire*.

54. Iklil Oya Selcuk, "State and Society in the Marketplace: A Study of Late Fifteenth-century Bursa", PhD dissertation, Harvard University, 2009, 234.

55. Wachtel, *The Balkans in World History*.

56. Selcuk, "State and Society in the Marketplace", esp. 277–284.

57. Brian L. Davies, *Warfare, State and Society on the Black Sea Steppe, 1500–1700*, Routledge, 2007, 24.

58. Alan Mikhail, *Under Osman's Tree: The Ottoman Empire, Egypt, and Environmental History*, University of Chicago Press, 2017.

59. Bruce Masters, "Trade in the Ottoman Lands to 1215/1800", in Maribel Fierro (ed.), *The New Cambridge History of Islam, Vol. 2* Cambridge University Press, 2010.

60. Sam White, "Ecology, Climate, and Crisis", 41.

61. Daniel Chirot, *Social Change in a Peripheral Society: The Creation of a Balkan Colony*, Academic Press, 1976, 47.

62. R. Haynes, *Moldova: A History*, I.B. Tauris, 2020, ch. 2.

63. Christine Philliou, "Communities on the Verge: Unraveling the Phanariot Ascendancy in Ottoman Governance", *Comparative Studies in Society and History*, 51, 2009, 151–181; Haynes, *Moldova*, ch. 4.

64. Antov, "Imperial Expansion, Colonization, and Conversion", ch. 5.

65. White, "Ecology, Climate, and Crisis".

66. Charles King, *The Black Sea. A History*, Oxford University Press, 2004, 115.

67. Masters, "Trade in the Ottoman Lands".

68. Greene, "Beyond the Northern Invasion".

69. Varlık, *Plague and Empire*, 178–179; Karen Barkey, *Empire of Difference: The Ottomans in Comparative Perspective*, Cambridge University Press, 2008, 239; Hathaway, *Arab Lands under Ottoman Rule*, 155; Fikret Adanır, "The Ottoman Peasantries, *c*.1360-*c*.1860", in Tom Scott (ed.), *The Peasantries of Europe: From the Fourteenth to the Eighteenth Centuries*, Longman, 1998, 269–310.

70. Bideleux and Jeffries, *A History of Eastern Europe*, 163.

71. Michael Brett and Elizabeth Fentress, *The Berbers*, Blackwell, 1996, 161; Emrah Safa Gürkan, "The Centre and the Frontier: Ottoman Cooperation with the North African Corsairs in the Sixteenth Century", *Turkish Historical Review*, 1, 2010, 125–163; Murphey, *Ottoman Warfare*, 10; Finkel, *Osman's Dream*, 10.

72. Davies, *Warfare, State and Society*, 6–8; James Forsyth, *The Caucasus: A History*, Cambridge University Press, 2013, 214.

73. Victor Ostapchuk, "The Ottoman Black Sea Frontier and the Relations of the Porte with the Polish-Lithuanian Commonwealth and Muscovy, 1622–1628", PhD thesis, Harvard University, 1989, 3.

74. Alan Fisher, "Chattel Slavery in the Ottoman Empire", *Slavery and Abolition*, 1:1, 1980, 25–45; Zübeyde Güneş-Yağcı, "The Black Sea Slave Trade According to the Istanbul Port Customs Register, 1606–1607", in Christoph Witzenrath (ed.), *Eurasian Slavery, Ransom and Abolition in World History, 1200–1860*, Taylor & Francis, 2015.

75. King, *The Black Sea*, 117–118; Alessandro Stanziani, "Serfs, Slaves, or Wage Earners? The Legal Status of Labour in Russia from a Comparative Perspective, from the Sixteenth to the Nineteenth Century", *Journal of World History*, 3, 2008, 183–202.

76. Hathaway, *Arab Lands under Ottoman Rule*, 52; Murat Yasar, "Evliya Celebi in the Circassian Lands: Vampires, Tree Worshippers, and Pseudo-Muslims", *Acta Orientalia Academiae Scientiarum Hung*, 67:1, 2014, 75–96; Michael Khodarkovsky, "The Non-Christian Peoples on the Muscovite Frontiers", in Maureen Perrie (ed.), *The Cambridge History of Russia, Vol. 1*, Cambridge University Press, 2006; Forsyth, *The Caucasus*.

77. Elena Inozemtseva, "On the History of Slave-Trade in Dagestan", *Iran and the Caucasus*, 10:2, 2006.

78. Davies, *Warfare, State and Society*, 17.

79. Mikhail B. Kizilov, "The Black Sea and the Slave Trade: The Role of Crimean Maritime Towns in the Trade in Slaves and Captives in the Fifteenth to Eighteenth Centuries", *International Journal of Maritime History*, 17:1, 2005, 211–235; Davies, *Warfare, State and Society*, 25.

80. Witzenrath (ed.), *Eurasian Slavery*, Editor's Intro.

81. Jamieson, *Lords of the Sea*, 29–30; Norman Housley, *The Later Crusades, 1274–1580. From Lyons to Alcazar*, Oxford University Press, 1992, 116.

82. Jamieson, *Lords of the Sea*, 29–30.

83. Gürkan, "The Centre and the Frontier".

84. Houari Touati, "The Ottoman Maghrib", in *The New Cambridge History of Islam, Vol. 2*.

85. Andrew Hess, *The Forgotten Frontier: A History of the Sixteenth-century Ibero-African Frontier*, Chicago University Press, 1978, 165.

86. Touati, "The Ottoman Maghrib".

87. Davis, *Christian Slaves, Muslim Masters*, 103; Frederico Cresti, "Algiers in the Ottoman Period; The City and Its Population", in Salma Khadra Jayyusi et al. (eds.), *The City in the Islamic World*, Brill, 2008.

88. Fatiha Loualich, "In the Regency of Algiers: The Human Side of the Algerine Corso", in Maria Fusaro, Colin Heywood, and Mohamed-Salah Omri (eds.), *Trade and Cultural Exchange in the Early Modern Mediterranean: Braudel's Maritime Legacy*, I.B. Tauris, 2010.

89. Jamieson, *Lords of the Sea*, 91, 150.

90. Michael Brett, "North Africa State and Society, 1056–1659", in Youssef M. Choueiri (ed.), *A Companion to the History of the Middle East*, Blackwell, 2005. Also see Phillip C. Naylor, *North Africa: A History from Antiquity to the Present*, University of Texas Press, 2005, 117–121.

91. Metin Kunt, "Ottomans and Safavids. States, Statecraft, and Societies, 1500–1800", in Choueiri (ed.), *A Companion to the History of the Middle East*.

92. Jamieson, *Lords of the Sea*, 39.

93. Ibid., 206.

94. Davis, *Christian Slaves, Muslim Masters*, 8, 45.

95. Ibid., 23.

96. Ronald C. Jennings, "Black Slaves and Free Blacks in Ottoman Cyprus, 1590–1640", *Journal of the Economic and Social History of the Orient*, 30:3, 1987.

97. John Wright, *The Trans-Saharan Slave Trade*, Routledge, 2007, 39, 53.

98. Hathaway, *Arab Lands under Ottoman Rule*, 16; Salih Ozbaran, "Ottoman Expansion in the Red Sea", in *The Cambridge History of Turkey, Vol. 2*.

99. Roland Oliver and Anthony Atmore, *Medieval Africa, 1250–1800*, Cambridge University Press revised edn, 2001, 130. Jennings, "Black Slaves and Free Blacks".

100. Ehud R. Toledano, "Enslavement in the Ottoman Empire in the Early Modern Period", in David Eltis and Stanley L. Engerman (eds.), *The Cambridge World History of Slavery Vol. 3*, Cambridge University Press, 2011.

101. Varlık, *Plague and Empire*, 155.

102. Selcuk, "State and Society in the Marketplace", 122, 129, concurring with the estimate of Halil Sahillioglu.

103. Charles L. Wilkins, "A Demographic Profile of Slaves in Early Ottoman Aleppo", in Witzenrath (ed.), *Eurasian Slavery*.

104. Davies, *Warfare, State and Society*.

105. Rhoads Murphey, "The Ottoman Resurgence in the Seventeenth-century Mediterranean: The Gamble and Its Results", *Mediterranean Historical Review*, 8:2, 1993, 186–200.

106. Mossensohn, "Medical Treatment in the Ottoman Navy".

107. Davies, *Warfare, State and Society*, 91.

108. Brian L. Davies, "The Prisoner's Tale: Russian Captivity Narratives and Changing Muscovite Perceptions of the Ottoman–Tatar Dar-al-Islam", in Witzenrath (ed.), *Eurasian Slavery*.

109. B. G. Martin, "Mai Idris of Bornu and the Ottoman Turks, 1576–78", *International Journal of Middle East Studies*, 3:4, 1972, 470–490. Also see Wright, *The Trans-Saharan Slave Trade*, 44.

110. David L. Mearns, David Parham, and Bruno Frohlich, "A Portuguese East Indiaman from the 1502–1503 Fleet of Vasco da Gama Off Al Hallaniyah Island, Oman: An Interim Report", *International Journal of Nautical Archaeology*, 45:2, 2016, 1–21.

111. Quoted in Thomas D. Boston, "Sixteenth-Century European Expansion and the Economic Decline of Africa", *Review of Black Political Economy*, 20:4, 1992, 5–38.

112. Monteiro, Saturnino, *Portuguese Sea Battles 1139–1975*, 2010, Oeiras, Vol. I, 233. Also see Sanjay Subrahmanyam, "The Birth-Pangs of Portuguese Asia: Revisiting the Fateful 'Long Decade' 1498–1509", *Journal of World History*, 2, 2007, 261–280.

113. Ozbaran, "Ottoman Expansion in the Red Sea"; Monteiro, *Portuguese Sea Battles*, Vol. 1, 329.

114. Ozbaran, "Ottoman Expansion in the Red Sea".

115. Claude Markovitz, *A History of Modern India 1480–1950*, trans. Nisha George and Maggy Hendry, Anthem Press, 2002 (orig. 1994), 43, 36; Sanjay Subrahmanyam, *Portuguese Empire in Asia, 1500–1700*, Wiley, 2012, 84–85.

116. N. R. Farooq, "An Overview of Ottoman Archival Documents and Their Relevance for Medieval Indian History", *Medieval History Journal*, 20:1, 2017.

117. Ibid.

118. Andelko Vlasic, "Georgius Huszthius, a Traveller from Croatia, and His Account of the Ottoman Naval Campaign in India (1538–1539)", *Acta Orientalia Academiae Scientiarum Hung.*, 68:3, 2015, 349–362.

119. Juan Cole, "Rival Empires of Trade and Imami Shi'ism in Eastern Arabia, 1300–1800", *International Journal of Middle East Studies*, 19:2, 1987, 177–204.

120. A. R. Disney, *A History of Portugal and the Portuguese Empire: From Beginnings to 1807*, Vol. 2, Cambridge University Press, 2009, 135–136.

121. Donald Crummey, "Ethiopia in the Early Modern Period: Solomonic Monarchy and Christianity", *Journal of Early Modern History*, 8:3, 2004, 191–209.

122. A.C.S. Peacock, "The Ottoman Empire and the Indian Ocean", *Oxford Research Encyclopedia of Asian History*, 2018; John Alexander, "Ottoman Frontier Policies in Northeast Africa, 1517–1914", in Peacock (ed.), *The Frontiers of the Ottoman World*.

123. Ozbaran, "Ottoman Expansion in the Red Sea".

124. A.C.S. Peacock, "The Ottomans and the Funj Sultanate in the Sixteenth and Seventeenth Centuries", *Bulletin of SOAS*, 75:1, 2012, 87–111.

125. Giancarlo Casale, *The Ottoman Age of Exploration*, Oxford University Press, 2010, 124; Pierre-Yves Manguin, "Of Fortresses and Galleys. The 1568 Acehnese Siege of Melaka, after a Contemporary Bird's-Eye View", *Modern Asian Studies*, 22:3, 1988, 607–628.

126. Robert M. Maxon, *East Africa: An Introductory History*, 3rd edn, University of West Virginia Press, 2009, 46; Peacock, "The Ottoman Empire and the Indian Ocean".

127. A.C.S. Peacock, "The Economic Relationship between the Ottoman Empire and Southeast Asia in the Seventeenth Century", in A.C.S. Peacock and Annabel Teh Gallop, *From Anatolia to Aceh. Ottomans, Turks and Southeast Asia*, Oxford University Press, 2015.

128. Gabor Agoston, "Firearms and Military Adaptation: The Ottomans and the European Military Revolution, 1450–1800", *Journal of World History*, 25:1, 2014, 85–124.

129. Jorge Santos Alves, "From Istanbul with Love: Rumours, Conspiracies, and Commercial Completion in Aceh-Ottoman Relations, 1550s–1570s", in Peacock and Gallop, *From Anatolia to Aceh*.

130. Casale, *The Ottoman Age of Exploration*. Also see Bernard Haykel, "Western Arabia and Yemen during the Ottoman Period", in *The New Cambridge History of Islam, Vol. 2*.

131. Peacock, "The Ottoman Empire and the Indian Ocean".

132. Viceroy Almeida, quoted in Subrahmanyam, "The Birth-Pangs of Portuguese Asia".

133. Ágoston, "Firearms and Military Adaptation".

134. Uyar and Erickson, *A Military History of the Ottomans*, 46.

135. John J. Jefferson, "The Ottoman-Hungarian Campaigns of 1442", *Journal of Medieval Military History*, 10, 2012; Pratyay Nath, *Climate of Conquest: War, Environment, and Empire in Mughal North India*, Oxford University Press, 2019, 32–33; Ágoston, *Guns for the Sultan*, 18.

136. Ágoston, *Guns for the Sultan*, 57, 151.

137. Philip T. Hoffman, "Prices, the Military Revolution, and Western Europe's Comparative Advantage in Violence", *Economic History Review*, 64, 2011, 39–59.

138. Ágoston, "Firearms and Military Adaptation".

139. Grant, "Rethinking the Ottoman 'Decline.'"

140. Murphey, *Ottoman Warfare*, 113–121; H. Burcu Ozguven, "Early Modern Military Architecture in the Ottoman Empire", *Nexus Network Journal*, 16:3, 2014, 737–749.

141. Philip Mansel, *Constantinople. City of the World's Desire, 1453–1924*, Penguin 1997, 46.

142. Uyar and Erickson, *A Military History of the Ottomans*, 32.

143. Ágoston, "Firearms and Military Adaptation"; Kelly De Vries, "The Effectiveness of Fifteenth-century Shipboard Artillery", *Mariner's Mirror*, 84:4, 1998.

144. Susan Rose, *Medieval Naval Warfare, 1000–1500*, Routledge, 2002, 112.

145. Jeffrey G. Royal and John M. McManamon, "Three Renaissance Wrecks from Turkey and Their Implications for Maritime History in the Eastern Mediterranean", *Journal of Maritime Archaeology*, 4:2, 2009, 103–129; Murphey, *Ottoman Warfare*, ch. 5; Husain, *Rivers of the Sultan*, ch. 4; Ágoston, "Firearms and Military Adaptation".

146. Ágoston, "Firearms and Military Adaptation"; Iqtidar Alam Khan, *Gunpowder and Firearms: Warfare in Medieval India*, Oxford University Press, 2004, 85, n.46.

147. Khan, *Gunpowder and Firearms*, 129; Ágoston, "Firearms and Military Adaptation".

148. Ágoston, "Firearms and Military Adaptation".

149. B. W. Diffie, *Foundations of the Portuguese Empire, 1415–1580*, University of Minnesota Press, 1977, 212.

150. Earnest W. Porta, "Morocco in the Early Atlantic World, 1415–1603", PhD dissertation, Georgetown University, 2018.

151. Casale, *The Ottoman Age of Exploration*, 11.

Chapter 12: The Dutch Puzzle and the Mobilisation of Eastern Europe

1. Alan Albery, "Woodland Management in Hampshire, 900 to 1815", *Agricultural History*, 22:2, 2011, 159–181.

2. Richard C. Hoffman, *An Environmental History of Medieval Europe*, Cambridge University Press, 2014, 187. Also see John Thomas Wing, "Roots of Empire: State Formation and the Politics of Timber Access in Early Modern Spain, 1556–1759", PhD dissertation, University of Minnesota, 2009; Paul Warde, *Ecology, Economy and State Formation in Early Modern Germany*, Cambridge University Press, 2005, 352; Wendy R. Childs, "Timber for Cloth; Changing Commodities in Anglo-Baltic Trade in the Fourteenth Century", in Lars Berggren et al. (eds.), *Cogs, Cargoes, and Commerce. Maritime Bulk Trade in Northern Europe, 1150–1400*, Pontifical Institute of Mediaeval Studies, 2002.

3. K. Hanecaa et al., "Provenancing Baltic Timber from Art Historical Objects: Success and Limitations", *Journal of Archaeological Science*, 32, 2005, 261–271. Also see Nils Hybel, "Early Commercial Contacts between England, Prussia, and Poland", in Richard W. Unger and Jakub Basista (eds.), *Britain and Poland-Lithuania: Contact and Comparison from the Middle Ages to 1795*, Brill, 2008; Tomasz Wazny, "Baltic Timber in Western Europe—An Exciting

Dendrochronological Question", *Dendrochronologia*, 20:3, 2002, 313–320; K. Haneca, K. Cufar, and H. Beeckman, "Oaks, Tree-Rings and Wooden Cultural Heritage: A Review of the Main Characteristics and Applications of Oak Dendrochronology in Europe", *Journal of Archaeological Science*, 36, 2009, 1–11; M. Bridge, "Locating the Origins of Wood Resources: A Review of Dendroprovenancing", *Journal of Archaeological Science*, 39, 2012, 2828–2834.

4. Wendy R. Childs, "England's Contacts with Poland-Lithuania in the Fourteenth to Sixteenth Centuries", in Unger and Basista (eds.), *Britain and Poland-Lithuania*. Also see Bridge, "Locating the Origins of Wood Resources".

5. Childs, "Timber for Cloth" and "England's Contacts with Poland-Lithuania".

6. Childs, "Timber for Cloth".

7. Mateusz Falkowski, "Fear and Abundance: Reshaping of Royal Forests in Sixteenth-Century Poland and Lithuania", *Environmental History*, 22:4, 2017, 618–642.

8. António dos Santos Pereira, "The Urgent Empire Portugal Between 1475 and 1525", *e-Journal of Portuguese History*, 4:2, 2006; Marian Małowist, *Western Europe, Eastern Europe and World Development 13th–18th Centuries: Essays of Marian Małowist*, J. Batou and H. Szlajfer (eds.), Brill, 2009, ch. 2; Jason W. Moore, "Madeira, Sugar, and the Conquest of Nature, in the 'First' Sixteenth Century; Part One: From 'Island of Timber' to Sugar Revolution, 1420–1506", *Review—Fernand Braudel Center*, 32:4, 2009, 345–390.

9. Wing, "Roots of Empire", 15.

10. Mary Fischer, "The Perfect Gentle Knight: Fourteenth-Century Crusaders in Prussia", *Travels and Mobilities in the Middle Ages: From the Atlantic to the Black Sea*, Marianne O'Doherty and Felicitas Schmieder (eds.), Brepols, 2015.

11. Saulius Suziedelis, *Historical Dictionary of Lithuania*, Scarecrow Press, 2011, 149.

12. Rasa Mazeika, "Of Cabbages and Knights. Trade and Trade Treaties with the Infidel on the Northern Frontier, 1200–1390", *Journal of Medieval History*, 20, 1994, 63–76.

13. S. C. Rowell, "Of Men and Monsters: Sources for the History of Lithuania in the Time of Gediminas (ca. 1315–1342)", *Journal of Baltic Studies*, 24:1, 1993, 73–112.

14. Aleksander Pluskowski, *The Archaeology of the Prussian Crusade. Holy War and Colonisation*, Routledge, 2013, 140. Also see Norman Davies, *God's Playground. A History of Poland, Volume One—The Origins to 1795*, Clarendon Press, 1981, 257; Markus Cerman, *Villagers and Lords in Eastern Europe, 1300–1800*, Palgrave Macmillan, 2012.

15. David Kirby, *Northern Europe in the Early Modern Period: The Baltic World 1492–1772*, Longman, 1990, 244; Imbi Sooman et al., "The Couronian Colony on Tobago in Past and Present", *Journal of Baltic Studies*, 44:4, 2013, 503–526.

16. Robert Frost, *The Oxford History of Poland-Lithuania: Vol. I*, Oxford University Press, 2015, 105–106, 203.

17. Małowist, *Western Europe, Eastern Europe and World Development*, ch. 2.

18. Jean W. Sedlar, *East Central Europe in the Middle Ages, 1000–1500*, University of Washington Press, 2011, ch. 11.

19. Pluskowski, *The Archaeology of the Prussian Crusade*, 223–227.

20. Childs, "England's Contacts with Poland-Lithuania". Also see Herman Van Der Wee, "The Western European Woollen Industries, 1500–1750", in David Jenkins (ed.), *The Cambridge History of Western Textiles, Vol. I*, Cambridge University Press, 2003, 412.

21. R. C. Hoffmann, "Strekfusz: A Fish Dish Links Jagiellonian Kraków to Distant Waters", in Piotr Górecki and Nancy Van Deusen (eds.), *Central and Eastern Europe in the Middle Ages: A Cultural History*, Tauris, 2009.

22. T. R. Slater, "Medieval and Renaissance Urban Morphogenesis in Eastern Poland", *Journal of Historical Geography*, 15:3, 1989, 239–259.

23. Milja Van Tielhof, "Grain Provision in Holland, ca. 1490–ca. 1570", in P. Hoppenbrouwers and J. Luiten van Zanden (eds.), *Peasants into Farmers? The Transformation of Rural Economy and Society in the Low Countries (Middle Ages–19th Century) in Light of the Brenner Debate*, Brepols, 2001; Jan De Vries and Ad Van Der Woude, *The First Modern Economy: Success, Failure, and Perseverance of the Dutch Economy, 1500–1815*, Cambridge University Press, 1997, 177–178; Cerman, *Villagers and Lords in Eastern Europe*, 44; Davies, *God's Playground*, 257.

24. Stefan Halikoswki Smith, "Demystifying a Change in Taste: Spices, Space, and Social Hierarchy in Europe, 1380–1750", *International History Review*, 29:2, 2007, 237–257. Also see Grzegorz Myśliwski, "Venice and Wrocław in the Later Middle Ages", in Górecki, Van Deusen and Knoll (eds.), *Central and Eastern Europe in the Middle Ages*; Zsigmond Pál Pach, "Hungary and the Levantine Trade in the 14th–17th Centuries", *Acta Orientalia Academiae Scientiarum Hungaricae*, 60:1, 2007, 9–31.

25. Alessandro Stanziani, "Serfs, Slaves, or Wage Earners? The Legal Status of Labour in Russia from a Comparative Perspective, from the Sixteenth to the Nineteenth Century", *Journal of World History*, 3, 2008, 183–202, and "Revisiting Russian Serfdom: Bonded Peasants and Market Dynamics, 1600s–1800s", *International Labor and Working-Class History*, 78, 2010, 12–27.

26. Edgar Melton, "The Agrarian East", in Hamish Scott (ed.), *The Oxford Handbook of Early Modern European History, 1350–1750: Vol. I*, Oxford University Press, 2015.

27. Cerman, *Villagers and Lords in Eastern Europe*, 75.

28. Frost, *Oxford History of Poland-Lithuania*, ch. 21.

29. Piotr Guzowski, "A Changing Economy: Models of Peasant Budgets in Fifteenth- and Sixteenth-century Poland", *Continuity and Change*, 20, 2005, 9–25.

30. Nerijus Babinskas, "Economic Challenges in Early Modern Ages and Different Responses of European Margins. Comparative Considerations Based on Historiography: The Cases of Polish-Lithuanian Commonwealth and Moldavian Principality", *Romanian Journal for Baltic and Nordic Studies*, 4:2, 2012, 51–62.

31. David Turnock, *The Making of Eastern Europe: From the Earliest Times to 1815*, Routledge, 1988, 214; Melton, "The Agrarian East".

32. Heli Huhtamaa, "Climatic Anomalies, Food Systems, and Subsistence Crises in Medieval Novgorod and Ladoga", *Scandinavian Journal of History*, 40:4, 2015, 562–590.

33. Mikołaj Malinowski, "East of Eden: Polish Living Standards in a European Perspective, ca. 1500–1800", Working Paper 6, Utrecht University, Centre for Global Economic History, 2013.

34. Jillian R. Smith, "Hanseatic Cogs and Baltic Trade: Interrelations between Trade Technology and Ecology", PhD dissertation, University of Nebraska–Lincoln, 2010.

35. Teresa Pac, "Churches at the Edge: A Comparative Study of Christianization Processes along the Baltic Sea in the Middle Ages: Gdańsk and Novgorod", PhD dissertation, State University of New York at Binghamton, 2005, 51.

36. Tom Scott, *The City-State in Europe, 1000–1600*, Oxford University Press, 2012, 60.

37. George Christakos et al., "Black Death: The Background", in *Interdisciplinary Public Health Reasoning and Epidemic Modelling: The Case of Black Death*, Springer-Verlag, 2005; Stephan A. Lutgert, "Victims of the Great Famine or the Black Death? The Archaeology of the Mass Graves Found in the Former Graveyard of the Holy Ghost Hospital in Lubeck (N. Germany), in the European Context", *Hikuin*, 27, 2000, 255–264.

38. Judith Potter, "Social Networks in Late Medieval Luebeck", PhD dissertation, New York University, 2001, 44–45.

39. Ibid., 27.

40. Rhiman A. Rotz, "The Lubeck Uprising of 1408 and the Decline of the Hanseatic League", *Proceedings of the American Philosophical Society*, 121:1, 1977, 1–45.

41. Potter, "Social Networks in Late Medieval Luebeck", 27.

42. Mike Burkhardt, "Kontors and Outposts", in Donald J. Harreld (ed.), *A Companion to the Hanseatic League*, Brill, 2015.

43. Ulf Christian Ewert and Stephan Selzer, "Social Networks", in Harreld (ed.), *Companion to the Hanseatic League*. Also see Potter, "Social Networks in Late Medieval Luebeck".

44. T. Jiří Bílý, "The Legal Position of the Dalmatian Merchants in Medieval Lübeck", *Journal on European History of Law*, 1, 2010, 62–66. Also see Timothy J. Runyan et al., "Notes on John D. Fudge, *Cargoes, Embargos, and Emissaries. The Commercial and Political Interaction of England and the German Hanse, 1450–1510*", *International Journal of Maritime History*, 8:1, 1996, 247–258.

45. Juhan Kreem, "The Business of War: Mercenary Market and Organisation in Reval in the Fifteenth and Early Sixteenth Centuries", *Scandinavian Economic History Review*, 49:2, 2001, 26–42; David Nicolle and G. A. and S. Embleton, *Forces of the Hanseatic League 13th–15th Centuries*, Osprey, 2014; David Potter, "The International Mercenary Market in the Sixteenth Century: Anglo-French Competition in Germany, 1543–50", *English Historical Review*, 111:440, 1996, 24–58; Sven Ekdahl, "The Teutonic Order's Mercenaries during the 'Great War' with Poland-Lithuania (1409–11)", in John France (ed.), *Mercenaries and Paid Men: The Mercenary Identity in the Middle Ages*, Brill, 2008, 345–362.

46. Nicolle et al., *Forces of the Hanseatic League*, 37.

47. Hans-Peter Baum, "Annuities in Late Medieval Hanse Towns", *Business History Review*, 59:1, 1985.

48. Carsten Jahnke, "The City of Lübeck and the Internationality of Early Hanseatic Trade", in Justyna Wubs-Mrozewicz and Stuart Jenks (eds.), *The Hanse in Medieval and Early Modern Europe*, Brill, 2013.

49. Scott, *The City-State in Europe*, 140. Also see Ulrich Müller, "Network of the Centres— Centres of the Networks? The Relations between 'Hanseatic' Medieval Towns and their Surroundings/Hinterlands", in *Town and Country in Medieval North Western Europe: Dynamic Interactions*, Alexis Wilkin et al. (eds.), Brepols, 2015.

50. Rotz, "The Lubeck Uprising of 1408"; K. H. Waldrow, "The Rise and Decline of a Saltern: Rent-seeking at Its Best", *Journal of European Economic History*, 22:3, 1993, 581–600.

51. E. Tiberg, *Moscow, Livonia and the Hanseatic League 1487–1550*. Acta Universitatis Stockholmiensis, 1995.

52. Ibid., 227–228.

53. Rotz, "The Lubeck Uprising of 1408"; Jürgen Sarnowsky, "The 'Golden Age' of the Hanseatic League", in Harreld (ed.), *Companion to the Hanseatic League*.

54. Mike Burkhardt, "Kontors and Outposts".

55. Sarnowsky, "The 'Golden Age' of the Hanseatic League".

56. Jan Glete, *Warfare at Sea, 1500–1650: Maritime Conflicts and the Transformation of Europe*, Routledge, 2000, 116.

57. Kirby, *Northern Europe in the Early Modern Period*, 7; Sverre Bagge, *Cross and Scepter: The Rise of the Scandinavian Kingdoms from the Vikings to the Reformation*, Princeton University Press, 2014.

58. Detlev Ellmers, "The Cog as Cargo Carrier", in Robert Gardiner and Richard W. Unger (eds.), *Cogs, Caravels and Galleons: The Sailing Ship 1000–1650*, Conway Maritime Press, 1994, 29–46, 44; Natascha Mehler and Mark Gardiner, "English and Hanseatic Trading and Fishing Sites in Medieval Iceland: Report on Initial Fieldwork", *Germania*, 85:2, 2007, 385–427.

59. Scott, *The City-State in Europe*, 62.

60. Erik Gøbel, "The Sound Toll Registers Online Project, 1497–1857", *International Journal of Maritime History*, 12:2, 2010, 305–324.

61. Kirby, *Northern Europe*, 59; Justyna Wubs-Mrozewicz, "Interplay of Identities: German Settlers in Late Medieval Stockholm", *Scandinavian Journal of History*, 29:1, 2004, 53–67.

62. Michael North, *The Expansion of Europe, 1250–1500*, Manchester University Press, 2012 (German original 2007), 335; Magdalena Naum, "Premodern Translocals: German Merchant Diaspora Between Kalmar and Northern German Towns (1250–1500)", *International Journal of Historical Archaeology*, 17, 2013, 376–400; Wubs-Mrozewicz, "Interplay of Identities".

63. Hans Antonson, "The Extent of Farm Desertion in Central Sweden During the Late Medieval Agrarian Crisis: Landscape as a Source", *Journal of Historical Geography*, 35, 2009, 619–641.

64. Johan Söderberg, "Prices and Economic Change in Medieval Sweden", *Scandinavian Economic History Review*, 55:2, 2007, 128–152.

65. Naum, "Premodern Translocals".

66. Mette Svart Kristiansen, "Fish for Peasants and Kings—A Danish Perspective", in Jan Klápště and Petr Sommer (eds.), *Processing, Storage, Distribution of Food. Food in the Medieval Rural Environment*, Brepols, 2011; Brian Fagan, *Fish on Friday: Feasting, Fasting and the Discovery of the New World*, Basic Books, 2006, 108; Thomas A. Quesenbery, "The Institutional Success of the German Hansa, 1158–1666", MA thesis, California State University, Dominguez Hills, 2000.

67. Justyna Wubs-Mrozewicz, *Traders, Ties and Tensions: The Interactions of Lübeckers, Overijsslers Hollanders in Late Medieval Bergen*, Uitgeverij Verloren, 2008, 15.

68. Sarnowsky, "The 'Golden Age' of the Hanseatic League".

69. Maren Sofie Løfsgård, "Immigration to Late Medieval Bergen—A Study of Names and Positions in an International City", Master's thesis, University of Bergen, 2016, 78.

70. Charlotte Masemann, "Cultivation and Consumption: Medieval Lübeck"s Gardens", in Lawrin Armstrong, Evana Elbl, and Martin M. Elbl (eds.), *Money, Markets and Trade in Late Medieval Europe*, Brill, 2007, 572–607.

71. Söderberg, "Prices and Economic Change in Medieval Sweden"; Jahnke, "The City of Lübeck".

72. David Gaimster, "A Parallel History: The Archaeology of Hanseatic Urban Culture in the Baltic c.1200–1600", *World Archaeology*, 37:3, 2005, 408–423; Natascha Mehler, "The Perception and Interpretation of Hanseatic Material Culture in the North Atlantic: Problems and

Suggestions", *Journal of the North Atlantic*, 2, 2009–2010, 89–108; Magdalena Naum, "Material Culture and Diasporic Experiences: A Case of Medieval Hanse Merchants in the Baltic", *Archaeological Papers of the American Anthropological Association*, 26, 2015, 72–86.

73. Alexander Cowan, "Cultural Traffic in Lubeck and Danzig in the Sixteenth and Seventeenth Centuries", *Scandinavian Journal of History*, 28, 2003, 175–185.

74. Richard W. Unger, "Beer: A New Bulk Good of International Trade", in Berggren et al. (eds.), *Cogs, Cargoes, and Commerce*, 118; Justyna Wubs-Mrozewicz, "Rules of Inclusion, Rules of Exclusion: The Hanseatic Kontor in Bergen in the Late Middle Ages and Its Normative Boundaries", *German History*, 29:1, 2011, 1–22.

75. Glete, *Warfare at Sea*, ch. 7, quotes 119 and 123.

76. Oscar Gelderblom and Joost Jonker, "Early Capitalism in the Low Countries", Working Paper 41, Utrecht University, Centre for Global Economic History, 2013.

77. W. P. Blockmans, "The Social and Economic Effects of Plague in the Low Countries: 1349–1500", *Revue belge de philologie et d'histoire*, 58:4, 1980, 833–863.

78. Joris Roosen and Daniel R. Curtis, "The 'Light Touch' of the Black Death in the Southern Netherlands: An Urban Trick?", *Economic History Review*, 72:1, 2019, 1–25.

79. Robert Stein and Judith Pollmann, *Networks, Regions and Nations: Shaping Identities in the Low Countries, 1300–1650*, Brill, 2010, 51–52.

80. James D. Tracy, *Holland under Habsburg Rule, 1506–156: The Formation of a Body Politic*, University of California Press, 1990, 12.

81. Jonathan Israel, *The Dutch Republic: Its Rise, Greatness, and Fall, 1477–1806*, Oxford University Press, 1995, 14.

82. Jessica Dijkman, *Shaping Medieval Markets: The Organisation of Commodity Markets in Holland, c.1200–c.1450*, Brill, 2011, 7–8, 11, concurring with Peter Hoppenbrouwers.

83. Dijkman, *Shaping Medieval Markets*, 7–8.

84. Various personal communications.

85. Ole J. Benedictow, *The Black Death 1346–1353: The Complete History*, Boydell Press, 2004, ch. 21.

86. S. Haensch et al., "Distinct Clones of *Yersinia pestis* Caused the Black Death", *PLoS Pathogens*, 6:10, 2010.

87. Jan Luiten Van Zanden, "A Third Road to Capitalism? Proto-Industrialisation and the Moderate Nature of the Late Medieval Crisis in Flanders and Holland, 1350–1550", in Hoppenbrouwers and van Zanden (eds.), *Peasants into Farmers?*

88. Blockmans, "The Social and Economic Effects of Plague"; P. J. van Dam, "Sinking Peat Bogs: Environmental Change in Holland, 1350–1550", *Environmental History*, 6:1, 2001, 32–45.

89. Jaco Zuijderduijn, "Living *la vita apostolica*. Life Expectancy and Mortality of Nuns in Late-Medieval Holland", Working Paper 44, Utrecht University, Centre for Global Economic History, 2013.

90. Bas J. P. van Bavel and Jan Luiten van Zanden, "The Jump-Start of the Holland Economy during the Late-Medieval Crisis, c.1350–c.1500", *Economic History Review*, 47:3, 2004, 513; Audrey M. Lambert, *The Making of the Dutch Landscape: An Historical Geography of the Netherlands*, Seminar Press, 1971, 212; Tim Soens, "The Origins of the Western Scheldt. Environmental Transformation, Storm Surges and Human Agency in the Flemish Coastal Plain (1250–1600)", in Erik

Thoen et al. (ed.), *Landscapes or Seascapes? The History of the Coastal Environment in the North Sea Area Reconsidered*, Brepols, 2013, 287–312.

91. James A. Galloway, "Storm Flooding, Coastal Defence and Land Use Around the Thames Estuary and Tidal River c.1250–1450", *Journal of Medieval History*, 35, 2009, 171–188.

92. Van Dam, "Sinking Peat Bogs: Environmental Change in Holland".

93. Tim Soens, "Flood Security in the Medieval and Early Modern North Sea Area: A Question of Entitlement?", *Environment and History*, 19, 2013, 209–232.

94. Lambert, *Making of the Dutch Landscape*, 117, 122–123.

95. Jan van Doesburg, "Archaeological Evidence for Pest Control in Medieval Rural Settlements in the Netherlands", in Jan Klápště and Petr Sommer (eds.), *Processing, Storage, Distribution of Food. Food in the Medieval Rural Environment*, Brepols, 2011, 31–43.

96. Erik Thoen and Tim Soens, "The Family or the Farm: A Sophie's Choice? The Late Medieval Crisis in Flanders", in John Drendel (ed.), *Crisis in the Later Middle Ages: Beyond the Postan-Duby Paradigm*, Brepols, 2015. 195–224; B.J.P. van Bavel, *Manors and Markets: Economy and Society in the Low Countries, 500–1600*, Oxford University Press, 2010, ch. 6.

97. Van Bavel and van Zanden, "The Jump-Start of the Holland Economy"; Van Zanden, "A Third Road To Capitalism".

98. Van Zanden, "A Third Road to Capitalism"; Zuijderduijn, "Living la vita apostolica"; Van Bavel and van Zanden, "The Jump-Start of the Holland Economy".

99. Dijkman, *Shaping Medieval Markets*, 320–1; Lambert, *Making of the Dutch Landscape*, 176.

100. S. Broadberry et al., *British Economic Growth, 1270–1870*, Cambridge University Press, 2015, 377, citing Carlos Alvarez-Nogal and colleagues.

101. Tracy, *Holland under Habsburg Rule*, 10, 12; Dijkman, *Shaping Medieval Markets*, 55.

102. Lambert, *Making of the Dutch Landscape*, 161–172.

103. Oscar Gelderblom, *Cities of Commerce: The Institutional Foundations of International Trade in the Low Countries, 1250–1650*, Princeton University Press, 2013, 35.

104. Dijkman, *Shaping Medieval Markets*, 6.

105. Richard W. Unger, "Beer: A New Bulk Good".

106. De Vries and Van der Woude, *First Modern Economy*, 93. Also see Koen Deconinck, Eline Poelmans, and Johan Swinnen, "How Beer Created Belgium (and the Netherlands): The Contribution of Beer Taxes to War Finance during the Dutch Revolt", *Business History*, 58:5, 2016, 694–724.

107. Koen et al., "How Beer Created Belgium".

108. R. C. Hoffman, "Frontier Foods for Late Medieval Consumers: Culture, Economy, Ecology", *Environment and History*, 7, 2001, 131–167. Also see Michael Scott Martin, "The Goal and the Goldmine: Constraints Management and the Dutch Herring Fishing Industry, 1400–1700", *Essays in Economic & Business History*, 27, 2009; Bo Poulsen, *Dutch Herring: An Environmental History, c.1600–1860*, Aksant, 2008; L. Sicking, "Protection Costs and Profitability of the Herring Fishery in the Netherlands in the Sixteenth Century, A Case Study", *International Journal of Maritime History*, 15:2, 2003, 265–277; Richard W. Unger, "Dutch Herring, Technology, and International Trade in the Seventeenth Century", *Journal of Economic History*, 40:2, 1980, 253–280.

109. Louis Sicking, *Neptune and the Netherlands: State, Economy, and War at Sea in the Renaissance*, 2004, Brill, ch. 3.

110. James D. Tracy, "Herring Wars: The Habsburg Netherlands and the Struggle for Control of the North Sea, ca. 1520–1560", *Sixteenth Century Journal*, 24:2, 1993, 249–272; De Vries and Van der Woude, *First Modern Economy*, 419; Poulsen, *Dutch Herring*, 46; W. Jeffrey Bolster, *The Mortal Sea: Fishing the Atlantic in the Age of Sail*, Belknap Press, 2012, 31.

111. Martin, "The Goal and the Goldmine".

112. Carla Rahn Phillips, *Six Galleons for the King of Spain. Imperial Defense in the Early 17th Century*, Johns Hopkins University Press, 1986, 35; Filipe Castro, "In Search of Unique Iberian Ship Design Concepts", *Historical Archaeology*, 42:2, 2008, 63–87; Cláudia Rei, "The Organization of Merchant Empires", PhD dissertation, Boston University, 2009, 78–79; De Vries and Van Der Woude, *The First Modern Economy*, 355.

113. Rei, "The Organization of Merchant Empires", 78–79.

114. De Vries and Van Der Woude, *The First Modern Economy*, 357.

115. Tracy, *Holland under Habsburg Rule*, 95.

116. Bart Lambert, "Merchants on the Margins: Fifteenth-Century Bruges and the Informal Market", *Journal of Medieval History*, 42:2, 2016), 226–253.

117. Tracy, *Holland under Habsburg Rule*, 177.

118. De Vries and Van Der Woude, *The First Modern Economy*, 353, 350.

119. C. Lesger, "Intraregional Trade and the Port System in Holland, 1400–1700", in K. Davids and L. Noordegraaf (eds.), *The Dutch Economy in the Golden Age*, Netherlands Economic History Archive, 1993; Bas Van Bavel et al., "The Organisation of Markets as a Key Factor in the Rise of Holland from the Fourteenth to the Sixteenth Century: A Test Case for an Institutional Approach", *Continuity and Change*, 27, 2012, 347–378; van Dam, "Sinking Peat Bogs"; Bavel, *Manors and Markets*, ch. 6; Van Tielhof, "Grain Provision in Holland"; Dijkman, *Shaping Medieval Markets*, 275–298; Davies, *God''s Playground*, 257; De Vries and Van Der Woude, *The First Modern Economy*, 177–178, 415.

120. Tracy, *Holland under Habsburg Rule*, 97.

121. Gelderblom, *Cities of Commerce*, 149; Sicking, *Neptune and the Netherlands*, ch. 1.

122. Glete, *Warfare at Sea*, ch. 7; Sicking, *Neptune and the Netherlands*, ch. 4.

123. Lambert, *The Making of the Dutch Landscape*; Israel, *The Dutch Republic*, 121.

124. Tracy, *Holland under Habsburg Rule*, 75.

125. Virginia Lunsford, *Piracy and Privateering in the Golden Age Netherlands*, Palgrave Macmillan, 2005, 89. See also 44–46.

126. Richard Paping, "General Dutch Population Development 1400–1850: Cities and Countryside", University of Groningen, paper presented at Conference of the European Society of Historical Demography, Sardinia, 25–27 September, 2014.

127. M. J. Rodríguez-Salgado, "The Spanish Story of the 1588 Armada Reassessed", *Historical Journal*, 33:2, 1990, 461–478.

128. Lunsford, *Piracy and Privateering*, 17, 110; De Vries and Van Der Woude, *The First Modern Economy*, 404; Louis Sicking and Adri P. van Vliet, "Our Triumph of Holland's War. Violence and the Herring Fishery of the Low Countries, c. 1400–1650", in *Beyond the Catch: Fisheries of the North Atlantic, the North Sea and the Baltic, 900–1850*, Sicking and Darlene Abreu-Ferreira (eds.), Brill, 2009.

129. Phillips, *Six Galleons for the King of Spain*, ch. 1.

130. Erik Odegard, "The Sixth Admiralty: The Dutch East India Company and the Military Revolution at Sea, c. 1639–1667", *International Journal of Maritime History*, 26, 2014, 669–684.

131. Rodríguez-Salgado, "The Spanish Story of the 1588 Armada Reassessed".

132. Mark Meuwese, *Brothers in Arms, Partners in Trade: Dutch-Indigenous Alliances in the Atlantic World, 1595–1674*, Brill, 2012, 20–21.

133. Silvia Marzagalli, "The French Atlantic and the Dutch, Late Seventeenth–Late Eighteenth Century," in Gert Oostindie and Jessica V. Roitman (eds.), *Dutch Atlantic Connections, 1680–1800: Linking Empires, Bridging Borders*, Brill, 2014, 103–118.

134. David J. Starkey and Michael Haines, "The Newfoundland Fisheries, c. 1500–1900: A British Perspective", in Poul Holm Starkey and Tim D. Smith (eds.), *The Exploited Seas: New Directions for Marine Environmental History*, International Maritime Economic History Association; Starkey, "The Development of Fishing Fleets in the North Atlantic Ocean", in Christian Buchet (ed.), *The Sea in History. The Early Modern World*, Boydell Press, 2017.

135. Peter C. Emmer, "The First Global War: The Dutch versus Iberia in Asia, Africa and the New World, 1590–1609", *e-Journal of Portuguese History*, 1, 2003, 1–14; Catia Antunes, "The Commercial Relationship between Amsterdam and the Portuguese Salt-Exporting Ports: Aveiro and Setubal, 1580–1715", *Journal of Early Modern History*, 12:1, 2008, 25–53; Konrad A. Andrzej, and Ma. Magdalena Antczak, "Risky Business: Historical Archaeology of the Dutch Salt Enterprise on La Tortuga Island, Venezuela (1624–38)", *Post-Medieval Archaeology*, 49:2, 2015, 189–219.

136. C. R. Boxer quoted in Lunsford, *Piracy and Privateering*, 69.

137. Quoted in Markus P. M. Vink, "Between Profit and Power: The Dutch East India Company and Institutional Early Modernities in the 'Age of Mercantilism'", in Charles H. Parker and Jerry H. Bentley (eds.), *Between the Middle Ages and Modernity: Individual and Community in the Early Modern World*, Rowman & Littlefield, 2007.

138. Peter Vanderford Lape, "Contact and Conflict in the Banda Islands, Eastern Indonesia 11th–17th Centuries", PhD dissertation, Brown University, 2000; Martine van Ittersum, "Empire by Treaty? The Role of Written Documents in European Overseas Expansion, 1500–1800", in Adam Clulow and Tristan Mostert (eds.), *The Dutch and English East India Companies: Diplomacy, Trade and Violence in Early Modern Asia*, Amsterdam University Press, 2018.

139. Pim De Zwart, "Globalization in the Early Modern Era: New Evidence from the Dutch-Asiatic Trade, c. 1600–1800", *Journal of Economic History*, 76:2, 2016.

140. Jaap R. Bruijn and Femme S. Gaastra, "The Dutch East India Company's Shipping, 1602–1795, in Comparative Perspective", in Jaap R. Bruijn and Femme S. Gaastra (eds.), *Ships, Sailors and Spices: East India Companies and Their Shipping in the 16th, 17th and 18th Centuries*, NEHA, 1993. Another source gives 4,600 British voyages, 1600–1833. Ian Barrow, *The East India Company, 1600–1858*, Hackett Publishing, 2017, 10.

141. Jeffrey Robertson and Warwick Funnell, "The Dutch East-India Company and Accounting for Social Capital at the Dawn of Modern Capitalism 1602–1623", *Accounting, Organizations and Society*, 37, 2012, 342–360.

142. Wim Klooster, *The Dutch Moment. War, Trade and Settlement in the Seventeenth-Century Atlantic World*, Cornell University Press, 2016, 24; Filipa Da Silva, "African Islands and the Formation of the Dutch Atlantic Economy: Arguin, Gorée, Cape Verde and São Tomé, 1590–1670", *International Journal of Maritime History*, 26:3, 2014, 549–567.

143. H M. Feinberg, "New Data on European Mortality in West Africa: The Dutch on the Gold Coast, 1719–1760", *Journal of African History*, 15:3, 1974, 357–371.

144. Victor Enthoven, "Dutch Crossings. Migration between the Netherlands and the New World, 1600–1800", *Atlantic Studies*, 2:2, 2005.

145. Meuwese, *Brothers in Arms*, 37.

146. Ibid., 259–260; Enthoven, "Dutch Crossings".

147. Wim Klooster, "Curaçao as a Transit Center to the Spanish Main and the French West Indies", in Oostindie and Roitman (eds.), *Dutch Atlantic Connections*.

148. De Vries and Van Der Woude, *The First Modern Economy*, 254.

149. Jean-Pierre Proulx, *Whaling in the North Atlantic: From Earliest Times to the Mid-19th Century*, Parks Canada, 1986, 54, 57 (making the usual allowance of 25% for whales killed but not utilized).

150. Deconinck et al., "How Beer Created Belgium"; Geert H. Janssen, "The Dutchness of the Dutch Golden Age", *Historical Journal*, 53, 2010, 805–817; David Parrott, *The Business of War. Military Enterprise and Military Revolution in Early Modern Europe*, Cambridge University Press, 2012, 321.

151. Lambert, *The Making of the Dutch Landscape*, 177.

152. Ibid., 178.

153. Ibid., 204; Dijkman, *Shaping Medieval Markets*, 318.

154. Lesger, "Intraregional Trade".

155. Israel, *The Dutch Republic*, 116–117.

156. J. L. van Zanden, "Economic Growth in the Golden Age. The Development of the Economy of Holland, 1500–1650", in Davids and Noordegraaf (eds.), *The Dutch Economy*, 30–31.

157. Israel, *The Dutch Republic*, 1178; Lambert, *Making of the Dutch Landscape*, 177.

158. Lesger, "Intraregional Trade".

159. Tracy, *Holland under Habsburg Rule*, 109.

160. Donald J. Harreld, *High Germans in the Low Countries: German Merchants and Commerce in Gold Age Antwerp*, Brill, 2004, 37.

161. Ibid. 183.

162. Oscar Gelderblom and Joost Jonker, "Completing a Financial Revolution: The Finance of the Dutch East India Trade and the Rise of the Amsterdam Capital Market, 1595–1612", *Journal of Economic History*, 64:3, 2004, 641–672; Oscar Gelderblom, "From Antwerp to Amsterdam: The Contribution of Merchants from the Southern Netherlands to the Rise of the Amsterdam Market (c. 1540–1609)", *Review Fernand Braudel Center*, 26:3 2003, 247–282.

163. Harreld, *High Germans in the Low Countries*, 89.

164. Christopher Ebert, *Between Empires: Brazilian Sugar in the Early Atlantic Economy, 1550–1630*, Brill, 2008, 72.

165. Ann Carlos and Larry Neal, "Amsterdam and London as Financial Centers in the Eighteenth Century", *Financial History Review*, 18:1, 2011, 21–46.

166. Gelderblom and Jonker, "Completing a Financial Revolution".

167. Ibid.

168. Julia Adams, *The Familial State. Ruling Families and Merchant Capitalism in Early Modern Europe*, Cornell University Press, 2005, 55; Wim Klooster and Gert Oostindie, *Realm between Empires: The Second Dutch Atlantic, 1680–1815*, Cornell University Press, 2019, ch. 2.

169. Parrott, *The Business of War*, 321; Tracy, "Herring Wars".

170. Scott, *The City-State in Europe*, 205.

171. Adams, *The Familial State*, 47.

172. Vink, "Between Profit and Power", 299.

173. Harreld, *High Germans in the Low Countries*, 4.

174. Soderberg, "Prices and Economic Change in Medieval Sweden".

175. Kirby, *Northern Europe*, 239.

176. Leos Müller, *The Merchant Houses of Stockholm, c.1640–1800: A Comparative Study of Early-Modern Entrepreneurial Behaviour*, Uppsala University Library, 1998.

177. J. T. Kotilaine, *Russia's Foreign Trade and Economic Expansion in the Seventeenth Century: Windows on the World*, Brill, 2005, 67.

178. Erik Lindberg, "Club Goods and Inefficient Institutions: Why Danzig and Lübeck Failed in the Early Modern Period", *Economic History Review*, 62:3 (2009), 604–628; Piotr Guzowski, "The Influence of Exports on Grain Production on Polish Royal Demesne Farms in the Second Half of the Sixteenth Century", *Agricultural History Review*, 59:2, 2011, 312–327.

179. De Vries and Van Der Woude, *The First Modern Economy*, 200.

180. Cowan, "Cultural Traffic in Lubeck and Danzig".

181. Cerman, *Villagers and Lords*, 102.

182. De Vries and Van Der Woude, *The First Modern Economy*, 177–178.

183. Christiaan van Bochove, *The Economic Consequences of the Dutch. Economic Integration around the North Sea, 1500–1800*, Aksant, 2008, ch. 6.

184. Lunsford, *Piracy and Privateering*, 69, citing Richard Unger.

185. Van Bochove, *The Economic Consequences of the Dutch*, ch. 5.

186. Ibid., 85.

187. Gustav Sætra, "The International Labour Market for Seamen, 1600–1900: Norway and Norwegian Participation". in Paul van Royen, Jaap Bruijn, and Jan Lucassen (eds.), *"Those Emblems of Hell": European Sailors and the Maritime Labour Market, 1570–1870*, International Maritime Economic History Association, 1997.

188. Jaap Bruijn and Els van Eyck van Heslinga, "Seamen's Employment in the Netherlands (c. 1600–c.1800)", *Mariners' Mirror*, 70:1, 1984.

189. Gyorgy Novaky, "Swedish Naval Personnel in the Merchant Marine and in Foreign Naval Service in the Eighteenth Century", in Richard Gorski (ed.), *Maritime Labour: Contributions to the History of Work at Sea, 1500–2000*, Aksant, 2007.

190. Jelle van Lottum, Jan Lucassen, and Lex Heerma van Voss, "Sailors, National and International Labour Markets and National Identity, 1600–1850", in Richard Unger (ed.), *Shipping and Economic Growth 1350–1850*, Brill, 2011.

191. Adam Clulow, "'Great help from Japan': The Dutch East India Company's Experiment with Japanese Soldiers", in Clulow and Mostert (eds.), *The Dutch and English East India Companies*.

192. Connie Kelleher, "Pirate Ports and Harbours of West Cork in the Early Seventeenth Century", *Journal of Maritime Archaeology*, 8, 2013, 347–366.

193. Lisa Jardine, *Going Dutch. How England Plundered Holland's Glory*, Harper, 2009, 23.

194. Jonathan Oates, "Dutch Forces in 18th Century Britain; A British Perspective", *Journal of the Society for Army Historical Research*, 85, 2007, 20–39.

195. Parrott, *The Business of War*, 201–202.

196. Van Bochove, *The Economic Consequences of the Dutch*.

197. Jardine, *Going Dutch*, 338.

198. Jonathan Scott, *England's Troubles: Seventeenth-Century English Political Instability in European Context*, Cambridge University Press, 2000, 486.

199. Larry Neal, *The Rise of Financial Capitalism. International Capital Markets in the Age of Reason*, Cambridge University Press, 1990, 161; De Vries and Van Der Woude, *The First Modern Economy*, 144–146.

200. Carlos and Neal, "Amsterdam and London as Financial Centers".

201. Om Prakash, *The New Cambridge History of India: European Commercial Enterprise in Pre-colonial India*, Cambridge University Press, 1998, 118.

Chapter 13: Muslim Colonial Empires

1. I find that Giancarlo Casale uses the same anecdote to open his chapter ,"The Islamic Empires of the Early Modern World", in Jerry H. Bentley, Sanjay Subrahmanyam, and Merry E. Wiesner-Hanks (eds.), *The Cambridge World History, vol. 6, The Construction of a Global World, 1400–1800 CE, Part 1: Foundations*, Cambridge University Press, 2015.

2. Weston F. Cook, *The Hundred Years' War for Morocco: Gunpowder and the Military Revolution in the Early Modern Muslim World*, Westview Press, 1994.

3. Earnest W. Porta, "Morocco in the Early Atlantic World, 1415–1603", PhD dissertation, Georgetown University, 2018, 146–147. On plague strikes, see ibid., 150, and Mercedes Garcia-Arenal, *Ahmad al-Mansur: The Beginnings of Modern Morocco*, One World, 2009, 7, 136.

4. Garcia-Arenal, *Ahmad al-Mansur*, 73; Porta, "Morocco in the Early Atlantic World", 224, 242; Vincent J. Cornell, "Socio-economic Dimensions of Reconquista and Jihad in Morocco: Portuguese Dukkala and the Sadid Sus, 1450–1557", *International Journal of Middle East Studies*, 22, 1990, 379–418; Andrew Hess, *The Forgotten Frontier: A History of the Sixteenth-century Ibero-African Frontier*, University of Chicago Press, 1978, 115.

5. Cornell, "Socio-economic Dimensions"; Amira Bennison, "Liminal States: Morocco and the Iberian Frontier between the Twelfth and Nineteenth Centuries", *Journal of North African Studies*, 6:1, 2001, 11–28.

6. Abderrahmane El Moudden, "Sharifs and Padishahs: Moroccan-Ottoman Relations from the 16th through the 18th Centuries. Contribution to the Study of a Diplomatic Culture", PhD dissertation, Princeton University, 1992; Porta, "Morocco in the Early Atlantic World", 259–262; Garcia-Arenal, *Ahmad al-Mansur*, 9.

7. Garcia-Arenal, *Ahmad al-Mansur*, 30. Also see Stephen Cory, "The Man Who Would Be Caliph: A Sixteenth-Century Sultan's Bid for an African Empire", *International Journal of African Historical Studies*, 42, 2, 2009.

8. Chris Gratien, "Race, Slavery, and Islamic Law in the Early Modern Atlantic: Ahmad Baba al-Tinbukti's Treatise on Enslavement", *Journal of North African Studies*, 18:3, 2013, 454–468.

9. Alice Louise Willard, "Rivers of Gold, Oceans of Sand: The Songhay in the West African World-System", PhD dissertation, Johns Hopkins University, 1999.

10. John Hunwick, "Secular Power and Religious Authority in Muslim Society: The Case of Songhay", *Journal of African History*, 37, 1996, 175–194.

11. Lansiné Kaba, "Archers, Musketeers, and Mosquitoes: The Moroccan Invasion of the Sudan and the Songhay Resistance (1591–1612)", *Journal of African History*, 22, 1981, 457–475.

12. Garcia-Arenal, *Ahmad al-Mansur*, 104–105.

13. Kaba, "Archers, Musketeers, and Mosquitoes"; Gratien "Race, Slavery, and Islamic Law".

14. Garcia-Arenal, *Ahmad al-Mansur*, 107–108.

15. Quoted in Stephen Cory, *Reviving the Islamic Caliphate in Early Modern Morocco*, Routledge, 2013, 128.

16. Gratien, "Race, Slavery, and Islamic Law".

17. Francisco Bethencourt, "Political Configurations and Local Powers", in Francisco Bethencourt and Diogo Ramada Curto (eds.), *Portuguese Oceanic Expansion, 1400–1800*, Cambridge University Press, 2007.

18. Gratien, "Race, Slavery, and Islamic Law".

19. Ibid.

20. Kaba, "Archers, Musketeers, and Mosquitoes".

21. Garcia-Arenal, *Ahmad al-Mansur*, 98; Porta, "Morocco in the Early Atlantic World", 342; John K. Thornton, *Warfare in Atlantic Africa, 1500–1800*, 1999, UCL Press, 22.

22. Juan Cole, "Rival Empires of Trade and Imami Shi'ism in Eastern Arabia, 1300–1800", *International Journal of Middle East Studies*, 19:2, 1987, 177–204.

23. Leonor Freire Costa, Pedro Lains, and Susana Munch Miranda, *An Economic History of Portugal, 1143–2010*, Cambridge University Press, 2016, 112.

24. Donald Hawley, "Some Surprising Aspects of Omani History", *Asian Affairs*, 13:1, 1982, 28–39; Glenn J. Ames, "The Straits of Hurmuz Fleets; Omani-Portuguese Naval Rivalry and Encounters, c. 1660–1680", *Mariner's Mirror*, 83:4, 1997, 398–409.

25. Sanjay Subrahmanyam, "Of Imarat and Tijarat: Asian Merchants and State Power in the Western Indian Ocean, 1400 to 1750", *Comparative Studies in Society and History*, 37:4, 1995, 750–780; Tonio Andrade, "Beyond Guns, Germs, and Steel: European Expansion and Maritime Asia, 1400–1750", *Journal of Early Modern History*, 14:1–2, 2010, 165–186.

26. Hawley, "Some Surprising Aspects"; Andrade, "Beyond Guns, Germs, and Steel"; Subrahmanyam, "Of Imarat and Tijarat".

27. Ames "The Straits of Hurmuz Fleets".

28. Subrahmanyam, "Of Imarat and Tijarat". Also see Andrade, "Beyond Guns, Germs, and Steel".

29. Hawley, "Some Surprising Aspects".

30. Marcus Vink, Review of Willem Floor, *The Persian Gulf: Dutch-Omani Relations: A Commercial and Political History 1651–1806*, 2014, *International Journal of Maritime History*, 27:4, 2015, 837–838.

31. M. Reda Bhacker, *Trade and Empire in Muscat and Zanzibar: Roots of British Domination*, Routledge, 2002, 9.

32. Risso, Patricia, "Cross-Cultural Perceptions of Piracy: Maritime Violence in the Western Indian Ocean and Persian Gulf Region during a Long Eighteenth Century", *Journal of World History*, 2001, 12:2, 293–319.

33. Andrade, "Beyond Guns, Germs, and Steel".

34. J. Jones and N. A. Ridout, *History of Modern Oman*, Cambridge University Press 2015, ch. 1.

35. Bhacker, *Trade and Empire in Muscat and Zanzibar*, 20.

36. B. Arunachalam, "Technology of Indian Sea Navigation (c. 1200–c. 1800)", *Medieval History Journal*, 11:2, 2008, 187–227; Aniruddha Bose, "Science and Technology in India: The Digression of Asia and Europe", *History Compass*, 5:2, 2007, 375–385; Sinnappah Arasaratnam, *Maritime India in the Seventeenth Century*, Oxford University Press, 1994, 75–76, 252–253, 258.

37. Pius Malekandathil, "Indian Ocean in the Shaping of Late Medieval India", *Studies in History*, 30:2, 2014, 125–149.

38. Martha Chaiklin, "Surat and Bombay; Ivory and Commercial Networks in Western India", in Adam Clulow and Tristan Mostert (eds.), *The Dutch and English East India Companies: Diplomacy, Trade and Violence in Early Modern Asia*, Amsterdam University Press, 2018; Jones and Ridout, *History of Modern Oman*, ch. 2.

39. Malekandathil, "Indian Ocean"; Bhacker, *Trade and Empire in Muscat and Zanzibar*, 14, 34.

40. Ibid., 3–4.

41. Subrahmanyam, "Of Imarat and Tijarat"; D. Anthony Low and Harold G. Marcus, "Eastern Africa", *Encyclopædia Britannica*, 2015.

42. Bhacker, *Trade and Empire in Muscat and Zanzibar*, 26.

43. Hawley, "Some Surprising Aspects".

44. N. Thomas Håkansson, "The Human Ecology of World Systems in East Africa: The Impact of the Ivory Trade", *Human Ecology*, 32:5, 2004, 561–591.

45. Sean Stilwell, *Slavery and Slaving in African History*, Cambridge University Press, 2014, 170.

46. Rudi Mathee, "The Safavid Economy as Part of the World Economy", in Willem M. Floor and Edmund Herzig (eds.), *Iran and the World in the Safavid Age*, I.B. Tauris, 2012.

47. David Bulbeck, Anthony Reid, Lay Cheng Tan, and Yigi Wu, *Southeast Asian Exports since the 14th Century: Cloves, Pepper, Coffee and Sugar*, KITLV Press/Institute of Southeast Asian Studies, 1998, 10; Hawley, "Some Surprising Aspects".

48. Sugata Bose, *A Hundred Horizons: The Indian Ocean in the Age of Global Empire*, Harvard University Press, 2006, 102.

49. R. D. McChesney, "The Chinggisid Restoration in Central Asia: 1500–1785", *Cambridge History of Inner Asia. The Chinggisid Age*, Nicola Di Cosmo, Allen J. Frank, and Peter B. Golden (eds.), Cambridge University Press, 2009. Also see Alisher Ilkhamov, "Archaeology of Uzbek Identity", *Central Asian Survey*, 23:3, 2004, 289–326; Stephen Dale, *Indian Merchants and Eurasian Trade, 1600–1750*, Cambridge University Press, 1994, 15, 21.

50. Bert Fragner, "The Safavid Empire and the Sixteenth- and Seventeenth-Century Political and Strategic Balance of Power within the World System", in Floor and Herzig (eds.), *Iran and the World*.

51. Sholeh A. Quinn, "Iran under Safavid Rule", in David O. Morgan and Anthony Reid (eds.),, *The New Cambridge History of Islam Vol. 3*, Cambridge University Press, 2010; Nikolay Antov, "Imperial Expansion, Colonization, and Conversion to Islam in the Islamic World's 'Wild West': The Formation of the Muslim Community in Ottoman Deliorman (N.E. Balkans), 15th–16th cc", PhD dissertation, University of Chicago, 2011, ch. 4; Rudi Matthee, "Was Safavid Iran an Empire?", *Journal of the Economic and Social History of the Orient*, 53, 2010, 233–265.

52. Roger Savory, *Iran under the Safavids*, Cambridge University Press, 1980, 65, 69.

53. Ibid., 43–44.

54. Ali Anooshahr, "The Rise of the Safavids According to Their Old Veterans: Amini Ha-ravi's Futuhat-e Shahi", *Iranian Studies*, 48:2, 2015, 249–267.

55. Andrew de la Garza, "Mughals at War: Babur, Akbar, and the Indian Military Revolution, 1500–1605", PhD dissertation, Ohio State University, 2010, 61; Metin Kunt, "Ottomans and Sa-favids States, Statecraft, and Societies, 1500–1800", in Youssef M. Choueiri (ed.), *A Companion to the History of the Middle East*, Blackwell, 2005.

56. Savory, *Iran under the Safavids*, 112.

57. Willem Floor and Patrick Clawson, "Safavid Iran's Search for Silver and Gold", *International Journal of Middle East Studies*, 32:3, 2000, 345–368.

58. Edmund M. Herzig, "The Volume of Iranian Raw Silk Exports in the Safavid Period", *Iranian Studies*, 25.1/2, 1992, 61–79; "Silk", *Encyclopedia Iranica*; Rudi Mathee, "The Safavid Economy as Part of the World Economy", Floor and Herzig (eds.), *Iran and the World*.

59. Amita Satyal, "The Mughal Empire, Overland Trade, and Merchants of Northern India, 1526–1707", PhD dissertation, University of California, Berkeley, 2008, 197.

60. Janet Martin, "Muscovite Travelling Merchants: The Trade with the Muslim East (15th and 16th centuries)", *Central Asian Survey*, 4:3, 1985, 21–38.

61. Richard Foltz, *Iran in World History*, Oxford University Press, 2016, 78.

62. Sebouh D. Aslanian, "From the Indian Ocean to the Mediterranean: Circulation and the Global Trade Networks of Armenian Merchants from New Julfa/Isfahan, 1605–1747", PhD dis-sertation, Columbia University, 2007; Bhaswati Bhattacharya, "Armenian European Relation-ship in India, 1500–1800: No Armenian Foundation for European Empire?", *Journal of the Eco-nomic and Social History of the Orient*, 48:2, 2005, 277–322.

63. Peter Good, "The East India Company and the Foundation of Persian Naval Power in the Gulf under Nader Shah, 1734–47", in Adam Clulow and Tristan Mostert (eds.), *The Dutch and English East India Companies: Diplomacy, Trade and Violence in Early Modern Asia*, Amster-dam University Press, 2018.

64. David Washbrook, "India in the Early Modern World Economy: Modes of Production, Reproduction and Exchange", *Journal of World History*, 2:1, 2007, 87–111; Tim Dyson, *A Popula-tion History of India: From the First Modern People to the Present Day*, Oxford University Press, 2018, 125.

65. Foltz, *Iran in World History*, 73.

66. Jos Gommans, "Warhorses and Post-nomadic Empire in Asia, c. 1000–1800", *Journal of World History*, 2, 2007, 1–21; Stephen Dale, *The Muslim Empires of the Ottomans, Safavids, and Mughals*, Cambridge University Press, 73 and "India under Mughal Rule". in *The New Cambridge History of Islam Vol. 3*; Pratyay Nath, "Through the Lens of War: Akbar's Sieges (1567–69) and Mughal Empire-Building in Early Modern North India", *South Asia: Journal of South Asian Stud-ies*, 41:2, 2018, 245–258.

67. Iqtidar Alam Khan, *Gunpowder and Firearms: Warfare in Medieval India*, Oxford Univer-sity Press, 2004, 44, and "Gunpowder and Empire: Indian Case", *Social Scientist*, 33.3/4, 2005, 54–65; Ali Anooshahr, *The Ghazi Sultans and the Frontiers of Islam*, Taylor & Francis, 2008, ch. 1; Garza, "Mughals at War".

68. Anooshahr, *The Ghazi Sultans*, 34.

69. Garza, "Mughals at War", 67–69.

70. Khan, *Gunpowder and Firearms*, 63.

71. Garza, "Mughals at War", 71.

72. Khan, *Gunpowder and Firearms*, 64–74, 97; John F. Richards, *The Mughal Empire*, Cambridge University Press, 1995, Ch. 1.

73. Khan, "Gunpowder and Empire".

74. Ibid.

75. Richard Eaton, *The Rise of Islam and the Bengal Frontier, 1204–1760*, University of California Press, 1993, 18. Also see Garza, "Mughals at War", ch. 4.

76. Pratyay Nath, *Climate of Conquest: War, Environment, and Empire in Mughal North India*, Oxford University Press, 2019, from which all quotes in this paragraph are drawn.

77. Khan, *Gunpowder and Firearms*, 47; Richard Eaton and Philip Wagoner, "Warfare on the Deccan Plateau, 1450–1600: A Military Revolution in Early Modern India?", *Journal of World History*, 25:1, 2014 .

78. Ibid.

79. Pushkar Sohoni, "From Defended Settlements to Fortified Strongholds: Responses to Gunpowder in the Early Modern Deccan", *South Asian Studies*, 31:1, 2015, 111–126.

80. Eaton and Wagoner, "Warfare on the Deccan Plateau".

81. Sohoni, "From Defended Settlements to Fortified Strongholds".

82. Brendan P. LaRocque, "Trade, State, and Religion in Early Modern India: Devotionalism and the Market Economy in the Mughal Empire", PhD dissertation, University of Wisconsin–Madison, 2004.

83. Muzaffar Alam, "Trade, State Policy and Regional Change: Aspects of Mughal-Uzbek Commercial Relations, c. 1550–1750", *Journal of the Economic and Social History of the Orient*, 1994, 37:3, 202–227; LaRocque, "Trade, State, and Religion in Early Modern India".

84. Michael H. Fisher, *A Short History of the Mughal Empire*, I.B Tauris, 2016, 103–104; Subah Dayal, "Making the 'Mughal' Soldier: Ethnicity, Identification, and Documentary Culture in Southern India, c. 1600–1700", *Journal of the Economic and Social History of the Orient*, 5–6, 2019, 856–924.

85. David Washbrook, "India in the Early Modern World Economy". Also see Ravi Palat, *The Making of an Indian Ocean World-Economy, 1250–1650. Princes, Paddy Fields, and Bazaars*, Palgrave Macmillan, 2015, 128–129; Douglas E. Streusand, *Islamic Gunpowder Empires: Ottomans, Safavids, and Mughals*, Westview Press, 2010, 274.

86. Rajat Datta, "Governing Agrarian Diversities: The State and the Making of an Early Modern Economy in Sixteenth-century Northern India", *Medieval History Journal*, 16, 2, 2013, 473–499. Also see Shireen Moosvi, *People, Taxation, and Trade in Mughal India*, Oxford University Press, 2008.

87. Sinnappah Arasaratnam, *Maritime India in the Seventeenth Century*, Oxford University Press, 1994.

88. LaRocque, "Trade, State, and Religion", 53.

89. Bose, "Science and Technology in India".

90. Eaton, *The Rise of Islam and the Bengal Frontier*, 203 n24.

91. Prasannan Parthasarathi, *Why Europe Grew Rich and Asia Did Not: Global Economic Divergence, 1600–1850*, Cambridge University Press, 2011, 48. Also see Moosvi, *People, Taxation, and Trade*, 48–49.

92. Ibid., xxvii, 45–49. Parthasarathi, *Why Europe Grew Rich and Asia Did Not*, 48; Claude Markovitz, *A History of Modern India 1480–1950*, trans. Nisha George and Maggy Hendry, Anthem Press, 2002 (orig. 1994), 19.

93. Nile Green, *Making Space: Sufis and Settlers in Early Modern India*, Oxford University Press, 2012, Intro.

94. Markovitz, *A History of Modern India*, 117; Streusand, *Islamic Gunpowder Empires*, 275.

95. Eaton, *The Rise of Islam and the Bengal Frontier*.

96. Catherine B. Asher and Cynthia Talbot, *India Before Europe*, Cambridge University Press, 2006, 280.

97. Sumit Guha, "Rethinking the Economy of Mughal India: Lateral Perspectives", *Journal of the Economic and Social History of the Orient*, 58:4, 2015, 532–575.

98. Guha, "Rethinking the Economy of Mughal India"; Stephen Broadberry, Johann Custodis, and Bishnupriya Gupta, "India and the Great Divergence: An Anglo-Indian Comparison of GDP per Capita, 1600–1871", *Explorations in Economic History*, 55, 2015, 58–75.

99. Dale, *Indian Merchants and Eurasian Trade*.

100. Quoted in Satyal, "The Mughal Empire, Overland Trade", 3.

101. Datta, "Governing Agrarian Diversities".

102. Broadberry, Custodis, and Gupta, "India and the Great Divergence".

103. Nath, *Climate of Conquest*, 188. Quoting, and agreeing with, the seventeenth-century Dutch observer Francesco Pelsaert.

104. Shireen Moosvi, "A 'State Sector' in Overseas Trade: The Imperial Mughal Shipping Establishment at Surat", *Studies in People's History*, 2:1, 2015, 71–75.

105. Kathryn Wellen, "The Danish East India Company's War against the Mughal Empire, 1642–1698", *Journal of Early Modern History*, 19, 2015, 439–461.

106. Adam Clulow, "European Maritime Violence and Territorial States in Early Modern Asia, 1600–1650", *Itinerario*, 33:3, 2009.

107. Scott C. Levi, "Commercial Linkages with Central Asia and Iran", in Richard M. Eaton and Ramya Sreenivasan (eds.), *The Oxford Handbook of the Mughal World*, Oxford University Press, 2020.

108. Fisher, *Short History of the Mughal Empire*, 6.

109. Richards, *The Mughal Empire*, Intro; Richard C. Foltz, *Mughal India and Central Asia*, Oxford University Press, 1998, 6.

110. Asher and Talbot, *India Before Europe*, 154.

111. Kaushik Roy, "Mughal Empire and Warfare in Afghanistan 1500–1810", in Kaushik Roy (ed.), *War and Society in Afghanistan. From the Mughals to the Americans, 1500–2013*, Oxford University Press, 2015.

112. Dale, *Indian Merchants and Eurasian Trade*.

113. Ibid.

114. Roy, "Mughal Empire and Warfare in Afghanistan".

115. Rudi Mathee, "Safavid Iran and the 'Turkish Question' or How to Avoid a War on Multiple Fronts", *Iranian Studies*, 52:3–4, 2019, 513–542.

116. Sanjay Subrahmanyam, *Portuguese Empire in Asia, 1500–1700*, Wiley, 2012, 24.

117. A.C.S. Peacock, "The Ottoman Empire and the Indian Ocean", *Oxford Research Encyclopedia of Asian History*, 2018.

118. Fisher, *Short History of the Mughal Empire*, 112.

119. Subrahmanyam, *Portuguese Empire in Asia*, 24.

120. Jos Gommans, *Mughal Warfare: Indian Frontiers and High Roads to Empire, 1500–1700*, Routledge, 2002, 41. Also see Ali Anooshahr, "Mughals, Mongols, and Mongrels: The Challenge of Aristocracy and the Rise of the Mughal State in the Tarikh-i Rashidi", *Journal of Early Modern History*, 18, 2014, 559–577; Foltz, *Mughal India and Central Asia*, 36.

121. Sanjay Subrahmanyam, "Iranians Abroad: Intra-Asian Elite Migration and Early Modern State Formation", *Journal of Asian Studies*, 51:2, 1992, 340–363.

122. Satyal, "The Mughal Empire, Overland Trade", 94.

123. Gommans, *Mughal Warfare*, 95.

124. Corinne Lefèvre, "Messianism, Rationalism and Inter-Asian Connections: The Majalis-i Jahangiri (1608–11) and the Socio-intellectual History of the Mughal 'ulama," *Indian Economic and Social History Review*, 54:3, 2017, 317–338.

125. Foltz, *Iran in World History*, 76; Fragner, "The Safavid Empire".

126. Lefèvre, "Messianism, Rationalism and Inter-Asian Connections".

127. LaRocque, "Trade, State, and Religion in Early Modern India", 20.

128. Gommans, "Warhorse and Post-nomadic Empire".

129. Richard M. Eaton, "'Kiss My Foot,' Said the King: Firearms, Diplomacy, and the Battle for Raichur, 1520", *Modern Asian Studies*, 43:1, 2009, 289–313; Markovitz, *A History of Modern India*, 66.

130. Alam, "Trade, State Policy and Regional Change"; Ali Bahrani Pour, "The Trade in Horses between Khorasan and India in the 13th–17th centuries", *The Silk Road*, 11, 2013, 123–138; Abhimanyu Singh Arha, "Hoofprint of Empire: An Environmental History of Fodder in Mughal India (1650–1850)", *Studies in History*, 32:2, 186–208; Gommans, *Mughal Warfare*, 116.

131. Gommans, *Mughal Warfare*, 25.

132. Alam, "Trade, State Policy and Regional Change".

133. Pour, "The Trade in Horses".

Chapter 14: Plague and Russian Expansion

1. Allen J. Frank, "The Western Steppe: Volga-Ural Region, Siberia and the Crimea", in Nicola Di Cosmo, Allen J. Frank, and Peter B. Golden (eds.), *The Cambridge History of Inner Asia: The Chinggisid Age*, Cambridge University Press, 2009.

2. Anna Reid, *The Shaman's Coat: A Native History of Siberia*, Weidenfeld and Nicolson, 2002, 3.

3. Erika Monahan, *The Merchants of Siberia. Trade in Early Modern Eurasia*, Cornell University Press, 2016, 335.

4. Richard Hellie, "The Peasantry", in Maureen Perrie (ed.), *The Cambridge History of Russia. Vol. I*, Cambridge University Press, 2006, 291.

5. Lawrence N. Langer, "Economic Stagnation or Depression: War and the Economy in the Reign of Vasilii II", *Russian History*, 42, 2015, 32–48.

6. David B. Miller, "Monumental Building as an Indicator of Economic Trends in Northern Rus' in the Late Kievan and Mongol Periods, 1138–1462", *American Historical Review*, 94:2, 1989, 360–390.

7. Charles J. Halperin, *Russia and the Golden Horde: The Mongol Impact on Medieval Russia*, Indiana University Press, 1987, 83–84.

8. Miller, "Monumental Building".

9. P. C. B. Armstrong, "Foreigners, Furs and Faith: Muscovy's Expansion into Western Siberia, 1581–1649", MA thesis, Dalhousie University, 1997, 140.

10. Marian Małowist, "The Trade of Eastern Europe in the Later Middle Ages", in M. M. Postan, Edward Miller, and Cynthia Postan (eds.), *The Cambridge Economic History of Europe*, Vol. 2, Cambridge University Press, 1987 .

11. Lyuba Grinberg, "From Mongol Prince to Russian Saint: A Neglected 15th-Century Russian Source on the Mongol Land Consecration Ritual, *Kritika*, 12:3, 2011; Elena Pavlova, "Private Land Ownership in Northeastern Russia during the Late Appanage Period", PhD dissertation, Chicago University, 1998, 65–66; Małowist, "The Trade of Eastern Europe".

12. "Rome of the Waterways" is quoted by E. Tiberg, *Moscow, Livonia and the Hanseatic League 1487–1550*, Acta Universitatis Stockholmiensis, 1995, 12.

13. Roman Konstantinovich Kovalev, "The Infrastructure of the Novgorodian Fur Trade in the Pre-Mongol Era (ca. 900–ca.1240), PhD thesis, University of Minnesota, 2003, 2.

14. Henrik Birnbaum, *Lord Novgorod the Great: Essays in the History and Culture of a Medieval City-State. Part One: The Historical Background*, Slavica, 1981, 137; Kovalev, "Infrastructure of the Novgorodian Fur Trade", 321.

15. Tatjana N. Jackson, "Novgorod the Great in Baltic Trade before 1300", *Acta Borealia*, 25:2, 2008, 83–92.

16. Valentin L. Yanin, "The Archaeology of Novgorod", *Scientific American*, 262.2, 1990; Mark Maltby, "From Bovid to Beaver: Mammal Exploitation in Medieval Northwest Russia", in Umberto Albarella et al. (eds.), *The Oxford Handbook of Zooarchaeology*, Oxford University Press, 2017.

17. Langer, "Economic Stagnation"; Miller, "Monumental Building"; Janet Martin, *Medieval Russia 980–1584*, 2nd edn, Cambridge University Press, 2007, 222–223; Birnbaum, *Lord Novgorod the Great*; Nancy Shields Kollmann, *The Russian Empire 1450–1801*, Oxford University Press, 2017, 28.

18. Eve Levin, "Muscovy and Its Mythologies. Pre-Petrine History in the Past Decade", *Kritika*, 12:4, 2011, 773–788.

19. Pavel V. Lukin, "The Veche and the 'Council of Lords' in Medieval Novgorod. Hanseatic and Russian Data", *Russian History*, 41, 2014, 458–503; Nicholas V. Riasanovsky, *A History of Russia*, 5th edn., Oxford University Press, 1993, 83.

20. Teresa Pac, "Churches at the Edge: A Comparative Study of Christianization Processes along the Baltic Sea in the Middle Ages: Gdańsk and Novgorod", PhD dissertation, State University of New York at Binghamton, 2005, 81.

21. Janet Martin, "North-eastern Russia and the Golden Horde (1246–1359)", in Perrie (ed.), *The Cambridge History of Russia. Vol I*.

22. Michael Christopher Paul, "'A Man Chosen by God': The Office of Archbishop in Novgorod, Russia (1165–1478)", PhD dissertation, University of Miami, 2003, 318. Also see Pac, "Churches at the Edge".

23. Paul, "'A Man Chosen by God'", 206.

24. Nikolai J. Dejevsky, *Novgorod in the Early Middle Ages: The Rise and Growth of an Urban Community*, Oxford Archaeopress, 2007, 108.

25. Małowist, "The Trade of Eastern Europe". Also see Birnbaum, *Lord Novgorod the Great*, 137, and Riasanovsky, *A History of Russia*, 79.

26. Tiberg, *Moscow, Livonia and the Hanseatic League*, 25.

27. Edgar Melton, "The Russian Peasantries, 1450–1860", in Tom Scott (ed.), *The Peasantries of Europe: From the Fourteenth to the Eighteenth Centuries*, Longman, 1998, 227–266; Lukin, "The Veche and the 'Council of Lords'". Another source gives 520,000. Paul Bushkovitch, "Change and Culture in Early Modern Russia", *Kritika*, 16:2, 2015, 291–316.

28. Lukin, "The Veche and the 'Council of Lords'", Pac, "Churches at the Edge", 335; Henrik Birnbaum, *Novgorod in Focus: Selected Essays*, Slavica, 1996, 72.

29. Miller, "Monumental Building".

30. Małowist, "The Trade of Eastern Europe".

31. Zofia Brzozowska, "Sophia—the Personification of Divine Wisdom in the Culture of Novgorod the Great from 13th to 15th Century", *Studia Ceranea*, 4, 2014, 13–26; Maltby, "From Bovid to Beaver".

32. Robert O. Crummey, *The Formation of Muscovy, 1304–1613*, 1987, Longman, 57 and ch. 7.

33. D. Ostrowski, "Troop Mobilization by the Muscovite Grand Princes, 1313–1533", in Eric Lohr and Marshall Poe (eds.), *Military and Society in Russia, 1450–1917*, Brill, 2002.

34. Marian Małowist, "The Trade of Eastern Europe" and *Western Europe, Eastern Europe and World Development 13th–18th Centuries: Essays of Marian Małowist*, J. Batou and H. Szlajfer (eds.), Brill, 2009, ch. 15. Also see Jukka Korpela, "The Baltic Finnic People in the Medieval and Pre-Modern Eastern European Slave Trade", *Russian History*, 41, 2014, 85–117; Boris Kagarlitsky, *Empire of the Periphery. Russia and the World System*, trans. Renfrey Clarke, Pluto Press, 2008.

35. Kagarlitsky, *Empire of the Periphery*, 70.

36. Lawrence N. Langer, "Slavery in the Appanage Era: Rus' and the Mongols", in Christoph Witzenrath (ed.), *Eurasian Slavery, Ransom and Abolition in World History, 1200–1860*, Taylor & Francis, 2015.

37. Jukka Korpela, "'. . . And They Took Countless Captives': Finnic Captives and the East European Slave Trade during the Middle Ages", in Witzenrath (ed.), *Eurasian Slavery*.

38. Arkadiy E.Tarasov, "The Religious Aspect of Labour Ethics in Medieval and Early Modern Russia", *International Review of Social History*, 56, 2011, 125–140.

39. Vladimir Klimenko, "Thousand-year History of Northeastern Europe Exploration in the Context of Climatic Change: Medieval to Early Modern Times", *The Holocene*, 26:3, 2016, 365–379. Also see Tora Hultgreen, "When Did the Pomors Come to Svalbard?" *Acta Borealia*, 19:2, 2002, 125–145; T. A. Shrader, "Across the Borders: the Pomor Trade", in T. N. Jackson and J. P. Nielsen (eds.), *Russia-Norway: Physical and Symbolic Borders*, Moscow, 2005.

40. Nancy Shields Kollmann, "Russia", in Christopher Allmand (ed.), *The New Cambridge Medieval History*, Vol. 7, Cambridge University Press, 1998, 748–770.

41. Kovalev, "Infrastructure of the Novgorodian Fur Trade".

42. Janet Martin, *Treasure of the Land of Darkness: The Fur Trade and Its Significance for Medieval Russia*, Cambridge University Press, 1986, 68.

43. Kovalev, "Infrastructure of the Novgorodian Fur Trade", 321.

44. Richard Vaughan, "The Arctic in the Middle Ages", *Journal of Medieval History*, 8, 1982, 313–342.

45. Janet Martin, "The Land of Darkness and the Golden Horde. The Fur Trade under the Mongols XIIIth–XIVth Centuries", *Cahiers du Monde Russe et Soviétique*, 19:4, 1978, 401–421.

46. Crummey, *The Formation of Muscovy*, 63. Also see Martin, *Treasure of the Land of Darkness*, 132–134.

47. Kollmann, *The Russian Empire*, 50; Janet Martin, "The Emergence of Moscow (1359–1462)", in Perrie (ed.), *The Cambridge History of Russia. Vol. I.*

48. Heli Huhtamaa, "Climatic Anomalies, Food Systems, and Subsistence Crises in Medieval Novgorod and Ladoga", *Scandinavian Journal of History*, 40:4, 2015, 562–590; Langer, "Economic Stagnation".

49. V. L. Yanin, "Medieval Novgorod", in Perrie (ed.), *The Cambridge History of Russia. Vol. 1*; Riasanovsky, *A History of Russia*, 104–105.

50. Langer, "Slavery in the Appanage Era".

51. Michael Rywkin, "Russian Colonial Expansion before Ivan the Dread: A Survey of Basic Trends", *Russian Review*, 32:3, 1973, 286–293.

52. Barbara Alpern Engel and Janet Martin, *Russia in World History*, Oxford University Press, 2015, 20; Martin, *Medieval Russia*, 248.

53. Crummey, *The Formation of Muscovy*, 54.

54. Langer "Slavery in the Appanage Era".

55. Frank, "The Western Steppe".

56. Langer, "Slavery in the Appanage Era" and "Economic Stagnation".

57. Carol Belkin Stevens, *Russia's Wars of Emergence, 1460–1730*, Pearson Education, 2007, 24; Mark Greengrass, *Christendom Destroyed. Europe 1617–1648*, Allen Lane, 2014, 173.

58. Andrew Gentes, *Exile to Siberia, 1590–1822*, 2008, Palgrave Macmillan, 30, citing Boivoj Plavsic; Christoph Witzenrath, *Cossacks and the Russian Empire, 1598–1725: Manipulation, Rebellion and Expansion into Siberia*, 2007, Routledge, 3, citing Andreas Kappeler.

59. Riasanovsky, *A History of Russia*, 110.

60. Monahan, *The Merchants of Siberia*.

61. Ibid., 121.

62. Ostrowski, "Troop Mobilization"; Bulat R. Rakhimzianov, "Meshchera as a Point of Political Interaction between Muscovy and the Tartar World", *Russian History*, 43, 2016, 373–393.

63. Brian Davis, "The Recovery of Fugitive Peasants from Muscovy's Southern Frontier: The Case of Kozlov, 1636–40", *Russian History*, 19:1–4, 1992, 29–56; Richard Hellie, "Slavery and Serfdom in Russia", in Abbot Gleason (ed.), *A Companion to Russian History*, Blackwell, 2009; Witzenrath (ed.), *Eurasian Slavery*, Editor's Intro; Alessandro Stanziani, "Serfs, Slaves, or Wage Earners? The Legal Status of Labour in Russia from a Comparative Perspective, From the Sixteenth to the Nineteenth Century", *Journal of World History*, 3, 2008, 183–202, and "Revisiting Russian Serfdom: Bonded Peasants and Market Dynamics, 1600s–1800s", *International Labor and Working-Class History*, 78, 2010, 12–27.

64. Hellie, "Slavery and Serfdom". Hellie was generally reluctant to concede Russians any innovations at all.

65. Tarasov, "The Religious Aspect of Labour Ethics"; Donald Ostrowski, "The Growth of Muscovy (1462 to 1533)", in Perrie (ed.), *The Cambridge History of Russia. Vol. I*; Hellie, "Slavery

and Serfdom"; Stanziani, "Slavery and Bondage"; Hans-Heinrich Nolte, "Iasyry: Non-Orthodox Slaves in Pre-Petrine Russia", in Witzenrath (ed.), *Eurasian Slavery*; Langer, "Slavery in the Appanage Era".

66. Brian L. Davies, *Warfare, State and Society on the Black Sea Steppe, 1500–1700*, Routledge, 2007, 43, and "Muscovy's Conquest of Kazan", *Kritika*, 15:4, 2014, 873–883. Also see Ostrowski, "The Growth of Muscovy"; A. M. Kleimola, "Holding On in the 'Stamped-Over District'—the Survival of a Political Elite: Riazan Landholders in the Sixteenth Century", *Russian History*, 19:1–4, 1992, 129–142; Michael C. Paul, "The Military Revolution in Russia, 1550–1682", *Journal of Military History*, 68:1, 2004, 9–45.

67. Birnbaum, *Novgorod in Focus*, 74. But see his own *Lord Novgorod the Great*, n.119 and V. L. Yanin, "Medieval Novgorod"; Charles J. Halperin, "Novgorod and the 'Novgorodian Land'", *Cahiers du Monde Russe*, 40:3, 1999, 345–363; Yanin, "The Archaeology of Novgorod".

68. Charles J. Halperin, "Three 'Hands' and Literacy in Muscovy during the Reign of Ivan IV", *Canadian-American Slavic Studies*, 51, 2017, 29–63. Also see Boris N. Mironov, "The Development of Literacy in Russia and the USSR from the Tenth to the Twentieth Centuries", *History of Education Quarterly*, 31:2, 1991, 229–252.

69. Pavlova, "Private Land Ownership", 14–15, 20 and passim.

70. Christoph Witzenrath, "Literacy and Orality in the Eurasian Frontier: Imperial Culture and Space in Seventeenth-Century Siberia and Russia", *Slavonic & East European Review*, 2009, 87:1, 53–77; Alexandra M. Haugh, "Indigenous Political Culture and Eurasian Empire. Russia in Siberia in the Seventeenth Century", PhD dissertation, University of California, Santa Cruz, 2005, 314.

71. Charles Halperin, "Muscovite Political Institutions in the 14th Century", *Kritika*, 1:2, 2000, 237–257.

72. Langer, "Economic Stagnation".

73. Matthew P. Romaniello, "Controlling the Frontier: Monasteries and Infrastructure in the Volga Region, 1552–1682", *Central Asian Survey*, 19:3–4, 2000, 426–440.

74. Monahan, *The Merchants of Siberia*, 161; Pavlova, "Private Land Ownership".

75. Pavlova, "Private Land Ownership", 59–60, 74, 149.

76. Matthew P. Romaniello, *The Elusive Empire: Kazan and the Creation of Russia, 1552–1671*, University of Wisconsin Press, 2012 and "Controlling the Frontier".

77. Pavlova, "Private Land Ownership".

78. Ostrowski, "The Growth of Muscovy".

79. Tiberg, *Moscow, Livonia and the Hanseatic League*, 48.

80. Langer, "Economic Stagnation". Note the immigration of Greek merchants, the Khovrins, from Sudak in the 1350s. Also see Małowist, "The Trade of Eastern Europe in the Later Middle Ages"; Monahan, *The Merchants of Siberia*.

81. Erika Monahan Downs, "Trade and Empire: Merchant Networks, Frontier Commerce and the State in Western Siberia, 1644–1728", PhD dissertation, Stanford University, 2007, 19. And see ch. 2, 5.

82. Monahan, *The Merchants of Siberia*, 38.

83. Langer, "Economic Stagnation".

84. Janet Martin, "Muscovite Travelling Merchants: The Trade with the Muslim East (15th and 16th Centuries)", *Central Asian Survey*, 4:3, 1985, 21–38; Mary Jane Maxwell, "Afanasii

Nikitin: An Orthodox Russian's Spiritual Voyage in the Dar al-Islam, 1468–1475", *Journal of World History*, 17:3, 2006, 243–266.

85. Langer "Slavery in the Appanage Era".

86. Romaniello, *The Elusive Empire*.

87. Frank, "The Western Steppe".

88. Michael Khodarkovsky, "Taming the 'Wild Steppe': Muscovy's Southern Frontier, 1480–1600", *Russian History*, 26:3, 1999, 241–297.

89. Christian Noack, "The Western Steppe: The Volga-Ural Region, Siberia and the Crimea under Russian Rule", in *The Cambridge History of Inner Asia*.

90. Gabor Agoston, "Military Transformation in the Ottoman Empire and Russia, 1500–1800", *Kritika*, 12.2, 2011, 281–319; Paul, "The Military Revolution in Russia".

91. Langer, "Economic Stagnation".

92. Paul, "The Military Revolution in Russia".

93. Stevens, *Russia's Wars of Emergence*, 47.

94. Romaniello, *The Elusive Empire*, 31.

95. Paul, "The Military Revolution in Russia".

96. Khodarkovsky, "Taming the 'Wild Steppe'".

97. Victor Ostapchuk, "The Ottoman Black Sea Frontier and the Relations of the Porte with the Polish-Lithuanian Commonwealth d Muscovy, 1622–1628", PhD thesis, Harvard University, 1989, 83.

98. Khodarkovsky, "Taming the 'Wild Steppe'".

99. Janet Marie Kilian, "Allies & Adversaries: The Russian Conquest of the Kazakh Steppe", PhD dissertation, George Washington University, 2013.

100. Shane O'Rourke, *The Cossacks*, Manchester University Press, 2007, 32; M. I. Chukhryaeva et al., "The Haplomatch Program for Comparing Y-Chromosome STR-Haplotypes and Its Application to the Analysis of the Origin of Don Cossacks", *Russian Journal of Genetics*, 52:5, 2016, 521–529.

101. Chukhryaeva et al., ". . . the Analysis of the Origin of Don Cossacks"; O'Rourke, *The Cossacks*, 27.

102. Rakhimzianov, "Meshchera as a Point of Political Interaction".

103. O'Rourke, *The Cossacks*, 52.

104. Brian J. Boeck, *Imperial Boundaries: Cossack Communities and Empire Building in the Age of Peter the Great*, Cambridge University Press, 2009, 35.

105. Maureen Perrie, "Folklore as Evidence of Peasant Mentalite: Social Attitudes and Values in Russian Popular Culture", *Russian Review*, 48:2, 1989, 119–143.

106. Witzenrath, *Cossacks and the Russian Empire*, 11, 41.

107. Davies, *Warfare, State and Society*, 39; O'Rourke, *The Cossacks*, 48–49.

108. Nicholas V. Feodoroff, *History of the Cossacks*, Nova Science, 1999; Boeck, *Imperial Boundaries*, 25, 43.

109. Murat Yaşar, "The North Caucasus between the Ottoman Empire and the Tsardom of Muscovy: The Beginnings, 1552–1570", *Iran and the Caucasus*, 20, 2016, 105–125.

110. Rudi Matthee, "Anti-Ottoman Politics and Transit Rights: The Seventeenth-Century Trade in Silk between Safavid Iran and Muscovy", *Cahiers du Monde Russe*, 35:4, 1994, 739–761.

111. Ostapchuk, "The Ottoman Black Sea Frontier", ch. 2–3; Davies, *Warfare, State and Society*, 32–33; Orest Subtelny, *Ukraine: A History*, 3rd edn, Toronto University Press, 2000, 106–113.

112. Davies, *Warfare, State and Society*, 89.

113. Stevens, *Russia's Wars of Emergence*, 89–90, 185.

114. Monahan, *The Merchants of Siberia*, 109.

115. Kilian. "Allies & Adversaries".

116. James Forsyth, *A History of the Peoples of Siberia. Russia's North Asian Colony, 1581–1900*, Cambridge University Press, 1992, 66.

117. Andrew Gentes, *Exile to Siberia, 1590–1822*, Palgrave Macmillan, 2008, 87; W. Bruce Lincoln, *Conquest of a Continent. Siberia and the Russians*, Cornell University Press, 1994, 63.

118. Jürgen Paul, "The Rise of the Khwajagan-Naqshbandiyya Sufi Order in Timurid Herat", in Nile Green (ed.), *Afghanistan's Islam: From Conversion to the Taliban*, University of California Press, 2016.

119. Haugh, "Indigenous Political Culture and Eurasian Empire", 70–71. My treatment of the khanate of Sibir is particularly indebted to this excellent thesis.

120. Monahan, *The Merchants of Siberia*, 77.

121. Haugh, "Indigenous Political Culture and Eurasian Empire", 70–71.

122. Craig G. Kennedy, "The Juchids of Muscovy: A Study of Personal Ties Between Emigre Tartar Dynasts and the Muscovite Grand Princes in the Fifteenth and Sixteenth Centuries", PhD dissertation, Harvard University, 1994.

123. Haugh, "Indigenous Political Culture and Eurasian Empire".

124. Monahan, *The Merchants of Siberia*, 78.

125. Haugh, "Indigenous Political Culture and Eurasian Empire".

126. S. F. Mataurov, "The Kuchumovichi in Tara's Cis-Irtysh Region and Storming the City of Tara in 1634", *Golden Horde Review*, 6:1, 2018, 134–144.

127. Janet M. Hartley, *Siberia: A History of the People*, Yale University Press, 2014, 35.

128. Monahan, *The Merchants of Siberia*, 292.

129. Raymond H. Fisher, *The Russian Fur Trade, 1550–1700*, University of California Press, 1943, 115.

130. Fisher, *The Russian Fur Trade*, 138. The 1595 gift numbers are accepted by later historians.

131. Oleg V. Bychkov, "Russian Hunters in Eastern Siberia in the Seventeenth Century: Lifestyle and Economy", trans. Mina A. Jacobs, *Arctic Anthropology*, 31:1, 1994, 72–85.

132. Lincoln *Conquest of a Continent*, 86 (and see map 1, x–xi) says 29 posts by 1640. Hartley, (*Siberia*, 11) says over 50 fortified villages by 1630.

133. Fisher, *The Russian Fur Trade*, 153.

134. J. T. Kotilaine, *Russia's Foreign Trade and Economic Expansion in the Seventeenth Century: Windows on the World*, Brill, 2005, 194.

135. Alexander Etkind, *Internal Colonization: Russia's Imperial Experience*, Polity, 2011, 80, citing the research of Oleg Vilkov. Also see Monahan, *The Merchants of Siberia*, 86.

136. Witzenrath, *Cossacks and the Russian Empire*, 45.

137. Dmitry Beyer, "Women, Gender and Sexuality in Tsarist Siberia, 1582–1906", MA thesis, University of Wisconsin–Milwaukee, 2013.

138. Forsyth, *Peoples of Siberia*, 76.

139. E. Bekmakhanova, quoted in Andrew A. Gentes, "'Licentious Girls' and Frontier Domesticators: Women and Siberian Exile from the Late 16th to the Early 19th Centuries", *Sibirica*, 3:1, 2003, 3–20; Forsyth, *Peoples of Siberia*.

140. Gentes, "'Licentious Girls'."

141. Beyer, "Women, Gender and Sxuality".

142. Witzenrath, *Cossacks and the Russian Empire*, 252.

143. Yuri Slezkine, "The Sovereign's Foreigners: Classifying the Native Peoples of 17th Century Siberia", *Russian History*, 19:1–4, 1992, 475–485; Martina Winkler, "Another America: Russian Mental Discoveries of the North-west Pacific Region in the Eighteenth and Early Nineteenth Centuries", *Journal of World History*, 7, 2012, 27–51.

144. Beyer, "Women, Gender and Sexuality", 52, citing D. J. Ostrowski.

145. Ibid., 98, 123.

146. Gwenn A. Miller, *Kodiak Kreol: Communities of Empire in Early Russian America*, Cornell University Press, 2010, 138. Also see Aron L. Crowell, "Russians in Alaska, 1784: Foundations of Colonial Society at Three Saints Harbor, Kodiak Island", *Kroeber Anthropological Society Papers*, 81, 1997, 10–41; Andrei V. Grinev, "A Fifth Column in Alaska: Native Collaborators in Russian America", Richard L. Bland, trans., *Alaska History*, 22, 2007, 1–21; Martha Ortega Soto, "Impact on the Spanish Empire of the Russian Incursion into the North Pacific, 1741–1821", in Danna A. Levin Rojo and Cynthia Radding (eds.), *The Handbook of Borderlands of the Iberian World*, Oxford University Press, 2019.

147. Ryan Tucker Jones, "A 'Havock Made among Them': Animals, Empire, and Extinction in the Russian North Pacific, 1741–1810", *Environmental History*, 16, 2011, 585–609.

148. Hartley, *Siberia*, ch. 4.

149. Brigitte Pakendorf et al., "Mitochondrial DNA Evidence for Admixed Origins of Central Siberian Populations", *American Journal of Physical Anthropology*, 120, 2003, 211–224; L. Tarskaia, "Surnames in Siberia: A Study of the Population of Yakutia through Isonymy", *American Journal of Physical Anthropology*, 138:2, 2009, 190–198.

150. David N. Collins, "Sexual Imbalance n Frontier Communities: Siberia and New France to 1760", *Sibirica*, 4:2, 2004, 162–185.

151. Collins, "Sexual Imbalance in Frontier Communities".

152. Tatiana Tairova, "Elite Women in the Ukrainian Hetmanate", *Canadian Slavonic Papers*, 60:1–2, 2018, 26–43; Boeck, *Imperial Boundaries*, 215.

153. Feodoroff, *History of the Cossacks*, 73.

154. Collins, "Sexual Imbalance in Frontier Communities".

155. Feodoroff, *History of the Cossacks*, 147.

156. Andrew Gentes, "'Licentious Girls.'"

157. Gentes, *Exile to Siberia*, 37, citing the research of Petr Slovtsov.

158. Shrader, "Across the Borders: The Pomor Trade".

159. Hultgreen, "When Did the Pomors Come to Svalbard?"

160. Raymond H. Fisher, "Mangazeia: A Boom Town of Seventeenth Century Siberia", *Russian Review*, 4:1, 1944, 89–99.

161. Hartley, *Siberia*, ch. 4.

162. Klimenko, "Thousand-year History of Northeastern Europe Exploration".

163. Collins, "Sexual Imbalance in Frontier Communities".

164. Pakendorf et al., "Mitochondrial DNA Evidence for Admixed Origins"..

165. E. F. Fursova, "Western Siberian Folk Art: Northern Russian and Ural Traditions in Distaff Decoration", *Archaeology, Ethnology & Anthropology of Eurasia*, 40:3, 2012, 103–113.

166. Hartley, *Siberia*, ch. 4.

167. Forsyth, *Peoples of Siberia*, 115; Noack, "The Western Steppe"; Beyer, "Women, Gender and Sexuality".

168. Hartley, *Siberia*, ch. 2; Reid, *The Shaman's Coat*, 2.

169. Kollmann, *The Russian Empire*, 29; Forsyth, *Peoples of Siberia*, 58; Peter C. Perdue, *China Marches West: The Qing Conquest of Central Asia*, Belknap Press, 2005, 91; Etkind, *Internal Colonization*, 77.

170. Kollmann, *The Russian Empire*, 29.

171. Beyer, "Women, Gender and Sexuality", 110–111, 124–125.

172. Andrei A. Znamenski, "'Vague Sense of Belonging to the Russian Empire'; The Reindeer Chukchi's Status in 19th Century Northeastern Siberia", *Arctic Anthropology*, 36, 1999, 19–36; Lincoln, *Conquest of a Continent*, 55.

173. Haugh, "Indigenous Political Culture and Eurasian Empire", 129–168; Hartley, *Siberia*, 40.

174. Alfred J. Rieber, "Russia in Asia", *Oxford Research Encyclopedia of Asian History*, 2018.

175. Kilian, "Allies & Adversaries"; Khodarkovsky, *Russia's Steppe Frontier*, 133; Noack, "The Western Steppe".

176. Jiger Janabel, "From Mongol Empire to Qazaq Juzder: Studies on the Steppe Political Cycle (13th–18th Centuries)", PhD dissertation, Harvard University, 1997, 99.

177. Perdue, *China Marches West*, 307.

178. Kilian, "Allies & Adversaries", ch. 2. Also see Monahan, *The Merchants of Siberia*, ch. 5.

179. Kilian, "Allies & Adversaries", 56–57.

180. Quoted in Hyeok Hweon Kang, "Big Heads and Buddhist Demons: The Korean Musketry Revolution and the Northern Expeditions of 1654 and 1658", *Journal of Chinese Military History*, 2, 2013, 127–189.

181. Kang, "Big Heads and Buddhist Demons". Also see Andrey V. Ivanov, "Conflicting Loyalties: Fugitives and 'Traitors' in the Russo-Manchurian Frontier, 1651–1689", *Journal of Early Modern History*, 13, 2009, 333–358; Hartley, *Siberia*, 15–16.

182. Ivanov, "Conflicting Loyalties".

183. Ibid.

184. Fisher, *The Russian Fur Trade*, 222–233.

185. Kollmann, *The Russian Empire*, ch. 8.

186. Fisher, *The Russian Fur Trade*, 237; Monahan, *The Merchants of Siberia*, 167.

187. Fisher, *The Russian Fur Trade*, 233.

188. Eva-Maria Stolberg, "Interracial Outposts in Siberia; Nerchinsk, Kiakhta, and the Russo-Chinese Trade in the Seventeenth/Eighteenth Centuries", *Journal of Early Modern History*, 4:3–4, 2000, 322–336.

189. Ibid.

190. Ibid.

191. Muping Bao, "Trade Centres (Maimaicheng) in Mongolia, and Their Function in Sino-Russian Trade Networks", *International Journal of Asian Studies*, 3:2, 2006, 211–237.

192. Lincoln, *Conquest of a Continent*, 145–146.

193. Ryan Jones, "Empire of Extinction: Nature and Natural History in the Russian North Pacific, 1739–1799", PhD dissertation, Columbia University, 2008.

194. Jones, "Empire of Extinction", 133–135.

195. Jones, "A 'Havock Made among Them.'"

196. Crowell, "Russians in Alaska".

197. Stuart Banner, *Possessing the Pacific: Land, Settlers, and Indigenous People from Australia to Alaska*, Harvard University Press, 2007, 291; Benson Bobrick, *East of the Sun: The Epic Conquest and Tragic History of Siberia*, Poseidon Press, 1992, ch. 11.

198. Andrei V. Grinev, "A Fifth Column in Alaska: Native Collaborators in Russian America", Richard L. Bland, trans., *Alaska History*, 22, 2007, 1–21.

199. Richard Ravalli, Kirsten Livingston, and Hannah Zimmerman, "A Revised List of Vessels Engaged in the California Sea Otter Trade, 1786–1847", *International Journal of Maritime History*, 24:2, 2012, 225. This study counts 50,000 skins, 1786–1847, but the great majority were taken before 1812, and at least half the ships involved left no count.

200. Kovalev, "Infrastructure of the Novgorodian Fur Trade", 105.

201. Ann M. Carlos and Frank D. Lewis, *Commerce by a Frozen Sea: Native Americans and the European Fur Trade*, University of Pennsylvania Press, 2010, 19; E. E. Rich, "Russia and the Colonial Fur Trade", *Economic History Review*, 7:3 (1955), 307–328.

202. Winkler, "Another America".

203. Monahan, *The Merchants of Siberia*, 338.

204. Fisher, *The Russian Fur Trade*, 220–221; Stephen Dale, *Indian Merchants and Eurasian Trade, 1600–1750*, Cambridge University Press, 1994, ch. 4.

Part IV: Expansion, Industry, and Empire

1. Faruk Tabak, *The Waning of the Mediterranean, 1550–1870: A Geohistorical Approach*, Johns Hopkins University Press, 2010, 18–19; Geoffrey Parker, *Global Crisis: War, Climate Change and Catastrophe in the Seventeenth Century*, Yale University Press, 2013, ch. 7.

2. John Thomas Wing, "Roots of Empire: State Formation and the Politics of Timber Access in Early Modern Spain, 1556–1759", PhD dissertation, University of Minnesota, 2009, 204.

3. Jonathan Grant, "Rethinking the Ottoman 'Decline': Military Technology Diffusion in the Ottoman Empire, Fifteenth to Eighteenth Centuries", *Journal of World History*, 10:1, 1999, 179–201.

4. Alan Mikhail, *Nature and Empire in Ottoman Egypt: An Environmental History*, Cambridge University Press, 2011, and *Under Osman's Tree: The Ottoman Empire, Egypt, and Environmental History*, University of Chicago Press, 2017.

5. Guido Alfani, "Economic Inequality in Northwestern Italy: A Long-Term View (Fourteenth to Eighteenth Centuries)", *Journal of Economic History*, 75:4, 2015, 1058–1096. Also see Alfani, "Plague in Seventeenth-Century Europe and the Decline of Italy: An Epidemiological Hypothesis", *European Review of Economic History*, 17, 2013, 408–430.

6. Jan Luiten van Zanden and Emanuele Felice, "Benchmarking the Middle Ages. XV Century Tuscany in European Perspective", Utrecht University Centre for Global Economic History, Working paper no. 81, 2017.

7. E. A. Ekert, "The Retreat of Plague from Central Europe, 1640–1720: A Geomedical Approach", *Bulletin of the History of Medicine*, 2000, 74, 1–28; Ruth Mackay, *Life in a Time of Pestilence: The Great Castilian Plague of 1596–1601*, Cambridge University Press, 2019.

8. Mikhail, *Under Osman's Tree*, 147; K. K. Karaman and S. Pamuk, "Ottoman State Finances in European Perspective, 1500–1914", *Journal of Economic History*, 70:3, 2010.

9. Sven Beckert, *Empire of Cotton. A New History of Global Capitalism*, Penguin, 2014, 27; Prasannan Parthasarathi, *Why Europe Grew Rich and Asia Did Not: Global Economic Divergence, 1600–1850*, Cambridge University Press, 2011, ch. 5; Giorgio Riello, *Cotton: The Fabric that Made the Modern World*, Cambridge University Press, 2013, 70–72.

10. Peer Vries, *State, Economy and the Great Divergence. Great Britain and China, 1680s–1850s*, Bloomsbury, 2015, 243, 249.

11. Regina Grafe and Maria Alejandra Irigoin, "A Stakeholder Empire: The Political Economy of Spanish Imperial Rule in America", *Economic History Review*, 65:2, 2012, 609–651; Alejandra Irigoin and Regina Grafe, "Bargaining for Absolutism: A Spanish Path to Nation-State and Empire Building", *Hispanic American Historical Review*, 88:2, 2006; Scott Eastman, "The Spanish Empire and Atlantic World History", *Journal of Colonialism and Colonial History*, 15:2, 2014.

12. Karaman and Pamuk, "Ottoman State Finances"; Sevket Pamuk, "Institutional Change and Economic Development in the Middle East, 700–1800", in Larry Neal and Jeffrey G., Williamson (eds.), *The Cambridge History of Capitalism. Vol. 1*, Cambridge University Press, 2014; Karen Barkey, *Empire of Difference: The Ottomans in Comparative Perspective*, Cambridge University Press, 2008, 257.

13. Gabor Ágoston, "Military Transformation in the Ottoman Empire and Russia, 1500–1800", *Kritika*, 12:2, 2011, 281–319.

Chapter 15: Empire? What Empire?

1. Roland Oliver and Anthony Atmore, *Medieval Africa, 1250–1800*, Cambridge University Press, revised edn, 2001, 7, 67–68, 81–89.

2. Núria Silleras-Fernández, "*Nigra Sum Sed Formosa*: Black Slaves and Exotica in the Court of a Fourteenth-Century Aragonese Queen", *Medieval Encounters*, 13, 2007, 546–565; Debra Blumenthal, *Enemies and Familiars: Slavery and Mastery in Fifteenth-Century Valencia*, Cornell University Press, 2009, 20–21; P. E. Russell, *A Social History of Black Slaves and Freedmen in Portugal*, 1441–1555, Cambridge University Press, 1982, 194; Joaquim Romero Magalhães, "Africans, Indians, and Slavery in Portugal", *Portuguese Studies*, 13, 1997, 143–151; William D. Phillips, "Slavery in the Atlantic Islands and the Early Modern Spanish Atlantic World", in David Eltis and Stanley L. Engerman (eds.), *The Cambridge World History of Slavery Volume 3*, Cambridge University Press, 2011.

3. Robin Blackburn, *The Making of New World Slavery. From the Baroque to the Modern, 1492–1800*, Verso, 2010 (orig. 1997), 114. Also see Christoph Witzenrath (ed.), *Eurasian Slavery, Ransom and Abolition in World History, 1200–1860*, Taylor & Francis. 2015, Editor's Intro.

4. Toby Green, *The Rise of the Trans-Atlantic Slave Trade in Western Africa, 1300–1589*, Cambridge University Press, 2012, 79–89; Trevor Paul Hall, "The Role of Cape Verde Islanders in Organizing nd Operating Maritime Trade Between West Africa And Iberian Territories, 1441–1616", PhD dissertation, Johns Hopkins University, 1993.

5. Hall, "The Role of Cape Verde Islanders ", 103–104.

6. John K. Thornton, *Warfare in Atlantic Africa, 1500–1800*, 1999, UCL Press, 81, 62.

7. W. A. Richards, "The Import of Firearms into West Africa in the Eighteenth Century", *Journal of African History*, 21:1, 1980, 43–59; Priya Satiya, *Empire of Guns: The Violent Making of the Industrial Revolution*, Penguin, 2018, esp. 189; Giacomo Macola, "An Africanist's Perspective on Priya Satia's Empire of Guns", *Journal of World History*, 14:3, 2019, 461–462.

8. Joseph Inikori, "The Import of Firearms into West Africa 1750–1807: A Quantitative Analysis", *Journal of African History*, 18:3, 1977, 339–368; Richards, "The Import of Firearms into West Africa".

9. Richards, "The Import of Firearms into West Africa"; Ralph A. Austen, "Imperial Reach Versus Institutional Grasp: Superstates of the West and Central African Sudan in Comparative Perspective", *Journal of Early Modern History*, 13, 2009, 509–541.

10. Warren C. Whatley, "The Gun-Slave Hypothesis and the 18th Century British Slave Trade", *Explorations in Economic History*, 67, 2018, 80–104.

11. Richard J. Follett, *The Sugar Masters: Planters and Slaves In Louisiana's Cane World, 1820–1860*, Louisiana State University Press, 2005; Michael Tadman, "The Demographic Cost of Sugar: Debates on Slave Societies and Natural Increase in the Americas", *American Historical Review*, 105:5, 2000, 1534–1575.

12. B. W. Higman, "The Sugar Revolution", *Economic History Review*, 53:2, 2000, 213–236; Richard S. Dunn, "The Demographic Contrast between Slave Life in Jamaica and Virginia, 1760–1865", *Proceedings of the American Philosophical Society*, 151:1, 2007, 43–60.

13. Ralph Davis, *The Rise of the Atlantic Economies*, Weidenfeld and Nicolson, 1973, 136.

14. A. W. Lawrence, *Trade Castles and Forts of West Africa*, Jonathan Cape, 1963.

15. Christopher R. DeCorse, "The Danes on the Gold Coast: Culture Change and the European Presence", *African Archaeological Review*, 11, 1993, 149–173.

16. Jennifer Lofkrantz and Paul E. Lovejoy, "Maintaining Network Boundaries: Islamic Law and Commerce from Sahara to Guinea Shores", *Slavery & Abolition*, 36:2, 2015, 211–232.

17. Rebecca Shumway, "Castle Slaves of the Eighteenth-Century Gold Coast (Ghana)", *Slavery & Abolition*, 35:1, 2014, 84–98.

18. P.E.H. Hair and Robin Law, "The English in Western Africa to 1700", in Nicholas Canny (ed.), *The Oxford History of the British Empire, Vol.1*, Oxford University Press, 1998.

19. Ousmane Traoré, "State Control and Regulation of Commerce on the Waterways and Coast of Senegambia, ca. 1500–1800", in Carina E. Ray and Jeremy Rich (eds.), *Navigating African Maritime History*, Liverpool University Press, 2009; Toby Green, *A Fistful of Shells: West Africa from the Rise of the Slave Trade to the Age of Revolution*, Allen Lane, 2019; Ray A. Kea, "Africa in World History, 1400 to 1800", in Jerry H. Bentley, Sanjay Subrahmanyam, and Merry E. Wiesner-Hanks (eds.), *The Cambridge World History, Vol. 6: The Construction of a Global World, 1400–1800 CE, Part 1: Foundations*, Cambridge University Press, 2015.

20. Hall, "The Role of Cape Verde Islanders". Also see Peter Mark, "The Evolution of 'Portuguese' Identity: Luso-Africans on the Upper Guinea Coast from the Sixteenth to the Early Nineteenth Century", *Journal of African History*, 40, 1999, 173–191; Natalie Everts, "Social Outcomes of Trade Relations: Encounters Between Africans and Europeans in the Hubs of the Slave Trade on the Guinea Coast", in Wim Klooster (ed.), *Migration, Trade, and Slavery in an Expanding World*, Brill, 2009.

21. Malyn Newitt, *Emigration and the Sea. An Alternative History of Portugal and the Portuguese*, C. Hurst, 2015, 215.

22. Hall, "The Role of Cape Verde Islanders", 158–159, 172.

23. Regions of Embarkation, Atlantic Slave Trade Database, http://www.slavevoyages.org/assessment/estimates

24. Mariana P. Candido, *An African Slaving Port and the Atlantic World. Benguela and Its Hinterland*, Cambridge University Press, 2013, 81. Also see Amaral Ferreira Roquinaldo, "Transforming Atlantic Slaving: Trade, Warfare and Territorial Control in Angola, 1650–1800", PhD dissertation, University of California, 2003; John Thornton, "The Art of War in Angola, 1575–1680", *Comparative Studies in Society and History*, 30:2, 1988, 360–378 and *Warfare in Atlantic Africa, 1500–1800*.

25. Russell-Wood, *The Portuguese Empire*, 69.

26. Sean Stilwell, *Slavery and Slaving in African History*, Cambridge University Press, 2014, 118–120.

27. Luiz Felipe de Alencastro, "The Economic Network of Portugal's Atlantic World", in Francisco Bethencourt and Diogo Ramada Curto (eds.), *Portuguese Oceanic Expansion, 1400–1800*, New York: Cambridge University Press, 2007.

28. Atlantic Slave Trade Database. Also see John Wood Sweet, "The Subject of the Slave Trade: Recent Currents in the Histories of the Atlantic, Great Britain, and Western Africa", *Early American Studies*, 7:1, 2009, 1–4; David Eltis, "The Volume and Structure of the Transatlantic Slave Trade: A Reassessment", *William and Mary Quarterly*, 58:1, 2001, 17–46.

29. Robin Blackburn came independently to a similar figure for embarkations 1500–1800 (8.34 million). *The Making of New World Slavery*, 377.

30. Pier Larson, "African Slave Trades in Global Perspective", in John Parker and Richard Reid (eds.), *Oxford Handbook of Modern African History*, Oxford University Press, 2013.

31. See Babacar M'Baye, "The Economic, Political, and Social Impact of the Atlantic Slave Trade on Africa", *The European Legacy*, 11:6, 2006, 607–622 and various works of Nathan Nunn.

32. Compare James Forsyth, *The Caucasus: A History*, Cambridge University Press, 2013 with Sean Stilwell, *Slavery and Slaving in African History*, Cambridge University Press, 2014.

33. Jordan Goodman, *Tobacco in History. The Cultures of Dependence*, Routledge, 1993, 51.

34. Ibid., 159; Stefan Halikoswki Smith, "Demystifying a Change in Taste: Spices, Space, and Social Hierarchy in Europe, 1380–1750", *International History Review*, 29:2, 2007, 237–257.

35. Blackburn, *The Making of New World Slavery*, 173. Also see Russell R. Menard, *Sweet Negotiations: Sugar, Slavery and Plantation Agriculture in Early Barbados*, University of Virginia Press, 2006; Christopher Ebert, *Between Empires: Brazilian Sugar in the Early Atlantic Economy, 1550–1630*, Brill, 2008; Jose Jobson De Andrade Arruda, "Colonies as Mercantile Investments: The Luso-Brazilian Empire, 1500–1808", in James D. Tracy (ed.), *The Political Economy of Merchant Empires: State Power and World Trade 1350–1750*, Cambridge University Press, 1991.

36. Max Savelle, *Empires to Nations: Expansion in America, 1713–1824*, University of Minnesota Press, 1974, 51. Also see Ralph A. Austen and Woodruff D. Smith, "Private Tooth Decay as Public Economic Virtue: The Slave-Sugar Triangle, Consumerism, and European Industrialization", *Social Science History*, 14, 1990, 95–115; Ahmed Reid, "Sugar, Slavery and Productivity in Jamaica, 1750–1807", *Slavery & Abolition*, 37:1, 2016, 59–182.

37. Norma J. Hall, "Northern Arc: The Significance of the Shipping and Seafarers of Hudson Bay, 1508–1920", PhD thesis, Memorial University of Newfoundland, 2009.

38. Ann M. Carlos and Frank D. Lewis, *Commerce by a Frozen Sea : Native Americans and the European Fur Trade*, University of Pennsylvania Press, 2010, 21–25.

39. Carlos and Lewis, *Commerce by a Frozen Sea*, 107, 25–26.

40. W. J. Eccles, "The Fur Trade and Eighteenth-Century Imperialism", *William and Mary Quarterly*, 40:3, 1983, 342–362. There is a vast literature on this issue. One seminal work is Richard White, *The Middle Ground: Indians, Empires, and Republics in the Great Lakes Region, 1650–1815*, Cambridge University Press, 1991.

41. Kris Lane, "Potosí Mines", in *Oxford Research Encyclopedia of Latin American History*, Oxford University Press, 2017.

42. John TePaske and Kendall Brown, *A New World of Gold and Silver*, Brill, 2010, 12–29; Harry E. Cross, "South American Bullion and Export, 1550–1750", in John Richards (ed.), *Precious Metals in the Later Medieval and Early Modern Worlds*, Carolina Academic Press, 1983.

43. Marcel Moussette, "A Universe Under Strain: Amerindian Nations in North-Eastern North America in the 16th Century", *Post-Medieval Archaeology*, 43:1, 2009, 30–47.

44. W. Jeffrey Bolster, *The Mortal Sea: Fishing the Atlantic in the Age of Sail*, Belknap Press, 2012, and "Putting the Ocean in Atlantic History: Maritime Communities and Marine Ecology in the Northwest Atlantic, 1500–1800", *American Historical Review*, 113:1, 2008, 19–47; David J. Starkey, "The Development of Fishing Fleets in the North Atlantic Ocean", in Christian Buchet (ed.), *The Sea in History. The Early Modern World*, Boydell Press, 2017.

45. James S. Olson et al. (eds.), *Historical Dictionary of the Spanish Empire, 1402–1975*, Greenwood Press, 1992, 308.

46. Daniel Vickers, "The Northern Colonies. Economy and Society, 1600–1775", in Stanley L. Engerman and Robert E. Gallman (eds.), *The Cambridge Economic History of the United States, Vol. 1*, Cambridge University Press, 1996.

47. Lynne Mackin Wolforth, "Smallpox Diffusion Between Small and Dispersed Historic Native American Populations", PhD thesis, University of Illinois at Urbana-Champaign, 1997, 8.

48. Chantal Cramaussel, "Population and Epidemics North of Zacatecas", in Danna A. Levin Rojo and Cynthia Radding (eds.), *The Handbook of Borderlands of the Iberian World*, Oxford University Press, 2019.

49. Robert McCaa, "The Peopling of Mexico from Origins to Revolution", in Michael R. Haines and Richard H. Steckel (eds.), *Population History of North America*, Cambridge University Press, 2000; Massimo Livi Bacci, *Conquest: The Destruction of the American Indios*, Polity Press, 2008 (orig. 2005), 126.

50. Bacci, *Conquest*, ch. 8.

51. Russell R. Menard, "Economic and Social Development of the South", in Engerman and Gallman, *Cambridge Economic History of the United States, Vol. 1*.

52. Susan Kellogg, "The Colonial Mosaic of Indigenous New Spain, 1519–1821", in William H. Beezley (ed.), *Oxford Research Encyclopedia of Latin American History*, Oxford University Press, 2014.

53. Noble David Cook, "The Corregidores of the Colca Valley, Peru: Imperial Administration in an Andean Region", *Anuario de Estudios Americanos*, 60:2, 2003, 413–439.

54. Rafael Dobado and Gustavo A. Marrero, "The Role of the Spanish Imperial State in the Mining-Led Growth of Bourbon Mexico's Economy", *Economic History Review*, 64:3, 2011, 855–884.

55. Quoted in David Hurst Thomas, "Honor and Hierarchies Long-Term Trajectories in the Pueblo and Mississippian Worlds", in Clay Mathers, Jeffrey M. Mitchem, and Charles M. Haecker (eds.), *Native and Spanish New Worlds: Sixteenth-Century Entradas in the American Southwest and Southeast*, University of Arizona Press, 2013.

56. David J. Weber, *Bárbaros: Spaniards and Their Savages in the Age of Enlightenment*, Yale University Press, 2005, 191.

57. Wayne E. Lee, "The Military Revolution of Native North America: Firearms, Forts, and Polities" in Lee (ed.), *Empires and Indigenes: Intercultural Alliance, Imperial Expansion, and Warfare in the Early Modern World*, New York University Press, 2011; Patrick M. Maloney, *The Skulking Way of War. Technology and Tactics among the New England Indians*, Johns Hopkins University Press, 1991; William A. Starna and José António Brandão, "From the Mohawk-Mahican War to the Beaver Wars: Questioning the Pattern", *Ethnohistory*, 51:4, 2004.

58. Gregory Dowd, *A Spirited Resistance: The North American Indian Struggle for Unity, 1745–1815*, Johns Hopkins University Press, 1992.

59. Weber, *Bárbaros*, 202–204.

60. Pekka Hämäläinen, *The Comanche Empire*, Yale University Press, 2008 and *Lakota America: A New History of Indigenous Power*, Yale University Press, 2019.

61. Vincent Clément, "Conquest, Natives, and Forest: How Did the Mapuches Succeed in Halting the Spanish Invasion of Their Land (1540–1553, Chile)?", *War in History*, 22:4, 2015, 428–447.

62. Dauril Alden, "Changing Jesuit Perceptions of the Brasis during the Sixteenth Century", *Journal of World History*, 3:2, 1992, 205–218.

63. Tim Lockley, "Runaway Slave Colonies in the Atlantic World", in *Oxford Research Encyclopedia of Latin American History*. Also see R. R. Kent, "Palmares: An African State in Brazil", in Joyce Lorimer (ed.), *Settlement Patterns in Early Colonization, 16th–18th Centuries*, Variorum, 1998.

64. Kathleen J. Higgins, "Masters and Slaves in a Mining Society: A Study of Eighteenth Century Sabara, Minas Gerais", *Slavery & Abolition*, 11:1, 1990, 58–73.

65. Hal Langfur, "Uncertain Refuge; Frontier Formation and the Origins of the Botocudo War in Late Colonial Brazil", *Hispanic American Historical Review*, 82, 2002, 215–256 and "Native Informants and the Limits of Portuguese Dominion in Late-Colonial Brazil", in Rojo and Radding (eds.), *The Handbook of Borderlands of the Iberian World*; Peter Mitchell, *Horse Nations. The Worldwide Impact of the Horse on Indigenous Societies Post-1492*, Oxford University Press, 2015, 244.

66. Weber, *Bárbaros*, 206.

67. Laura E. Matthew and Michel R. Oudijk, *Indian Conquistadors: Indigenous Allies in the Conquest of Mesoamerica*, University of Oklahoma Press, 2007.

68. Raphael B. Folsom, *Yaquis and the Empire: Violence, Spanish Imperial Power, and Native Resilience in Colonial Mexico*, Yale University Press, 2015.

69. Weber, *Bárbaros*, 162. Also see Michel R. Oudijk, "The Conquest of Mexico", in Deborah L. Nichols (ed.), *The Oxford Handbook of Mesoamerican Archaeology*, Oxford University

Press, 2012; Kevin Terraciano, "Indigenous Peoples in Colonial Spanish American Society", in Thomas H. Holloway (ed.), *A Companion to Latin American History*, Wiley-Blackwell, 2011.

70. Mitchell, *Horse Nations*, ch. 17.

71. Alistair Hennessy, "Argentines, Anglo-Argentines and Others", in Alistair Hennessy and John King (eds.), *The Land that England Lost. Argentina and Britain, a Special Relationship*, British Academic Press, 1992, 14.

72. Maria Andrea Campetella, "At the Periphery of Empire: Indians and Settlers in the Pampas of Buenos Aires, 1580–1776", PhD thesis, Rutgers University, 2008, 103.

73. See, for example, Stephen Dale, *The Muslim Empires of the Ottomans, Safavids, and Mughals*, Cambridge University Press, 2010, 248, 257.

74. Matthias Van Rossum, "A 'Moorish World' within the Company. The VOC, Maritime Logistics and Subaltern Networks of Asian Sailors", *Itinerario*, 36:3, 2012.

75. Claude Markovitz, *A History of Modern India 1480–1950*, trans. Nisha George and Maggy Hendry, Anthem Press, 2002, orig .1994.

76. For recent optimism see Tirthankar Roy, "Economic Conditions in Early Modern Bengal: A Contribution to the Divergence Debate", *Journal of Economic History*, 70:1, 2010, 179–194; Prasannan Parthasarathi, *Why Europe Grew Rich and Asia Did Not: Global Economic Divergence, 1600–1850*, Cambridge University Press, 2011. For pessimism see Bishnupriya Gupta and Debin Ma, "Europe in an Asian Mirror: The Great Divergence", in S. N. Broadberry and K. H. O'Rourke (ed.), *The Cambridge Economic History of Modern Europe. Vol. 1, 1700–1870*, 2010; Stephen Broadberry, Johann Custodis, and Bishnupriya Gupta, "India and the Great Divergence: An Anglo-Indian Comparison of GDP Per Capita, 1600–1871", *Explorations in Economic History*, 55, 2015.

77. Philip J. Stern, *The Company-State: Corporate Sovereignty and the Early Modern Foundation of the British Empire in India*, Oxford University Press, 2011, ch. 1; Bhaswati Bhattacharya, "Armenian European Relationship in India, 1500–1800: No Armenian Foundation for European Empire?" *Journal of the Economic and Social History of the Orient*, 48:2, 2005, 277–322.

78. Bhattacharya, "Armenian European Relationship in India" and Lakshmi Subramanian, "Seths and Sahibs: Negotiated Relationships between Indigenous Capital and the East India Company", in H. V. Bowen, Elizabeth Mancke, and John G. Reid (eds.), *Britain's Oceanic Empire: Atlantic and Indian Ocean Worlds, c.1550–1850*, Cambridge University Press, 2012; Ghulam A. Nadri, "The English and Dutch East India Companies and Indian Merchants in Surat in the Seventeenth and Eighteenth Centuries. Interdependence, Competition and Contestation", in Adam Clulow and Tristan Mostert (eds.), *The Dutch and English East India Companies: Diplomacy, Trade and Violence in Early Modern Asia*, Amsterdam University Press, 2018.

79. Clulow et al., *The Dutch and English East India Companies*.

80. Tirthankar Roy, "Capitalism in India in the Very Long Run", in Larry Neal and Jeffrey G., Williamson (eds.), *The Cambridge History of Capitalism. Vol. 1*, Cambridge University Press, 2014.

81. Rajat Datta, "The Commercial Economy of Eastern India Under Early British Rule", in Bowen, Mancke, and Reid (eds.), *Britain's Oceanic Empire*.

82. Om Prakash, *The New Cambridge History of India: European Commercial Enterprise in Pre-colonial India*, Cambridge University Press 1998, 203, 240.

83. Kaushik Roy, "Military Synthesis in South Asia: Armies, Warfare, and Indian Society, c. 1740–1849", *Journal of Military History*, 69:3, 2005, 651–690.

84. Kaushik Roy, "Mughal Empire and Warfare in Afghanistan 1500–1810", in Roy (ed.), *War and Society in Afghanistan. From the Mughals to the Americans, 1500–2013*, Oxford University Press, 2015.

85. Roy, "Military Synthesis"; Douglas M. Peers, "Army Discipline, Military Cultures, and State-Formation in Colonial India, c.1780–1860", in Bowen, Mancke, and Reid (eds.), *Britain's Oceanic Empire*; Douglas M. Peers, "Gunpowder Empires and the Garrison State: Modernity, Hybridity, and the Political Economy of Colonial India, circa 1750–1860", *Comparative Studies of South Asia, Africa and the Middle East*, 27:2, 2007, 245–258; Mesrob Vartavarian, "An Open Military Economy: The British Conquest of South India Reconsidered, 1780–1799", *Journal of the Economic and Social History of the Orient*, 57, 2014, 486–510.

86. Lilach Gilady and Joseph MacKay, "Bringing the Insurgents Back In: Early Wars in British India", *Terrorism and Political Violence*, 27:5, 2015, 797–817; G. J. Bryant, "British Logistics and the Conduct of the Carnatic Wars (1746–1783)", *War in History*, 11:3, 2004.

87. Contemporary quoted in G. J. Bryant, *Emergence of British Power in India, 1600–1784: A Grand Strategic Interpretation*, Boydell & Brewer, 2013, 258.

88. Datta, "The Commercial Economy".

89. Ian Barrow, *The East India Company, 1600–1858*, Hackett, 2017, 57.

90. Bryant, *Emergence of British Power*, 75; William Dalrymple, *The Anarchy: The Relentless Rise of the East India Company*, Bloomsbury, 2019, Locs. 1082–97.

91. Stephen Broadberry and Bishnupriya Gupta, "Lancashire, India, and Shifting Competitive Advantage in Cotton Textiles, 1700–1850: The Neglected Role of Factor Prices", *Economic History Review*, 62:2, 2009, 279–305; Prakash, *New Cambridge History of India*, 240.

92. Bryant, *Emergence of British Power*, 193.

93. Datta, "The Commercial Economy".

94. Dalrymple, *The Anarchy*, Locs. 4604–4606. Also see Locs. 9148–9149 for Dalrymple's discussion with leading expert Peter Marshall.

95. Bryant, *Emergence of British Power*, 12.

96. R.G.S. Cooper, "Culture, Combat, and Colonialism in Eighteenth- and Nineteenth-Century India", *International History Review*, 27:3, 2005, 534–549.

97. Prakash, *New Cambridge History of India*, 346; Vartavarian, "An Open Military Economy"; G. J. Bryant, "Indigenous Mercenaries in the Service of European Imperialists: The Case of the Sepoys in the Early British Indian Army, 1750–1800", *War in History*, 7:1–2, 2000, 2–28; Kaushik Roy, "The Hybrid Military Establishment of the East India Company in South Asia: 1750–1849", *Journal of World History*, 6, 2011, 195–218; Barrow, *The East India Company*, 82. Also see Dirk Kolff's writings on the military market in India.

98. Dalrymple, *The Anarchy*, Locs. 4806–4807.

99. Peer Vries, *State, Economy and the Great Divergence. Great Britain and China, 1680s–1850s*, Bloomsbury, 2015, 342.

100. Javier Cuenca-Esteban, "India's Contribution to the British Balance of Payments, 1757–1812", *Explorations in Economic History*, 44:1, 2007, 154–176.

101. Emily Erickson, *Between Monopoly and Free Trade. The English East India Company, 1600–1757*, Princeton University Press, 2014.

102. Prakash, *New Cambridge History of India*, 242.

103. Leonard Spencer Austin, "A Fit o Absence of Mind? Illiberal Imperialism and the Founding of British India, 1757–1776", PhD dissertation, University of Chicago, 2010, 118.

104. Michael Herbert Fisher, *Counterflows to Colonialism: Indian Travellers and Settlers in Britain, 1600–1857*, 2004, Permanent Black, 72.

105. Gijs Dreijer, "The Afterlife of the Ostend Company, 1727–1745", *Mariner's Mirror*, 105:3, 2019, 275–287.

106. Cuenca-Esteban, "India's Contribution".

107. H. V. Bowen, "Bullion for Trade, War, and Debt-Relief: British Movements of Silver to, Around, and from Asia, 1760–1833", *Modern Asian Studies*, 44:3, 2010, 445–475; Shireen Moosvi, *People, Taxation, and Trade in Mughal India*, Oxford University Press, 2008, 19–20.

108. Dalrymple, *The Anarchy*.

109. Javier Cuenca Esteban, "The British Balance of Payments, 1772–1820: India Transfers and War Finance", *Economic History Review*, 54:1, 2001, 58–86 (Sinha's estimate for Bengal); Datta, "The Commercial Economy".

110. Bryant, *Emergence of British Power*, ch. 8.

111. Datta, "The Commercial Economy".

112. William T. Rowe, *China's Last Empire. The Great Qing*, Harvard University Press, 2009; Evelyn S. Rawski, *Early Modern China and Northeast Asia. Cross-border Perspectives*, Cambridge University Press, 2015; Dan Shao, "Manchuria in Modern East Asia, 1600s–1949", *Oxford Research Encyclopedia of Asian History*, Oxford University Press, 2017.

113. Ding Yizhuang and Mark Elliott, "How to Write Chinese History in the Twenty-First Century: The Impact of the 'New Qing History' Studies and Chinese Responses", *Chinese Studies in History*, 51:1, 2018.

114. Vries, *State, Economy and the Great Divergence*, 271. Also see Rowe, *China's Last Empire*, ch. 2; Lawrence Zhang, "Power for a Price: Office Purchase, Elite Families, and Status Maintenance in Qing China", PhD dissertation, Harvard University, 2010.

115. Ronald C. Po, *The Blue Frontier: Maritime Vision and Power in the Qing Empire*, Cambridge University Press, 2018, ch. 4.

116. Kwangmin Kim, "Saintly Brokers: Uyghur Muslims, Trade, and the Making of Qing Central Asia, 1696–1814", PhD dissertation, University of California, Berkeley, 2008; Nicola di Cosmo, "The Qing and Inner Asia: 1636–1800", in Nicola Di Cosmo, Allen J. Frank, and Peter B. Golden (eds.), *The Cambridge History of Inner Asia: The Chinggisid Age*, Cambridge University Press, 2009; Peter C. Perdue, *China Marches West: The Qing Conquest of Central Asia*, Belknap Press, 2005.

117. Po, *The Blue Frontier*, ch. 3; Dahpon David Ho, "Sealords Live in Vain: Fujian and the Making of a Maritime Frontier in Seventeenth-Century China", PhD dissertation, University of California, San Diego, 2011; Xing Hang, "Between Trade and Legitimacy, Maritime and Continent: The Zheng Organization in Seventeenth-Century East Asia", PhD dissertation, University of California, Berkeley, 2010; Tonio Andrade, "Beyond Guns, Germs, and Steel: European Expansion and Maritime Asia, 1400–1750", *Journal of Early Modern History*, 14:1–2, 2010, 165–186, *Lost Colony: The Untold Story of China's First Great Victory over the West*, Princeton University Press, 2011, and "An Accelerating Divergence? The Revisionist Model of World History and the Question of Eurasian Military Parity: Data from East Asia", *Canadian Journal of Sociology*, 36:2, 2011.

118. Rowe, *China's Last Empire*, 123.

119. Lillian M. Li and Alison Dray-Novey, "Guarding Beijing's Food Security in the Qing Dynasty: State, Market, and Police", *Journal of Asian Studies*, 58:4, 1999, 992–1032; Li Bozhong, *Fazhan yu zhiyue: Ming Qing Jiangnan shengchanli yanjiu (Development and Constraint: Productivity in Jiangnan in the Ming and Qing Dynasties)*, Lianjing, 2002, 368. All Chinese-language works in this chapter were translated for me by Dr. Joe Lawson.

120. Timothy Brook, *The Troubled Empire: China in the Ming and Yuan Dynasties*, Belknap Press, 2010, 5; Rowe, *China's Last Empire*, 91.

121. Richard von Glahn, "Beyond the Great Divergence: Current Scholarship on the Economic History of Premodern China", in Michael Szonyi (ed.), *A Companion to Chinese History*, John Wiley, 2017. Also see Rowe, *China's Last Empire*; Sucheta Mazumdar, *Sugar and Society in China. Peasants, Technology, and the World Market*, Harvard University Press, 1998; Wang Yuquan 王毓铨, Liu Zhongri 刘重日, and Zhang Xianqing 张显清. *Zhongguo jingji tongshi (xia)* 中国经济通史. 明代经济卷（上）*General History of the Chinese Economy. The Ming Dynasty I*, Zhongguo shehui kexue yuan, 2007; Bin Wong, *China Transformed* and "China Before Capitalism", in Neal and Williamson, *The Cambridge History of Capitalism Vol. 1*. For more pessimistic views, see Vries, *State, Economy and the Great Divergence*; Bishnupriya Gupta and Debin Ma, "Europe in an Asian Mirror: The Great Divergence", in Broadberry and O'Rourke (eds.), *The Cambridge Economic History of Modern Europe. Vol. 1*.

122. Vries, *State, Economy and the Great Divergence*, 371.

123. Ouyang Zongshu 欧阳宗书. *Haishang renjia: haiyang yuye jingji yu yumin shehui* 海上人家：海洋渔业经济与渔民社会 *(Ocean People: The Maritime Fishing Economy and Fishing Communities)*. Nanchang: Jiangxi gaoxiao chubanshe, 1998, 59. Also see Máñez K. Schwerdtner, and S.C.A. Ferse, "The History of Makassan Trepang Fishing and Trade", *PLoS one*, 5:6, 2010; Sean Anderson et al., "Serial Exploitation of Global Sea Cucumber Fisheries", *Fish and Fisheries*, 12:3, 2011; Kwee Hui Kian, "The Expansion of Chinese Inter-Insular and Hinterland Trade in Southeast Asia, c. 1400–1850", in David Henley and Henk Schulte Nordholt (eds.), *Environment, Trade and Society in Southeast Asia*, Brill, 2015; Daryl Wesley et al., "Sails Set in Stone: A Technological Analysis of Non-indigenous Watercraft Rock Art Paintings in North Western Arnhem Land", *Journal of Maritime Archaeology*, 7:2, 2012.

124. Rawski, *Early Modern China*, 65.

125. Rowe, *China's Last Empire*, 14.

126. Quoted by Vries, *State, Economy and the Great Divergence*, 315.

127. Carl A. Trocki, *Opium, Empire and the Global Political Economy: A Study of the Asian Opium Trade 1750–1950*, Routledge, 1999, 76.

128. Luke Clossey, "Merchants, Migrants, Missionaries, and Globalization in the Early-Modern Pacific", *Journal of World History*, 1, 2006, 41–58; Russell-Wood, *The Portuguese Empire*, 168; Mazumdar, *Sugar and Society*, 255.

129. Kent G. Deng, "Miracle or Mirage? Foreign Silver, China's Economy and Globalization from the 16th to the 19th centuries", *Pacific Economic Review*, 13:3, 2008, 320–358.

130. Birgit Tremml, "The Global and the Local: Problematic Dynamics of the Triangular Trade in Early Modern Manila", *Journal of World History*, 23:3, 2012, 555–586.

131. Andrew Christian Peterson, "Making the First Global Trade Route; The Southeast Asian Foundations of the Acapulco-Manila Galleon Trade, 1519–1650", PhD dissertation, University

of Hawaii at Manoa, 2014, 3; Alejandra Irigoin, "A Trojan Horse in Daoguang China? Explaining the Flows of Silver In and Out of China", LSE Working Papers No. 173/13, 2013.

132. John L. Cranmer-Byng and John E. Wills, Jr., "Trade and Diplomacy with Maritime Europe, 1644–c. 1800", in Wills (ed.), *China and Maritime Europe, 1500–1800: Trade, Settlement, Diplomacy, and Missions*, Cambridge University Press, 2011, 191; Jorge Morais Barros Amândio, "The Manila Galleon, Macao and International Maritime and Commercial Relations, 1500–1700", *International Journal of Maritime History*, 29:1, 2017, 123–137.

133. Trocki, *Opium, Empire and the Global Political Economy*; Yangwen Zheng, "Opium in China", *Oxford Research Encyclopedia of Asian History*; Bowen, "Bullion for Trade, War, and Debt-Relief".

134. Maxine Berg, "Britain, Industry and Perceptions of China: Matthew Boulton, 'Useful Knowledge' and the Macartney Embassy to China 1792–94", *Journal of World History*, 1, 2006, 269–288.

135. Kwee Hui Kian, "The Expansion of Chinese Inter-Insular and Hinterland Trade"; Heather Sutherland, "Pursuing the Invisible Makassar, City and Systems", in Henley and Nordholt (eds.), *Environment, Trade and Society*.

136. Martine van Ittersum, "Empire by Treaty? The Role of Written Documents in European Overseas Expansion, 1500–1800", in Clulow and Mostert (eds.), *The Dutch and English East India*.

137. Peter Boomgaard, "Technologies of a Trading Empire: Dutch Introduction of Water- and Windmills in Early Modern Asia, 1650s–1800", *History and Technology*, 24:1, 2008, 41–59.

138. Channa Wickremesekera, *Kandy at War: Indigenous Military Resistance to European Expansion in Sri Lanka 1594–1818*, Manohar, 2004.

139. James Boyajian, quoted in Leonard Y. Andaya, "The 'Informal Portuguese Empire' and the Topasses in the Solor Archipelago and Timor in the Seventeenth and Eighteenth Centuries", *Journal of Southeast Asian Studies*, 41:3, 2010, 391–420.

140. Reid, "Sugar, Slavery and Productivity in Jamaica"; W. A. Green, "The Planter Class and British West Indian Sugar Production, before and after Emancipation", *Economic History Review*, 26:3, 1973, 448–463.

141. Jonathan M. Chu, "An Independent Means: The American Revolution and the Rise of a National Economy", *Journal of Interdisciplinary History*, 31, 2000, 63–71. Also see James Belich, *Replenishing the Earth. The Settler Revolution and the Rise of the Anglo-World, 1780s–1920s*, Oxford University Press, 2009, ch. 2.

142. Belich, *Replenishing the Earth*, 50

143. John Bostoce, "From Davis Strait. to Bering Strait: The Arrival of the Commercial Whaling Fleet in North America's Western Arctic", *Arctic*, 37:4, 1984, 528–532; Louwrens Hacquebord, "Three Centuries of Whaling and Walrus Hunting in Svalbärd and Its Impact on the Arctic Ecosystem", *Environment and History*, 7, 2001, 169–185; Robert C. Allen and Ian Key, "Bowhead Whales in the Eastern Arctic, 1611–1911: Population Reconstruction with Historical Whaling Records", *Environment and History*, 12, 2006, 89–113; Jean-Pierre Proulx, *Whaling in the North Atlantic: From Earliest Times to the Mid-19th Century*, Parks Canada, 1986; Chesley W. Sanger, "'Oil Is an Indispensable Necessity of Life': The Impact of Oscillating Oil and Baleen (Bone) Prices on Cyclical Variations in the Scale and Scope of Northern Commercial Whaling, 1600–1900", *International Journal of Maritime History*, 15:2, 2003, 147–157; Daniel Vickers, "Nantucket

Whalemen in the Deep-Sea Fishery: The Changing Anatomy of an Early American Labor Force", *Journal of American History*, 72:2, 1985, 277–296; T. D. Smith et al., "Spatial and Seasonal Distribution of American Whaling and Whales in the Age of Sail", *PLoS one*, 7:4, 2012.

144. Boris Mironov and Gregory Freeze, *The Standard of Living and Revolutions in Imperial Russia, 1700–1917*, Routledge, 2012, ch. 4. Also see Gabor Ágoston, "Military Transformation in the Ottoman Empire and Russia, 1500–1800", *Kritika*, 12:2, 2011, 281–319; Dominic Lieven (ed.), *The Cambridge History of Russia: Vol. 2*, Cambridge University Press, 2006.

145. Silvia Marzagalli, "Economic and Demographic Developments", in David Andress (ed.), *Oxford Handbook of the French Revolution*, Oxford University Press, 2015; Jeff Horn, "Lessons of the Levant: Early Modern French Economic Development in the Mediterranean", *French History*, 29:1, 2015.

146. Silvia Marzagalli, "The French Atlantic World in the Seventeenth and Eighteenth Centuries", in Nicholas Canny and Philip Morgan (eds.), *The Oxford Handbook of the Atlantic World: 1450–1850*, Oxford University Press, 2011.

147. James Pritchard, *In Search of Empire: The French in the Americas, 1670–1730*, Cambridge University Press, 2004, ch. 8.

148. Marzagalli, "Economic and Demographic Developments". Also see Gwynne Lewis, "Proto-industrialization in France", *Economic History Review*, 47:1, 1994, 150–164; R. W. Unger, "The Tonnage of Europe's Merchant Fleets, 1300–1800", *American Neptune*, 52:4, 1992, 247–261.

149. Francois Crouzet, *A History of the European Economy, 1000–2000*, University of Virginia Press, 2001, 72–73 and *Britain Ascendant; Comparative Studies in Franco-British Economic History*, Cambridge University Press, 1990; Catherine Casson and Mark Dodgson, "Designing for Innovation: Cooperation and Competition in English Cotton, Silk, and Pottery Firms, 1750–1860", *Business History Review*, 93, 2019, 247–273; Brendan Simms, "Britain and Napoleon" (review article), *Historical Journal*, 41:3, 1998, 885–894.

150. H. V. Bowen, "Britain in the Indian Ocean Region and Beyond: Contours, Connections, and the Creation of a Global Maritime Empire", in Bowen, Mancke, and Reid (eds.), *Britain's Oceanic Empire*; Robert DuPlessis, *The Material Atlantic: Clothing, Commerce, and Colonization in the Atlantic World, 1650–1800*, Cambridge University Press, 57–58.

151. Erickson, *Between Monopoly and Free Trade*, 149; DuPlessis, *The Material Atlantic*, 57.

152. C. R. Boxer, "Brazilian Gold and British Traders in the First Half of the Eighteenth Century", *Hispanic American Historical Review*, 49:3, 1969, 454–472.

153. C. R. Boxer, *The Portuguese Seaborne Empire 1415–1825*, Hutchinson, 1969, 181,

154. Stephen J. Hornsby, "Geographies of the British Atlantic World" in Bowen, Mancke, and Reid (eds.), *Britain's Oceanic Empire*.

155. Jose Jobson De Andrade Arruda, "Colonies as Mercantile Investments: The Luso-Brazilian Empire, 1500–1808", in James D. Tracy (ed.), *The Political Economy of Merchant Empires: State Power and World Trade 1350–1750*, Cambridge University Press, 1991, 394. Also see A. R. Disney, *A History of Portugal and the Portuguese Empire: From Beginnings to 1807. Vol. 1*, Cambridge University Press, 2009, 262; Leonor Freire Costa, Pedro Lains, and Susana Munch Miranda, *An Economic History of Portugal, 1143–2010*, Cambridge University Press, 2016, 205; A.J.R. Russell-Wood, "The Portuguese Atlantic World, c. 1650–c. 1760", in Canny and Morgan (eds.), *The Oxford Handbook of the Atlantic World*; Malyn Newitt, *Emigration and the Sea*, Oxford University Press, 2015, ch. 2.

Chapter 16: Plaguing Britain

1. Michael Haupert, "A Brief History of Cliometrics and the Evolving View of the Industrial Revolution", *European Journal of the History of Economic Thought*, 26:4, 2019, 738–774.

2. Robert C. Allen, *The British Industrial Revolution in Global Perspective*, Cambridge University Press, 2009, ch. 7.

3. Charles K. Hyde, "The Adoption of Coke-Smelting by the British Iron Industry, 1709–1790", *Explorations in Economic History*, 10.4, 1973, 397–418; Allen, *The British Industrial Revolution*, ch. 9; William J. Ashworth, *The Industrial Revolution. The State, Knowledge, and Global Trade*, Bloomsbury, 2017, 170.

4. Mark Bailey, *After the Black Death: Economy, Society, and the Law in Fourteenth-century England*, Oxford University Press, 2021, 5; S. Broadberry et al., *British Economic Growth, 1270–1870*, Cambridge University Press, 2015, 366; Also see Allen, *The British Industrial Revolution*, 21.

5. Bailey, *After the Black Death*, 24.

6. Ibid., ch. 6; *Oxford English Dictionary*, "Yeoman" II.4.a.

7. This summary draws on Bailey, *After the Black Death*, and other works by the same author; Robert Allen, *Enclosure and the Yeoman: The Agricultural Development of the South Midlands 1450–1850*, Oxford University Press, 1992; Broadberry et al., *British Economic Growth*; Mark Overton, *Agricultural Revolution in England. The Transformation of the Agrarian Economy 1500–1800*, Cambridge University Press, 1996; Jane Whittle, *The Development of Agrarian Capitalism: Land and Labour in Norfolk 1440–1580*, Oxford University Press, 2000; Edward Miller (ed.), *The Agrarian History of England and Wales. Vol III*, Cambridge University Press, 1991; Alexandra Shepard and Judith Spicksley, "Worth, Age, and Social Status in Early Modern England", *Economic History Review*, 64:2, 2011, 493–530; Craig Muldrew, *Food, Energy and the Creation of Industriousness: Work and Material Culture in Agrarian England, 1550–1780*, Cambridge University Press, 2011.

8. Spencer Dimmock, *The Origin Of Capitalism in England, 1400–1600*, Brill, 2014. Also see M. A. Žmolek, "'Compelled to Sell All': Proletarianization, Agrarian Capitalism and the Industrial Revolution", in Lafrance, Xavier (ed.), *Case Studies in the Origins of Capitalism*, Palgrave Macmillan, 2019; Shami Ghosh, "Rural Economies and Transitions to Capitalism: Germany and England Compared (c.1200–c.1800)", *Journal of Agrarian Change*, 16:2, 2016, 255–290 and the works of Robert Brenner.

9. Frederic Aparisi, "Village Entrepreneurs: The Economic Foundations of Valencian Rural Elites in the Fifteenth Century", *Agricultural History*, 89:3, 2015, 336–357. William W. Hagen, "European Yeomanries: A Non-Immiseration Model of Agrarian Social History, 1350–1800", *Agricultural History Review*, 59:2, 2011, 259–265.

10. John Oldland, "Wool and Cloth Production in Late Medieval and Early Tudor England", *Economic History Review*, 67.1, 2014, 125–147; Broadberry et al., *British Economic Growth*, 106.

11. Eleanor Quinton and John Oldland, "London Merchant's Cloth Exports, 1350–1500", in Robin Netherton and Gale R. Owen-Crocker (eds.), *Medieval Clothing and Textiles*, Vol. 7, Boydell & Brewer, 2011. Also see John H. Munro, "Medieval Woollens: The Western European Woollen Industries and Their Struggles for International Markets, c. 1000–1500", and Herman Van Der Wee, "The Western European Woollen Industries, 1500–1750", both in David Jenkins (ed.), *The Cambridge History of Western Textiles, Vol. I*, Cambridge University Press, 2003; John H. Munro, "The Symbiosis of Towns and Textiles: Urban Institutions and the Changing

Fortunes of Cloth Manufacturing in the Low Countries and England, 1270–1570", *Journal of Early Modern History*, 3:1, 1999, 1–74; Rees Davies and Brendan Smith, *Lords and Lordship in the British Isles in the Late Middle Ages*, Oxford University Press, 2009, ch. 6.

12. Allen, *The British Industrial Revolution*, 19, also see 109, 121; Martin Rorke, "English and Scottish Overseas Trade, 1300–1600", *Economic History Review*, 59:2, 2006, 265–288; Carole Shammas, "The Decline of Textile Prices in England and British America Prior to Industrialization", *Economic History Review*, 47:3, 1994, 483–507; Richard A. Goldthwaite, *The Economy of Renaissance Florence*, Johns Hopkins University Press, 2009, 39, 265–282; Daniel R. Curtis, "Florence and Its Hinterlands in the Late Middle Ages: Contrasting Fortunes in the Tuscan Countryside, 1300–1500", *Journal of Medieval History*, 38:4, 201, 472–499.

13. Robin Ward, *The World of the Medieval Shipmaster: Law, Business, and the Sea, c.1350–1450*, Boydell Press, 2009, 4.

14. Maryanne Kowaleski, "The Expansion of the South-Western Fisheries in Late Medieval England", *Economic History Review*, 53, 2000, 429–454 and "The Commercialization of the Sea Fisheries in Medieval England and Wales", *International Journal of Maritime History*, 15:2, 2003, 177–231.

15. Evan T. Jones, "Charting the World of English Fishermen in Early Modern Iceland", *The Mariner's Mirror*, 90:4, 2004, 398–409; Natascha Mehler and Mark Gardiner, "English and Hanseatic Trading and Fishing Sites in Medieval Iceland: Report on Initial Fieldwork", *Germania*, 8:2, 2007, 385–427.

16. Ward, *The World of the Medieval Shipmaster*, 4.

17. Wendy R. Childs, "England's Contacts with Poland-Lithuania in the Fourteenth to Sixteenth Centuries", in Richard W. Unger and Jakub Basista (eds.), *Britain and Poland-Lithuania: Contact and Comparison from the Middle Ages to 1795*, Brill, 2008, and "Timber for Cloth; Changing Commodities in Anglo-Baltic Trade in the Fourteenth Century", in Lars Berggren et al. (eds.), *Cogs, Cargoes, and Commerce. Maritime Bulk Trade in Northern Europe, 1150–1400*, Pontifical Institute of Medieval Studies, 2002; Erik Gøbel, "The Sound Toll Registers Online Project, 1497–1857", *International Journal of Maritime History*, 22:2, 2010, 305–324.

18. Ronald Hope, *A New History of British Shipping*, John Murray, 1990, 69–70; Bruce E. Gelsinger, *Icelandic Enterprise: Commerce and Economy in the Middle Ages*, University of South Carolina Press, 1981.

19. Matthew W. Betts et al., "Zooarchaeology of the Historic Cod Fishery in Newfoundland and Labrador, Canada", *Journal of the North Atlantic*, 24, 2014, 1–21.

20. Derek Keene, "Changes in London's Economic Hinterland as Indicated By Debt Cases in the Court of Common Pleas", in James A. Galloway (ed.), *Trade, Urban Hinterlands and Market Integration c.1300–1600*, IHR Centre for Metropolitan History WP series no. 3, 2000.

21. Bailey, *After the Black Death*, ch. 7.

22. Caroline M. Barron, *London in the Later Middle Ages: Government and People 1200–1500*, Oxford University Press, 2010 (orig. 2004), ch. 5; Rorke, "English and Scottish Overseas Trade, 1300–1600".

23. Quinton and Oldland, "London Merchant's Cloth Exports".

24. Keene, "Changes in London's Economic Hinterland".

25. Geoffrey Parker, *Global Crisis: War, Climate Change and Catastrophe in the Seventeenth Century*, Yale University Press, 2013, 59.

26. E. A. Wrigley, "Urban Growth in Early Modern England: Food, Fuel, and Transport", *Past & Present*, 225, 2014.

27. D. C. North, J. J. Wallis, and B. R. Weingast, "A Conceptual Framework for Interpreting Recorded Human History", National Bureau of Economic Research, 2006.

28. Jan Luiten van Zanden, Sarah Carmichael, and Tine De Moor, *Capital Women: The European Marriage Pattern, Female Empowerment and Economic Development in Western Europe 1300–1800*, Oxford University Press 2019.

29. Tracy Dennison and Sheilagh Ogilvie, "Does the European Marriage Pattern Explain Economic Growth?", *Journal of Economic History*, 74:3, 2014; Jeremy Edwards and Sheilagh Ogilvie, "Did the Black Death Cause Economic Development by 'Inventing' Fertility Restriction?", CESIFO Working Papers, No. 7016, 2018, and "What Can We Learn from a Race with One Runner? A Comment on Foreman-Peck and Zhou, 'Late Marriage as a Contributor to the Industrial Revolution in England'", *Economic History Review*, 72:4, 2019, 1439–1446.

30. van Zanden, Carmichael, and De Moor, *Capital Women*, ch. 5. Also see Alexandra M. de Pleijt and Jan Luiten van Zanden, "Accounting for the 'Little Divergence'. What Drove Economic Growth in Pre-industrial Europe, 1300–1800?", Working Paper 43, Utrecht University, Centre for Global Economic History, 2013; Jan Luiten van Zanden, "The Road to the Industrial Revolution: Hypotheses and Conjectures about the Medieval Origins of the 'European Miracle'", *Journal of World History*, 3, 2008, 337–359; James Foreman-Peck and Peng Zhou, "Late Marriage as a Contributor to the Industrial Revolution in England", *Economic History Review*, 71:4, 2018, 1073–1099.

31. John Brewer, *The Sinews of Power: War, Money and the English State 1688–1783*, Routledge, 1989, 205.

32. Niall Ferguson, *The Cash Nexus: Money and Power in the Modern World, 1700–2000*, Allen Lane, 2001, 20.

33. D. G. Wright, *Democracy and Reform, 1815–1885*, Longman, 1970, 195.

34. Nicholas Vincent, "Past Imperfect" [Review of Clyve Jones (ed.), *A short history of Parliament*], *Times Literary Supplement*, 9 April 2010, 27.

35. Brewer, *The Sinews of Power*, 94.

36. Kenneth Morgan, "Anglo-Dutch Economic Relations in the Atlantic World, 1688–1783", in Gert Oostindie and Jessica V. Roitman (eds.), *Dutch Atlantic Connections, 1680–1800: Linking Empires, Bridging Borders*, Brill, 2014, 119–138.

37. Peer Vries, *State, Economy and the Great Divergence: Great Britain and China, 1680s–1850s*, Bloomsbury, 2015, 121.

38. N.A.M. Rodger, "War as an Economic Activity in the 'Long' Eighteenth Century", *International Journal of Maritime History*, 22:2, 2010, 1–18.

39. Brewer, *The Sinews of Power*, 58.

40. Apart from Brewer, see Anthony Page, *Britain and the Seventy Years' War, 1744–1815*, Palgrave Macmillan, 2015, and Ashworth, *The Industrial Revolution*.

41. N.A.M. Rodger, *The Command of the Ocean: A Naval History of Britain, 1649–1815*, Penguin 2005, Loc. 8930–8931. *The Diary of Samuel Pepys*, Robert Latham and William Mathews (eds.), 10 vols., Harper Collins, 1971.

42. Brewer, *The Sinews of Power*, ch. 5.

43. Rodger, *The Command of the Ocean*, Locs. 6536–6537, 8877–8878.

44. Brewer, *The Sinews of Power*, 358.

45. For the Venetian origin of patents before 1474, see Christine MacLeod and Allesandro Nuvolari, "Technological Change", in William Doyle (ed.), *Oxford Handbook of the Ancien Régime*, Oxford University Press, 2012.

46. George Ramsay, "Thomas More, Joint Keeper of the Exchange: A Forgotten Episode in the History of Exchange Control in England", *Historical Research*, 84:226, 2011; Ole Peter Grell, "The Creation of a Transnational, Calvinist Network and Its Significance for Calvinist Identity and Interaction in Early Modern Europe", *European Review of History*, 16:5, 2009, 619–636; "Palavicio, Horatio", and "Cromwell, Sir Oliver", *New Dictionary of National Biography*, Oxford University Press, 2004.

47. Ramsay, "Thomas More".

48. Broadberry et al., *British Economic Growth*, 370.

49. F. J. Fisher, "The Development of the London Food Market, 1540–1640", in F. J. Fisher, *London and the English Economy, 1500–1700* ed. P.J. Corfield and N.B. Harte, Hambledon Press, 1990.

50. Dimmock, *The Origin of Capitalism in England*, ch. 6.

51. Walter M. Stern, "Cheese Shipped Coastwise to London towards the Middle of the 18th Century", *Guildhall Miscellany*, 4, 1973, 207–221; J. A. Yelling, "Agriculture 1500–1730", in R. A. Dodgshon and R. A. Butlin (eds.), *An Historical Geography of England and Wales*, Academic Press, 1978, 163. Also see David Barnett, *London: Hub of the Industrial Revolution—A Revisionary History, 1775–1825*, London, 1998, 131.

52. Derrick Rixson, *The History of Meat Trading*, Nottingham University Press, 2000, 94, 198, 259.

53. Denis O'Hearn, *The Atlantic Economy. Britain, the US, and Ireland*, Manchester University Press, 2001; Cormac Ó' Grada, *Ireland: A New Economic History, 1780–1939*, Oxford University Press, 1994; Brinley Thomas, "Feeding England during the Industrial Revolution: A View from the Celtic Fringe", *Agricultural History*, 56, 1982, 328–342; Frank Geary, "The Act of Union, British-Irish Trade, and Pre-famine Deindustrialization", *Economic History Review*, 48, 1995, 68–88; Peter M. Solar, "Shipping and Economic Development in Nineteenth Century Ireland", *Economic History Review*, 59, 2006, 717–742.

54. Brinley Thomas, *The Industrial Revolution and the Atlantic Economy: Selected Essays*, Routledge, 1993, 64.

55. David Garrioch, "1666 and London's Fire History; A Re-evaluation", *Historical Journal*, 59:2, 2016, 219–338; Hope, *British Shipping*, 223–224; Hans Chr. Johansen, "Scandinavian Shipping in the Late Eighteenth Century in a European Perspective", *Economic History Review*, 45:3, 1992, 479–493.

56. Geoffrey Scammell, "British Merchant Shipbuilding, c.1500–1750", *International Journal of Maritime History*, 11:1, 1999, 27–52.

57. Joseph E. Inikori, "Africans and the Industrial Revolution. A Round Table Response", *International Journal of Maritime History*, 15:2, 2003, 330–361.

58. Nicholas R. Amor, *Late Medieval Ipswich: Trade and Industry*, Boydell & Brewer, 2011, 7.

59. Martin Gilbert, *The Routledge Atlas of British History*, 5th edn, London, 2011, 75.

60. Broadberry et al., *British Economic Growth*, 272.

61. Allen, *The British Industrial Revolution*, 148.

62. Joel Mokyr, *The Enlightened Economy. An Economic History of Britain 1700–1850*, Yale University Press, 2012, ch. 6.

63. Allen, *The British Industrial Revolution*, 161.

64. Ibid., 2.

65. Broadberry et al., *British Economic Growth*, 261.

66. Ulrich Pfister, "The Timing and Pattern of Real Wage Divergence in Pre-Industrial Europe: Evidence from Germany, c. 1500–1850", *Economic History Review*, 70:3, 2017, 701–729.

67. Emma Griffin "Diets, Hunger and Living Standards during the British Industrial Revolution", *Past & Present*, 239, 2018; Broadberry et al., *British Economic Growth*, 293–294, 295, table 5.05; Jane Humphries, "The Lure of Aggregates and the Pitfalls of the Patriarchal Perspective: A Critique of the High Wage Economy Interpretation of the British Industrial Revolution", *Economic History Review*, 66:3, 2013, 693–714.

68. Leonardo Ridolfi, "Six Centuries of Real Wages in France from Louis IX to Napoleon III: 1250–1860", *Journal of Economic History*, 79:3, 2019.

69. David Richardson, "The Slave Trade, Sugar, and British Economic Growth, 1748–1776", *Journal of Interdisciplinary History*, 17:4, 1987, 739–769.

70. Griffin, "Diets, Hunger and Living Standards".

71. Broadberry et al., *British Economic Growth*, 275.

72. Jessica Hanser, "Teatime in the North Country. Consumption of Chinese Imports in North-east England", *Northern History*, 49:1, 2012, 51–74.

73. Matthew R. Greenhall, "'Three of the Horsemen': The Commercial Consequences of Plague, Fire and War on British East Coast Trade, 1660–1674", *International Journal of Maritime History*, 24: 97, 2012, citing E. A. Wrigley.

74. Matthew R. Greenhall, " 'Three of the Horsemen.'"

75. David Jacks, "Foreign Wars, Domestic Markets: England, 1793–1815", *European Review of Economic History*, 15, 2011, 277–311.

76. Ibid.

77. Cheryl Fury, "The First English East India Company Voyage, 1601–1603: The Human Dimension", *International Journal of Maritime History*, 24:2, 2012, 69.

78. P. J. Marshall, "The English in Asia to 1700", P.E.H. Hair and Robin Law, "The English in Western Africa to 1700", both in Nicholas Canny (ed.), *The Oxford History of the British Empire*, Vol. 1, Oxford University Press, 1998.

79. Nuala Zahedieh, *The Capital and the Colonies: London and the Atlantic Economy, 1660–1700*, Cambridge University Press, 2010, 138.

80. Stephen J. Hornsby, "Geographies of the British Atlantic World", in H. V. Bowen, Elizabeth Mancke, and John G. Reid (eds.), *Britain's Oceanic Empire: Atlantic and Indian Ocean Worlds, c.1550–1850*, Cambridge University Press, 2012.

81. Francois Crouzet, *A History of the European Economy, 1000–2000*, University of Virginia Press, 2001, 54.

82. Patrick O'Brien, "European Economic Development; The Contribution of the Periphery", *Economic History Review*, 35:1, 1982, 1–18 and personal communications.

83. Anne E. McCants, "Poor Consumers as Global Consumers: The Diffusion of Tea and Coffee Drinking in the Eighteenth Century", *Economic History Review*, 61, 2008, 172–200.

84. Mokyr, *The Enlightened Economy*, locs. 3696–8.

85. Vries, *State, Economy and the Great Divergence*, 388.

86. Eric Williams, *Capitalism and Slavery*, Andre Deutsch, 1964 (orig. 1944).

87. Ahmed Reid, "Sugar, Slavery and Productivity in Jamaica, 1750–1807", *Slavery & Abolition*, 37.1, 2016, 159–182.

88. Robin Blackburn, *The Making of New World Slavery. From the Baroque to the Modern, 1492–1800*, Verso, 2010 (orig. 1997); Joseph E. Inikori, *Africans and the Industrial Revolution in England: A Study in International Trade and Development*, Cambridge University Press, 2002.

89. Sven Beckert, *Empire of Cotton. A New History of Global Capitalism*, Penguin, 2014, 37, 54.

90. Beckert, *Empire of Cotton*, 88–94; T.A.Z. Pereira, "The Rise of the Brazilian Cotton Trade in Britain during the Industrial Revolution", *Journal of Latin American Studies*, 50:4, 2018, 919–949.

91. Sidney W. Mintz, *Sweetness and Power: The Place of Sugar in Modern History*, Penguin, 1986; Ralph A. Austen and Woodruff D. Smith, "Private Tooth Decay as Public Economic Virtue: The Slave-Sugar Triangle, Consumerism, and European Industrialization", *Social Science History*, 14, 1990, 95–115; Kenneth Pomeranz, *The Great Divergence: China, Europe, and the Making of the Modern World Economy*, Princeton University Press, 2000, 274–275.

92. David Richardson, "The Slave Trade, Sugar, and British Economic Growth, 1748–1776", *Journal of Interdisciplinary History*, 17:4, 1987, 739–769. Per capita consumption figures from 1780 are lower because of a shift in the statistics from England to all Britain.

93. Sucheta Mazumdar, *Sugar and Society in China: Peasants, Technology, and the World Market*, Harvard Asia Center, 1998, 375.

94. Klas Rönnbäck, "On the Economic Importance of the Slave Plantation Complex to the British Economy During the Eighteenth Century: A Value-Added Approach", *Journal of World History*, 13, 2018, 309–327.

95. Kevin H. O'Rourke, Leandro Prados de la Escosura, and Guillaume Daudin, "Trade and Empire", in S. N. Broadberry and K. H. O'Rourke (eds.), *The Cambridge Economic History of Modern Europe. Vol 1*, Cambridge University Press, 2010, tables 4.1 and 4.5, assuming that half of all overseas trade was colonial. The authors estimate that it was 49% in 1784–86.

96. Blackburn, *The Making of New World Slavery*, 528–529; Mokyr, *The Enlightened Economy*, ch. 12.

97. Douglas A. Farnie, "The Role of Merchants as Prime Movers in the Expansion of the Cotton Industry, 1760–1990", in Farnie and David J. Jeremy (eds.), *The Fibre That Changed the World: The Cotton Industry in International Perspective, 1600–1990s*, Oxford University Press, 2004; Beckert, *Empire of Cotton*, ch. 3.

98. Giorgio Riello, *Cotton: The Fabric That Made the Modern World*, Cambridge University Press, 2013, ch. 8.

99. Mokyr, *The Enlightened Economy*, ch. 8.

100. Calculated from O'Rourke et al., "Trade and Empire", table 4.1.

101. Blackburn, *The Making of New World Slavery*, 70.

102. Ibid., 521–522.

103. O'Rourke et al., "Trade and Empire".

104. Simon Hill, "The Liverpool Economy during the War of American Independence, 1775–83", *Journal of Imperial and Commonwealth History*, 44:6, 2016, 835–856.

105. Allen, *The British Industrial Revolution*, 127.

106. Larry Neal, *The Rise of Financial Capitalism. International Capital Markets in the Age of Reason*, Cambridge University Press, 1990, 17.

107. Leonor Freire Costa, Pedro Lains, and Susana Munch Miranda, *An Economic History of Portugal, 1143–2010*, Cambridge University Press, 2016, 205.

108. Jose Jobson De Andrade Arruda, "Colonies as Mercantile Investments: The Luso-Brazilian Empire, 1500–1808", in James D. Tracy (ed.), *The Political Economy of Merchant Empires: State Power and World Trade 1350–1750*, Cambridge University Press, 1991, 393.

109. Stuart B. Schwartz, "The Economy of the Portuguese Empire", in Francisco Bethencourt and Diogo Ramada Curto (eds.), *Portuguese Oceanic Expansion, 1400–1800*, Cambridge University Press, 2007.

110. Harry E. Cross, "South American Bullion and Export, 1550–1750", in John Richards (ed.), *Precious Metals in the Later Medieval and Early Modern Worlds*, Carolina Academic Press, 1983.

111. K. K. Karaman and S. Pamuk, "Ottoman State Finances in European Perspective, 1500–1914", *Journal of Economic History*, 70:3, 2010.

112. Joseph E. Inikori, "Africa and the Globalization Process: Western Africa, 1450–1850", *Journal of World History*, 2, 2007, 63–86.

113. David Hancock, "The Intensification of Atlantic Maritime Trade (1492–1815)", in Christian Buchet (ed.), *The Sea in History. The Early Modern World*, Boydell Press, 2017.

114. Vries, *State, Economy and the Great Divergence*, 374.

115. Giorgio Riello, "Nature, Production and Regulation in Eighteenth-Century Britain and France: The Case of the Leather Industry", *Historical Research*, 81:211, 2008, 77–99.

116. Broadberry et al., *British Economic Growth*, table 4.05.

117. J. T. Kotilaine, *Russia's Foreign Trade and Economic Expansion in the Seventeenth Century: Windows on the World*, Brill, 2005, 194.

118. James S. Olson et al. (eds.), *Historical Dictionary of the Spanish Empire, 1402–1975*, Greenwood Press, 1992, 305.

119. E. A. Wrigley, "The Transition to an Advanced Organic Economy: A Half Millennium of English Agriculture", *Economic History Review*, 59:3, 2006, 435–480.

120. Scammell, "British Merchant Shipbuilding"; Emily Erickson, *Between Monopoly and Free Trade. The English East India Company, 1600–1757*, Princeton University Press, 2014, 67.

121. James W. Frey, "The Indian Saltpeter Trade, the Military Revolution and the Rise of Britain as a Global Superpower", *Historian*, 71:3, 2009, 507–554.

122. Gábor Ágoston, *Guns for the Sultan: Military Power and the Weapons Industry in the Ottoman Empire*, Cambridge University Press, 2005, 97, n.3.

123. Frey, "The Indian Saltpeter Trade".

124. Ibid.

125. Cuenca-Esteban, "The British Balance of Payments".

126. Quoted in O'Rourke, "The Worldwide Economic Impact".

127. R. Cole Harris and John Warkentin, *Canada Before Confederation. A Study in Historical Geography*, Oxford University Press, 1974, 86.

128. Sven-Erik Astrom, "Britain's Timber Imports from the Baltic, 1775–1930; Some New Figures And Viewpoints", *Scandinavian Economic History Review*, 37, 1989, 57–71; Graeme Wynn, *Timber Colony: A Historical Geography of Early 19th-century New Brunswick*, University of Toronto Press, 1981; T. W. Acheson, *Saint John. The Making of a Colonial Urban Community*, University of Toronto Press, 1985; L.C.A. Knowles and C. M. Knowles, *The Economic Development of the Overseas Empire*, Routledge, 3 vols., 1924–36, vol. 2 (revised edn, 1928), 164.

129. Patrick O'Brien, "The Nature and Historical Evolution of an Exceptional Fiscal State and Its Possible Significance for the Precocious Commercialization and Industrialization of the British Economy from Cromwell to Nelson", *Economic History Review*, 64:2. 2011, 408–446.

130. Priya Satia, *Empire of Guns. The Violent Making of the Industrial Revolution*, Duckworth, 2018, 2.

131. Philip T. Hoffman, "Prices, the Military Revolution, and Western Europe's Comparative Advantage in Violence", *Economic History Review*, 64, 2011, 39–59.

132. N.A.M. Rodger, "From the 'Military Revolution' to the 'Fiscal-Naval State'", *Journal for Maritime Research*, 13:2, 2011, 119–128. Brewer, *The Sinews of Power*, 27.

133. Larry Neal, *The Rise of Financial Capitalism* and "The Finance of Business during the Industrial Revolution", in R. Floud and D. McCloskey (eds.), *The Economic History of Britain since 1700*, 2nd edn, Cambridge University Press, 1994; P. K. O'Brien, "The French Wars and Capital Formation in Britain", in Anne Digby et al. (eds.), *New Directions in Economic and Social History*, Vol. 2, Macmillan, 1992; Peter Temin and Hans-Joachim Voth, "Credit Rationing and Crowding Out During the Industrial Revolution: Evidence from Hoare's Bank, 1702–1862", *Explorations in Economic History*, 30, 2005; Elise S. Brezis, "Foreign Capital Flows in the Century of Britain's Industrial Revolution: New Estimates Controlled Conjectures", *Economic History Review*, 48, 1995, 46–67; R. C. Nash, "The Balance of Payments and Foreign Capital Flows in the 18th Century England: A Comment", *Economic History Review*, 50, 1997, 110–128; Erik Banks, *The Rise and Fall of the Merchant Banks*, Kogan Page, 1999.

134. Broadberry et al., *British Economic Growth*, table 5.04.

135. O'Rourke, "The World-Wide Impact".

136. Ronald Hope, *A New History of British Shipping*, John Murray, 1990, 235.

137. Jacks, "Foreign Wars, Domestic Markets".

138. Satia, *Empire of Guns*, 172; Vries, *State, Economy and the Great Divergence*, 317.

139. James Pritchard, *In Search of Empire: The French in the Americas, 1670–1730*, Cambridge University Press, 2004, 393.

140. Glen O'Hara, *Britain and the Sea. Since 1600*, Palgrave Macmillan, 2010, 28, 387. Also see David J. Starkey, "Quantifying British Seafarers, 1789–1828", in Richard Gorski (ed.), *Maritime Labour: Contributions to the History of Work at Sea, 1500–2000*, Aksant, 2007.

141. Michael Duffy, *Soldiers, Sugar and Seapower: The British Expeditions to the West Indies and the War against Revolutionary France*, Clarendon Press, 1987, 387.

142. Peter Earle, *Sailors: English Merchant Seamen 1650–1775*, Methuen, 1998, 203.

143. Denver Brunsman, "Men of War: British Sailors and the Impressment Paradox", *Journal of Early Modern History*, 14, 2010, 9–44.

144. John Bostoce, "From Davis Strait to Bering Strait: The Arrival of the Commercial Whaling Fleet in North America's Western Arctic", *Arctic*, 37:4, 1984, 528–532.

145. Page, *Britain and the Seventy Years' War*, 108; Vries, *State, Economy and the Great Divergence*, 48–49; Roger B. Manning, *An Apprenticeship in Arms: The Origins of the British Army 1585–1702*, Oxford University Press, 2006, 419; Glen O'Hara, *Britain and the Sea*, 28.

146. Broadberry et al., *British Economic Growth*, 342.

147. Mokyr, *The Enlightened Economy*, ch. 13.

148. Steven King and Geoffrey Timmins, *Making Sense of the Industrial Revolution: English Economy and Society 1700–1850*, Manchester University Press, 2001, 47.

149. Allen, *The British Industrial Revolution*, 182

150. Stephen Broadberry and Bishnupriya Gupta, "Lancashire, India, and Shifting Competitive Advantage in Cotton Textiles, 1700–1850: The Neglected Role of Factor Prices", *Economic History Review*, 62:2, 2009, 279–305.

151. Ibid.; Serge Chassagne, "Calico Printing in Europe before 1780", in David Jenkins (ed.), *The Cambridge History of Western Textiles, Vol. I*, Cambridge University Press, 2003.

152. E.g., C. Knick Harley, "Cotton Textile Prices Revisited: A Response to Cuenca Esteban", *Economic History Review*, 52:4, 1999, 756–765.

153. Riello, *Cotton*, ch. 10; Beckert, *Empire of Cotton*, 73.

154. Brian Spear, "Textile Patents and the GB Industrial Revolution", *World Patent Information*, 44, 2016, 53–56.

155. Prasannan Parthasarathi, *Why Europe Grew Rich and Asia Did Not: Global Economic Divergence, 1600–1850*, Cambridge University Press, 2011, 109.

156. King and Timmins, *Making Sense of the Industrial Revolution*, 50; Mary B. Rose, *Firms, Networks, and Business Values: The British and American Cotton Industries since 1750*, Cambridge University Press, 2000, 30.

157. Spear, "Textile Patents"; Harley, "Cotton Textile Prices"; Keith Sugden, "An Occupational Study to Track the Rise of Adult Male Mule Spinning in Lancashire and Cheshire, 1777–1813", *Textile History*, 48:2, 2017.

158. Broadberry and Gupta, "Lancashire, India, and Shifting Competitive Advantage".

159. Indrajit Ray, "Identifying the Woes of the Cotton Textile Industry in Bengal: Tales of the Nineteenth Century", *Economic History Review*, 62, 2009, 857–892. Also see Ray's *Bengal Industries and the British Industrial Revolution (1757–1857)*, Routledge, 2011.

160. David J. Jeremy, "International Changes in Cotton-Manufacturing Productivity, 1830–1950s", in Farnie and Jeremy (eds.), *The Fibre That Changed the World*; Stephen Broadberry, Johann Custodis, and Bishnupriya Gupta, "India and the Great Divergence: An Anglo-Indian Comparison of GDP Per Capita, 1600–1871", *Explorations in Economic History*, 55, 2015.

161. J.K.J. Thomson, "Explaining the 'Take-Off' of the Catalan Cotton Industry", *Economic History Review*, 58:4, 2005, 701–735; Riello, *Cotton*, ch. 8.

162. Riello, *Cotton*, ch. 10.

163. Spencer Austin Leonard, "A Fit of Absence of Mind? Illiberal Imperialism and the Founding of British India, 1757–1776", PhD thesis, University of Chicago, 2010.

164. Riello, *Cotton*, ch. 7. Also see Beckert, *Empire of Cotton*, 49–51; Catherine Casson and Mark Dodgson, "Designing for Innovation: Cooperation and Competition in English Cotton, Silk, and Pottery Firms, 1750–1860", *Business History Review*, 93, 2019, 247–273; Maxine Berg, "Useful Knowledge, 'Industrial Enlightenment', and the Place of India", *Journal of World History*, 8, 2013, 117–141.

165. Hanser, "Teatime in the North Country". Also see Francesca Bray, "Technological Transitions", in Jerry H. Bentley, Sanjay Subrahmanyam, and Merry E. Wiesner-Hanks (eds.), *The Cambridge World History, Vol. 6: The Construction of a Global World, 1400–1800 CE, Part 1: Foundations*, 2015.

166. H. V. Bowen, "Britain in the Indian Ocean Region and Beyond: Contours, Connections, and the Creation of a Global Maritime Empire", in Bowen, Mancke, and Reid (eds.), *Britain's Oceanic Empire*; Susan Nort, "The Physical Manifestation of an Abstraction: A Pair of 1750s Waistcoat

Shapes", *Textile History*, 39:1, 2008, 92–104; Broadberry and Gupta, "Cotton Textiles and the Great Divergence"; Barrow, *East India Company*, 28; Ashworth, *The Industrial Revolution*, 182–183.

167. Broadberry and Gupta, "Lancashire, India, and Shifting Competitive Advantage", table 2.

168. John Singleton, "The Lancashire Cotton Industry, the Royal Navy and the British Empire, c.1700–c.1960", in Farnie and Jeremy (eds.), *The Fibre That Changed the World*.

169. Bowen, "Britain in the Indian Ocean Region and Beyond". Also see Nort, "The Physical Manifestation of an Abstraction"; Broadberry and Gupta, "Cotton Textiles and the Great Divergence"; Barrow, *East India Company*, 28; Ashworth, *The Industrial Revolution*, 182–183.

170. Carole Shammas, "The Decline of Textile Prices in England and British America Prior to Industrialization", *Economic History Review*, 47:3, 1994, 483–507; B. R. Mitchell, *International Historical Statistics: Europe, 1750–2005*, 6th edn, Palgrave Macmillan, 2007, 546.

171. Nort, "The Physical Manifestation of an Abstraction".

172. Norman Biggs, "A Tale Untangled: Measuring the Fineness of Yarn", *Textile History*, 35:1, 2004, 120–129.

173. Jeremy, "International Changes in Cotton-Manufacturing Productivity".

174. Harley, "Cotton Textile Prices".

175. I draw the numbers from Broadberry and Gupta, "Lancashire, India, and Shifting Competitive Advantage".

176. Chassagne, "Calico Printing in Europe", in T. C. Curtis and G. D. Smith (eds.), *Cotton's Renaissance. A Study in Market Innovation*, Cambridge University Press, 2001.

177. Sugden, "An Occupational Study".

178. Riello, *Cotton*, ch. 10.

179. Broadberry and Gupta, "Cotton Textiles and the Great Divergence".

180. Cuenca-Esteban, "India's Contribution".

181. Ray, "Identifying the Woes of the Cotton Textile Industry".

182. Ashworth, *The Industrial Revolution*, 142.

183. Cuenca-Esteban, "India's Contribution".

Conclusion

1. Pita Kelekna, *The Horse in Human History*, Cambridge University Press, 2009, 65; B. I. Sandor, "Tutankhamun's Chariots: Secret Treasures of Engineering Mechanics", *Fatigue & Fracture of Engineering Materials & Structures*, 27.7, 2004, 637–646; David W. Anthony, *The Horse, the Wheel and Language: How Bronze-Age Riders From the Eurasian Steppes Shaped the Modern World*, Princeton University Press, 2007, 462; Maria Pogrebova, "The Emergence of Chariots and Riding in the South Caucasus", *Oxford Journal of Archaeology*, 22:4, 2003, 397–409.

2. Murat Iyigun, *War, Peace, and Prosperity in the Name of God: The Ottoman Role in Europe's Socioeconomic Evolution*, University of Chicago Press, 2015.

3. Walter Scheidel, *Escape from Rome: The Failure of Empire and the Road to Prosperity*, Princeton University Press, 2019.

4. Eric Mielants, *The Origins of Capitalism and the 'Rise of the West'*, Temple University Press, 2007.

5. Quoted in Lisa Jardine, *Going Dutch. How England Plundered Holland's Glory*, Harper, 2009, 336.

6. Barry Cunliffe, *Europe between the Oceans. Themes and Variations, 9000 BC–AD 1000*, Yale University Press, 2008, viii.

7. J. Belich, *Replenishing the Earth. The Settler Revolution and the Rise of the Anglo-World, 1780s–1920s*, Oxford University Press, 2009.

8. Ibid., and J. Belich, *Paradise Reforged: A History of the New Zealanders from the 1880s to the Year 2000*, Penguin, 2001.

9. Paul Freedman, "Rural Society", in Michael Jones (ed.), *The New Cambridge Medieval History, Vol. IV*, Cambridge University Press, 2000, 92.

10. Peregrine Horden, "Mediterranean Plague in the Age of Justinian", in Michael Maas (ed.), *The Cambridge Companion to the Age of Justinian*, Cambridge University Press, 2005.

11. John L. Brooke, *Climate Change and the Course of Global History. A Rough Journey*, Cambridge University Press, 2014, 1–2.

INDEX

Barcelona, 93, 120, 131, 245

Basques, 90, 108–9, 164, 306

Basra, 273, 284, 285

Batavia, 240, 403

Bavaria, 89, 90

Beckert, Sven, 425

Bedouin, 41, 158, 195, 200

Behrendt, Stephen, 384

Benedictow, Ole, 37, 72, 302

Bengal: British conquest and exploitation, 393–99, cotton manufacture and British economy, 434–40; Mughal conquest and exploitation, 332–33, 335, 340; opium, 403; trade with China, 232

Berbers, 41, 200, 321

Bering Strait, 370

Bihar, 430

Bijaya, 120

Birmingham, 420, 431

birth-rates, 50–51, 149, 167, 249

Blackburn, Robin, 425

Black Death. *See* plague

"Black Portuguese", 148, 257–58, 393

Black Sea: Cossack, 357; Genoese, 115, 204, 243, 246; Golden Horde, 115; littoral, 36; Ottoman, 121, 248, 276; plague dispersal, 66; Russians, 358

Blockmans, Wim, 302

Bonaparte, Napoleon, 248

Bornu, Sultanate of, 282

Borsch, Stuart, 44

Botocudo, 391

Brazil, 375, 384; Dutch attempted conquest, 311, 314; diseases, 149, 153; gold, 165, 387, 407, 429; native "Indians", 386, 389, 391; Portuguese migration, settlement, and racial attitudes, 143, 147–48, 155, 255; slavery, 384, 390–91; sugar, 260, 386

Bretons, 161, 174. *See also* Brittany

Brewer, John, 415, 417

Bristol, 247, 413

Britain, British Empire, 140, 144, 179, 183, 240, 310, 408–40, 445; Chinese, relations with, 240, 403, 437–38, 440; Dutch,

relations with, 317–18, 407, 417, 429; "entwining" with other empires, 326, 406–7; "French wars", 406–7, 430–33; fur trade, 386–87, 402; Genoese influence, 244, 247, 418; in India, 393–99; migration and settlement, 149–57, 165; Omani, relations with, 326; Portuguese, relations with, 407, 429; rats, 66; USA, relations with, 340, 389, 405–6, 434; slavery, 381–85, 425–26; sugar, 386, 423, 425–26; whaling, 405–6. *See also* Bengal; British East India Company; England; Ireland; London; Scotland; Ulster; Wales

British East India Company (EIC), 393–94, 438–39; Bengal, 396–97; China trade, 403, 439–40; Dutch investment, 318; private trading, 398, 438; wars, 395, 397, 424

Brittany, 80, 161, 179. *See also* Bretons

Bruges, 244, 298, 306, 313

building booms, 39, 93

Bukhara/Bukharan, 359–60, 367

Bulgar (city on Volga), 346, 349

Bulgaria, 246, 269, 275, 277

Bulgars, 27

Bulliet, Richard, 211

bullion, 16, 19, 117; Americas, 265–6, 387; banking, 251; "bullion famine" of 14th century, 84, 93–4; Chinese, 234; "Dutch disease", 267; expansion, impact on, 429; as expansive trade, 107; inflation, impact on, 104; Ottoman, 273, 375. *See also* gold; silver

Burgos, 91

Burgundy, 80, 159, 172, 260

Burke, Peter, 217

Burkhardt, Jacob, 103

Bursa, 206–7, 276, 281, 445

Byzantines, 17, 22, 29, 132, 205, 245, 269, 276

Cabot, John, 244

Caffa, 36, 250; Genoese, 120, 245–46; Ottoman, 248, 278; slave trade, 278–79

Calicut, 228, 229, 238

camels, 8, 11, 22–23, 117–18; as gun carriers, 321, 394–95; as plague carriers, 45, 62–63

wars: of American Independence ("American War"), 406–7, 433; Anglo-Dutch, 317; Anglo-French ("second hundred years' war"), 406; of the Bosporus, 243, 250; of Chioggia , 243, 250; "Eighty Years", 308–9; English Civil, 317, 410, 416, 419;"French" (1793–1815), 406, 430, 433; Hundred Years, 244; post-plague, 171, 176; Seven Years, 406, 417, 433; of Spanish Succession, 309, 433; Thirty Years, 157, 266
Watt, James, 421
West Eurasia, 10, 19–22; maps, 9, 21
whaling, 108–9, 167, 311, 405–6
"whiteness": introduced, 143–45, negotiated, 145, 147–48; "White" Portuguese, 148, 384
women, European: dominate crew regions, 105, 165–67, 272, 364; "female formula", 150–51; and industrial revolution, 414–15; as "settler fore-mothers", 105, 144–46, 149–58, 164, 363–65; as slaves, 120; wages, 97–98, 152, 436; wet nursing, 203, 249; work, 97–98; 105, 114, 125, 159, 422, 436.

See also birth rates; European Marriage Pattern; marriage
women, non-European: African, 382–84, 426; Guanche, 145; indigenous Siberian 363, 370; Muslim, 24, 158, 194, 226
work animals, 14, 87–88, 212, 334, 374
"worlds", sub-planetary, 8. *See also* globalisation, scales of

Yacqui, 186, 392
Yamnaya, 12, 13
Yamysh, salt lake, 366
yellow fever, 149, 184, 389,
Yemen, 44, 196, 224–26, 284
Yersinia pestis, Y. pestis. See plague pathogen
Yersinia Pseudo-tuberculosis. *See* plague: prehistory
Yuan Dynasty, 56–58, 220. *See also* China; Mongols

Zamorin, 228, 238
Zanzibar, 226–27, 325–26, 404
Zhungars, 366–67, 369
Zimbabwe, 227, 260

A NOTE ON THE TYPE

This book has been composed in Arno, an Old-style serif typeface in the classic Venetian tradition, designed by Robert Slimbach at Adobe.